PENGUIN REFERENCE

The *Puzzler* Crossword Solver's Dictionary

The name *Puzzler* is synonymous with enjoyable puzzles. *Puzzler* is the oldest and best known of all puzzle magazines, and the company is renowned for its puzzle expertise. As the largest puzzle publisher in the UK, and probably the world, *Puzzler* Media now publishes sixty titles in more than twenty countries.

The *Puzzler* Crossword Solver's Dictionary

Puzzler

PENGUIN BOOKS

PENGUIN BOOKS

Published by the Penguin Group
Penguin Books Ltd, 80 Strand, London WC2R 0RL, England
Penguin Group (USA) Inc., 375 Hudson Street, New York, New York 10014, USA
Penguin Group (Canada), 90 Eglinton Avenue East, Suite 700, Toronto, Ontario,
Canada M4P 2Y3 (a division of Pearson Penguin Canada Inc.)
Penguin Ireland, 25 St Stephen's Green, Dublin 2, Ireland
(a division of Penguin Books Ltd)
Penguin Group (Australia), 250 Camberwell Road, Camberwell,
Victoria 3124, Australia (a division of Pearson Australia Group Pty Ltd)
Penguin Books India Pvt Ltd, 11 Community Centre,
Panchsheel Park, New Delhi – 110 017, India
Penguin Group (NZ), 67 Apollo Drive, Rosedale, North Shore 0632,
New Zealand (a division of Pearson New Zealand Ltd)
Penguin Books (South Africa) (Pty) Ltd, 24 Sturdee Avenue,
Rosebank, Johannesburg 2196, South Africa

Penguin Books Ltd, Registered Offices: 80 Strand, London WC2R 0RL, England

www.penguin.com

First published 2007
1

Copyright © Puzzler, 2007
All rights reserved

The moral right of the author has been asserted

Printed in England by Clays Ltd, St Ives plc

ISBN: 978-0-141-02746-3

Introduction

The Puzzler Crossword Solver's Dictionary is the ideal resource for crossword solvers and a treasure trove for all lovers of the English language. Here you'll find those words that often prove elusive because they have several meanings. The clue 'Stick', for example, could lead to several answers, as you'll see if you look it up on page 325. The meanings given alongside each word will lead you to the answer you're after, or at least give you that memory jog in the right direction.

You'll also find a list of phrases, expressions, places and titles containing the word, so if you spot that an answer contains 'love' or 'night', you can refer to the list for possible answers that contain the word.

Definitions of the word are given first – they're in alphabetical order based on part of speech (first noun, then verb, adjective, and any others).

As an added bonus, some words are accompanied by a box containing a more extensive list of places and other proper nouns. These words are more specialised and appear in thematic and tougher puzzles.

Whether you're a crossword addict, a quiz buff, or just someone who enjoys browsing, you'll find the *The Puzzler Crossword Solver's Dictionary* an invaluable addition to your reference collection.

Dictionary Abbreviations

al	album of songs	nr	nursery rhyme
b	book	o	opera
bal	ballet	pa	painting
cl	classical piece	pan	pantomime
com	comic strip	pl	play
f	film	po	poem
ga	video or computer game	r	radio programme
h	hymn	s	song
mag	magazine	sc	sculpture, statue
mus	musical	tv	television programme
n	newspaper		

The *Puzzler* Crossword Solver's Dictionary

A

abandon lack of inhibition; leave, stop; abandon ship

abandoned deserted, uninhibited

abandonment desertion, relinquishment

abbey monastery; UK bank; Abbey Road, Fountains Abbey, Glastonbury Abbey, Westminster Abbey, Woburn Abbey; *Northanger Abbey* (b)

Abbey
Bath, Battle, Beaulieu, Buckfast, Fountains, Glastonbury, Hexham, Jervaulx, Kelso, Kirkstall, Lacock, Medmenham, Melrose, Mottisfont, Netley, Rievaulx, Selby, Shrewsbury, Sweetheart, Tintern, Waltham, Westminster, Whitby, Woburn

---

abbot monastery head; Newton Abbot

abdicate give up, renounce a throne

abdication renunciation; 1936 royal crisis

abet assist in crime; aid and abet

abhors hates; nature abhors a vacuum

abide continue, endure, live, (by) obey; *Abide with Me* (h)

abiding *see* abide; law-abiding

ablaze excited, on fire, very colourful

able competent, intelligent; get-at-able; able seaman, able-bodied

abnormal unnatural; abnormal load

aboard on a ship or plane; all aboard

abode home; right of abode

abolition scrapping; ending of slavery in the USA

abominable repulsive; Abominable Snowman

about approximately, around, concerning; bring about, come about, hang about, how about?, knock about, lark about, man about town, mess about, muck about, right about, turn about; about-face, about-turn; about time too, beat about the bush, green about the gills, have a thing about, make no bones about, nothing to write home about, tell me about it, that's about the size of it, throw your weight about; *About a Boy* (b/f), *About Schmidt* (f), *All about Eve* (f), *How about That?* (s), *Mad about the Boy* (s), *Man about the House* (tv), *Much Ado about Nothing* (f/pl), *Tell Her about It* (s), *There's Something about Mary* (f), *The Truth about Cats and Dogs* (f), *The Truth about Charlie* (f)

above aforementioned, higher, over; over and above, a cut above; above all, above all else, above board, above suspicion; punch above your weight; *Above Suspicion* (f), *Above Us the Waves* (f), *Heavens Above* (f)

abroad foreign places; in another country; go abroad; *An Englishman Abroad* (pl), *The Innocents Abroad* (b)

abrupt curt, sudden

absence lack, non-attendance; absence makes the heart grow fonder, conspicuous by one's absence

absent away, inattentive; absent friends, absent-minded; *The Absent-Minded Professor* (f)

absinthe green liqueur; *The Absinthe Drinker* (pa)

absolute total, unlimited; decree absolute; absolute majority, absolute temperature, absolute zero; *Absolute Beginners* (b/f), *Absolute Power* (f/tv)

absolutely completely, indeed; *Absolutely Fabulous* (tv)

absorbed soaked up; engrossed; self-absorbed

absorbing soaking up; gripping

absorption assimilation, engrossment, soaking up; self-absorption

abstract summary; remove, summarise; theoretical; abstract art

abstraction concept, preoccupied state, removal

absurd ridiculous; Theatre of the Absurd; *Absurd Person Singular* (pl)

academic don; scholarly, theoretical

academy college; military academy; Academy Award, Royal Academy, Royal Academy of Arts; *Fame Academy* (tv), *Police Academy* (f)

accede agree, become a member, take office

accent diacritic, emphasis, mode of pronunciation; emphasise; acute accent, grave accent

accept receive, say yes, take as true

acceptance affirmative reply, receipt

accepted *see* accept; customary

access admission, entry; enter, retrieve (computing); Microsoft package

accessible approachable, easy to understand, within reach

accession addition, coming to office, formal entry to an organisation

accessory accomplice, extra, small fashion item; supplementary

accident chance, crash, mishap; accident and emergency, accident-prone; an accident waiting to happen

accidental musical sign; subsidiary, unintentional; *Accidental Death of an Anarchist* (pl), *The Accidental Tourist* (b/f)

accidents *see* accident; chapter of accidents

accommodate fit in with, provide lodging for

accommodating *see* accommodate; obliging

accommodation housing, settlement; accommodation address

accompany escort, provide musical backing for

accomplished achieved; skilled

accord agreement; be consistent, bestow; Honda model; of your own accord, with one accord

according *see* accord; corresponding (to); according to schedule, cut your coat according to your cloth; *The World according to Garp* (b/f)

account importance, invoice, report; bank account, bring to account, call to account, charge account, current account, deposit account, expense account, joint account, on account of, on no account, profit and loss account, savings account, take account of, turn to account; *Joint Account* (tv)

accountant book-keeper; chartered accountant, turf accountant

accounting *see* account; keeping of financial records; cost accounting, creative accounting; there's no accounting for taste

accounts *see* account; financial records; by all accounts

accredited attributed; officially authorised

accumulator betting system, electric cell

accurate correct, precise

accused defendant; indicted; *The Accused* (f)

ace expert, playing-card, tennis serve; excellent; within an ace of; ace up your sleeve; *Ace in the Hole* (f), *Ace of Spades* (s), *Ace Ventura: Pet Detective* (f)

acerbic scathing, sour

aces *see* ace; hold all the aces; *Aces High* (f), *Aces Wild* (f)

ache pain, yearning; hurt, yearn; stomach ache

acid LSD; non-alkali, sour; acetic acid, amino acid, citric acid, hydrochloric acid, lactic acid, sulphuric acid; acid bath, acid drops, acid house, acid rain, acid test

acknowledge admit, confirm receipt of, express gratitude for, greet, recognise officially

acorn fruit of the oak; *Acorn Antiques* (tv)

acorns *see* acorn; great oaks from little acorns grow

acquaintance casual friend, familiarity; nodding acquaintance

acquainted familiarised; familiar

acquired obtained; acquired taste

acquit absolve, perform; acquit yourself

acre land measure; Israeli port; God's acre; *God's Little Acre* (b)

across crossword clue type; spanning; come across, get across, put across; across country, across the board; shot across the bows; *Across the Pacific* (f), *Ferry across the Mersey* (s)

act deed, law, play section, performance, pretence; behave, make a move, play a role, pretend, take effect; class act, disappearing act, double act, high-wire act, old pals' act, play-act; act of contrition, act of God, act of grace, act out, act up, act your age; caught in the act, get in on the act, read the Riot Act to; Act of Settlement, Act of Union, Official Secrets Act, Riot Act; *Act of Will* (b), *Sister Act* (f)

acting *see* act; drama; stand-in; method acting, play-acting

action armed conflict, deed, effect,

excitement, film director's command, lawsuit, physical effort; deal with; affirmative action, direct action, industrial action, live action, pump-action, rearguard action; action-packed, action painting, action replay, action stations; in action, out of action, suit the action to the word; Action Man; *Solid Gold Easy Action* (s), *World in Action* (tv)

actions *see* action; actions speak louder than words

active verb voice; energetic, functioning, involved, liable to erupt; retro-active; active service, active volcano

activity bustle, functioning, occupation, recreational pursuit; displacement activity

actor dramatic performer; character actor, method actor; actor-manager

acts *see* act; New Testament book; *Between the Acts* (b)

actual real; in actual fact

actually in reality; *Love Actually* (f)

acute type of accent or angle; severe, sharp; acute accent

adapt get used (to), modify

add append, say more, tot up; add on, add-ons, add up; add insult to injury

added *see* add; value-added, value added tax

adder snake; death adder, puff adder; adder's tongue

addict drug user, enthusiast; drug addict; *System Addict* (s)

addicts *see* addict; *Telly Addicts* (tv)

adding *see* add; adding machine

addition supplement, totting up; in addition

addled confused, rotten

address detailed location, speech; deal with, speak to, write location details on; accommodation address, forwarding address, home address, public address system

adequate passable, sufficient

adhere (to) obey, stick

adherent devotee; sticking

adhesive glue; sticking; self-adhesive

adjourn go elsewhere, suspend

adjust get used (to), modify; *Do Not Adjust Your Set* (tv)

administer dispense, manage

administration government in power, management of paperwork

admirable worthy of respect; *The Admirable Crichton* (f/pl)

admiral senior naval officer; rear admiral, red admiral, vice-admiral, white admiral; Admiral of the Fleet, Admiral's Cup

admission acknowledgement, entrance fee, entry, new hospital patient; no admission

admit allow in, confess

ado fuss; *Much Ado about Nothing* (f/pl)

adolescent teenager; teenage

adopt choose, espouse, take as your own child

adoration deep love, worship; *The Adoration of the Magi* (pa)

adored loved, worshipped; *My Eyes Adored You* (s)

advance loan, progress, writer's upfront payment; lend, move forward, put forward; prior; advance guard; in advance

advanced *see* advance; ahead of the times; Advanced Level

advances *see* advance; sexual approaches

advantage benefit, superiority, tennis

score; Boots loyalty card; take advantage

advent   arrival; pre-Christmas period; Advent calendar

adventure   exciting experience, excitement; adventure playground; *An Awfully Big Adventure* (f), *The Poseidon Adventure* (f)

adventures   *see* adventure; *The Adventures of Augie March* (b), *The Adventures of Huckleberry Finn* (b), *The Adventures of Robin Hood* (f/tv), *The Adventures of Robinson Crusoe* (f), *The Adventures of Roderick Random* (b), *The Adventures of Tom Sawyer* (b/f)

advertise   announce publicly, promote; *Murder Must Advertise* (b)

advertising   *see* advertise; commercial publicity; subliminal advertising; advertising agency, advertising campaign; *How to Get Ahead in Advertising* (f)

advice   suggestions; Citizens' Advice Bureau

advised   gave counsel, informed, suggested; ill-advised, well advised

advocate   Scottish barrister, proponent; recommend; devil's advocate; Lord Advocate; *The Devil's Advocate* (b/f)

aerial   antenna; taking place above ground; 2005 Kate Bush album; aerial view

affair   event, matter, romantic liaison; love affair; *The End of the Affair* (b/f), *Love Affair* (f), *The Thomas Crown Affair* (f)

affairs   *see* affair; state of affairs; *Family Affairs* (tv), *Internal Affairs* (f)

affect   assume, feign, have an impact on, move emotionally

affected   *see* affect; pretentious

affection   fondness; *The Object of My Affection* (f)

affiliate   linked organisation; attach as a member

affirmative   positive statement; positive; affirmative action; in the affirmative

afford   have enough money for, provide

afield   at a distance; far afield

afraid   frightened, sorry; *Who's Afraid of Virginia Woolf?* (f/pl)

aft   at the rear of a ship; fore and aft

after   following, in pursuit of, in the style of, next to; later; look after, sought after, take after; after-effect, after a fashion, after all, after the fact, after you; after word comes weird, be wise after the event, one after another, one after the other, throw good money after bad; *After Henry* (f/r/tv), *After Hours* (f), *After Many a Summer* (b), *After the Fall* (pl), *After the Gold Rush* (al), *The Day after Tomorrow* (f), *Ever After* (f), *Night after Night* (f), *Time after Time* (s)

afternoon   time of day; good afternoon; *Death in the Afternoon* (b), *Dog Day Afternoon* (f), *Seance on a Wet Afternoon* (f), *Sunny Afternoon* (s)

aga   Eastern ruler; make of cooker; Aga Khan

again   moreover, once more; born-again; again and again, but then again, come again, every now and again, here we go again, now and again, once again, same again, yet again, you can say that again; *Destry Rides Again* (f), *Hello Again* (f), *Here Comes the Rain Again* (s), *Home Again* (tv), *Let's Twist Again* (s), *Never Say Never Again* (f), *On the Road*

Again (s), *Play It Again, Sam* (f), *So You Win Again* (s), *We'll Meet Again* (s), *You Win Again* (s)

against abutting, opposed to, unfavourable to; over against, race against time, strike a blow against, up against it; against all odds, against expectation, against the grain, against the stream, against the Sun; hope against hope, kick against the pricks; *Against All Odds* (f/s)

age epoch, stage of life, very long time; get older; golden age, jazz age, middle age, middle-age spread, New Age music, old age, old-age pension, old-age pensioner, over age, reading age, space age, third age, under-age; age group, age-old; act your age, come of age, of an age; Age of Aquarius, Age of Reason, Bronze Age, Ice Age, Iron Age, New Age, Stone Age; *The Age of Innocence* (b/f), *The Age of Reason* (b), *The Awkward Age* (b), *Ice Age* (f), *Thirty Is a Dangerous Age, Cynthia* (f)

aged of a specified number of years, old; got older; *The Secret Diary of Adrian Mole Aged 13¾* (b)

agency bureau; advertising agency, dating agency, estate agency, intelligence agency, news agency, travel agency; Child Support Agency

agenda list of items; hidden agenda

agent cause, representative, spy; double agent, estate agent, land agent, press agent, secret agent, shipping agent, special agent, travel agent; agent provocateur; Agent Orange; *Agent Cody Banks* (f), *The Confidential Agent* (b), *The Secret Agent* (b/f)

ages *see* age; a long time; dark ages; Middle Ages; *Rock of Ages* (h)

aggravate annoy, make worse

aggregate builder's mix, collection, total; combined

aggrieved injured; resentful

agile nimble, quick-witted

ago in the past; long ago, years ago

agony terrible pain; early 1980s Maureen Lipman sitcom; agony aunt, agony column; *The Agony and the Ecstasy* (b/f)

agree concur, consent, tally; agree to differ

agreeable pleasant, willing

agreement concord, pact; gentleman's agreement, prenuptial agreement; Good Friday Agreement; *Gentleman's Agreement* (f)

ahead further forward, in front, in the lead; get ahead, go-ahead, press ahead, streets ahead; ahead of, ahead of time; ahead of its time, ahead of the game, full speed/steam ahead; *How to Get Ahead in Advertising* (f), *The Way Ahead* (f)

aid assistance; assist; first aid, hearing aid, in aid of, legal aid; aid and abet; what's all this in aid of?; Band Aid, Band-Aid, Live Aid

aide assistant; aide-de-camp, aide-memoire

aim objective; intend, point (a weapon); take aim

ain't dialect for am or is not; if it ain't broke, don't fix it; *Ain't Misbehavin'* (s), *Ain't Nobody* (s), *Ain't No Doubt* (s), *Ain't No Mountain High Enough* (s), *Ain't No Pleasing You* (s), *Ain't That a Shame* (s), *He Ain't Heavy, He's My Brother* (s), *It Ain't Half Hot Mum* (tv)

air atmosphere, manner, tune; broadcast, give vent to, ventilate;

change of air, clear the air, compressed air, float on air, fresh air, hang in the air, hot air, hot-air balloon, in the air, in the open air, mid-air, nip in the air, off the air, on air, on the air, open-air, rend the air, surface-to-air, take the air, up in the air, walk on air; air ambulance, air bag, air bed, air brakes, air-bubble, air chief marshal, air commodore, air-conditioned, air-conditioning, air corridor, air cushion, air display, air-drop, air force, air freight, air freshener, air guitar, air gun, air hole, air hostess, air kiss, air line, air marshal, air pistol, air pocket, air pump, air quality, air-raid, air-raid shelter, air-raid warden, air rifle, air sac, air-sea rescue, air terminal, air traffic control, air traffic controller, air vice-marshal; breath of fresh air, castles in the air, vanish into thin air, with your nose in the air; Air France, Air Miles, Bel Air, Royal Air Force; *Air Force One* (f), *Air on a G String* (cl), *Coming up for Air* (b), *Con Air* (b/f), *The Fresh Prince of Bel-Air* (tv)

aircraft flying vehicle; anti-aircraft gun; aircraft carrier

airport place to catch a plane; Arthur Haley novel, 1970 Burt Lancaster film, late 1990s documentary series; Gatwick Airport, Heathrow Airport

airs *see* air; pretentiousness; airs and graces

airy ethereal, light hearted, well ventilated; airy-fairy

aisles passageways; rolling in the aisles

alarm warning device; disquiet, frighten; false alarm, fire alarm, smoke alarm; alarm bell, alarm clock

alas cry of dismay; *Alas Smith and Jones* (tv)

album blank book, collection of recordings; concept album, photograph album, stamp album

alchemist medieval scientist; *The Alchemist* (pl)

alcoholic person dependent on booze; intoxicating; non-alcoholic

alcoholics *see* alcoholic; Alcoholics Anonymous

ale beer; Adam's ale, brown ale, cakes and ale, ginger ale, light ale, pale ale, real ale, yard of ale; *Cakes and Ale* (b)

alert period of vigilance; warn of danger; vigilant; red alert

alias assumed name; otherwise known as; Jennifer Garner tv series; *Alias Smith and Jones* (tv)

alight get off a vehicle, land and settle; on fire; set alight

aligned affiliated, arranged in order; non-aligned; Non-Aligned Movement

alike similar; similarly; look alike; great minds think alike, share and share alike

alive animated, existing; alive and kicking, alive and well; *Staying Alive* (f/s)

all each one, everyone, the whole; above all, above all else, after all, against all odds, and all that, and all that jazz, at all costs, be all ears, by all accounts, by all means, catch-all, cure-all, first of all, free-for-all, in all but name, in all conscience, in all directions, in all probability, jack of all trades, know all the answers, know-all, not at all, of all time, on all fours, once and for all, one and all, to all appearances, warts and all, with all your might; all aboard, all along, all-American, all and sundry, all at once, all at sea, all-clear, all fingers and thumbs, all-important, all-in, all in all, all in good time, all-in-one, all-in wrestling, all manner, all night, all-nighter, all of a doodah, all of a piece, all of a sudden, all of a tremble, all-out, all-out war, all over, all right, all-round, all-rounder, all-seater, all-singing all-dancing, all square, all systems go, all-terrain vehicle, all the best, all the rage, all the same, all the time, all the time in the world, all there, all things considered, all thumbs, all-ticket, all-time, all together, all told, all very well; all good things come to an end, all hell breaks loose, all in a day's work, all mouth and trousers, all over bar the shouting, all roads lead to Rome, all's fair in love and war, all that glitters is not gold, all the way down the line, carry all before you, don't put all your eggs in one basket, firing on all cylinders, have all the answers, hold all the aces, hold all the cards, it takes all sorts to make a world, it's all Greek to me, jack of all trades and master of none, let it all hang out, not all it's cracked up to be, pull out all the stops, put all your eggs in one basket, to all intents and purposes, to cap it all, what's all this in aid of, when all is said and done, written all over one's face; All Blacks, All Fools' Day, All Hallows, All Saints' Day, All Souls' Day, Primate of All England; *A Man for All Seasons* (f/pl), *All about Eve* (f), *All along the Watchtower* (s), *All around the World* (s), *All Creatures Great and Small* (tv), *All Cried Out* (s), *All Gas and*

Gaiters (tv), *All I Have to Do Is Dream* (s), *All My Loving* (s), *All of Me* (f), *All or Nothing* (s), *All Quiet on the Western Front* (b/f), *All Right Now* (s), *All Shook Up* (s), *All Stood Still* (s), *All That Jazz* (f), *All the King's Men* (b/f), *All the President's Men* (f), *All the Things She Said* (s), *All Things Bright and Beautiful* (h), *All Together Now* (s), *All You Need Is Love* (s), *All's Well That Ends Well* (pl), *And All That Jazz* (s), *Goodbye to All That* (b), *Greatest Love of All* (s), *I Drove All Night* (s), *I'm All Right Jack* (f), *June Is Bustin' Out All Over* (s), *Loser Takes All* (b/f), *Love Is All Around* (s), *Open All Hours* (tv), *Rocking All Over the World* (s), *Some Guys Have All the Luck* (s), *The Sum of All Fears* (b/f), *1066 and All That* (b), *They Think It's All Over* (tv), *To Serve Them All My Days* (tv), *The Way of All Flesh* (b), *We Have All the Time in the World* (s), *Winner Takes All* (tv), *The Winner Takes It All* (s)

alley lane; blind alley, bowling alley, skittle alley; alley cat; Tin Pan Alley; *Tin Pan Alley* (mus)

alligator reptile; alligator pear

allow admit, permit

allowance amount permitted, regular pocket money; maternity allowance, mobility allowance, subsistence allowance

allowances *see* allowance; make allowances for

allure attraction; entice

alluring *see* allure; attractive

ally associate, partner in war; join by treaty; *Ally McBeal* (tv)

almond variety of nut; almond oil, almond paste

almost nearly; *Almost Famous* (f)

aloe bitter plant; aloe vera

alone exclusively, solitary, solo; go it alone, leave alone, leave well alone, let alone, let well alone, stand-alone; *Home Alone* (f), *I Think We're Alone Now* (s), *You'll Never Walk Alone* (s)

along from one to another, lengthwise, onward motion; all along, come along, jog along, muddle along, play along, sail along, string along; along with; get along like a house on fire; *All along the Watchtower* (s), *Along Came a Spider* (f), *Along Came Polly* (f)

aloud audibly; read aloud, think aloud

alpha Greek letter, police code word; alpha and omega; Alpha Centauri

alphabet set of letters in order; alphabet soup; *Alphabet Street* (s)

also too; also-ran; *The Sun Also Rises* (b)

altar church table; high altar; altar boy; lead to the altar.

alter change; alter ego

alternate take turns; every other

alternating *see* alternate; alternating current

alternative option; other, unconventional; alternative energy, alternative medicine, alternative therapy; *The Devil's Alternative* (b)

altitude height; altitude sickness

altogether completely, in total, on the whole; in the altogether

always every time, for eternity, in any event; 1989 Steven Spielberg film; the customer is always right; *Always Look on the Bright Side of Life* (s), *Always on My Mind* (s), *It's Always Fair Weather* (f), *The Postman Always Rings Twice* (f)

amateur sportsperson who doesn't get paid; non-professional; 1994 Hal Hartley film; amateur dramatics; *The Amateur Cracksman* (b)

amazing surprising; impressive; *Amazing Grace* (s)

ambassadors senior diplomats; *The Ambassadors* (b/pa)

amber orange-yellow colour, resin; *Forever Amber* (f), *The Amber Spyglass* (b)

ambulance medical vehicle; air ambulance; ambulance driver, ambulance-chaser; St John Ambulance

ambush surprise attack; lie in wait and attack

amendment modification; Fifth Amendment

amends reparation; adjusts; make amends, offer of amends

amiss slightly wrong; go amiss, take it amiss

among between, included in, surrounded by; first among equals, put the cat among the pigeons; *First among Equals* (b)

amorous in loving mood; *The Amorous Prawn* (f/pl)

amount quantity; be equivalent; any amount

amusement fun diversion, hilarity; amusement arcade, amusement park

amusing making laugh; funny

anaesthetic numbing agent; general anaesthetic, local anaesthetic

analgesic painkiller; painkilling

analysis critical examination, psychotherapy; systems analysis

anarchist anti-establishment activist; *Accidental Death of an Anarchist* (pl)

anatomy body structure; *The Anatomy Lesson* (pa)

ancestral inherited; ancestral home

anchor cornerstone, ship's mooring device, US broadcaster; brand-name butter; moor (a ship); crown and anchor, sea anchor, up-anchor, weigh anchor; anchor leg; at anchor

anchors *see* anchor; *Anchors Aweigh* (mus)

ancient bygone, very old; ancient demesne, ancient monument; The Ancient of Days; *The Rime of the Ancient Mariner* (po)

anemone windflower; sea anemone, wood anemone

angel divine messenger, financial backer, paragon of virtue; US tv vampire series; fallen angel, guardian angel; angel cake, angel-fish; Angel Falls, Hell's Angel; *Angel and the Badman* (f), *An Angel at My Table* (f), *Angel Eyes* (s), *Angel Heart* (f), *Angel of Harlem* (s), *Angel of the Morning* (s), *Angel of the North* (sc), *Angel Pavement* (b), *The Blue Angel* (f), *The Exterminating Angel* (f), *Fallen Angel* (s), *I'm No Angel* (f/s), *Jacob Wrestling with the Angel* (pa), *Tenth Avenue Angel* (f)

angels *see* angel; angels on horseback; on the side of the angels, fools rush in where angels fear to tread; *Angels and Demons* (b), *Angels in America* (pl), *Angels with Dirty Faces* (f), *Charlie's Angels* (f/tv), *Desolation Angels* (al/b/f), *Hark the Herald Angels Sing* (h), *Hell's Angels* (f), *Little Angels* (tv), *Only Angels Have Wings* (f), *Rage of Angels* (b), *Where Angels Fear to Tread* (f)

anger rage; infuriate; anger management; *Anger Management* (f), *Look Back in Anger* (pl), *The Upside of Anger* (f)

angle degree of inclination, intersection of two lines, viewpoint; go fishing; right angle, wide-angle, wide-angle lens; angle bracket, angle of inclination

angler fisherman; angler fish; *The Compleat Angler* (b)

angora species of cat, goat or rabbit, wool; angora cat, angora rabbit

angry furious; Angry Young Men; *Twelve Angry Men* (f)

animal creature; pack animal; animal kingdom, animal liberation, animal magnetism, animal reserve, animal trainer; *Animal Crackers* (f), *Animal Farm* (b), *Animal Hospital* (tv), *I Am Not an Animal* (tv)

animated in cartoon form, lively

animation cartoon-making, liveliness; suspended animation

ankle foot and leg joint; ankle-biter

annexe building extension; granny annexe

annexes *see* annexe; adds, takes possession of

annoyed made cross; cross

annual yearbook; yearly; annual general meeting

anon author unknown; soon; ever and anon

anonymous nameless; Alcoholics Anonymous

anorak nerd, waterproof jacket

another a different one; one more; one another; another place, another time; another mouth to feed, another string to your bow, as one door closes another opens, have another think coming, one after another, one good turn deserves another, one man's meat is another's poison, tomorrow is another day; *Another Brick in the Wall* (s), *Another Country* (b/f/pl),

Another One Bites the Dust (s), *Stay Another Day* (s), *The Thing from Another World* (f)

answer response, solution; be responsible, respond; dusty answer; answer back

answering *see* answer; answering machine, answering service

answers *see* answer; have/know all the answers

ant insect; fire ant, leafcutter ant, white ant; ant-hill

ante stake; ante meridiem; raise/up the ante

anteater South American mammal; scaly anteater, spiny anteater

anthem song; national anthem

anti against; anti-aircraft gun, anti-hero, anti-heroine, anti-inflammatory, anti-roll bar, anti-static, anti-vivisectionist

antic silly prank; *Antic Hay* (b)

anticipate act as a precursor of, expect

antique old valuable item; old

antiques *see* antique; *Acorn Antiques* (tv), *Antiques Roadshow* (tv)

anxiety worry; *Status Anxiety* (b)

anxious apprehensive, eager

any some, whichever; any amount, any time; any minute now, at any cost, at any moment, at any price, at any rate, by any chance, by any means, in any event; *Alice Doesn't Live Here Any More* (f), *Any Dream Will Do* (s), *Any Number Can Play* (f), *Any Old Iron* (s), *Any Questions?* (r)

anybody no person in particular; anybody's guess

anyhow carelessly, whichever way

anyone no person in particular; *Anyone Who Had a Heart* (s)

anything whatever; like anything; anything but; anything in trousers; *Anything Goes* (mus/s), *Anything You Can Do* (s)

apart in pieces, separated, separately; drift apart, fall apart, joking apart, poles apart, take apart, tear apart; apart from; come/fall apart at the seams

apartment flat; *The Apartment* (f)

ape primate; imitate; Barbary ape, great ape; *I Go Ape* (s)

apes *see* ape; *Planet of the Apes* (f)

apocalypse destruction on an awesome scale; *Apocalypse Now* (f), *Whoops Apocalypse* (f)

apostle disciple; apostle spoon

appalling causing extreme dismay to; terrible

apparatus equipment, structure

apparent obvious, ostensible; heir apparent

appeal attraction, charity's request, earnest request; attract, implore, request earnestly; court of appeal, sex appeal; appeal court; Lord of Appeal

appear come into sight, seem, turn up; appear in print, appear on the scene

appearance arrival, outward aspect; make an appearance, personal appearance, put in an appearance

appearances *see* appearance; keep up appearances; to all appearances; *Keeping Up Appearances* (tv)

appendix body sac, supplementary section of a book

appetite predilection, wish for food

applaud clap, praise

apple fruit; Beatles' record label, computer manufacturer; Adam's apple, cooking-apple, crab apple, custard apple, eating apple, love apple, oak apple, rotten apple, toffee apple; apple-cheeked, apple of your eye, apple pie, apple-pie bed, apple-pie order, apple sauce, apple strudel, apple tree; an apple a day keeps the doctor away, in apple-pie order, upset the apple cart; Big Apple, Oak-Apple Day; *The Apple Cart* (pl)

apples *see* apple; bob for apples, apples and pears

appliance domestic machine, putting into operation

application diligence, formal request, putting into operation, putting on of a substance

apply be relevant, put into practice, spread (a substance) on, request formally

appointed furnished, nominated; self-appointed, well appointed

appointment job, meeting, nomination; by appointment; *Appointment with Danger* (f), *Appointment with Death* (b/f), *Appointment with Venus* (f)

appreciate be grateful for, estimate highly, increase in value, understand

appreciation gratitude, increase in value, recognition of value, sympathetic critical review

apprehend arrest, understand

apprehension ability to understand, arrest

apprentice learner of a trade; *The Apprentice* (tv), *The Good Apprentice* (b), *The Sorcerer's Apprentice* (cl)

approach arrival, means of access; deal with, draw near

appropriate steal, take for your own use; suitable

approval acceptance; on approval, seal of approval, stamp of approval

approved agreed to, believed to be good; approved school

apricot fruit, orange-yellow colour; apricot brandy

approximate be close (to); estimated

apron pinafore; apron strings, apron-stage

apropos pertinent; with regard to; apropos of nothing

apt liable, suitable

aqua light turquoise colour, Latin for 'water'; sub-aqua; aqua vitae

arc curve; arc lamp, arc welding; Arc de Triomphe, Prix de L'Arc de Triomphe

arcade amusement centre, covered walkway, row of shops; amusement arcade, shopping arcade

arch curve, curved building feature, prefix meaning 'principal'; roguish; arch-enemy; Admiralty Arch, Marble Arch

archers bowmen; *The Archers* (r)

arches *see* arch; fallen arches; *Underneath the Arches* (s)

architect building designer; *The Belly of an Architect* (f)

archives old records; files away

area district, domain, surface measurement; catchment area, goal area, grey area, local area network, motorway service area, no-go area, penalty area, service area; area code

arena scene, stadium; tv arts programme

argue contend, quarrel; argue the toss

argument quarrel, reasoning; for the sake of argument

ark boat, holy chest; out of the ark; Ark of the Covenant, Ark Royal, Noah's Ark; *Raiders of the Lost Ark* (f), *Schindler's Ark* (b)

arm branch, limb; supply with weapons; chance your arm, side arm, strong-arm, twist your arm; arm in arm, arm-twisting, arm-wrestling; cost an arm and a leg, keep at arm's length, the long arm of the law; *The Long Arm of the Law* (s), *The Man with the Golden Arm* (b/f)

armed supplied weapons to; carrying weapons; one-armed bandit; armed forces; armed to the teeth

armies *see* army; *The Armies of the Night* (b)

armistice truce; Armistice Day

armour weapon-proof plating; body armour; armour-plated; knight in shining armour

armoured having a protective metal layer; armoured car

arms *see* arm; heraldic insignia, weapons; babe in arms, brothers in arms, call to arms, coat of arms, gentleman-at-arms, passage of arms, present arms, reverse arms, secure arms, serjeant-at-arms, shoulder arms, slope arms, small arms, trail arms, under arms, up in arms, with open arms; arms control, arms race; in the arms of Morpheus; Cardiff Arms Park, College of Arms; *Arms and the Man* (pl), *Babes in Arms* (mus), *A Farewell to Arms* (b/f), *Men at Arms* (b), *Open Arms* (s)

army fighting force, horde; army camp; Eighth Army, New Model Army, Red Army, Salvation Army, Territorial Army; *The Army Game* (tv), *Dad's Army* (tv), *Oliver's Army* (s), *Secret Army* (tv), *Seven Nation Army* (s), *You're in the Army Now* (f)

around approximately, here and there, on all sides; hang around, play around, run around, run rings around, shop around, turn around, wrap-around; around the clock, around the world; green around the gills, just around the corner, money makes the world go around, throw your weight around, what goes around comes around; *All around the World* (s), *Around the World in Eighty Days* (b/f), *I Get Around* (s), *Love Is All Around* (s), *Rock around the Clock* (f/s)

arouse awaken, excite, provoke

arranging adapting (music), organising, putting into order; flower-arranging

arrears money owed; in arrears

arrest detention in custody; stop, take into custody; citizen's arrest, house arrest, under arrest, wrongful arrest; arrest of judgement; *Cardiac Arrest* (f/tv)

arresting *see* arrest; eye-catching

arrive happen, reach a destination; arrive on the scene

arrow archer's missile, pointer; bow and arrow, an arrow in the quiver; Golden Arrow; *Broken Arrow* (f), *The Flame and the Arrow* (f), *Time's Arrow* (b)

arsenal arms store; London football team, Tube station

arsenic poisonous element; *Arsenic and Old Lace* (f)

art creative activity, knack; Yasmina Reza play; abstract art, body art, clip art, commercial art, fine art, martial art, noble art, objet d'art, op art, performance art, pop art, state-of-the-art, work of art; art form, art gallery, art historian, art history, art house; art for art's sake, the art of the possible, get down to a fine art, the noble art of self-defence; Art Deco, Art Nouveau; *Art Attack* (tv), *Art for Art's Sake* (s), *O Brother, Where Art Thou?* (f)

artery blood vessel, main transport route; pulmonary artery

artichoke vegetable; globe artichoke, Jerusalem artichoke

article grammatical determiner, item; newspaper piece; definite article, indefinite article, leading article; article of faith

articles *see* article; period of apprenticeship

articulate put into words; composed of distinct parts, eloquent

articulated put into words; hinged

artificial insincere, synthetic; artificial fertiliser, artificial intelligence, artificial respiration

artillery heavy weapons; Royal Artillery

artist painter, performer; graphic artist, make-up artist, pavement artist, performance artist, trapeze artist; artist in residence; *A Portrait of the Artist as a Young Man* (b)

arts *see* art; creative pursuits, non-scientific subjects; beaux arts, black arts, fine arts, graphic arts, liberal arts, martial arts, performing arts; arts and crafts; Arts and Crafts Movement, Bachelor of Arts, Royal Academy of Arts

ascend rise; ascend the throne

ascendant on the way up; in the ascendant

ascension act of rising; Ascension Day, Ascension Island

ascent upward climb, upward slope; *The Ascent of Man* (tv)

ash burnt remains, timber, tree; bone ash, fly ash, mountain ash; ash

blonde, ash-can; Ash Wednesday

ashes *see* ash; cricketing trophy; dust and ashes, sackcloth and ashes; ashes to ashes; rake over the ashes, rise from the ashes; *Ashes to Ashes* (s)

aside stage whisper; in reserve, separately; brush aside, set aside; aside from

ask enquire, invite, request; ask for trouble; I ask you

asking *see* ask; asking price; for the asking

asleep slumbering; fast asleep

aspect appearance, facet, outlook, viewpoint

aspects *see* aspect; *Aspects of Love* (mus)

asphalt bituminous substance; *The Asphalt Jungle* (f)

aspidistra house plant; *Keep the Aspidistra Flying* (b), *The Biggest Aspidistra in the World* (s)

ass beast of burden, fool; *The Devil Is an Ass* (pl)

assault physical attack; attack violently; assault course; *Assault on Precinct 13* (f)

assemble congregate, put together

assembly gathering of people, putting together; general assembly, legislative assembly, self-assembly; assembly line, assembly rooms; National Assembly, Welsh Assembly; *Riotous Assembly* (b)

assent agreement; agree; royal assent

assessment evaluation; continuous assessment, self-assessment, standard assessment task

asset advantage, item of value; asset-stripping

assets *see* asset; trader's property; fixed assets

assign allocate, appoint

assignment allocation, allotted task, legal process of transfer

assistance help; National Assistance

assistant helper, shop worker; laboratory assistant, personal assistant, sales assistant, shop assistant

assisted helped; power-assisted; assisted place

associate colleague; connect, hobnob

association connection, society; free association, guilt by association, housing association, word association; association football; Football Association

assume pretend to have, suppose, undertake

assumption acceptance, pretence, supposition; Roman Catholic feast day

assurance certainty, confidence, life cover, promise; life assurance, self-assurance

assure convince, guarantee, make certain, provide life cover for

astray into trouble, missing; go astray, lead astray

astringent cosmetic toning lotion; harsh

astronomer person who studies the stars; Astronomer Royal

astronomical celestial, gigantic

asymmetric unevenly balanced; asymmetric bars

ate *see* eat; Greek goddess

athlete sportsperson; athlete's foot

athletic sporty; part of a football team name; Charlton Athletic, Oldham Athletic, Wigan Athletic

atlas bodybuilder, book of maps; mountain range, Titan in Greek mythology; Atlas Mountains; *Atlas Shrugged* (b)

atmoshere air, ambience

atmospheric relating to the air, with an ambience; atmospheric pressure

atom particle of matter, very small quantity, atom bomb

atonement act of reparation; Ian McEwan novel; Day of Atonement

atrophy wasting away; waste away

attaché embassy official; cultural attaché, military attaché; attaché case

attached joined; fond; no strings attached

attachment affection, email enclosure, extra part, legal seizure, attachment of earnings

attack criticism, offensive move; assault, criticise; counter-attack, heart attack, panic attack; *Art Attack* (tv)

attacks *see* attack; *Mars Attacks!* (f)

attempt effort; try

attend be present, listen, wait on

attendance number present, presence; dance attendance on, in attendance

attendant aide, worker in a cloakroom etc; accompanying; cloakroom attendant, lift attendant

attention care, mental concentration, notice; pay attention, stand to attention

attentive alert, considerate

attic roof space; relating to Athens; *Cash in the Attic* (tv)

attorney legal proxy, US lawyer; district attorney, power of attorney; Attorney-General

attraction lure, magnetic pull, place that draws visitors; chemical attraction; *Fatal Attraction* (f), *The Main Attraction* (s)

attractive appealing, good-looking

attribute feature; assign

aubergine eggplant, purple colour;

aubergine parmigiana

auction sale; sell; Dutch auction; auction bridge, auction room; on the auction block; *House Auction* (tv)

audience formal interview, viewers or listeners

audio relating to sound; audio typist, audio-visual

audit inspection of accounts; check the accounts of; National Audit Office

audition job interview for actors; take part in such an interview

aught anything; for aught I know

augur soothsayer; foretell

august venerable; month; *August is a Wicked Month* (b), *The Teahouse of the August Moon* (f)

aunt parent's sister; agony aunt, great-aunt, maiden aunt; Aunt Sally; *Charley's Aunt* (pl), *Travels with My Aunt* (b)

auntie *see* aunt; the BBC

aura atmosphere, human energy field

auspices patronage, portentous signs; under the auspices of

author writer; be the writer of; budding author, co-author; *Six Characters in Search of an Author* (pl)

authorised gave official permission to; officially approved; Authorised Version

authoritative reliable, self-confident

authority expert, legal power; local authority, unitary authority

auto car; concerning cars; auto-exposure, auto-suggestion; *Auto-da-Fe* (b), *Grand Theft Auto* (ga)

autograph signature; autograph hunter

automated mechanised; automated teller machine

automatic type of car transmission; involuntary, self-operating; semi-automatic; automatic pilot, automatic writing

auxiliary assistant; supplementary

avengers those seeking retribution; *The Avengers* (tv)

avenue method of approach, wide road; Fifth Avenue, Warwick Avenue; *Electric Avenue* (s), *The Prisoner of Second Avenue* (f), *Tenth Avenue Angel* (f)

Avenue
Electric, Fifth, Madison, Park, Pennsylvania, Shaftesbury, Warwick

average arithmetic mean; calculate the mean of; ordinary average wage

averages *see* average; law of averages

aviator pilot; *The Aviator* (f)

avoid circumvent, refrain from, shun

avoidance circumvention, eschewal; tax avoidance

avowed solemnly swore; self-confessed

awake rouse from sleep; no longer asleep; wide awake

awakening arousal; rousing from sleep; *Spring Awakening* (pl)

award prize; give a prize to; discretionary award; Academy Award

aware conscious, well informed; self-aware

away absent, at a distance, on the opponents' ground; beaver away, break away, carried away, explain away, far and away, fire away, frighten away, fritter away, get away, give away, give-away, go away, miles away, put away, right away, run away, stow away, straight away, take away, throw away, waste away, wear away, while away, whisk away, whittle away; an apple a day keeps the doctor away, blow away the cobwebs, get away with (blue) murder, get away with it, a heartbeat away, take your breath away, when the cat's away the mice will play; *Away in a Manger* (h), *Blown Away* (f), *Cast Away* (f), *Home and Away* (tv), *Not Fade Away* (s), *Since You Went Away* (f), *Walk Away Renee* (s)

awe   fearful respect; fill with fearful respect; awe-inspiring

aweigh   off the seabed; *Anchors Aweigh* (mus)

awfully   very, very badly; *An Awfully Big Adventure* (f)

awkward   difficult, inconvenient, unco-operative, ungainly; *The Awkward Age* (b)

awry   askew, amiss

axe   chopper; discontinue; UK river; battle-axe, ice axe, have an axe to grind; *So I Married an Axe Murderer* (f)

axis   centre line; WWII alliance

aye   for always, old word for yes; aye-aye, aye aye

B

babble   idle talk, murmur of a brook; gibber

babe   infant, term of endearment; 1995 film about a pig; *Babe: Pig in the City* (f), *I Got You Babe* (s)

babes   *see* babe; *Babes in Arms* (mus), *The Babes in the Wood* (pan)

babies   *see* baby; jelly babies; *The Water-Babies* (b)

baby   infant, term of endearment; mollycoddle; cry-baby, newborn baby, tar baby, test-tube baby, war baby; baby boom, baby boomer, baby-bouncer, baby buggy, baby doll, baby-doll nightdress, baby face, baby food, baby grand, baby walker; throw the baby out with the bathwater, wet the baby's head; Baby Bio; *The Baby and the Battleship* (f), *Baby Come Back* (s), *Baby Doll* (f), *Baby Face* (f), *Baby It's Cold Outside* (s), *Baby Love* (s), *Bringing Up Baby* (f), *Bye Baby Bunting* (s), *Bye Bye Baby* (s), *Cry-Baby* (f), *Dream Baby* (s), *Maybe Baby* (f/s), *Million Dollar Baby* (f), *Rosemary's Baby* (f), *See My Baby Jive* (s), *Someone Else's Baby* (s), *Sugar Baby Love* (s), *Tar Baby* (b), *Three Men and a Baby* (f), *What Ever Happened to Baby Jane?* (f)

bachelor   unmarried man; bachelor boy, bachelor party; Bachelor of Arts, Bachelor of Law, Bachelor of Music; *Bachelor Boy* (s), *Bachelor Mother* (f), *Bachelor Party* (f)

back   football defender, rear, reverse side, spine; accompany musically, place a bet on, reverse, sponsor, support; ago; answer back, bounce back, centre back, claw back, come back, cut back, double back, draw back, fall back, fight back, go back, go back on, hang back, hold back, keep back, kick back, knock back, laid-back, left back, money-back guarantee, play back, plough back, pull back, right back, roll back, set back, short back and sides, slap on the back, small of the back, stab in the back, take back, think back, throw back, tie-back, turn back; back and forth, back-bencher, back benches, back boiler, back-breaking, back door, back down, back end, back number, back of beyond, back off, back out, back pay, back room, back row, back seat, back slang, back straight, back street, back up, back-heel, back-pedal, back-projection, back-rest, back-seat, back-seat driver, back-stabbing, back-to-nature; back to back, back to front, back to square one, back to the drawing board, be glad to *see* the back of, bring back down to earth, by the back door, fed up to the back teeth, get your own back, make a rod for your own back, off the back of a lorry, on the back burner, a pat on the back, pin your ears back, put back the clock, take a back seat, the shirt off your back, watch your back, water off a duck's back; Hog's Back; *Baby Come Back* (s), *Back in the USSR* (s), *Back Off Boogaloo* (s), *Back to Life* (s), *Back to the Future* (f), *The Boys Are Back in Town* (s), *The Empire Strikes Back* (f), *Get Back* (s), *Holding Back the Years* (s), *How Stella Got Her Groove Back* (f), *Jay and Silent Bob Strike Back* (f), *Look Back in Anger* (pl), *Walk Right Back* (s), *Working My Way Back to You* (s)

backing   *see* back; musical accompaniment, rear layer, sponsorship, support; backing track

backwards   in a reverse direction; know backwards; backwards and forwards, bend over backwards

bacon   meat; English philosopher; smoky bacon; bacon and egg;
bring home the bacon, save your bacon

bad   naughty, rotten, unpleasant, wicked; go bad; bad blood, bad break, bad debt, bad egg, bad faith, bad form, bad hair day, bad luck, bad manners, bad-mouth, bad news, bad patch, bad-tempered, bad timing; bad news travels fast, a bad workman blames his tools, best of a bad bunch, in a bad way, make the best of a bad job, throw good money after bad, with bad grace; *The Bad and the Beautiful* (f), *Bad Boys* (f), *Bad Company* (f), *Bad Day at Black Rock* (f), *Bad Girls* (tv), *Bad Moon Rising* (s), *The Bad News Bears* (f), *Bad Timing* (f), *The Good, the Bad and the Ugly* (f), *Very Bad Things* (f)

badge   emblem; 1969 Cream hit; *The Red Badge of Courage* (f)

badger   nocturnal animal; harass; honey badger; badger-baiting

badly   *see* bad; badly off; *Men Behaving Badly* (tv)

badminton   racket game; Gloucestershire horse trials venue; badminton court

baffle   noise-reducer; perplex

bag   holdall; grab; air bag, bin bag, carpet bag, carrier bag, clutch bag, diplomatic bag, doggy bag, duffel bag, Gladstone bag, golf bag, goody bag, grow-bag, Jiffy bag, kit-bag, lucky bag, mixed bag, plastic bag, polythene bag, school bag, shopping bag, shoulder bag, sleeping bag, sponge bag, string bag, tea bag, toilet bag, tool-bag, tote bag, work-bag; bag and baggage, bag lady, bag of nerves, bag of tricks; in the bag, let the cat out of the bag

baggage   suitcases; bag and baggage, excess baggage; *Excess Baggage* (f/r)

baggy   loose-fitting; *Baggy Trousers* (s)

bags   *see* bag; circles under the eyes, lots; Oxford bags; pack your bags

bail   part of a wicket, surety money; secure the release of; jump bail, released on bail, stand bail, surrender to bail; bail-bond, bail out

bailey   castle wall; sea area; motte and bailey; bailey bridge; Old Bailey; *Rumpole of the Bailey* (tv)

bailiff   landlord's agent, sheriff's officer; civic head of the Channel Islands

bait   enticement, fish lure; taunt; rise to the bait

baiting   *see* bait; badger-baiting, bear-baiting

bake   cook, harden by heat; bake blind; *Can She Bake a Cherry Pie?* (f)

baked   *see* bake; half-baked, sun-baked; baked Alaska, baked beans

baker   bread supplier; baker's dozen; Baker Street; *Baker Street* (s), *The Fabulous Baker Boys* (f)

baking   *see* bake; sweltering; baking powder, baking soda

balaclava   woollen hood; 1854 Crimean battle; balaclava helmet

balance   amount of money, equilibrium, weighing device; equalise; spring balance; balance of payments, balance of power, balance of trade, balance sheet, balance wheel; catch off balance, in the balance, on balance, redress the balance, strike a balance, tip the balance

balcony   platform alongside a room; theatre gallery

bald   blunt, hairless; bald eagle, bald-headed, bald-pated; (as) bald as a coot

balderdash   nonsense; *Balderdash and Piffle* (tv)

bale   bundle, evil

ball   dance, sphere; beach ball, billiard ball, cricket ball, crystal ball, cue ball, fancy-dress ball, golf ball, have a ball, masked ball, medicine ball, no-ball, play ball, rugby ball, tennis ball, wrecking ball; ball and chain, ball-and-socket joint, ball-bearing, ball game, ball of the foot, ball of the thumb; the ball is in your court, get/keep/set/start the ball rolling, keep your eye on the ball, on the ball, spot the ball, the whole ball of wax; *Ball of Fire* (f), *Monster's Ball* (f)

ballad   narrative song; *The Ballad of John and Yoko* (s), *The Ballad of Davy Crockett* (s), *The Ballad of Peckham Rye* (b), *The Ballad of Reading Gaol* (po), *The Ballad of the Sad Cafe* (f)

ballads   *see* ballad; *Barrack-Room Ballads* (po)

ballerina   dancer; prima ballerina

ballet   form of dance; corps de ballet; ballet dancer, ballet shoes; *Ballet Shoes* (b)

ballistic   relating to projectiles; go ballistic; ballistic missile

balloon   inflatable sac; increase, swell out; barrage balloon, hot-air balloon, Montgolfier balloon, observation balloon, weather balloon; balloon whisk; go down like a lead balloon, when the balloon goes up; *The Moon's a Balloon* (b)

balloons   *see* balloon; *Ninety-Nine Red Balloons* (s)

ballot   voting occasion; organise a

vote among; second ballot, secret ballot; ballot box, ballot paper

ballroom   dance venue; ballroom dancing; *Ballroom Blitz* (s), *Strictly Ballroom* (f)

balls   *see* ball; *Great Balls of Fire* (mus/s)

balm   ointment; lemon balm, tiger balm

bamboo   tropical grass; *House of Bamboo* (f)

ban   prohibition; prohibit; ban the bomb

banana   fruit; banana belt, banana boat, banana republic, banana skin, banana split; *The Banana Boat Song* (s), *Banana Republic* (s), *The Banana Splits* (tv)

bananas   *see* banana; crazy; 1971 Woody Allen film; go bananas; *Herbie Goes Bananas* (f)

band   group, pop group, stripe, wavelength; come together; Alice band, beat the band, big band, brass band, citizens' band, dance band, elastic band, jazz band, jug band, one-man band, rubber band, steel band; Band Aid, Band-Aid; *Alexander's Ragtime Band* (s), *Band of Brothers* (tv), *Band of Gold* (tv), *Band on the Run* (s), *The Band Wagon* (mus), *Black Velvet Band* (s), *One-Man Band* (s), *Sgt Pepper's Lonely Hearts Club Band* (al/s)

bandage   medical dressing; dress (a wound)

bandit   outlaw; one-armed bandit; *The Kissing Bandit* (f), *Smokey and the Bandit* (f)

bandits   *see* bandit; *Time Bandits* (f)

bandy   exchange (words); bow-legged; bandy words, bandy-bandy

bane   poison, scourge; *Precious Bane* (b)

bang   loud noise; knock loudly, make a loud noise; precisely; slap bang, whizz-bang; bang on, bang the drum, bang up; with a bang; Big Bang; *Boom Bang-a-Bang* (s), *Chitty Chitty Bang Bang* (f)

bangers   old cars, sausages; bangers and mash

bangs   *see* bang; fringe; *She Bangs* (s)

bank   financial institution, mound, river's edge, store; depend (on), pay in, tilt in flight; London Tube station; blood bank, bottle bank, break the bank, central bank, clearing bank, fog bank, investment bank, merchant bank, piggy-bank, savings bank; bank account, bank card, bank clerk, bank draft, bank holiday, bank loan, bank manager, bank on, bank rate, bank statement; Bank of England, Dogger Bank, Jodrell Bank, Left Bank, National Savings Bank, South Bank, West Bank; *The Bank Dick* (f), *The South Bank Show* (tv)

banker   betting certainty, board-game dealer, financier, Newfoundland boat; Dick Francis novel; merchant banker; banker's draft, banker's order

bankrupt   insolvent; bankrupt stock

bankruptcy   insolvency; bankruptcy court

banks   *see* bank; *Agent Cody Banks* (f)

banner   flag; Star-Spangled Banner; *Star-Spangled Banner* (s)

banqueting   feasting; banqueting hall; Banqueting House

baptism   christening; baptism of fire

bar   bolt, drinking venue, drinks counter, lawyers as a group, slab, unit of atmospheric pressure; prohibit;

except for; anti-roll bar, bull bar, cocktail bar, coffee bar, crush bar, five-bar gate, heel bar, lounge bar, milk bar, public bar, scroll bar, space bar, wine bar; bar billiards, bar chart, bar code, bar line, bar mitzvah, bar none, bar stool; all over bar the shouting, called to the bar; *A Bar at the Folies-Bergère* (pa)

barb   aquarium fish, cutting remark, fish-hook; *Barb Wire* (f)

barbarian   brutish person; brutish; neither a Greek nor a Roman

barbecue   outdoor meal; grill over charcoal; barbecue sauce

barbed   covered with spikes, deliberately hurtful; barbed wire; *A Bouquet of Barbed Wire* (b/tv)

barber   hairdresser; barber's pole, barber-shop; *The Barber of Seville* (o)

barbican   fortified entrance; London arts complex; London Tube station

bare   naked; uncover; lay bare; bare bones, bare-knuckle; with your bare hands; *Night on a Bare Mountain* (cl), *The Bare Necessities* (s)

barefoot   not wearing shoes; *Barefoot in the Park* (f/pl), *The Barefoot Contessa* (f)

bargain   good deal; negotiate a price; drive a hard bargain, plea bargain, strike a bargain; bargain-hunter; *Bargain Hunt* (tv)

bargaining   *see* bargain; collective bargaining, plea-bargaining

barge   canal boat; shove; barge in

bark   sound of a dog; tree-trunk covering; make a noise like a dog; bark beetle; bark up the wrong tree, his bark is worse than his bite

barking   *see* bark; bonkers; London suburb; Barking and Dagenham

barley   cereal; lemon barley, pearl barley; barley mow, barley sugar, barley water, barley wine; *The Barley Mow* (s), *Nathan Barley* (tv)

barn   farm building; Dutch barn, tithe barn; barn dance, barn door, barn owl

barnacle   crustacean; barnacle goose; *Barnacle Bill* (f)

baron   nobleman; robber baron; baron of beef; Baron's Court

barrack   jeer; barrack-room lawyer; *Barrack-Room Ballads* (po)

barracks   *see* barrack; soldiers' housing

barrage   artificial dam, bombardment; barrage balloon

barred   marked with stripes, prohibited; no holds barred

barrel   keg, tube of a gun; put into vats; biscuit barrel, scrape the barrel; barrel-chested, barrel organ, barrel roll, barrel vault; the bottom of the barrel, (have) over a barrel, lock stock and barrel

barrels   *see* barrel; with both barrels

barren   lifeless, unproductive; *Those Barren Leaves* (b)

barrier   hurdle, protective rail; crash barrier, crush barrier, sound barrier; barrier cream, barrier reef; Great Barrier Reef, Thames Flood Barrier

barrow   ancient burial mound, pushcart; barrow-boy; Barrow-in-Furness

bars   *see* bar; asymmetric bars, behind bars, monkey bars, parallel bars, wall bars; Stars and Bars; *Stars and Bars* (b/f)

bartered   traded; *The Bartered Bride* (o)

base   foundation, headquarters, rounders position; establish, locate;

low; cloud base, touch base; base camp, base jumping, base metal, base rate

baseball us game; baseball cap

based *see* base; water-based

bash party; hit hard; have a bash; bash on

bashing *see* bash; Bible-bashing, spud-bashing, square-bashing

basic fundamental, unadorned; computer language; basic wage; *Basic Instinct* (f)

basin cooking bowl, natural hollow in the earth, sink; pudding basin; Minas Basin

basket shopping carrier; linen basket, Moses basket, picnic basket; basket of currencies; (don't) put all your eggs in one basket

basking species of shark; wallowing; basking shark

basque bodice; European language; relating to a Spanish/French region; Basque Country

bass fish, male voice; double bass, drum and bass, sea bass; bass clef, bass drum; Bass Strait

baste moisten when cooking, use tacking stitches

bat flying mammal, racket; play at the wicket; cricket bat, fruit bat, horseshoe bat, vampire bat; bat mitzvah, bat-eared fox; blind as a bat, off your own bat; *Bat out of Hell* (s)

batch quantity of goods; arrange in sets

bath tub; wash in a tub; English city; acid bath, bird-bath, blanket bath, bubble bath, dust bath, early bath, hip bath, steam bath, Turkish bath; Bath bun, bath chair, bath cubes,

bath mat, bath salts, bath-house; send for an early bath; Bath Oliver, Companion of the Bath, Order of the Bath

bathe swim, wash

bathing *see* bath and bathe; bathing costume, bathing machine, bathing suit

bathroom washing area; bathroom scales

baths *see* bath; swimming pool

batman officer's valet; 1960s superhero tv series, 1989 superhero film; *Batman Begins* (f), *Batman Forever* (f), *Batman Returns* (f)

baton stick; take up the baton; Baton Rouge

bats *see* bat; have bats in the belfry

batten strip of wood; strengthen with strips of wood; batten down the hatches

batter flour, egg and milk mixture, one hitting the ball in a game; hit repeatedly

battering *see* batter; battering ram

battery artillery emplacement, intensive farming system, portable source of electricity

batting *see* bat; cotton wadding; without batting an eyelid

battle military conflict; flight; Sussex town; ding-dong battle, join battle, losing battle, pitched battle, running battle, battle on, battle royal, battle stations, battle-axe, battle-cruiser; Battle of Bannockburn, Battle of Britain, Battle of the Bulge

battlefield war arena; *Battlefield Earth* (f)

battleship war vessel; *The Baby and the Battleship* (f), *The Battleship Potemkin* (f)

baulk   area of a billiard table; flinch
bay   alcove, coastal inlet, parking space, reddish-brown horse, shrub, type of window; howl; Dublin Bay prawns, keep at bay, loading bay, sick bay; bay for blood, bay leaf, bay window; at bay; Aboukir Bay, Algeciras Bay, Bantry Bay, Bay of Bengal, Bay of Biscay, Bay of Pigs, Botany Bay, Colwyn Bay, Galway Bay, Herne Bay, Hudson Bay, Robin Hood's Bay, San Francisco Bay, Tiger Bay; *The Stag at Bay* (pa)

> **Bay**
> Aboukir, Alum, Baffin, Bantry, Botany, Cardigan, Colwyn, Galway, Hawke, Herne, Hudson, Lyme, Morecambe, Robin Hood's, San Francisco, Tampa, Tiger

beach   shore; land on the shore; beach ball, beach buggy, beach-head; Palm Beach; *The Beach* (b/f), *Echo Beach* (s), *On the Beach* (b/f), *The Palm Beach Story* (f)
beacon   warning light or fire; Belisha beacon, radar beacon
beacons   *see* beacon; Brecon Beacons
bead   globule, necklace ball; *The Glass Bead Game* (b)
beads   *see* bead; worry beads
beagle   hound; Darwin's ship; British-built Mars probe
beak   bird's bill, magistrate, schoolmaster
beaker   tumbler; Beaker Folk
beam   joist, ray of light, widest part of a ship; smile broadly; cross-beam, full beam, laser beam, off beam; beam engine
bean   legume; 1997 Rowan Atkinson

film; black bean sauce, old bean; bean counter, bean curd, bean sprouts
beans   *see* bean; baked beans, black-eyed beans, borlotti beans, broad beans, butter beans, cannellini beans, cocoa beans, fava beans, French beans, garbanzo beans, jelly beans, jumping beans, kidney beans, lima beans, mung beans, pinto beans, refried beans, runner beans, soya beans, string beans; beans on toast; full of beans, spill the beans
bear   grizzly animal; carry, tolerate; black bear, brown bear, cave bear, grizzly bear, honey-bear, koala bear, Kodiak bear, polar bear, teddy bear, woolly bear; bear a grudge, bear-baiting, bear-cat, bear cub, bear fruit, bear hug, bear ill will, bear in mind, bear market, bear pit, bear up, bear witness; bring to bear, grin and bear it, like a bear with a sore head; Great Bear
beard   facial hair; old man's beard, Vandyke beard
bearing   *see* bear; demeanour, deportment, direction, heraldic device, relevance; ball-bearing, child-bearing
bears   *see* bear; *The Bad News Bears* (f)
beast   animal, brute; beast of burden; the nature of the beast; The Beast; *Beauty and the Beast* (b/f), *The Number of the Beast* (al/b/s)
beat   patrol area, rhythm; defeat, hit, outstrip, pulsate, whisk; dead beat, pound the beat; beat generation, beat hollow, beat it, beat the band, beat the bounds, beat the clock, beat the rap, beat time, beat up; beat a (hasty) retreat, beat about the bush, if you

can't beat them join them; Mersey Beat; *Beat It* (s), *Beat the Devil* (f)

beaten *see* beat; weather-beaten; off the beaten track

beater old carpet cleaner, person who disturbs grouse, whisking appliance; egg beater, panel beater, world-beater

beau dandy, suitor; French for 'attractive'; beau geste, beau monde; *Beau Geste* (f)

beautiful very attractive; *All Things Bright and Beautiful* (h), *The Bad and the Beautiful* (f), *The Beautiful and Damned* (b), *A Beautiful Mind* (f), *Beautiful Noise* (s), *Beautiful Stranger* (s), *Life Is Beautiful* (f), *My Beautiful Laundrette* (f), *Oh What a Beautiful Mornin'* (s), *Oh You Beautiful Doll* (s), *Small Is Beautiful* (b), *Together We Are Beautiful* (s), *Wonderful World, Beautiful People* (s), *You're Beautiful* (s)

beauty attractiveness, attractive woman; Camberwell beauty; beauty contest, beauty parlour, beauty queen, beauty salon, beauty sleep, beauty spot; beauty is in the eye of the beholder, beauty is only skin deep; *American Beauty* (f), *Beauty and the Beast* (b/f), *Beauty Shop* (f), *Black Beauty* (b), *Fatal Beauty* (f), *Sleeping Beauty* (b/f), *Stage Beauty* (f), *Weak in the Presence of Beauty* (s)

beaux *see* beau; beaux arts; *The Beaux' Stratagem* (pl)

beaver rodent, very young member of the Scouting movement; work hard; eager beaver; beaver away

because for the reason that; because of; *Because I Love You* (s), *Because the Night* (s), *I Love You Because* (s)

beck small stream; at your beck and call

becomes develops into, suits; *Death Becomes Her* (f), *Mourning Becomes Electra* (pl), *What Becomes of the Broken-Hearted?* (s)

becoming developing into; appropriate, flattering

bed bottom of the sea or river, flower patch, place to sleep; air bed, apple-pie bed, breakfast in bed, camp-bed, day-bed, double bed, feather bed, flower-bed, four-poster bed, go to bed, put to bed, reed bed, sofa bed, test bed, truckle bed; bed and board, bed and breakfast, bed of nails, bed of roses, bed-warmer; and so to bed, get out of bed on the wrong side, reds under the bed

bedding sheets and blankets etc, straw for animals to sleep on; planting out; bedding plant

bedroom sleeping chamber; bedroom farce; *Bedroom Farce* (pl), *Bedroom in Arles* (pa)

beds *see* bed; bunk-beds, twin beds

bedside area next to a sleeping place; bedside lamp, bedside manner

bee buzzing insect, spelling contest; bumble-bee, honey-bee, queen bee, spelling bee; bee orchid, bee-eater; bee in your bonnet, the bee's knees, busy as a bee; *Flight of the Bumble-Bee* (cl)

beech tree, wood; copper beech

beef meat from a cow; complain; baron of beef, bully beef, corned beef, roast beef; beef tea, beef tomato, beef up, beef Wellington

been (had) existed; has-been; *It's Been Nice* (s), *I've Been Wrong Before* (s), *Never Been Kissed* (f), *Since You've Been Gone* (f/s), *You've Been Framed* (tv)

beer ale; ginger beer, guest beer, ice

beer, root beer, small beer; beer and skittles, beer belly, beer cellar, beer garden, beer hall, beer mat, beer money

bees *see* bee; killer bees; the birds and the bees

beetle dice game, insect; Volkswagen model; overhang, scurry; bark beetle, carpet beetle, Colorado beetle, death-watch beetle, dung beetle, goliath beetle, rhinoceros beetle, stag beetle; beetle-browed, beetle-crushers, beetle drive, beetle off

beetroot dark red vegetable; (as) red as a beetroot

before ahead of, earlier than, previously; leg before wicket; before long, before the mast, before the wind; business before pleasure, carry all before you, cast pearls before swine, (don't) put the cart before the horse, learn to walk before you run, look before you leap, you have to crawl before you can walk; *Before She Met Me* (b), *Before Sunrise* (f), *Before Sunset* (f), *Before Winter Comes* (f), *A Kiss Before Dying* (f)

beg ask for money, implore; beg the question, beg to differ; I beg your pardon

beggar mendicant; beggar belief, beggar-my-neighbour; *Beggar-My-Neighbour* (tv), *The Beggar's Opera* (o)

beggars *see* beggar; beggars can't be choosers

begging *see* beg; go begging; begging letter

begin start; *Begin the Beguine* (s)

beginner novice; beginner's luck

beginners *see* beginner; *Absolute Beginners* (b/f)

begins *see* begin; charity begins at home, life begins at forty; *Batman Begins* (f), *Life Begins* (tv), *Life Begins at Forty* (tv)

behaved acted, acted correctly; well behaved

behaving *see* behaved; *Men Behaving Badly* (tv)

beheading method of execution; decapitating; *Invitation to a Beheading* (b)

behind posterior; at the back (of), in arrears; come from behind, fall behind; behind bars, behind closed doors, behind line, behind the scenes, behind time; wet behind the ears; *Behind a Painted Smile* (s)

being creature, existence; existing; human being, well-being; for the time being; *Are You Being Served?* (tv), *Being John Malkovich* (f), *Being There* (f), *The Importance of Being Earnest* (f/pl), *The Unbearable Lightness of Being* (b/f)

bel unit of sound; Bel Air, Bel Paese; *Bel-Ami* (b)

belfry church tower; Birmingham golf venue; have bats in the belfry

belief doctrine, faith, opinion; beggar belief, beyond belief

believe have confidence in, hold to be true, think; 1998 Cher hit; make-believe; *I Believe* (s), *Reason to Believe* (s)

believer adherent of a religion; non-believer; *Daydream Believer* (s), *I'm a Believer* (s)

believing *see* believe; seeing is believing; *Seeing Is Believing* (s)

bell chime; alarm bell, Canterbury bell, diving bell, division bell, dumb-bell, ring a bell; bell, book and candle, bell-bottoms, bell curve, bell jar, bell-ringing, bell tent, bell the cat, bell tower; (as) sound as a bell, clear as a bell, saved by the bell; Lutine Bell; *The Bell* (b), *The Bell Jar* (b), *For Whom the Bell Tolls* (b/f), *Ring My Bell* (s)

belle beautiful woman; belle époque; *Belle de Jour* (f), *La Belle Hélène* (o), *Memphis Belle* (f)

belles *see* belle; belles-lettres

bellows air pump; roars; centrifugal bellows

bells *see* bell; church bells, hell's bells, sleigh bells; bells and whistles; Bow Bells; *Jingle Bells* (s), *Summoned by Bells* (b), *Tubular Bells* (cl), *When Eight Bells Toll* (b/f)

belly stomach; beer belly, Delhi belly, pot belly, yellow-belly; belly button, belly dance, belly-flop, belly laugh, belly up; *The Belly of an Architecht* (f)

bellyful sufficiency; have a bellyful

belongs is part of; *Tomorrow Belongs to Me* (s)

beloved sweetheart; adored; Toni Morrison novel; dearly beloved; *Cry the Beloved Country* (b)

below further down, inferior to, less than, under; below decks, below par, below stairs, below the belt; sit below the salt

belt waistband, zone; hit hard; banana belt, black belt, cartridge belt, chastity belt, conveyor belt, fan belt, green belt, safety belt, seat belt, shoulder belt, stockbroker belt, suspender belt, tighten your belt; belt and braces, belt out, belt up; below the belt, under your belt; Bible Belt, Lonsdale Belt, Orion's Belt, Van Allen Belt

ben mountain; Ben Nevis; *Ben-Hur* (f)

bench judges collectively, long seat;

work table; cross bench, front bench, park bench, treasury bench; bench press, bench test; Queen's Bench

benches *see* bench; back benches

bend curve; make curved, stoop; carrick bend, hairpin bend, sheet bend; bend over, bend over backwards, bend sinister, bend the elbow, bend the knee; (go) round the bend; *Bend It Like Beckham* (f), *Bend Me, Shape Me* (s), *Bend Sinister* (b)

bender drinking binge; gender bender, mind-bender

bends *see* bend; decompression sickness

beneath at a lower level, inferior to, under; beneath contempt

benefit advantage, social security payment; be of use to; child benefit, cost-benefit, fringe benefit, sickness benefit, supplementary benefit, unemployment benefit; benefit match, benefit of the doubt

bent *see* bend; penchant; corrupt; hell-bent

beret soft flat hat; Green Beret, Red Beret; *Raspberry Beret* (s)

berry small fruit; brown as a berry

berth bunk on a ship, docking place; give a wide berth to

beside adjacent to, apart from; beside yourself

besides apart from, in addition

best outwit; finest, to the highest degree; get the best of, make the best of, man's best friend, personal best, second best, six of the best, Sunday best, the best of three, the best part; best bet, best bib and tucker, best bitter, best boy, best man, best of a bad bunch, best-selling, best wishes; all the best, at best, at the best of times, the best of both worlds, the best thing since sliced bread, the best things in life are free, do your level best, for the best, give it your best shot, honesty is the best policy, laughter is the best medicine, make the best of a bad job, may the best man win, put your best foot forward, to the best of my knowledge, with the best will in the world; *Best Friends* (f), *The Best Man* (f/pl), *The Best Things in Life Are Free* (s), *The Best Years of Our Lives* (f), *Diamonds Are a Girl's Best Friend* (s), *My Best Friend's Wedding* (f), *Personal Best* (f), *Your Hundred Best Tunes* (r)

bet   wager; place(d) a wager; best bet, each-way bet, safe bet; bet your bottom dollar, you bet, you can bet your boots; Shin Bet

beta   Greek letter, second-class mark; beta blocker, beta-carotene

bets   *see* bet; hedge your bets

betrayal   act of treachery; 1983 Jeremy Irons film

better   improve, surpass; finer, more suitable, recovered from illness; get better, get the better of, the better part; better half, better off; better late than never, better safe than sorry, better the devil you know, for better or worse, go one better, half a loaf is better than no bread/none, it is better to give than to receive, prevention is better than cure, so much the better, think better of it, two heads are better than one; *Better the Devil You Know* (s), *Nobody Does It Better* (s)

betting   *see* bet; spread betting; betting shop, betting slip

between   drive a wedge between, go-between; between a rock and a hard place, between ourselves, between you and me, betwixt and between, fall between two stools, few and far between, in between times, just between ourselves, read between the lines; *Between the Acts* (b), *Between the Lines* (tv), *The Go-Between* (b/f), *Just between Ourselves* (pl)

beware   watch out; beware of the dog; *Sailor Beware* (f), *Women Beware Women* (pl)

bewitched   captivated; under a spell; 1960s sitcom; 2005 Nicole Kidman film

beyond   apart from, further off than, further on, later than; back of beyond; beyond a joke, beyond belief, beyond description, beyond doubt, beyond measure, beyond recall, beyond reproach, beyond the pale; *Beyond the Fringe* (tv), *Beyond the Sea* (f), *One Step Beyond* (s)

bias   fabric's diagonal line, prejudice; bias binding

bib   baby's neck-cloth, top part of an apron; best bib and tucker

bible   any book regarded as authoritative, holy book; Bible-bashing, Bible-thumping; Bible Belt, Gideon Bible, Holy Bible, King James' Bible

bicycle   pedal-powered vehicle; ride a pedal-powered vehicle; bicycle pump, bicycle race, bicycle tyres; *Bicycle Race* (s), *Bicycle Thieves* (f)

bid   auction or other offer, bridge call; command, make an offer

bidding   *see* bid; procedure in whist or bridge; force the bidding

bide   stay; bide your time

big   important, large; 1988 Tom Hanks film; talk big, the big E, the big screen, the big time, think big; big band, big break, big business, big cat, big cheese, big deal, big dipper, big enchilada, big end, big fish, big game, big-game hunter, big girl's blouse, big gun, big-headed, big league, big money, big mouth, big noise, big shot, big time, big toe, big top, big wheel; big fish in a small pond, in a big way, too big for your boots; Big Apple, Big Bang, Big Ben, Big Bertha, Big Easy, Big Sur, Little Big Horn, Mr Big; *An Awfully Big Adventure* (f), *Big Break* (tv), *Big Brother* (tv), *Big Business* (f), *The Big Chill* (f), *The Big Country* (f), *The Big Easy* (f), *Big Girls Don't Cry* (s), *Big Impression* (tv), *The Big Issue* (mag), *Big Jake* (f), *The Big Kill* (b), *The Big Parade* (f), *The Big Sleep* (f), *Big Spender* (s), *Big Sur* (b), *Big Train* (tv), *Big Trouble in Little China* (f), *Big Yellow Taxi* (s), *Bright Lights, Big City* (b/f), *Little Big Man* (f), *My Big Fat Greek Wedding* (f)

bigger *see* big; have bigger fish to fry; *A Bigger Splash* (pa)

biggest *see* big; *The Biggest Aspidistra in the World* (s)

bike cycle; dirt bike, exercise bike, mountain bike, quad bike, trail bike; on your bike

bikini bathing suit; Pacific atoll; bikini briefs; *Itsy Bitsy Teeny Weeny Yellow Polka Dot Bikini* (s)

bill banknote, beak, draft law, invoice, poster, promontory; send an invoice to; double bill, electricity bill, fit the bill, foot the bill, gas bill, pay the bill, private member's bill, telephone bill, top the bill; bill and coo, bill of exchange, bill of fare, bill of lading, bill of rights, bill of sale; Old Bill; *Barnacle Bill* (f), *The Bill* (tv), *Bill & Ted's Bogus Journey* (f), *Kill Bill* (f)

billet bar of iron or steel, note, troops' quarters; billet-doux

billiards three-ball game; bar billiards

billion large number; *Billion Dollar Brain* (b/f)

billy goat; silly-billy; billy goat; like billy-o; Puffing Billy; *Billy Budd* (b/f/o), *Billy Don't Be a Hero* (s), *Billy Elliot* (f), *Billy Liar* (f/pl)

bin garbage can, storage container; throw away; bread bin, litter bin, sin bin, swing-bin, wheelie bin; bin bag, bin-end, bin-liner

bind annoyance; place under an obligation, tie, unite, wrap tightly

binder cementing agent, document holder; ring binder

binding *see* bind; book's cover; obligatory; bias binding, perfect binding

bingo numbers game; bingo hall

birch corporal punishment instrument, tree, wood; silver birch

bird feathered creature; 1988 Clint Eastwood film; butcher-bird, cage bird, diving bird, do bird, early bird, frigate bird, game bird, get the bird, give the bird, home bird, pilot bird, rare bird, secretary bird, water-bird; bird-bath, bird-brained, bird-call, bird-eating spider, bird-house, bird's nest, bird's-eye chilli, bird's-eye view, bird's-foot trefoil, bird's-nest soup, bird of paradise, bird of passage, bird of prey, bird-table; the early bird catches the worm, eat like a bird, not a dicky bird; *The Blue Bird* (f), *Bremner, Bird and Fortune* (tv), *I Know Why the Caged Bird*

Sings (b), *The Secretary Bird* (pl), *Sweet Bird of Youth* (f/pl)

birdie child's word for a feathered creature, one under par, in golf; watch the birdie; *Bye Bye Birdie* (mus), *The Birdie Song* (s)

birds *see* bird; birds of a feather flock together, fine feathers make fine birds, kill two birds with one stone, strictly for the birds, the birds and the bees; *Birds of a Feather* (tv), *Birds of America* (b), *The Birds* (f), *The Liver Birds* (tv), *The Thorn Birds* (b/tv)

birth arrival into the world, origin; 2004 Nicole Kidman film; date of birth, give birth, water birth; birth certificate, birth control, birth mother, birth rate, birth sign; *The Birth of a Nation* (f), *The Birth of Venus* (pa)

birthday annual celebration; official birthday; birthday cake, birthday card, birthday party, birthday present, birthday suit; Birthday Honours; *Birthday Girl* (f), *The Birthday Party* (pl)

biscuit beige colour, cookie, unglazed pottery; dog biscuit, sea biscuit, ship's biscuit, water biscuit; biscuit barrel, biscuit tin; take the biscuit

bishop chessman, church dignitary, mulled wine; Bishop Auckland, Bishop Rock, Bishop's Stortford

bit *see* bite; part of a bridle, part of a drill, small amount, unit of computing information; brace and bit, threepenny bit, two-bit; bit on the side, bit part; a bit much, a bit of all right, bit by bit, the biter bit, champ at the bit, hair of the dog that bit you, quite a bit; *A Bit of a Do* (tv)

bitch female dog; criticise; *Switch Bitch* (b), *The Bitch* (f)

bite mouthful, piquant flavour, snack, wound from a dog or insect; begin to take effect, sink the teeth into, sting; sound bite; bite the bullet, bite the dust, bite your tongue; bite off more than you can chew, bite the hand that feeds you, his bark is worse than his bite; *Love at First Bite* (f)

bites *see* bite; *Another One Bites the Dust* (s), *Reality Bites* (f)

biting *see* bite; freezing cold, sarcastic; nail-biting

bits *see* bit; thrilled to bits; *Bits and Pieces* (s)

bitten *see* bite; flea-bitten, hard-bitten; the biter bitten, bitten by the bug, once bitten, twice shy; *Once Bitten, Twice Shy* (s)

bitter variety of beer; acrimonious. resentful, sharp-tasting, very cold; best bitter, keg bitter, mild and bitter; bitter lemon, bitter orange, bitter pill, bitter-sweet; to the bitter end; *Bitter Moon* (f), *Bitter-Sweet* (mus), *Bitter Sweet Symphony* (s), *The Bitter Tears of Petra Von Kant* (f)

black colour; gloomy; jet black, pitch-black; black and blue, black and tan, black and white, black arts, black bean sauce, black bear, black belt, black bottom, black box, black bread, black cap, black cat, black coffee, black comedy, black economy, black eye, black-eyed beans, black-eyed peas, black-eyed Susan, black flag, Black Forest gateau, black friar, black grouse, black hole, black ice, black looks, black magic, black Maria, black mark, black market, black night, black out, black pudding, black sheep, black spot, black swan, black tie, black velvet, black widow; in the black, look on the black side; Black Country, Black Death, Black Forest, Black Hole of Calcutta, Black Magic, Black Monday, Black Russian, Black Sea, Black Watch, Penny Black; *Bad Day at Black Rock* (f), *Black Beauty* (b/f), *Black Books* (tv), *The Black Dwarf* (b), *Black Eyed Boy* (s), *Black Hawk Down* (f), *Black Magic Woman* (s), *Black Narcissus* (f), *Black Night* (s), *Black or White* (s), *The Black Prince* (b), *Black Rain* (f), *Black Spring* (b), *The Black Swan* (f), *The Black Tower* (b), *The Black Tulip* (b), *Black Velvet Band* (s), *The Boys from the Black Stuff* (tv), *The Bride Wore Black* (f), *Men in Black* (f), *Paint It Black* (s), *Pot Black* (tv), *White Hunter Black Heart* (f)

blackberry   soft fruit; hand-held email device; *Blackberry Way* (s)

blackbird   member of the thrush family; *Bye-Bye Blackbird* (s)

blackboard   teacher's writing surface; *The Blackboard Jungle* (b/f)

blacksmith   farrier; *The Chant of Jimmie Blacksmith* (f)

bladder   internal organ; gall bladder, swim bladder

blade   cutting edge, grass leaf, part of an ice skate; 1998 Wesley Snipes film; razor blade, shoulder blade; *Blade Runner* (f)

blame   responsibility; hold responsible; to blame; *Blame It on Rio* (f), *Blame It on the Bellboy* (f), *Blame It on the Boogie* (s), *Blame It on the Weatherman* (s)

blames   *see* blame; a bad workman blames his tools

bland   dull, tasteless; *The Tale of Pigling Bland* (b)

blandish   flatter; *No Orchids for Miss Blandish* (b), *Serena Blandish* (b)

blank   dummy bullet; empty, expressionless; draw a blank, point blank; blank cheque, blank verse; at point-blank range; *Blankety Blank* (tv), *Grosse Point Blank* (f), *Point Blank* (f)

blanket   bedcover; across the board; christening blanket, electric blanket, security blanket, wet blanket; blanket bath, blanket stitch

blare   loud, harsh sound; sound loudly

blarney   flattering talk; Irish castle; Blarney Stone

blast   explosion, strong rush of wind; use explosives; mild expletive; full blast; blast furnace, blast off

blaze   fire, mark on an animal's face; burn; blaze a trail; *Blaze of Glory* (s)

blazes   *see* blaze; go to blazes, like blazes

blazing   *see* blaze; *Blazing Saddles* (f)

bleach   whitening agent; whiten

bleak   cheerless; *Bleak House* (b/tv)

bleary   unfocused; bleary-eyed

bleed   drain, lose vital fluid, seep (of ink); bleed like a stuck pig

bleeding   *see* bleed; love-lies-bleeding; bleeding heart

blemish   flaw, pimple; spoil

blend   mixture; go together harmoniously, mix; Gold Blend

bless   confer divine favour on, consecrate; bless you; *Bless Me Father* (tv), *Bless This House* (tv), *God Bless America* (s)

blessing   *see* bless; approval, benediction, boon, divine favour; mixed blessing; blessing in disguise

blessings   *see* bless; count your blessings

blew *see* blow; *Honey, I Blew Up the Kids* (f), *Just Blew In from the Windy City* (s)

blight bane, plant disease; spoil

blimp airship; Colonel Blimp; *The Life and Death of Colonel Blimp* (f)

blind window covering; deprive of sight; exitless, unable to see; Austrian blind, bake blind, colour-blind, eff and blind, festoon blind, roller blind, Roman blind, sun-blind, swear blind, venetian blind; blind alley, blind date, blind drunk, blind man's buff, blind side, blind spot, blind stitch; blind as a bat, turn a blind eye; *Blind Date* (tv), *Three Blind Mice* (nr)

blinded *see* blind; *Blinded by the Light* (s)

blindness inability to see; night blindness, snow blindness, word blindness

blink flicker; in the blink of an eye, on the blink

bliss heavenly joy; British composer; Peter Carey novel

blithe carefree; *Blithe Spirit* (f/pl)

blitz bombardment, intense campaign; saturation bombing of London during WW2; the Blitz; *Ballroom Blitz* (s)

blob droplet; *The Blob* (f)

block group of flats, lump, obstacle, obstruction; obstruct; brake block, breeze block, chock-a-block, knife block, mental block, stumbling block, tower block, writer's block; block and tackle, block-booking, block capitals, block letters, block vote; chip off the old block, on the auction block, put your head on the block; *Prisoner: Cell Block H* (tv)

blocks *see* block; starting blocks

blonde fair-haired woman; fair-haired; ash blonde, bottle blonde, dumb blonde, platinum blonde, strawberry blonde; blonde bombshell; *Blonde Fist* (f), *Blonde Venus* (f), *Legally Blonde* (f), *My Favorite Blonde* (f), *Platinum Blonde* (f)

blondes *see* blonde; *Gentlemen Prefer Blondes* (b/f)

blood body fluid; bad blood, bay for blood, blue blood, fresh blood, give blood, prince of the blood, princess of the blood, red blood cells, rush of blood (to the head), spill blood, spit blood, sweat blood, young blood; blood and thunder, blood-and-thunder tale, blood bank, blood brother, blood count, blood-curdling, blood donor, blood feud, blood group, blood money, blood orange, blood poisoning, blood pressure, blood relation, blood sport, blood sugar, blood, sweat and tears, blood vessel; blood is thicker than water, have blood on your hands, in cold blood, in your blood, like getting blood out of a stone, make your blood boil, make your blood curdle, make your blood run cold; *Blood and Sand* (f), *Blood Brothers* (mus), *Blood Simple* (f), *Captain Blood* (f), *First Blood* (f), *Harry Potter and the Half-Blood Prince* (b), *In Cold Blood* (b/f), *Theatre of Blood* (f), *Wise Blood* (b/f)

bloody gory; bloody-minded; Bloody Mary; *Sunday Bloody Sunday* (f)

bloom flower; be in flower, thrive

blossom flower of trees; be in flower, prosper; *Cotton Blossom* (s)

blot eyesore, ink mark; tarnish; ink-blot test; blot out; blot your copybook

blouse   woman's shirt; big girl's blouse
blow   hard stroke, setback; exhale sharply, gust, pant, spend recklessly, waft; body blow, puff and blow, soften the blow, strike a blow against, strike a blow for; blow a fuse, blow a gasket, blow a hole in, blow-by-blow, blow-dry, blow fly, blow it, blow off steam, blow-out, blow over, blow the gaff, blow the socks off, blow the whistle on, blow up, blow your top; blow away the cobwebs, blow hot and cold, blow out of all proportion, blow your own trumpet; *Blow Fly* (b)
blowing   *see* blow; glass-blowing, mind-blowing, whistle-blowing
blown   *see* blow; full-blown; *Blown Away* (f)
blows   *see* blow; come to blows
blue   colour; Oxbridge sportsman; depressed; Adonis blue, black and blue, bolt from the blue, boys in blue, Cambridge blue, cobalt blue, Danish blue, electric blue, Kerry blue, midnight blue, navy blue, Oxford blue, powder blue, Prussian blue, royal blue, saxe blue, sky-blue, true blue; blue blood, blue-blooded, blue cheese, blue-chip, blue-collar, blue ensign, blue-eyed boy, blue flag, blue-green algae, blue helmet, blue lamp, blue moon, blue pencil, blue riband, blue rinse, blue-sky, blue tit, blue whale; Blue John, Blue Vinny; *The Blue Angel* (f), *The Blue Bird* (f/pl), *The Blue Boy* (pl), *The Blue Danube* (cl), *Blue Eyes* (s), *Blue Hawaii* (f), *Blue Is the Colour* (s), *The Blue Lagoon* (f), *The Blue Lamp* (f), *The Blue Max* (f), *Blue Murder at St Trinian's* (f), *Blue Peter* (tv), *The Blue Planet* (tv), *Blue Skies* (mus/s), *Blue Sky* (f), *Blue Steel* (f), *Blue Suede Shoes* (s), *Blue Velvet* (f), *Deep Blue Sea* (f), *The Deep Blue Sea* (f), *Devil in a Blue Dress* (f), *Electra Glide in Blue* (f), *Forever in Blue Jeans* (s), *Little Boy Blue* (nr), *Mr Blue Sky* (s), *NYPD Blue* (tv), *A Patch of Blue* (f), *Porterhouse Blue* (tv), *Rhapsody in Blue* (cl), *Soldier Blue* (f), *The Thin Blue Line* (tv), *True Blue* (al/s), *Union City Blue* (s), *Visions in Blue* (s)
blueberry   small soft fruit; *Blueberry Hill* (s)
blues   Oxbridge sportsmen, state of melancholy, style of music; rhythm and blues; *The Blues Brothers* (f), *Even Cowgirls Get the Blues* (f), *GI Blues* (f), *Hill Street Blues* (tv), *I Guess That's Why They Call It the Blues* (s), *Lovesick Blues* (s), *Summertime Blues* (s)
bluff   cliff, deception; deceive, pretend; plain-spoken; double bluff; *Call My Bluff* (tv)
blunder   mistake; make a mistake
blunt   lacking sharpness, outspoken
blurt   speak hastily; blurt out
blush   go red; at first blush
boa   feathered scarf, snake; boa constrictor
boar   male hedgehog or badger, pig; wild boar
board   game-playing surface, meals in lodgings, panel of directors, piece of timber; get on a vehicle, lodge; above board, across the board, bed and board, boogie board, bulletin board, circuit board, diving board, draining board, drawing board, emery board, full board, half board, idiot board, ironing board, leader board, mortar board, on board, ouija board, running-board, sandwich board,

skirting-board, sounding board, take on board, wobble-board; board meeting, board-game; back to the drawing board, go by the board, sweep the board; Board of Trade, Milk Marketing Board

boarding   *see* board; boarding card, boarding house, boarding kennels, boarding party, boarding pass, boarding school

boards   *see* board; theatre stage; tread the boards

boat   sailing craft, sauce dish; banana boat, canal boat, dragon boat, dragon-boat festival, E-boat, ferry boat, flying boat, gravy boat, mail boat, rowing boat, sailing boat, sauce boat, torpedo boat, U-boat; boat people, boat race, boat train; (don't) rock the boat, in the same boat, miss the boat, push the boat out; *The Banana Boat Song* (s), *The Boat That I Row* (s), *Don't Rock the Boat* (s/tv), *On a Slow Boat to China* (s), *Rock the Boat* (s), *Show Boat* (mus), *Three Men in a Boat* (b), *When the Boat Comes In* (tv)

bob   hairstyle, old shilling; duck down; plumb bob, ski-bob; bob and weave, bob for apples; Bob's your uncle; *Bob the Builder* (tv)

bobble   woolly ball; bobble hat

bobby   police officer; bobby-dazzler, bobby pin, bobby socks, bobby-soxer; *Bobby Dazzler* (tv)

bodice   dress-top, woman's undergarment; liberty bodice; bodice-ripper

bodies   *see* body; *Vile Bodies* (b)

body   corpse, fullness, human form, main part, organisation, tight-fitting garment, torso; foreign body, governing body, heavenly body, out-of-body experience; body and soul, body armour, body art, body blow, body-check, body clock, body double, body language, body piercing, body politic, body-popping, body scrub, body shop, body snatchers, body stocking, body warmer, body wave, body wrap; in a body, keep body and soul together, over my dead body; Body Shop; *Body Double* (f), *The Body in the Library* (b), *The Body Snatcher* (f), *Invasion of the Body Snatchers* (f)

bodyguard   minder; *The Bodyguard* (f)

bog   marsh; peat-bog; bog-standard

bogus   fake; *Bill & Ted's Bogus Journey* (f)

boil   carbuncle; cook in hot water, simmer; make your blood boil

boiled   *see* boil; hard-boiled, soft-boiled; boiled egg, boiled sweet

boiler   steam-generating vessel, tough old chicken; back boiler, pot-boiler; boiler suit

boiling   *see* boil; very hot; boiling point; keep the pot boiling

boils   *see* boil; a watched pot never boils

bold   fearless, heavily printed; bold as brass; *Bold as Brass* (tv)

boll   cotton seed pod; boll weevil

bolster   pillow; strengthen

bolt   crossbow arrow, nut's counterpart, roll (of cloth); eat hurriedly, lock, run off; coach bolt; bolt upright, bolt-hole; bolt from the blue, make a bolt for

bolts   *see* bolt; nuts and bolts

bomb   explosive device, lot of money; fail; atom bomb, buzz bomb, dive-bomb, incendiary bomb, sex bomb,

stink bomb, time bomb; bomb
disposal, bomb site, bomb squad; ban
the bomb, go down a bomb, go like a
bomb; *Sex Bomb* (s)

bomber warplane; dive-bomber;
bomber jacket

bombshell attractive woman, sudden
surprising news; 1933 Jean Harlow
film; blonde bombshell

bonanza big stroke of luck; classic tv
western series

bond close relationship, pledge; glue,
unite; bail-bond, junk bond; Bond
Street, Premium Bond

bondage servitude; *Of Human
Bondage* (b)

bonded *see* bond; warehoused;
bonded warehouse

bone corset stiffener, part of a
skeleton; fillet; funny bone, knuckle
bone, neck-bone, off the bone, on
the bone, rag-and-bone man, skin
and bone, T-bone steak, thigh bone,
to the bone; bone ash, bone china,
bone dry, bone idle, bone marrow,
bone of contention; close to the
bone, pare to the bone, work your
fingers to the bone; *The Bone
People* (b), *The Bone Collector* (f)

bones *see* bone; bare bones, make no
bones about; put flesh on the bones

bonfire outdoor blaze; Bonfire Night;
The Bonfire of the Vanities (b/f)

bongo drum; *Expresso Bongo* (f)

bonnet car engine cover, hat; Easter
bonnet, Scotch bonnet, sun bonnet;
bee in your bonnet

bonny pretty; *My Bonny Lies over the
Ocean* (s)

bonus extra gift; no-claims bonus

boo cry of disapproval; jeer; tickety-
boo; wouldn't say boo to a goose

boob slip-up; make a small error;
boob tube

booby silly person; booby prize,
booby-trap

boogie jazz music; dance to jazz;
boogie board; *Boogie Wonderland* (s),
Blame It on the Boogie (s), *Boogie
Nights* (f), *Born to Boogie* (f), *Broadway
Boogie-Woogie* (pl), *Get Up and
Boogie* (s), *I Love to Boogie* (s), *Yes Sir, I
Can Boogie* (s)

book printed work; reserve; cash
book, closed book, coffee-table book,
cookery book, double-book, exercise
book, guest book, hymn-book, map
book, open a book, open book,
phone book, phrase book, picture
book, pillow book, prompt book,
rent book, service book, statute book,
stud book, talking book, telephone
book; book club, book-ends, book in,
book-keeper, book-keeping, book of
hours, book token, book up; bell,
book and candle, bring to book, by
the book, don't judge a book by its
cover, every trick in the book, in my
book, oldest trick in the book, throw
the book at; Book of Kells, Domesday
Book; *The Book and the
Brotherhood* (b), *The Jungle Book* (b/f),
The Pillow Book (f), *Talking Book* (al)

booking *see* book; advance
reservation, referee's punishment;
block-booking; booking office

books *see* book; cook the books, on
the books, turn-up for the books;
Black Books (tv), *Prospero's Books* (f)

boom explosive sound, microphone
pole, sail support, time of prosperity;
bellow, reverberate, thrive; baby
boom, sonic boom; *Boom Bang-a-
Bang* (s), *Boom Boom* (s)

boon blessing; 1980s tv series; Mills and Boon

boost sudden surge; uplift

booster additional dose of vaccine, auxiliary rocket motor; booster seat

boot item of footwear, luggage compartment in a car; kick, start (a computer); car boot sale; boot camp; the boot is on the other foot, get the boot, put the boot in, to boot

booth kiosk; phone booth, polling booth, toll-booth; *Phone Booth* (f)

boots *see* boot; bovver boots, Chelsea boots, desert boots, moon boots, snow-boots, thigh boots, wellington boots; (as) tough as old boots, too big for your boots, you can bet your boots; *Puss in Boots* (pan), *These Boots Are Made for Walkin'* (s)

booty swag; *Car Booty* (tv), *Shake Your Booty* (s)

booze liquor; drink a lot; booze-up

bop dance; *Be Bop a Lula* (s)

bopper disco dancer; teeny-bopper

border edge, frontier; be adjacent to; herbaceous border; Border collie, border on

bore firearm's calibre, tedious activity or person, tidal wave; drill, stultify; smooth-bore

bored *see* bore; fed up; bored stiff; bored out of your mind

born brought into the world; first born, natural-born; born and bred, born-again; born to the purple, I wasn't born yesterday, to the manner born; *Born and Bred* (tv), *Born Free* (f/s), *Born in the USA* (s), *Born on the Fourth of July* (f), *Born to Be Wild* (s), *Born to Boogie* (f), *Born Yesterday* (f), *First Born* (f/tv), *Natural Born Killers* (f), *A Star Is Born* (f), *To the Manor Born* (tv), *Unto Us a Child Is Born* (s)

borough local government division; rotten borough

borrow slope on a putting green; take on loan

borrowed *see* borrow; live on borrowed time

bosom chest; bosom buddies

boss leader, raised stud; lord it over

botany merino (wool), study of plants; Botany Bay

both the two; burn the candle at both ends, have it both ways, keep both feet on the ground, the best of both worlds, with both barrels, you can't have it both ways; *Both Sides Now* (s)

bother ado; pester

bothered *see* bother; hot and bothered

bottle glass vessel, nerve; hot-water bottle, ink bottle, milk bottle; bottle bank, bottle blonde, bottle-feed, bottle green, bottle-opener, bottle out, bottle up; hit the bottle; *Message in a Bottle* (s), *The Bottle Factory Outing* (b)

bottom lowest point, rump; 1990s sitcom; black bottom, rock bottom; bottom drawer, bottom line, bottom out; at bottom, bet your bottom dollar, the bottom of the barrel, from the bottom of my heart, get to the bottom of; *Voyage to the Bottom of the Sea* (f)

boulder large stone; Colorado city

boulevard avenue; *Sunset Boulevard* (mus)

bounce elasticity; be returned by a bank (of a cheque), jump up and down; bounce back

bouncer cricket delivery, doorman; baby-bouncer

bouncy exuberant, springy; bouncy castle

bound *see* bind; leap; certain, obliged; desk-bound, homeward bound, muscle-bound, outward bound, pot-bound, spiral-bound; bound over; *Homeward Bound* (s), *Prometheus Bound* (pa/pl)

boundary cricket hit, frontier

bounds *see* bound; beat the bounds, in leaps and bounds, know no bounds, out of bounds; Bounds Green

bountiful abundant; Lady Bountiful

bounty reward; ship famous for a mutiny, brand-name chocolate bar; bounty hunter; *Bounty Hunter* (ga), *Mutiny on the Bounty* (f)

bouquet bunch of flowers, fragrance; bouquet garni; *A Bouquet of Barbed Wire* (b/tv)

bourbon chocolate biscuit, whiskey; French dynasty

bourgeois middle-class; petit bourgeois

bout boxing match, short period

bow act of bending the head, arrow-firing weapon, front of a ship, knot, violin rod; bend; Cupid's bow, dicky bow, ox-bow; bow and arrow, bow-fronted, bow-legged, bow out, bow tie, bow window, bow-wow; another string to your bow, bow and scrape, take a bow; Bow Bells, Bow Street, Bow Street Runners

bowl dish, US stadium; pitch, in cricket; dust bowl, finger bowl, goldfish bowl, rose bowl; bowl over; life is just a bowl of cherries; *The Golden Bowl* (b), *Life Is Just a Bowl of Cherries* (s)

bowler cricketer, hat; fast bowler, pace bowler, seam bowler, spin bowler; bowler hat

bowling *see* bowl; seam bowling, spin bowling, tenpin bowling; bowling alley, bowling green

bows *see* bow; shot across the bows; *Buttons and Bows* (s)

box container, evergreen shrub; cuff on the ear, put in a container, spar; ballot box, black box, call-box, cardboard box, cash box, chocolate box, Christmas box, cigar box, coin box, collecting box, cool box, dead letter box, dispatch box, fuse box, goggle-box, jack-in-the-box, junction box, jury box, letter-box, loose box, lunch-box, money box, music box, penalty box, phone box, pillar-box, PO box, police box, poor box, press box, royal box, sentry box, shadow-box, signal box, squeeze-box, telephone box, tuck-box, voice box, window box, wine box, witness box; box camera, box clever, box junction, box kite, box number, box-office, box pew, box pleat, box spanner; out of your box, think outside the box; Box Hill; *Juke Box Jury* (tv), *Musical Box* (tv), *Music Box* (f), *The Music Box* (f), *Pandora's Box* (f), *The Wrong Box* (f)

boxer breed of dog, fighter in a ring; Chinese rebellion; kick-boxer; boxer shorts

boxing fighting as a sport; kick-boxing, shadow-boxing; boxing gloves, boxing ring; Boxing Day

boy male child; altar boy, barrow-boy, best boy, blue-eyed boy, cabin-boy, golden boy, old boy, old boy network, page boy, paper boy, principal boy, rude boy, Teddy boy, toy boy, whipping boy, wide boy;

boy racer, boy wonder; boy meets girl; Boy Scout; *About a Boy* (b/f), *Bachelor Boy* (s), *Black Eyed Boy* (s), *The Blue Boy* (pa), *The Boy Friend* (mus), *A Boy from Nowhere* (s), *Boy on a Dolphin* (f), *Circus Boy* (tv), *Danny Boy* (s), *Elephant Boy* (f), *The Last Boy Scout* (f), *Mad about the Boy* (s), *Mary's Boy Child* (s), *My Boy Lollipop* (s), *Oh Boy* (tv), *Old Boy Network* (tv), *Shy Boy* (s), *Small Town Boy* (s), *Sonny Boy* (s), *Tell Them Willie Boy Is Here* (f), *The Winslow Boy* (f/pl)

boycott   refuse to deal with; punitive ban

boys   male children; boys in blue; boys will be boys, jobs for the boys; *Bad Boys* (f), *The Boys Are Back in Town* (s), *Boys Don't Cry* (f), *The Boys from the Black Stuff* (tv), *Boys' Town* (f), *Boys Will Be Boys* (f), *Catholic Boys* (f), *The Fabulous Baker Boys* (f), *The Lost Boys* (f), *The Sunshine Boys* (f), *Two Little Boys* (s), *Where the Boys Are* (f/s)

brace   old carpentry tool, orthodontic device, pair, strong support; strengthen; brace and bit

bracelet   wrist ornament; charm bracelet, friendship bracelet

braces   *see* brace; trouser straps; belt and braces

bracket   parenthesis, shelf support; link together; angle bracket

braid   bind with a ribbon; plait

brain   clever person, thinking organ; hit hard on the head; feather-brain, pea-brain; brain drain, brain-teaser; (have) on the brain; *Billion Dollar Brain* (b)

brains   *see* brain; intelligence; brains trust; rack your brains

brake   slowing-down device; decelerate; disc brake; brake block, brake horsepower, brake lining, brake pad, brake shoe

brakes   *see* brake; air brakes

bran   cereal fibre; bran tub

branch   limb of a tree, subdivision; divide (of a road); olive branch, root and branch; branch line, branch out; Special Branch; *Special Branch* (tv)

brand   mark of ownership, particular type, tradename; mark with a hot iron, stigmatise; own brand; brand leader, brand name, brand new; *I've Got a Brand New Combine Harvester* (s)

branding   *see* brand; branding iron

brands   *see* brand; Brands Hatch

brandy   cognac; apricot brandy, cherry brandy, Napoleon brandy, peach brandy; brandy butter, brandy glass, brandy snap

brass   copper/zinc alloy, effrontery, money, orchestra section; 1980s tv comedy series; top brass; brass band, brass monkey, brass tacks, brass-rubbing; bold as brass, get down to brass tacks, with brass knobs on; *Bold as Brass* (tv), *Brass Eye* (tv), *Brass in Pocket* (s)

brat   unruly child; brat pack; *Brat Camp* (tv), *Brat Farrar* (b)

brave   courageous; Native American warrior; *Brave New World* (b/f), *None but the Brave* (f), *Scotland the Brave* (cl)

bravo   cry of approval, radio code word; *Juliet Bravo* (tv), *Rio Bravo* (f)

brawn   meat product, physical strength

bray   cry of a donkey; speak loudly and harshly; County Wicklow resort, Berkshire village; *The Vicar of Bray* (s)

breach   infringement; violate; breach

of promise, breach of the peace; step into the breach

bread money, staple food; Carla Lane sitcom; black bread, break bread, brown bread, French bread, granary bread, laver bread, rye bread, soda bread, white bread; bread and butter, bread-and-butter, bread and wine, bread bin, bread knife, bread roll, bread sauce; the best thing since sliced bread, cast bread upon the waters, half a loaf is better than no bread; *Bread of Heaven* (h)

breadth distance across; hair's breadth

break fracture, interruption, short holiday; cease to function, fall to bits, make public, smash; bad break, big break, commercial break, even break, leg break, off-break, point break, tax break, tea break, tie-break; break away, break bread, break camp, break cover, break-dance, break dancer, break down, break even, break free, break in, break of day, break off, break out, break point, break ranks, break sweat, break the bank, break the habit, break the ice, break the law, break the mould, break through, break up, break-up; break a leg, break it up, break new ground, break your duck, break your heart, make or break; *Big Break* (tv), *Break On Through* (s), *I Want to Break Free* (s), *Never Give a Sucker an Even Break* (f), *Point Break* (f), *Prison Break* (tv)

breakdown collapse, decomposition, explanatory analysis, mechanical failure; *19th Nervous Breakdown* (s)

breaker car dismantler, large wave; circuit-breaker, ground-breaker, ice-breaker, jaw-breaker, record-breaker, safe-breaker, strike-breaker, tie-breaker; *Breaker Morant* (f)

breakers *see* breaker; *The Ghost Breakers* (f)

breakfast morning meal; to have your morning meal; bed and breakfast, continental breakfast, dog's breakfast, English breakfast, wedding breakfast; breakfast in bed; *Breakfast at Tiffany's* (b/f), *Breakfast in America* (s), *The Breakfast Club* (f)

breaking *see* break; back-breaking, ground-breaking, law-breaking, record-breaking, safe-breaking; breaking and entering, breaking point; *Breaking Glass* (mus), *Breaking Point* (b/ga), *Breaking Up Is Hard to Do* (s), *Don't Go Breaking My Heart* (s)

breaks *see* break; all hell breaks loose; *The Missouri Breaks* (f)

breast part of the body; chimney breast; make a clean breast of it

breath inhalation or exhalation, puff (of air), slight trace; draw breath, take breath; breath test; breath of fresh air, catch your breath, don't hold your breath, hold your breath, out of breath, save your breath, take your breath away, under your breath, waste your breath; *Every Breath You Take* (s)

breathe respire, whisper; breathe freely, breathe new life into; breathe down your neck, breathe your last, live and breathe

breathing *see* breathe; circular breathing; breathing space; as natural as breathing

bred *see* breed; born and bred, ill-bred, pure-bred, well-bred; *Born and Bred* (tv)

breed group within a species; bring

up, generate, reproduce; cross-breed; *This Happy Breed* (f/pl)

breeding   *see* breed; pedigree, refinement; breeding ground

breeds   *see* breed; familiarity breeds contempt

breeze   gentle wind; sea breeze; breeze block

breezy   casual, pleasantly windy; bright and breezy

brevity   succinctness; brevity is the soul of wit

brew   be in the offing, make (tea/ beer); concoction; home brew; brew up

bribe   corrupting gift; buy off

brick   clay-fired slab, trustworthy person; chicken brick; brick red, brick wall; *Another Brick in the Wall* (s), *Brick Lane* (b), *Goodbye Yellow Brick Road* (s)

bricks   *see* brick; bricks and mortar; like a cat on hot bricks, like a ton of bricks

bridal   nuptial; bridal suite

bride   new wife; Irish saint; *The Bartered Bride* (o), *Bride and Prejudice* (f), *The Bride of Frankenstein* (f), *The Bride of Lammermoor* (b), *The Bride Wore Black* (f), *The Bride Wore Red* (f), *Corpse Bride* (f), *Father of the Bride* (f), *I Was a Male War Bride* (f), *The Mourning Bride* (pl), *The Princess Bride* (f), *Runaway Bride* (f)

bridge   card game, ship's captain's platform, structure spanning a river; reach across; auction bridge, Bailey bridge, bascule bridge, contract bridge, duplicate bridge, humpback bridge, pontoon bridge, railway bridge, suspension bridge, swing bridge, toll-bridge; bridge of the nose, bridge roll, bridge-building; bridge the gap, water under the bridge; Bridge of Sighs, Clifton Suspension Bridge, Forth Bridge, Humber Bridge, London Bridge, Saltash Bridge, Stamford Bridge, Tower Bridge, Trent Bridge; *The Bridge* (pl), *The Bridge of San Luis Rey* (b), *The Bridge on the River Kwai* (f), *Bridge over Troubled Water* (al/s), *A Bridge Too Far* (f), *Composed Upon Westminster Bridge* (po), *A View from the Bridge* (pl)

Bridge
Albert, Barnes, Battersea, Blackfriars, Brooklyn, Charles, Chelsea, Chiswick, Clifton Suspension, Forth, Golden Gate, Hammersmith, Humber, Hungerford, Kew, Lambeth, London, Menai, Millennium, Putney, Richmond, Saltash, Severn, Southwark, Stamford, Sydney Harbour, Tay, Tower, Trent, Twickenham, Vauxhall, Wandsworth, Waterloo, Westminster

---

bridges   *see* bridge; burn your bridges; *The Bridges of Madison County* (f)

bridging   *see* bridge; bridging loan

bridle   horse's headgear item; curb, toss the head in anger; bridle path

brief   lawyer's instructions; instruct thoroughly; short; in brief, watching brief; hold a/no brief for; *Brief Encounter* (f), *The Brief* (tv), *The Pelican Brief* (f)

briefs   *see* brief; knickers; bikini briefs

brig   ship, ship's jail

brigade   military unit; fire brigade;

Light Brigade; *Fire Brigade* (s), *The Charge of the Light Brigade* (po)

bright clever, shining, sunny, vivid; honour bright; bright spark; (as) bright as a button, bright and breezy, bright and early, bright-eyed and bushy-tailed, look on the bright side; *All Things Bright and Beautiful* (h), *Always Look on the Bright Side of Life* (s), *Bright Eyes* (s), *Bright Lights* (f), *Bright Lights, Big City* (b/f), *Ring of Bright Water* (b/f)

brilliant diamond; extremely clever, shining with light; *My Brilliant Career* (f)

brim edge; reach the point of overflow; full to the brim

brimstone sulphurous mineral, yellow butterfly; fire and brimstone; *Brimstone and Treacle* (f/pl)

bring fetch; bring about, bring and buy sale, bring down, bring into question, bring out, bring to account, bring to bear, bring to book, bring to heel, bring to justice, bring to light, bring to pass, bring up; bring back down to earth, bring down the curtain, bring home the bacon, bring the house down, bring up the rear; *Bring Me Sunshine* (s), *Bring Me the Head of Alfredo Garcia* (f), *Bring on the Empty Horses* (b)

bringing *see* bring; *Bringing Up Baby* (f)

briny the sea; salty

brisk invigorating, quick

bristle stiff hair; show indignation

brittle nutty sweet; fragile

broach chisel; raise (a subject)

broad wide; broad beans, broad gauge, broad-minded; in broad daylight; Broad Church

broadcast radio or tv programme; scatter/scattered (seeds), transmit/transmitted; outside broadcast; *Broadcast News* (f)

broadens gets wider; travel broadens the mind

brogue regional accent, strong shoe ·

broke *see* break; penniless; flat broke, stony broke; go for broke, if it ain't broke don't fix it

broken *see* break; utterly demoralised; broken-down, broken-hearted; rules are made to be broken; *Broken Arrow* (f), *Morning Has Broken* (s), *What Becomes of the Broken-Hearted?* (s)

broker agent; honest broker, insurance broker, power broker

bronze copper/ tin alloy, third-place medal; bronze medal, bronze medallist; Bronze Age

brood group of baby fowl; ponder sadly

broody motherly (of a hen), pensive, wanting to have a baby

brook small stream; tolerate; Becher's Brook, Stamford Brook

broom brush, shrub; new broom; a new broom sweeps clean

broth soup; Scotch broth; too many cooks spoil the broth

brother fellow unionist, male sibling, male member of a religious order; blood brother, half-brother, lay brother, twin brother; brother-in-law; *Big Brother* (tv), *Brother, Can You Spare a Dime* (s), *Brother Sun, Sister Moon* (f), *He Ain't Heavy, He's My Brother* (s), *O Brother Where Art Thou?* (f), *Oh Brother* (tv)

brothers *see* brother; brothers in arms; *Blood Brothers* (mus), *The Blues Brothers* (f), *The Brothers*

Karamazov (b), *Super Mario Brothers* (f)

brow   crest (of a hill), forehead

brown   colour; grill; meadow brown; brown ale, brown bear, brown Betty, brown bread, brown coal, brown goods, brown rat, brown rice, brown sauce, brown sugar, brown trout; brown as a berry, how now brown cow, in a brown study; Brown Owl; *Brown Girl in the Ring* (s), *Brown Sugar* (s), *Father Brown* (f), *Golden Brown* (s), *The Innocence of Father Brown* (b), *Jackie Brown* (f), *Mrs Brown* (f), *Tom Brown's Schooldays* (b/f)

browned   *see* brown; browned off

brownie   chocolate cake; junior Guide; brownie points

browning   *see* brown; English poet; *The Browning Version* (pl)

browns   *see* brown; hash browns

browser   casual reader or shopper, internet-surfing program

bruise   contusion; contuse

brush   broom, fox's tail; dandy brush, nail brush, scrubbing brush, wire brush; brush aside, brush-up; daft as a brush, tar with the same brush; *Brush Strokes* (tv)

brute   cruel person; brute force

bubble   trapped pocket of air; fizz; air-bubble, hubble-bubble; bubble and squeak, bubble bath, bubble-car, bubble wrap

bubbles   *see* bubble; Millais painting; *Charlie Bubbles* (f)

buck   dollar, male deer or other animal, vaulting horse; kick against; Regency buck; buck-teeth; the buck stops here, buck up your ideas, (make) a fast buck, pass the buck; *Buck Rogers in the 25th Century* (f), *Regency Buck* (b), *Uncle Buck* (f)

bucket   pail; rain heavily; rust-bucket; bucket and spade, bucket seat, bucket shop; kick the bucket; *There's a Hole in My Bucket* (s)

buckets   *see* bucket; sweat buckets

buckle   strap fastener; warp; buckle down, buckle under

bud   plant shoot; begin to sprout; cotton bud, taste bud; nip in the bud

buddies   friends; bosom buddies

budding   *see* bud; budding author

buddy   friend; stage musical

budget   plan of expenditure, sum of money available; organise your finances; Budget Day

buds   *see* bud; *The Darling Buds of May* (b/tv)

buff   aficionado, fawn colour, leather with a velvety surface; polish; blind man's buff, film buff; in the buff

buffalo   bison; US city; water buffalo; buffalo wings; *American Buffalo* (f/pl), *Buffalo Girls* (b/f), *Buffalo Soldier* (f)

buffers   old codgers, shock absorbers; hit the buffers

buffet   cafe, self-service meal; beat against; buffet car

bug   insect, listening device, virus; eavesdrop on; May bug; bug-eyed; bitten by the bug; *A Bug's Life* (f), *The Love Bug* (f)

buggy   carriage, pushchair, small vehicle; baby buggy, beach buggy

bugle   small bead, small trumpet, wild flower; bugle call

build   physique; construct; self-build; build-up

builder   construction worker; *Bob the Builder* (tv), *The Master Builder* (pl)

building   *see* build; edifice; bridge-building, empire-building, jerry-building, sick building syndrome;

building site, building society; Empire State Building

built   *see* build; clinker-built, custom-built, in-built, jerry-built; built-in, built-in obsolescence, built-up; Rome wasn't built in a day

bulb   corm, light fixture; light bulb

bulge   protuberance; protrude; Battle of the Bulge

bulging   *see* bulge; bulging at the seams

bulk   majority, size; bulk buying

bull   centre of a target, male animal, nonsense, papal edict; cock-and-bull story, pit bull (terrier), Staffordshire bull terrier; bull bar, bull market, bull-mastiff, bull terrier; bull in a china shop, like a bull at a gate, (like) a red rag to a bull, take the bull by the horns; John Bull; *Bull Durham* (f), *John Bull's Other Island* (pl), *Little White Bull* (s), *Raging Bull* (f)

bulldog   stocky canine; bulldog clip; *Bulldog Drummond* (b/f)

bulldoze   demolish, force through

bullet   projectile; 1996 Mickey Rourke film; bullet train; bite the bullet

bulletin   newsletter, report; news bulletin; bulletin board

bullets   *see* bullet; rubber bullets; *Rubber Bullets* (s)

bullseye   target centre; darts tv quiz show

bully   intimidator; intimidate; bully beef, bully off; bully for her/him/you

bumble   drone, move in a clumsy way; bumble-bee; *Flight of the Bumble-Bee* (cl)

bump   minor collision, swelling; collide with; speed bump; bump into, bump off, bump-start

bumper   car's protective bar, cricket

bouncer, full glass; abundant; bumper car, bumper-to-bumper

bun   coil of hair, small cake; Bath bun, Chelsea bun, choux bun, currant bun, hot cross bun; have a bun in the oven; *Honey Bun* (s)

bunch   group; group together; bunch of fives; best of a bad bunch; *I've Got a Lovely Bunch of Coconuts* (s), *The Brady Bunch* (tv), *The Wild Bunch* (f)

bunches   *see* bunch; pigtails

bundle   loose parcel; wrap; bundle of nerves; a bundle of fun, go a bundle on

bung   football bribe, stopper; chuck, close with a stopper

bunged   *see* bung; bunged up

bungle   mismanagement; botch

bunk   bed; bunk-beds; do a bunk

bunker   coal container, golf sand trap, underground shelter; Bunker Hill

bunny   rabbit; Easter bunny; bunny girl, bunny-hop, bunny rabbit

bunting   songbird, stream of flags; corn bunting, reed bunting, snow bunting; *Bye Baby Bunting* (s)

buoy   floating marker; cheer up

buoyant   capable of floating, cheerful

burden   load; weigh down; beast of burden; burden of proof

bureau   agency, writing-desk; bureau de change; Citizens Advice Bureau

burglar   housebreaker; cat burglar

buried   *see* bury; dead and buried

burn   injury caused by fire, small stream; copy data (to a CD), go up in flames, scorch, set fire to; Chinese burn, first-degree burn, slash-and-burn; burn down, burn out, burn rubber, burn to a crisp; burn a hole in your pocket, burn the candle at both ends, burn the midnight oil, burn your bridges, burn your fingers; *First-Degree Burn* (b)

burner stove ring; Bunsen burner, incense burner; on the back burner

burning *see* burn; burning bush, burning desire, burning question; my ears are burning; *Babylon's Burning* (s), *London's Burning* (tv), *Mississippi Burning* (f), *The Lady's Not for Burning* (pl)

burns *see* burn; fiddle while Rome burns

burnt *see* burn; burnt ochre, burnt offering, burnt-out, burnt sienna, burnt to a cinder; get your fingers burnt; *A Burnt-Out Case* (b)

burr lilt, prickly seed-case, rough edge

burrow hole; excavate

burst explosion, rupture; explode, split open

bursting *see* burst; bursting at the seams

bury inter; Greater Manchester town; bury the hatchet, bury your head in the sand; Bury St Edmunds

bus public vehicle; transport in a public vehicle; bus conductor, bus driver, bus fare, bus lane, bus pass, bus shelter, bus station, bus stop, bus terminus; miss the bus; *Bus Stop* (f/s), *The Runaway Bus* (b)

buses *see* bus; *On the Buses* (tv)

bush shrub, wild scrubland; burning bush, gooseberry bush, mulberry bush, rose bush; bush fire, bush telegraph; beat about the bush; Shepherd's Bush; *The Bush Tucker Man* (tv), *Here We Go round the Mulberry Bush* (f/s)

bushel old eight-gallon measure; hide your light under a bushel

bushy shaggy; bright-eyed and bushy-tailed

business commerce, commercial company, concern, line of work; big business, funny business, in business, in the business of, mean business, monkey business, show business; business card, business park, business proposition, business studies; business as usual, business before pleasure, like nobody's business, mind your own business; *Big Business* (f), *The Business* (f), *Death Is a Lonely Business* (b), *Monkey Business* (f), *Show Business* (f), *A Small Family Business* (pl)

busk corset stay; perform in the street

busman PSV driver; busman's holiday

bust bosom, sculpture; shatter; bankrupt; bust a gut, bust-up; fit to bust; *Bognor or Bust* (tv), *Monte Carlo or Bust* (f)

busy police officer; occupied, over-ornate; busy Lizzie; busy as a bee

but except for, however; anything but, in all but name, nothing but, slow but sure; but then again; close but no cigar, it never rains but it pours

butch aggressively masculine; *Butch Cassidy and the Sundance Kid* (f)

butcher seller of meat; slaughter; butcher-bird; have a butcher's

butler servant; what the butler saw; *What the Butler Saw* (pl)

buts objections; ifs and buts

butt cask, cigarette end, end of a gun/snooker cue, target (of ridicule); hit with the head or horns, be joined end to end; water butt; butt in

butter dairy spread; brandy butter, bread and butter, bread-and-butter, cocoa butter, coconut butter, peanut butter, rum butter, shea butter; butter beans, butter-cream, butter-dish, butter muslin, butter up; fine words butter no parsnips

butterfly swimming stroke, winged insect; 1982 Orson Welles film; peacock butterfly; butterfly bush, butterfly effect, butterfly net, butterfly nut, butterfly stroke; *Madame Butterfly* (o)

button fastener; do up (a garment); belly button, panic button, snooze button, tummy button; button it, button mushroom; (as) bright as a button, button your lip, on the button; *Button Moon* (tv)

buttonhole small slit in a garment for fastening, flower in the lapel; detain in conversation; buttonhole stitch

buttons *see* button; pantomime character; *Buttons and Bows* (s)

buy bribe, purchase; bring and buy sale; buy and sell, buy off, buy time; buy a pig in a poke, buy a pup; *Can't Buy Me Love* (s)

buyer purchaser; first-time buyer; buyer's market

buying *see* buy; bulk buying, impulse buying

buzz atmosphere of excitement, humming sound, rumour; hum like a bee; buzz bomb, buzz off, buzz saw;

buzzard large hawk; Leighton Buzzard

bye direct transfer to the next round, extra cricket run; cheerio; leg bye; bye-bye; *Bye Baby Bunting* (s), *Bye Bye Baby* (s), *Bye Bye Birdie* (mus), *Bye-Bye Blackbird* (b/s), *Bye Bye Blues* (s), *Bye Bye Love* (s)

bygones relics of the past; let bygones be bygones

bypass relief road; go round

C

cab   taxi, trucker's compartment; hackney cab, hansom cab; cab driver, cab rank

cabaret   floor show; 1972 Liza Minelli musical film

cabbage   leafy vegetable; red cabbage; cabbage moth, cabbage white

caber   Highland pole; tossing the caber

cabin   berth, chalet; log cabin; cabin-boy, cabin class, cabin crew, cabin cruiser, cabin fever; *Cabin in the Sky* (f), *Uncle Tom's Cabin* (b)

cabinet   assembly of government ministers, cupboard; filing cabinet, kitchen cabinet, shadow cabinet; cabinet meeting, cabinet minister, cabinet pudding; *The Cabinet of Dr Caligari* (f)

cable   cord, telegram; send a telegram; cable-car, cable railway, cable stitch, cable television; *The Cable Guy* (f)

cackle   raucous laugh, sound of a chicken; laugh raucously; cut the cackle

cactus   spiny plant; Christmas cactus; *Cactus Flower* (f)

cadet   junior officer, trainee soldier; sea cadet, space cadet

cadge   scrounge; on the cadge

cafe   eatery; transport cafe; café au lait, café noir, cafe society; *Baghdad Cafe* (f), *The Ballad of the Sad Cafe* (f), *Cafe Society* (f), *Cafe Terrace at Night* (pa), *Fried Green Tomatoes at the Whistle Stop Cafe* (f)

cage   enclosure; imprison; gilded cage, safety cage; cage bird, cage in

caged   *see* cage; *I Know Why the Caged Bird Sings* (b)

cake   slab, sweet baked dough; encrust; angel cake, barm cake, Battenberg cake, birthday cake, Christmas cake, cream cake, devil's food cake, Dundee cake, Eccles cake, fairy cake, fish-cake, Genoa cake,

Kendal mint cake, lardy cake, layer cake, linseed cake, Madeira cake, marble cake, pat-a-cake, piece of cake, Pontefract cake, pound cake, rock cake, seed cake, simnel cake, sponge cake, tea-cake, tipsy cake, upside-down cake, wedding cake; the icing on the cake, a piece of cake, you can't have your cake and eat it; *Layer Cake* (f)

cakes *see* cake; cakes and ale; sell like hot cakes; *Cakes and Ale* (b)

calamity disaster; *Calamity Jane* (f)

calculated worked out; deliberate

calculating working out; scheming, shrewd

calculation assessment, mathematical determination, shrewdness

calendar 365 days on a chart, almanac; Advent calendar, Gregorian calendar, Julian calendar, perpetual calendar; calendar month, calendar year; *Calendar Girls* (f)

calf part of the leg, young of various animals; fatted calf, golden calf, in calf; calf love, calf's meat; kill the fatted calf

calibre degree of excellence, internal diameter of a gun's bore

call bridge bid, shout, summons; cry aloud, hail, name, phone, summon, visit; bird-call, bugle call, clarion call, close call, cold call, curtain call, house call, local call, on call, photo call, port of call, roll-call, trunk call; call a halt, call-box, call by, call centre, call off, call out, call sign, call to arms, call up; at your beck and call, call a spade a spade, call it a day, call it quits, call the tune, call to account, what-d'you-call-it; *Call Me Madam* (f), *Call My Bluff* (tv), *Call Off the Search* (al), *I Guess That's Why They Call It the Blues* (s), *I Just Called to Say I Love You* (s), *The Call of the Wild* (b), *You Can Call Me Al* (s)

called *see* call; so-called; called to the bar; *A Fish Called Wanda* (f), *A Man Called Horse* (f), *A Thing Called Love* (s), *A Town Called Malice* (s)

calling *see* call; vocation; calling card; *The Calling of St Matthew* (pl)

calls *see* call; he who pays the piper calls the tune; *An Inspector Calls* (pl), *House Calls* (f)

calm peace; pacify; peaceful, still; keep calm; calm down; (as) calm as a millpond; *Dead Calm* (f)

came *see* come; *Along Came a Spider* (f), *Along Came Polly* (f), *Father Came Too!* (f), *The Man Who Came to Dinner* (f), *The Rains Came* (f), *The Spy Who Came In from The Cold* (b/f)

camel humped animal; Cornish river; US cigarette brand; Bactrian camel; camel hair; *Carry On...Follow That Camel* (f)

cameo brief acting role, brooch; cameo role

camera device for taking photographs; box camera, in camera, off camera, pinhole camera, speed camera, video camera; camera obscura, camera-ready, camera shy; *Candid Camera* (tv), *I Am a Camera* (f), *My Camera Never Lies* (s)

camomile medicinal plant; *The Camomile Lawn* (b/tv)

camp faction, temporary settlement; pitch a tent; flamboyantly theatrical; aide-de-camp, army camp, base camp, boot camp, break camp, holiday camp, labour camp, nudist camp, prison camp, refugee camp, summer camp, work camp; camp commandant, camp-bed, camp-follower, camp out; Camp David; *Brat Camp* (tv)

campaign crusade, series of planned activities; electioneer; advertising campaign, smear campaign, whispering campaign

camper motor-home, person sleeping in a tent; more flamboyantly theatrical

campus university grounds; *Sweetheart of the Campus* (f)

can metal container; containerise, is able to, put an end to; ash-can, garbage can, in the can, petrol can, tin can, trash can, watering can; can of worms, can-do, can-opener; beggars can't be choosers, bite off more than you can chew, carry the can, catch-as-catch-can, if you can't be good be careful, if you can't beat them join them, a leopard can't change his spots, two can play at that game, you can bet your boots, you can say that again, you can't have it both ways, you can't have your cake and eat it, you can't teach an old dog new tricks, you have to crawl before you can walk; *Any Number Can Play* (f), *Anything You Can Do* (s), *Any Which Way You Can* (f), *Brother, Can You Spare a Dime?* (s), *Can-Can* (mus), *Can She Bake a Cherry Pie?* (f), *Can't Buy Me Love* (s), *Can the Can* (s), *Can You Forgive Her?* (b), *Catch Me If You Can* (f), *The Girl Can't Help It* (f), *Heaven Can Wait* (f), *I Can See for Miles* (s), *More Than I Can Say* (s), *Never Can Say Goodbye* (s), *Only Two Can Play* (f), *We Can Work It Out* (s), *Yes Sir, I Can Boogie* (s), *You Can Call Me Al* (s), *You Can't Hurry Love* (s), *You Can't Take It with You* (f)

canal artificial waterway, duct that conveys a fluid; alimentary canal, root canal, ship canal; canal boat; Caledonian Canal, Grand Canal, Kiel Canal, Panama Canal Suez Canal

Canal
Caledonian, Corinth, Grand, Grand Union, Kennet and Avon, Kiel, Manchester Ship, Panama, Suez

canary yellow songbird; canary yellow; Canary Islands, Canary Wharf; *The Cat and the Canary* (f)

cancel call off; cancel out

candid outspoken; *Candid Camera* (tv)

candidate applicant for a post, person seeking office; *The Candidate* (f), *The Manchurian Candidate* (f)

candle source of light; Roman candle; candle-holder; bell, book and candle, burn the candle at both ends, not worth the candle; *Candle in the Wind* (s)

candy American confectionery; preserve in sugar; Terry Southern novel, 1968 film based on a Terry Southern novel; eye candy; candy-striped; *Candy Man* (s)

cane bamboo, rod, sugar plant, wickerwork material; beat with a rod; sugar cane; cane fruit, cane sugar, cane toad

canine dog, sharp front tooth; concerning dogs; canine tooth

caning *see* cane; old form of school punishment, severe defeat, wickerwork

canned   preserved in a tin, recorded in advance

cannery   tinning factory; *Cannery Row* (b/f)

canning   *see* can; Canning Town

cannon   old heavy gun, snooker or billiards stroke; collide; 1970s US private-eye tv series; loose cannon, water cannon; cannon fodder; Cannon Street

canon   cathedral clergyman, church decree, general rule, major literary works; brand-name camera, office-products company; canon law

cant   humbug, hypocrisy, inclination from the level, language of thieves; tilt

canter   horse's pace; gallop gently; at a canter

canvas   heavy fabric, oil painting, surface for a painting, winning margin in rowing; under canvas

canyon   deep gorge; Grand Canyon, Torrey Canyon; *Grand Canyon* (f)

cap   award for playing for your country, brimless hat, lid, mushroom top; go one better than, put a ceiling on; baseball cap, black cap, cloth cap, cradle cap, death-cap, dunce's cap, filler cap, flat cap, fool's cap, forage cap, hub-cap, ice cap, ink cap, jockey cap, knee-cap, liberty cap, mob-cap, percussion cap, polar cap, rate-cap, screw cap, thinking cap, yachting cap; cap in hand, cap sleeve; feather in your cap, if the cap fits wear it, put on your thinking cap, to cap it all; *Red Cap* (tv)

capacity   ability, volume; cubic capacity

cape   cloak, headland; Cape Canaveral, Cape Cod, Cape Dutch, Cape Horn, Cape of Good Hope, Cape Town, Cape Verde; *Cape Fear* (f)

Cape
Canaveral, Cod, Finisterre, Horn, Town, Verde, Wrath, York

caper   amusing or far-fetched film, pickled flower bud, prank; frolic; cut a caper

capital   assets, country's main city, large letter, start-up money; excellent, punishable by death; venture capital, working capital; capital expenditure, capital gains, capital gains tax, capital letter, capital offence, capital punishment, capital transfer tax; make capital out of

capitalise   begin (a word) with an upper-case letter, convert (debt) into stock or shares, exploit

capitalist   magnate, supporter of free-market economics; relating to free enterprise; venture capitalist

capitals   *see* capital; block capitals

capped   *see* cap; chosen to play for your country, closed with a lid, covered (tooth); snow-capped

caprice   fickleness, whim; 1967 Doris Day film

capsule   detachable compartment, gelatine case for medicine; space capsule, time capsule; capsule hotel

captain   military rank, sports team's leader; command (a ship); group captain; captain's table; *Captain Blood* (f), *Captain Brassbound's Conversion* (pl), *Captain Corelli's Mandolin* (b/f), *Captain Pugwash* (tv), *Captain Scarlet and the Mysterons* (tv), *The Captain's Table* (f), *Sky Captain and the World of Tomorrow* (f)

captains *see* captain; *Captains Courageous* (f)
captivity confinement; in captivity
capture arrest, seizure; seize, take prisoner, win control of; data capture; *I Capture the Castle* (b/f)
car automobile, railway coach; armoured car, bubble-car, buffet car, bumper car, cable-car, club car, company car, dining car, estate car, hire car, motor car, pace car, panda car, patrol car, police car, Pullman car, racing car, restaurant car, saloon car, sleeping car, sports car, squad car, stock car, stock-car racing, touring car, used car, veteran car, vintage car; car boot sale, car crash, car dealer, car ferry, car park, car phone, car-pool, car-sick, car wash; *Car Booty* (tv), *Car Wash* (f/s), *Car 54, Where Are You?* (tv), *Fast Car* (s)
caramel burnt sugar, toffee-like sweet; crème caramel
caravan home on wheels, line of pack animals; caravan park, caravan site; *Caravan of Love* (s)
carbon element; carbon copy, carbon dating, carbon dioxide, carbon fibre, carbon monoxide, carbon paper
carbuncle large pimple, red precious stone
card ace of hearts etc, eccentric person, greetings token, stiff paper; comb (raw wool); bank card, birthday card, boarding card, business card, calling card, cash card, charge card, cheque card, cheque guarantee card, Christmas card, cigarette card, court-card, credit card, cue card, debit card, donor card, green card, greetings card, ID card, key card, loyalty card, place card, playing-card, red card,

report card, smart card, store card, swipe card, tarot card, test card, three-card trick, trump card, visiting card, warrant card, wild card, yellow card; card-carrying member, card game, card index, card player, card punch, card sharp, card swipe, card table, card vote; have a card up your sleeve; *Green Card* (f)
cardboard box-making material; flimsy; cardboard box
cardiac relating to the heart; *Cardiac Arrest* (f/tv)
cardigan button-up jumper; W Wales town
cardinal compass point, high-ranking RC priest, N American finch, shade of red; paramount; cardinal number, cardinal point, cardinal sin
cards *see* card; deck of cards, house of cards, marked cards, on the cards, pack of cards; hold all the cards, lay your cards on the table, play your cards right; *House of Cards* (b/tv), *Play Your Cards Right* (tv)
care concern, custody, heedfulness, worry; be concerned, give a hoot; day care, devil-may-care, in care, primary care, respite care, take care (of); care label; care in the community; Care Bears
career profession, progress through life; rush headlong; *My Brilliant Career* (b/f)
careful cautious; if you can't be good be careful
careless clumsy, negligent; careless driving; *Careless Hands* (s), *Careless Whisper* (s)
caretaker janitor; temporary (government); *The Caretaker* (pl)
cargo freight; cargo pants

caring   *see* Care; considerate

carnal   sexual; *Carnal Knowledge* (f)

carnival   fiesta; carnival queen; Notting Hill Carnival; *The Carnival Is Over* (s)

carol   Christmas song; sing Christmas songs, sing in a chirpy way; Christmas carol; carol-singers; *A Christmas Carol* (b), *Mickey's Christmas Carol* (f)

carp   freshwater fish; complain; crucian carp

carpenter   woodworker; *If I Were a Carpenter* (s), *The Walrus and the Carpenter* (po)

carpet   floor covering; cover a floor, reprimand; Axminster carpet, fitted carpet, magic carpet, Persian carpet, red carpet; carpet bag, carpet beetle, carpet slippers, carpet-sweeper; on the carpet, sweep under the carpet; *The Phoenix and the Carpet* (b)

carriage   deportment, horse-drawn vehicle, train coach; gun carriage, hackney carriage, horseless carriage, railway carriage; carriage and pair, carriage clock, carriage return

carriageway   road; dual carriageway

carrier   airline, goods conveyor, luggage rack, shopping bag, trained pigeon, transmitter of disease; aircraft carrier, people carrier, personnel carrier, troop carrier; carrier bag, carrier pigeon

carrion   dead flesh; carrion crow

carrot
incentive, root vegetable; carrot and stick

carry   approve by a vote, transport from one place to another; cash and carry; carry away, carry off, carry on, carry out, carry over, carry weight;
carry all before you, carry a torch for, carry the can, carry the day, fetch and carry; *Carry On at Your Convenience* (f), *Carry On Cleo* (f), *Carry On Constable* (f), *Carry On Cowboy* (f), *Carry On Cruising* (f), *Carry On ... Follow That Camel* (f), *Carry On Matron* (f), *Carry On Nurse* (f), *Carry On Regardless* (f), *Carry On Sergeant* (f), *Carry On Teacher* (f), *Carry On Up the Khyber* (f)

carrying   *see* carry; card-carrying member

cars   *see* car; *Z Cars* (tv)

cart   trailer, wagon; lug; horse and cart, in the cart; (don't) put the cart before the horse, upset the apple cart

cartoon   animated film, comic strip, satirical drawing; strip cartoon; *Cartoon Heroes* (s)

cartridge   bullet casing, container; cartridge belt, cartridge paper

carve   sculpt, slice; carve up; *Carve Her Name with Pride* (f), *What a Carve Up!* (b)

carving   *see* carve; sculpture; carving knife

case   container, example, grammatical inflection, lawsuit, luggage item, matter being investigated by the police, medical instance; check out (a joint); attaché case, display case, head-case, in any case, in case, just in case, long-case clock, lower case, meet the case, on my case, open-and-shut case, packing-case, slip case, special case, test case, upper case, vanity case; case history, case law, case study, case the joint; *A Burnt-Out Case* (b), *A Slight Case of Murder* (f)

cash   money; convert into ready

money; hard cash, petty cash; cash and carry, cash book, cash box, cash card, cash cow, cash crop, cash desk, cash dispenser, cash down, cash flow, cash in, cash in hand, cash on delivery, cash register, cash surrender value; cash in your chips, strapped for cash; *Cash in the Attic* (tv), *Tango & Cash* (f)

cashier   bank teller, checkout operator; discharge dishonourably

casing   protective covering; checking out (a joint)

casino   gambling establishment; 1995 Martin Scorsese film; *Casino Royale* (b/f)

cassette   container for a reel of film, tape; cassette deck, cassette player

cast   actors in a play, squint; appoint (an actor), fling, mould, scatter; die-cast, open-cast, plaster cast, worm cast; cast a spell, cast away, cast iron, cast lots, cast off; cast bread upon the waters, cast pearls before swine, the die is cast, ne'er cast a clout till may be out; *Cast a Dark Shadow* (f), *Cast a Giant Shadow* (f), *Cast Away* (f)

castaway   shipwrecked person; 1986 Oliver Reed film

castaways   *see* castaway; *In Search of the Castaways* (f)

casting   *see* cast; casting couch, casting vote

castle   fortress, rook in chess; move a king/rook in chess; bouncy castle; Arundel Castle, Edinburgh Castle, Elephant and Castle, Glamis Castle, King of the Castle, Maiden Castle, Windsor Castle; *Castle Rackrent* (b), *Crotchet Castle* (b), *I Capture the Castle* (b/f), *Queenie's Castle* (tv),

Takeshi's Castle (tv), *The Castle* (b), *The Castle of Otranto* (b)

Castle
Alnwick, Arundel, Balmoral, Bamburgh, Barnard, Blarney, Bodiam, Caernarfon, Carisbrooke, Colditz, Conwy, Donnington, Dover, Edinburgh, Fotheringhay, Glamis, Harlech, Hever, Kenilworth, Leeds, Ludlow, Maiden, Pevensey, Restormel, Richmond, Stormont, Tintagel, Warwick

---

castles   *see* castle; castles in the air

castor   swivelled furniture wheel; one of the 'Heavenly Twins'; castor oil; Castor and Pollux

casual   indifferent, informal, temporary (worker); casual labour

casualty   accident victim, A&E; tv hospital series; casualty ward

cat   feline, old naval punishment; alley cat, angora cat, bear-cat, big cat, black cat, Burmese cat, cat's eye, fat cat, Manx cat, Persian cat, scaredy-cat, Siamese cat, tabby cat; cat and fiddle, cat and mouse, cat burglar, cat flap, CAT scan, cat-o'-nine-tails, cat's cradle, cat's pyjamas, cat's whisker; bell the cat, cat in hell's chance, a cat may look at a king, the cat's whiskers, curiosity killed the cat, let the cat out of the bag, like a cat on a hot tin roof, like a cat on hot bricks, like a scalded cat, no room to swing a cat, put the cat among the pigeons, see which way the cat jumps, there's more than one way to skin a cat, when the cat's away the mice will play; Kit Cat Club; *Cat Ballou* (f), *Cat on a Hot Tin Roof* (pl), *The Cat and the*

Canary (f), *Felix the Cat* (f), *Top Cat* (tv)

catalogue   mail-order book; list; mail-order catalogue

catch   angler's haul, door-securing device, snag; arrest, become infected with, seize; safety catch; catch a cold, catch a crab, catch-all, catch fire, catch on, catch up; catch-as-catch-can, catch off balance catch your breath, catch your death of cold, first catch your hare, set a thief to catch a thief, a sprat to catch a mackerel; *Catch Me If You Can* (f), *To Catch a Thief* (f)

catcher   baseball player, trapper; rat-catcher; *The Catcher in the Rye* (b)

catches   *see* catch; the early bird catches the worm

catching   *see* catch; infectious; eye-catching

catchphrase   slogan; tv game show hosted by Roy Walker

caterpillar   butterfly or moth larva, steel track on a vehicle

cathedral   chief church; *Murder in the Cathedral* (pl)

catholic   member of the Church of Rome; wide-ranging; is the Pope a catholic; His Catholic Majesty, Roman Catholic, Roman Catholic Church; *Catholic Boys* (f)

cats   *see* cat; Lloyd Webber musical; rain cats and dogs; *Cats and Dogs* (f), *CATS Eyes* (tv), *Cool for Cats* (s), *The Truth about Cats and Dogs* (f)

cattle   cows; Highland cattle; cattle grid, cattle market, cattle thief

caught   *see* catch; caught up; caught in a cleft stick, caught in the act, caught red-handed, caught short, caught with your pants/trousers down

cauliflower   vegetable; cauliflower cheese, cauliflower ear

cause   ideal, reason; bring about; lost cause, root cause; cause and effect, cause célèbre, cause trouble; *Rebel without a Cause* (f)

causeway   raised path for crossing water or marshland; Giant's Causeway

caustic   corrosive, scathing; caustic soda

caution   circumspection, warning; advise (against), warn; err on the side of caution, throw caution to the wind

cautionary   admonitory; cautionary tales; *Cautionary Tales* (b)

cavalier   courtly gentleman; offhand; royalist in the English Civil War, Vauxhall saloon model; *The Laughing Cavalier* (pa)

cavalry   mounted soldiers; cavalry twill; Household Cavalry

cavalcade   parade; Noël Coward play

cave   underground chamber; go potholing; Latin for 'beware'; Aladdin's cave; cave bear, cave in, cave paintings; cave canem; *Fingal's Cave* (cl)

cavern   large underground chamber; Cavern Club

caving   *see* cave; mining method, speleology

cavity   hole, tooth hollow; cavity wall

cayenne   red pepper; capital of French Guiana; cayenne pepper

cease   stop; without cease; wonders will never cease

cedars   evergreen trees; *Snow Falling on Cedars* (b/f)

ceiling   room's inner roof, upper limit; glass ceiling, suspended ceiling;

Dancing on the Ceiling (s)

celebrated   made merry, marked a special occasion; illustrious

celebration   ceremony, honouring, party; 70s hit for Kool and the Gang

celebrity   fame, famous person; *Celebrity Fit Club* (tv), *Celebrity Squares* (tv), *I'm a Celebrity..., Get Me Out of Here!* (tv)

cell   battery compartment, jail room, smallest unit of an organism, small group of terrorists; dry cell, padded cell, prison cell, red blood cell, stem cell, white cell; cell-mate; *Prisoner: Cell Block H* (tv)

cellar   basement, salt container, wine store; store (wine); beer cellar, coal cellar, salt cellar, wine cellar

cellular   having holes that trap air; 2004 Kim Basinger film

cement   building material; join firmly; Portland cement; cement mixer; *The Cement Garden* (b)

cent   US coin; fifty per cent, hundred per cent, per cent; *The Seven-Per-Cent Solution* (f)

central   middle, principal; central bank, central heating, central locking, central nervous system, central reservation; Central African Republic, Central America, Central Line, Central Park, Finchley Central, Grand Central, Massif Central; *By Grand Central Station I Sat Down and Wept* (b)

centre   focus, middle; put in the middle; call centre, city centre, civic centre, community centre, day centre, dead centre, detention centre, garden centre, health centre, job centre, law centre, leisure centre, music centre, nerve centre, shopping centre; centre back, centre forward, centre of excellence, centre of gravity, centre spread, centre stage; right, left and centre; Centre Court, Metro Centre; *Journey to the Centre of the Earth* (b)

centred   *see* centre; child-centred, self-centred, soft-centred

centurion   Roman army officer; make of tank

century   100 years, 100 runs in cricket, Roman army unit; half-century; *Buck Rogers in the 25th Century* (f), *Sale of the Century* (tv)

ceremonies   *see* ceremony; master of ceremonies

ceremony   pomp, ritual; initiation ceremony, tea ceremony, without ceremony; stand on ceremony

cert   sure thing; dead cert

certain   particular, sure; make certain; for certain; *A Certain Smile* (b/f)

certainty   firm conviction, pre-determined event

certificate   proficiency document; provide with an official document; birth certificate, marriage certificate, medical certificate, self-certificate

certify   attest, declare insane

chaff   banter, corn husks; tease

chain   22 yards, set of links, string of islands or mountains; shackle; ball and chain, choke chain, daisy chain, food chain, paper-chain, watch chain; chain gang, chain letter, chain mail, chain reaction, chain-smoker, chain stitch, chain store; *Chain Gang* (s), *Chain Reaction* (s), *Puppet on a Chain* (b/f)

chains   *see* chain; *Take These Chains from My Heart* (s)

chainsaw   power-driven cutting tool;

The Texas Chainsaw Massacre (f)

chair professorship, seat; preside over (a meeting); bath chair, dentist's chair, easy chair, high-chair, rocking chair, sedan chair, swivel chair, Windsor chair, wing chair

chairman committee boss, company president; vice-chairman

chairs *see* chair; easy chairs, musical chairs; *The Twelve Chairs* (b/f)

chalice religious cup; poisoned chalice

chalk blackboard marker, calcium carbonate; write on a blackboard; late 1990s sitcom; French chalk; chalk and cheese, chalk and talk; by a long chalk; *The Caucasian Chalk Circle* (pl)

challenge accusation, test of abilities; dare, compete against, object to, stimulate; peremptory challenge; *Challenge Anneka* (tv), *University Challenge* (tv)

challenger champion's opponent, questioner; US space shuttle

chamber assembly room, compartment; decompression chamber, echo chamber, lower chamber, second chamber, torture chamber, upper chamber; chamber music, chamber of commerce, chamber of horrors, chamber pot

chambers *see* chamber; barristers' offices; Edinburgh-based dictionary publishers

chameleon inconstant person, lizard; *Karma Chameleon* (s)

champ N Irish potato dish, winner; munch; champ at the bit; *The Champ* (f)

champagne sparkling wine; champagne socialist; *Champagne Supernova* (s)

champions winners; defends; European Champions Cup; *We Are the Champions* (s)

championship sporting contest, strong advocacy; league championship; County Championship

champs *see* champ; Champs Elysées

chance destiny, luck, opportunity; risk; accidental; fighting chance, outside chance, sporting chance, treble chance; by any chance, cat in hell's chance, chance your arm, a fat chance, half a chance, on the off chance, stand a chance, take a chance, take your chance; *The Main Chance* (tv), *Take a Chance on Me* (s)

chancellor German head of government, senior state official, honorary university head; vice-chancellor; Chancellor of the Exchequer, Lord Chancellor

chancer opportunist, risk-taker; 1990s Clive Owen tv drama series

change alternation, loose coins; alter, put fresh clothes on; bureau de change, gear change, loose change, sea change, short-change, small change; change colour, change gear, change hands, change of air, change of scene, change over, change-ringing, change step; a change is as good as a rest, change your tune, chop and change, don't change horses in midstream, for a change, a leopard can't change his spots, plus ça change, plus c'est la meme chose

changes *see* change; permutations (in bell-ringing); 1975 David Bowie hit, 1987 Danielle Steel novel; ring the changes; *Mr Norris Changes Trains* (b)

changing *see* change; chopping and

changing; *Changing Rooms* (tv), *Changing Places* (f)

channel broad strait, duct, tv station; pay channel; Channel swimmer, channel-hopper; cross the Channel; Bristol Channel, Channel Islands, Channel Tunnel, English Channel, St George's Channel

chant cry of a crowd, incantation; sing; Gregorian chant; *The Chant of Jimmie Blacksmith* (f)

chaparral dense, tangled brushwood; *The High Chaparral* (tv)

chap bloke, cracked skin patch

chapel small church, trade union branch; lady chapel; Sistine Chapel; *Crying in the Chapel* (s)

chaps blokes, cowboy breeches

chapter book division, organised branch of a society, phase; chapter house; chapter of accidents, chapter and verse

char cleaner, tea, trout-like fish; scorch

character distinguishing feature, humorous or eccentric person, moral qualities, personality, person in a book or film, symbol; character actor, character assassination; out of character, strength of character

characters *see* character; *Six Characters in Search of an Author* (pl)

charade mime within a game, ridiculous pretence; 1963 Cary Grant thriller

charades popular parlour-game, ridiculous pretences

charge attack, cost, load, person or thing entrusted to someone's care; accuse formally, demand as a price, fill completely, storm forward; community charge, cover charge,

depth charge, drink-driving charge, service charge; charge account, charge card, chargé d'affaires, charge nurse; free of charge, in charge, put on a charge, take charge; *The Charge of the Light Brigade* (po)

charger battery replenisher, large serving dish, warhorse; knight on a white charger

charges *see* charge; press charges, reverse the charges

chariot ancient two-wheeled carriage; *Swing Low Sweet Chariot* (s)

chariots *see* chariot; *Chariots of Fire* (f)

charity philanthropy, theological virtue; charity begins at home; *Sweet Charity* (f)

charlie nincompoop, radio code word; perfume popular in the 1970s; tail-end Charlie; Checkpoint Charlie; *Charlie's Angels* (f/tv), *Charlie and the Chocolate Factory* (b/f) *Charlie Bubbles* (f)

charm appeal, talisman; attract, captivate; lucky charm; charm bracelet, charm offensive, charm school

charmed *see* charm; tv series about three sisters with magic powers

charmer attractive person, sorcerer; snake charmer; *The Charmer* (tv)

charming *see* charm; delightful; Prince Charming; *Prince Charming* (s)

chart diagram, map; plot; bar chart, flip chart, flow chart, pie chart, wall-chart

charter bill of rights, formal deed; hire; charter flight; Citizen's Charter

chartered *see* charter; chartered accountant

chase pursuit; pursue; paper chase,

wild-goose chase; chase the dragon, give chase, go and chase yourself

chaser drink taken after another, tracker; ambulance-chaser

chastity sexual abstinence; chastity belt

chat informal talk; talk casually; weekly women's magazine; chit-chat, fireside chat, langue de chat; chat room, chat show

chats *see* chat; *Fireside Chats* (r)

chattels belongings; goods and chattels

chatter uncontrollable rattle of teeth; talk rapidly

chattering *see* chatter; the chattering classes

cheap contemptible, inexpensive, shoddy; dirt cheap; cheap rate; cheap and nasty, on the cheap

cheats swindlers; deceives; cheats never prosper

check pattern of squares; curb, inspect; body-check, cross-check, double-check, Prince of Wales check, rain check, security check, sound-check, spot check; check in, check out, check up, check-up; in check, keep a check on, take a rain check

checkpoint manned border crossing, place on a race route; Checkpoint Charlie

cheek effrontery, side of the face; tongue-in-cheek; cheek by jowl, cheek to cheek, turn the other cheek

cheeky impudent; cheeky monkey

cheer cry of approval, gladness; applaud, gladden, shout for joy; cheer up

cheerful merry; *Reasons to be Cheerful* (s)

cheers *see* cheer; toast before

drinking; , 1980s American sitcom set in a bar; three cheers

cheese dairy product; big cheese, blue cheese, cauliflower cheese, Cheddar cheese, Cheshire cheese, cottage cheese, cream cheese, curd cheese, hard cheese, macaroni cheese, Monterey Jack cheese, Parmesan cheese, Swiss cheese, Swiss cheese plant; cheese and onion, cheese plant, cheese straws, cheese-paring; chalk and cheese, say cheese

chef restaurant cook; Lenny Henry 1990s tv comedy series; commis chef; chef-d'oeuvre; *The Naked Chef* (tv)

chemical lab substance; chemical attraction, chemical compound, chemical dependency, chemical engineer, chemical formula

chemist druggist, scientist; dispensing chemist, research chemist

chemistry attraction, physical science; chemistry set

cheque bank draft; blank cheque, traveller's cheque; cheque card, cheque guarantee card

chequebook pad of bank orders; chequebook journalism

chequered mixed (career), variegated; chequered flag

chequers divides into different coloured squares; country residence of the prime minister; Chinese chequers

cherries *see* cherry; nickname of Bournemouth FC; (life is just a) bowl of cherries; *Life Is Just a Bowl of Cherries* (s)

cherry new ball in cricket, small red fruit; cherry brandy, cherry-pick, cherry pie, cherry tomato; *Can She*

Bake a Cherry Pie? (f), *The Cherry Orchard* (pl)

chess   board-game; 1986 Tim Rice/Benny Andersson musical; chess club; *The Chess Players* (f)

chest   front upper body, set of drawers, trunk; community chest, sea chest, tea chest, treasure chest, war chest; chest of drawers

chestnut   edible tree-fruit, old joke, reddish-brown colour; horse chestnut, old chestnut, water chestnut

chew   munch; bite off more than you can chew, chew the cud, chew the fat

chewing   *see* chew; chewing gum

chi   22nd Greek letter, vital energy in Eastern medicine; tai chi; Ho Chi Minh City

chicken   poultry bird, white meat, youthful person; cowardly; coronation chicken, spring chicken; chicken à la king, chicken brick chicken-feed, chicken run, chicken-livered, chicken tikka masala, chicken wire; chicken and egg situation, chicken out, like a headless chicken; Mother Carey's Chicken; *Chicken Little* (f), *Chicken Run* (f), *The Chicken Song* (s)

chicks   young hens; *White Chicks* (f)

chief   leader; principal; air chief marshal, colonel-in-chief, commander-in-chief; chief constable chief inspector, chief of staff, chief petty officer, chief technician, chief whip; Lord Chief Justice

child   offspring, youngster; latchkey child, love child; child-bearing, child benefit, child-centred, child guidance clinic, child's play, child star; with child; Child Support Agency; *Child of Our Time* (tv), *Five Children and It* (b),

The Golden Child (f), *Love Child* (s), *Mary's Boy Child* (s), *Mother and Child Reunion* (s), *Sweet Child o' Mine* (s), *Unto Us a Child Is Born* (s)

children   *see* child; Save the Children Fund; *Children of a Lesser God* (f), *Children of the New Forest* (b), *Children of the Revolution* (s), *Methuselah's Children* (b), *Midnight's Children* (b), *Mother Courage and Her Children* (pl), *The Railway Children* (b/f)

chill   coldness, numbing fear, slight fever; refrigerate; cook-chill, wind-chill (factor); chill factor, chill out; *The Big Chill* (f)

chiller   cold cabinet, horror film; spine-chiller

chilli   hot dish, hot-tasting capsicum pod; bird's-eye chilli; chilli con carne, chilli powder

chilling   *see* chill; spooky; spine-chilling

chime   ringing sound; peal; chime in

chimes   *see* chime; tubular bells; wind chimes

chimney   smokestack; chimney breast, chimney pot, chimney stack, chimney sweep; smoke like a chimney

chin   front of the lower jaw; double chin; chin-chin, chin up; keep your chin up, take it on the chin; *Chu Chin Chow* (f)

china   porcelain; Asian country; bone china; china clay, China rose, China syndrome, China tea; bull in a china shop; Great Wall of China, Indo-China, South China Sea; *Big Trouble in Little China* (f), *China Doll* (f), *China Girl* (s), *On a Slow Boat to China* (s), *The China Syndrome* (f), *Visions of China* (s)

chink   narrow opening, noise made by coins

chinless   ineffectual, without a defined jawline; chinless wonder

chip   French fry, gambling counter, golf shot, piece of silicon in computers, small fragment, surface flaw; pare; blue-chip, chocolate-chip cookie, silicon chip; chip in; chip off the old block, have a chip on your shoulder

chipper   machine that turns timber into small pieces, potato-slicing machine; cheerful and lively

chipping   *see* chip; Chipping Norton

chippy   shop selling fried food; quarrelsome

chips   *see* chip; egg and chips, fish and chips; cash in your chips, chips with everything, when the chips are down; *Chips with Everything* (pl), *Curry and Chips* (tv), *Goodbye Mr Chips* (b/f)

chisel   carving tool; carve, cheat; cold chisel

chit   girl or young woman, receipt; chit-chat

chitty   receipt; *Chitty Chitty Bang Bang* (f)

chock   wedge; chock-a-block, chock-full

chocolate   dark-brown colour, sweet foodstuff; drinking chocolate, hot chocolate, milk chocolate, plain chocolate; chocolate box, chocolate egg, chocolate-chip cookie; *Charlie and the Chocolate Factory* (b/f), *Strawberry and Chocolate* (f), *Willie Wonka and the Chocolate Factory* (f)

choice   preference, selection; excellent; Hobson's choice, multiple-choice; spoilt for choice; *Sophie's Choice* (b/f)

choir   church singers, vocal group; choir practice

choke   engine valve; stifle; choke chain

choked   *see* choke; disappointed

choker   hard thing to accept, tight-fitting necklace

choose   select; pick and choose

choosy   fussy; brand-name cat food

chop   karate blow, meat cut; hack; karate chop, lamb chop, mutton-chop whiskers, pork chop; chop-chop, chop logic, chop suey, chop up; chop and change; *Pork Chop Hill* (f)

chopper   axe, helicopter, high-handlebarred motorcycle

chord   group of musical notes sounded together; strike a chord

chorus   backing singers, repeated part of a song; dawn chorus; chorus girl, chorus line; *A Chorus Line* (f), *A Chorus of Disapproval* (pl)

chow   Chinese breed of dog, nosh; chow mein; *Chu Chin Chow* (f)

christening   baptism; baptising, using for the first time; christening blanket

chronic   appalling, habitual, long-lasting (illness)

chronicles   annals; records; *The Anglo-Saxon Chronicles* (b), *The Martian Chronicles* (b)

chuck   device for holding a tool in a drill, word of endearment; throw; chuck it down, chuck it in; *Chuck E's in Love* (s)

chuffed   made the noise of a steam engine; very pleased

chump   blockhead; off your chump; *A Chump at Oxford* (f)

church   holy building, religious

organisation; ecclesiastical; church bells, church mouse, church school; Broad Church, Church Commissioners, Church of England, Church of Scotland, Episcopal Church, Free Church, Greek Orthodox Church, High Church, Low Church, Orthodox Church, Reformed Church, Roman Catholic Church, Russian Orthodox Church, Unification Church

churn butter machine, large milk can; agitate; churn out

chutney pickle of Indian origin; mango chutney

cider alcoholic apple drink; *The Cider House Rules* (b/f), *Cider with Rosie* (b)

cigar roll of tobacco leaves for smoking; cigar box; close but no cigar

cigarette tobacco product; cigarette card, cigarette holder, cigarette paper

cinch certainty, easy task, saddle girth

cinder ember; burnt to a cinder

cinema films, film theatre; cinema-goer, cinéma verité; *Cinema Paradiso* (f)

cipher code, zero

circle ring, social set, theatre seating area; go round; corn circle, crop circle, dress circle, magic circle, stone circle, vicious circle; come full circle, circle the wagons; Antarctic Circle, Arctic Circle, Circle Line; *The Caucasian Chalk Circle* (pl), *Circle of Friends* (f), *The First Circle* (b), *Full Circle* (tv)

circles *see* circle; go/run round in circles; *Ever Decreasing Circles* (tv)

circuit electrical route, lap, judge's round, round tour; closed-circuit, television, printed circuit, short circuit; circuit board, circuit-breaker,

circuit judge, circuit training; *Short Circuit* (f)

circular advertising leaflet; recurring in a cycle, round in shape; court circular; circular breathing, circular saw

circulation blood flow, periodicals sold, public availability; out of circulation

circus large traffic junction in a city, show with clowns and acrobats; three-ring circus; Oxford Circus, Piccadilly Circus; *Circus Boy* (tv), *Monty Python's Flying Circus* (tv)

citadel fortress, Salvation Army hall; *The Citadel* (b/f)

cities *see* city; *A Tale of Two Cities* (b/f), *Alice in the Cities* (f)

citizen native inhabitant of a country, urban resident; senior citizen; citizen's arrest; *Citizen Kane* (f), *Citizen Smith* (tv)

citizens *see* citizen; citizens' band; Citizens' Advice Bureau, Citizens' Charter

city big town; garden city, holy city, inner city; city centre, city desk, city farm, city hall, city slicker; Atlantic City, Carson City, City of London, City Technology College, Coventry City, Dodge City, Emerald City, The Eternal City, Ho Chi Minh City, Hull City, Jefferson City, Leicester City, Mexico City, Salt Lake City, Universal City, Vatican City, Welwyn Garden City, White City, Windy City; *Atlantic City* (f), *Babe: Pig in the City* (f), *Bright Lights, Big City* (b/f), *The City and the Stars* (b), *The City Gardener* (tv), *The City Heiress* (pl), *City Hospital* (tv), *City Lights* (f), *City Slickers* (f), *Holby City* (tv), *Just Blew*

In from the Windy City (s), *Sex and the City* (tv), *Sin City* (f), *Spin City* (tv), *Summer in the City* (s), *Union City Blue* (s)

> **City**
> Atlantic, Birmingham, Bristol, Carson, Coventry, Dodge, Emerald, Hull, Jefferson, Leicester, Manchester, Mexico, Norwich, Oklahoma, Salt Lake, Stoke, Universal, Vatican, Welwyn Garden, Windy

civic municipal; Honda model; civic centre

civil of the state, non-criminal (of law cases), polite; civil defence, civil disobedience, civil engineer, civil law, civil liberties, civil marriage, civil partnership, civil rights, civil servant, civil service, civil war; English Civil War, Civil List; *The Naked Civil Servant* (b/tv)

claim demand; allege, call for, profess; lay claim to, stake a claim

claims *see* claim; no-claims bonus, small claims court

clam bivalve shellfish; clam up

clamp gripping device, wheel lock; grip tightly; wheel clamp; clamp down

clanger blunder; drop a clanger

clap peal (of thunder), sudden blow; applaud; clap in irons

clapped *see* clap; clapped-out

clarion medieval trumpet; clarion call

clasp fastener; embrace, grip tightly; clasp knife

class category, group of pupils, social status, sophistication; cabin class, club class, first class, first-class post, high-class, middle class, second class, tourist class, upper class, working class, world-class; class act, class-conscious, class struggle; *A Touch of Class* (f), *The Ruling Class* (f)

classes *see* class; the chattering classes

classical music by old masters; influenced by Greek or Roman forms or principles, of lasting style; classical education

clause contract proviso, part of a sentence; escape clause, let-out clause, main clause, sub-clause, subordinate clause; *The Santa Clause* (f)

claw animal's nail; scratch (at); claw back, claw hammer

claws *see* claw; get your claws into

clay fine earth, potter's raw material; china clay, fire-clay; clay pigeon, clay pigeon shooting, clay pipe; feet of clay; *Concrete and Clay* (s)

clean purify; dirt-free; come clean, dry-clean, spring-clean, squeaky clean; clean and jerk, clean and tidy, clean bill of health, clean-cut, clean-shaven, clean sheet, clean slate, clean sweep, clean up; (as) clean as a whistle, keep a clean sheet, keep your hands clean, keep your nose clean, make a clean breast of it, make a clean sweep, a new broom sweeps clean, wipe the slate clean; *How Clean Is Your House?* (tv)

cleaner dirt remover, domestic help; less dirty; dry-cleaner, pipe cleaner, vacuum cleaner, window cleaner; *Confessions of a Window Cleaner* (f)

cleaners *see* cleaner; take to the cleaners

clear absolve, jump over, tidy up, unblock; cloudless, empty, obvious, transparent; all-clear, crystal clear; clear-cut, clear off, clear out, clear-sighted, clear up; (as) clear as a bell/crystal/mud, clear the air, the coast is clear, in the clear, keep clear, steer clear of; *Clear and Present Danger* (f)

clearance discharge (of a debt), official permission to go ahead, removal of contents; clearance sale

clearing *see* clear; forest glade; clearing bank, clearing house

clef musical notation symbol; alto clef, bass clef, roman-à-clef, treble clef

cleft rift; (caught) in a cleft stick

clementine small citrus fruit; *My Darling Clementine* (s)

clenched pressed tightly together; clenched-fist salute

clerical relating to office work, relating to church ministers; clerical collar, clerical error

clerk office worker; articled clerk, bank clerk, filing clerk, sales clerk, town clerk; clerk of the course, clerk of the court, clerk of the works

clever brainy, ingenious; clever clogs, clever Dick; box clever, too clever by half

click short sharp sound; fall into place, hit it off, snap (your fingers), use a computer mouse; clickety-click

climate atmosphere, general weather conditions; continental climate, Mediterranean climate; climate control; *Love in a Cold Climate* (b)

climb ascent; ascend, scale; climb down; *Climb Ev'ry Mountain* (s)

climber mountaineer, tall clinging plant; rock climber, social climber

climbing *see* climb; rock climbing; climbing frame, climbing wall; climbing the walls

clinch embrace; hug, settle (a deal)

cling variety of peach; hold on tightly

clinical cold, hospital-like, pertaining to the treatment of patients; clinical psychologist, clinical psychology, clinical thermometer, clinical trial

clinker brick with a vitrified surface, red powder used to polish steel, stony residue from burnt coal, wrong musical note; clinker-built; *The Expedition of Humphry Clinker* (b)

clip fastener, hairgrip, short extract; curtail, trim; bulldog clip, crocodile clip, jubilee clip, paper-clip, tie clip, toe-clip; clip art, clip-clop, clip joint, clip-on; clip the wings of

clipping *see* clip; newspaper cutting

clipper cutter, old sailing ship; tea clipper

cloak large cape; conceal, disguise; cloak-and-dagger

cloakroom hall closet for garments, lavatory; cloakroom attendant

clobber gear; hit

clock timepiece; attain (a time or speed), hit; alarm clock, biological clock, body clock, carriage clock, cuckoo clock, dandelion clock, grandfather clock, long-case clock, speaking clock, twenty-four-hour clock, water clock; clock golf, clock in, clock off, clock out, clock radio, clock tower, clock-watcher; around the clock, beat the clock, punch the clock, put back the clock, round the clock, watch the clock; *Rock around the Clock* (f/s)

clockwork timepiece mechanism; as regular as clockwork, like clockwork; *A Clockwork Orange* (b/f)

clog wooden shoe; block; clog dance

clogs   *see* clog; clever clogs; pop your clogs

cloister   covered walkway, place of religious retreat; seclude; *The Cloister and the Hearth* (b)

close   dead-end road, ending; end, shut; nearby, humid, stuffy; close by, close call, close down, close finish, close-fisted, close harmony, close in, close-knit, close-mouthed, close off, close ranks, close-run thing, close season, close shave, close thing, close up, close-up; at close quarters, at close range, sail close to the wind, too close for comfort, close at hand, close but no cigar, close the gap, close to the bone, close to home, close to the mark, close to your heart; *At Close Range* (b), *Close Encounters of the Third Kind* (f), *A Close Shave* (f), *Close (to the Edit)* (s), *Close to You* (s), *Up Close and Personal* (f)

closed   *see* close; shut; closed book, closed-circuit television, closed shop; behind closed doors

closes   *see* close; as one door closes another opens

closet   cupboard; secrete; covert; water closet; skeleton in the closet

closing   *see* close; early closing, early-closing day; closing date, closing down, closing time

cloth   (the) clergy, fabric, rag; face-cloth, floor-cloth, J-cloth, tea cloth; cloth cap, cloth-ears; cut from the same cloth, cut your coat according to your cloth, man of the cloth

clothes   garments; covers; plain-clothes man, swaddling clothes; clothes hanger, clothes-horse, clothes-line, clothes peg, clothes-prop; *The Clothes Show* (tv), *The Emperor's New Clothes* (b)

clothing   garments; covering; a wolf in sheep's clothing

clotted   congealed; clotted cream

cloud   haze, mass of water droplets in the sky; obscure; mushroom cloud, storm cloud; cloud base, cloud cover, cloud cuckoo land, cloud over; every cloud has a silver lining, on cloud nine, under a cloud; Morning Cloud; *Get Off of My Cloud* (s)

clouded   *see* cloud; clouded yellow; *The Clouded Yellow* (f)

clouds   *see* cloud; war clouds; Clouds Hill; *Obscured by Clouds* (s)

clout   blow, influence, nail with a large flat head; hit; ne'er cast a clout till May be out

clove   aromatic spice, section of garlic; clove hitch

clover   trefoil plant; four-leaf clover; in clover

clown   buffoon, circus funny man, joker; behave comically; *Cathy's Clown* (s), *Death of a Clown* (s), *The Tears of a Clown* (s)

clowns   *see* clown; *Send in the Clowns* (s)

club   playing-card, cudgel, golf iron, society; bludgeon; book club, chess club, country club, fan club, golf club, job club, supporters club, yacht club, youth club; club car, club class, club sandwich, club secretary, club soda, club together; in the club, in the pudding club; Darby and Joan Club, Hellfire Club, Jockey Club, Kennel Club, Kit Cat Club, Rotary Club; *The Breakfast Club* (f), *Buena Vista Social Club* (f), *Celebrity Fit Club* (tv), *Club Tropicana* (s), *The Cotton Club* (f), *Fight Club* (f), *The*

First Wives Club (f), *The Paradise Club* (tv), *Sgt Pepper's Lonely Hearts Club Band* (al/s)

clue   hint; provide a hint; *Give Us a Clue* (tv), *I'm Sorry I Haven't a Clue* (r)

clued   provided a hint; clued up

clutch   grasp, part of a car's transmission, set of bird's eggs; grip tightly; clutch bag; clutch at straws

coach   bus, carriage, private tutor, sports teacher; train; coach and horses, coach bolt, coach house, coach station, coach tour, coach trip

coaching   *see* coach; coaching inn

coal   carbon fuel; brown coal; coal cellar, coal dust, coal-face, coal-hole, coal-pit, coal scuttle, coal tar, coal tit; *Coal Miner's Daughter* (f), *King Coal* (b)

coalition   alliance of political parties; rainbow coalition

coals   *see* coal; coals to Newcastle, haul over the coals, rake over old coals

coarse   rough, vulgar; coarse fishing

coast   shore; freewheel; 2005 BBC documentary series; hug the coast, the coast is clear; Coral Coast, Gold Coast, Ivory Coast, Sunshine Coast; *The Mosquito Coast* (b/f)

coat   animal's fur, layer, outer garment; overlay; Afghan coat, dress coat, duffel coat, frock coat, fur coat, morning coat, pea coat, sugar-coat, trench coat; coat dress, coat hanger, coat of arms, coat of paint, coat-rack, coat-stand, coat-tails; cut your coat according to your cloth, trail your coat

coated   *see* coat; sugar-coated; *Sugar Coated Iceberg* (s)

cob   head of maize, loaf of bread,

lump of coal, male swan, strong sturdy horse; corn cob, corn on the cob; cob-loaf

cobra   snake; 1986 Sylvester Stallone film; king cobra, spitting cobra; *Cobra Verde* (f), *King Cobra* (f)

cobwebs   spiders' snares; blow away the cobwebs

cock   rooster; tilt; cock-a-doodle-doo, cock-a-hoop, cock-a-leekie, cock-and-bull story, cock-eyed, cock-up; at full cock, at half cock, cock of the walk

cockles   shellfish; warm the cockles of your heart

cocktail   mixed drink, mixture; 1988 film starring Tom Cruise; fruit cocktail, grapefruit cocktail, Molotov cocktail, prawn cocktail; cocktail bar, cocktail stick; *The Cocktail Party* (pl)

cocoa   hot drink; cocoa beans, cocoa butter

coconut   palm fruit; coconut butter, coconut ice, coconut shy

cocoon   chrysalis sheath, secure place; protect (from); 1985 sci-fi film

cod   fish, pay-as-you-get money terms (COD as abbrev); inauthentic; cod-liver oil; Cape Cod

coddle   cook gently over water, pamper

code   body of laws, cipher; area code, bar code, dialling code, genetic code, morse code, zip code; code-name; Green Cross Code, Highway Code; *The Da Vinci Code* (b/f)

coffee   beverage; black coffee, espresso coffee, Gaelic coffee, instant coffee, Irish coffee, Turkish coffee; coffee bar, coffee grounds, coffee morning, coffee pot, coffee shop, coffee table, coffee-table book; *Cream in My Coffee* (tv)

coffin   burial casket; nail in the coffin

coin   metal item of currency; invent (a word or phrase); coin box, coin it, coin-op; to coin a phrase

coins   *see* coin; *Three Coins in the Fountain* (f/s)

cold   chill, common illness; chilly, unemotional, unfriendly; common cold, leave cold; cold-blooded, cold call, cold chisel, cold comfort, cold cream, cold cuts, cold feet, cold frame, cold front, cold-hearted, cold shoulder, cold sore, cold storage, cold store, cold turkey, cold war; blow hot and cold, catch a cold, catch your death of cold, cold hands, warm heart, the cold light of day, feed a cold, starve a fever, go hot and cold, in a cold sweat, in cold blood, (leave) out in the cold, make your blood run cold; *Baby It's Cold Outside* (s), *Cold Comfort Farm* (b), *Cold Feet* (tv), *Cold Mountain* (f), *Ice Cold in Alex* (f), *In Cold Blood* (b/f), *Love in a Cold Climate* (b), *The Spy Who Came In from the Cold* (b/f)

collar   pet's neck band, shirt top; accost, arrest; blue-collar, clerical collar, dog collar, Eton collar, flea collar, mandarin collar, shawl collar, white-collar, wing collar; hot under the collar; *Lipstick on Your Collar* (s/tv)

collateral   assets pledged against a loan; additional but secondary; 2004 Tom Cruise film; collateral damage, collateral security

collected   gathered; unperturbed

collecting   amassing, fetching; stamp collecting; collecting box

collection   accumulation, couturier's new range, group of things; stamp collection; collection plate

collective   co-operative enterprise; aggregate, common to the members of a group; collective bargaining, collective farm, collective noun, collective ownership, collective unconscious

collector   person who amasses things; debt collector, stamp collector, tax collector, ticket collector; *The Bone Collector* (f), *The Collector* (b/f)

college   educational institution; Buster Keaton 1927 classic; electoral college, sixth-form college, staff college, technical college, training college; City Technology College, College of Arms, Eton College

collie   breed of sheepdog; Border collie

collision   conflict, crash; head-on collision; collision course

cologne   perfume; German city; eau de cologne

colonel   military rank; lieutenant colonel; colonel-in-chief; Colonel Blimp; *Colonel Bogey* (s), *The Life and Death of Colonel Blimp* (f)

colony   community (of ants, eg), outpost of an empire; Crown Colony

colour   hue; blush, exaggerate, stain; change colour, complementary colour, local colour, off-colour, primary colour, secondary colour; colour-blind, colour-fast, colour scheme, colour sergeant, colour supplement; troop the colour; *Blue Is the Colour* (s)

coloured   *see* colour; multi-coloured; coloured pencil; *Multi-Coloured Swap Shop* (tv)

colours   *see* colour; ensigns of a particular regiment; primary colours; nail your colours to the mast, sail under false colours, show your true colours, with flying colours

column   line of troops, pillar, regular newspaper article, row; agony column, fifth column, gossip column, personal column, spinal column, steering column; Nelson's Column; *Nelson's Column* (tv)

columnist   feature writer; fifth columnist, gossip columnist, newspaper columnist

coma   unconscious state; 1978 Michael Douglas thriller

comb   fleshy crest of some birds, hair-care tool; groom (hair), scour (the area); curry-comb, fine-tooth comb; comb out

combat   battle; fight, resist; hors de combat, single combat; combat fatigue, combat trousers

combination   mixture, number sequence which opens a lock, state of being joined; combination garment, combination lock

combinations   *see* combination; old-fashioned undergarment

combine   company; blend; combine harvester; *I've Got a Brand New Combine Harvester* (s)

combustion   process of burning; internal-combustion engine, spontaneous combustion

come   arrive, hail (from); johnny-come-lately, things to come; come about, come across, come again, come along, come back, come clean, come down, come forward, come from behind, come-hither, come home, come in, come into, come nowhere, come of age, come off it, come on, come-on, come to, come to blows, come to grief, come to life, come to light, come to naught, come

to pass, come to rest, come true, come unstuck, come-uppance; all good things come to an end, come a cropper, come apart at the seams, come full circle, come hell or high water, come in handy, come into question, come into your own, come on strong, come on the scene, come out in the wash, come out of the woodwork, come out of your shell, come to a grinding halt, come to a sticky end, come to terms with, come to that, come to think of it, come to your knowledge, come under the hammer, come up smelling of roses, come up trumps, come what may, first come first served, how come? till kingdom come, till the cows come home, to kingdom come, what goes up must come down; *Baby Come Back* (s), *Cathy Come Home* (tv), *Come as You Are* (s), *Come Dancing* (tv), *Come On Eileen* (s), *Come Together* (s), *Johnny Come Lately* (f), *Lassie Come Home* (f), *The Shape of Things to Come* (b), *Some Day My Prince Will Come* (s), *Strictly Come Dancing* (tv)

comedian   funny entertainer, joker; stand-up comedian

comedians   *see* comedian; *The Comedians* (f)

comedy   amusing play or programme, humour; black comedy, low comedy, musical comedy, situation comedy, slapstick comedy; comedy of manners; *The Comedy of Errors* (pl), *The Divine Comedy* (pl), *The King of Comedy* (f)

comes   *see* come; after word comes weird, if the worst comes to the worst, what goes around comes around, when push comes to shove, when your ship comes in; *Before Winter Comes* (f), *Here Comes Mr Jordan* (f), *Here Comes Summer* (s), *Here Comes the Night* (s), *Here Comes the Rain Again* (s), *Here Comes the Sun* (s), *When the Boat Comes In* (tv)

comet   celestial object; chain of electrical shops; Halley's Comet

comfort   ease, solace; console, soothe; cold comfort; comfort station; too close for comfort; Southern Comfort; *Cold Comfort Farm* (b), *Southern Comfort* (f)

comforter   baby's dummy, person or thing providing consolation, US warm quilt, woollen scarf; Job's comforter

comforts   *see* comfort; things that make life easy and pleasant; creature comforts; *Creature Comforts* (f)

comic   amusing person, children's magazine; humorous; comic opera, comic relief, comic strip; Comic Relief

coming   *see* come; imminent; up and coming; have another think coming, have it coming, see someone coming; Second Coming; *Coming Home* (f), *Coming to America* (f), *Coming Up for Air* (b), *Guess Who's Coming to Dinner* (f), *The Second Coming* (po)

comma   butterfly species, punctuation mark; inverted comma

command   authority, directive; govern, order; high command, (royal) command performance, second-in-command; command module

commandant   former S African army rank, POW camp's chief officer; camp commandant

commander   high-ranking police officer, military leader, Salvation Army administrator; lieutenant commander, wing commander; commander-in-chief; *Master and Commander* (b/f)

commanding   *see* command; having an air of authority

commandment   edict, religious rule for living by; eleventh commandment

commandments   *see* commandment; The Ten Commandments; *The Ten Commandments* (f)

comment   observation; make a remark; no comment

commentary   spoken account of an event; running commentary

commerce   trade; chamber of commerce, e-commerce

commercial   tv advertisement; intended to make a profit, relating to trade; commercial art, commercial break, commercial traveller, commercial vehicle

commission   agent's percentage, officer status, official body entrusted to carry out a task, special order; appoint, order specially, put into service; high commission; European Commission, Royal Commission

commissioner   EU top official, police chief, representative of the supreme authority in an area; county commissioner, police commissioner; commissioner for oaths; High Commissioner

commit   carry out (a crime), consign, pledge

committal   burial ceremony, imprisonment, pledge; non-committal

committed   *see* commit; dedicated

committee   board of appointed

persons; management committee, select committee, steering committee; committee stage

common area of public land; average, belonging to the whole community, mutual, vulgar, widespread; in common, junior common room, lowest common denominator, lowest common multiple, senior common room; common cold, common denominator, common ground, common knowledge, common law, common lodging-house, common market, common-or-garden, common room, common sense; out of the common; Clapham Common, Common Entrance, Court of Common Pleas, Ealing Common, Streatham Common; *Common as Muck* (tv), *Common People* (s), *Fanfare for the Common Man* (cl)

> **Common**
> Clapham, Ealing, Putney, Streatham, Wandsworth, Wimbledon

commons *see* Common; lower house of the UK parliament; House of Commons

commonwealth group of states, organisation of former British dependencies, republican period in Britain, 1649-60; Commonwealth Games, the Commonwealth

commune group of people sharing living arrangements and goods, radical Parisian group in the French Revolution; feel in close spiritual contact (with)

communicating getting in touch, passing on (information); *Communicating Doors* (pl)

communication connecting passage or channel, exchanging of information, message, social contact; communication cord

communications *see* communication; lines of contact; line of communications; communications satellite

communion holy sacrament, sharing of intimate thoughts; 1990 Christopher Walken film; communion wafer; Anglican Communion

community body of people living in one place, society; community centre, community charge, community chest, community policeman, community service, community singing; care in the community

commute journey to work; reduce (a term of punishment), travel a distance to work

compact agreement, face-powder case; consolidate; concise, dense; early 1960s soap opera; compact disc

companion escort, friend, one of a pair; stable companion; companion set; Companion of Honour, Companion of the Bath

companions *see* companion; *The Good Companions* (b)

company assembly, associates, business enterprise, crew of a ship; young women's glossy magazine; holding company, joint-stock company, keep company, limited company, livery company, management company, part company, private company, public company, public limited company, repertory company, shell company, ship's company, trust company; company car, company director; in company with, keep company with, misery loves company, two's company (three's a crowd); *Bad Company* (f), *The Company of Wolves* (f), *Two's Company* (tv)

compare contrast, equate, liken; without compare; compare notes

compares *see* compare; *Nothing Compares 2 U* (s)

compartment separate section of a container, train section; glove compartment, smoking compartment

compass direction indicator; compass rose

compasses *see* compass; instruments for drawing circles; pair of compasses

compassion sympathy; compassion fatigue

compassionate showing concern for others, merciful; compassionate leave

complaint ailment, grievance

complementary alternative (medicine), enhancing another's qualities, forming a whole; complementary colour, complementary medicine

complete finish; fully equipped, utter, whole

complex collection of interrelated buildings, neurosis; intricate, problematic; guilt complex, inferiority complex, Oedipus complex, persecution complex, superiority complex

compliment flattering remark; express admiration; return the compliment

compliments *see* compliment; compliments slip

composed wrote music; calm and collected, consisting (of); *Composed upon Westminster Bridge* (po)

compost soil fertiliser; potting compost; compost heap

compound alloy; aggravate, intensify; consisting of several parts; chemical compound; compound fracture

comprehensive type of school; providing cover for most risks, wide in scope; comprehensive school

compress lint pad; flatten, force into a small space

compressed *see* compress; compressed air

compromise half-measure, negotiated agreement; bring into disrepute, reach an understanding; Missouri Compromise

compulsory mandatory; compulsory purchase

computer data processor; personal computer; computer dating, computer game, computer-literate, computer science, computer virus; *OK Computer* (al)

con prisoner, scam; deceive, study carefully, swindle; chilli con carne, ex-con; con man, con trick; *Con Air* (f)

conceit arrogance

conceive become pregnant, envisage

concentrate liquid which needs dilution before use; condense, focus attention (on)

concentrated *see* concentrate; gathered; undiluted

concentration amount of a substance in a solution, gathering (of people), single-mindedness

concept idea; concept album

conception creation of an embryo,

idea, understanding; Immaculate Conception

concern anxiety, business; relate to, worry; going concern; to whom it may concern; Age Concern

concert agreement, musical event; in concert, live concert, promenade concert; concert-goer, concert grand, concert hall, concert party, concert performance, concert pianist, concert pitch

concerto orchestral piece with a solo; Honda saloon model; *The Warsaw Concerto* (cl)

concession act of yielding, adjustment, allowance, business within the premises of a larger enterprise

conclusion end, inference; foregone conclusion; in conclusion

conclusions *see* conclusion; jump to conclusions

concrete building material; definite; reinforced concrete; concrete jungle, concrete mixer; *Concrete and Clay* (s), *Concrete Junction* (ga/s)

concubine mistress; *Farewell My Concubine* (f)

condensed abridged, concentrated; condensed milk

condition clause, medical problem, prerequisite, state; accustom; necessary condition; in a delicate condition, in mint condition, on condition, out of condition

conditional type of clause or verb form; based on stipulations, depending on other factors; conditional discharge

conditioned *see* condition; brought into the desired state for use, trained; air-conditioned, cask-conditioned

condor large S American vulture; *Three Days of the Condor* (f)

conduct behaviour; escort, lead an orchestra; disorderly conduct, safe conduct

conducted *see* conduct; conducted tour

conductor orchestra leader, fare-taker on public transport, transmitter of electricity; bus conductor, lightning conductor

cone circular pyramid, fruit of the pine tree, ice-cream holder, roadworks marker, volcanic peak; fir cone, nose-cone, pine cone

confectioner seller of sweets; confectioner's custard

confer consult together, grant

conference meeting for discussion, variety of pear; news conference, press conference; in conference

confession admission, statement of religious belief; deathbed confession

confessions *see* confession; *Confessions of a Nazi Spy*, *Confessions of a Window Cleaner* (f)

confidence feeling of certainty, secret, self-assurance; 1880 Henry James novel; self-confidence, vote of (no) confidence; confidence trick; in confidence

confident optimistic, self-assured; self-confident

confidential private, secret; *Kitchen Confidential* (b), *LA Confidential* (f), *The Confidential Agent* (b)

confinement custody, pregnancy, restraint, segregation; solitary confinement

confirmation Christian rite of passage, verification

conflict argument, war; be in

opposition; conflict resolution; conflict of interest; *The Final Conflict* (f)

conformist adherent of the established church, follower of social norms; relating to established practices; *The Conformist* (b/f)

confused jumbled, perplexed; *Dazed and Confused* (f)

congeniality friendliness, natural affinity; *Miss Congeniality* (f)

congress meeting; Indian political party, US legislative body; Trades Union Congress

conjunction alignment, simultaneous occurrence, word used to connect sentences; in conjunction

conjure perform magic; conjure up; a name to conjure with

connecting joining; connecting rod

connection association, link; in connection with, in this connection; French Connection; *The French Connection* (f)

conning *see* con; conning tower

conquer master, overcome; divide and conquer; *She Stoops to Conquer* (pl)

conquering *see* conquer; *Hail the Conquering Hero* (f)

conquest act of acquiring by force, victory; Norman Conquest

conquests *see* conquest; *The Norman Conquests* (pl)

cons *see* con; arguments against; mod cons, pros and cons

conscience sense of right and wrong; prisoner of conscience; in all conscience

conscientious diligent, relating to a sense of right and wrong; conscientious objector

conscious awake, aware, deliberate; class-conscious, health-conscious, self-conscious, semi-conscious

consciousness awareness, perception, state of being awake; black consciousness, self-consciousness, stream of consciousness

conscript person forced into military service; force into service

consent agreement; permit; informed consent

consequence direct result, importance, social distinction; in consequence

conservation care and repair (of historic sites), environmental protection; nature conservation

conservatory hothouse, school of music

consider think over; *Consider Yourself* (s)

consideration motive, payment, thoughtfulness; in consideration of take into consideration, under consideration

considered *see* consider; all things considered

consolation comfort after loss; consolation prize

console panel with dials, switches etc, key desk of an organ; give sympathy to

consonant non-vowel; in harmony (with)

consort monarch's spouse, partner; keep company (with); prince consort

conspicuous eye-catching, prominent; conspicuous by one's absence

conspiracy plot; conspiracy of silence, conspiracy theory; *Conspiracy Theory* (f)

constable police officer; chief constable, high constable, police constable, special constable; Lord High Constable; *Carry On Constable* (f)

constant faithful, unchanging; *Constant Craving* (s), *The Constant Gardener* (b/f), *The Constant Nymph* (b/f)

constituent component part, resident of an electoral district; forming a part

constitution natural condition of the body or mind, structure, written embodiment of political principles; Constitution Hill

constrictor compression muscle, large snake; boa constrictor

construct subjective theory; build, compile

constructive derived by inference, helpful and useful (of advice or criticism); constructive dismissal

consul country's representative abroad, ancient Roman magistrate; *The Honorary Consul* (b/f)

consulate embassy department; brand of cigarettes

consumer user of goods and services; consumer durables, consumer resistance

consuming eating or drinking, using up; time-consuming

consummate complete (a transaction), make (a marriage) legally complete; highly skilled, perfect of its kind

consumption amount used up, eating and drinking, pulmonary tuberculosis

contact connection, communication, useful person in times of need; get in touch with; 1997 sci-fi film starring Jodie Foster; contact lenses, contact sport

contained curbed, held, included; self-contained

contemplation reflective thought; navel-contemplation

contempt disdain, disregard of a law; beneath contempt; contempt of court; familiarity breeds contempt, hold in contempt

content internal substance; satisfied; to your heart's content

contention assertion, disagreement; bone of contention; in contention

contest competition, conflict; oppose; beauty contest; no contest

continental inhabitant of mainland Europe; belonging to a large land-mass, of the European mainland; continental breakfast, continental climate, continental drift, continental quilt, continental shelf; *The Continental* (s)

contingent detachment or section (of soldiers, eg); incidental, subject to chance

continuing carrying on; continuing education

continuity commentary linking broadcast items, maintenance of consistent detail between film scenes, unbroken progression; continuity announcer

continuous non-stop; continuous assessment

contour line on a map, outline; contour line

contract written business agreement; catch (an illness), shrink; maintenance contract, social contract; contract bridge; *The Draughtsman's Contract* (f), *The Social Contract* (b)

contradiction paradox, statement asserting the opposite; contradiction in terms

contrary opposite; perverse; on the contrary, quite the contrary, to the contrary

contrast evident difference; be at variance, show differences between

contributory involving a fund which you pay into, playing a part in; non-contributory pension

contrition remorse; act of contrition

contrived arranged; artificial

control direction, restraint; be in charge of, regulate; air traffic control, arms control, birth control, climate control, cruise control, dual control, ground control, quality control, remote control, self-control; control tower; in control, out of control, under control; *Ground Control* (f)

controller person in charge, regulator; air traffic controller, quality controller

controlling *see* control; controlling interest

convenience handiness, labour-saving device, lavatory, suitability; flag of convenience, marriage of convenience; convenience food, convenience store; at your convenience; *Carry On at Your Convenience* (f)

convent nuns' residence, school run by nuns; *The Convent* (f/tv)

convention agreement between states, generally accepted practice, large meeting; national convention

conversation talk; conversation piece, conversation stopper; *The Conversation* (f)

converse opposite; talk

conversion adoption of a new faith, building adapted to a new purpose, process of change, rugby kick scoring two points; *Captain Brassbound's Conversion* (pl)

convert person who adopts a new faith; transform

conveyance transference of property ownership, vehicle

conveyor moving production-line part, transporter; conveyor belt

convict prisoner; pronounce guilty

convoy line of vehicles; accompany for protection; 1978 film about truckers; in convoy

coo dove's call; murmur affectionately; bill and coo

cook person who prepares meals; prepare food; pastry-cook; cook-chill, cook's tour; cook the books, cook your goose; Cook Islands, Cook Strait; *The Cook, the Thief, His Wife and Her Lover* (f), *Ready Steady Cook* (tv)

cooked *see* cook; pre-cooked

cooker oven, grill and hob, variety of apple; gas cooker, pressure cooker, slow cooker

cookery food preparation; cookery book

cookie biscuit, packet of data used to identify an internet user; chocolate-chip cookie, fortune cookie; the way the cookie crumbles; *The Fortune Cookie* (f)

cooking *see* cook; cuisine; home cooking; cooking-apple; what's cooking?

cooks *see* cook; too many cooks spoil the broth

cool chill, self-control; calm, refrigerate; chilly, indifferent, trendy, unruffled;

cool box, cool customer, cool it, cool off; (as) cool as a cucumber; *Be Cool* (f), *Cool for Cats* (s), *Cool Hand Luke* (f), *Cool World* (f), *Daddy Cool* (s)

cooler chilling device, prison; less warm; water cooler; *The Cooler* (f)

cooling *see* cool; cooling tower, cooling-off period

coop business where profits are shared, poultry pen; enclose (hens); hen-coop

cooped *see* coop; cooped up

coot aquatic bird; (as) bald as a coot

cop police officer; catch; cop it, cop out, cop shop; cop hold of, it's a fair cop, not much cop; *Beverly Hills Cop* (f), *Kindergarten Cop* (f)

cope ecclesiastical vestment; deal (with), get by

coping *see* cope; covering of masonry on a wall; coping saw, coping stone

copper metallic element, old penny, police officer; copper beech, copper-bottomed, copper's nark

copy material for a newspaper writer, replica; duplicate, emulate, plagiarise; carbon copy, fair copy, hard copy, top copy; copy editor, copy typist

copybook collection of handwriting to imitate; conventional, hackneyed; blot your copybook

copyright inventor's patent; copyright library

coral marine reef growth, orange-pink colour; fire coral; coral snake; *The Coral Island* (b)

cord thick string; communication cord, sash cord, spinal cord, umbilical cord

cordon police line, ribbon of honour, system of road blocks; seal (off); cordon bleu, cordon off, cordon sanitaire

cords *see* cord; vocal cords

core innermost part; hard core, to the core; core time

cork stopper; Irish county and city; stop up (a wine bottle)

corked *see* cork; tainted state of wine

corn cereal crop, dated humour, toe complaint; Indian corn; corn bunting, corn circle, corn cob, corn dolly, corn exchange, corn-fed, corn oil, corn on the cob

corner angle, cranny, free kick in football; trap; tight corner; corner shop; corner the market, fight your corner, in a corner, just around the corner, turn the corner; Hyde Park Corner, Poets' Corner, Speakers' Corner; *The House at Pooh Corner* (b)

cornered trapped; *The Three-Cornered Hat* (bal)

corners *see* corner; cut corners

coronation investiture of a monarch; coronation chicken; *Coronation Street* (tv)

coroner inquest official; coroner's court

coronets small crowns; *Kind Hearts and Coronets* (f)

corporal military rank; physical (punishment); lance corporal; corporal punishment

corporate of a large company, shared by all the members of a group; corporate image, corporate raider

corporation large business, pot belly, town council; corporation tax

corps body of people, military unit; diplomatic corps, esprit de corps; corps de ballet

corpse dead body; forget your lines or laugh on stage; *Corpse Bride* (f)

corpus body of literature; habeas

corpus; corpus delicti; Corpus Christi

correct amend; accurate, proper; politically correct

correction amendment; house of correction; correction fluid

correspondence harmony, letter writing, similarity; correspondence course

correspondent regular letter-writer, reporter on a particular subject; agreeing; foreign correspondent, lobby correspondent, racing correspondent; *From Our Own Correspondent* (r)

corresponding writing letters; analogous; corresponding member

corridor passageway; air corridor

corridors *see* corridor; corridors of power; *The Corridors of Power* (b)

cosmetic beauty product; affecting only the appearance; cosmetic surgery

cosmic of the universe; cosmic dust, cosmic rays; *Cosmic Girl* (s)

cost detriment, expense, price; put a price on; cost accounting, cost-benefit, cost-effective, cost-efficient, cost of living, cost price; at any cost, cost an arm and a leg, cost a pretty penny, cost the earth, count the cost, to my cost

costs *see* cost; fixed costs, running costs; at all costs

costume actor's clothes, attire; dress; bathing costume, national costume, swimming costume; costume drama, costume jewellery

cosy teapot insulator; homely, snug; tea cosy

cottage country dwelling, small house; thatched cottage, tied cottage; cottage cheese, cottage garden,

cottage hospital, cottage industry, cottage loaf, cottage pie; Craven Cottage, Dove Cottage, Swiss Cottage; *Return to River Cottage* (tv)

cotton fabric, thread; sea-island cotton; cotton bud, cotton on, cotton-picking, cotton reel, cotton wool; wrap in cotton wool; *Cotton Blossom* (s), *The Cotton Club* (f)

couch coarse grass, settee; express in language of a particular style; casting couch, studio couch; couch potato

cough accompaniment to a cold; clear the throat, splutter; hacking cough, whooping cough; cough drop, cough mixture, cough up

could was able to, would be able to; *Could You Be Loved?* (s), *I Wish I Could Fly* (s)

council committee, local government body; county council, parish council, town council, works council; council house, council of war, council tax; Privy Council

counsel advice, adviser, barrister; advise; counsel of despair, counsel of perfection; keep your own counsel, take counsel; Queen's Counsel

counselling *see* counsel; advice and support, psychotherapy; marriage counselling

counsellor professional adviser, psychotherapist; marriage counsellor, privy counsellor

count nobleman, tally; add up, deem to be, include, rely (on), signify; blood count, head count, keep count, lose count, pollen count; count on, count sheep, count the cost, count the days, count the hours; count your blessings, out for the count; *The Count of Monte Cristo* (b/f)

countdown ten seconds before a rocket launch; Channel 4 word game; *The Final Countdown* (s)

countenance face, facial expression; approve; keep your countenance, out of countenance

counter casino chip, shop's serving table; contradict, oppose; bean counter, Geiger counter, over the counter, rev counter, under the counter; counter-accusation, counter-attack, counter-declaration, counter-espionage, counter-insurgency, counter-intelligence, counter-intuitive, counter-revolution, counter-tenor; Counter-Reformation; *Point Counter Point* (b)

counties *see* county; Home Counties

counting *see* count; counting house

countries nations; Low Countries

country nation, rural area; rural; across country, cross-country, developing country, go to the country, line of country, mother country, the old country, up-country; country and western, country club, country dance, country dancing, country house, country mile, country music, country seat; Basque Country, Black Country, West Country; *Another Country* (b/f/pl), *The Big Country* (f), *The Country Girl* (f), *The Country Girls* (b), *Country Mile* (s), *The Country Wife* (pl), *Cry the Beloved Country* (b), *The Far Country* (f), *A Month in the Country* (b/f/pl), *North Country* (f), *Take Me Home Country Road* (s), *Wild in the Country* (f)

counts *see* count; *Every Second Counts* (tv)

county local government division,
shire, US state division; metropolitan county; county commissioner, county council, county court, county cricket, county town; County Championship, Derby County; *The Bridges of Madison County* (f), *Coward of the County* (s), *Orange County* (f)

coup master stroke, putsch; coup de foudre, coup de grâce, coup d'état, coup de théâtre

couple pair; link together; *A Couple of Swells* (s), *The Odd Couple* (f)

coupon voucher; reply coupon

courage bravery; Dutch courage, take courage; *Courage under Fire* (f), *Mother Courage and Her Children* (pl), *The Red Badge of Courage* (f)

courageous brave; *Captains Courageous* (f)

course circuit, one part of a meal, path, racetrack, session of lessons on a particular subject; hunt (hares); assault course, clerk of the course, collision course, correspondence course, crash course, damp course, foundation course, golf course, main course, matter of course, off course, on course, sandwich course; as a matter of course, the course of nature, in due course, in the course of, of course, par for the course, stay the course

courses *see* course; horses for courses

court enclosed space or yard, monarch's entourage, playing area for racket sports, trial venue; seek, woo; appeal court, badminton court, bankruptcy court, clerk of the court, contempt of court, coroner's court, county court, friend at court, grass court, hard court, high court, high court judge, juvenile court, kangaroo court, law court, out-of-court, sheriff court, small claims court, squash court, tennis court, ward of court; court-card, court circular, court disaster, court martial, court of appeal, court order, court shoes; the ball is in your court, laugh out of court, pay court to, silence in court; Baron's Court, Centre Court, Court of Common Pleas, Court of Session, Court of St James's, Crown Court, Earl's Court, Hampton Court, High Court of Justice, Inns of Court, Supreme Court, Tottenham Court Road; *The Court Jester* (f), *Crown Court* (tv), *In the Court of the Crimson King* (al)

courtesy   act of civility or respect, politeness; courtesy light, courtesy of

courts   *see* court; Royal Courts of Justice

cousin   offspring of your aunt or uncle; country cousin, distant cousin, first cousin, second cousin; *Cousin Bette* (b), *My Cousin Rachel* (f), *My Cousin Vinny* (f), *My Perfect Cousin* (s)

cove   fellow, sheltered bay; Lulworth Cove

covenant   agreement; stipulate; deed of covenant, restrictive covenant; Ark of the Covenant; *The Holcroft Covenant* (b/f)

cover   binding of a book, blanket, camouflage, insurance protection, mask; clothe, insure, protect; break cover, cloud cover, dust cover, extra cover, first-day cover, ground cover, re-cover, take cover, under cover; cover charge, cover note, cover point, cover up; don't judge a book by its cover; *Cover Me* (s)

covering   *see* cover; covering letter

covers   *see* cover; loose covers

cow   bovine animal, female of other animals; intimidate; cash cow, holy cow, Jersey cow, mad cow disease, sacred cow, sea cow; cow-house, cow parsley; how now brown cow; *Poor Cow* (b/f)

coward   person who lacks courage; *Coward of the County* (s)

cowboy   shoddy tradesman, Wild West cattle herder; *Carry On Cowboy* (f), *Drugstore Cowboy* (f), *Midnight Cowboy* (f), *Rhinestone Cowboy* (s), *Urban Cowboy* (f)

cowl   chimney cover, monk's hood; cowl neck

cows   *see* cow; till the cows come home; *Mad Cows* (b/f)

cox   rowing boat pilot; English apple

coyote   wild dog; *Coyote Ugly* (f)

crab   crustacean, Cancer star sign symbol, wild sour apple; Boston crab, dressed crab, fiddler crab, hermit crab, horseshoe crab, king crab, spider crab; crab apple, crab stick; catch a crab; Crab Nebula

crack   fissure, form of cocaine, joke, sudden sharp explosive sound; break into (a safe), break open, collapse under pressure, solve; first-rate; crack down, crack of dawn, crack of doom, crack up; crack a joke, crack the whip, fair crack of the whip, hard/tough nut to crack

cracked   *see* crack; bonkers; cracked wheat; not all it's cracked up to be

cracker   biscuit, Christmas party novelty, firework; Robbie Coltrane crime series; cream cracker, prawn cracker, safe-cracker; cracker barrel

crackers   *see* cracker; bonkers; *Animal*

Crackers (f), *Animal Crackers in My Soup* (s), *A Cream Cracker under the Settee* (tv)

cracking   *see* crack; excellent; get cracking

cracks   *see* crack; paper over the cracks

cradle   baby's bed; embrace protectively; cat's cradle; cradle cap, cradle-snatcher; *The Hand that Rocks the Cradle* (f)

craft   cunning, handiwork, skill, skilled trade, vessel; construct, fashion; landing craft

crafts   *see* craft; objects made by hand; arts and crafts; Arts and Crafts Movement

craftsman   artisan; master craftsman

cram   stuff, swot

cramp   muscle pain; restrict; writer's cramp; cramp your style

crane   long-necked wading bird, lifting device; stretch (the neck); 1960s adventure tv series starring Patrick Allen

crank   eccentric person, starting-handle; start (a motor engine) with a handle

cranny   crevice; every nook and cranny

crash   collapse, collision; computer breakdown, noise of things breaking; clatter, collide; controversial 1996 Cronenberg film; 2004 Oscar-winning film; car crash; crash barrier, crash course, crash helmet, crash-land, crash-landing, crash test; Wall Street Crash; *48 Crash* (s)

craven   coward; cowardly; Craven Cottage

craving   desire; yearning; *Constant Craving* (s)

craw   pouch in a bird's gullet; stick in your craw

crawl   swimming stroke; grovel, move slowly, walk on all fours; pub crawl; make your flesh crawl, you have to crawl before you can walk

crawler   baby's overall, sycophant; crawler lane

crazy   bonkers, very enthusiastic (about); Patsy Cline song; stir crazy; crazy golf, crazy paving; Crazy Horse; *Crazy People* (f), *Dirty Mary Crazy Larry* (f), *Girl Crazy* (f), *Stir Crazy* (f), *You Drive Me Crazy* (s)

cream   dairy product, elite, off-white colour; skim (off), work (butter etc) to a smooth consistency; barrier cream, butter-cream, Chantilly cream, clotted cream, cold cream, Devonshire cream, double cream, foundation cream, full-cream, ice cream, ice-cream parlour, ice-cream soda, Neapolitan ice cream, peaches and cream, salad cream, shaving cream, single cream, sour cream, sun-cream, vanishing cream, whipping cream; cream cake, cream cheese, cream cracker, cream horn, cream of tartar, cream puff, cream sherry, cream soda, cream tea; *A Cream Cracker under the Settee* (tv), *Cream in My Coffee* (tv)

crease   batsman's mark, fold or wrinkle (in clothes, eg); fold, pucker

creative   artistic, showing imagination; creative accounting

creature   animate being; creature comforts; *Creature Comforts* (f)

creatures   *see* creature; *Heavenly Creatures* (f)

credibility   trustworthiness; credibility gap

credit   approval, loan facility, merit;

ascribe, believe; do credit, family credit, in credit, letter of credit, on credit; credit card, credit rating, credit transfer, credit union; to your credit

creed dogma, profession of faith, set of principles; Nicene Creed

creek small inlet; up the creek (without a paddle); *Dawson's Creek* (tv), *Frenchman's Creek* (b/f) *Jonathan Creek* (tv), *The Miracle of Morgan's Creek* (f)

creep unpleasant person, yes-man; move stealthily; make your flesh creep

creeper climbing plant, low ball in cricket, soft-soled shoe; Virginia creeper

creepers *see* creeper; brothel creepers; jeepers creepers; *Jeepers Creepers* (f)

creeping *see* creep; creeping Jenny

creepy spooky; creepy-crawly

creole language of mixed origins; early Louisiana settler; *King Creole* (f/s)

crêpe French pancake, light wrinkled fabric, thin paper used for decorations; crêpe de Chine, crêpe paper; crêpe Suzette

crescent curving street, narrow curved shape, moon phase; Mornington Crescent, Red Crescent

cress salad vegetable grown with mustard; mustard and cress

crest apex, heraldic insignia, hill ridge, tuft of feathers on a bird's head; surmount; on the crest of a wave; *Falcon Crest* (tv)

crew band of people, workforce of a ship or aircraft; man (a ship or aircraft); cabin crew; crew cut, crew neck

crib baby's bed, cattle stall; copy illicitly

cricket jumping insect, summer sport; county cricket, French cricket, test cricket; cricket ball, cricket bat; not cricket; *The Cricket on the Hearth* (b)

cried *see* cry; *All Cried Out* (s)

crime illegal act; partners in crime, scene of the crime; crime sheet; *Crime and Punishment* (b), *Crime School* (f), *Crime Sheet* (tv), *True Crime* (f)

crimes *see* Crime; war crimes; *Crimes and Misdemeanors* (f)

criminal lawbreaker; against the law; criminal law; *Law & Order: Criminal Intent* (tv)

crimson shade of red; *Crimson Tide* (f), *In the Court of the Crimson King* (al)

crisis predicament, turning point; charity which helps the homeless; identity crisis, midlife crisis; Cuban Missile Crisis

crisp thin slice of fried potato; brittle, terse; burn to a crisp

critic nit-picker, reviewer; literary critic

critical fault-finding, decisive, vital; critical mass, critical temperature

criticism analysis and judgement of an artistic work, fault-finding; literary criticism

crock battered old car, decrepit person, earthenware vessel; crock of gold

crocodile alligator-like reptile; crocodile clip, crocodile tears; Crocodile River; *Crocodile Dundee* (f), *Crocodile Rock* (s), *Crocodile Shoes* (tv)

croft small Scottish farm; *Lara Croft: Tomb Raider* (f)

crook bishop's or shepherd's staff, criminal; by hook or by crook

crooked askew, dishonest; *There Was a Crooked Man* (f)

crop bird's dilated oesophagus, farmer's harvest, riding whip, short haircut; cut short; cash crop, hunting crop, riding crop; crop circle, crop dusting, crop-spraying, crop top, crop up

cropper plant to be marketed, small printing machine, species of pigeon; come a cropper

croquet lawn game; croquet mallet

cross boxing punch, Christian symbol, teacher's mark for 'wrong'; fold (the arms or legs), interbreed, intersect, mark with an 'X', traverse; annoyed; Celtic cross, criss-cross, double-cross, Greek cross, hot cross bun, Latin cross, Maltese cross, rally-cross; cross-beam, cross-bencher, cross-breed, cross-check, cross-country, cross-current, cross-cut, cross-dress, cross-examination, cross-examine, cross-fade, cross-fertilisation, cross hairs, cross-hatching, cross index, cross-legged, cross over, cross-ply, cross-pollination, cross-question, cross reference, cross section, cross stitch; at cross purposes, cross the Channel, cross the rubicon, cross your heart, dot the i's and cross the t's; Banbury Cross, Charing Cross, George Cross, Green Cross Code, Hatton Cross, Iron Cross, King's Cross, King's Cross St Pancras, King's Cross Thameslink, Military Cross, Red Cross, St Andrew's Cross, St George's Cross, Stations of the Cross, Victoria Cross; *Never a Cross Word* (tv), *The Sign of the Cross* (f)

crossed *see* cross; star-crossed

crosses *see* cross; noughts and crosses

crossing *see* cross; intersection,

journey over water; level crossing, pedestrian crossing, pelican crossing, zebra crossing; *Crossing Delancey* (f), *Miller's Crossing* (f)

crossword puzzle; crossword puzzle

crotchet note equal to half a minim, perverse fancy; *Crotchet Castle* (b)

crouching squatting; *Crouching Tiger, Hidden Dragon* (f)

crow raven-like bird; boast; carrion crow, hooded crow; crow's feet crow's nest; as the crow flies; *As the Crow Flies* (b), *The Crow* (f), *The Crow Road* (b)

crowd attendance, large group of people; cluster, jostle; in-crowd; crowd-puller; two's company, three's a crowd; *The Crowd* (f), *A Face in the Crowd* (f), *Far from the Madding Crowd* (b/f), *The IT Crowd* (tv)

crown artificial replacement for a tooth, five shillings, royal head-dress; add a finishing touch to, hit on the head, invest as monarch; half-a-crown, half-crown, jewel in the crown, triple crown; crown and anchor, crown green, crown of thorns, crown prince, crown princess, crown prosecutor; Crown Colony, Crown Court, Crown Derby, Crown Jewels, Minister of the Crown; *Crown Court* (tv), *Crown Imperial* (cl), *The Jewel in the Crown* (b/tv), *The Thomas Crown Affair* (f)

crows *see* crow; stone the crows; *Wheat Field with Crows* (pa)

crude oil before treatment; primitive, untreated, vulgar; crude oil

cruel brutal; *Cruel Intentions* (f), *Cruel Summer* (s), *The Cruel Sea* (b/f)

cruelty brutality; mental cruelty; *Intolerable Cruelty* (f)

cruise leisurely sea voyage, type of missile; sail to and fro, travel at a sedate pace; cruise control, cruise missile

cruiser fast warship; battle-cruiser, cabin cruiser

cruising *see* cruise; controversial 1980 Al Pacino film; *Carry On Cruising* (f)

crumbles desserts of stewed fruit with crusty toppings; disintegrates, pulverises; the way the cookie crumbles

crumple collapse, scrunch up; crumple zone

crunch crispy sound, critical situation; chew noisily, grind (underfoot)

crunching *see* crunch; processing large quantities of (numbers); number crunching

crush drink made from pressed fruit, infatuation, squeeze; compress, suppress; crush bar/barrier

crushed *see* crush; crushed velvet

crust hard outer layer; Earth's crust, upper crust

crux decisive moment, essential part; crux of the matter

cry loud sound of grief, shout; be in tears, shriek; a far cry, far cry, hue and cry, war cry; cry-baby, cry off, cry out, cry wolf; cry for the moon, cry stinking fish, don't cry over spilt milk, shoulder to cry on; *Big Girls Don't Cry* (s), *Boys Don't Cry* (f), *Cry-Baby* (f/s), *Cry Freedom* (f), *Cry the Beloved Country* (b), *Cry Wolf* (b/s), *Don't Cry for Me Argentina* (s), *Hue and Cry* (f), *The War Cry* (mag)

crying *see* cry; for crying out loud; *Crying in the Chapel* (s), *The Crying Game* (f/s)

crystal clear quartz, cut glass; lead crystal, liquid crystal (display); crystal ball, crystal clear, crystal-gazing, crystal set; (as) clear as crystal; Crystal Palace; *The Crystal Maze* (tv)

cub junior reporter, junior Scout, young of various animals; bear cub, lion cub; cub reporter; Wolf Cub

cube six-sided solid object; chop into small squares; bath cube, ice cube, Rubik's cube, stock cube, sugar cube; cube root

cubed *see* cube; raised to the power of three

cuckoo bird; slightly crazy; cloud cuckoo land; cuckoo clock, cuckoo pint, cuckoo spit; *One Flew Over the Cuckoo's Nest* (f), *The Cuckoo Waltz* (tv)

cuckoos *see* cuckoo; *The Midwich Cuckoos* (b)

cucumber long green salad vegetable; sea cucumber; (as) cool as a cucumber

cud chewed food of a ruminant; chew the cud

cudgels coshes; bludgeons; take up the cudgels

cue actor's prompt, rod for billiards or snooker; on cue; cue ball, cue card

cuff clout, end of a sleeve; clip round the ear; off the cuff

cuisine cookery; haute cuisine, nouvelle cuisine

culottes divided skirt; sans-culottes

cultivated devoted attention to, fostered (an association), prepared (land) for crops; educated, refined

cultivation attention to detail, growing (of crops), fostering (of an association), refinement

cultural relating to the arts; cultural attache; Cultural Revolution

culture arts and customs, crop of experimentally-grown bacteria; pop culture; culture shock, culture vulture; *The Culture Show* (tv)

cultured propagated in an artificial medium; refined

cup competition trophy, drinking vessel, fruit drink, golf hole, shaped bra section; make a hollow with the hands; egg cup, fruit cup, gold cup, loving cup, stirrup cup; cup and saucer, cup-bearer, cup match, cup of tea, cup-tie; not my cup of tea; Admiral's Cup, Cheltenham Gold Cup, Cup Final, Davis Cup, European Champions Cup, FA Cup, Ryder Cup, World Cup; *Tin Cup* (f)

cupboard closet; fume cupboard; cupboard love; skeleton in the cupboard

curate parish priest; manage museum collections; curate's egg

curd cheese part of milk; bean curd, lemon curd; curd cheese

curdle coagulate; make your blood curdle

curdling *see* curdle; blood-curdling

curds solid parts of milk; curds and whey

cure remedy; heal, preserve (meat); rest cure, water cure; cure-all; prevention is better than cure

curiosity desire to know or learn, strange or unusual object or fact; curiosity killed the cat; *The Old Curiosity Shop* (b)

curious nosey, peculiar

curl loop of hair, spiral; bend round, twist in a circular shape; kiss curl;

curl up; curl your lip, make your hair curl, make your toes curl

curlew wading bird; stone curlew

curling *see* curl; curling tongs

curly wavy; curly endive; *Curly Top* (f)

currant small dried grape; currant bun

currencies monetary systems; basket of currencies

currency money, prevalence; decimal currency

current flow of electricity or water; present; alternating current, cross-current, direct current, rip current; current account, current liabilities

curriculum courses offered by a school or college; curriculum vitae; National Curriculum

curry spiced Indian dish; groom (a horse); curry-comb curry favour, curry leaves, curry plant, curry powder; *Curry and Chips* (tv)

curse evil spell, expletive; damn, swear

cursory hasty and superficial; cursory glance

curtain drape, end of a play; screen; safety curtain; curtain call, curtain-raiser, curtain-up; bring down the curtain; Iron Curtain; *Torn Curtain* (f)

curve arc; gently sweep; bell curve, learning curve

cushion pillow, shock absorber; alleviate (a blow), pad; air cushion, whoopee cushion

cushions *see* cushion; scatter cushions

custard yellow sauce for puddings; confectioner's custard, egg custard; custard apple, custard pie, custard tart

custody detention, guardianship; protective custody

custom habit, patronage, tradition; made to order; custom house, custom-built, custom-made

customer client; cool customer; the customer is always right

customs *see* custom; government border controls on movements of goods; customs union

cut flesh wound, hairdo, reduction, share; abridge, cease filming, censor, deliberately ignore, divide (a pack of cards), reduce, use scissors or a knife; clean-cut, clear-cut, crew cut, cross-cut, feather-cut, half-cut, power cut, razor cut, rough cut, scissor cut, short cut, straight-cut; cut and dried, cut and paste, cut and run, cut and thrust, cut back, cut corners, cut glass, cut loose, cut no ice, cut off, cut out, cut-price, cut short, cut-throat, cut-throat razor, cut to ribbons, cut up; a cut above, cut a caper, cut a dash, cut a swathe through, cut down to size, cut from the same cloth, cut it fine, cut it out, cut off your nose to spite your face, cut the cackle, cut the mustard, cut to the quick, cut your coat according to your cloth, to cut a long story short; *The First Cut Is the Deepest* (s), *In the Cut* (f), *Prime Cut* (f), *Rough Cut* (f)

cutlet small piece of meat; nut cutlet

cuts *see* cut; cold cuts; *Short Cuts* (f)

cutter coastal motor launch, knife, tailor; daisy-cutter; *Cutter's Way* (f)

cutting *see* cut; newspaper clipping, piece of a plant removed for propagation; incisive, sarcastic; railway cutting, wood-cutting; cutting edge; *Cutting It* (tv)

cyanide poison; *Sparkling Cyanide* (b)

cycle pushbike, regular sequence; ride a bike; life cycle, song cycle

cyclist bike rider; trick cyclist

cylinder engine's piston-housing, geometrical tube shape; cylinder head

cylinders *see* cylinder; firing on all cylinders

D

dab flatfish, small brush stroke; pat gently; dab hand

dabs *see* dab; fingerprints

dabble get involved superficially, shake about in water

dad father; 1990s George Cole sitcom; *Dad's Army* (tv)

daddy father; sugar daddy; daddy-long-legs; *Daddy Cool* (s), *Daddy Long Legs* (mus)

daft silly; (as) daft as a brush

dagger big knife; cloak-and-dagger

daggers *see* dagger; at daggers drawn, look daggers

daily charwoman, newspaper; every 24 hours; daily dozen, daily paper; *Daily Mirror* (n), *Daily Telegraph* (n), *Daily Worker* (n)

daisies *see* daisy; pushing up daisies

daisy wild flower; Michaelmas daisy, ox-eye daisy; daisy chain, daisy wheel, daisy-cutter; fresh as a daisy; *Daisy Miller* (b), *Driving Miss Daisy* (f), *Princess Daisy* (b/tv)

dale valley; *Mrs Dale's Diary* (r)

dally dawdle; dilly-dally

dam mother of a horse, river barrier; *The Dam Busters* (f)

damage harm; cause harm to; 1992 Louis Malle film; collateral damage; what's the damage?

damaged *see* damage; damaged goods

damages *see* damage; punitive damages

damask fabric, variety of rose; damask rose, damask steel

dame non-hereditary title, pantomime character; grande dame; Notre Dame; *The Hunchback of Notre Dame* (f), *Notre Dame de Paris* (b), *There Is Nothin' Like a Dame* (s)

damn put a curse on, revile; exclamation of annoyance; as near as damn it, damn with faint praise, not worth a damn; *Damn Yankees* (f)

damned eternally cursed; *The Beautiful and Damned* (b), *Village of* *the Damned* (f), *Voyage of the Damned* (f)

damp moisture; moist; rising damp; damp course, damp squib, damp-proof; *Rising Damp* (tv)

damper depressive influence, draught regulator, shock absorber; more moist; put a damper on

dance movement to music; move to music; barn dance, belly dance, break-dance, clog dance, country dance, dinner-dance, fan dance, folk dance, ice dance, line dance, morris dance, round dance, square dance, tap-dance, tea dance, war dance; dance band, dance floor, dance hall, dance of the seven veils; dance attendance on, dance to your tune, lead a merry dance, a song and dance; Floral Dance; *A Dance to the Music of Time* (b), *Dance with a Stranger* (f), *The Floral Dance* (cl), *Invitation to the Dance* (b/cl), *I Won't Dance* (s), *Let's Face the Music and Dance* (s), *Sabre Dance* (cl), *Save the Last Dance for Me* (s), *Shall We Dance?* (s), *Strictly Dance Fever* (tv), *A Time to Dance* (b/tv)

dancer person who moves to music; Santa's reindeer; ballet dancer, belly dancer, break dancer, clog dancer, go-go dancer, lap dancer, morris dancer, tap dancer; *Private Dancer* (s)

dances *see* dance; *Dances with Wolves* (f)

dancing *see* dance; ballroom dancing, belly dancing, break-dancing, clog dancing, country dancing, folk dancing, formation dancing, ice dancing, lap-dancing, line dancing, morris dancing, old-time dancing, sequence dancing, square-dancing,

tap-dancing; dancing girl; all-singing all-dancing; *Come Dancing,* (tv), *Dancing at Lughnasa* (f/pl), *Dancing in the Dark* (s), *Dancing in the Street* (s), *Dancing on Ice* (tv), *Dancing on the Ceiling* (s), *Dancing Queen* (s), *Dirty Dancing* (f), *Strictly Come Dancing* (tv)

dandelion wild flower; dandelion clock

dandy fop; children's comic; dandy brush; fine and dandy; *Yankee Doodle Dandy* (f)

danger peril; danger money; in danger, on the danger list; *Appointment with Danger* (f), *Clear and Present Danger* (f), *Danger Man* (tv)

dangerous risky; *Dangerous Liaisons* (f), *Dangerous Moonlight* (f), *These Dangerous Years* (f), *Thirty Is a Dangerous Age, Cynthia* (f)

dare challenge, have the courage; I dare say; *Where Eagles Dare* (b/f)

dares *see* Dare; who dares wins; *Who Dares Wins* (f)

dark absence of light; evil, gloomy, swarthy, unlit; in the dark, keep dark; dark horse; dark night of the soul, leap in the dark, shot in the dark, stab in the dark, tall, dark and handsome, whistle in the dark; Dark Ages; *Cast a Dark Shadow* (f), *Dancing in the Dark* (s), *The Dark of the Matinee* (s), *Dark Star* (f), *Dark Victory* (f), *Dark Water* (f), *His Dark Materials* (b), *Near Dark* (f), *A Shot in the Dark* (f), *Wait until Dark* (f)

darken become blacker; never darken my door

darkness absence of light, state of ignorance; Prince of Darkness; *Darkness at Noon* (b), *Edge of Darkness* (tv), *Heart of Darkness* (b), *Prince of Darkness* (f)

darling   sweetheart; 1965 Julie Christie film; *The Darling Buds of May* (b/tv), *Move Over Darling* (f/s), *My Darling Clementine* (f)

darn   sewn repair; mend; mild expletive; *Too Darn Hot* (s)

darning   *see* darn; darning needle

dart   arrow, garment tuck; move quickly; Devon river

darts   *see* dart; pub game; darts player

dash   elan, punctuation mark, small amount, sprint; sportswear brand; hurry, ruin, throw to the ground; pebble-dash; cut a dash

data   information; data processing, data protection

date   palm fruit, romantic meeting, specific time; become outmoded, establish the age of, go out with; blind date, closing date, out of date, post-date, pre-date, release date, sell-by date, up to date, use-by date; date of birth, date stamp; to date; (International) Date Line; *Blind Date* (tv)

dating   *see* date; carbon dating, computer dating, post-dating, pre-dating, radiocarbon dating; dating agency

daub   clumsy brush stroke; paint roughly; wattle and daub

daughter   girl child; god-daughter; daughter-in-law; *Coal Miner's Daughter* (f), *Mistral's Daughter*, (b/tv), *Not without My Daughter* (f), *The Prodigal Daughter* (b), *Ryan's Daughter* (f), *The Surgeon's Daughter* (b)

daughters   *see* daughter; *Wives and Daughters* (b)

dawn   beginning, sunrise; Rider Haggard novel; crack of dawn; dawn chorus; *Dawn of the Dead* (f), *Red Dawn* (f), *Zulu Dawn* (f)

day   24-hour period; a year and a day, bad hair day, break of day, duvet day, early-closing day, feast day, first-day cover, flag day, good day, high day, holy day, latter-day, market day, name day, off day, one day, open day, pay day, polling day, present-day, quarter day, rag day, rainy day, red-letter day, saint's day, some day, speech day; day and night, day-bed, day care, day centre, day labourer, day-long, day of obligation, day of reckoning, day of rest, day off, day out, day release, day return, day room, day school, day trip, day tripper; all in a day's work, an apple a day keeps the doctor away, call it a day, carry the day, day by day, day in day out, every dog has its day, from day to day, have a field day, have a nice day, late in the day, many happy returns of the day, name the day, pass the time of day, Rome wasn't built in a day, save the day, seize the day, that will be the day, the cold light of day, to my dying day, tomorrow is another day, win the day; All Fools' Day, All Saints' Day, All Souls' Day, April Fool's Day, Armistice Day, Ascension Day, Bastille Day, Boxing Day, Budget Day, Christmas Day, Day of Atonement, Day of Judgement, Day-Glo, D-Day, Easter Day, Empire Day, Father's Day, Groundhog Day, Independence Day Innocents' Day, Judgement Day, Labour Day, Lady Day, Latter-Day Saints, The Lord's Day, May Day, Midsummer Day, Mother's Day, New Year's Day, Oak-Apple Day, Pancake

Day, Poppy Day, Remembrance Day, Seventh-Day Adventist, Six Day War, St Andrew's Day, St David's Day, St George's Day, St Patrick's Day, St Swithin's Day, St Valentine's Day, Thanksgiving Day, VJ Day; *Bad Day at Black Rock* (f), *The Day after Tomorrow* (f), *A Day at the Races* (f), *Day for Night* (f), *A Day in the Death of Joe Egg* (pl), *Day of the Dead* (f), *The Day of the Jackal* (b/f), *The Day of the Locust* (b/f), *The Day of the Triffids* (b/f), *The Day the Earth Stood Still* (f), *The Day Today* (tv), *Day Tripper* (s), *Dog Day Afternoon* (f), *Every Day Hurts* (s), *Ferris Bueller's Day Off* (f), *A Grand Day Out* (f), *Groundhog Day* (f), *A Hard Day's Night* (f/s), *Independence Day* (f), *Isn't This a Lovely Day* (s), *Lady for a Day* (f), *The Last Day of Pompeii* (pa), *Light of Day* (f), *Long Day's Journey into Night* (f/pl), *The Longest Day* (b/f/s), *Lovely Day* (s), *Many a New Day* (s), *Match of the Day* (tv), *Night and Day* (b/mus/pl/s), *One Fine Day* (f/s), *The Remains of the Day* (b/f), *Seize the Day* (b), *Some Day My Prince Will Come* (s), *Some Day You'll Be Sorry* (s), *Stay Another Day* (s), *That'll Be the Day* (f/s)

daydream musing; be lost in thought; *Daydream Believer* (s)

daylight period between dawn and dusk; 1996 Sylvester Stallone film; daylight robbery; in broad daylight, see daylight

days *see* day; dog days, early days, feast days, glory days, salad days, the old days, these days; count the days, the good old days, high days and holidays, my days are numbered, nine-days' wonder, one of these days,

one of those days; The Ancient of Days, Ember Days, Rogation Days; *Anne of the Thousand Days* (f), *Around the World in Eighty Days* (b/f/tv), *Burmese Days*, (b), *Days of Heaven* (f), *Days of Thunder* (f), *Days of Wine and Roses* (f/s), *Days with Sir Roger de Coverley* (b), *Eight Days a Week* (s), *End of Days* (f), *The Good Old Days* (tv), *The Happiest Days of Your Life* (f), *Happy Days* (tv), *How to Lose a Guy in Ten Days* (f), *The Last Days of Pompeii* (b), *Radio Days*, (f), *Salad Days* (mus), *Seven Days in May* (f), *These Days* (s), *Those Were the Days* (s), *To Serve Them All My Days* (tv), *Three Days of the Condor* (f)

daze confused state; knock senseless

dazed *see* daze; *Dazed and Confused* (f)

dazzle blind with light, impress; razzle-dazzle

dazzler impressive person or thing; bobby-dazzler; *Bobby Dazzler* (tv)

dead complete, lifeless, numb; completely; drop-dead gorgeous; dead beat, dead centre, dead cert, dead duck, dead end, dead giveaway, dead-head, dead heat, dead leg, dead letter, dead letter box, dead loss, dead man's handle, dead reckoning, dead ringer, dead set, dead shot, dead time, dead wood, dead-head; (as) dead as a doornail, be the dead spit of, dead and buried, dead as a dodo, dead in the water, dead men tell no tales, the dead of night, dead on your feet, dead to the world, flog a dead horse, left for dead, make a dead set at, over my dead body; Dead Sea, Dead Sea Scrolls; *Dawn of the Dead* (f), *Day of the Dead* (f), *The Dead* (b), *Dead Calm* (f), *Dead End* (f), *Dead Man Walking* (f),

Dead Men Tell No Tales (b), *Dead Ringer* (f), *Dead Ringer for Love* (s), *Dead Ringers* (f/r/tv), *Dead Souls* (b), *The Dead Zone* (b/f), *Drop the Dead Donkey* (tv), *The House of the Dead* (b), *The Naked and the Dead* (b/f), *Night of the Living Dead* (f), *The Quick and the Dead* (f), *The Return of the Living Dead* (f), *Shaun of the Dead* (f), *Waking the Dead* (tv)

deadlier *see* deadly; *Deadlier than the Male* (b/f)

deadly lethal; seven deadly sins; deadly nightshade, deadly sin; *Kiss Me Deadly* (b/f)

deaf unable to hear; tone-deaf; deaf as a post, fall on deaf ears, turn a deaf ear

deal business transaction, wood type; buy and sell, cope (with), give out playing-cards; Kent town; big deal, good deal, great deal, package deal, raw deal, square deal; deal out; it's a deal, wheel and deal; New Deal; *Deal or No Deal* (tv), *Raw Deal* (f)

dealer person who gives out playing-cards, trader; car dealer, wheeler-dealer

dealing *see* deal; double-dealing, insider dealing, wheeler-dealing; wheeling and dealing

dean cathedral dignitary, university official; Forest of Dean

dear beloved, expensive; dear John letter; dear me, dear to your heart, for dear life, oh dear; Dear Madam, Dear Sir; *Dear John* (tv), *Dear Me* (b), *Dear Prudence* (s), *Father Dear Father* (tv)

dearly at a high price, fondly, very much; pay dearly; dearly beloved

death cessation of life, fatality; kiss of death, near-death experience, sudden death; death-cap, death's head hawkmoth, death knell, death mask, death penalty, death trap, death warrant, death-watch beetle, death wish; as sure as death, at death's door, catch your death of cold, death by misadventure, dice with death, die a death, do to death, fate worse than death, hold on for grim death, in at the death, life and death, like death warmed up, matter of life and death, put to death, sentence to death, tickled to death; Black Death, Death Star, Death Valley, Wall of Death; *Accidental Death of an Anarchist* (pl), *Appointment with Death* (b/f), *A Day in the Death of Joe Egg* (pl), *Death and the Maiden* (f), *Death Becomes Her* (f), *Death in the Afternoon* (b), *Death in Venice* (b/f), *Death Is a Lonely Business* (b), *Death of a Clown* (s), *Death of a Salesman* (f/pl), *Death of an Expert Witness* (b/tv), *The Death of Marat* (pl), *Death on the Nile* (b/f), *Death Race 2000* (f), *Death Wish* (f), *Kiss of Death* (f), *The Life and Death of Colonel Blimp* (f), *Love and Death on Long Island* (f), *A Matter of Life and Death* (f), *Sudden Death* (f), *A Taste for Death* (b), *The Triumph of Death* (pa), *Till Death Us Do Part* (tv)

debate discussion; discuss; under debate

debauched corrupted; dissolute

debit sum owed; take from an account; direct debit; debit card

debrief questioning after a mission; question after a mission

debt sum owed; bad debt, national debt; debt collector, debt of gratitude, debt of honour; in debt

decay decomposition; decompose

deceased person who has died; recently died

decimal   fraction; denoting a numerical system; decimal currency, decimal point

decimate   execute one in ten, reduce heavily

decision   resolution; split decision; *Executive Decision* (f)

deck   floor of a ship, pack of cards; adorn festively, punch to the ground; cassette deck, flight deck, lower deck, promenade deck, sun deck, tape deck; deck-hand, deck of cards; *Deck of Cards* (s)

decks   *see* deck; below decks

declare   announce; declare an interest

decline   reduction; diminish, refuse; on the decline; *Decline and Fall* (b), *The History of the Decline and Fall of the Roman Empire* (b)

decompression   expansion (of computer data), reduction in the force of air; decompression chamber, decompression sickness

decorating   adorning, applying wallpaper and paint; interior decorating

decoration   adornment, medal; interior decoration

decorations   garlands and ornaments; Xmas decorations

decorator   painter and paper-hanger; interior decorator

decoy   artificial bird, item used as a lure; entice

decrease   reduction; reduce

decreasing   *see* decrease; *Ever Decreasing Circles* (tv)

decree   edict, judicial decision; ordain; decree absolute, decree nisi

dedicated   committed, inscribed; loyally focused; *Dedicated Follower of Fashion* (s)

dedication   commitment, inscription

deductible   US insurance excess; can be subtracted; tax-deductible

deed   feat, legal document; deed of covenant, deed poll; *Judge John Deed* (tv)

deeds   *see* deed; title deeds; *Mr Deeds Goes to Town* (f)

deep   sea; extending far down, intense, low in pitch; knee-deep, rapture of the deep, skin-deep; deep end, deep-felt, deep-freeze, deep-fry, deep-rooted, deep-sea diving, deep-seated, deep-set, deep space; beauty is only skin deep, drink deep, go off the deep end, in at the deep end, in deep water, jump in at the deep end, still waters run deep; Deep South; *The Deep* (f), *Deep Blue Sea* (f), *The Deep Blue Sea* (pl), *Deep Impact* (f), *In Deep* (tv), *River Deep Mountain High* (s), *Still Waters Run Deep* (s)

deepest   *see* deep; *The First Cut Is the Deepest* (s)

deeply   *see* deep; *Truly Madly Deeply* (f)

deer   antlered creature or creatures; fallow deer, mouse deer, red deer, roe deer; deer park; *The Deer Hunter* (f)

default   fail to pay; failure to pay, pre-selected option in computing; by default, in default, judgement by default

defeat   loss; conquer, thwart; *A Fairly Honourable Defeat* (b)

defect   flaw; switch allegiance

defence   barricade, protection, vindication; civil defence, self-defence; defence mechanism, defence minister; the noble art of self-defence; *Defence of the Realm* (f)

defend   protect, stick up for

defender   non-attacking player,

protector; Defender of the Faith

defensive self-justifying, serving to protect; on the defensive

defer capitulate, postpone

deficit shortfall; trade deficit

defined gave the meaning of; demarcated; ill-defined

definite certain, specific; definite article

definition meaning, sharpness of outline; by definition

deflated discouraged, emptied of air

defuse calm (a situation), make safe (a bomb)

defy challenge, disobey; defy description

degenerate immoral person; grow worse; immoral

degrade break down chemically, humiliate, lower the quality of

degree level, measuring unit for temperature and angles, university qualification; first degree, first-degree burn, third degree; to a degree, to the nth degree; *First-Degree Burn* (b)

degrees *see* degree; by degrees; *Six Degrees of Separation* (f)

delay temporary hold-up; hold up

delegate conference attendee, representative; hand over (a task)

delegation group of representatives, handing over work to others

deliberate consider carefully; intentional, unhurried

delicate exquisite, fragile, sensitive, sickly; in a delicate condition

delicious tasty; Golden Delicious

delight pleasure; make happy; Turkish delight; red sky at night, shepherd's delight

delights *see* delight; *The Garden of Earthly Delights* (pa)

delinquent offender; failing in one's duty, tending to commit crimes; juvenile delinquent

delirium frenzy, madness; delirium tremens

deliver convey, fulfil, give birth to, rescue; deliver the goods, stand and deliver; *Stand and Deliver* (s)

delivery birth of a baby, consignment, manner of speaking in public, throw of a cricket ball; cash on delivery, express delivery, recorded delivery, special delivery; delivery man, delivery note, delivery room, delivery van; take delivery of

dell small valley; computer manufacturer; commedia dell'arte

delta Greek letter, radio code word, river-mouth; delta wing; *Delta Lady* (s), *Delta Wedding* (b), *The Delta Force* (f)

deluge flood; inundate

demand insistent request, need; ask insistently, claim as a right, require; final demand, supply and demand; in demand, in great demand, on demand

demanding asking insistently; difficult

democrat believer in social equality; member of a US political party; social democrat; Liberal Democrat

demolition knocking down; *Demolition Man* (f)

demon evil spirit; like a demon

demons *see* demon; *Angels and Demons* (b)

demonstrate protest in public, show

demonstration display, public protest

den hideout, lair, place of vice; gambling den, opium den, the lion's

den; den of iniquity, den of thieves; *Dragons' Den* (tv)

denier disowner, old French coin, unit of yarn fineness

denominator number below the line in a fraction; (lowest) common denominator

dense stupid, tightly packed

dent slight hollow; make concave

dental concerning teeth; dental floss, dental nurse, dental surgeon, dental surgery, dental technician

dentist tooth doctor; dentist's chair, dentist's drill

deny contradict, refuse

depart digress, leave; depart this life

department subdivision; maternity department, ordnance department; department store; State Department; *Department S* (tv)

departure act of leaving, digression; point of departure; departure lounge

dependency overseas territory, reliance; chemical dependency

depending being contingent, relying; depending on

depleted used up; depleted uranium

deposit initial payment, money in the bank, sediment; put down, put into a bank account; safety deposit; deposit account; lose one's deposit

depress push down, sadden

depression economic downturn, hollow, region of low atmospheric pressure, state of melancholy

deprivation hardship, withholding; sensory deprivation

deprived divested; needy

depth downward distance, intensity; in depth; depth charge; out of your depth

depths point far beneath the surface, remote place; hidden depths; *The Lower Depths* (pl)

derail cause to leave the tracks, leave the tracks, scupper

derby local match, type of hat; Epsom horse race, English city; donkey derby, local derby; derby hat; Crown Derby, The Derby, Derby County, Kentucky Derby, Sage Derby

dereliction abandoned state, neglect (of duty)

derivative investment contract, product based on another source, word obtained from another; lacking originality

descale clean (a fish), remove lime deposits from

descant treble melody; descant recorder

describe give an account of, trace in outline

description variety, word picture; job description; beyond description, defy description

desert arid region; abandon; ship of the desert; desert boots, desert island; rats desert a sinking ship; Desert Fox, Desert Rats, Gobi Desert, Kalahari Desert, Mojave Desert, Sahara Desert; *Desert Island Discs* (r) *The Desert Fox* (f/ga), *The Desert Song* (f), *Sons of the Desert* (f)

> **Desert**
> Arabian, Atacama, Gibson, Gobi, Kalahari, Mojave, Namib, Negev, Nubian, Sahara, Simpson, Sinai

deserts *see* desert; just deserts

deserves merits; one good turn deserves another

design blueprint, purpose; draw up;

graphic design, interior design; by
design; *Design for Living* (pl)

designated specified; designated
driver

designer creator; having a prestigious
fashion label, upmarket; graphic
designer, industrial designer, interior
designer; designer stubble

designs *see* design; have designs on;
Grand Designs (tv)

desire ardent wish; want; burning
desire, heart's desire; *A Streetcar
Named Desire* (f/pl), *Wings of Desire* (f)

desired wanted; leave a lot to be
desired

desk writing table; cash desk, city
desk, reception desk, roll-top desk,
writing-desk; desk job, desk-bound

desktop basic computer screen with
icons, type of computer publishing,
working surface of a table; desktop
publishing

desolate bleak, miserable,
uninhabited

desolation emptiness, misery;
Desolation Angels (al/b/f)

despair loss of hope; lose hope;
counsel of despair

desperate dire, distraught; *Desperate
Housewives* (tv), *Desperate Remedies*
(b/f)

desperately *see* desperate; *Desperately
Seeking Susan* (f)

despite regardless of; despite yourself

dessert sweet course; dessert wine

destination journey's end; *Final
Destination* (f)

destiny fate; man of destiny; *The Man
of Destiny* (s), *You Are My Destiny* (s)

destroyer killer, warship; *Conan the
Destroyer* (f)

destroying wrecking; soul-destroying

detached unfastened; dispassionate,
standing apart; semi-detached

detail minor point; itemise; devil's in
the detail, go into detail, in detail;
The Last Detail (f)

details *see* detail; the gory details

detect discern, discover, investigate

detective police investigator; private
detective; detective inspector,
detective story; *Ace Ventura: Pet
Detective* (f), *The Chinese Detective* (tv),
The Singing Detective (pl/tv)

detectives *see* detective; *The
Detectives* (tv), *Emil and the
Detectives* (b), *Watching the
Detectives* (s)

detention after-school punishment,
custody; detention centre

determined ascertained, resolved;
resolute

deuce two in cards, 40-40 in tennis;
Deuce Bigalow: Male Gigolo (f)

devastate disappoint greatly, lay
waste

developing converting (land),
evolving, processing (photos);
developing country, developing
solution

development building project,
evolution, new stage in a situation,
treatment of photographic film;
housing development, ribbon
development; research and
development

deviation divergence; standard
deviation

devices gadgets, heraldic emblems,
schemes; left to your own devices

devil evil spirit, Satan; dust devil,
printer's devil, she-devil, Tasmanian
devil; devil-may-care, devil's
advocate, devil's dozen, devil's food

cake, devil-worshipper; be a devil, better the devil you know, devil's in the detail, the devil to pay, give the devil his due, like the devil, play the devil with, speak/talk of the devil; Devil's Island; *Beat the Devil* (f), *Better The Devil You Know* (s), *Devil Gate Drive* (s), *Devil in a Blue Dress* (f), *Devil in Disguise* (s), *The Devil Is an Ass* (pl), *The Devil Rides Out* (b/f), *The Devil's Advocate* (b/f), *The Devil's Alternative* (b), *The Devil's Disciple* (pl), *Devil's Island* (f), *Flesh and the Devil* (f), *The Life and Loves of a She-Devil* (b), *She-Devil* (f), *Shout at the Devil* (f), *Sympathy for the Devil* (s), *The White Devil* (pl)

devils evil spirits; devils on horseback; Red Devils; *The Devils* (f), *The Old Devils* (b)

devoted committed; loving; *Hopelessly Devoted to You* (s)

dew morning moisture; dew point

dewy moist, youthful; dewy-eyed

diagnosis identification of illness; *Diagnosis Murder* (tv)

dial clock face; start a telephone call; Dial-a-Ride; *Dial M for Murder* (f)

dialling telephoning (a number); direct dialling; dialling code, dialling tone

dialogue conversation; meaningful dialogue

diamond baseball pitch, gemstone; 60th; industrial diamond, rough diamond; diamond jubilee, diamond mine, diamond rattlesnake, diamond ring, diamond wedding

diamonds *see* diamond; cards suit; *Diamonds Are a Girl's Best Friend* (s), *Diamonds Are Forever* (f/s), *The Eustace Diamonds* (b), *Lucy in the Sky with Diamonds* (s)

diaphragm contraceptive device, sheet of muscle

diaries *see* diary; *The Princess Diaries* (f)

diary daily journal; *Bridget Jones's Diary* (b/f), *The Diary of a Nobody* (b), *The Diary of Anne Frank* (b), *Lytton's Diary* (tv), *Mrs Dale's Diary* (r), *The Secret Diary of Adrian Mole Aged 13¾* (b)

dice gaming cubes; chop into cubes; liar dice, no dice, poker dice; dice with death, load the dice

dick detective; clever Dick, spotted dick; every Tom, Dick and Harry; *Dick Tracy* (f), *Dick Whittington*, (pan), *Moby Dick* (b), *The Bank Dick* (f), *Tom, Dick or Harry* (s)

dicky back seat of a car, false shirt-front; unreliable; dicky bow; not a dicky bird

dictate command, speak as someone else writes

dictator absolute ruler; *The Great Dictator* (f)

die gaming cube; pass away; do-or-die; die-cast, die down, die out; die a death, the die is cast, never say die, old habits die hard, straight as a die, to die for; *Die Hard* (f), *Dreams Die Fast* (b), *Fools Die* (b), *Live and Let Die* (f/s), *Never Say Die* (al/f), *The Pope Must Die* (f)

dies *see* die; *Tomorrow Never Dies* (f)

diesel liquid fuel, type of engine; fashion label; diesel engine

diet eating regimen; eat less; vegetarian diet

differ be unalike, fail to agree; agree to differ, beg to differ

difference lack of similarity, quarrel; goal difference, same difference; split the difference, with a difference

different separate, unalike; a different kettle of fish; *A Different World* (tv)

difficulty problem; technical difficulty

dig archaeological excavation, mocking remark, prod; excavate, like; infra dig; dig in, dig up; dig in your heels, dig up dirt, dig your own grave, dig yourself into a hole

digs *see* dig; lodgings

digest compilation of stories; absorb (food or information); *Reader's Digest* (mag)

digestion mental assimilation, processing of food

digestive biscuit; relating to gut action

digger excavating machine, miner, soldier; gold-digger, grave-digger

digit finger or toe, number

digital numerical, of the fingers; digital audiotape, digital compression; *Digital Fortress* (b)

dignity decorum, personal honour; stand on your dignity

dilemma quandary; on the horns of a dilemma; *The Doctor's Dilemma* (pl)

dill herb; dill pickle

dim become obscure; poorly lit, slow-witted; dim sum, dim-witted; take a dim view of

dime US coin; dime a dozen, dime store; *Brother, Can You Spare a Dime* (s)

dimension aspect, size; fourth dimension

dimmer *see* dim; dimmer switch

din noise; instil; *Gunga Din* (f/po)

dine eat; dine out

diner person who eats, US cafe; Barry Levinson film of 1982

ding bell's sound; ding-a-ling, ding-dong, ding-dong battle

dining *see* dine; dining car, dining room, dining table, dining-room table

dinner main meal; dog's dinner, tv dinner; dinner-dance, dinner jacket, dinner lady, dinner party, dinner service, dinner set; *Dinner at Eight* (f), *Guess Who's Coming to Dinner* (f), *The Man Who Came to Dinner* (f)

dinosaurs prehistoric creatures; *One of Our Dinosaurs Is Missing* (f)

dint hollow; by dint of

dip brief immersion, creamy savoury sauce, downward slope, pickpocket, quick swim; immerse briefly, pick pockets, suddenly drop; lucky dip, sheep-dip, skinny-dip; dip out, dip switch

diplomacy art of international relations, tact; gunboat diplomacy, megaphone diplomacy, shuttle diplomacy

diplomatic skilful in negotiation, tactful; diplomatic bag, diplomatic corps, diplomatic immunity

dipper headlights switch, scoop, water-bird; big dipper; Big Dipper

dire calamitous, very serious; dire straits

direct aim, control, indicate a route, supervise actors; in a straight line, non-stop, plain-spoken; direct action, direct current, direct debit, direct dialling, direct-grant school, direct hit, direct mail, direct marketing, direct speech, direct tax

directions instructions, routes; stage directions; in all directions

director board member, film boss; company director, film director, funeral director; director-general

directory phone book, reference book; ex-directory, telephone directory; directory enquiries

dirt filth, malicious gossip; pay-dirt; dirt bike, dirt cheap, dirt track; dig up dirt, dish the dirt, eat dirt

dirty filthy; play dirty; dirty look, dirty money, dirty weekend, dirty work; do the dirty on, get your hands dirty, quick and dirty, you dirty rat; *Angels with Dirty Faces* (f), *Dirty Dancing* (f), *The Dirty Dozen* (f), *Dirty Harry* (f), *Dirty Mary Crazy Larry* (f), *Dirty Pretty Things* (f), *Dirty Rotten Scoundrels* (f), *Dirty Weekend* (f), *Dirty Work* (f/pl)

disappearing vanishing; disappearing act

disapproval unfavourable opinion; *A Chorus of Disapproval* (pl)

disarmament withdrawal of weapons; nuclear disarmament

disaster calamity; court disaster; disaster movie

disc flat round object, pop record; compact disc, gold disc, slipped disc, tax disc; disc brake, disc jockey

discs *see* disc; *Desert Island Discs* (r)

discharge firing of a gun, leak; fire (a gun), pay off (a debt), release; conditional discharge, dishonourable discharge, honourable discharge

disciple follower; *The Devil's Disciple* (pl)

discipline branch of learning, controlled behaviour; chastise, train; military discipline, self-discipline

discount price reduction; reduce the price of, reject as unimportant; trade discount; discount house, discount store

discretionary judgement, tact; discretionary award, discretionary grant, discretionary income

discrimination ability to tell one thing from another, good taste, policy of prejudice; positive discrimination

discus round object for throwing; *The Discus Thrower* (sc)

disease illness; Dutch elm disease, foot-and-mouth disease, mad cow disease

disgrace ignominy, outrage; bring shame upon; in disgrace

disguise conceal one's identity, dress up; false appearance; blessing in disguise

dish food item or course, handsome person, plate; butter-dish, Petri dish, satellite dish, side dish, soap dish; dish out, dish up; dish the dirt; *The Dish* (f)

dishonourable shameful; dishonourable discharge

disk computer storage device; floppy disk, hard disk; disk drive

dismissal bowling-out (in cricket), sacking from a job; constructive dismissal

disobedience failure to comply; civil disobedience

disorder ailment, untidiness; seasonal affective disorder

disorderly unruly, untidy; disorderly conduct; drunk and disorderly

dispatch do away with, send off; dispatch box, dispatch rider

dispenser pharmacist, vending machine; cash dispenser

dispensing giving out; dispensing chemist, dispensing optician

disperse scatter widely, thin out and vanish

display exhibition; exhibit; air display, liquid crystal display, visual display unit; display case

disposable throwaway; disposable income

disposal riddance; bomb disposal, waste-disposal unit; at your disposal

dispose arrange; dispose of

disposed arranged; having a tendency; ill-disposed, well disposed

dispute argument; argue; demarcation dispute

dissent difference in opinion; express a different opinion

distance aloofness, space between two points; make remote; long-distance, middle-distance; distance learning, distance runner; go the distance, keep your distance, stay the distance; *The Loneliness of the Long Distance Runner* (b/f)

distant aloof, remote; distant cousin; *Distant Drums* (s), *Distant Voices, Still Lives* (f)

distinction contrast, excellence

distinguished recognised as different; acclaimed

distracted drew the attention of; inattentive

distraction agitation, amusement; drive to distraction

distress adversity, anguish; cause suffering to; distress signal

district region; red-light district; district attorney, district auditor, district nurse; District Line, Lake District, Peak District; *District Nurse* (tv)

disturbed interrupted; emotionally upset

disturbing interrupting; emotionally upsetting

ditch drainage channel; get rid of, make a forced landing; last-ditch

dive seedy bar; plunge; duck and dive, swallow dive; dive-bomb, dive-bomber

diver swimmer who plunges in head first; deep-sea diver, pearl diver, scuba diver, skin-diver

divert distract, reroute

divide separate into parts, share out; great divide; divide and conquer, divide and rule

dividend payout; final dividend, peace dividend

dividends benefits, payouts

divine discover by guesswork; godly; divine right of kings; to err is human, to forgive divine; *The Divine Comedy* (pl), *The Divine Right of Kings* (po), *Divine Secrets of the Ya-Ya Sisterhood* (b/f)

diving pool sport; plunging; deep-sea diving, pearl diving, scuba diving, skin-diving; diving bell, diving bird, diving board, diving suit

divinity holiness, religious studies

division cleft, section (army, soccer league), sharing out; long division; division bell, division of labour

divorce ending of a marriage; split up; *Divorce American Style* (f), *Le Divorce* (f)

divorced severed; no longer married

dizzy light-headed; dizzy heights, dizzy spell

dock common weed, defendant's stand, harbour; come into port, cut short; dry dock; dock strike; in dock, in the dock; *Dixon of Dock Green* (tv), *Hickory Dickory Dock* (nr)

doctor physician; falsify; family doctor, flying doctor, spin doctor, witch doctor; doctor of philosophy; an apple a day keeps the doctor away, what the doctor ordered; *Doctor at Large* (f), *Doctor at Sea* (f), *Doctor Dolittle* (f), *Doctor Faustus* (b), *Doctor in Love* (f), *Doctor in the House* (tv), *Doctor Jekyll and Mr Hyde* (b), *The Doctor's Dilemma* (pl), *Doctor Who* (tv), *Doctor Zhivago* (b/f), *The Flying Doctor* (tv), *The Island of Dr Moreau* (f)

doctors *see* doctor; doctors make the worst patients

doctrine set of beliefs; Monroe Doctrine

document written report; record (information)

dodge evade; Dodge City

dodo extinct bird; (as) dead as a dodo

doe female deer or rabbit; doe-eyed; John Doe; *Meet John Doe* (f)

does *see* doe; accomplishes; handsome is as handsome does

doesn't *see* does; *Alice Doesn't Live Here Any More* (f)

dog canine; follow; a dog's life, guard dog, guide dog, gun dog, hot dog, hunting dog, Mexican hairless dog, police dog, prairie dog, pug dog, pye-dog, sausage dog, Scottie dog, sea dog, shaggy-dog story, sniffer dog, top dog, tracker dog; dog biscuit, dog collar, dog days, dog kennel, dog rose, dog show, dog star, dog tag, dog-eared, dog-end, dog-leg, dog's breakfast, dog's dinner, dog's life, dog-tired, dog-tooth, dog-watch; beware of the dog, dog eat dog, dog in the manger, every dog has its day, hair of the dog (that bit you), you can't teach an old dog new tricks; *Dog Day Afternoon* (f), *Hound Dog* (s),

It's Me or the Dog (tv), *My Dog Skip* (f), *Wag the Dog* (f)

doggy puppy; fond of canines; doggy bag, doggy-paddle

doghouse kennel; in the doghouse

dogs *see* dog; go to the dogs, let sleeping dogs lie, rain cats and dogs; Battersea Dogs' Home, Isle of Dogs; *Cats and Dogs* (f), *The Dogs of War* (b/f), *The Plague Dogs* (b/f), *Reservoir Dogs* (f), *Straw Dogs* (f), *The Truth about Cats and Dogs* (f)

doing *see* does; evil-doing, nothing doing; doing well

dole unemployment benefit; mete (out); on the dole; *Love on the Dole* (f)

doll plaything; baby-doll nightdress, Barbie doll, Kewpie doll, rag doll, Russian doll; doll's house; *Baby Doll* (f), *China Doll* (f), *A Doll's House* (pl), *Living Doll* (s), *Oh, You Beautiful Doll* (s), *Rag Doll* (s)

dollar currency unit; dollar sign; bet your bottom dollar; *Billion Dollar Brain* (b/f), *Million Dollar Baby* (f), *The Six Million Dollar Man* (tv)

dollars see dollar; *A Fistful of Dollars* (f), *For a Few Dollars More* (f)

dolls see doll; *Guys and Dolls*, (mus), *Valley of the Dolls* (b/f)

dolly easy catch in cricket, washtub pole, wheeled platform; cloned sheep; corn dolly; dolly mixtures, dolly tub, Dolly Varden; *Hello Dolly* (f/s)

dolphin marine mammal; bottlenose dolphin; *Boy on a Dolphin* (f)

dome cupola; Greenwich millennium structure; onion dome; *Welcome to the Pleasure Dome* (s)

domestic servant; relating to home;

gross domestic product; domestic science

domino priest's cloak, spotted playing-piece; Keira Knightley film; domino effect

don mafia boss, Spanish title, university lecturer; English river, Russian river; put on; Don Juan; *And Quiet Flows the Don* (b), *Don Carlos* (o), *Don Giovanni* (o), *Don Juan* (po), *Don Quixote* (b)

done (had) accomplished; well done; done for, done in, done up; do as you would be done by, done and dusted, easier said than done, easily done, have done with, over and done with, when all is said and done, a woman's work is never done; *She Done Him Wrong* (f)

dong sound of a bell, Vietnamese currency unit; ding-dong, ding-dong battle

donkey children's card game, horse-like animal; nodding donkey; donkey derby, donkey jacket, donkey work, donkey's years; talk the hind leg off a donkey; *Drop the Dead Donkey* (tv)

donor giver (of blood or funds); blood donor; donor card

don't; don't change horses in midstream, don't cry over spilt milk, don't hold your breath, don't judge a book by its cover, don't look a gift horse in the mouth, don't mention it, don't put all your eggs in one basket, don't put the cart before the horse, don't rock the boat, I don't mind telling you, if it ain't broke don't fix it, two wrongs don't make a right, you don't say; *Big Girls Don't Cry* (s), *Billy Don't be a Hero* (s), *Boys Don't Cry* (f), *Don't Cry for Me Argentina* (s), *Don't Fear the Reaper* (s), *Don't Give Up* (s), *Don't Give Up on Us* (s), *Don't Go Breaking My Heart* (s), *Don't Let the Sun Go Down on Me* (s), *Don't Look Now* (b/f), *Don't Rock the Boat* (s/tv), *Don't Say a Word* (f), *Don't Wait Up* (tv), *Don't You Want Me* (s), *I Don't Like Mondays* (s), *Papa Don't Preach* (s), *Please Don't Tease* (s), *They Shoot Horses Don't They* (f)

doodle scribble aimlessly; aimless sketch; cock-a-doodle-doo; *Yankee Doodle Dandy* (f)

doom dreadful fate; consign to ruin; crack of doom; *Indiana Jones and the Temple of Doom* (f)

door room access; back-door, barn door, fire door, next door, next door to, patio door, revolving door, stable door, stage door, swing door; door furniture, door handle, door-knocker; as one door closes another opens, at death's door, by the back door, foot in the door, keep the wolf from the door, never darken my door; *The Door in the Floor* (f), *Green Door* (s), *Living Next Door to Alice* (s), *My Wife Next Door* (tv), *Stage Door* (f)

doornail ornamental stud; (as) dead as a doornail

doors accesses to rooms; French doors; behind closed doors, out of doors; *Communicating Doors* (pl), *The Doors* (f), *Early Doors* (tv), *Sliding Doors* (f), *The Doors of Perception* (b)

doorstep thick slice of bread, threshold; peddle; on the doorstep

dope cannabis, fool, information; administer drugs to

dory fish, small boat; hunky dory; John Dory; *Hunky Dory* (al)

The *Puzzler* Crossword Solver's Dictionary

dose measure of medicine; give
medicine to; like a dose of salts

dot tiny speck; on the dot, polka dot,
the year dot; dot matrix; dot the i's
and cross the t's; *Itsy Bitsy Teeny
Weeny Yellow Polka Dot Bikini* (s)

dotted placed at irregular intervals,
speckled; dotted line

double large shot of spirits, lookalike,
replica, twice the amount; multiply
by two; body double; double act,
double agent, double back, double-
barrelled, double bass, double
bassoon, double bed, double bill,
double bluff, double-book, double-
breasted, double-check, double chin,
double cream, double-cross, double-
dealing, double-decker, double-
declutch, double Dutch, double
eagle, double-edged, double
entendre, double-entry, double
exposure, double fault, double
feature, double figures, double first,
double-fronted, double-glazed,
double glazing, double helix, double
jeopardy, double-jointed, double
negative, double-park, double quick,
double standards, double take,
double time, double top, double up,
double vision, double whammy,
double white line; at the double, in
double quick time, double or
nothing, double or quits; Double
Gloucester; *Body Double* (f), *Double
Indemnity* (b/f), *Double Jeopardy* (f),
Double Your Money (tv), *The Double-
Dealer* (pl)

doubles *see* double; game for two
pairs; mixed doubles

doubt uncertainty; feel unsure; self-
doubt; benefit of the doubt, beyond
doubt, in doubt, no doubt; *Ain't No*

Doubt (s), *Shadow of a Doubt* (f)

doubting *see* doubt; Doubting
Thomas

dough money, uncooked bread;
Mouldy Old Dough (s)

doughnut fried cake ring; jam
doughnut

dove bird; collared dove, ring-dove,
turtle dove; Dove Cottage; *Wings of a
Dove* (s), *The Wings of the Dove* (b/f)

down feathers; Northern Ireland
county; to or on a lower level;
dejected; drink; back down, bogged
down, break down, bring down,
broken-down, buckle down, burn
down, calm down, cash down, chuck
it down, clamp down, climb down,
close down, come down, crack down,
die down, dress down, dress-down
Friday, dressing-down, fall down, flag
down, hand down, hold down,
knock down, knuckle down, lay
down, let down, lie down, low-down,
mark down, mown down, nail down,
pin down, pipe down, play down,
put down, rain down, rub down, run
down, settle down, shut down,
simmer down, sit down, sit-down
strike, slow down, stand down, step
down, strike down, take down, tear
down, tie down, tone down, top-
down, touch down, track down, turn
down, two-up two-down, upside
down, upside-down cake, wash
down, water down, wear down;
down and out, down at heel, down
in the dumps, down in the mouth,
down on your luck, down payment,
down the hatch, down the road,
down to earth, down tools; batten
down the hatches, breathe down
your neck, bring back down to earth,

bring down the curtain, bring the house down, caught with your pants/trousers down, cut down to size, eyes down, force down your throat, get down to a fine art, get down to brass tacks, go down a bomb, go down a storm, go down like a lead balloon, go down like ninepins, go/walk down memory lane, go down the drain, go down the pan, go down the plughole, go down the tubes, go down the wire, lay down the law, let your hair down, look down your nose at, put down roots, put your foot down, sell down the river, shoot down in flames, suit down to the ground, take down a peg or two, take down the law, take lying down, throw down the gauntlet, what goes up must come down, when the chips are down, whistle down the wind; Down Under; *Black Hawk Down* (f), *By Grand Central Station I Sat Down and Wept* (b), *Don't Let the Sun Go Down on Me* (s), *Down and Out in Beverly Hills* (f), *Down and Out in Paris and London* (b), *Down in the Groove* (al), *Down to Earth* (tv), *Down Under* (s), *Falling Down* (f), *Flying Down to Rio* (f), *Igby Goes Down* (f), *Sit Down* (s), *The Stars Look Down* (b/f), *Tie Me Kangaroo Down, Sport* (s), *Two Up Two Down* (tv), *Upside Down* (s), *Watership Down* (b/f), *Whistle Down the Wind* (b/f)

downs upland area; drinks; hand-me-downs, ups and downs; South Downs

downstairs on a lower storey; *Upstairs Downstairs* (tv)

dozen twelve; baker's dozen, daily dozen, devil's dozen, half a dozen; dime a dozen, talk nineteen to the dozen; *The Dirty Dozen* (f)

drab dull; olive drab

drabs military clothing, slovenly women; in dribs and drabs

draft money order, preliminary version, US conscription; draw up an outline; bank draft, banker's draft

drag drumming pattern, clothing of the opposite sex, tiresome thing; haul, pass by tediously; drag king, drag on, drag queen, drag racing; drag through the mud, drag your feet

dragon mythical creature; komodo dragon; dragon boat, dragon-boat festival; chase the dragon; *Crouching Tiger, Hidden Dragon* (f), *Enter the Dragon* (f), *Pete's Dragon* (f), *Puff the Magic Dragon* (s), *Red Dragon* (b/f), *The Year of the Dragon* (f)

dragons see dragon; *Dragons' Den* (tv), *Dungeons and Dragons* (f)

dragoon cavalryman; coerce

drain sewage pipe; draw off (liquid), exhaust, flow away; brain drain, storm drain; go down the drain, laugh like a drain

draining see drain; draining board

drakes male ducks; (play) ducks and drakes

drama art of writing and presenting plays, crisis, stage play; costume drama, kitchen-sink drama; drama school

dramatic relating to plays, striking, theatrical, thrilling

dramatics theatrical behaviour; amateur dramatics

drape curtain; hang loosely

draught current of air, swig of a drink; served from a cask; draught-proof; on draught, sleeping draught

draughtsman person skilled at

technical drawing; *The Draughtsman's Contract* (f)

draw attraction, lottery, tied score; attract, finish level, pull, sketch; draw back, draw breath, draw lots, draw up; draw a blank, draw a veil over, draw in your horns, draw the line, draw the short straw, luck of the draw, quick on the draw; *The Quick Draw McGraw Show* (tv)

drawer person issuing a cheque, sketcher, sliding box; bottom drawer, top-drawer; refer to drawer

drawers *see* drawer; chest of drawers

drawing *see* draw; picture; line drawing, mechanical drawing; drawing board, drawing room, drawing-pin; back to the drawing board

drawl lazy style of speech; speak lazily

drawn (had) attracted, finished level, pulled, sketched; long-drawn-out; drawn-out; at daggers drawn

dread terror; be in fear of

dreadful terrible; penny dreadful

dream cherished hope, vision while asleep; imagine whilst asleep; pipe dream, the American dream; dream ticket, dream up; like a dream; *All I Have to Do Is Dream* (s), *A Midsummer-Night's Dream* (pl), *Any Dream Will Do* (s), *Dream Baby* (s), *Dream Lover* (s), *I Dream of Jeannie* (tv), *I Have a Dream* (s), *Requiem for a Dream* (b/f), *Silver Dream Machine* (s), *Silver Dream Racer* (f), *Theme for a Dream* (s)

dreams *see* dream; *Dreams Die Fast* (b), *Electric Dreams* (f/s), *Field of Dreams* (f), *Island of Dreams* (s), *Sweet Dreams* (f), *Sweet Dreams (Are Made of This)* (al/s), *Together in Electric Dreams* (s)

dredge clear (a river-bed), sprinkle (with sugar or flour)

dregs most useless part, residue

dress clothing, frock; decorate, put on clothes, treat (a wound); coat dress, cross-dress, evening dress, fancy dress, fancy-dress ball, head-dress, Highland dress, mini-dress, morning dress, pinafore dress, service dress, shirt dress, wedding dress; dress circle, dress coat, dress down, dress rehearsal, dress sense, dress shirt, dress up, dress-down Friday; *Devil in a Blue Dress* (f), *Red Dress* (s)

dressed clothed, decorated, put on clothes; dressed crab, dressed up; dressed to kill, dressed (up) to the nines, mutton dressed as lamb; *Dressed to Kill* (f)

dresser kitchen sideboard, wardrobe assistant; cross-dresser, Welsh dresser; *The Dresser* (f)

dressing decorating, putting on clothes; salad sauce, wound cover; French dressing, salad dressing, top-dressing, well dressing, window dressing; dressing-down, dressing-gown, dressing-room, dressing table; Thousand Island dressing

dribble run with the football, slaver

dried removed moisture from; dried-up; cut and dried

drift deviation from a course, gist, heap of snow; float aimlessly; continental drift; drift apart, drift net; North Atlantic Drift

drifter vagrant; *High Plains Drifter* (f)

drill baboon, fabric, hole-boring tool, marching practice, seed trench; bore a hole, instil, instruct; dentist's drill, electric drill, fire drill, hammer drill, kerb drill, pack drill, pneumatic drill; drill hall, drill sergeant; no names, no pack drill

drink imbibe; beverage; drink deep, drink up, drink-driver, drink-driving; drink like a fish, drink the health of, drink under the table, I'll drink to that, the worse for drink; *Eat Drink Man Woman* (f)

drinker person who likes a tipple; *The Absinthe Drinker* (pa)

drinking imbibing; drinking chocolate, drinking fountain, drinking song, drinking-up time

drip slow trickle, wimp; trickle; non-drip; drip-dry, drip feed

drive access road, ambition, avenue, car trip, golf stroke; control a vehicle, hit a golf ball, propel; beetle drive, disk drive, fly-drive, four-wheel drive, front-wheel drive, left-hand drive, off drive, rear-wheel drive, right-hand drive, test-drive, whist drive; drive home, drive out, drive-in, drive-in movie, drive-through; drive a hard bargain, drive a wedge between, drive to distraction, drive up the wall; *Devil Gate Drive* (s), *Mulholland Drive* (f), *They Drive by Night* (f), *You Drive Me Crazy* (s)

driven *see* drive; as pure as the driven snow

driver chauffeur, golf club; ambulance driver, back-seat driver, bus driver, cab driver, co-driver, designated driver, drink-driver, engine driver, L-driver, learner driver, lorry driver, owner-driver, racing driver, slave-driver, Sunday driver, taxi driver, tractor driver, truck driver; in the driver's seat; *Taxi Driver* (f)

driving *see* drive; careless driving, drink-driving, drink-driving charge; driving lesson, driving licence, driving range, driving test; in the driving seat; *Driving Miss Daisy* (f)

drone humming sound, male bee; hum

drop lozenge, reduction, steep downward slope; abandon, fall, let fall, reduce; acid drop, air-drop, cough drop, ear drop, eye-drop, lemon drop, name-drop, pear-drop; drop by, drop goal, drop handlebars, drop in, drop kick, drop off, drop out, drop scone, drop shot, drop shoulder, drop waist, drop zone, drop-dead gorgeous; drop a clanger, a drop in the ocean, drop like flies, ready to drop; *Drop the Dead Donkey* (tv), *Drop Zone* (f), *The Lemon Drop Kid* (f)

dropped *see* drop; the penny dropped

dropping *see* drop; jaw-dropping, name-dropping

drops *see* drop; knockout drops

drove *see* drive; *I Drove all Night* (s)

drown flood, muffle, perish in water; drown your sorrows

drug narcotic; put under sedation; truth drug; drug addict; *Love Is the Drug* (s)

drum cylindrical container, percussion instrument; beat with the fingers; bass drum, oil drum, side drum, snare drum, steel drum; drum and bass, drum kit, drum major, drum majorette, drum pad, drum roll; bang the drum; *The Tin Drum* (b)

drummer percussionist; *The Little Drummer Girl* (b/f)

drums *see* drum; *Distant Drums* (s)

drunk   inebriated; blind drunk, punch-drunk; (as) drunk as a lord, drunk and disorderly; *Punch-Drunk Love* (f)

dry   parched, uninteresting, without alcohol, without water; desiccate, parch; blow-dry, bone dry, drip-dry, freeze-dry, scrunch-dry, spin-dry, tumble-dry; dry cell, dry-clean, dry dock, dry-eyed, dry fly, dry-fry, dry goods, dry ice, dry land, dry Martini, dry rot, dry run, dry sherry, dry slope, dry-stone walling, dry up; hang out to dry, high and dry, home and dry, like watching paint dry; *Dry Rot* (f/pl), *A Dry White Season* (b/f)

dryer   domestic appliance; spin dryer, tumble-dryer, washer-dryer

dual   consisting of two parts; dual carriageway, dual control

dub   add a soundtrack to, give a nickname to, invest with a knighthood

dubious   open to suspicion, uncertain

duchess   female aristocrat; grand duchess; *The Duchess of Duke Street* (tv), *The Duchess of Malfi* (pl)

duchy   nobleman's territory; grand duchy

duck   strong fabric, waterfowl, zero in cricket; bob down, evade; Bombay duck, dead duck, eider duck, lame duck, mandarin duck, Muscovy duck, Peking duck, roast duck, sitting duck, wild duck; duck pond, duck-billed platypus; break your duck, duck and dive, like a duck to water, out for a duck, water off a duck's back; *Duck Soup* (f)

ducking   *see* duck; ducking stool

duckling   baby waterfowl; ugly duckling; *The Ugly Duckling* (b/s)

ducks   *see* duck; ducks and drakes; play ducks and drakes with

duct   channel; tear duct

dude   US guy; dude ranch

due   expected, fitting, owed; rightful treatment; due east, due north, due process, due south, due to, due west; give the devil his due, in due course; *Due South* (tv)

duel   fight on a matter of honour; 1971 Spielberg film

dues   fees; pay your dues

duff   of poor quality; flour pudding; plum duff; duff up

duffel   coarse cloth; duffel bag, duffel coat

duke   male aristocrat; grand duke; Duke Ellington; Iron Duke; *The Duchess of Duke Street* (tv)

dull   drab, overcast, tedious

dumb   unable to speak; dumb blonde, dumb waiter, dumb-bell; *The Dumb Waiter* (pl)

dummy   baby's comforter, tailor's model; fake; tailor's dummy; dummy run; sell a dummy to

dump   rubbish tip, unpleasant place; get rid of, set down heavily; *Stig of the Dump* (b)

dumper   lorry; dumper truck

dumps   *see* dump; down in the dumps

dunce   poor learner; dunce's cap

dune   sand-hill; Frank Herbert novel, 1984 David Lynch film; sand dune

dung   manure; dung beetle

dungeons   underground prison cells; *Dungeons and Dragons* (f)

dunk   dip into liquid; basketball goal; slam dunk

dupe   cheated person; hoodwink

duplicate   replica; make a copy of; duplicate bridge

duration   length of time; for the duration

dust   finely powdered earth; wipe (furniture); coal dust, cosmic dust, gold dust; dust and ashes, dust bath, dust bowl, dust cover, dust devil, dust jacket, dust sheet, dust storm, dust-up; bite the dust, kick up dust, when the dust settles; Dust Bowl; *Another One Bites the Dust* (s), *A Handful of Dust* (b), *Heat and Dust* (b/f), *Red Dust* (f)

dusted   see dust; done and dusted

duster   cleaning cloth; feather duster; Red Duster

dusting   wiping (furniture); crop dusting; dusting powder

dusty   covered in fine powder; dusty answer

duty   obligation, task, tax on imports; bounden duty, heavy-duty, on duty, point duty, stamp duty, tour of duty; duty free, duty-paid; *Duty Free* (tv), *Tour of Duty* (tv)

duvet   eiderdown; duvet day

dwarf   undersized; small person, small star; red dwarf, white dwarf; *Red Dwarf* (tv), *The Black Dwarf* (b)

dwarfs   see dwarf; *Snow White and the Seven Dwarfs* (b/f)

dye   colourant; change the colour of; tie-dye

dyed   artificially coloured; dyed in the wool

dying   expiring; to my dying day; *A Kiss Before Dying* (f), *As I Lay Dying* (b), *Dying Swan* (cl), *Dying Young* (f)

dyke   ditch, flood prevention wall; Foss Dyke, Offa's Dyke

dynamics   forces which stimulate change, study of motion under the action of forces; group dynamics

dynamo   energy converter; human dynamo

dynasty   line of heredity rulers; 1980s US series starring Joan Collins

E

each every one; individually; each-way (bet); at each other's throats each and every one

eager keen; over-eager; eager beaver; eager to please

eagle bird of prey, two under par in golf; 1950s boys' comic; bald eagle, double eagle, fish eagle, golden eagle, harpy eagle, legal eagle, sea eagle, spread eagle; eagle-eyed; *The Eagle Has Landed* (b/f), *The Eagle of the Ninth* (b)

eagles *see* eagle; *Legal Eagles* (f), *Where Eagles Dare* (b/f)

ear auditory organ, blade of corn, musical perception; cauliflower ear, dog-ear, give ear, glue ear, inner ear, middle ear, pig's ear, play by ear; ear drops, ear lobes, ear-flaps, ear-piercing, ear-splitting, ear-trumpet; flea in your ear, get a thick ear, give a thick ear to, have a tin ear, keep an ear to the ground, lend an ear, make a pig's ear of, out on your ear, play it

by ear, turn a deaf ear; the War of Jenkins's Ear; *A Flea in Her Ear* (pl)

earl nobleman; Earl Grey, Earl's Court; *My Name Is Earl* (tv)

earlier beforehand; earlier on

earliest first to arrive, most primitive; at the earliest

early premature, primitive; ahead of time, in good time; early bath, early bird, early closing, early-closing day, early days, early music; bright and early, the early bird catches the worm, send for an early bath; Early Modern English; *Early Doors* (tv)

earn bring in (money), deserve; pay as you earn

earned *see* earn; well earned

earnest sincere, serious; in earnest; *The Importance of Being Earnest* (pl)

earring item of jewellery; *Girl with a Pearl Earring* (b/f)

ears *see* ear; cloth-ears; be all ears, fall on deaf ears, music to your ears, my ears are burning, pin your ears back, walls have ears, wet behind the ears; *Prick Up Your Ears* (b/f)

earth one of the ancient elements, planet, soil; connect (a conductor) with the ground, drive (a fox, eg) to its lair; down to earth, fuller's earth, rare earth, scorched earth, scorched-earth policy; earth mother, earth sciences, earth's crust, earth-shattering, earth tremor; bring back down to earth, cost the earth, go to earth, like nothing on earth, move heaven and earth, the salt of the earth; Earth Summit, Friends of the Earth; *Battlefield Earth* (f), *The Day the Earth Stood Still* (f), *Down to Earth* (tv), *The Good Earth* (b/f), *The Greatest Show on Earth* (f), *Heaven Is a Place on Earth* (s), *Journey to the Centre of the Earth* (b), *Life on Earth* (tv), *The Man Who Fell to Earth* (f), *Night on Earth* (f)

earthly terrestrial, worldly; not stand an earthly; *Earthly Powers* (b), *The Garden of Earthly Delights* (pa)

earwig informer, pincered insect; listen in

ease comfort, leisure; alleviate, facilitate; at ease, hearts-ease, ill at ease; ease off; stand at ease

easier simpler; easier said than done

easily simply; easily done, easily led

East
Africa, Anglia, Bergholt, End, Fife, Finchley, Grinstead, Ham, India Company, Indies, Kilbride, Lothian, Stirlingshire, Sussex, Timor

---

east compass direction; the Orient; due east, north-east, north-north-east, south-east; Dutch East Indies, East Anglia, East Berlin, East End, East Grinstead, East Kilbride, East Midlands, East Sussex, East Timor, Far East, Middle East, Near East; *East Is East* (f), *East of Eden* (b/f), *East Lynne* (b)

eastern of the Orient; north-eastern, south-eastern; eastern hemisphere; Eastern Bloc, Eastern Standard Time, Far Eastern, Great Eastern, Middle Eastern

easy comfortable, simple; stand easy; easy chair, easy-going, easy listening, easy meat, easy money, easy-peasy, easy street, easy terms; (as) easy as falling off a log, (as) easy as winking, easy on the eye, free and easy, go easy on, of easy virtue, take it easy; Big Easy; *The Big Easy* (f), *Easy Lover* (s), *Easy Rider* (f), *Easy Street* (f), *Five Easy Pieces* (f), *It's So Easy* (s), *Mr Midshipman Easy* (b), *Solid Gold Easy Action* (s)

eat take in food; eat dirt, eat out; dog eat dog, eat humble pie, eat like a bird, eat like a horse, eat your words, I'll eat my hat, you are what you eat, (you can't) have your cake and eat it; *Eat Drink Man Woman* (f), *Eat the Peach* (f), *You Are What You Eat* (tv)

eaten sea eat; moth-eaten, worm-eaten

eater consumer, someone having a meal; bee-eater, fire-eater, lotus-eater, meat-eater; *The Pumpkin Eater* (b/f)

eating *see* eat; bird-eating spider, fire-eating, man-eating; eating apple; what's eating you?; *Eating People Is Wrong* (b), *What's Eating Gilbert Grape* (f)

eats *see* eat; *Fear Eats the Soul* (f)

eau French for 'water'; eau de cologne, eau de toilette, eau de vie; Eau de Nil

ebb   receding tide; subside; ebb and flow, ebb tide; at a low ebb; *Ebb Tide* (f)

ebony   black hardwood; *Ebony and Ivory* (s), *Ebony Eyes* (s)

eccentric   device on a revolving shaft, oddball; quirky

echo   radio code word, reverberated sound; common local newspaper name; resound, say again; echo chamber, echo-sounder; *Echo Beach* (s)

eclipse   blotting out of the Sun or Moon, overshadowing; block the light of, outshine; lunar eclipse, partial eclipse, solar eclipse, total eclipse; *Total Eclipse of the Heart* (s)

economic   costing less money, fiscal, to do with budgets and finances; economic efficiency

economical   thrifty; economical with the truth

economics   financial aspects, science of the production and distribution of wealth; home economics

economist   finance expert; political economist; *The Economist* (mag)

economy   financial and commercial structure of a country, money management, thrift; black economy, false economy, mixed economy, planned economy, political economy; economy of scale

ecstasy   rapture, recreational drug; *The Agony and the Ecstasy* (b/f)

edge   blade's sharpened side, border, brink, slight advantage; advance slowly; cutting edge, leading edge, on edge, straight edge; on a knife edge, set your teeth on edge; *Bridget Jones: the Edge of Reason* (b/f), *Edge of Darkness* (tv), *Jagged Edge* (f), *On*

Wenlock Edge (po), *The Edge of Heaven* (s), *Postcards from the Edge* (f), *The Razor's Edge* (b)

edged   *see* edge; deckle-edged, double-edged, gilt-edged

edges   *see* edge; rough edges

edgeways   sidelong; get a word in edgeways

edible   fit to be eaten; *The Edible Woman* (b)

edit   amend text; copy-edit; *Close (to the Edit)* (s)

edition   copies of a book published at one time; first edition, omnibus edition

editor   head of a newspaper or magazine, person who prepares books for publication; copy editor, features editor, managing editor

educated   taught; cultured, learned; self-educated; educated guess

educating   *see* educated; *Educating Archie* (r), *Educating Rita* (f/pl)

education   process of learning; classical education, co-education, continuing education, further education, higher education, physical education; *Sentimental Education* (b)

educational   academic; co-educational

eel   long slippery fish; conger eel, electric eel, moray eel

eels   *see* eel; jellied eels

effect   impression, result; accomplish; butterfly effect, cause and effect, domino effect, Doppler effect, for effect, greenhouse effect, in effect, knock-on effect, placebo effect, side effect

effective   capable, causing the required outcome, serviceable; cost-effective

effects *see* effect; belongings; after-effects, personal effects, sound effects, special effects

efficiency competence, productivity; economic efficiency

efficient competent, productive; cost-efficient

egg hen's produce, ovum; bacon and egg, bad egg, boiled egg, chocolate egg, curate's egg, Easter egg, hard-boiled egg, nest egg, Scotch egg; egg and chips, egg-and-spoon race, egg beater, egg cup, egg custard, egg-flip, egg-nog, egg on, egg on toast, egg-timer, egg-whisk, egg white; chicken and egg situation, over-egg the pudding, with egg on your face; *A Day in the Death of Joe Egg* (pl), *The Egg and I* (f)

eggs *see* egg; scrambled eggs; eggs Benedict; as sure as eggs is eggs, (don't) put all your eggs in one basket, teach your grandmother to suck eggs

eggshells containers of yolks and albumen; walk on eggshells

ego amour propre, self-esteem; alter ego; ego trip; et in arcadia ego; *Et in Arcadia Ego* (pl)

eight even number; figure of eight, pieces of eight, seventy-eight; have one over the eight, one over the eight; After Eight; *Dinner at Eight* (f), *Eight and a Half* (f), *Eight Days a Week* (s), *Eight Men Out* (f), *Forty-Eight Hours* (f), *When Eight Bells Toll* (b/f)

eighth half of a quarter; Eighth Army; *King Henry the Eighth* (pl)

eightsome four couples, octet; eightsome reel

eighty four score; *Around the World in Eighty Days* (b/f/tv), *Nineteen Eighty-Four* (b/f)

elaborate go into details; complex; over-elaborate

elastic stretchy material; flexible; elastic band

elbow arm joint; jostle; tennis elbow; elbow grease, elbow-room; bend the elbow, give the elbow to, more power to your elbow

elbows *see* elbow; up to your elbows

elder church official, community leader, forefather, shrub with white flowers; first-born, senior; ground elder; elder statesman; *The Sons of Katie Elder* (f)

elderberry small black fruit; elderberry wine

elect chosen ones; vote for; re-elect

election voting occasion; 1999 Reese Witherspoon film; by-election, general election, re-election

electoral concerning voting; electoral college, electoral roll

electric charged with current, thrilling, using the mains or a battery; electric-arc welding, electric blanket, electric blue, electric drill, electric eel, electric fence, electric fire, electric guitar, electric shaver, electric shock, electric storm, electric toothbrush, electric typewriter; *Are Friends Electric?* (s), *Electric Avenue* (s), *Electric Dreams* (f/s), *The Electric Horseman* (f), *Electric Ladyland* (al), *Together in Electric Dreams* (s)

electrical mains or battery powered; electrical engineer, electrical fault, electrical resistance

electricity energy from charged particles, state of high excitement; electricity bill

electrify pass a current through, thrill

electronic operating with microchips; electronic notebook, electronic publishing, electronic shopping

element   essential part, heating coil, substance listed in the periodic table; trace element; *The Fifth Element* (f)

elementary   fundamental, simple; elementary particle, elementary school

elephant   largest living land animal; African elephant, Indian elephant, rogue elephant, white elephant; elephant grass, elephant seal, elephant shrew; Elephant and Castle; *Elephant Boy* (f), *Elephant Song* (b), *The Elephant Man* (f), *Nellie the Elephant* (s)

elephants   *see* elephant; pink elephants

eleven   odd number; eleven-plus; *Ocean's Eleven* (f)

eleventh   last man at cricket, ordinal number; eleventh commandment; at the eleventh hour; *Eleventh Hour* (tv)

elk   largest of all living deer; elk hound

elm   tree; Dutch elm disease, slippery elm, wych elm; *A Nightmare on Elm Street* (f)

else   besides, instead; something else; above all else, or else; *Someone Else's Baby* (s), *Something Else* (s)

elsewhere   in another place; *St Elsewhere* (tv)

ember   small piece of burnt-out coal; Ember Days

emerald   green gemstone, shade of green; emerald green; Emerald City, Emerald Isle

emergency   crisis, urgent medical case; accident and emergency, state of emergency; emergency exit; *Emergency Ward 10* (tv)

emery   abrasive substance; emery board, emery paper, emery wheel

eminence   renown; eminence grise

emirates   Arab states; United Arab Emirates

emotional   expressing feelings, impassioned; over-emotional; *Emotional Rescue* (s)

emperor   ruler of a great dominion, species of large butterfly; purple emperor; emperor moth, emperor penguin; *The Emperor's New Clothes* (b), *The Last Emperor* (f)

empire   colonial power, extensive dominion; famous old Glasgow theatre, monthly film magazine; empire-building, empire line; British Empire, Empire Day, Empire State Building, Holy Roman Empire, Ottoman Empire, Roman Empire; *Empire of the Sun* (b/f), *The Empire Strikes Back* (f), *The History of the Decline and Fall of the Roman Empire* (b)

Empire
Austro-Hungarian, British, Holy Roman, Ottoman, Roman

---

employment   occupation, work; self-employment; employment exchange

empress   female ruler; *The Scarlet Empress* (f)

empty   containing nothing; unload; empty nester, empty-handed, empty-headed; empty vessels make most noise, running on empty; Empty Quarter; *Bring on the Empty Horses* (b), *Running on Empty* (f)

emulsion   suspension of one liquid in another, water-based paint; emulsion paint

enactment   depiction, passing of a bill

into law, performance; re-enactment society

enchanted bewitched, delighted; *Some Enchanted Evening* (s)

enchilada Mexican dish; big enchilada; the whole enchilada

encounter confrontation; meet; *Brief Encounter* (f)

encounters *see* encounter; *Close Encounters of the Third Kind* (f)

encyclopedia reference volume; walking encyclopedia

end close, extremity, finale, goal, terminus; complete, conclude, finish, stop; back end, big end, bin-end, dead end, deep end, dog-end, fag end, scrag-end, tail end, tail-end Charlie, the end, up-end; end product, end up, end-user; the die is cast, all good things come to an end, at a loose end, at an end, be-all and end-all, come to a sticky end, the end justifies the means, end of the line, the end of the road, go off the deep end, in at the deep end, in the end, jump in at the deep end, make your hair stand on end, a means to an end, on the receiving end, put an end to, thin end of the wedge, to the bitter end; East End, Land's End, West End, World's End; *Dead End* (f), *End Game* (f), *End of Days* (f), *The End of the Affair* (b/f), *Howard's End* (b/f), *Peril at End House* (b), *The Restaurant at the End of the Universe* (b)

endearment affectionate utterance; *Terms of Endearment* (f)

ended *see* end; open-ended

ending *see* end; finale; happy ending, never-ending; *My Happy Ending* (s)

endive salad plant similar to chicory; curly endive

endless infinite, unceasing; *Endless Love* (f)

endowment bequest, insurance policy linked to a mortgage; endowment mortgage, endowment policy

ends *see* end; book-ends, odds and ends, split ends; burn the candle at both ends, make ends meet; *All's Well That Ends Well* (pl), *Loose Ends* (r)

enduring putting up with; hard-wearing, lasting; *Enduring Love* (b/f)

enemy foe; arch-enemy, public enemy; *An Enemy of the People* (pl), *Enemy at the Gates* (f), *Enemy of the State* (f), *The Public Enemy* (f), *Sleeping with the Enemy* (f)

energy power, vigour; alternative energy, kinetic energy, potential energy, solar energy

enforcement application (of a law, eg); law enforcement; enforcement notice

enforcer user of strong-arm methods; *The Enforcer* (f)

engagement betrothal, commitment; engagement ring

engine power unit; beam engine, diesel engine, fire engine, internal-combustion engine, jet engine, search engine, steam engine, tank engine, traction engine; engine driver, engine room; *Ivor the Engine* (tv), *Thomas the Tank Engine* (b/tv)

engineer expert technician; manipulate, mastermind; chemical engineer, civil engineer, electrical engineer, mechanical engineer, sound engineer, structural engineer

engineers *see* engineer; Royal Engineers

engraving   etched drawing; drawing by cutting; steel engraving, wood engraving

enjoy   take pleasure in; enjoy yourself

enough   sufficient; sufficiently; man enough; enough is enough, enough said, fair enough, sure enough; *Ain't No Mountain High Enough* (s)

enquiries   official investigations, questions; directory enquiries

ensign   military or naval flag; blue ensign, red ensign, white ensign

entente   international understanding; Entente Cordiale, Triple Entente

enter   become a member of, gain access to, go in, record; enter the lists; *Enter Laughing* (f), *Enter the Dragon* (f)

entering   *see* enter; breaking and entering

enterprise   firm, initiative; *Star Trek* series, starship in *Star Trek*; free enterprise, private enterprise; enterprise zone

entertainer   showbiz personality; *The Entertainer* (f/pl)

entertaining   considering (an idea), giving pleasure to, receiving as a guest; amusing; *Entertaining Mr Sloane* (f/pl)

entirety   totality; in its entirety

entrance   way in; delight, place under a spell; entrance hall; Common Entrance

entry   access, competition attempt, diary insertion; double-entry, no entry, port of entry; entry form, entry-level, entry permit

envelope;   self-addressed envelope; push the envelope

environmental   green, of your surroundings, relating to the natural world; environmental audit

envoy   diplomat, messenger; peace envoy

envy   jealousy; be jealous of; green with envy

epoch   era, significant point in time; epoch-making

equal   peer; add up to; identical, level; equal opportunities; equal to the occasion

equals   *see* equal; equals sign; first among equals; *First among Equals* (b)

equatorial   relating to the tropics; equatorial doldrums; Equatorial Guinea

equilibrium   balance; 2002 Christian Bale sci-fi thriller

equity   impartiality, total assets of a company; actors' union; negative equity, personal equity plan

era   major division of time; Christian era

ermine   white stoat fur, used on ceremonial robes; Ermine Street

err   blunder, stray; err on the right side, err on the side of caution, to err is human, to forgive divine

errand   task involving a short journey; fool's errand; errand of mercy

errant   in the wrong, roving in search of adventure; knight errant

error   mistake; clerical error, in error, margin of error, trial and error; by trial and error, see the error of your ways

errors   *see* error; *The Comedy of Errors* (pl)

escape   evasion, getaway; evade, flee, leak; fire escape, narrow escape; escape clause, escape mechanism, escape route, escape valve; *Escape from New York* (f), *Escape to Victory* (f), *The Great Escape* (f)

espionage spying; counter-espionage, industrial espionage

esprit vivacious quality; make of Lotus car; esprit de corps

essence concentrated extract, intrinsic nature, vital element; in essence, of the essence; time is of the essence

essential leading principle; vital; non-essential; essential oil

establishment business premises, foundation, institution, society's elite

estate area of housing, country house and grounds, effects and affairs of the deceased, long-bodied car; fourth estate, housing estate, industrial estate, real estate, third estate, trading estate; estate agency, estate agent, estate car

esteem admiration; hold in high regard; self-esteem

estuary mouth of a river; Estuary English

eternal constant, without end; eternal triangle; hope springs eternal; the Eternal City; *Eternal Flame* (s), *Eternal Sunshine of the Spotless Mind* (f)

eternity time everlasting; 2001 Robbie Williams chart-topper; eternity ring; *From Here to Eternity* (f)

ethic attitude, moral principle; (Protestant) work ethic

ethnic of a racial group; multi-ethnic; ethnic minority

evangelical based upon the gospels, missionary, zealous in advocating something; evangelical prophet

evaporated disappeared; thick sweetened (milk); evaporated milk

evasion avoidance; tax evasion

eve day before, nightfall; Christmas Eve, New Year's Eve; *All about Eve* (f), *The Lady Eve* (f), *The Three Faces of Eve* (f)

even balanced, divisible by two, equal, flat, steady; yet; break even; even break, even money, even out, even up, even-handed, even-stevens; honours are even, on an even keel, even so, even though; *Even Cowgirls Get the Blues* (f), *Never Give a Sucker an Even Break* (f)

evening nightfall; good evening; evening dress, evening out, evening primrose, evening star; *The Evening Star* (f), *Some Enchanted Evening* (s)

event occurrence, sporting occasion; field event, happy event, non-event, throwing event, track event; be wise after the event, in any event, in the event; *Event Horizon* (f), *The Main Event* (f)

ever always, at any time; ever since, ever so; ever and anon; *Did You Ever* (s), *Ever After* (f), *Ever Decreasing Circles* (tv), *Ever Fallen in Love* (s), *What Ever Happened to Baby Jane?* (f)

every each one; each and every one; every inch, every man jack, every other, every time; every cloud has a silver lining, every dog has its day every nook and cranny, every now and again, every now and then, every once in a while, every picture tells a story, every so often, every Tom, Dick and Harry, every trick in the book, every which way; *Every Breath You Take* (s), *Every Day Hurts* (s), *Every Home Should Have One* (f), *Every Loser Wins* (s), *Every Man in His Humour* (pl), *Every Picture Tells a Story* (al), *Every Second Counts* (tv), *Every Which Way but Loose* (f)

everybody   each person; *C'mon
Everybody* (s), *Everybody Hurts* (s),
Everybody Loves Raymond (tv),
Everybody Wants to Rule the World (s)

everything   all, the lot; chips with
everything, money isn't everything;
Chips with Everything (pl), *Everything I
Do (I Do It for You)* (s), *Life, The
Universe and Everything* (b)

evidence   courtroom testimony,
indication, proof; hearsay evidence,
in evidence; turn Queen's evidence;
Inadmissible Evidence (f)

evident   indisputable, obvious; self-
evident

evil   wickedness; sinful; king's evil, the
evil eye, the evil one; evil eye, evil-
doer, evil-minded, evil spirit; speak evil
of; *Evil Under the Sun* (b/f), *Resident Evil*
(f/ga), *Touch of Evil* (f), *Touching Evil* (tv)

examination   careful perusal,
educational or medical test; medical
examination

examine   analyse, inspect, test; cross-
examine

example   case in point, paradigm; for
example; make an example of

excellence   greatness, perfection;
centre of excellence, par excellence

exception   departure from the rule;
take exception; the exception proves
the rule

excess   extravagance, surfeit; over the
limit; in excess of; excess baggage;
Excess Baggage (f/r)

exchange   bandy (words), swap; bill
of exchange, corn exchange,
employment exchange, foreign
exchange, labour exchange, rate of
exchange, stock exchange, telephone
exchange; exchange rate

exchequer   old state department in

charge of revenue; Chancellor of the
Exchequer

excise   customs duty; cut out

exclamation   outcry, surprised
utterance; exclamation mark

exclusion   barring of a child from
school, item not covered by an
insurance policy, leaving out;
exclusion order

exclusive   newspaper scoop; classy,
restricted

excuse   lame explanation; forgive, free
from obligation, justify (a fault);
lame excuse; excuse me, excuse my
French

execute   carry out, kill

execution   capital punishment,
carrying out, performance; stay of
execution

executioner   person who carries out a
death sentence; *Mine Own
Executioner* (f)

executive   governing branch, high-
level manager; managing, official;
executive officer, executive privilege;
Executive Decision (f), *Executive
Stress* (f)

exercise   physical activity, task; work
out (in a gym, eg); five-finger
exercise; exercise bike, exercise book,
exercise yard

exhaust   waste gases expelled via a
pipe; tire out, use up; exhaust pipe,
exhaust system

exhibition   allowance as a
scholarship, demonstration, public
display; Great Exhibition

exile   banishment, refugee; banish; tax
exile; *Exile on Main Street* (al)

existence   life, survival; peaceful co-
existence, pre-existence

exit   way out; depart; emergency exit;

exit poll; *Last Exit to Brooklyn* (b/f)

exorcist person who drives away evil spirits; *The Exorcist* (f)

expectancy anticipation, hope; life expectancy

expectation assumption, hope; against expectation

expectations *see* expectation; *Great Expectations* (b/f)

expedition journey of exploration, speed; foraging expedition; *The Expedition of Humphry Clinker* (b)

expense cost, outlay; expense account; at the expense of, no expense spared, spare no expense

experience event which leaves an impression, knowledge and skill acquired; feel (an emotion), go through; near-death experience, out-of-body experience, overseas experience, work experience; *Songs of Innocence and Experience* (po)

expert specialist; knowledgeable; *Death of an Expert Witness* (b/tv), *The Expert* (tv)

experts *see* expert; *The Experts* (f)

explain account for, clarify, solve; explain away

explosive dynamite, eg; volatile; high explosive, plastic explosive

exposure baring of skin to the elements, photographic access to light, publicity, revelation; auto-exposure, double exposure; exposure meter; *Indecent Exposure* (b), *Northern Exposure* (tv)

express fast train; give voice to, symbolise; rapid; express delivery, express train; American Express, Orient Express, Pony Express; *Express Yourself* (s), *Midnight Express* (f), *Murder on the Orient Express* (b/f), *The*

Polar Express (f), *Shanghai Express* (f), *Starlight Express* (mus), *Von Ryan's Express* (f)

expression common term, facial posture, representation; self-expression

extended enlarged, lengthened; extended family

extinct defunct, vanished (species); extinct volcano

extinguisher device for putting out a fire; fire extinguisher

extra crowd-scene actor; additional cricket run; additional, surplus; 1990s Renault van; extra cover, extra-curricular, extra-sensory, extra-sensory perception, extra-special, extra time, extra virgin; go the extra mile

extras *see* extra; Ricky Gervais sitcom

eye centre of a storm, hole in a needle, hook's fastening counterpart, seed bud of a potato, sight organ; look at; bird's-eye chilli, bird's-eye view, black eye, eagle eye, evil eye, fish-eye, glad eye, glass eye, hook and eye, lazy eye, magic eye, mind's eye, ox-eye, ox-eye daisy, private eye, rapid eye movement, red eye, rib-eye, shut-eye, the evil eye, tiger's-eye, worm's-eye view; eye candy, eye-catching, eye-drop, eye level, eye-level grill, eye of a storm, eye-opener, eye strain, eye-teeth, eye up, eye-witness; apple of your eye, beauty is in the eye of the beholder, easy on the eye, an eye for an eye, give the glad eye to, give your eye teeth, here's mud in your eye, I spy with my little eye, in the blink/wink of an eye, in the twinkling of an eye, keep a weather eye on, keep an eye on, keep your eye on the ball, leap to the eye, look straight in the eye, see eye to eye, to the naked eye, turn a blind eye; *Brass Eye* (tv), *Eye of the Beholder* (f), *Eye of the Needle* (b/f), *Eye of the Tiger* (b/f)/s, *Private Eye* (mag), *Queer Eye for the Straight Guy* (tv), *Red Eye* (f), *Reflections in a Golden Eye* (f)

eyeball globe of the visual organ; confront; eyeball to eyeball

eyebrow arc of facial hair; eyebrow pencil; raise an eyebrow

eyed *see* eye; looked at; black-eyed beans, black-eyed peas, black-eyed Susan, bleary-eyed, blue-eyed boy, bug-eyed, cock-eyed, dewy-eyed, doe-eyed, dry-eyed, eagle-eyed, gimlet-eyed, goggle-eyed, green-eyed monster, hawk-eyed, pie-eyed, pop-eyed, square-eyed, starry-eyed, wall-eyed, wide-eyed; bright-eyed and bushy-tailed; *Black Eyed Boy* (s), *Wide Eyed and Legless* (s)

eyelashes cilia; false eyelashes

eyelid facial feature used for blinking; without batting an eyelid

eyes *see* eye; cat's-eyes, snake eyes, square eyes; eyes down; feast your eyes on, make sheep's eyes at; *Angel Eyes* (s), *Bette Davis Eyes* (s), *Blue Eyes* (s), *Bright Eyes* (s), *CATS Eyes* (tv), *Ebony Eyes* (s), *Eyes Wide Shut* (f), *For Your Eyes Only* (b/f), *I Only Have Eyes for You* (s), *Ma He's Making Eyes at Me* (s), *My Eyes Adored You* (s), *Smoke Gets in Your Eyes* (s), *Snake Eyes* (f), *The Man with the X-Ray Eyes* (f)

F

fabulous wonderful; *Absolutely Fabulous* (tv), *The Fabulous Baker Boys* (f)

face dial, visage; confront, look out on; about-face, baby face, coal-face, full-face, in-your-face, long face, lose face, poker-face, rock face, save face, straight face, to my face, volte-face; face-cloth, face facts, face-lift, face mask, face off, face pack, face paints, face powder, face-saving, face-to-face, face value; cut off your nose to spite your face, face the music, fly in the face of, keep a straight face, look someone in the face, on the face of it, slap in the face, with egg on your face, written all over one's face; *A Face in the Crowd* (f), *Baby-Face* (f), *Face-Off* (f), *Face the Music* (al/tv), *Funny Face* (f), *Let's Face the Music and Dance* (s), *The Man without a Face* (f)

faced *see* face; hatchet-faced, long-faced, moon-faced, po-faced, poker-faced, red-faced, stony-faced, two-faced, whey-faced

faces *see* face; *Angels with Dirty Faces* (f), *New Faces* (tv), *The Three Faces of Eve* (f)

facial beauty treatment; of the physiognomy

facility amenity, ease (of action or performance)

fact reality, true statement; after the fact, in fact, (as a) matter of fact, in actual fact, in point of fact, it's a fact of life

factor aspect, business agent, determinant; chill factor, load factor, rhesus factor, wind-chill factor; Max Factor; *The Human Factor* (b/f), *The Krypton Factor* (tv), *The X Factor* (tv)

factory industrial plant; factory farming, factory floor, factory ship, factory shop; *Charlie and the Chocolate Factory* (b/f), *The Bottle Factory Outing* (b), *The Wasp Factory* (b), *Willie Wonka and the Chocolate Factory* (f)

facts *see* fact; face facts; the facts of life

faculty ability, university department

fade die away, grow pale; cross-fade; fade out; *Not Fade Away* (s)

fag ciggie, public school runner, tiresome chore; fag end

fail be unsuccessful; without fail; fail-safe; Fianna Fail; *Fail Safe* (f)

faint swoon; pass out; barely visible, faint-hearted; damn with faint praise, faint heart never won fair lady

fair carnival, expo; attractive, equitable, light-haired, moderate; the fair sex, world fair; fair copy, fair dinkum, fair dos, fair game, fair-haired, fair-minded, fair play, fair to middling, fair trade, fair trial, fair-weather friend; all's fair in love and war, faint heart never won fair lady, fair and square, fair crack of the whip fair enough, fair's fair, (it's) a fair cop; Fair Isle, Goose Fair, Office of Fair Trading; *Bartholomew Fair* (pl), *The Fair Maid of Perth* (b), *Fair Stood the Wind for France* (b), *It's Always Fair Weather* (f), *My Fair Lady* (f), *Scarborough Fair* (s), *State Fair* (mus), *Vanity Fair* (b)

fairly justly, moderately, fairly and squarely; *A Fairly Honourable Defeat* (b)

fairy magical being; airy-fairy, tooth fairy; fairy cake, fairy godmother, fairy lights, fairy ring, fairy story, fairy tale; Fairy Liquid, Sugar Plum Fairy; *Fairy Tale of New York* (s)

faith belief, loyalty; 1987 George Michael album; article of faith, bad faith, multi-faith; faith healer, faith healing; in good faith; Defender of the Faith; *Keep the Faith* (s)

faithful loyal; Old Faithful

faithfully accurately, in a loyal manner; yours faithfully

falcon bird of prey; peregrine falcon; *Falcon Crest* (tv), *The Maltese Falcon* (b/f)

fall collapse, decline, original sin, US autumn; be killed in battle, diminish, drop down, sin; free fall; fall apart, fall back, fall behind, fall down, fall guy, fall-off, fall out, fall over; fall apart at the seams, fall between two stools, fall by the wayside, fall on deaf ears, fall on stony ground, fall on your feet, fall victim to; *After the Fall* (pl), *Decline and Fall* (b), *The Fall and Rise of Reginald Perrin* (tv), *The Fall Guy* (tv), *The Fall of the House of Usher* (b), *The History of the Decline and Fall of the Roman Empire* (b), *Legends of the Fall* (f), *Night Must Fall* (f), *When I Fall in Love* (s), *Why Do Fools Fall in Love?* (s)

fallen *see* fall; those killed in battle, fallen angel, fallen arches; *Ever Fallen in Love* (s), *Fallen Angel* (s), *The Fallen Idol* (f)

falling *see* fall, falling star; as easy as falling off a log; *Falling Down* (f), *Snow Falling on Cedars* (b/f)

fallow uncultivated (land), fallow deer

falls *see* fall; cascades; Angel Falls, Iguazu Falls, Niagara Falls, Sioux Falls, Victoria Falls

> **Falls**
> Angel, Horseshoe, Iguazu, Niagara, Reichenbach, Sioux, Victoria

false artificial, bogus, mistaken; one false move, play false; false alarm, false consciousness, false economy, false eyelashes, false friend, false pretences, false start, false step, false teeth; sail under false colours; *One False Move* (b/f)

fame   celebrity, renown; film and tv series about a showbiz school; hall of fame, ill fame; *Fame Academy* (tv), *Fame Is the Spur* (b/f)

familiar   witch's companion; acquainted (with), unceremonious, well known

familiarity   intimacy, offensive informality, recognition; familiarity breeds contempt

families   *see* family; happy families

family   group of relatives, related group; extended family, nuclear family; family credit, family doctor, family life, family name, family planning, family reunion, family ties, family tree, family values; in the family way; Holy Family; *Addams Family Values* (f), *The Addams Family* (f/tv), *A Family at War* (tv), *Family Affairs* (tv), *Family Fortunes* (tv), *Family Life* (f), *The Family Reunion* (pl), *Family Ties* (tv), *The Family Way* (f), *The Grove Family* (tv), *My Family* (tv), *The Partridge Family* (tv), *The Royle Family* (tv), *A Small Family Business* (pl), *The Swiss Family Robinson* (b), *We Are Family* (s)

famine   severe food shortage; Potato Famine

famished   ravenous; *The Famished Road* (b)

famous   well known; world-famous, famous last words; *Almost Famous* (f), *Rich and Famous* (f), *When Will I Be Famous?* (s)

fan   air-circulator, enthusiast; cool with moving air; extractor fan; fan belt, fan club, fan dance, fan-jet, fan mail, fan out, fan-tailed; *Cosi Fan Tutte* (o), *Lady Windermere's Fan* (pl)

fancy   inclination, whim; be attracted to, imagine; ornamental; flight of fancy; fancy dress, fancy-dress ball, fancy-free, fancy goods, fancy man, fancy woman, fancy-work; just fancy, take a fancy to; *Fancy Pants* (f)

fanfare   trumpet flourish; *Fanfare for the Common Man* (cl)

fang   animal's sharp tooth; *White Fang* (b/f)

fantastic   wonderful; trip the light fantastic; *Fantastic Four* (f), *Fantastic Voyage* (b/f)

fantasy   daydream, delusion; *Fantasy Football League* (tv), *Fantasy Island* (tv)

far   distant; to a great extent; a far cry, by far, go far, go too far, in so far as, so far; far afield, far and away, far and wide, far cry, far-fetched, far-flung, far gone, far-off, far out, far-reaching, far-seeing, far-sighted; far be it for me, few and far between; Far East; *A Bridge Too Far* (f), *Far and Away* (f), *The Far Country* (f), *Far from Heaven* (f), *Far from the Madding Crowd* (b/f), *The Far Pavilions* (b/tv)

farce   absurd situation, outlandish comedy; bedroom farce; *Bedroom Farce* (pl)

fare   food and drink, price of travel, taxi passenger; cope, get on; bill of fare, bus fare

fares   *see* fare; fares please

farewell   goodbye; *A Farewell to Arms* (b/f), *Farewell My Concubine* (f), *Farewell My Lovely* (b/f), *So Long Farewell* (s)

The *Puzzler* Crossword Solver's Dictionary

farm   agricultural unit; cultivate land; city farm, collective farm, fish-farm, health farm, home farm, sewage farm, stud farm, wind farm; farm out; *Animal Farm* (b), *Cold Comfort Farm* (b), *The Farm* (tv), *Maggie's Farm* (s), *The Olive Farm* (b), *Rebecca of Sunnybrook Farm* (f)

farmer   agriculturist; gentleman farmer, pig farmer, tenant farmer; *Leon the Pig Farmer* (f)

farming   *see* farm; agriculture; factory farming, subsistence farming

farthing   old British coin; penny-farthing

farthings   *see* farthing; *A Kid for Two Farthings* (f)

fashion   current style, trend; shape; 1980 David Bowie song; Bristol fashion, in fashion, out of fashion, parrot-fashion; fashion show, fashion victim; after a fashion; *Dedicated Follower of Fashion* (s)

fashioned   *see* fashion; fully-fashioned, old-fashioned

fast   period without food; go without food; firmly fixed, quick; a fast buck, colour-fast, hard and fast, hold fast, make fast, thick and fast; fast and loose, fast asleep, fast bowler, fast food, fast forward, fast-talk, fast track; bad news travels fast, make a fast buck, pull a fast one; *Dreams Die Fast* (b), *Fast and Loose* (f/tv), *The Fast and the Furious* (f), *Fast Car* (s), *The Fast Show* (tv)

fastener   connecting device; zip-fastener

fat   adipose tissue, cooking grease; overweight; puppy fat, wool-fat; fat cat, fat hen; a fat chance, chew the fat, live off the fat of the land; *Fat*

Friends (tv), *Fat Is a Feminist Issue* (b), *My Big Fat Greek Wedding* (f), *One Fat Englishman* (b), *Two Fat Ladies* (tv)

fatal   deadly; *Fatal Attraction* (f), *Fatal Beauty* (f), *The Fatal Shore* (b)

fate   chance, destiny; destine; tempt fate, fate worse than death, seal your fate; *A Simple Twist of Fate* (f)

fated   destined; ill-fated

father   Catholic priest, male parent, originator; beget; father figure, father-in-law; how's your father, like father like son; Father Christmas, Father's Day, Father of the House, God the Father, Holy Father, Old Father Time, Our Father; *Bless Me Father* (tv), *Father Brown* (b/f), *Father Came Too!* (f), *Father Dear Father* (tv), *Father of the Bride* (f), *Father Ted* (tv), *The Innocence of Father Brown* (b), *In the Name of the Father* (f), *Son of My Father* (s), *A Voyage round My Father* (pl/tv)

fathers   *see* father; founding fathers, Pilgrim Fathers

fathom   nautical unit of measurement; understand, work out

fatigue   exhaustion; tire; combat fatigue, compassion fatigue, information fatigue

fatigues   military garments; tires

fatty   greasy, fatty acids

fault   culpability, error, flaw, geological rift; blame; at fault, double fault, electrical fault, find fault, foot fault, to a fault; fault-finder

favour   act of kindness, bias; prefer, smile upon; in favour, in favour of, out of favour, curry favour, grace and favour, without fear or favour

favoured   *see* favour; approved; most favoured nation status

favourite   likely winner, pet; preferred to all others; firm favourite, hot favourite, odds-on favourite; favourite son; *My Favourite Things* (s)

fawn   young deer; behave obsequiously

fear   dread; be afraid of; fools rush in where angels fear to tread, never fear, no fear, put the fear of God into, without fear or favour; *Cape Fear* (f), *Fear and Loathing in Las Vegas* (b/f), *Fear Eats the Soul* (f), *Fear Is the Key* (b), *Fear of Flying* (b), *Journey into Fear* (f), *Primal Fear* (f), *The Ministry of Fear* (b/f), *The Wages of Fear* (f)

fearing   *see* fear; God-fearing

fears   *see* fear; *The Sum of All Fears* (b/f)

feast   banquet; have a lavish meal; chocolate ice-cream, lolly brand; midnight feast, movable feast; feast day; feast your eyes on, ghost/skeleton at the feast; Feast of Tabernacles; *Babette's Feast* (f), *Belshazzar's Feast* (cl/pa)

feather   part of a bird's plumage; fur and feather, tar and feather, white feather; feather bed, feather-brained, feather-cut, feather duster; (as) light as a feather, birds of a feather (flock together), feather in your cap, feather your nest, *Birds of a Feather* (tv), *White Feather* (f)

feathers   *see* feather; fine feathers make fine birds; *Horse Feathers* (f), *The Four Feathers* (f)

feature   distinctive quality, facial element, magazine highlight, special attraction; present prominently; double feature

featured   *see* feature; sharp-featured

features   *see* feature; features editor

fed   gave a meal to, given a good supply; corn-fed, well fed; fed up; fed up to the back teeth

federal   concerning a group of states; Federal Reserve

federation   alliance of states; Russian Federation

fee   price charged for a service; parking fee, registration fee, search fee, transfer fee, fee fi fo fum

feed   give nourishment to, take nourishment; bottle-feed, chicken-feed, drip feed, spoon-feed, another mouth to feed, feed a cold, starve a fever

feeding   *see* feed; feeding frenzy

feeds   *see* feed; bite the hand that feeds you

feel   sense, texture; get the impression, touch, feel small, feel-good; feel the pinch, feel the pulse, get a feel for, have a feel for; *I Feel Fine* (s), *Never Mind the Quality, Feel the Width* (tv)

feeler   antenna, probe; feeler gauge

feeling   *see* feel; awareness, emotion; tactile; fellow feeling, sinking feeling, that sinking feeling, the feeling is mutual; *That Same Old Feeling* (s), *That Sinking Feeling* (f)

fees   *see* fee; school fees

feet   body extremities, fractions of a yard; cold feet, crow's feet; feet of clay; dead on your feet, drag your feet, fall on your feet, find your feet, get/have itchy feet, have two left feet, keep both feet on the ground, land on your feet, put your feet up, six feet under, under your feet, vote with your feet; *Cold Feet* (tv), *Six Feet Under* (tv), *Tiger Feet* (s)

fell   *see* fall; moorland hill; cut down (a tree), fell-walking; in one fell swoop; *The Man Who Fell to Earth* (f)

fellow associate, chap, fellow feeling, fellow-traveller; hail-fellow-well-met; *The Quare Fellow* (pl)

felt *see* feel; thick compact woollen cloth; deep-felt; felt-tip pen; make your presence felt

female girl or woman, female impersonator; *Single White Female* (f)

feminist campaigner for women's rights; concerning women's rights; post-feminist; *Fat Is a Feminist Issue* (b)

fence palisade, receiver of stolen goods; fight with swords; electric fence, over the fence, ring fence, sit on the fence; *Rabbit-Proof Fence* (f)

fences *see* fence, mend fences, rush your fences

fern bracken; tree fern

ferry passenger and car ship, shuttle boat; transport to and fro; car ferry; ferry boat; *Ferry across the Mersey* (s)

festival celebration; dragon-boat festival, film festival, harvest festival, pop festival; Aldeburgh Festival, Festival of Britain, Festival of Lights, Royal Festival Hall

Festival
Aldeburgh, Bayreuth, Cannes, Chichester, Edinburgh, Glastonbury, Glyndebourne, Montreux, Reading, Salzburg, Three Choirs

festoon garland; hang (with garlands), festoon blind

fetch go and get, sell for, fetch and carry

fetched *see* fetch; far-fetched

fetching *see* fetch; attractive

fête outdoor charity bazaar, fête champêtre; *Jour de Fête* (f)

feud dispute; blood feud

fever disease marked by high temperature; 1950s Peggy Lee song; cabin fever, glandular fever, hay fever, jungle fever, marsh fever, rheumatic fever, scarlet fever, swamp fever, swine fever, yellow fever; fever pitch; feed a cold, starve a fever; *Fever Pitch* (b/f), *Hay Fever* (pl), *Jungle Fever* (f), *Night Fever* (s), *Saturday Night Fever* (f), *Sea Fever* (po), *Strictly Dance Fever* (tv)

few small amount; a good few, precious few, quite a few, few and far between; *A Few Good Men* (f), *For a Few Dollars More* (f)

fewer a smaller number of, no fewer than

fiat decree, judge's warrant; Italian make of car; fiat lux

fibre any fine material, dietary roughage, strand; carbon fibre, glass fibre; fibre optics

fiction invention, made-up story or novel; non-fiction, pulp fiction, science fiction; truth is stranger than fiction; *Pulp Fiction* (f)

fiddle petty swindle, violin; falsify, tinker (with); cat and fiddle, fiddle while Rome burns, fiddle-de-dee, fit as a fiddle, on the fiddle, play second fiddle

fiddler species of crab, swindler, violinist, fiddler crab; *Fiddler on the Roof* (mus)

fidelity faithfulness; high fidelity, *High Fidelity* (b/f)

field grassy area, sphere; deal with, select (a team or individual) to play; force field, gravitational field, ice-field, left field, level playing field, magnetic field, open-field system, paddy field; field archaeologist, field

event, field glasses, field goal, field
hospital, field marshal, field mice,
field of vision, field officer, field test,
field trial, field trip; have a field day,
hold the field, in the field, play the
field, take the field; Bosworth Field;
Field of Dreams (f), *Lilies of the
Field* (f), *Wheat Field with Crows* (pa)

fields *see* field, Lincoln's Inn Fields, St
Martin-in-the-Fields; *Fresh Fields* (tv),
The Killing Fields (f), *London Fields* (b),
Strawberry Fields Forever (s)

fifteen odd number; Jamie Oliver's
restaurant; *Fifteen to One* (tv)

fifth harmonic interval in music,
twenty per cent as a fraction, fifth
columnist; take the fifth; Fifth
Amendment, Fifth Avenue; *King
Henry the Fifth* (pl), *The Fifth
Element* (f)

fifty half a century, fifty pence, fifty
per cent, fifty-fifty, fifty-pence piece;
Fifty Ways to Leave Your Lover (s)

fig sticky tropical fruit, fig-leaf, fig roll

fight battle; enter into combat; pillow
fight, straight fight, sword fight; fight
back, fight off; fight fire with fire,
fight or flight, fight shy of, fight to
the finish, fight tooth and nail, fight
your corner, pick a fight; *Fight
Club* (f)

fighter combatant, pugilist; freedom
fighter; fighter pilot; *Street Fighter* (f)

fighting *see* fight; hostilities, fighting
chance, fighting fit; *Kung Fu
Fighting* (s), *The Fighting Temeraire* (pa)

figs *see* fig; syrup of figs

figure numeral, shape of the body;
calculate, reckon; ballpark figure,
father figure; figure of eight, figure of
speech, figure out, figure-skating;
figure it out

figures double figures

file tool, collection of data, column,
dossier, folder for papers, rasp; store
away in order, walk in a line; Indian
file, nail-file, on file, rank and file,
single file; *The Ipcress File* (b/f), *The
Odessa File* (b/f)

files *see* file; *The X-Files* (tv)

filing *see* file; filing cabinet, filing
clerk

fill glut; load to capacity, occupy the
whole of, repair (a tooth), fill in, fill
up

filler padding, paste to repair cracks
in walls; stocking filler; filler cap

fillet boneless joint, narrow band;
remove the bones from; fillet steak

filling *see* fill; contents (of a sandwich
or pie), tooth amalgam; substantial
or satisfying (food), filling station

film cinema, movie, photographic
material, thin coating; record on
celluloid, take pictures of; horror
film, on film, silent film; film buff,
film director, film festival, film-goer,
film noir, film premiere, film set, film
star; *Film Fun* (mag), *Girls on Film* (s)

filter one end of a cigarette, strainer;
percolate, purify; oil filter; filter-
tipped

filth dirt, obscenity; Irvine Welsh
novel

fin fish's steering organ, thin
projecting edge; dorsal fin, pectoral
fin, tail fin; fin de siècle

final end, last stage of a knockout
competition; conclusive, last;
quarter-final, semi-final, the final
straw; final demand, final dividend,
final score, Cup Final; *The Final
Conflict* (f), *The Final Countdown* (s),
Final Destination (f), *Final Score* (tv)

finals *see* final; exams taken in the last year of university

finance money matters; provide money for; high finance

financial concerned with money matters; financial modelling, financial year; *Financial Times* (n)

find discovery; discover, locate (a lost object); find fault, find out, find the lady; find your feet, find your tongue

finder camera lens device, discoverer; fault-finder

finding *see* find; *Finding Nemo* (f)

fine money penalty; impose a monetary penalty on; bright (weather), delicate, excellent; fine and dandy, fine art, fine print, fine-spun, fine-tooth comb, fine-tune; cut it fine, fine feathers make fine birds, fine kettle of fish, fine words butter no parsnips, get down to a fine art, not to put too fine a point on it; Fine Gael; *A Fine Romance* (tv), *I Feel Fine* (s), *One Fine Day* (f/s)

finger hand digit; touch, toy with; five-finger exercise, index finger, little finger, ring finger, trigger finger; finger bowl, finger food, finger-painting, finger roll; have a finger in the pie, have your finger on the pulse, lay a finger on, lift a finger, pull your finger out, put the finger on; *The Magic Finger* (b)

fingered *see* finger; green-fingered, light-fingered, nimble-fingered, sticky-fingered

fingers *see* finger; fish fingers, green fingers, ladies' fingers, sticky fingers, all fingers and thumbs, burn your fingers, get your fingers burnt, snap your fingers, work your fingers to the bone; *Sticky Fingers* (s)

fingertips ends of the hand digits; at/to your fingertips

finish conclusion, surface texture; conclude; close finish, grandstand finish, photo-finish; finish off, finish with; fight to the finish

finishing *see* finish; finishing post, finishing school, finishing touch

fir coniferous tree; Douglas fir; fir cone

fire blaze, domestic heater, one of four elements in astrology, passion; bake or dry in a kiln, dismiss, shoot (a gun); No.1 hit for the Crazy World of Arthur Brown in 1968; baptism of fire, bush fire, catch fire, electric fire, forest fire, hang fire, log fire, on fire, open fire, quick-fire, set fire to, St Elmo's fire, sure-fire, under fire; fire alarm, fire and brimstone, fire ant, fire away, fire brigade, fire-clay, fire coral, fire door, fire drill, fire-eating, fire engine, fire escape, fire extinguisher, fire irons, fire-raising, fire risk, fire sale, fire starter, fire station, fire stone, fire trap, fire-walking, fire warden; fight fire with fire, get along like a house on fire, get on like a house on fire, go through fire and water, have other irons in the fire, no smoke without fire, play with fire, set the Thames/world on fire; Great Fire (of London), Pacific Ring of Fire; *Ball of Fire* (f), *Chariots of Fire* (f), *Courage under Fire* (f), *Fire and Rain* (s), *Fire Brigade* (s), *Fire over England* (f), *Great Balls of Fire* (mus/s), *Harry Potter and the Goblet of Fire* (b/f), *In the Line of Fire* (tv), *Light My Fire* (s), *St Elmo's Fire* (f), *Setting the World on Fire* (b), *This Wheel's on*

Fire (s), *We Didn't Start the Fire* (s)

fired   *see* fire; oil-fired; fired up

fireman   emergency-service worker, old train-driver's assistant, fireman's lift

fireside   domestic hearth; fireside chat; *Fireside Chats* (r)

firing   *see* fire, firing line, firing squad; firing on all cylinders

firm   company; fix solidly; resolute, secure, solid; firm favourite, firm hand; on firm ground; *The Firm* (b/f), *The Long Firm* (b/tv)

first   outset, winner; earliest, initial, leading; at first, double first, head first, modern first edition, safety first; first aid, first born, first class, first-class post, first cousin, first-day cover, first degree, first-degree burn, first-footer, first fruits, first-hand, first impressions, first lady, first lieutenant, first light, first mate, first name, first night, first off, first offender, first officer, first order, first person, first-person shooter, first position, first post, first principles first-rate, first reading, first refusal, first thing, first-time buyer, first up; at first blush, at first hand, at first instance, at first sight, first among equals, first and foremost, first and last, first catch your hare, first come first served, first of all, first past the post, first things first, a fox smells its own lair first, in the first instance, in the first place, of the first magnitude/order/water, on first-name terms; First International, First Minister, First World, Glorious First of June; *First among Equals* (b), *First Blood* (f), *First Born* (f/tv), *The First Circle* (b), *The First Cut Is the Deepest* (s), *First-*

Degree Burn (b), *First Knight* (f), *The First Wives Club* (f), *Love at First Bite* (f)

fiscal   monetary, relating to public revenue; procurator fiscal; fiscal year

fish   aquatic vertebrate; go angling; angel-fish, angler fish, big fish, flying fish, gefilte fish, lantern-fish, wet fish, white fish; fish and chips, fish-cake, fish eagle, fish-eye, fish-farm, fish fingers, fish hawk, fish kettle, fish knife, fish-pond, fish slice, fish-tank; big fish in a small pond, cry stinking fish, a different kettle of fish, drink like a fish, fine/pretty kettle of fish, fish out of water, have bigger/other fish to fry, like a fish out of water; *A Fish Called Wanda* (f), *Big Fish* (f), *Rumble Fish* (f)

fisherman   angler, Fisherman's Friend; *The Shoes of the Fisherman* (b/f)

fishing   *see* fish; angling; coarse fishing, fly fishing, pearl fishing; fishing line, fishing rod, fishing tackle; *Gone Fishing* (s)

fist   clenched hand; clenched-fist salute; an iron fist in a velvet glove, make a fist of; *Blonde Fist* (f), *Fist of Fury* (f)

fistful   as much as a hand can hold; *A Fistful of Dollars* (f)

fit   involuntary convulsions, tantrum; be the right size, instal; healthy, suitable; fighting fit, hissy fit, keep fit, match fit, see fit, think fit; fit in, fit the bill, fit to bust, fit up, fit-up; fit as a fiddle, fit as a flea, fit like a glove, fit to be tied; *Celebrity Fit Club* (tv)

fits   *see* fit, fits and starts; if the cap fits, wear it

fitted   *see* fit; fitted carpet

fitter   garage mechanic, machine

assembler, person who alters clothes; more appropriate, more healthy; gas fitter

fittest   *see* fit, survival of the fittest

fitting   *see* fit; trying-on session with a dressmaker; apt, fitting room

five   odd number; forty-five, high five, nine to five, take five; five-a-side, five-bar gate, five eighths, five-finger exercise, five o'clock shadow, five-spice, five-star; *Anna of the Five Towns* (b), *Five Children and It* (b), *Five Easy Pieces* (f), *Five Graves to Cairo* (f), *A Five-Year Sentence* (b), *Nine to Five* (f/s), *Six-Five Special* (tv), *Slaughterhouse-Five* (b/f), *Take Five* (s)

fives   ball game played with the gloved hand; bunch of fives, rugby fives

fix   spot of bother; fasten firmly, predetermine the result of, repair; quick fix, get a fix on, if it ain't broke, don't fix it; *Jim'll Fix It* (tv)

fixed   *see* fix; immovable, fixed assets, fixed costs, fixed income, fixed odds

fixer   person who makes arrangements, photographic solution; *The Fixer* (b/f)

fizzle   splutter, fizzle out

flag   banner, paving stone, plant belonging to the iris family; begin to tire, mark (an item) for attention; black flag, blue flag, chequered flag, house flag, marker flag, red flag, Union flag, white flag, yellow flag; flag day, flag down, flag of convenience; fly the flag, hoist the flag; *The Red Flag* (s), *Under Two Flags* (f), *White Flag* (s)

flags   *see* flag, put the flags out; *Put Out More Flags* (b)

flak   anti-aircraft fire, criticism; flak jacket

flake   particle of snow; come away in slivers; Cadbury's chocolate bar; flake white

flaky   crumbly, eccentric; flaky pastry

flame   finger of fire, sweetheart; burn brightly; naked flame, old flame; flame gun, flame tree, flame-thrower; *Eternal Flame* (s), *The Flame and the Arrow* (f), *The Flame Trees of Thika* (b/tv), *His Latest Flame* (s)

flames   *see* flame; shoot down in flames

flamingo   long-legged, pink wading bird; *Pretty Flamingo* (s)

flank   cut of meat, outer part of the thigh, wing of an army; attack or protect the side of, be either side of

flannel   face cloth, waffle, woollen fabric; soft-soap

flap   hinged cover, state of agitation; move (wings), panic unnecessarily; cat flap, ear-flap

flare   illuminated distress signal, sudden burst of light, widening; blaze up, widen out like a bell; solar flare; flare path, flare up

flash   burst of lightning, camera light, instant in time, momentary gleam of light; sparkle momentarily; showy, flash flood; flash in the pan, in a flash, quick as a flash; *Flash Gordon* (f), *Jumpin' Jack Flash* (s)

flask   liquid container, thermos; hip flask, Thermos flask, vacuum flask

flat   apartment, level; expired (battery), fixed (rate), low-heeled (shoes), monotonous, out of tune, smooth; granny flat, studio flat; flat broke, flat cap, flat-footed, flat of the hand, flat out, flat-packed, flat racing, flat spin, flat-top, flat tyre; (as) flat as a pancake, in a flat spin;

Tortilla Flat (b/f)

flats *see* flat; salt flats

flatter pay compliments to; more level

flavour taste of food; add seasoning to, flavour of the month

flaw defect; tragic flaw

flea jumping, biting insect; flea-bitten, flea collar, flea market; fit as a flea, flea in your ear; *A Flea in Her Ear* (pl), *Spanish Flea* (s)

fleece sheep's coat, warm woollen jacket; overcharge; Golden Fleece; *The Golden Fleece* (b)

fleet group of ships; nimble, rapid; Hampshire town, river running below London; Admiral of the Fleet, Fleet Prison, Fleet Street; *Follow the Fleet* (f)

fleeting momentary, transient; fleeting moment

flesh edible part of animals or fruit, soft part of the body; 1968 Warhol film; pound of flesh; flesh out, flesh wound; in the flesh, make your flesh crawl/creep, put flesh on the bones, the way of all flesh, thorn in the flesh; *Flesh and the Devil* (f), *The Way of All Flesh* (b), *The Devil in the Flesh* (b/f)

flew *see* fly; *One Flew Over the Cuckoo's Nest* (b/f)

flick light tap, movie; browse (through), tap with your nail; flick knife

flies *see* fly; as the crow flies, drop like flies, no flies on me, time flies when you're having fun; *As the Crow Flies* (b), *Lord of the Flies* (b/f)

flight air journey, dart's feathered end, escape, exodus, movement through the air, series of steps; charter flight, free flight, in-flight, maiden flight, scheduled flight, take flight, test flight, top flight; flight deck, flight lieutenant, flight line, flight of fancy, flight of stairs, flight path, flight recorder, flight simulator; fight or flight, in full flight; *Flight of the Bumble-Bee* (cl), *Flight of the Navigator* (f)

fling brief affair, Highland dance, wild spree; hurl; Highland fling

flint hard stone; former county of N Wales; *Our Man Flint* (f)

flip somersault; get angry, turn quickly over; egg-flip; flip chart, flip side, flip-flops, flip-top; flip your lid

flit sudden escape; abscond, dart about; moonlight flit

float carnival vehicle, cash kitty, cistern ball, fishing-line attachment, milk van, raft; be buoyant in water, hover, offer (stock in a company); milk float, float on air

floating *see* float; adrift, free to fluctuate (of a currency), suspended in a liquid; free-floating; floating population, floating rib, floating voter

flock group of birds or sheep, large crowd, fine wool giving a raised surface to cloth, stuffing material; gather (together), go with the crowd; flock of sheep, flock wallpaper; birds of a feather (flock together)

floe large drifting mass of ice; ice floe

flog beat with a whip, sell; flog a dead horse, *Flog It* (tv)

flood water excess; inundate; flash flood; flood plain, flood tide; in full flood; Thames Flood Barrier

floor level, lower limit, lower surface of a room, storey; knock down, stump; dance floor, factory floor, ground floor, sea floor, shop floor; floor-cloth, floor show; wipe the floor with; *The Door in the Floor* (f)

flop failure; be unsuccessful, droop, hang limply; belly-flop, flip-flop, Fosbury flop

floppy droopy; floppy disk

floral covered with blooms; Floral Dance; *The Floral Dance* (cl)

floss dental thread, fluffy mass of fibres; use string for cleaning teeth; candy floss, dental floss; *The Mill on the Floss* (b)

flotation buoyancy, launch of a public company on the stock market; flotation tank

flotsam goods lost by shipwreck found in the sea; flotsam and jetsam

flounce gathered strip sewn to the hem of a dress, impatient and disgusted movement; move abruptly with impatience and disgust

flounder species of flatfish; struggle with violent and awkward movments

flour finely ground grain; plain flour, self-raising flour

flourish showy splendour; brandish exuberantly, thrive

flow steady continuous stream; circulate, gush; cash flow, ebb and flow; flow chart; go with the flow, in full flow; Scapa Flow; *Let Your Love Flow* (s), *Orinoco Flow* (s)

flower best of anything, blossom on a plant; flourish; Bach flower remedies, in flower, orange flower water, passion flower; flower-arranging flower-bed, flower girl, flower people, flower power; *Cactus Flower* (f)

flowers *see* flower; *Flowers in the Rain* (s), *Our Lady of the Flowers* (b)

flown (had) travelled by air; high-flown

flows *see* flow; *And Quiet Flows the Don* (b)

flu viral illness; gastric flu, yuppie flu

fluff fault in a performance, soft down; bungle, make soft

fluid liquid; flowing, unstable; amniotic fluid, correction fluid; fluid ounce

flung *see* fling; far-flung

fluorescent strip (light), vividly colourful; fluorescent lighting

flush poker hand, rosy glow; chase or wash out, cleanse a lavatory, redden; level; royal flush, straight flush

flute tall narrow wine glass, vertical groove, wind instrument; sing or whistle melodiously; whistle and flute; *The Magic Flute* (o)

fly winged insect; move swiftly, travel through the air; knowing; blow fly, dry fly, fruit fly, let fly, no-fly zone, Spanish fly, tsetse fly; fly a kite, fly agaric, fly ash, fly at, fly by, fly-by-night, fly-drive, fly fishing, fly half, fly high, fly in, fly out, fly-past, fly-posting, fly solo, fly swat, fly-spray, fly-tipping; fly in the face of, fly into a rage, fly off the handle, fly on the wall, fly the flag, the fur will fly, pigs might fly; *Blow Fly* (b), *The Fly* (f), *Fly Me to the Moon* (s), *Wish I Could Fly* (s)

flyer advert, air traveller, aviator; high-flyer; Cheltenham Flyer

flying *see* fly; airborne, hasty; high-flying, kite-flying; flying boat, flying buttress, flying doctor, flying fish, flying fox, flying jacket, flying lemur, flying lizard, flying officer, flying picket, flying saucer, flying squad, flying squirrel, flying start, flying suit, flying trapeze, flying visit; with flying colours; Flying Dutchman, Flying Scotsman; *Fear of Flying* (b), *The Flying Doctor* (tv), *Flying Down to Rio* (f), *The Flying Nun* (tv), *Keep the Aspidistra Flying* (b), *Monty Python's Flying Circus* (tv), *Those Magnificent Men in Their Flying Machines* (f/s)

foal young horse; in foal

foam cushion sponge, lather; foam at the mouth

fob attachment to a key-ring, small pocket watch and chain; fob off, fob-watch

focal central, focal point

focus point of attention, point of convergence or origin, sharp definition of an image; adjust to ideal sight range; soft focus; focus group

fodder feed for livestock; cannon fodder

foe enemy; friend or foe

fog mist; befuddle; fog bank, fog lamp; *The Fog* (b/f), *Fog on the Tyne* (s), *Fog over Frisco* (f)

foil fencing sword, metal food wrap; frustrate, outwit

folk people, traditional community-based music; folk dance, folk music, folk rock, folk singer, folk song, folk tale; there's nowt so queer as folk; Beaker Folk; *The Folk Singer* (s), *My Ain Folk* (f), *Poor Folk* (b), *Queer as Folk* (tv)

follies absurdities, variety shows; *Rock Follies* (tv), *Ziegfeld Follies* (f)

follow ensue, obey, pursue, follow-my-leader, follow on, follow suit, follow through, follow up, follow your nose; *Carry On ... Follow that Camel* (f), *Follow the Fleet* (f)

follower attendant, supporter, successor; camp-follower; *Dedicated Follower of Fashion* (s)

folly madness, useless ornamental building

fonder more affectionate; absence makes the heart grow fonder

food nourishment; baby food, convenience food, devil's food cake, fast food, finger food, health food, junk food, soul food; food chain, food poisoning, food processor, food value; food for thought

fool court jester, creamy dessert, idiot; bamboozle; April fool; fool's errand, fool's gold, fool's mate, fool's paradise; a fool and his money are soon parted, make a fool of, more fool you, nobody's fool, there's no fool like an old fool; *The Fool on the Hill* (s), *Fool's Gold* (s), *A Fool Such as I* (s), *Nobody's Fool* (f), *What Kind of Fool Am I?* (s)

foolish silly; penny wise and pound foolish; *These Foolish Things* (s)

fools *see* fool; All Fools' Day, April Fools' Day; *Fools Die* (b), *Only Fools and Horses* (tv), *Ship of Fools* (b/f/pa), *Why Do Fools Fall in Love?* (s)

foot body part, twelve inches; pay (a bill); athlete's foot, ball of the foot, bird's-foot trefoil, first-foot, flat foot, on foot, wrong-foot; foot fault, foot rot, foot soldier, foot the bill, foot-and-mouth disease; the boot/shoe is on the other foot, foot in the door, get/start off on the right/wrong foot, my foot, (not to) put a foot right, one foot in the grave, put your best foot forward, put your foot down, put your foot in it; *My Left Foot* (f), *One Foot in the Grave* (tv)

football soccer; American football,

association football, Gaelic football, table football; football hooligan, football match, football pools, Football Association; *Fantasy Football League* (tv)

footer soccer, colloquially, text at the base of a page; fiddle about; first-footer

footing *see* foot; basis, toehold; first-footing, lose your footing

footlight stage lamp; *Footlight Parade* (f)

forage cattle feed; hunt for food, rummage, forage cap

forbid ban; God forbid

forbidden banned; forbidden fruit

force army, compulsion, power; compel; air force, brute force, centrifugal force, centripetal force, electromotive force, in force, labour force, land force, life force, police force, strike force, task force, tour de force, vital force; force field, force majeure; by force of, by main force, force down your throat, force the bidding, force the issue, force the pace; Royal Air Force; *Air Force One* (f), *The Delta Force* (f), *Ground Force* (tv), *Magnum Force* (f), *Ultimate Force* (tv)

forced *see* force; forced landing, forced march

forces *see* force; armed services; armed forces, join forces

fore front, golfer's warning cry, fore and aft; to the fore

forecast prediction; predict; weather forecast

foregone past, previously determined; foregone conclusion

foreign alien, of another country; foreign body, foreign correspondent, foreign exchange, foreign minister; (French) Foreign Legion, Foreign Office, Foreign Secretary

foremost first in rank and dignity, first in time or place; leading, first and foremost

forensic relating to scientific methods for solving crime; forensic medicine

forest extensive woodland; cover with trees; organisation that supports smokers; forest fire, forest ranger, Black Forest, Black Forest gateau, Epping Forest, New Forest, Nottingham Forest, Sherwood Forest; *Children of the New Forest* (b), *Once Upon a Forest* (f)

> **Forest**
> Ashdown, Black, Charnwood, Epping, New, Nottingham, Savernake, Sherwood

forever always, constantly; *Batman Forever* (f), *Diamonds Are Forever* (f), *Forever Amber* (f), *Forever in Blue Jeans* (s), *Forever Young* (f), *Strawberry Fields Forever* (s)

forewarned alerted in advance; forewarned is forearmed

forge smithy; counterfeit, weld together; Valley Forge

forget fail to remember; forget-me-not; forget it, forgive and forget

forgive absolve; forgive and forget, to err is human to forgive divine; *Can You Forgive Her?* (b)

forgot *see* forget; *The Land That Time Forgot* (f)

forgotten *see* forget; consigned to oblivion; never-to-be-forgotten

fork cutlery item, divide in a road, pronged digging tool; branch, pay (out); knife and fork, toasting fork, tuning fork; fork out, fork-lift truck

forked   *see* fork; forked lightning

forlorn   pitiful; forlorn hope

form   bench, class in school, outward appearance, type; create, shape, take shape; art form, bad form, entry form, free-form, good form, life form, on form, on good form, order form, out of form, sixth form, sixth-form college, true to form

formation   arrangement, pattern; formation dancing

forming   *see* form; habit-forming

formula   list of ingredients, mathematical equation, procedure, set of chemical symbols; chemical formula; Formula One, Formula Two Formula Three

fort   citadel; hill fort, hold the fort; Fort Knox, Fort Lauderdale, Fort William; *Fort Apache* (f)

forth   onwards; Scottish river and bridge, sea area south of Cromarty; and so forth, back and forth; Forth Bridge

fortress   citadel; *Digital Fortress* (b)

fortune   destiny, huge sum of money, luck; a small fortune, good fortune, hostage to fortune, soldier of fortune; fortune cookie, fortune-hunter, fortune teller; tell your fortune; *Bremner, Bird and Fortune* (tv), *The Fortune* (f), *The Fortune Cookie* (f), *Wheel of Fortune* (b/tv)

fortunes   *see* fortune

forty   number; forty winks, forty-eight hours, forty-five, forty-niner, forty-something; life begins at forty; *Ali Baba and the Forty Thieves* (pan), *Forty-Eight Hours* (f), *The 40 Year Old*

Virgin (f), *Life Begins at Forty* (tv)

forum   discussion place, Roman marketplace; Blandford Forum; *A Funny Thing Happened on the Way to the Forum* (f)

forward   attacking player; send on; away from the back, brazen, progressive; centre forward, come forward, fast forward, full forward, go forward, lock forward, prop forward; forward-looking; put your best foot forward; *Pay It Forward* (f)

forwarding   *see* forward; forwarding address

forwards   *see* forward; backwards and forwards

fossil   antiquated leftover, prehistoric relic hardened into rock; fossil fuel

foster   be a temporary parent, cherish (a hope), encourage; foster-parent

foul   Infringement of soccer rules; dirty, offensive; professional foul; foul play, foul-mouthed, foul up; *Foul Play* (f)

found   *see* find; establish

foundation   basis, base of a building, charitable endowment, cosmetic preparation, establishment (of an organisation), priming substance for a canvas; foundation course, foundation cream, foundation garment, foundation stone

founder   creator; sink; founder-member

founding   establishing; founding father

fountain   decorative water spray; drinking fountain, soda fountain; fountain pen; Trevi Fountain; *Three Coins in the Fountain* (f/s)

four   even number; petit four, twenty-four-hour clock; four-in-hand, four-leaf clover, four-letter word, four-minute mile, four-poster (bed), four-seater, four-sided, four-square, four-star, four-wheel drive; to the four winds; *Fantastic Four* (f), *The Four Seasons* (cl), *Four Weddings and a Funeral* (f), *Nineteen Eighty-Four* (b/f), *The Four Feathers* (f), *The Four Just Men* (b/f), *The Sign of Four* (b/f), *Twenty-Four* (tv)

fours quartets, races for boats with small crews, teams each comprising two pairs; plus fours, on all fours

fourth ordinal number, quarter; fourth dimension, fourth estate; Fourth International, Fourth of July; *Born on the Fourth of July* (f), *The Fourth Estate* (b), *The Fourth Protocol* (b/f)

fowl any bird kept for its eggs and flesh, poultry; guinea fowl

fox carnivorous animal with a bushy tail; baffle; Arctic fox, bat-eared fox, flying fox; fox terrier, fox-hunting; a fox smells its own lair first; *The Desert Fox (f/ga)*, *Reynard the Fox* (po)

foxes *see* fox; *The Little Foxes* (f/pl)

fraction part of a whole number; improper fraction, vulgar fraction

fracture bone-break; compound fracture, Pott's fracture

frame border, one game of snooker, supporting structure; encircle; formulate, lay blame on (an innocent person); A-frame, climbing frame, cold frame, freeze-frame, time frame, window frame, Zimmer frame; frame of mind, frame of reference, frame tent, frame-up; in the frame, out of the frame

framed *see* frame; timber-framed;

Who Framed Roger Rabbit? (f), *You've Been Framed!* (tv)

frank stamp (pre-paid post); candid; *The Diary of Anne Frank* (b)

franking *see* frank; franking machine

fray scuffle; become ragged at the edges

freak aberration; behave wildly; abnormal; freak out; *Le Freak* (s)

freaky weird; *Freaky Friday* (f)

free release; at large, generous, gratis, vacant, willing; break free, duty free, fancy-free, hands-free, interest-free, lead-free petrol, post-free, scot-free, set free, tax-free; free and easy, free association, free enterprise, free fall, free flight, free-floating, free-form, free-for-all, free hand, free house, free kick, free-living, free love, free market, free of charge, free pardon, free parking, free port, free radicals, free-range, free rein, free ride, free sample, free skating, free-standing, free throw, free time, free trade, free translation, free verse, free vote, free will; the best things in life are free, make free with; Free Church, Irish Free State, Orange Free State; *The Best Things in Life Are Free* (s), *Born Free* (f/s), *Duty Free* (tv), *Free Willy* (f), *I Want to Break Free* (s), *Set Me Free* (s), *Young Hearts Run Free* (s)

freedom liberty, freedom fighter, *Cry Freedom* (f), *Land and Freedom* (f), *Long Walk to Freedom* (b), *The Roads to Freedom* (b)

freely generously, willingly, without restriction; breathe freely

freeze chill; get very cold, stand perfectly still, turn to ice; deep-freeze; freeze-dry, freeze-frame, freeze up

freezer cold-storage cabinet; fridge-freezer

freezes *see* freeze; until hell freezes over

freezing *see* freeze; bitterly cold, freezing point

freight cargo; air freight; freight train

frenzy agitation; 1972 Hitchcock thriller; feeding frenzy

frequency number of radio vibrations, rate of occurrence; high frequency, low frequency, radio frequency, ultra-high frequency; frequency modulation

fresh cheeky, new, newly made; fresh air, fresh blood, fresh out of; breath of fresh air, fresh as a daisy; *Fresh Fields* (tv), *The Fresh Prince of Bel-Air* (tv)

fret ridge on the fingerboard of a guitar; feel anxious

friar wandering monk, friar's balsam; Black Friar, Grey Friar, White Friar

fridge cold food store; fridge-freezer

fried cooked in a pan using fat, sweltered; French fried potatoes, southern-fried, stir-fried; fried rice; *Fried Green Tomatoes at The Whistle Stop Cafe* (f), *The Kentucky Fried Movie* (f)

friend ally, chum; boy friend, fair-weather friend, false friend, man's best friend, pen-friend; friend at court, friend or foe; a friend in need is a friend indeed; Fisherman's Friend; *The Boy Friend* (mus), *Diamonds Are a Girl's Best Friend* (s), *My Best Friend's Wedding* (f), *Our Mutual Friend* (b), *You've Got a Friend* (s), *You've Got a Friend in Me* (s)

friendly amicable; eco-friendly, ozone-friendly, user-friendly; friendly society; Friendly Islands

friends *see* friend; Jennifer Aniston

sitcom; absent friends, best friends, good friends, just good friends, make friends with; Friends of the Earth; *Are Friends Electric?* (s), *Best Friends* (f), *Circle of Friends* (b/f), *Fat Friends* (tv), *Just Good Friends* (tv), *Such Good Friends* (f), *Thomas the Tank Engine and Friends* (tv), *With a Little Help from My Friends* (s)

friendship amity; friendship bracelet

fries *see* fry; chips; French fries

frigate naval escort vessel; frigate bird

fright sudden scare, terror; look a fright, stage fright, take fright; *Stage Fright* (f)

frighten terrify; frighten away, frighten off

frilled provided with ruffles; frilled lizard

frills embellishments, ruffles; no-frills

fringe decorative edging, forehead hair; form a border; Celtic fringe, lunatic fringe; fringe benefit; *Beyond the Fringe* (tv), *The Surrey with the Fringe on Top* (s)

frisk do a body-search, leap playfully

fritter foodstuff coated in batter; squander (away); fritter away

frock dress; frock coat

frog amphibian; Goliath frog, leap-frog; tree frog; have a frog in your throat

front façade, forward part, seaside promenade, show, vanguard; be the lead performer in a band, face forwards, meet face to face; back to front, cold front, in front, occluded front, out front, popular front, up front, warm front; front bench, front line, front-line troops, front of house, front-runner, front-wheel drive; in front of the sticks; National Front; *All*

Quiet on the Western Front (b/f), *The Front Page* (f), *Front Row* (r), *A Son at the Front* (b), *Up the Front* (f)

frontal relating to the fore part of anything, relating to the forehead or façade of a building; frontal lobe

fronts *see* front; Y-fronts

frost coldness, deposit of ice crystals; coat with sugar, cover with rime; ground frost, hoar frost; *Frost in May* (b), *The Frost Report* (tv), *A Touch of Frost* (tv)

frown furrowing of the brow; scowl; frown on

frozen *see* freeze; extremely cold, preserved at a very low temperature; frozen shoulder, frozen stiff

fruit edible part of a plant, rewards of labours or efforts; bear fruit, cane fruit, citrus fruit, forbidden fruit, kiwi fruit, old fruit, passion fruit, sharon fruit, soft fruit, stone fruit, Ugli fruit; fruit bat, fruit cocktail, fruit cup, fruit fly, fruit juice, fruit-machine, fruit salad, fruit sugar; *Strange Fruit* (s)

fruitcake eccentric person, large confection with currants, raisins and cherries; (as) nutty as a fruitcake

fruits *see* fruit; first fruits

fry young fishes; cook in hot fat; deep-fry, dry-fry, pan-fry, small fry, stir-fry; fry-up; have bigger/other fish to fry

frying *see* fry; frying pan

fudge soft buttery sweet, unpopular compromise; conceal the truth, manipulate (facts)

fuel power source; incite, inflame; fossil fuel, nuclear fuel, smokeless fuel; fuel gauge, fuel-injected, fuel tank

fugitive escapee; on the run; *The Fugitive* (f/tv)

fulfilling achieving; satisfying; self-fulfilling prophecy

fulfilment completion, satisfaction; non-fulfilment, wish-fulfilment

full crammed to capacity, replete, top (speed); chock-full; full beam, full blast, full-blooded, full-blown, full board, full-bodied, full circle, full-cream, full dress rehearsal, full-face, full forward, full house, full-length portrait, full marks, full moon, full nelson, full of beans, full quota, full-scale, full stop, full-time, full-timer, full toss, full up, full whack; at full cock, at full pelt, at full stretch, at full tilt, come full circle, the full monty, full of the joys of spring, full speed/steam ahead, full to the brim, in full flight, in full flood/flow, in full view, not the full quid/shilling; *Full Circle* (tv), *Full Metal Jacket* (f), *The Full Monty* (f), *A Pocket Full of Rye* (s)

fuller *see* full; old cloth-worker; fuller's earth

fullness completion, rounded shape (face), satiated feeling; in the fullness of time

fully completely; fully grown, fully-fashioned, fully-fledged

fume vapour; be in a rage, give off smoke, seethe; fume cupboard

fun amusement; enjoyable; having fun, in fun; fun fur, fun run; a bundle of fun, make fun of, poke fun at, time flies when you're having fun; *Film Fun* (mag), *Fun with Dick and Jane* (f), *Girls Just Want to Have Fun* (s), *House of Fun* (s)

function purpose, social event, use; be operative, work; *A Private Function* (f)

fund supply of money; provide capital for; managed fund, slush fund, trust fund; fund-holding, fund-raising; Save the Children Fund

funds *see* fund; available money; in funds

funeral ceremony for the deceased; funeral director, funeral parlour; it's your funeral; *Four Weddings and a Funeral* (f), *Funeral in Berlin* (b/f)

funnel implement to aid pouring, smokestack; guide (liquid) through; funnel-web spider

funny amusing, odd; funny bone, funny business, funny ha-ha, funny money, funny peculiar; *Funny Face* (f), *Funny Girl* (f), *A Funny Thing Happened on the Way to the Forum* (f), *My Funny Valentine* (s)

fur animal's pelt, hard deposit found in boilers etc; fun fur; fur and feather, fur coat, fur seal; the fur will fly

furious angry; *The Fast and the Furious* (f)

furnace industrial oven; blast furnace

furnishings contents of a house; soft furnishings

furniture household goods; door furniture, street furniture; furniture van; part of the furniture

further promote; additional; in addition, further education, further to; until further notice

fury rage; female spirit in Greek myth; 1936 Spencer Tracy drama; like fury, hell hath no fury like a woman scorned; *Fist of Fury* (f), *The Sound and the Fury* (b)

fuse bomb's wick, circuit breaker; join by melting, overload safeguard in an electrical circuit; fuse box, fuse wire; blow a fuse, short fuse

future time ahead; forthcoming; in future; future perfect, future-proofing; *Back to the Future* (f), *Future Shock* (b)

fuzzy blurred, woolly; warm and fuzzy

G

gab chatter; gift of the gab

gables roof-ends; *Anne of Green Gables* (b), *The House of the Seven Gables* (b/f)

gadget ingenious device; *Inspector Gadget* (f/tv)

gaff fishing hook; blow the gaff

gaffer boss; gaffer tape

gag joke, mouth restraint; retch, silence

gain profit; acquire; gain ground; gain the upper hand

gained *see* gain; nothing ventured nothing gained

gains *see* gain; capital gains (tax), ill-gotten gains

gaiters ankle coverings; *All Gas and Gaiters* (tv)

gal US lass; *For Me and My Gal* (mus), *My Gal Sal* (f)

gala fête, swimming tournament; Royal Gala

galaxy star system; brand of chocolate; US Ford saloon model; *The Hitch-Hiker's Guide to the Galaxy* (b/r/tv)

gall annoyance, fungal-like growth on plants, impudence; annoy; gall bladder, gall-stones

gallery art exhibition space, golf spectators, long balcony, top seats in a theatre; art gallery, observation gallery, portrait gallery, press gallery, rogues' gallery, shooting gallery; play to the gallery; National Gallery, National Portrait Gallery, Whispering Gallery

galley kitchen on a ship, printer's proof, Roman ship; galley slave

gallon imperial liquid measure; ten-gallon hat

gallop fastest pace of a horse; ride a horse fast

gallows frame for hangings; gallows humour

galore in abundance; *Whisky Galore* (f)

gamble bet, risky undertaking; make bets, take a risk

gambling   *see* gamble; gambling den

game   hunted animals, pastime, sporting event; willing; ball game, big game, big-game hunter, board-game, card game, computer game, end game, fair game, indoor game, numbers game, panel game, parlour game, video game, wall game, war game; game bird, game plan, game point, game preserve, game show, game warden; ahead of the game, the game is up, a mug's game, the name of the game, play the game, two can play at that game; *The Army Game* (tv), *The Crying Game* (f), *End Game* (f), *The Game* (f), *The Generation Game* (tv), *The Glass Bead Game* (b), *Harry's Game* (b/tv), *Master of the Game* (b), *The Name of the Game* (s), *Ripley's Game* (b/f), *The Pajama Game* (f), *The Power Game* (tv), *Spy Game* (f)

games   *see* game; mind games; Commonwealth Games, Highland Games, Olympic Games; *House of Games* (f), *Patriot Games* (b/f), *The Games* (tv), *War Games* (f)

gaming   betting; war gaming

gamma   Greek letter, radioactivity-emitting (rays); gamma rays

gamut   entire range; run the gamut

gander   male goose; Newfoundland airport

gang   group, work crew; chain gang, press-gang; gang show, gang up; Gang of Four; *Chain Gang* (s)

gangs   *see* gang; *Gangs of New York* (f)

gannet   greedy person, seabird

gantry   bridge-like structure; *Elmer Gantry* (b/f)

gap   interval, opening, space between two things: US clothing chain; credibility gap, generation gap, trade gap; gap year; bridge the gap, close the gap, mind the gap; *Cumberland Gap* (s)

garage   building for a car, urban music genre; garage sale

garbage   rubbish; garbage can; garbage in, garbage out

garden   land around a house; plant flowers, weed and dig; beer garden, botanic garden, common-or-garden, cottage garden, herb garden, kitchen garden, knot garden, market garden, rock garden, roof garden, rose garden, tea garden, winter garden, zoological garden; garden centre, garden city, garden gnome, garden of remembrance, garden party, garden peas, garden wall; Covent Garden, Garden of Eden, Garden State, Hampstead Garden Suburb, Welwyn Garden City; *The Cement Garden* (b/f), *The Garden of Earthly Delights* (pa), *Garden State* (f), *I Never Promised You a Rose Garden* (f), *Rose Garden* (s), *The Secret Garden* (b)

gardener   horticulturist; landscape gardener, market gardener; *The City Gardener* (tv), *The Constant Gardener* (b/f)

gardeners   *see* gardener; *Gardeners' World* (tv)

gardening   horticultural hobby; tending plants; landscape gardening, market gardening

gardens   *see* garden; Hanging Gardens, Kensington Gardens, Kew Gardens, Lost Gardens of Heligan, Victoria Tower Gardens, Winter Gardens

garland   chain of flowers; adorn with flowers

garment item of clothing; combination garment, foundation garment

garnish decoration for food; decorate (food)

garrison military outpost; furnish with soldiers

garter highest knighthood order, stocking support; garter snake, garter stitch

garters *see* garter; have your guts for garters

gas airy matter, domestic fuel, US petrol; talk idly; CS gas, calor gas, greenhouse gas, inert gas, laughing gas, marsh gas, mustard gas, natural gas, nerve gas, noble gas, rare gas, tear gas; gas bill, gas fitter, gas guzzler, gas lamp, gas mask, gas meter, gas turbine, gas-permeable; *All Gas and Gaiters* (tv)

gash laceration; lacerate

gasket engine seal; head gasket; blow a gasket

gasp sudden breath; draw breath sharply; last-gasp

gastric pertaining to the stomach; gastric flu, gastric juices

gate airport boarding point, attendance figures, entrance; five-bar gate, kissing gate, sluice gate, starting gate, toll-gate, water gate; gate money; like a bull at a gate; Brandenburg Gate, Golden Gate, Notting Hill Gate; *Devil Gate Drive* (s)

gates *see* gate; *Enemy at the Gates* (f)

gateau cake; Black Forest gateau

gather assemble, collect, tuck (fabric), understand; gather round, gather up, gather way, gather your wits

gathering *see* gather; assembly; wool-gathering

gathers *see* gather; a rolling stone gathers no moss

gauge measuring device, railway track's width; estimate, measure; broad gauge, feeler gauge, fuel gauge, marking gauge, narrow gauge, rain gauge, tyre gauge, wind gauge

gauntlet heavy glove; take up/throw down the gauntlet; *Red Gauntlet* (b)

gay homosexual, lively; Gay Gordons; *The Gay Divorcee* (f)

gaze steady look; stare fixedly

gazelle antelope; Thomson's gazelle

gazing *see* gaze; crystal-gazing, navel-gazing

gear clothes, equipment, toothed wheel; change gear, high gear, landing gear, reverse gear, riot gear, top gear; gear change, gear lever, gear up; *Top Gear* (tv)

gee exclamation of surprise; hasten (a horse); gee-gee, gee up, gee whiz

geese waterfowl; *The Wild Geese* (f)

geisha Japanese hostess; geisha girl; *Memoirs of a Geisha* (b/f)

gel viscous substance; come together well, solidify; silica gel

gen information; gen up

gene DNA unit; gene pool

general high army rank; non-specific, widespread; annual general meeting, director-general, inspector general, major general, postmaster general, surgeon general; general anaesthetic, general assembly, general election, general headquarters, general pardon, general practice, general practitioner, general-purpose general staff, general store, general strike; in general; Adjutant General, Attorney-General, General Synod, Governor General, Lord Justice-General,

Paymaster-General, Quartermaster General, Secretary General, Solicitor General; *The General* (f), *Witchfinder General* (f)

generation age group, production (of power); beat generation, lost generation, second-generation; generation gap; Generation X; *The Generation Game* (tv), *Star Trek: the Next Generation* (tv)

generator energy converter; Van de Graaff generator

genetic hereditary; genetic code, genetic engineering, genetic fingerprinting

genius brilliant natural talent, very clever person; stroke of genius

gentle mild, tender; gentle giant; *Gentle on My Mind* (s), *The Gentle Touch* (tv)

gentleman cultured and courteous male; gentleman-at-arms, gentleman cricketer, gentleman farmer, gentleman-in-waiting, gentleman of leisure, gentleman of the road, gentleman's agreement, gentleman's gentleman; Gentleman's Relish; *Gentleman Jim* (f), *Gentleman's Agreement* (f), *An Officer and a Gentleman* (f)

gentlemen *see* gentleman; *Gentlemen Prefer Blondes* (b/f), *The League of Gentlemen* (f/tv), *Officers and Gentlemen* (b), *The Two Gentlemen of Verona* (pl)

gently *see* gentle; *While My Guitar Gently Weeps* (s)

genuine authentic, sincere

germ malign micro-organism, seed; germ warfare

gesture expressive movement; give a sign

get become, fetch, obtain, understand; get across, get ahead, get-at-able, get away, get back, get better, get by, get cracking, get hitched, get ideas, get lost, get nowhere, get off, get on, get out, get outside of, get over, get ready, get results, get somewhere, get spliced, get through, get together, get up, get-up, get-up-and-go, get weaving; get a feel for, get a fix on, get a grip on, get a move on, get a thick ear, get a word in edgeways, get along like a house on fire, get away with blue murder, get away with it, get away with murder, get down to a fine art, get down to brass tacks, get in on the act, get in the way, get it in the neck, get it together, get itchy feet, get off on the right/wrong foot, get off the ground, get on like a house on fire, get on your nerves, get on your wick, get out of bed on the wrong side, get rich quick, get shot of, get stuck in, get the ball rolling, get the best of, get the better of, get the bird, get the boot, get the hang of, get the hump, get the measure of, get the message, get the nod, get the picture, get the push, get the shove, get to grips with, get to sleep, get to the bottom of, get up steam, get up your nose, get well soon, get wind of, get your claws into, get your fingers burnt, get your goat, get your hands dirty, get your hooks into, get your knickers in a twist, get your own back, get your skates on, get your teeth into, get your tongue round; *Annie Get Your Gun* (mus), *Get Back* (s), *Get Carter* (f), *Get It Together* (s), *Get Ready* (s), *Get Shorty* (f), *Get Smart* (tv), *Get Up and*

Boogie (s), *How to Get Ahead in Advertising* (f), *I Get a Kick Out of You* (s), *I Get Around* (s), *I'm a Celebrity…, Get Me Out of Here!* (tv)

gets   see get; *As Good as It Gets* (f), *Smoke Gets in Your Eyes* (s)

getting   see get; go-getting; getting on for, like getting blood out of a stone; *The Getting of Wisdom* (b/f), *Getting to Know You* (s)

ghetto   deprived city area; ghetto blaster; *In the Ghetto* (s)

ghost   phantom; 1990 Demi Moore film; ghost-like, ghost story, ghost town, ghost train; give up the ghost, ghost at the feast, the ghost in the machine; Holy Ghost, Silver Ghost; *The Ghost Breakers* (f), *Ghost Busters* (f), *The Ghost Goes West* (f), *The Ghost Sonata* (pl), *Ghost Story* (f), *Ghost Town* (s), *The Ghost Train* (f/pl), *Ghost World* (f)

giant   huge person; very large; 1956 James Dean film; gentle giant, red giant; giant-killer, giant panda, giant slalom, giant squid, giant toad; Giant's Causeway; *Cast a Giant Shadow* (f), *The Iron Giant* (b/f), *James and the Giant Peach* (b)

giants   see giant; *Standing on the Shoulders of Giants* (al)

giddy   dizzy; giddy-up; play the giddy goat

gift   natural talent, present; God's gift; gift token, gift voucher, gift-wrapped; (don't) look a gift horse in the mouth, gift of the gab, the gift of tongues; *The Gift* (f), *Humboldt's Gift* (b), *It's a Gift* (f)

gig   old carriage, pop concert

gild   coat with precious metal, give a false brilliance to; gild the lily

gilded   see gild; gilded cage

gill   fish's breathing organ, quarter-pint measure

gills   see gill; green about/around the gills, to the gills

gilt   coated with precious metal; young sow; gilt-edged; take the gilt off the gingerbread

gin   clear spirit; pink gin, sloe gin; gin and tonic, gin rummy, gin sling, gin trap

ginger   hot spice; red-haired; stem ginger; ginger ale, ginger beer, ginger nut, ginger snap, ginger tom; *Ginger and Fred* (f), *The Ginger Man* (b)

gingerbread   spicy cake; gingerbread man; take the gilt off the gingerbread

gird   encircle, fasten with a belt

girl   young female; big girl's blouse, bunny girl, chorus girl, dancing girl, flower girl, geisha girl, it girl, land-girl, old girl; girl Friday; boy meets girl; *Birthday Girl* (f), *Brown Girl in the Ring* (s), *China Girl* (s), *Cosmic Girl* (s), *The Country Girl* (f), *Diamonds Are a Girl's Best Friend* (s), *Funny Girl* (mus), *Georgy Girl* (f), *The Girl Can't Help It* (f), *Girl Crazy* (f), *The Girl from Ipanema* (s), *The Girl on a Motorcycle* (f), *Girl with a Pearl Earring* (b/f), *The Goodbye Girl* (f), *Gregory's Girl* (f), *His Girl Friday* (f), *Jersey Girl* (f), *The Little Drummer Girl* (b), *The Little Match Girl* (b), *Material Girl* (s), *Me and My Girl* (tv), *My Girl* (f/s), *Not That Sort of Girl* (b), *One Hundred Men and a Girl* (f), *A Pretty Girl Is Like a Melody* (s), *Sunday Girl* (s), *Take a Girl Like You* (b), *Tank Girl* (f), *There's a Girl in My Soup* (f), *The White Girl* (pa), *Who's That Girl* (f/s), *Working Girl* (f)

girls   see girl; *Bad Girls* (tv), *Big Girls Don't Cry* (s), *Buffalo Girls* (f), *Calendar Girls* (f), *California Girls* (s), *The Country Girls* (b), *Girls in Uniform* (f), *The Girls of Slender Means* (b), *Girls on Film* (s), *Girls on Top* (tv), *Girls Just Want to Have Fun* (s), *The Golden Girls* (tv), *The Land Girls* (f), *Mean Girls* (f), *The Trouble with Girls* (f)

give   donate, provide with; give away, give-away, give birth, give blood, give chase, give ear, give ground, give in, give notice, give odds, give out, give up, give way; give a shout to, give a thick ear to, give a wide berth to, give and take, give it a miss, give it a whirl, give it your best shot, give pause for thought, give the bird, give the devil his due, give the elbow to, give the glad eye to, give the lie to, give the nod, give the push, give the slip, give up the ghost, give your eye teeth, it is better to give than to receive; *Don't Give Up* (s), *Don't Give Up on Us* (s), *Give Us a Clue* (tv), *Never Give a Sucker an Even Break* (f)

glacé   sugar-coated; marron glacé; glacé icing

glad   pleased; glad eye, glad hand, glad rags; be glad to see the back of, give the glad eye to

glade   woodland clearing; brand-name air-freshener

gladiator   Roman fighter; 2000 Russell Crowe film

glamour   allure; young women's magazine

glance   quick look; quickly look; cursory glance

gland   secreting structure in the body; sebaceous gland

glass   tumbler, window-pane material; brandy glass, cut glass, Lalique glass, looking-glass, magnifying glass, optical glass, plate glass, safety glass, shot glass, stained glass, volcanic glass, Waterford glass, weather glass, wine glass; glass-blowing, glass ceiling, glass eye, glass fibre, glass slipper, glass wool; *Breaking Glass* (mus), *The Glass Bead Game* (b), *The Glass Menagerie* (f/pl), *The Glass Slipper* (b/f), *Heart of Glass* (s), *Through the Looking-Glass* (b)

glasses   spectacles, tumblers; field glasses, granny glasses, opera glasses

glaze   pottery coating; coat with a glossy substance, put in windows

gleam   lustre; shine

glean   learn gradually, reap

glen   valley; *Glengarry Glen Ross* (f/pl), *Monarch of the Glen* (tv), *The Monarch of the Glen* (pa)

glide   effortless movement; fly a plane without an engine, move smoothly; *Electra Glide in Blue* (f)

gliding   see glide; hang-gliding

glimmer   brief light; twinkle

glint   brief flash of light; sparkle

glitter   tiny sparkly particles; sparkle

glittering   see glitter; *The Glittering Prizes* (b/tv)

glitters   see glitter; all that glitters is not gold

global   worldwide; global village, global warming

globe   orb, sphere representing the Earth; Shakespeare's playhouse; globe artichoke; Golden Globe

gloom   sadness, semi-darkness

glorious   wonderful; Glorious Twelfth

glory   fame and honour; knickerbocker glory, morning glory;

glory box, glory days, glory hole; go to glory; Old Glory; *Blaze of Glory* (s), *Hope and Glory* (f/tv), *Land of Hope and Glory* (al/s), *Morning Glory* (al/s), *Paths of Glory* (f), *The Power and the Glory* (b), *The Real Glory* (f), *Tunes of Glory* (f)

gloss shiny finish; give a shine to; lip-gloss; gloss over, gloss paint

glove covering for the hand; oven glove; glove compartment, glove puppet; fit like a glove, an iron fist in a velvet glove,

gloves *see* glove; boxing gloves, kid gloves, rubber gloves; handle with kid gloves

glow brightness; give off light or warmth; glow-worm

glue adhesive substance; stick together; glue ear

glutton greedy person; a glutton for punishment

gnome financier, goblin; garden gnome

goal eventual aim, football score; drop goal, field goal, golden goal, own goal; goal area, goal difference, goal kick, goal line; score a goal

goalposts football net supports; move the goalposts

goat horned animal; billy goat, mountain goat, nanny-goat; get your goat, play the giddy goat; *The Goat or Who Is Sylvia* (pl)

goatherd minder of animals; *The Lonely Goatherd* (s)

gobble eat greedily; sound of a turkey; gobble up

goblet glass or cup; *Harry Potter and the Goblet of Fire* (b/f)

god deity, supreme being; act of God, honest-to-God, man of God, play God, sun god; God forbid, God willing, god-daughter, God-fearing, God's acre, God's gift; for the love of God, put the fear of God into; God the Father, House of God, Lamb of God; *Children of a Lesser God* (f), *God Bless America* (s), *God Save the Queen* (s), *God's Little Acre* (b), *Waiting for God* (tv)

goddess female deity; Green Goddess

godfather mafia boss, male sponsor at a christening; *The Godfather* (b/f)

godmother female sponsor at a christening; fairy godmother

gods *see* god; household gods; in the lap of the gods; *Gods and Monsters* (f)

goer energetic person, project likely to succeed; cinema-goer, concert-goer, film-goer, movie-goer, party-goer, play-goer, race-goer, theatre-goer

goes board-game turns; departs, is working, travels; here goes; as the saying goes, the story goes, that goes without saying, what goes around comes around, what goes up must come down, when the balloon goes up, who goes there?; *Anything Goes* (mus/s), *As Time Goes By* (s/tv), *Herbie Goes Bananas* (f), *Igby Goes Down* (f), *Mr Deeds Goes to Town* (f), *Mr Smith Goes to Washington* (f), *The Ghost Goes West* (f)

goggle stare wide-eyed; goggle-box, goggle-eyed

goggles *see* goggle; protective spectacles; night-vision goggles

going riding conditions; departing, travelling; in working order; easy-going, heavy going; going abroad, going away, going back, going bad, going concern, going in, going mad, going off, going out, going-over, going straight, going strong, going wrong; going for a song, going to ground, going to press, while the going is good; *Going for a Song* (tv), *Going for Gold* (tv), *Going Live* (tv), *Going My Way* (f), *Going Straight* (tv), *Is She Really Going Out with Him?* (s), *Sixteen Going on Seventeen* (s)

gold Olympic first prize, precious metal; crock of gold, fool's gold, old gold, pot of gold, rolled gold, solid gold, white gold; gold-digger, gold disc, gold dust, gold leaf, gold medal, gold medallist, gold mine, gold miner, gold-mining, gold plate, gold record, gold reserve, gold standard; all that glitters is not gold, (as) good as gold, have a heart of gold, worth your weight in gold; Cheltenham Gold Cup, Gold Coast, the Gold Rush; *After the Gold Rush* (al), *Band of Gold* (s/tv), *Fool's Gold* (s), *Going for Gold* (tv), *The Gold Rush* (f), *Good as Gold* (b), *Solid Gold, Easy Action* (s),

golden made of precious metal; golden age, golden boy, golden calf, golden eagle, golden goal, golden goose, golden hamster, golden handcuffs, golden handshake, golden jubilee, golden mean, golden oldie, golden orfe, golden parachute, golden pheasant, golden retriever, golden rod, golden rule, golden syrup, golden wedding; silence is golden; Golden Arrow, Golden Delicious, Golden Fleece, Golden Gate, Golden Globe, Golden Hind; *The Golden Bowl* (b/f), *Golden Brown* (s), *The Golden Child* (f), *The Golden Fleece* (b), *The Golden Girls* (tv), *The Golden Shot* (tv), *The*

Man with the Golden Arm (b/f), *The Man with the Golden Gun* (f), *On Golden Pond* (f), *Reflections in a Golden Eye* (f), *Silence Is Golden* (s)

goldfish aquatic pet; goldfish bowl

golf outdoor game, radio code word; clock golf, crazy golf; golf bag, golf ball, golf club, golf course, golf links

golly soft doll; expression of surprise; *Good Golly Miss Molly* (s)

gondoliers Venetian boatmen; *The Gondoliers* (o)

gone (had) departed, past, used up; far gone; gone away, gone off; gone for a burton; *Gone Fishing* (s), *Gone in Sixty Seconds* (f), *Gone with the Wind* (b/f), *Since You've Been Gone* (f/s)

good benefit; excellent, virtuous; feel-good, for good, a good few, a good job, a good many, no good, on good form, pretty good, very good; good afternoon, good day, good deal, good evening, good form, good-for-nothing, good fortune, good friends, good gracious, good grief, good health, good hiding, good-humoured, good-looking, good loser, good morning, good-natured, good-neighbourliness, good riddance, good Samaritan, good thinking, good-time, good turn; all good things come to an end, a change is as good as a rest, all in good time, (as) good as gold, (as) good as new, be on to a good thing, for good measure, the good old days, the great and the good, had a good innings, if you can't be good be careful, in good faith, in good health, in good shape, in good standing, in good time, just good friends, make good time, a miss is as good as a mile, much good may it do you, no news is good news, one good turn deserves another, throw good money after bad, while the going is good, with good grace; Cape of Good Hope, Good Friday, Good Friday Agreement; *A Few Good Men* (f), *As Good as It Gets* (f), *The Good Apprentice* (b), *Good as Gold* (b), *The Good Companions* (b/f), *The Good Earth* (b/f), *Good Golly Miss Molly* (s), *A Good Heart* (s), *The Good Life* (tv), *Good Morning* (s), *Good Morning Vietnam* (f), *Good Night and Good Luck* (f), *The Good Old Days* (tv), *The Good Soldier* (b), *The Good Terrorist* (b), *The Good, the Bad and the Ugly* (f), *Good Vibrations* (s), *Good Will Hunting* (f), *Good Wives* (b), *Good Year for the Roses* (s), *I'm into Something Good* (s), *It's Good News Week* (s), *Just Good Friends* (tv), *Lady Be Good* (mus), *On the Good Ship Lollipop* (s), *The Long Good Friday* (f), *No Good* (s), *Such Good Friends* (f)

goodbye word of farewell; *Goodbye Columbus* (b/f), *The Goodbye Girl* (f), *Goodbye Mr Chips* (b/f), *Goodbye to All That* (b), *Goodbye to Berlin* (b), *Goodbye Yellow Brick Road* (s), *Hello Goodbye* (s), *The Long Goodbye* (b/f), *Never Can Say Goodbye* (s)

goodness virtue; exclamation of surprise; honest-to-goodness, thank goodness; goodness knows, goodness me

goodnight word of farewell at bedtime; goodnight, sleep tight; *Goodnight Sweetheart* (tv), *The Long Kiss Goodnight* (f)

goods wares; brown goods, damaged goods, dry goods, fancy goods, white goods, worldly goods; goods and chattels, goods train; deliver the goods

goody childish expression of pleasure; goody bag, goody two shoes, goody-goody

goon nickname for a German prison guard in WWII, hired thug, silly person; *The Goon Show* (r)

goose large water-bird; barnacle goose, brent goose, Canada goose, golden goose, snow goose, wild-goose chase; goose pimples, goose-grass, goose-step; cook your goose, wouldn't say boo to a goose; Goose Fair; *Mother Goose* (pan), *Mother Goose Suite* (cl), *Old Mother Goose* (nr), *The Snow Goose* (b)

gooseberry hairy green fruit, unwanted third person; Chinese gooseberry; gooseberry bush; play gooseberry

gore blood and guts, skirt panel; impale; Gore-Tex

gorge deep ravine; overeat; Cheddar Gorge

gorgeous very attractive; drop-dead gorgeous

gory involving bloodshed; the gory details

gossip tittle-tattle; indulge in tittle-tattle; gossip column, gossip columnist

got *see* get; *Have I Got News for You?* (tv), *How Stella Got Her Groove Back* (f), *I Got Rhythm* (s), *I Got You Babe* (s), *I've Got a Brand New Combine Harvester* (s), *I've Got a Lovely Bunch of Coconuts* (s), *I've Got My Love to Keep Me Warm* (s), *Peggy Sue Got Married* (f), *'Ullo John, Got a New Motor?* (s), *You Really Got Me* (s),

You've Got a Friend (s), *You've Got a Friend in Me* (s), *You've Got Mail* (f)

governing ruling; self-governing; governing body

government political administration, rule; local government, minority government, national government, self-government; government-financed, government property, government surplus, government whip; Government House; *The Government Inspector* (pl)

governor leader, member of a school board; Governor General

gown robe; dressing-gown

grab take forcibly; smash and grab

grabs *see* grab; up for grabs

grace divine mercy, elegance, short prayer before a meal; act of grace, coup de grâce, saving grace, state of grace; grace note; grace and favour, with bad grace, with good grace; *Amazing Grace* (s), *Saving Grace* (f), *State of Grace* (f), *Will and Grace* (tv)

graces Daughters of Zeus; airs and graces; *The Three Graces* (pa/sc)

gracious courteous, tasteful; good gracious

grade level, US school year; categorise; make the grade; Standard Grade

graduate person with a degree; obtain an academic degree; *The Graduate* (f)

graffiti wall drawings; *American Graffiti* (f)

graft corruption, hard work; transplant, work hard

grail cup of Christ; holy grail; *Monty Python and the Holy Grail* (f)

grain cereal crop, seed from a cereal crop, small particle, tiny amount, wood pattern; against the grain

grammar structure of a language; grammar school

granary bread variety, wheat storehouse; granary bread

grand exalted, splendid; £1000; baby grand, concert grand; grand cru, grand duchess, grand duchy, grand duke, grand jury, grand larceny, grand master, grand opera, grand piano, grand slam, grand style, grand total, grand tour; Grand Canal, Grand Canyon, Grand Central, Grand Marnier, Grand National, Grand Prix; *By Grand Central Station I Sat Down and Wept* (b), *Grand Canyon* (f), *A Grand Day Out* (f), *Grand Designs* (tv), *Grand Hotel* (f), *Grand Theft Auto* (ga), *Le Grand Meaulnes* (b)

grandeur magnificence; delusions of grandeur

grandfather parent's male parent, style of clock; great-grandfather; grandfather clause, grandfather clock

grandmother parent's female parent; great-grandmother; teach your grandmother to suck eggs

grandstand seating area at a stadium; former BBC sports programme; grandstand finish

grange country house; *Grange Hill* (tv)

granny parent's female parent, familiarly; granny annexe, granny flat, granny glasses, granny knot; Granny Smith

grant allow, bestow, concede; subsidy; direct-grant school, discretionary grant; grant-maintained

granted *see* grant; take for granted

grape vine fruit; grape hyacinth; *What's Eating Gilbert Grape?* (f)

grapefruit   citrus fruit; grapefruit cocktail, grapefruit juice

grapes   *see* grape; sour grapes; *The Grapes of Wrath* (b/f)

graphic   diagram; vividly descriptive; graphic artist, graphic arts, graphic design, graphic designer, graphic equaliser, graphic novel

grappling   tussling; grappling hook

grasp   take hold of firmly, understand; grasp the nettle

grasping   *see* grasp; avaricious

grass   informer, lawn covering; tell on; elephant grass, goose-grass, lemon grass, marram grass, pampas grass, rye grass; grass court, grass roots, grass skirt, grass snake, grass widow; keep off the grass, put out to grass, snake in the grass; *The Grass Is Singing* (b), *Green Green Grass of Home* (s), *Whispering Grass* (s)

grasshopper   cocktail, insect; knee-high to a grasshopper

grate   fireplace; irritate, make a rasping sound, shred (food)

gratitude   appreciation; debt of gratitude

grave   burial place, type of accent; serious; grave accent, grave robber, grave-digger; dig your own grave, one foot in the grave; *One Foot in the Grave* (tv)

gravel   small pebbles; gravel-voiced

graven   carved, deeply fixed; graven image

graves   *see* grave; war graves; *Five Graves to Cairo* (f)

graveyard   burial ground; graveyard shift

gravity   falling force, seriousness; centre of gravity, specific gravity; *Gravity's Rainbow* (b)

gravy   meat sauce; gravy boat, gravy train

graze   skin injury; feed in the open (of animals), lightly touch, scrape (the skin)

grease   oily substance; lubricate; 1978 John Travolta musical; elbow grease; grease gun, grease monkey; grease the palm of

greased   lubricated; like greased lightning

greasy   oily; greasy pole, greasy spoon

great   big, eminent, fantastic; great ape, great auk, great crested grebe, great Dane, great deal, great divide, great scott, great tit, great white shark, great-aunt, great-grandchild, great-granddaughter, great-grandfather, great-grandmother, great-grandson, great-nephew, great-niece, great-uncle; go great guns, the great and the good, great minds think alike, great oaks from little acorns grow, the great unwashed, in great demand, no great shakes, time is a great healer; Alexander the Great, Alfred the Great, Great Barrier Reef, Great Bear, Great Britain, Great Eastern, Great Exhibition, Great Fire (of London), Great Lakes, Great Malvern, Great Ormes Head, Great Plague of London, Great Portland Street, Great Smoky Mountains, Great Wall (of China), Great Western Railway, Great Yarmouth; *All Creatures Great and Small* (tv), *Great Balls of Fire* (mus/s), *The Great Caruso* (f), *The Great Dictator* (f), *The Great Escape* (f), *Great Expectations* (b/f), *The Great Gatsby* (b/f), *The Great Lie* (f), *The Great Pretender* (s), *The Great Race* (f), *The Great Ziegfeld* (f),

Tamburlaine the Great (pl)

greater   *see* great; Greater Antilles, Greater Manchester

greatest   *see* great; *Greatest Love of All* (s), *The Greatest Show on Earth* (f)

green   colour, grassy area; ecology-conscious, inexperienced; blue-green algae, bottle green, bowling green, crown green, emerald green, jade green, lime green, Lincoln green, little green men, olive green, pea green, putting green, rub of the green, sage-green, village green; green belt, green card, green-eyed monster, green fingers, green jersey, green-keeper, green light, green man, green pepper, green room, green tea, green woodpecker; green about/around the gills, green with envy; Bounds Green, Golders Green, Green Beret, Green Cross Code, Green Goddess, Green Mountain State, Green Park, Green Paper, Green Party, Gretna Green, Kensal Green, Turnham Green, Wood Green; *Anne of Green Gables* (b), *Camberwick Green* (tv), *Dixon of Dock Green* (tv), *Fried Green Tomatoes at the Whistle Stop Cafe* (f), *Green Card* (f), *Green Door* (s), *Green Green Grass of Home* (s), *The Green Man* (b/f), *The Green Mile* (b/f), *Green Tambourine* (s), *Green Wing* (tv), *How Green Was My Valley* (b/f), *Linda Green* (tv)

greenhouse   garden structure; greenhouse effect, greenhouse gas

greens   *see* green; vegetables; spring greens

greeting   welcoming; salutation

greetings   words of goodwill; greetings card

grenade   small bomb; hand grenade

grenadier   guardsman; Grenadier Guards

grey   colour; overcast; grey area, grey matter, grey seal, grey squirrel; Earl Grey, Grey Friar; *Agnes Grey* (b), *Little Grey Rabbit* (b), *The Old Grey Whistle Test*

greyhound   tall, slim dog; greyhound racecourse, greyhound racing

grid   network; cattle grid, national grid

grief   sorrow; grief-stricken; come to grief, good grief

grill   cook under heat, interrogate; part of a cooker; eye-level grill, mixed grill; grill room

grim   bleak, ghastly; hold on for grim death; Grim Reaper

grime   filth; *A Life of Grime* (tv)

grin   smile broadly; grin and bear it

grind   pulverise, sharpen; drudgery; grind to a halt, have an axe to grind

grinder   back tooth, food mill; knife-grinder, organ-grinder

grinding   *see* grind; harsh and tedious; come to a grinding halt, grinding to a halt

grindstone   tool-sharpening device; nose to the grindstone

grip   handshake, mode of holding, travelling bag; hold spellbound, hold tightly; key grip, kirby grip; get a grip on

gripe   colic in babies, complaint; complain; gripe water

grips   *see* grip; get to grips with

grist   brewing malt, corn for grinding; grist to the mill

grit   pluckiness, small particles; clench (teeth); millstone grit; *True Grit* (f)

grits   maize kernels; clenches (teeth); hominy grits

gritty determined, gravelly; nitty-gritty

grizzly fretful; grizzly bear

groom man getting married, person who looks after horses; smarten up

groove rut; tongue and groove; in the groove; *Down in the Groove* (al), *How Stella Got Her Groove Back* (f), *Into the Groove* (s)

gross twelve dozen; excluding deductions, flagrant, obese, vulgar; gross domestic product, gross national product

ground earth, sporting area; prevent from flying or going out; pulverised; breeding ground, common ground, gain ground, give ground, go to ground, (happy) hunting ground, lose ground, middle ground, parade ground, proving ground, recreation ground, stamping ground, testing ground; ground-breaking, ground control, ground cover, ground elder, ground floor, ground frost, ground rent, ground rule, ground speed, ground squirrel; break new ground, fall on stony ground, get off the ground, hit the ground running, keep an ear to the ground, keep both feet on the ground, on firm ground, on the ground, on your own ground, shift your ground, stand your ground, suit down to the ground, thin on the ground; Boleyn Ground; *Ground Control* (f), *Ground Force* (tv)

groundhog woodchuck; Groundhog Day; *Groundhog Day* (f)

grounds *see* ground: dregs, land around a mansion, reasons; coffee grounds

group pop band, set of people or things; categorise; age group, blood group, focus group, peer group, pressure group, skiffle group, splinter group; group captain, group dynamics, group therapy; Bloomsbury Group; *The Group* (b)

grouse complaint, game bird; complain; black grouse, red grouse; grouse shooting

grove cluster of trees; Arnos Grove, Lime Grove; *Byker Grove* (tv), *Laburnum Grove* (pl), *The Grove Family* (tv)

grow become larger, develop; grow-bag, grow up; absence makes the heart grow fonder, great oaks from little acorns grow

growing *see* grow; growing pains

grown *see* grow; fully grown, home-grown; grown-up

growth development, increase; growth industry, growth ring

grub food, insect larva; Grub Street; *New Grub Street* (b)

grudge feeling of resentment; allow unwillingly; bear a grudge

grumpy crotchety; Disney dwarf; *Grumpy Old Men* (tv), *Grumpy Old Women* (tv)

guarantee written assurance; ensure; cheque guarantee card, money-back guarantee

guard train official, sentry, warder; watch over; advance guard, life guard, mount guard, old guard, praetorian guard, security guard, stand guard, take guard; guard dog, guard of honour, guard rail, guard's van; Home Guard, National Guard, Swiss Guard, Yeoman of the Guard; *The Yeomen of the Guard* (o)

guarded *see* guard; cautious

guardian keeper; British newspaper;

legal guardian; guardian angel
guards *see* guard; Grenadier Guards, Horse Guards, Household Guards, Scots Guards, Welsh Guards
guess rough estimate; estimate; anybody's guess, educated guess, second-guess; *Guess Who's Coming to Dinner* (f), *I Guess That's Why They Call It the Blues* (s)
guest invited visitor; paying guest; guest beer, guest book, guest house, guest of honour; be my guest
guidance directional advice; marriage guidance
guide tour courier; girl Scout; lead the way; pocket guide, rough guide; guide dog; Girl Guide, Queen's Guide; *The Hitch-Hiker's Guide to The Galaxy* (b/r/tv), *Rough Guide* (tv)
guided *see* guide; guided missile
guild trade association; Townswomen's Guild
guilt culpability, self-reproach; guilt complex, guilt trip; guilt by association; *A Sense of Guilt* (b/tv)
guilty conscience-stricken, culpable
guinea old English coin; West African republic; guinea fowl, guinea pig; Equatorial Guinea, Guinea-Bissau, New Guinea, Papua New Guinea
guitar stringed instrument; air guitar, electric guitar, Hawaiian guitar, pedal steel guitar, slide guitar, Spanish guitar; *The Guitar Player* (pa), *Spanish Guitar* (s), *While My Guitar Gently Weeps* (s)
gulf abyss, deep inlet; Gulf of Aqaba, Gulf of Bothnia, Gulf of Mexico, Gulf Stream, Gulf War, Persian Gulf
gull seabird; herring gull
gum adhesive substance, chewy sweet, part of the mouth; large Moscow store; chewing gum, red gum, wine gum; gum arabic, gum tree; up a gum tree
gun firearm; air gun, anti-aircraft gun, Bren gun, flame gun, Gatling gun, grease gun, hired gun, Lewis gun, machine gun, radar gun, ray gun, six-gun, smoking gun, spray gun, staple gun, Sten gun, stun gun, sub-machine gun, tommy gun; gun carriage, gun dog; jump the gun, son of a gun; *Annie Get Your Gun* (mus), *Have Gun Will Travel* (tv), *The Man with the Golden Gun* (f), *The Naked Gun* (f), *This Gun for Hire* (b/f), *Top Gun* (f)
gunboat small warship; gunboat diplomacy
gunpowder explosive; Gunpowder Plot
guns *see* gun; big guns; go great guns, stick to your guns; *The Guns of Navarone* (b/f), *Young Guns* (f)
gushing flowing copiously; effusive
gut fibre made from intestines, intestine; remove the innards from; gut-rot; bust a gut
guts *see* gut; entrails, determination; worry-guts; have your guts for garters
gutter inner margin of a book, kerbside channel; gutter press
guy bloke, bonfire effigy, tent rope; fall guy, wise guy; guy-rope; penny for the guy; Guy Fawkes Night; *The Cable Guy* (f), *The Fall Guy* (tv), *Guy Mannering* (b), *How to Lose a Guy in Ten Days* (f), *Jealous Guy* (s), *No More Mr Nice Guy* (s), *Queer Eye for the Straight Guy* (tv), *Sweet Talkin' Guy* (s), *The Tall Guy* (f)
guys *see* guy; *Guys and Dolls* (mus), *Some Guys Have All the Luck* (s), *Tough*

Guys (f), *Wise Guys* (f)
guzzler   greedy eater; gas guzzler
gym   exercise hall; gym shoe
gymnastics   acrobatic sport; rhythmic
  gymnastics

gypsy   Romany; Natalie Wood film;
  gypsy moth; *The Gypsy Moths* (f), *The
  Virgin and the Gypsy* (b/f)

H

habit custom, mannerism, monk's or nun's garment, regular behaviour; riding habit; habit-forming; break the habit, kick the habit

habits *see* habit; old habits die hard

hacking horse-riding; chopping, gaining unauthorised access to computers, hitting illegally with the foot during sport; persistent (cough); hacking cough, hacking jacket

hackles cock's neck feathers, combs for flax, dog's neck hair; make your hackles rise

hackney carriage horse, carriage let out for hire; East London borough; hackney cab, hackney carriage

hail old greeting, rain falling as ice; greet exaltedly; hail a taxi; hail-fellow-well-met; Hail Mary; *Hail the Conquering Hero* (f)

hair bristle, tresses; 1960s musical; bad hair day, camel hair; hair oil, hair-raising, hair restorer, hair's breadth, hair shirt, hair-splitting, hair trigger; hair of the dog (that bit you), keep your hair on, let your hair down, lose your hair, make your hair curl, make your hair stand on end, neither hide nor hair, not turn a hair, tear your hair out

hairpin coiffure fastener; very sharp (bend); hairpin bend

hairs bristles; cross hairs, split hairs

half one of two equal parts; better half, fly half, other half, scrum half, stand-off half, time and a half; half a chance, half-a-crown, half a dozen, half-and-half, half an hour, half-baked, half board, half-brother, half-century, half-cocked, half-crown, half-cut, half-hearted, half hitch, half-hour, half-hourly, half-hunter, half-inch, half-life, half-light, half-marathon, half mast, half measure, half-moon, spectacles, half-nelson, half-sovereign, half-term (holiday), half-timbered, half-time, half-tone, half-truth, half-volley, half-yearly; at half cock, at half mast, half a loaf is better than none/no bread, half a mo, half a tick, half seas over, not half, too clever by half; *Eight and a Half* (f), *Half a Sixpence* (f), *Hancock's Half Hour* (tv), *Harry Potter and the Half-Blood Prince* (b), *How the Other Half Loves* (pl), *It Ain't Half Hot Mum* (tv), *Nine and a Half Weeks* (f)

halfpenny former UK coin; shove-halfpenny, twopenny-halfpenny

halfway intermediate position; at the mid point; meet halfway; halfway house; *Halfway to Paradise* (s)

hall entrance lobby, meeting room; banqueting hall, beer hall, bingo hall, city hall, concert hall, dance hall, drill hall, entrance hall, lecture hall, mess hall, music hall, town hall, village hall; hall of fame, hall of justice, hall of mirrors, hall porter; Eaton Hall, Lower Loxley Hall, Royal Albert Hall, Royal Festival Hall, Tammany Hall; *Annie Hall* (f), *Locksley Hall* (po), *The Tenant of Wildfell Hall* (b), *Toad of Toad Hall* (pl)

Hall

Apethorpe, Benthall, Berrington, Brangwyn, Campion, Carnegie, Clare, County, Drill, Dunham Massey, Felbrigg, Free Trade, Greyfriar's, Hanbury, Hardwick, Hovingham, Hughes, Ilam, Kedleston, Lady Margaret, Leith, Melford, New, Oxburgh, Queen Elizabeth, Royal Albert, Royal Festival, Speke, St Benet's, St Edmund, St George's, Sudbury, Tammany, Tatton, Toad, Trinity, Wigmore, Wildfell, Wimpole

---

hallows consecrates; All Hallows

halt small railway station, standstill; stop; lame; call a halt, come to a grinding halt, grind to a halt

halter rope for holding an animal; halter neck

halved divided into two; a trouble shared is a trouble halved

ham cured pork, radio enthusiast, terrible actor; overact; Parma ham, radio ham; ham-fisted; West Ham

hammer nail-hitting tool, Olympic throwing event; drive (home), hit with a mallet, trounce; British horror-film company; claw hammer; hammer and sickle, hammer and tongs, hammer drill, hammer home, hammer thrower, hammer-toed; come under the hammer; *If I Had a Hammer* (s), *Mike Hammer* (tv)

hamper food basket; impede; picnic hamper

hamster rodent often kept as a pet; golden hamster

hand body part, bunch (of bananas), pointer on a clock, round of applause, set of cards, share in performance, side, unit of horse measurement, worker; give; at hand, by hand, cap in hand, cash in hand, close at hand, dab hand, deck-hand, firm hand, first-hand, flat of the hand, four-in-hand, free hand, glad hand, in hand, left-hand drive, lend a hand, minute hand, near at hand, old hand, red hand, right hand, right-hand drive, right-hand man, second hand, second-hand shop, sleight of hand, the whip hand; hand down, hand grenade, hand in hand, hand-me-down, hand on, hand out, hand over, hand-pick, hand-picked, hand-sewn, hand-to-hand, hand-towel; at first hand, at second hand, bite the hand that feeds you, gain/have the upper hand, in the palm of your hand, on the other hand, overplay your hand, play a lone hand, put your hand in your pocket, strengthen your hand, take in hand, throw your hand in, try your hand at; *Cool Hand Luke* (f), *Hand on Your Heart* (s), *The Hand That Rocks the Cradle* (f), *I Want to Hold Your Hand* (s), *Second Hand Rose* (s), *The Upper Hand* (tv)

handbags   women's holdalls; criticises stridently; handbags at ten paces; *Handbags and Gladrags* (s)

handcuffs   wrist shackles; puts wrist shackles on; golden handcuffs

handed   *see* hand; cack-handed, empty-handed, even-handed, free-handed, heavy-handed, high-handed, left-handed, mob-handed, open-handed, red-handed, right-handed, short-handed, single-handed; caught red-handed

handful   quantity contained in the fist, small quantity, unruly child; *A Handful of Dust* (b)

handkerchief   cloth for the nose; pocket handkerchief; handkerchief pocket

handle   carrying-strap, doorknob, hilt, name; deal with, feel; dead man's handle, door handle; fly off the handle, handle with kid gloves, too hot to handle; *Hard to Handle* (s)

handlebar   bicycle part; very wide (moustache); handlebar moustache

handlebars   *see* handlebar; drop handlebars

handles   *see* handle; love handles

hands   *see* hand; change hands, shake hands, show of hands; hands-free, hands up; cold hands, warm heart, get your hands dirty, have blood on your hands, keep your hands clean, lay hands on, many hands make light work, put your hands together, put your hands up, putty in your hands, rub your hands, take your life in your hands, throw up your hands, wash your hands of, with your bare hands, wring your hands; *Careless Hands* (s)

handshake   common mode of greeting; golden handshake

handsome   generous, good-looking (of a man), substantial; handsome is as handsome does, tall, dark and handsome

handwriting   penmanship; joined-up handwriting

handy   convenient, useful; come in handy; *Handy Man* (s)

hang   drape; execute using a rope, suspend; strap-hang; hang about, hang around, hang back, hang fire, hang-glider, hang-gliding, hang loose, hang on, hang out, hang together, hang tough, hang up; get the hang of, hang by a thread, hang in the air, hang out to dry, let it all hang out, a peg to hang a matter on; Hang Seng index; *Hang 'Em High* (f), *Let's Hang On* (s)

hanger   hook; clothes hanger, coat hanger; hanger-on

hanging   *see* hang; execution with a rope, wall tapestry; wall hanging; hanging on, hanging up; Hanging Gardens; *Hanging on the Telephone* (s), *Picnic at Hanging Rock* (f)

hangover   after-effect of alcohol; *Hangover Square* (b/f)

hanky   cloth or tissue for the nose; hanky panky; *Hanky Panky* (s)

happen   occur; an accident waiting to happen

happened   *see* happen; *A Funny Thing Happened on the Way to the Forum* (mus), *It Happened One Night* (f), *It Happened Tomorrow* (f), *Something Happened* (b), *What Ever Happened to Baby Jane?* (f)

happens   *see* happen; as it happens

happiest   *see* happy; *The Happiest Days of Your Life* (f)

happiness   joy; *The Inn of the Sixth Happiness* (f)

happy   contented, joyful; slap-happy, trigger happy; Happy Christmas, happy ending, happy event, happy families, happy-go-lucky, happy hour, happy hunting ground, happy medium, Happy New Year; happy as a sandboy, many happy returns, many happy returns of the day; *Happy Days* (tv), *Happy Gilmore* (f), *Happy Talk* (s), *Happy Together* (s), *Happy Valley* (b), *I Whistle a Happy Tune* (s), *My Happy Ending* (s), *This Happy Breed* (f/pl), *Trigger Happy* (tv)

harbour   place of refuge, place of shelter for ships; entertain (a thought or feeling), shelter; mulberry harbour; harbour master; *Harbour Lights* (tv)

hard   difficult, firm, tough; die-hard; hard-bitten, hard-boiled, hard-boiled egg, hard cash, hard cheese, hard copy, hard core, hard court, hard disk, hard hat, hard-headed, hard-hearted, hard labour, hard line, hard lines, hard luck, hard-luck story, hard man, hard-nosed, hard pad, hard-pressed, hard rain, hard rock, hard sell, hard shoulder, hard standing, hard tack, hard times, hard to please, hard up, hard-wired, hard-won; between a rock and a hard place, drive a hard bargain, hard and fast, hard as nails, hard nut to crack, old habits die hard, school of hard knocks; *A Hard Day's Night* (f/s), *Breaking Up Is Hard to Do* (s), *Die Hard* (f), *Hard Rain* (f), *Hard Times* (b), *Hard to Handle* (s), *Spy Hard* (f)

hardest   *see* hard; *Sorry Seems to Be the Hardest Word* (s)

hare   swift rabbit-like animal; run quickly; March hare, mouse hare; hare-brained; first catch your hare; Hare Krishna

hark   pay attention; hark who's talking; *Hark the Herald Angels Sing* (h)

harm   damage, injury; hurt; out of harm's way

harmony   accord, melodiousness; close harmony; harmony of the spheres

harness   set of straps for a horse; control, rein, utilise; in harness

harp   large plucked musical instrument; keep (on about); lager brand name; aeolian harp, Celtic harp, Jew's harp, Welsh harp

harpy   fierce woman, mythical female monster; harpy eagle

harrow   farming implement; cause distress, haunt; famous public school

harrier   bird of prey, cross-country runner, hunting dog; vertical take-off plane; hen harrier, marsh harrier

hart   deer; hart's tongue; White Hart Lane; *Hart's War* (f), *Hart to Hart* (tv)

harvest   crop yield; gather in crops; Neil Young album; harvest festival, harvest home, harvest moon, harvest mouse; *Cornish Harvest* (b), *Red Harvest* (b)

harvester   reaper; combine harvester; *I've Got a Brand New Combine Harvester* (s)

hash   dish of chopped meat and vegetables, jumble, telephone keypad symbol; chop up; hash browns; make a hash of, settle your hash

haste   hurry; post-haste; haste makes waste, more haste less speed

hasty   hurried, speedy; beat a hasty retreat

hat   headgear item; bobble hat, bowler hat, cocked hat, derby hat, hard hat, high-hat, old hat, opera hat, panama hat, paper hat, pork pie hat, stovepipe hat, sun hat, ten-gallon hat, tin hat, top hat; hat-peg, hat-pin, hat-trick; I'll eat my hat, keep under your hat, knock into a cocked hat, my hat, pass the hat (round), pick out of a hat, take your hat off to, talk through your hat, throw your hat into the ring; *The Three-Cornered Hat* (bal), *Top Hat* (f)

hatch   serving aperture, nautical entranceway; devise (a plot), emerge from an egg, incubate; down the hatch; Brands Hatch

hatches   *see* hatch; batten down the hatches, under the hatches

hatchet   small axe; hatchet-faced, hatchet job, hatchet man; bury the hatchet

hatching   *see* hatch; shading in fine lines; cross-hatching

hate   intense loathing; dislike intensely; pet hate

hatter   milliner; mad as a hatter; Mad Hatter's Tea Party

haul   drag, fisherman's catch; pull or drag forcibly, take goods by truck; long haul, short haul; haul over the coals, over the long haul

haunt   favourite place; pester from beyond the grave, play on your mind, visit frequently

haunted   inhabited by ghosts; haunted house; *The Haunted Mansion* (f)

have   be equipped with, experience, possess; must-have; have-a-go, have-nots; have a ball, have a bash, have a bellyful, have a bun in the oven, have a butcher's, have a card up your sleeve, have a chip on your shoulder, have a feel for, have a field day, have a finger in the pie, have a frog in your throat, have a go, have a heart, have a heart of gold, have all the answers, have an axe to grind, have a nice day, have another think coming, have ants in your pants, have a plum in one's mouth, have a screw loose, have a soft spot for, have a stab, have a thick/thin skin, have a thin time, have a thing about, have a tin ear, have a whale of a time, have a will of your own, have bats in the belfry, have bigger fish to fry, have blood on your hands, have designs on, have done with, have it both ways, have it coming, have it in for, have it out, have itchy feet, have kittens, have no idea, have on, have on the brain, have one over the eight, have other fish to fry, have other irons in the fire, have over a barrel, have the hots for, have the hump, have the last laugh, have the upper hand, have two left feet, have what it

155

takes, have words, have your finger on the pulse, have your guts for garters, have your head screwed on, have your heart in your mouth, walls have ears, you can't have it both ways, you can't have your cake and eat it, you have to crawl before you can walk; *All I Have to Do Is Dream* (s), *Every Home Should Have One* (f), *Girls Just Want to Have Fun* (s), *Have Gun Will Travel* (tv), *Have I Got News for You?* (tv), *Have I the Right* (s), *Have You Seen Her?* (s), *I Have a Dream* (s), *I'm Sorry I Haven't a Clue* (r) *I Only Have Eyes for You* (s), *Some Guys Have All the Luck* (s), *To Have and Have Not* (f), *We Have All the Time in the World* (s)

haven place of refuge; tax haven; New Haven

having *see* have; not having any of it, time flies when you're having fun

havoc chaos; play havoc with, wreak havoc

haw red hedgerow fruit; hum and haw

hawk bird of prey, warmonger; clear the throat noisily, peddle goods; fish hawk, sea hawk, sparrow-hawk; hawk-eyed; *Black Hawk Down* (f), *Hudson Hawk* (f), *The Sea Hawk* (f)

hay dried grass; hay fever; hit the hay, make hay while the sun shines; *Antic Hay* (b), *Hay Fever* (pl) *The Hay Wain* (pa)

haystack pile of dried grass; needle in a haystack

hazard danger; dare; occupational hazard

hazel light-brown colour, nut variety; witch hazel

head body part, chief, froth on beer, most senior teacher; aim (for), command; senior; beach-head, big-head, cross-head screw, cylinder head, dead-head, death's head hawkmoth, loose-head prop, talking head, tight head, Turk's head, well head; head-case, head count, head-dress, head first, head gasket, head-hunted, head of state, head office, head on, head-on collision, head over heels, head start, head teacher, head-to-head, head-turning, head waiter; bury your head in the sand, by a short head, have your head screwed on, hide your head, hit the nail on the head, knock on the head, like a bear with a sore head, price on your head, put your head in a noose, put your head on the block, rush of blood to the head, scratch your head, wet the baby's head, win by a short head; Flamborough Head, Great Ormes Head, Nag's Head, The Bodley Head; *A Severed Head* (b), *Bring Me the Head of Alfredo Garcia* (f)

Head
Beachy, Dunnet, Duncansby, Flamborough, Great Ormes, Spurn, St Bees, St David's

headed *see* head; bald-headed, big-headed, empty-headed, hard-headed, hot-headed, level-headed, light-headed, muddle-headed, pig-headed, shock-headed, thick-headed, wrong-headed

heading *see* head; article or book section's title, navigational direction; sub-heading

heads *see* head; heads and/or tails; two heads are better than one; *Talking Heads* (pl/tv)

healer physician; faith healer; time is a great healer

health   state of being well; good health, ill health, occupational health; health centre, health-conscious, health farm, health food, health resort, health service, health visitor; clean bill of health, drink the health of, in good/poor health; *In Sickness and in Health* (tv)

heap   untidy pile; pile up; compost heap, scrap heap, slag heap

hear   detect sound, listen to, receive news; hear Mass, hear things; hear hear

hearing   *see* hear; ability to perceive sounds, judicial investigation or trial; hearing aid

hearsay   rumour; hearsay evidence

heart   body organ, centre, red playing-card, shape used to mean 'love', spirit; at heart, bleeding heart, by heart, lose heart, purple heart, take to heart, young at heart; heart attack, heart-rending, heart's desire, heart-searching, heart-stopping, heart-throb, heart-to-heart, heart-warming; absence makes the heart grow fonder, break your heart, close to your heart, cold hands warm heart, cross your heart, dear to your heart, faint heart never won fair lady, from the bottom of my heart, have a heart, have a heart of gold, have your heart in your mouth, home is where the heart is, in my heart of hearts, to your heart's content, warm the cockles of your heart, wear your heart on your sleeve; *Angel Heart* (f), *Anyone Who Had a Heart* (s), *Don't Go Breaking My Heart* (s), *A Good Heart* (s), *Hand on Your Heart* (s), *Heart and Soul* (s), *Heart of Darkness* (b), *Heart of Glass* (s), *The Heart Is a Lonely Hunter* (b), *The Heart*

of Midlothian (b), *The Heart of the Matter* (b), *I Lost My Heart to a Starship Trooper* (s), *My Heart Will Go On* (s), *Rhythm of My Heart* (s), *Take These Chains from My Heart* (s), *This Old Heart of Mine* (s), *Total Eclipse of the Heart* (s), *Where the Heart Is* (tv), *White Hunter Black Heart* (f), *Wild at Heart* (f), *Wooden Heart* (s), *Young at Heart* (f/s)

heartbeat   bodily pulse; ITV drama set in Aidensfield, 1959 Buddy Holly single, 1992 Nick Berry single; a heartbeat away

heartbreak   grief; *Heartbreak Hotel* (s), *Heartbreak House* (pl)

heartburn   indigestion; *Heartburn Hotel* (tv)

hearth   part of a fireplace; hearth-rug; *The Cloister and the Hearth* (b), *The Cricket on the Hearth* (b)

hearts   *see* heart; cards suit; Edinburgh-based soccer club; lonely hearts, purple hearts; hearts-ease; in my heart of hearts; *Kind Hearts and Coronets* (f), *Sgt Pepper's Lonely Hearts Club Band* (al/s), *Two Hearts* (s), *Young Hearts Run Free* (s)

heat   extreme warmth, form of energy, preliminary round of a contest; warm up; 1995 Al Pacino/Robert De Niro crime thriller; dead heat, pack heat, prickly heat, white heat; heat rash, heat-resistant, heat-seeking, heat shield, heat treatment; in the heat of the moment, turn the heat on; *Heat and Dust* (b/f), *In the Heat of the Night* (f), *Red Heat* (f), *White Heat* (f)

heater   warming device; immersion heater, (night) storage heater

heath   barren open country; Hampstead Heath, Haywards Heath

heating *see* heat; domestic warmth, temperature control system; central heating, induction heating

heave lift or pull with difficulty; heave-ho

heaven paradise; 1985 Bryan Adams single; heaven-sent; heaven forfend, in seventh heaven, move heaven and earth, stink to high heaven; *Bread of Heaven* (s), *Days of Heaven* (f), *The Edge of Heaven* (s), *Far from Heaven* (f), *Heaven Can Wait* (f), *Heaven Is a Place on Earth* (s), *Kingdom of Heaven* (f), *Pennies from Heaven* (tv), *Three Steps to Heaven* (s)

heavenly blissful, celestial, divine; heavenly body, heavenly host; *Heavenly Creatures* (f)

heavens firmament, skies; the heavens opened, thank heavens; *Heavens Above* (f)

heavy ponderous, weighty; hot and heavy, top-heavy; heavy-duty, heavy going, heavy-handed, heavy industry, heavy metal, heavy water; make heavy weather of, take a heavy toll; *He Ain't Heavy, He's My Brother* (s)

heavyweight class of boxer, person of influence or importance; light heavyweight

hedge fence made of shrubs; avoid commitment; hedge-hopping, hedge sparrow; hedge your bets

hedgehog small prickly animal; *Sonic the Hedgehog* (ga)

heed pay attention to; take heed

heel cad, command to a dog, end of a violin bow, foot part, rear of a shoe; list; Achilles' heel, back-heel, bring to heel, Cuban heel, down at heel; heel bar; turn on your heel

heeled *see* heel; well heeled

heels *see* heel; kitten heels; dig in your heels, head over heels, hot on the heels of, kick up your heels, on the heels of, take to your heels

heights altitudes, uplands, utmost degrees; dizzy heights; Golan Heights, Jackson Heights; *Pacific Heights* (f), *Wuthering Heights* (b/f/s)

heir person in line to inherit, successor; heir apparent, heir presumptive, heir to the throne

heiress female due to inherit, female successor; *The City Heiress* (pl), *The Heiress* (f)

helix spiral shape; double helix

hell Devil's domain, place of suffering; raise hell; hell-bent; all hell breaks loose, cat in hell's chance, come hell or high water, hell's bells, hell for leather, hell hath no fury like a woman scorned, (just) for the hell of it, play merry hell, there will be hell to pay, until hell freezes over; Hell's Angels; *Bat out of Hell* (s), *Hell's Kitchen* (tv), *The Pure Hell of St Trinian's* (f)

hellfire eternal flames for the wicked; Hellfire Club

hello common word of greeting; glossy celebrity magazine, 1984 Number One hit for Lionel Richie; *Hello Again* (f), *Hello Dolly* (f/s), *Hello Goodbye* (s), *Hello Mary Lou* (s), *Hello Young Lovers* (s)

helmet protective hat; balaclava helmet, blue helmet, crash helmet, pith helmet

help assistance; assist; Beatles film and song; home help, self-help; help out; so help me, there is no help for it; *The Girl Can't Help It* (f), *Help Me Rhonda* (s), *Somebody Help Me* (s),

With a Little Help from My Friends (s)
helper
 assistant; mother's little helper;
 Mother's Little Helper (s)
hem garment edge; sew the edge of (a
 garment); hem in
hemisphere half of the globe, one of
 the two brain divisions; eastern
 hemisphere, northern hemisphere,
 southern hemisphere, western
 hemisphere
hemp cannabis-yielding plant, plant
 used in making rope; Indian hemp
hen domestic fowl; fat hen, French
 hen; hen-coop, hen harrier, hen
 night, hen party
herald College of Arms official,
 messenger; proclaim; Triumph
 Herald; *Hark the Herald Angels Sing* (h)
herb plant used for flavouring or in
 medicine; pot-herb; herb garden
herbal plant-based (medicine); herbal
 tea
herd animal group; group together;
 herd instinct
here in or to this place; the buck
 stops here, here and now, here and
 there, here goes, here we go again,
 here's mud in your eye, Kilroy was
 here, neither here nor there, same
 here, see here; *Alice Doesn't Live Here
 Any More* (f), *From Here to Eternity* (f),
 Here Comes Mr Jordan (f), *Here Comes
 Summer* (s), *Here Comes the Night* (s),
 Here Comes the Rain Again (s), *Here We
 Go round the Mulberry Bush* (f/s), *I'm a
 Celebrity … Get Me Out of Here!* (tv),
 Neither Here Nor There (b), *Take It from
 Here* (r) *Tell Them Willie Boy Is
 Here* (f), *Wish You Were Here* (al/f/tv)
heritage national history, patrimony;
 English Heritage, World Heritage Site

hermit recluse, species of crab; hermit
 crab
hero courageous person, idol, principal
 male character; 1992 Dustin Hoffman
 film; anti-hero, war hero; hero-
 worship; *Billy Don't Be a Hero* (s), *Hail
 the Conquering Hero* (f), *Holding Out for
 a Hero* (s), *Local Hero* (f), *My Hero* (tv)
heroes *see* hero; 1977 David Bowie
 song; *Cartoon Heroes* (s), *Cockleshell
 Heroes* (f), *The Heroes of Telemark* (f),
 Hogan's Heroes (tv), *No More Heroes* (s)
heroic courageous; heroic verse
heroine brave woman, principal
 female character; anti-heroine
herring edible sea fish; red herring;
 herring gull; *Albert Herring* (o)
hesitates pauses in uncertainty; he
 who hesitates is lost
hewn chiselled, chopped down;
 rough-hewn
hey call for attention; hey presto; *Hey
 Joe* (s), *Hey Jude* (s)
hidden concealed; hidden agenda,
 hidden depths, hidden reserves;
 Crouching Tiger, Hidden Dragon (f)
hide animal pelt, concealed place
 from which to observe wildlife;
 conceal, keep out of view; hide and
 seek, hide out; hide your head, hide
 your light under a bushel, neither
 hide nor hair; *Hide and Seek* (f)
hiding *see* hide; thrashing; good
 hiding, on a hiding to nothing
high elevated or intoxicated state;
 drunk or drugged, elevated, shrill,
 tall; fly high, knee-high, ultra-high
 frequency; high altar, high and dry,
 high and mighty, high-chair, high-
 class, high command, high
 commission, high constable, high
 court, high court judge, high day,

high explosive, high fidelity, high finance, high five, high-flown, high-flyer, high-flying, high frequency, high gear, high-handed, high-hat, high-impact, high jinks, high jump, high-level, high life, high mass, high-minded, high noon, high-octane, high-pitched, high-powered, high priest, high-rise, high road, high roller, high school, high seas, high season, high sheriff, high society, high-speed train, high-spirited, high spirits, high spot, high street, high table, high tea, high-tech, high tide, high treason, high-up, high-water mark, high wire, high-wire act; come hell or high water, for the high jump, high as a kite, high days and holidays, hit the high spots, knee-high to a grasshopper, live high on the hog, stink to high heaven; High Church, High Commissioner, High Court of Justice, High Street Kensington, High Wycombe, Lord High Chancellor, Lord High Constable; *A High Wind in Jamaica* (b), *Aces High* (f), *Ain't No Mountain High Enough* (s), *Hang 'Em High* (f), *The High Chaparral* (tv), *High Fidelity* (b/f), *High Hopes* (f/s), *The High Life* (tv), *High Noon* (f), *High Plains Drifter* (f), *High Sierra* (f), *High Society* (f), *River Deep, Mountain High* (s), *Romy and Michele's High School Reunion* (f), *Sweet Valley High* (tv), *Take the High Road* (tv), *The Tide Is High* (s)

higher *see* high; further up, greater, superior; higher education

highland mountainous area; Highland cattle, Highland dress, Highland fling; Highland Games, West Highland terrier

highly greatly, immensely; highly strung

highway main route, road; 1980s religious programme hosted by Sir Harry Secombe; information highway; Highway Code; *Lost Highway* (f), *No Highway* (b)

hike cross-country walk, upwards jerk; jerk upwards, ramble; hitch-hike; take a hike

hiker rambler; hitch-hiker; *The Hitch-Hiker's Guide to the Galaxy* (b/f/r)

hill large mound, steep slope; ant-hill; hill figure, hill fort, hill station, hill-walking; over the hill; Biggin Hill, Broken Hill, Bunker Hill, Clouds Hill, Constitution Hill, Notting Hill, Notting Hill Gate, Parliament Hill, Sudbury Hill, Tower Hill, Tulse Hill; *Blueberry Hill* (s), *The Benny Hill Show* (tv), *The Folks That Live on the Hill* (b/s), *The Fool on the Hill* (s), *Grange Hill* (tv), *The Hill* (f), *Hill Street Blues* (tv), *The Lavender Hill Mob* (f), *Notting Hill* (f), *Pork Chop Hill* (f)

Hill
Biggin, Bunker, Capitol, Clouds, Constitution, Highgate, Nob, Notting, Parliament, Silbury, Sudbury, Tower

---

hills *see* hill; (as) old as the hills; Beverly Hills, Mendip Hills; *A Pale View of Hills* (b), *Beverly Hills Cop* (f)

Hills
Beverly, Black, Cheviot, Chiltern, Malvern, Mendip, Ochil, Quantock

---

hilt dagger or sword handle; up to the hilt

hind   female deer; rear; hind legs; talk the hind leg off a donkey; Golden Hind

hindrance   obstacle; without let or hindrance

hindsight   wisdom after an event; with hindsight

hint   innuendo, tip; imply, suggest; hint at

hip   fruit of the dog rose, pelvic joint; trendy; hip bath, hip flask, hip hop; shoot from the hip

hire   charter, rental; engage, lease; for hire; hire car, hire out, hire purchase; *This Gun for Hire* (f)

hired   *see* hire; hired gun

history   all past events, study of the past; art history, case history, modern history, natural history, oral history; history repeats itself, the rest is history; Natural History Museum; *The History Man* (b/tv), *The History of Mr Polly* (b), *The History of the Decline and Fall of the Roman Empire* (b)

hit   blow, strike, successful record; strike with a blow or missile; direct hit, one-hit wonder, smash hit; hit-and-miss, hit home, hit list, hit man, hit on, hit out at, hit parade; hit for six, hit it off, hit the bottle, hit the buffers, hit the ground running, hit the hay, hit the high spots, hit the jackpot, hit the nail on the head, hit the right note, hit the road, hit the roof, hit the sack, hit the skids, hit the spot, hit the wall, hit the wrong note; *Hit Me with Your Rhythm Stick* (s), *Hit the Road Jack* (s)

hitch   snag, variety of knot; hook up, thumb a lift; 2005 Will Smith comedy; clove hitch, half hitch; hitch-hike, hitch-hiker; hitch your

wagon to a star; *The Hitch-Hiker's Guide to the Galaxy* (b/f/r)

hitched   *see* hitch; get hitched

hither   in this direction, to this place; come-hither; hither and thither

hive   bee colony; hive off

hoar   frost; greyish-white; hoar frost

hob   male ferret, stove top

hobble   faltering walk; walk with a limp; hobble skirt

hobby   pastime, small falcon; hobby horse

hock   horse's leg joint, joint of meat, white German wine; put in pawn; in hock

hockey   game played with curved sticks; ice hockey; hockey stick

hoe   promontory, weeding tool; Dutch hoe; Plymouth Hoe

hog   greedy person, large powerful motorbike, pig; be selfish with; road hog; hog-tied; go the whole hog, live high on the hog; Hog's Back; *Hog Wild* (f)

hoist   lifting apparatus; lift; hoist by your own petard, hoist the flag

hold   cargo area, grip; contain, grasp, keep; on hold; hold back, hold down, hold fast, hold off, hold on, hold out, hold over, hold sway, hold up; cop hold of, don't hold your breath, hold a/no brief for, hold all the aces, hold all the cards, hold in contempt, hold on for grim death, hold the field, hold the fort, hold the purse strings, hold the record, hold the ring, hold the stage, hold to ransom, hold your breath, lay hold of, leave hold of, quit hold of; *I Want to Hold Your Hand* (s)

holder   custodian, gripping implement, owner; candle-holder,

The *Puzzler* Crossword Solver's Dictionary

cigarette holder, pen-holder

holding *see* hold; property owned; fund-holding, road-holding; holding company, holding pattern; *Holding Back the Years* (s), *Holding Out for a Hero* (s)

holds *see* hold; no holds barred

hole aperture, cavity, golf target; air hole, black hole, bolt-hole, coal-hole, cubby-hole, glory hole, hidey-hole, mouse-hole, nineteenth hole, pigeon-hole, priest's hole, toad-in-the-hole, top-hole, watering hole; hole in one, hole in the wall, hole up; blow a hole in, burn a hole in your pocket, dig yourself into a hole, a square peg in a round hole; Black Hole of Calcutta; *Ace in the Hole* (f), *Hole in My Shoe* (s), *There's a Hole in My Bucket* (s), *Towed in a Hole* (f)

holes *see* hole; nine holes; pick holes in

holiday religious festival, vacation; 1984 Madonna hit, 1938 George Cukor film; bank holiday, busman's holiday, half-term holiday, on holiday, package holiday, summer holiday; holiday camp; Holiday Inn; *Busman's Holiday* (tv), *Dreadlock Holiday* (s), *Holiday Inn* (f), *Monsieur Hulot's Holiday* (f), *Roman Holiday* (f), *Summer Holiday* (f/s)

holidays *see* holiday; high days and holidays

holier *see* holy; holier-than-thou

hollow cavity, indentation; scoop (out); concave, empty, meaningless; beat hollow; *The Hollow Men* (po), *Sleepy Hollow* (f), *The Legend of Sleepy Hollow* (b)

holt copse, otter's den, woody hill; *Felix Holt, the Radical* (b)

holy blessed, sacred; holy city, holy cow, holy day, holy grail, holy mackerel, holy of holies, holy orders, holy roller, holy war, holy water; Holy Bible, Holy Family, Holy Father, Holy Ghost, Holy Island, Holy Joe, Holy Roman Empire, Holy See, Holy Spirit, Holy Week, Holy Writ; *Holy Roller* (s), *Holy Smoke!* (f), *The Legend of the Holy Drinker* (f), *Monty Python and the Holy Grail* (f)

homage reverence, tribute; *Homage to Catalonia* (b)

home abode, habitat; indoors; David Storey play; ancestral home, at home, close to home, come home, down-home, drive home, hammer home, harvest home, hit home, mobile home, motor home, near to home, nursing home, old folks' home, rest home, show home, starter home, stately home, strike home, take-home pay; home address, home and dry, home bird, home brew, home cooking, home economics, home farm, home from home, home-grown, home help, home improvement, home in on, home loan, home-made, home movie, home office, home page, home rule, home run, home straight, home stretch, home town, home truth; bring home the bacon, charity begins at home, home is where the heart is, nothing to write home about, there's no place like home, till the cows come home; Battersea Dogs Home, Home Counties, Home Guard, Home Secretary; *At Home with the Braithwaites* (tv), *Cathy Come Home* (tv), *Coming Home* (f), *Every Home Should Have One* (f), *Green Green Grass of Home* (s), *Home Again* (tv),

Home and Away (tv), *Home Alone* (f), *Home to Roost* (tv), *Home Truths* (r) *Lassie Come Home* (f), *Run for Home* (s), *Sweet Home Alabama* (f), *Take Me Home Country Roads* (s)

homeward in the direction of your house; homeward bound; *Homeward Bound* (s)

honest incorruptible, truthful; honest broker, honest-to-God, honest-to-goodness; make an honest woman of, turn an honest penny

honesty sincerity, truthfulness; honesty is the best policy

honey bee's produce, term of endearment; milk and honey; honey badger, honey-bear, honey-bee; *Honey Bun* (s), *Honey for Tea* (tv), *Honey, I Blew Up the Kid* (f), *Honey, I Shrunk the Kids* (f), *Honey, We Shrunk Ourselves* (f), *A Taste of Honey* (f/pl)

honeydew melon variety, sweet sticky substance found on leaves; honeydew melon

honorary discretionary, in title only, unpaid (position); *The Honorary Consul* (b/f)

honour distinction, great respect, special award, virtue; show respect; debt of honour, guard of honour, guest of honour, in honour of, lap of honour, maid of honour, matron of honour, point of honour; honour bright; on your honour, upon my honour; Companion of Honour

honourable illustrious; MP's title; right honourable; honourable discharge, honourable mention; *A Fairly Honourable Defeat* (b), *The Honourable Schoolboy* (b)

honoured *see* honour; time-honoured

honours *see* honour; military

honours; honours list; do the honours, honours are even; Birthday Honours

hooch illicitly distilled alcohol; *Turner and Hooch* (f)

hood gangster, head-covering, US car bonnet; Robin Hood's Bay; *The Adventures of Robin Hood* (f/tv), *Boyz N the Hood* (f), *Little Red Riding Hood* (b)

hooded cloaked and masked; hooded crow

hoof foot of a horse, cow etc; cloven hoof, on the hoof

hoofed *see* hoof; cloven-hoofed

hook boxing punch, clasp, coat peg, curved piece of metal, poor golf shot; fasten, trap; small town east of Basingstoke; Spielberg Peter Pan film; grappling hook, off the hook; hook and eye, hook-nosed, hook up; by hook or by crook, hook, line and sinker, sling your hook

hooks *see* hook; get your hooks into

hooligan lout; football hooligan

hoop circular band, croquet arch; encircle; cock-a-hoop, hula-hoop; hoop-la

hoops *see* hoop; hula-hoops; go through hoops, put through the hoops; Hula Hoops

hoot call of an owl, real laugh, sound of a car's horn; cry like an owl, jeer, laugh, sound (a horn)

hooter car's horn, nose, siren

hop one-legged jump, plant used in beer-making, village dance; jump on one leg, leap; bunny-hop, channel-hop, hip hop, long hop, on the hop; hop, skip and jump, hop, step and jump, hop-picking; hop it; *At the Hop* (s)

hope   aspiration, expectation, optimism; be optimistic, expect, wish (for); forlorn hope; hope against hope, hope springs eternal, not a hope, some hope, while there's life there's hope; Cape of Good Hope; *Chicago Hope* (tv), *Hope and Glory* (f/tv), *Land of Hope and Glory* (s)

hopelessly   in a despairing way; *Hopelessly Devoted to You* (s)

hopes   *see* hope; pin your hopes on; *High Hopes* (f/s)

hopper   container for a bulk material, young locust; channel-hopper

hopping   *see* hop; hedge-hopping, island-hopping; hopping mad

horizon   juncture of Earth and sky, limit of your experience; BBC science documentary programme; on the horizon; *Event Horizon* (f), *Lost Horizon* (b/f)

hormone   gland secretion; hormone replacement therapy

horn   antler, bone on a bull's head, brass instrument, hooter; cream horn, French horn, hunting horn, on the horn, post horn; horn of plenty, horn-rimmed; Cape Horn, Little Big Horn

horned   having antlers; horned toad

hornet   large wasp-like insect; hornet's nest; stir up a hornets' nest

hornpipe   nautical dance; sailors' hornpipe

horns   *see* horn; lock horns; draw in your horns, on the horns of a dilemma, take the bull by the horns

horror   fear, fright, repugnance, scary film genre; horror film, horror-stricken, horror-struck; *The Rocky Horror Show* (mus), *The Rocky Horror Picture Show* (mus)

horrors   *see* horror; chamber of horrors; Chamber of Horrors; *Little Shop of Horrors* (mus)

horse   equine animal; clothes-horse, dark horse, hobby horse, iron horse, one-horse race, one-horse town, pommel horse, rocking horse, shire horse, stalking horse, the horse's mouth, two-horse race, vaulting horse, white horse; horse and cart, horse chestnut, horse laugh, horse racing, horse riding, horse sense, horse-trading; (don't) look a gift horse in the mouth, (don't) put the cart before the horse, eat like a horse, flog a dead horse, from the horse's mouth; Crazy Horse, Horse Guards, Quarter Horse, Trojan Horse; *Horse Feathers* (f), *The Horse's Mouth* (b), *The Horse Whisperer* (b/f), *A Horse with No Name* (s), *A Man Called Horse* (f), *The Wooden Horse* (f)

horseman   rider; *The Electric Horseman* (f)

horsepower   unit measuring the rate of work of an engine; brake horsepower

horses   *see* horse; coach and horses, white horses; don't change horses in midstream, horses for courses; *Bring on the Empty Horses* (b), *Only Fools and Horses* (tv), *They Shoot Horses, Don't They?* (f), *White Horses* (s)

horseshoe   curved metal plate for an equine foot; horseshoe bat, horseshoe crab, horseshoe moustache

hose   garden watering tube, stockings or tights; hose-reel

hospital   infirmary; cottage hospital, field hospital, teaching hospital; hospital trust; *Animal Hospital* (tv), *Britannia Hospital* (f), *City Hospital* (tv)

host bread consecrated in the Christian Eucharist, compère, multitude, party-giver; give (a party), present (a tv programme); heavenly host, mine host

hostage person held to ransom; 2005 Bruce Willis negotiation drama film; hostage to fortune

hostel lodging place for travellers or students; youth hostel

hostess female party giver or compère; air hostess; hostess trolley

hot recently stolen, spicy, very warm; in hot pursuit, in hot water, piping hot, red hot, red-hot poker, white-hot; hot air, hot-air balloon, hot and bothered, hot and heavy, hot-blooded, hot chocolate, hot cross bun, hot-desking, hot dog, hot favourite, hot gospeller, hot-headed, hot key, hot pants, hot potato, hot rod, hot seat, hot shoe, hot spot, hot spring, hot stuff, hot tap, hot-tempered, hot ticket, hot toddy, hot tub, hot up, hot water, hot-water bottle, hot-wire; blow/go hot and cold, hot off the press, hot on the heels of, hot under the collar, like a cat on a hot tin roof, like a cat on hot bricks, sell like hot cakes, strike while the iron is hot, too hot to handle; *Cat on a Hot Tin Roof* (f/pl), *Hot Metal* (tv), *The Hot Spot* (f), *Hot Stuff* (s), *I'm the Last of the Red-Hot Mammas* (s), *It Ain't Half Hot Mum* (tv), *The Long Hot Summer* (f), *Some Like It Hot* (f), *The Hot Rock* (f), *Too Darn Hot* (s)

hotel residence for paying guests; capsule hotel, maître d'hôtel, temperance hotel; *Grand Hotel* (f), *Heartbreak Hotel* (s), *Heartburn*

Hotel (tv), *Hotel Babylon* (tv), *Hotel California* (s), *Hotel du Lac* (b/tv), *The Hotel New Hampshire* (b/f), *Hotel Paradiso* (pl), *Hotel Rwanda* (f), *The White Hotel* (b)

hound dog used in hunting or tracking; pursue; Afghan hound, basset hound, elk hound; *Hound Dog* (s), *The Huckleberry Hound Show* (tv), *The Hound of the Baskervilles* (b/f)

hour measure of time; eleventh hour, half an hour, half-hour, happy hour, lunch hour, man-hour, miles per hour, on the hour, quarter of an hour, rush hour, the eleventh hour, twenty-four-hour clock, witching hour, zero hour; at the eleventh hour; *Eleventh Hour* (tv), *Hancock's Half Hour* (tv), *Happy Hour* (s), *In the Midnight Hour* (s), *One Hour Photo* (f), *One Hour with You* (f), *Rush Hour* (f), *24 Hour Party People* (f), *Zero Hour* (f)

hourly every sixty minutes; half-hourly

hours *see* hour; after hours, book of hours, count the hours, small hours; *After Hours* (f), *Forty-Eight Hours* (f), *The Hours* (f), *Open All Hours* (tv)

house bingo winner's cry, dwelling, dynasty, group within a school, style of popular dance music, theatre audience; contain, give shelter to; medical tv series starring Hugh Laurie; acid house, art house, bath-house, bird-house, boarding house, chapter house, clearing house, coach house, common lodging-house, council house, counting house, country house, cow-house, custom house, discount house, doll's house, free house, front of house, full house, guest house, halfway house, haunted house, in-house, keep house, lodging house, lower house, man of the house, manor house, meeting house, oast house, on the house, open house, opera house, post-house, pot-house, public house, road house, rooming house, safe house, senate house, summer house, town house, tree house, upper house, Wendy house; house arrest, house call, house flag, house-hunter, house-hunting, house husband, house in multiple occupation, house lights, house martin, house of cards, house of correction, house party, house plant, house-proud, house-sitter, house sparrow, house-to-house, house-train, house-warming; bring the house down, get along/on like a house on fire, put your house in order; Admiralty House, Banqueting House, Burghley House, Father of the House, Government House, Hatfield House, House of Commons, House of God, House of Keys, House of Lords, House of Representatives, Mansion House, Mansion House Dinner, Mansion House Speech, Maxwell House, Random House, Sydney Opera House, Trinity House, White House; *Bleak House* (b/tv), *Bless This House* (tv), *The Cider House Rules* (b/f), *Doctor in the House* (b/f/tv), *A Doll's House* (pl), *The Fall of the House of Usher* (b), *Heartbreak House* (pl), *The House at Pooh Corner* (b), *House Auction* (tv), *House Calls* (f), *House of Bamboo* (f), *House of Cards* (b/tv), *House of Fun* (s), *House of Games* (f), *The House of Mirth* (b/f), *The House of the Dead* (b), *House of the Rising Sun* (s), *The House of the Seven Gables* (b/f), *The House of the Spirits* (b/f), *The House on the Strand* (b), *House of Wax* (f), *How Clean Is Your House?* (tv), *I Want That House* (tv), *Little House on the Prairie* (b), *Man about the House* (tv), *The Man of the House* (f), *Noel's House Party* (tv), *Peril at End House* (b), *Road House* (f), *The Russia House* (b/f), *This Ole House* (s)

House
Admiralty, Apsley, Banqueting, Bleak, Burghley, Clarence, Government, Harewood, Hatfield, Lancaster, Mansion, Maxwell, Osborne, Random, Somerset, Sydney Opera, Trinity, White

household domicile, family living together; household gods, household management, household name, household word; Household Cavalry, Household Guards

housemaid female servant; housemaid's knee

houses *see* house; go round the houses; Houses of Parliament; *Widowers' Houses* (pl)

housewives home-makers, small sewing cases; *Desperate Housewives* (tv)

housing *see* house; accommodation, cover; sheltered housing; housing association, housing development, housing estate

hover float on air, vacillate, wait close at hand; hover-mower

how in what manner?; Native American greeting; children's tv science show hosted by Fred

Dinenage; and how, know-how; how about, how come, how many, how much; the how and why, how do you do, how now brown cow, how say you?, how's that, how's tricks, how's your father, see how the land lies; *How about That* (s), *How Clean Is Your House?* (tv), *How Green Was My Valley* (b/f), *How I Won the War* (f), *How Stella Got Her Groove Back* (f), *How the Other Half Loves* (pl), *How the West Was Won* (f), *How to Get Ahead in Advertising* (f), *How to Lose a Guy in Ten Days* (f), *How to Make an American Quilt* (f), *How to Marry a Millionaire* (f), *How to Murder Your Wife* (f), *How to Save Your Own Life* (b), *How to Steal a Million* (f)

howler blunder, breed of noisy South American monkey; schoolboy howler

hub focus, wheel's centre; hub-cap

huckleberry American shrub bearing soft, blue-black fruit; *The Adventures of Huckleberry Finn* (b), *The Huckleberry Hound Show* (tv)

hue aspect, colour; hue and cry; *Hue and Cry* (f)

huff fit of pique; blow out loudly, take an opponent's piece in draughts; Hank Azaria tv series

hug cuddle, keep close to; bear hug; hug the coast

hula Hawaiian dance; hula-hoop; Hula Hoops

hulk rusty old ship; 2003 film starring Eric Bana; *The Incredible Hulk* (tv)

hull green part of a strawberry, outer covering of a seed, ship's framework; remove the seeds or shells from; Humberside city

hum bee's sound, droning sound; be a hive of activity, sing with closed lips, smell unpleasant; hum and haw

human being of the genus homo; genial, mortal, of mankind; human being, human dynamo, human interest, human nature, human race, human rights; to err is human, to forgive divine; *The Human Factor* (b/f), *Human Nature* (f), *The Human Stain* (b/f), *Of Human Bondage* (b)

humble lowly, meek, unpretentious; eat humble pie

humour comedy, fun; indulge; aqueous humour, gallows humour, ill humour, out of humour, vitreous humour; *Every Man in His Humour* (pl)

humoured *see* humour; tempered; good-humoured, ill-humoured

hump bulge, camel's appendage, fit of moroseness, sleeping policeman; carry (a heavy load); road hump; get/have the hump, over the hump

hunch feeling; bend the top of the body forward

hundred number, old shire subdivision; one hundred per cent; hundred per cent; *One Hundred and One Dalmatians* (f), *One Hundred Men and a Girl* (f), *One Hundred Years of Solitude* (b), *Your Hundred Best Tunes* (r)

hundreds *see* hundred; lots; hundreds and thousands; Chiltern Hundreds; *The Chiltern Hundreds* (f), *Hundreds and Thousands* (al)

hung *see* hang; hung jury, hung up, hung-over

hunger appetite, need and desire for food; Knut Hamsun novel; hunger march, hunger strike; *The Hunger* (f)

hunky fit and attractive (of a man); hunky-dory; *Hunky Dory* (al)

hunt   chase, pursuit; go after prey, search (for); fox-hunt, treasure hunt, witch hunt; hunt saboteur, hunt the thimble; National Hunt; *Bargain Hunt* (tv), *The Hunt for Red October* (b/f), *Treasure Hunt* (tv), *Witch Hunt* (f)

hunted   *see* hunt; head-hunted

hunter   horse attending meets, predator, stalker, style of pocket watch; British fighter plane introduced in 1956; autograph hunter, bargain-hunter, big-game hunter, bounty hunter, fortune-hunter, fox-hunter, half-hunter, house-hunter; hunter-gatherer, hunter's moon; *Bounty Hunter* (ga), *The Deer Hunter* (f), *The Heart Is a Lonely Hunter* (b), *The Night of the Hunter* (f), *White Hunter Black Heart* (f), *Will Success Spoil Rock Hunter?* (f)

hunting   *see* hunt; autograph hunting, fox-hunting, happy hunting ground, house-hunting; hunting crop, hunting dog, hunting ground, hunting horn; *Good Will Hunting* (f), *The Hunting of the Snark* (po)

hurricane   violent windstorm; WWII fighter plane; hurricane lamp; *The Hurricane* (f)

hurry   hasten, rush; in a hurry; hurry up; *You Can't Hurry Love* (s)

hurts   aches; *Everybody Hurts* (s), *Every Day Hurts* (s), *Love Hurts* (tv)

husband   male spouse; use sparingly; house husband; *An Ideal Husband* (f/pl), *Somebody Killed Her Husband* (f)

husbands   *see* husband; *Hollywood Husbands* (b), *Husbands and Wives* (f), *The Man Who Made Husbands Jealous* (b)

hush   silence; make (someone) be quiet; song recorded by Deep Purple and Kula Shaker; hush-hush, hush money, hush up; Hush Puppies

husky   Arctic dog; gruff-voiced

hustle   frenzied activity, fraud; pressurise, push roughly, sell aggressively, swindle; tv drama series about a team of confidence tricksters; 1975 Burt Reynolds/Catherine Deneuve film; *The Hustle* (s)

hustler   aggressive salesperson, con man; *The Hustler* (f)

hut   shack; Nissen hut; Pizza Hut

hutch   small animal cage; rabbit hutch; *Starsky and Hutch* (f/tv)

hyacinth   fragrant flowering bulb; grape hyacinth, wild hyacinth

hydraulic   operated by water pressure; hydraulic jack

hydrogen   gas which combines with oxygen to make water; hydrogen peroxide, hydrogen sulphide

hymn   religious song; hymn-book

hype   publicity; create publicity for; hype up

hysterics   panic attacks, wild outbursts of laughter or tears; in hysterics

I

ice cold formality, criminal slang for diamonds, frozen sweet, frozen water; decorate with frosting, freeze over; black ice, choc-ice, coconut ice, de-ice, dry ice, Neapolitan ice cream, on ice, on thin ice, pack ice, sheet of ice, water ice; ice axe, ice beer, ice-breaker, ice cap, ice cream, ice-cream parlour, ice-cream soda, ice cube, ice dance, ice dancing, ice-field, ice floe, ice hockey, ice lolly, ice over, ice pack, ice pick, ice plant, ice rink, ice shelf, ice show, ice skates, ice-skating; break the ice, cut no ice; Ice Age; *Dancing on Ice* (tv), *Ice Age* (f), *Ice Cold in Alex* (f), *Ice Station Zebra* (b/f), *The Ice Storm* (f)

iceberg frozen floating block at sea, variety of lettuce; iceberg lettuce; the tip of the iceberg; *Sugar Coated Iceberg* (s)

iced *see* ice; iced tea

icing *see* ice; sugary cake topping; glacé icing, royal icing; icing sugar; the icing on the cake

idea plan, thought; no idea, rough idea; have no idea, that's the idea, the very idea

ideal paradigm; perfect; Ideal Home Exhibition; *An Ideal Husband* (f/pl)

ideas *see* idea; get ideas; buck up your ideas

identical exactly the same; identical twins

identity individuality, persona; 2003 thriller with Ray Liotta; identity crisis, identity parade; *The Bourne Identity* (b/f)

idiot fool; idiot board; *The Idiot* (b)

idle inactive, lazy; tick over; bone idle

idol hero, image of a god; matinee idol; *Pop Idol* (tv), *The Fallen Idol* (f)

ignition act of setting on fire, car's starting mechanism; ignition key

ignorant unaware, uneducated; pig-ignorant

iguana large tropical lizard; *The Night of the Iguana* (f)

ill harm, injury; unwell; badly; bear ill will, speak ill of, think ill of; ill-advised, ill-assorted, ill at ease, ill-bred, ill-defined, ill-disposed, ill fame, ill-fated, ill-gotten, ill-gotten gains, ill health, ill humour, ill-informed, ill-mannered, ill-natured, ill starred, ill-tempered, ill-timed, ill-treat, ill-use, ill-will, ill wind

illiterate person who is unable to read or write; unable to read or write; functionally illiterate

illuminated decorated (a manuscript), lit up; illuminated manuscript

illusion deceptive appearance, magic trick; optical illusion; *FX: Murder by Illusion* (f), *Just an Illusion* (s), *La Grande Illusion* (f), *Use Your Illusion* (al)

illustrated accompanied by pictures; *The Illustrated Man* (b/f)

image idol, likeness, mental picture, picture, public persona; form a likeness of; corporate image, graven image, mirror image, self-image, spitting image, the living image; *Spitting Image* (tv)

immaculate pure; Immaculate Conception

immersion baptism, preoccupation, type of water heater; immersion heater

immunity exemption, resistance to (disease); diplomatic immunity

impact collision, strong effect; collide, make an impression; high-impact, low-impact; *Deep Impact* (f), *Sudden Impact* (f)

imperfect verb's continual past tense; faulty, flawed

imperial Small tufted beard popularised by Napoleon III, system of weights and measures; majestic, of a vast dominion, regal; Imperial Mints, Imperial War Museum; *Crown Imperial* (cl)

impersonator mimic; female impersonator

import item purchased from abroad, meaning, significance; bring (goods) from overseas, signify

importance significance, value; self-importance; *The Importance of Being Earnest* (pl), *A Woman of No Importance* (pl)

imposing being a nuisance; distinguished-looking

impossible unable to be done; *Mission: Impossible* (f)

impression effect on the mind, feeling, graphic representation; *Big Impression* (tv), *Impression: Sunrise* (pa)

impressions *see* impression; first impressions

imprisonment detention in jail; life imprisonment

improper unseemly; improper fraction

improvement change for the better; home improvement, self-improvement; room for improvement; *Room for Improvement* (tv)

impulse stimulus, sudden whim; brand-name perfume; impulse buying

inadmissible prohibited in court; *Inadmissible Evidence* (f)

incendiary arsonist, troublemaker; explosively causing fire, tending to stir up conflict; incendiary bomb

incense aromatic smoke; anger; incense burner

inch small measure of length; edge

forward slowly; every inch, half-inch; inch by inch

incident event; incident room; *The Oxbow Incident* (f), *Yangtse Incident* (f)

incidental accompanying, of secondary importance; incidental music

inclination bend or bow (of the head or body), gradient, liking, tilt; angle of inclination

incline ramp, slope; lean, tend

income earnings; discretionary income, disposable income, fixed income, private income, unearned income; income support, income tax

incredible unbelievable; *The Incredible Hulk* (tv)

indecent lewd, unseemly; *Indecent Exposure* (b), *Indecent Proposal* (f)

indeed actually; is that so?; a friend in need is a friend indeed

indefinite unspecific; indefinite article

indemnity legal exemption from penalties, security from damage or loss; *Double Indemnity* (b/f)

independence autonomy, self-sufficiency; Independence Day; *Independence Day* (f)

independent autonomous, self-supporting; independent inquiry; *The Independent* (n)

index alphabetical list, forefinger; catalogue (contents of a book, eg); card index, cross index, retail price index, share index, thumb index; index finger, index-linked; Dow Jones index, FT index, FTSE index, Hang Seng index, Nikkei index

indicator car's flasher, gauge, signpost; universal indicator

indirect circuitous, oblique; indirect object, indirect question

indoor within a building; indoor game, indoor sport

induction admission, course of initial training; induction heating, induction loop

industrial concerning manufacturing, used in manufacture; industrial action, industrial designer, industrial diamond, industrial espionage, industrial estate, industrial relations, industrial revolution, industrial-strength, industrial tribunal

industry diligence, economic activity, manufacturing; cottage industry, growth industry, heavy industry, light industry, service industry

inert chemically unreactive, passive; inert gas

infant baby or young child; infant school

infantry foot soldiers; light infantry

inferiority low rank or quality; inferiority complex

inferno hell, raging fire; first part of Dante's *The Divine Comedy*; *The Towering Inferno* (f)

infinitive basic form of a verb; split infinitive

inflammatory arousing violent feelings, causing swelling and pain; anti-inflammatory

influence effect; under the influence

information data, news or knowledge; information fatigue, information highway, information officer, information overload, information retrieval, information science, information superhighway, information technology; *The Information* (b)

informed grassed, told;

knowledgeable; ill-informed, well informed; informed consent

informer stool pigeon; *The Informer* (b/f)

inheritance legacy; inheritance tax

inheritors heirs, successors; *The Inheritors* (b)

iniquity gross injustice, vice; den of iniquity

initiation admission, beginning; initiation ceremony

initiative ability to act without prompting, first step, proposal; on your own initiative

injected introduced via a syringe; fuel-injected

injection medical jab; fuel injection, hypodermic injection; injection moulding

injury damage to the body; repetitive strain injury; injury time; add insult to injury

ink squid's weapon, printing and writing fluid; Indian ink, invisible ink, pen and ink; ink-blot test, ink bottle, ink cap, ink in, ink-jet printer, ink pen

inland away from the coast; inland sea; Inland Revenue

inn old coaching house, small hotel or pub; coaching inn; Lincoln's Inn Fields; *Holiday Inn* (f), *The Inn of the Sixth Happiness* (f), *Jamaica Inn* (b)

inner part of a target next to the bullseye; closer to the centre, hidden (feelings); inner city, inner ear, inner man, inner sanctum, inner space, inner tube; Inner Hebrides; *Inner Space* (f)

innings batting period in cricket; had a good innings

innocence artlessness, lack of guilt;

The Age of Innocence (b/f), *The Innocence of Father Brown* (b), *Songs of Innocence and of Experience* (po)

innocent naive person; free of guilt, naive; *The Innocent* (f), *An Innocent Man* (s), *Young and Innocent* (f)

innocents *see* innocent; young children slaughtered by Herod; Innocents Day; *The Innocents Abroad* (b)

inns *see* inn; Inns of Court

inquiry exploration, formal investigation; independent inquiry

insect six-legged invertebrate; stick insect

inside confidential (information), doing time, indoors, internal; privately; inside job, inside leg, inside out; know inside out; *The Kick Inside* (al), *Step Inside Love* (s)

insider person in the know, someone belonging to a certain organisation; insider dealing; *The Insider* (f)

inspection check-up, examination; kit inspection

inspector examiner, high-ranking police officer; chief inspector, detective inspector, police inspector, ticket inspector; inspector general, inspector of schools, inspector of taxes; *The Government Inspector* (pl), *An Inspector Calls* (pl), *Inspector Gadget* (f/tv), *Inspector Morse* (tv)

inspiring breathing in, encouraging; awe-inspiring

instance example, occurrence; cite as an example; for instance; at first instance, in the first instance

instant moment; immediate; instant coffee; this instant; *Instant Karma* (s)

instead alternatively; instead of

instinct natural impulse, sixth sense;

herd instinct, killer instinct; *Basic Instinct* (f), *Killer Instinct* (ga)

institute academy, guild; establish, set in motion; Women's Institute

instrument agency, device for producing musical sounds, formal legal document, tool; musical instrument, statutory instrument, wind instrument

insulating lagging (pipes), preventing the passage of electricity, sealing off; insulating tape

insulation lagging (of pipes), protection against heat or electricity; insulation material

insult offensive remark; treat with contempt; add insult to injury

insurance coverage against loss; life insurance; insurance broker, insurance policy; National Insurance

integrated amalgamated, co-ordinated; integrated circuit

intellectual cultured, educated person; brainy, highbrow; intellectual property

intelligence cleverness, information, secret services; artificial intelligence, counter-intelligence; intelligence agency, intelligence officer, intelligence quotient, intelligence service; *The Intelligence Men* (f)

intensive concentrated, thorough, unremitting; labour-intensive; intensive care

intent meaning, purpose; determined, eager, occupied; with intent; loiter with intent; *Law & Order: Criminal Intent* (tv)

intentional done on purpose; intentional fallacy

intentions plans; *Cruel Intentions* (f)

inter bury; inter-parliamentary; inter

alia, primus inter pares; Inter Milan

interest attentiveness, concern, curiosity, hobby, premium paid on borrowed money; concern deeply, engage the attention of; conflict of interest, controlling interest, human interest, love interest, self-interest, vested interest; interest-free; declare an interest

interests *see* interest; outside interests; in the interests of

interior central part; indoor, remote from the coast; interior decoration, interior design, interior monologue

internal domestic (of a country), emotional; internal-combustion engine internal market; *Internal Affairs* (f)

international global; international law, international style; Amnesty International, First International, Fourth International, International Date Line; *International Velvet* (f)

interpersonal of human relationships; interpersonal skills

interpreter oral translator; *The Interpreter* (f), *The Russian Interpreter* (b)

intervals breaks during performances, pauses; at intervals

interview consultation; *Interview with the Vampire* (f)

intestine part of the digestive system; large intestine, small intestine

intolerable unbearable; *Intolerable Cruelty* (f)

intuitive perceived without reasoning, spontaneous; counter-intuitive

invaders occupying forces; *Space Invaders* (ga)

invasion mass encroachment, seizure

and takeover (of a country); tv sci-fi
drama series with Sheriff Underlay;
Invasion of the Body Snatchers (f)

invention brainchild, originality;
necessity is the mother of invention

inverse antithesis; opposite in effect;
inverse proportion

inverted changed the order of,
turned upside down; inverted
commas, inverted snobbery

investment money put into an
enterprise, thing likely to increase in
value; inward investment;
investment bank, investment trust

invisible impossible to see; invisible
ink; *The Invisible Man* (b/f), *Invisible
Touch* (f)

invitation request to attend,
temptation; *Invitation to a
Beheading* (b), *Invitation to the Dance*
(cl/f), *Invitation to the Waltz* (b/cl)

inward private,
unexpressed (thought); inward
investment, inward-looking

iron branding instrument, common
metallic element, laundry appliance,
numbered golf club; press (clothes);
branding iron, cast iron, pig iron,
pump iron, rod of iron, sand iron,
soldering iron, steam iron, waffle
iron, wrought iron; iron-clad, iron
horse, iron maiden, iron man, iron
ore, iron out, iron oxide, iron rations;
an iron fist in a velvet glove rule with
a rod of iron, strike while the iron is
hot; Iron Age, Iron Cross, Iron
Curtain; *Any Old Iron* (s), *The Iron
Giant* (b/f), *The Iron Petticoat* (f), *The
Man in the Iron Mask* (b/f), *Pumping
Iron* (f)

ironing *see* iron; ironing board

irons *see* iron; shackles; fire irons, in

irons, leg-irons; clap in irons, have
other irons in the fire

Island
Ascension, Baffin, Barry, Bear,
Canvey, Christmas, Devil's, Easter,
Ellis, Fraser, Hayling, Holy, Long,
Lundy, Pitcairn, Portland, Prince
Edward, Rhode, Robben, Staten,
Three Mile, Vancouver, Walney

island territory surrounded by water;
desert island, Rhode Island red, sea-
island cotton, Thousand Island
dressing, traffic island; no man is an
island; Baffin Island, Bear Island,
Christmas Island, Devil's Island,
Easter Island, Holy Island, Long
Island, Prince Edward Island, Rhode
Island, Robben Island, Staten Island,
Three Mile Island; *Bear Island* (b/f),
The Coral Island (b), *Cutthroat
Island* (f), *Desert Island Discs* (r),
Devil's Island (f), *Fantasy Island* (tv),
Gilligan's Island (tv), *Island in the
Sun* (s), *Island of Dreams* (s), *The
Island of Dr Moreau* (f), *John Bull's
Other Island* (pl), *Love and Death on
Long Island* (f), *Treasure Island* (b)

Islands
Aleutian, Andaman, Aran, Balearic,
Canary, Cayman, Channel, Cook,
Falkland, Farne, Friendly,
Galapagos, Leeward, Marshall,
Orkney, Shetland, Society,
Solomon, Thousand, Windward

islands *see* island; archipelago;
Aleutian Islands, Andaman Islands,
Aran Islands, Balearic Islands, Blasket
Islands, Cayman Islands, Channel

Islands, Cook Islands Falkland Islands, Friendly Islands, Galapagos Islands, Lipari Islands, Marshall Islands, Nicobar Islands, Orkney Islands, Shetland Islands, Society Islands, Solomon Islands; *Islands in the Stream* (s)

isle   area of land surrounded by water; Apple Isle, Emerald Isle, Fair Isle, Isle of Dogs, Isle of Ely, Isle of Man, Isle of Skye, Isle of Thanet, Isle of Wight

isles   *see* isle; British Isles

isolation   detachment, loneliness, remoteness; in isolation

issue   edition, offspring, outcome, topic of discussion; emanate, put into circulation; at issue, rights issue, side issue; force the issue, make an issue of, take issue with; *The Big Issue*

(mag), *Fat Is a Feminist Issue* (b)

itch   restless craving, skin irritation; cause irritation, crave; *The Seven Year Itch* (f)

itching   *see* itch; impatient (for); itching palm, itching powder

itchy   in need of a scratch, restless; get itchy feet, have itchy feet

item   newspaper article, part of a list, thing; be an item

ivories   elephants' tusks, piano keys; tickle the ivories

ivory   elephant tusk substance, piano key, yellowish-white colour; ivory tower; Ivory Coast; *Ebony and Ivory* (s)

ivy   evergreen climbing plant; poison ivy; Ivy League; *Poison Ivy* (f)

J

jab injection, quick punch; poke sharply

jack court card, lifting device, small ball in bowls; every man jack, hydraulic jack, jumping jack, Monterey Jack cheese; jack in, jack-in-the-box, jack-knife, jack-o'-lantern, jack rabbit, Jack tar, Jack the Lad; jack of all trades (and master of none); Jack Frost, Jack Russell, Jack Sprat, Monterey Jack, Union Jack; *Hit the Road Jack* (s), *I'm All Right Jack* (f), *Jack and Jill* (nr), *Jack and the Beanstalk* (pan), *Jumpin' Jack Flash* (s), *Little Jack Horner* (nr)

jackal dog-like wild animal; *The Day of the Jackal* (b/f)

jackass fool, male donkey; laughing jackass

jacket book's cover, short coat; bomber jacket, dinner jacket, donkey jacket, dust jacket, Eton jacket, flak jacket, flying jacket, hacking jacket, leather jacket, life-jacket, mandarin jacket, matinee jacket, Norfolk jacket, puffa jacket, pyjama jacket, reefer jacket, safari jacket, smoking jacket, sports jacket, waxed jacket; jacket potato; *Full Metal Jacket* (f), *The Jacket* (f)

jackpot top prize; hit the jackpot

jade green gemstone, worn-out horse; jade green

jagged rough-edged; *Jagged Edge* (f)

jail prison; send to prison

jam fruit conserve, sticky situation, traffic tailback; become stuck, wedge in; raspberry jam, strawberry jam, traffic jam; jam doughnut, jam-jar, jam-packed, jam tart; jam tomorrow, money for jam

jams *see* jam; jim-jams

jar glass container; grate on, jolt; bell jar, jam-jar, kilner jar; *The Bell Jar* (b), *Whiskey in the Jar* (s)

jasmine fragrant shrub; jasmine tea

javelin light spear; javelin thrower

jaw chin bone; talk a lot; lantern jaw;

jaw-breaker, jaw-dropping

jazz musical style; Dixieland jazz, trad jazz, traditional jazz; jazz age, jazz band; and all that jazz; *All That Jazz* (mus), *And All That Jazz* (s), *The Jazz Singer* (f), *Tales of the Jazz Age* (b)

jealous envious, mistrustful in love; *Jealous Guy* (s), *Jealous Mind* (s), *The Man Who Made Husbands Jealous* (b)

jeans denim trousers; *Forever in Blue Jeans* (s)

jeepers expression of surprise; jeepers creepers; *Jeepers Creepers* (f)

jellied set in aspic; jellied eels

jelly wobbly dessert; petroleum jelly, royal jelly; jelly babies, jelly beans

jenny female donkey, spinning machine; creeping Jenny, spinning jenny

jeopardy danger; double jeopardy; in jeopardy; *Double Jeopardy* (f)

jerk sudden pull; pull sharply; marinated in spices; knee-jerk; clean and jerk; *The Jerk* (f)

jerking *see* jerk; tear-jerking

jerks *see* jerk; physical jerks

jersey sweater; breed of cow, largest of the Channel Islands; green jersey, yellow jersey; Jersey cow; New Jersey; *Jersey Girl* (f)

jester court fool; *The Court Jester* (f)

jet aircraft, ornamental black lignite, stream of liquid; fly very fast; deep black; fan-jet, ink-jet printer, jumbo jet, jump-jet, prop jet; jet black, jet engine, jet lag, jet-lagged, jet plane, jet-propelled, jet propulsion, jet set, jet-setter, jet ski, jet stream; *Leavin' on a Jet Plane* (s)

jetsam goods thrown overboard; flotsam and jetsam

jewel gemstone; jewel in the crown;

Jewel of the Nile (f), *The Jewel in the Crown* (b/tv)

jewellery personal ornaments; costume jewellery

jewels *see* jewel; Crown jewels

jiffy moment; brand-name padded envelope; Jiffy bag; in a jiffy

jig lively dance; move about jerkily; in jig time

jiggered exhausted; I'll be jiggered

jigsaw picture puzzle, tool for cutting curved lines; chain of fashion stores; 1962 Jack Warner film, Barbara Cartland's first novel; jigsaw puzzle

jill female ferret; *Jack and Jill* (nr)

jingle advertising tune, tinkling sound; make a tinkling sound; *Jingle Bells* (s)

jinks sudden changes of direction; dodges nimbly; high jinks

jive 1950s dance; perform a 1950s dance; *Jive Talkin'* (s), *See My Baby Jive* (s)

job occupation, task; Old Testament book, Old Testament character; a good job, desk job, hatchet job, inside job, nose job, odd job, odd-job man, put-up job; job centre, job club, job description, job lot, job satisfaction, Job's comforter, job-share; just the job, make the best of a bad job, on the job; *The Italian Job* (f), *An Unsuitable Job for a Woman* (b/tv)

jobs *see* job; jobs for the boys

jockey competitive horse rider; manoeuvre to gain an advantage; disc jockey; jockey cap; Jockey Club

joey baby marsupial; tv spin-off from *Friends*; *Pal Joey* (mus)

jog gentle run; run at an easy pace; jog along

join   connect; seam; join battle, join forces, join in, join up; if you can't beat them join them

joined   *see* join; joined-up handwriting

joint   large piece of meat, place where bones meet, reefer; shared; ball-and-socket joint, clip joint, Sunday joint, universal joint; joint account, joint-stock company; case the joint, out of joint, put one's nose out of joint; *Joint Account* (tv)

jointed   composed of segments; double-jointed

joke   funny story; talk humorously; in-joke, no joke, practical joke, standing joke; be no joke, beyond a joke, crack a joke

joker   humorist, wild playing-card; practical joker; the joker in the pack; *The Joker Is Wild* (f)

joking   *see* joke; joking apart

jolly   cheerful; Jolly Roger

joss   religious statue; joss stick

jot   tiny amount; make a brief note of

journal   diary, news publication; *Journal of the Plague Year* (b), *The Thief's Journal* (b), *Wall Street Journal* (n)

journalism   press reporting; chequebook journalism

journey   trip; travel; *Bill & Ted's Bogus Journey* (f), *Felicia's Journey* (f), *Journey into Fear* (f), *Journey to the Centre of the Earth* (b), *Long Day's Journey into Night* (f/pl), *A Sentimental Journey* (b), *Such a Long Journey* (b)

jowl   loose skin on the neck; cheek by jowl

joy   great pleasure; traveller's joy; jump for joy, pride and joy

joys   sources of pleasure; full of the joys of spring

jubilee   special anniversary; 1977 Derek Jarman film; diamond jubilee, golden jubilee, silver jubilee; Jubilee clip; Jubilee Line

judge   legal arbiter; deem; circuit judge, high court judge, touch judge; (as) sober as a judge, don't judge a book by its cover; *Judge Dredd* (f), *Judge John Deed* (tv)

judgement   discernment, legal verdict; arrest of judgement, pass judgement, value judgement; judgement by default; Day of Judgement, Judgement Day, Last Judgement; *Last Judgement* (pa)

judicial   relating to the law; judicial review, judicial separation

jug   container for pouring, prison; toby jug, water jug; jug band

jugular   neck vein; jugular vein; go for the jugular

juice   electrical power, liquid from a fruit, petrol; fruit juice, grapefruit juice, jungle juice, lemon juice, lime juice, orange juice, pineapple juice; stew in your own juice

juices   *see* juice; gastric juices

juicy   succulent, titillating

jumble   untidy mess, unwanted household goods; jumble sale

jumbo   very large; large plane; mumbo-jumbo; jumbo jet

jump   leap up, react in surprise; act of leaping; bungee jump, high jump, long jump, parachute jump, ski jump, triple jump, water jump; jump bail, jump leads, jump-jet, jump-off, jump-start; for the high jump, hop, skip and jump, hop, step and jump, jump for joy, jump in at the deep end, jump the gun, jump the queue, jump to conclusions

jumped *see* jump; jumped-up
jumper person or animal which leaps, sweater; bungee jumper, high jumper, long jumper, polo-neck jumper, queue-jumper, ski jumper, triple jumper
jumping *see* jump; base jumping, bungee-jumping, queue-jumping, ski-jumping; jumping bean, jumping beans, jumping jack
jumps *see* jump; see which way the cat jumps
junction electronic contact point, road intersection; box junction, T-junction; junction box; Clapham Junction, Watford Junction, Willesden Junction; *Tuxedo Junction* (s), *Up the Junction* (f)

Junction
Beckenham, Burscough, Clapham, Effingham, Limerick, Llandudno, Mitcham, Norwood, St Helen's, Tuxedo, Watford, Willesden

jungle tropical forest; concrete jungle; jungle fever, jungle juice; the law of the jungle; *The Asphalt Jungle* (f), *The Blackboard Jungle* (b/f), *Concrete Jungle* (ga/s), *The Jungle Book* (b/f), *Jungle Fever* (f), *King of the Jungle* (f), *Welcome to the Jungle* (f)
junior person with a low rank; 1994 Schwarzenegger film; lower in rank, younger; junior common room, junior school; *Junior Bonner* (f)
juniper gin-flavouring berry; *Jennifer Juniper* (s)
junk Chinese boat, worthless stuff; Mervyn Burgess novel; junk bonds, junk food, junk mail, junk shop

jury adjudicating panel; grand jury, hung jury; jury box; the jury is out; *I, The Jury* (b), *Juke Box Jury* (tv), *Runaway Jury* (b/f), *Trial by Jury* (f/o)
just deserved, morally right; exactly, only, very recently; only just; just a minute, just deserts, just fancy, just in case, just in time, just married, just right, just so; just around the corner, just between ourselves, just for the hell of it, just good friends, just like mother makes, just like that, just the job, just the same, just-in-time, life is just a bowl of cherries; *The Four Just Men* (b/tv), *Girls Just Want to Have Fun* (s), *I Just Called to Say I Love You* (s), *Just a Minute* (r), *Just an Illusion* (s), *Just Between Ourselves* (pl), *Just Blew In from the Windy City* (s), *Just Good Friends* (tv), *Just Like a Pill* (s), *Just Like a Woman* (s), *Just One of Those Things* (s), *Just So Stories* (b), *Just the Way You Are* (s), *Just William* (b), *Life Is Just a Bowl of Cherries* (s)
justice fairness; do justice to, hall of justice, poetic justice, rough justice; bring to justice, miscarriage of justice, scales of justice; High Court of Justice, Justice of the Peace, Lord Chief Justice, Lord Justice, Lord Justice-General, Royal Courts of Justice
justifiable defensible; justifiable homicide
justifies *see* justify; the end justifies the means
justify line up (written text), prove to be right; *Justify My Love* (s)
juvenile young person; childish; juvenile court, juvenile delinquent

K

kangaroo   marsupial; DH Lawrence novel; kangaroo court, kangaroo rat; *Tie Me Kangaroo Down, Sport* (s)

karaoke   sing-along entertainment; karaoke machine

karate   martial art; karate chop; *The Karate Kid* (f)

karma   Hindu and Buddhist spiritual law; *Instant Karma* (s), *Karma Chameleon* (s)

kebab   food cooked on a skewer; doner kebab, shish kebab

keel   bottom of a ship; keel over; on an even keel

keen   eager, sharp; mad keen; as keen as mustard

keep   castle's tower; feed, clothe and house, preserve, remain fresh, retain; keep at bay, keep back, keep calm, keep clear, keep company, keep count, keep dark, keep fit, keep house, keep mum, keep off, keep pace with, keep posted, keep quiet, keep rank, keep sweet, keep tabs on, keep the peace, keep track, keep up, keep watch; keep a check on, keep a clean sheet, keep a lookout for, keep a low profile, keep a secret, keep a straight face, keep a tight rein on, keep a weather eye on, keep an ear to the ground, keep an eye on, keep at arm's length, keep body and soul together, keep both feet on the ground, keep Britain tidy, keep company with, keep off the grass, keep the ball rolling, keep the pot boiling, keep the wolf from the door, keep under your hat, keep up appearances, keep your chin up, keep your countenance, keep your distance, keep your eye on the ball, keep your hair on, keep your hands clean, keep your mouth shut, keep your nose clean, keep your nose out, keep your options open, keep your own counsel, keep your pecker up, keep your shirt on, keep your temper; *I've Got My Love to Keep Me Warm* (s),

Keep on Running (s), *Keep the Aspidistra Flying* (b), *Keep the Faith* (s)

keeper attendant, custodian, person behind the wicket, zoo worker; book-keeper, green-keeper, lock-keeper, park-keeper, wicket-keeper

keepers *see* keeper; peace-keepers; finders keepers

keeping *see* keep; care, custody, guardianship; book-keeping, in keeping with, safe keeping; keeping up appearances, keeping up with the Joneses; *Keeping Up Appearances* (tv)

keeps *see* keep; an apple a day keeps the doctor away, for keeps

keg cask; powder keg; keg bitter

kennel dog house; dog kennel; kennel-maid; Kennel Club

kennels *see* kennel; boarding kennels

kept *see* keep; kept woman

kerb pavement edge; kerb drill

kettle kitchen water heater; fish kettle, pretty kettle of fish, tea kettle; a different kettle of fish, fine kettle of fish

key explanation on a map, lock opener, low-lying island, middle stone of an arch, musical pitch, one of the levers on a typewriter, part of a piano, solution; enter (data to a computer); vitally important; hot key, ignition key, low-key, master key, off-key, out of key, pass key, skeleton key; key card, key grip, key in, key signature, key-ring; under lock and key; Allen key; Key Largo, Key Stage, Key West; *Fear Is the Key* (b), *Key Largo* (f)

keyhole part of a lock; keyhole surgery; *Through the Keyhole* (tv)

keys *see* key; House of Keys

kick footballing action, recoil of a gun, thrill; hit with the foot; drop kick, free kick, goal kick, penalty kick, place kick, spot kick; kick back, kick-boxing, kick off, kick out, kick pleat, kick-start, kick up; kick against the pricks, kick in the teeth, kick over the traces, kick the bucket, kick the habit, kick up dust, kick up your heels, kick upstairs; *I Get a Kick out of You* (s), *The Kick Inside* (al)

kicking *see* kick; alive and kicking

kicks *see* kick; *Teenage Kicks* (s)

kid child, young goat; joke; whizz-kid; kid gloves; handle with kid gloves; *Butch Cassidy and the Sundance Kid* (f), *The Cincinnati Kid* (f), *The Cisco Kid* (tv), *Honey, I Blew Up the Kid* (f), *The Karate Kid* (f), *A Kid for Two Farthings* (f), *The Kid from Brooklyn* (f), *Kid Galahad* (f), *The Kid* (f), *The Kid Stays in the Picture* (f), *The Lemon Drop Kid* (f)

kidding *see* kid; no kidding

kidney renal organ; kidney beans, kidney-stone

kids *see* kid; kids' stuff; *Honey, I Shrunk the Kids* (f), *Kids in America* (s), *Spy Kids* (f)

kill homicide; murder; kill time; dressed to kill, go for the kill, in at the kill, kill the fatted calf, kill two birds with one stone; *The Big Kill* (b), *Dressed to Kill* (f), *Kill Bill* (f), *Licence to Kill* (f), *A Time to Kill* (b/f), *To Kill a Mockingbird* (b/f), *A View to a Kill* (f)

killed *see* kill; curiosity killed the cat; *Somebody Killed Her Husband* (f), *Video Killed the Radio Star* (s)

killer murderer; impressive, 1990 hit for Adamski; giant-killer; killer bees, killer instinct, killer whale; *Killer Instinct* (ga), *Killer Queen* (s), *Killer's Kiss* (f)

killers   *see* killer; *The Killers* (f), *Natural Born Killers* (f)

killing   *see* kill; large financial gain, slaughter; hilarious; giant-killing; make a killing; *The Killing Fields* (f), *The Killing of Sister George*

kin   blood relatives; kith and kin, next of kin; *Next of Kin* (f), *The Next of Kin* (f)

kind   type; considerate, generous; in kind, of a kind, of its kind; kind of, kind-hearted; not the marrying kind, nothing of the kind, one of a kind; *Close Encounters of the Third Kind* (f), *Kind Hearts and Coronets* (f), *A Kind of Loving* (b/f), *A Kind of Magic* (s), *Three of a Kind* (tv), *What Kind of Fool Am I?* (s)

kindergarten   nursery; *Kindergarten Cop* (f)

kindly   good-natured; generously; look kindly on, thank someone kindly

kindred   blood relationship; like-minded, matching, related; kindred spirit

kinetic   relating to movement; kinetic energy

king   male sovereign, court-card, vital chess piece; chicken à la king, drag king, pearly king; king cobra, king crab, king prawn, king's evil, king's ransom, king-sized; a cat may look at a king, king of the castle; King Charles Spaniel, King James Bible, King's Cross, King's Cross St Pancras, King's Cross Thameslink, King's Lynn, King of Kings; *All the King's Men* (b/f), *In the Court of the Crimson King* (al), *Jason King* (tv), *The King and I* (mus), *King Arthur* (f), *King Coal* (b), *King Cobra* (f), *King Creole* (f/s), *The Fisher King* (b/f), *King Henry the Eighth* (pl), *King Henry the Fifth* (pl), *King John* (pl), *King Kong* (f), *King Lear* (pl), *King Midas in Reverse* (s), *The King of Comedy* (f), *King of the Jungle* (f), *King of the Road* (s), *King Rat* (b/f), *King Richard the Second* (pl), *King Richard the Third* (pl), *King Solomon's Mines* (b), *The Lion King* (f), *The Madness of King George* (f), *The Waltz King* (f), *Your Love Is King* (s)

kingdom   state governed by a monarch; animal kingdom; till/to kingdom come; United Kingdom; *Campbell's Kingdom* (f), *Kingdom of Heaven* (f)

kings   *see* king; divine right of kings, the sport of kings; King of Kings, Valley of the Kings; *The Divine Right of Kings* (po), *Kings Row* (f), *Three Kings* (f), *Valley of the Kings* (f), *We Three Kings* (s)

kinsmen   male relatives; *The Two Noble Kinsmen* (pl)

kiosk   booth; telephone kiosk

kipper   smoked herring; kipper tie

kiss   affectionate greeting; caress with the lips, touch gently; air kiss, French kiss; kiss curl, kiss me, kiss of death, kiss of life; kiss and tell, kiss-me-quick, kiss the rod; *It Started with a Kiss* (s), *Killer's Kiss* (f), *The Kiss* (f/pa/sc), *A Kiss before Dying* (f), *Kiss from a Rose* (s), *Kiss Kiss* (b), *Kiss Me Deadly* (b/f), *Kiss Me Kate* (mus/tv), *Kiss of Death* (f), *The Long Kiss Goodnight* (f), *Sealed with a Kiss* (s)

kissed   *see* kiss; sun-kissed; *Never Been Kissed* (f), *Then He Kissed Me* (s)

kisses   *see* kiss; *Save Your Kisses for Me* (s)

kissing   *see* kiss; kissing cousin, kissing

gate; *French Kissing in the USA* (s), *The Kissing Bandit* (f), *Kissing Jessica Stein* (f)

kit   outfit, set of equipment; drum kit, survival kit, tool kit; kit inspection, kit-bag; Kit Cat Club

kitchen   food-preparation room; soup kitchen; kitchen cabinet, kitchen garden, kitchen roll, kitchen sink, kitchen-sink drama; *Hell's Kitchen* (tv), *Kitchen Confidential* (b)

kite   airborne toy on a string, reddish-brown hawk; write (a cheque) before you have sufficient funds in the bank to cover it; box kite, fly a kite; kite-flying; high as a kite

kitten   young cat; kitten heels; (as) weak as a kitten

kittens   *see* kitten; have kittens

kiwi   flightless bird of New Zealand, green hairy fruit; kiwi fruit

knack   flair, skill; knick-knack; *The Knack* (f)

knee   leg joint; strike with the patella; bend the knee, housemaid's knee; knee-cap, knee-deep, knee-high, knee-jerk, knee-length, knee-pad; knee-high to a grasshopper, on bended knee; Wounded Knee; *Claire's Knee* (f)

knees   *see* knee; knock knees; knees-up; the bee's knees, weak at the knees

knell   solemn ring of a bell; death knell

knew   *see* know; *He Knew He Was Right* (b/tv), *If You Knew Susie* (s), *The Man Who Knew Too Much* (f), *What Maisie Knew* (b)

knickers   ladies' underpants; directoire knickers, French knickers; get your knickers in a twist

knife   bladed weapon, cutlery item;

stab; bowie knife, bread knife, carving knife, clasp knife, fish knife, flick knife, jack-knife, palette knife, paper-knife, pocket knife, sheath knife, Stanley knife; knife and fork, knife block, knife-grinder; on a knife edge, stick the knife in, under the knife; *Knife in the Water* (f), *Mack the Knife* (s)

knight   chess piece, medieval gentleman-soldier, nobleman addressed as 'Sir'; dub; white knight; knight errant; knight in shining armour, knight of the road, knight on a white charger; Knight of the Thistle; *First Knight* (f), *Knight Rider* (tv), *The Knight of the Burning Pestle* (pl), *A Knight's Tale* (f)

knights   *see* knight; Knights Templars

knit   weave; make with needles and wool, wrinkle (the brow); close-knit, tight-knit

knitting   *see* knit; woollen garment-making activity; knitting needles

knives   *see* knife; knives and forks; Night of the Long Knives

knobs   door handles, rounded lumps; with brass knobs on

knock   bang on a door, blow; criticise, strike (a door); postman's knock; knock about, knock back, knock-down, knock-kneed, knock off, knock-on, knock-on effect, knock up; knock for six, knock into a cocked hat, knock into shape, knock it off, knock on the head, knock on wood, knock spots off, knock the socks off, knock the stuffing out of; *Knock on Wood* (s), *Knock Three Times* (s)

knocker   critic, door rapper; door-knocker; on the knocker

knockout   tournament, emphatic

boxing victory, very attractive person; technical knockout; knockout drops, knockout punch; *It's a Knockout* (tv)

knocks *see* knock; school of hard knocks; *Opportunity Knocks* (tv)

knot cluster, entanglement, intertwining of rope or string, nautical mile per hour; entangle, tie securely; Gordian knot, granny knot, reef knot, running knot, slip knot, Windsor knot; knot garden; tie the knot

knots *see* knot; at a rate of knots, tie up in knots; *Knots Landing* (tv)

knotty complicated, gnarled; knotty problem

know be acquainted with, be aware (of); know-all, know-how; better the devil you know, for aught I know, in the know, know all the answers, know backwards, know by sight, know inside out, know no bounds, know the ropes, know the score, know what's what, know your onions, know your own mind, what do you know; *Better the Devil You Know* (s), *Getting to Know You* (s), *I Know Him So Well* (s), *I Know Why the Caged Bird Sings* (b), *You Oughta Know* (s), *Your Mother Should Know* (s)

knowing *see* know; astute; there is no knowing

knowledge information, learning, taxi driver's test, understanding; common knowledge, tree of knowledge; come to your knowledge, to the best of my knowledge; *Carnal Knowledge* (f)

known *see* know; familiar; well-known

knows *see* know; goodness knows

knuckle hand joint; bare-knuckle, white-knuckle; knuckle bone, knuckle down, knuckle sandwich; near the knuckle

knuckles *see* knuckle; rap on/over the knuckles

L

label fashion company's trademark, tag; attach a description to; care label

laboratory scientist's workroom; language laboratory; laboratory assistant

labour hard work, process of childbirth, workforce; work hard; political party; casual labour, hard labour, manual labour, slave labour, sweated labour, unskilled labour; labour camp, labour exchange, labour force, labour-intensive, labour-saving; division of labour, labour of love, labour the point; Labour Day, Labour Party, New Labour; *Labour of Love* (s), *Love's Labour's Lost* (pl)

labourer manual worker; casual labourer, day labourer

labours *see* labour; Labours of Hercules; *The Labours of Hercules* (b)

laburnum shrub with yellow flowers; *Laburnum Grove* (f/pl)

lace delicate fabric, shoe-tie; Shirley Conran novel; entwine, tie (shoes); Chantilly lace, Honiton lace, Mechlin lace; *Arsenic and Old Lace* (f), *Chantilly Lace* (s), *Lavender and Old Lace* (b)

laced *see* lace; flavoured (with alcohol); strait-laced

lack insufficiency; be without

lad boy; Jack the Lad, stable lad; *A Shropshire Lad* (po)

ladder run in tights, set of steps; snag (tights); Jacob's ladder, property ladder, rope ladder; *Jacob's Ladder* (f), *Property Ladder* (tv)

ladders *see* ladder; snakes and ladders

ladies *see* lady; ladies' fingers, ladies' man, ladies' night, ladies' room; lords and ladies; *Ladies in Lavender* (f), *Ladies' Night* (s), *Two Fat Ladies* (tv)

lading cargo; taking cargo aboard; bill of lading

ladle soup spoon; spoon out

lads *see* lad; *The Likely Lads* (tv)

lady   refined woman, titled woman; bag lady, dinner lady, first lady, leading lady, lollipop lady, my lady, painted lady, tea lady; lady chapel, lady of the bedchamber, lady-in-waiting, lady's maid; faint heart never won fair lady, find the lady; Lady Bountiful, Lady Day, Lady Mayoress, Lady Muck, Our Lady, White Lady; *Delta Lady* (s), *The Lady* (mag), *Lady and the Tramp* (f), *Lady Be Good* (f/s), *Lady Chatterley's Lover* (b), *The Lady Eve* (f), *Lady for a Day* (f), *The Lady from Shanghai* (f), *Lady Madonna* (s), *The Lady of Shalott* (po), *The Lady of the Lake* (po), *Lady Seated at a Virginal* (pa), *The Lady's Not for Burning* (pl), *The Lady Vanishes* (f), *Lady Windermere's Fan* (pl), *My Fair Lady* (mus), *Our Lady of the Flowers* (b), *Silver Lady* (s), *The Portrait of a Lady* (b/f), *Three Times a Lady* (s), *The Wicked Lady* (b/f)

lag   old convict; fall behind, insulate; jet lag, old lag, time lag

lager   light beer; lager lout

lagoon   inland sea; *The Blue Lagoon* (f)

laid   *see* lay; new-laid; laid-back

lair   animal's den; a fox smells its own lair first; *The Lair of the White Worm* (b/f)

Lake
Annecy, Baikal, Coniston, Constance, District, Erie, Garda, Geneva, Huron, Ladoga, Michigan, Ontario, Placid, Superior, Titicaca, Victoria, Windermere, Winnipeg

---

lake   body of water, reddish pigment; oxbow lake, salt lake; Lake Baikal, Lake District, Lake Erie, Lake Geneva, Lake Huron, Lake Ladoga, Lake Michigan, Lake Ontario, Lake Poets, Lake Superior, Lake Windermere, Salt Lake City; *Swan Lake* (bal), *The Lady of the Lake* (po)

lakes   *see* lake; Great Lakes

lama   Buddhist spiritual leader; Dalai Lama

lamb   baby sheep, red meat; leg of lamb; lamb chop, lamb's lettuce, lamb's-tails; in two shakes of a lamb's tail, mutton dressed as lamb; Lamb of God

lambs   *see* lamb; *The Silence of the Lambs* (f)

lame   unable to walk properly; fabric interwoven with metallic threads (lamé); lame duck, lame excuse

lamp   mobile light; Aladdin's lamp, arc lamp, bedside lamp, Davy lamp, fog lamp, gas lamp, hurricane lamp, infrared lamp, lava lamp, oil lamp, safety lamp, spirit lamp, standard lamp, street lamp, tilley lamp; lamp-post, lamp standard; *The Blue Lamp* (f)

lance   thrusting weapon; cut open; fer de lance; lance corporal; *Fer-de-Lance* (b)

lancer   cavalry soldier; *The Lives of a Bengal Lancer* (f)

land   country, German state, terrain; touch down; cloud cuckoo land, crash-land, dry land, never-never land, no-man's-land, promised land; land agent, land bridge, land force, land-girl, land-mass, land-mine, land of Nod, land on your feet, land-owning; in the land of the living, lie of the land, live off the fat of the land, see how the land lies, spy out the land; Land Rover, Land's End,

Van Diemens Land; *Land and Freedom* (f), *The Land Girls* (f), *Land of Hope and Glory* (s), *The Land that Time Forgot* (f), *Stranger in a Strange Land* (b), *The Waste Land* (po), *Wonderful Land* (s)

landed *see* land; *The Eagle Has Landed* (b/f)

landing *see* land; area at the top of stairs; crash-landing, forced landing; landing craft, landing gear, landing-net, landing stage, landing strip; *Knots Landing* (tv)

landscape country scenery, painting of the countryside; redesign (a garden); landscape architect, landscape gardener; *Blott on the Landscape* (b/tv)

lane small road; bus lane, crawler lane, lovers' lane, memory lane, sea lane; go/ walk down memory lane; Drury Lane, Park Lane, Rayners Lane, Turnpike Lane, White Hart Lane; *Brick Lane* (b), *Penny Lane* (s), *Spring in Park Lane* (f)

> **Lane**
> Bramall, Brick, Drury, Park, Penny, Pudding, Rayners, Turnpike, White Hart

language human speech, nation's tongue; body language, sign language; language laboratory; speak the same language; *Mind Your Language* (tv)

lantern portable light; Chinese lantern, jack-o'-lantern, Japanese lantern, magic lantern; lantern-fish, lantern jaw

lap lick up, overtake in a race, wash up; circuit of a track, thighs of a seated person; lap-dancing, lap of honour, lap of luxury, lap up; in the lap of luxury, in the lap of the gods

lapse period of time gone by, slight mistake; become void, slip by; time-lapse

larceny theft; grand larceny

lardy fat; lardy cake

large big; writ large; large intestine, large-scale; as large as life, at large, by and large, in large measure, in large part; *Doctor at Large* (b/f)

larger *see* large; larger than life

lark silly escapade, songbird; lark about; up with the lark; *Lark Rise to Candleford* (b), *The Navy Lark* (r)

laser intense beam of light; laser beam, laser printer

lash blow from a whip; tie down with rope, whip

lashing *see* lash; tongue-lashing

lassie Scottish girl; famous screen dog; *Lassie Come Home* (f)

last cobbler's mould; endure; final; at last, at long last; last-ditch, last-gasp, last minute, last name, last night, last orders, last post, last resort, last rites, last thing; at the last minute, breathe your last, famous last words, first and last, have the last laugh, he who laughs last laughs longest, the last straw, the last word, lender of last resort, on your last legs; Last Judgement, Last Supper; *At Long Last Love* (f), *Fermat's Last Theorem* (b), *I'm the Last of the Red-Hot Mammas* (s), *Krapp's Last Tape* (pl), *The Last Boy Scout* (f), *Last Christmas* (s), *The Last Day of Pompeii* (pa), *The Last Days of Pompeii* (b), *The Last Detail* (f), *The Last Emperor* (f), *Last Exit to Brooklyn* (b/f), *Last Judgement* (pa),

Last Night a DJ Saved My Life (s), *The Last of England* (f/pa), *The Last of the Mohicans* (b/f), *Last of the Summer Wine* (tv), *Last Orders* (b/f), *The Last Picture Show* (f), *The Last Precinct* (b), *The Last Samurai* (f), *The Last Seduction* (f), *The Last Supper* (pa), *Last Tango in Paris* (f), *The Last Temptation of Christ* (f), *The Last Time* (s), *Last Train to Clarksville* (s), *The Last Waltz* (s), *The Last Wave* (f), *Last Year at Marienbad* (f), *The Lay of the Last Minstrel* (po), *Save the Last Dance for Me* (s), *Suddenly Last Summer* (f/pl)

latch door-closing device; latch on to; on the latch

late recently deceased, tardy; behind schedule; better late than never, late in the day, of late; *It's Too Late* (s), *The Late Show* (f)

lately recently; johnny-come-lately; *Johnny Come Lately* (f)

later at some future time; Jools Holland tv programme; later on; sooner or later

latest most up to date; at the latest; *His Latest Flame* (s)

latitude east-west map line, leeway

latter concluding, second-mentioned; latter-day; Latter-Day Saints

lattice trellis; lattice window

laugh expression of amusement; show amusement; belly laugh, horse laugh; laugh off; have the last laugh, a laugh a minute, laugh like a drain, laugh out of court, laugh up your sleeve; *Laugh-in* (tv), *Only When I Laugh* (tv)

laughing *see* laugh; laughing gas, laughing jackass, laughing stock; no/ not a laughing matter; *Enter Laughing* (f), *The Laughing Cavalier* (pa)

laughs *see* laugh; he who laughs last laughs longest

laughter audible sign of amusement; laughter is the best medicine; *Laughter in Paradise* (f), *Present Laughter* (pl)

launch powerboat, take-off; officially begin, send forth

launching *see* launch; launching pad

laureate person honoured with an award; poet laureate

laurel aromatic shrub

laurels *see* laurel; look to your laurels, rest on your laurels

lava molten rock; lava lamp

lavender fragrant plant; lavender water; *Ladies in Lavender* (f), *Lavender and Old Lace* (b), *The Lavender Hill Mob* (f)

Law
Boyle's, Charles', Faraday's, Gresham's, Hubble's, Murphy's, Newton's, Ohm's, Parkinson's, Salic, Sod's

---

law jurisprudence, ruling, scientific principle; brother-in-law, canon law, case law, civil law, common law, criminal law, daughter-in-law, father-in-law, in-law, international law, martial law, mob law, mother-in-law, mother-in-law's tongue, natural law, Roman law, rule of law, sister-in-law, son-in-law, statute law; law-abiding, law-breaking, law centre, law court, law lord, law-making; be a law unto yourself, break the law, law and order, law of averages, the law of the jungle, lay down the law, the long arm of the law; Bachelor of Law, Boyle's Law, Charles' Law, Murphy's Law, Ohm's Law, Parkinson's Law,

Salic Law, Sod's Law; *LA Law* (tv), *Law & Order: Criminal Intent* (tv), *The Long Arm of the Law* (s)

lawn area of cultivated grass, fine cotton fabric; lawn tennis; *The Camomile Lawn* (b/tv)

lawyer person in the legal profession; barrack-room lawyer

lay minstrel's song; non-clerical, non-professional; produce eggs, set down, was recumbent; lay bare, lay brother, lay-by, lay down, lay odds, lay off, lay on, lay reader, lay up; lay a finger on, lay claim to, lay down the law, lay hands on, lay hold of, lay it on the line, lay on with a trowel, lay siege to, lay to rest, lay your cards on the table; *As I Lay Dying* (b), *The Lay of the Last Minstrel* (po)

layer egg-producing bird, stratum, tier; mine-layer, ozone layer, plate-layer; layer cake; *Layer Cake* (f)

laying *see* lay; mine-laying

lazy idle; lazy eye, lazy Susan

lead cord, heavy metal, title role; go in front, guide; lead astray, lead crystal, lead-free (petrol), lead in, lead on, lead pencil, lead piping, lead poisoning, lead the way, lead time; all roads lead to Rome, go down like a lead balloon, lead a merry dance, lead to the altar

leader boss, newspaper editorial, one in front; brand leader, follow-my-leader, loss-leader, squadron leader, youth leader; leader board; *Leader of the Pack* (s)

leading *see* lead; foremost; leading article, leading edge, leading lady, leading light, leading man, leading question, leading the way; *Liberty Leading the People* (pa)

leads *see* lead; jump leads

leaf page of a book, piece of foliage; flick through; bay leaf, fig-leaf, four-leaf clover, gold leaf, loose-leaf, maple leaf; leaf mould, leaf spot, leaf through; turn over a new leaf; *Maple Leaf Rag* (s)

league alliance, association of teams, nautical measure; big league, major league, rugby league; league championship, league tables; in league, not in the same league; Arab League, Hanseatic League, Ivy League, League of Nations; *Fantasy Football League* (tv), *The League of Gentlemen* (f/tv)

leagues *see* league; *Twenty Thousand Leagues under the Sea* (b/f)

leak disclosure of secret information, seepage; seep, divulge (secret information); leak out; spring a leak

lean be at an angle; meagre, without superfluous fat; lean on, lean-to

leaning *see* lean; Leaning Tower of Pisa

leap big jump; jump; quantum leap; leap-frog, leap year; leap in the dark, leap to the eye, look before you leap; *Quantum Leap* (tv)

leaps *see* leap; in leaps and bounds

learn acquire knowledge; learn the ropes, learn to walk before you run

learned *see* learn; scholarly

learner novice; learner driver

learning *see* learn; knowledge; accelerated learning, distance learning; learning curve

lease rental contract; rent; a new lease of life

least smallest amount; to the smallest degree; not least; at least, at the very least, not in the least, the line/path of least resistance, to say the least

leather   tanned hide; thrash; Morocco leather, patent leather; leather jacket; hell for leather

leave   time off; abandon, bequeath, depart; compassionate leave, French leave, maternity leave, shore leave, sick leave; leave alone, leave cold, leave go, leave hold of, leave out, leave standing, leave-taking; leave a lot to be desired, leave in the lurch, leave it at that, leave no stone unturned, leave out in the cold, leave well alone, leave your options open, take it or leave it, take your leave; *Fifty Ways to Leave Your Lover* (s), *If You Leave Me Now* (s), *Leave It to Charlie* (tv), *Love Me or Leave Me* (f), *Shore Leave* (s)

leaves   *see* leaf and leave; Chinese leaves, curry leaves, tea leaves; *Those Barren Leaves* (b)

leaving   *see* leave; *Leaving Las Vegas* (f)

lecture   educational talk; deliver an educational talk; lecture hall, lecture tour

led   *see* lead; easily led

ledge   shelf; window ledge

lee   sheltered side; US Civil War general, SW Irish river; lee tide; Rosie Lee

leer   lascivious look; ogle

leeway   room for manoeuvre, sideways drift; make up leeway

left   *see* leave; port side; remaining; left back, left field, left-hand drive, left-handed, left luggage, left off, left out, left wing, left-winger,; have two left feet, left for dead, left to your own devices, left to yourself, right left and centre; Left Bank; *My Left Foot* (f)

leg   lower limb, stage of an event; anchor leg, cabriole leg, dead leg, dog-leg, hind leg, inside leg, long leg, peg leg, square leg; leg break, leg bye, leg-irons, leg it, leg of lamb, leg-of-mutton sleeve, leg of pork, leg-pull, leg slip, leg spin, leg-spinner, leg-up, leg warmers,; break a leg, (cost) an arm and a leg, leg before wicket, shake a leg, talk the hind leg off a donkey

legal   lawful; street legal; legal aid, legal eagle, legal guardian, legal separation, legal tender; *Boston Legal* (tv), *Is It Legal?* (tv), *Legal Eagles* (f)

legally   *see* legal; *Legally Blonde* (f)

legend   traditional story; 1985 Tom Cruise film; *The Legend of Bagger Vance* (f), *The Legend of Sleepy Hollow* (f), *The Legend of the Holy Drinker* (f), *The Legend of Xanadu* (s)

legends   *see* legend; *Legends of the Fall* (s)

legion   body of Roman soldiers, great number; British Legion, (French) Foreign Legion

legislative   having the power to make laws; legislative assembly

legitimate   make lawful; born to married parents, conforming to the law

legs   *see* leg; 1985 ZZ Top hit; daddy-long-legs, sea legs; on your last legs, stretch your legs; *Daddy Long Legs* (mus)

leisure   recreation; gentleman of leisure; leisure centre; at leisure, at your leisure

lemon   citrus fruit, shade of yellow; bitter lemon; lemon balm, lemon barley, lemon curd, lemon drops, lemon grass, lemon juice, lemon sole, lemon squash, lemon-squeezer, lemon tea, lemon verbena; *The Lemon Drop Kid* (f)

lemonade fizzy drink; lemonade powder

lemur Madagascan primate; flying lemur, ring-tailed lemur

lend give temporarily; lend a hand, lend an ear

lending *see* lend; minimum lending rate, public lending right; lending library

length end-to-end distance; full-length portrait, knee-length; at length, keep at arm's length

lens optical glass, part of the eye behind the iris; contact lens, fisheye lens, single-lens reflex, telephoto lens, wide-angle lens, zoom lens

lent *see* lend; period before Easter; Lent lily

leopard large spotted cat; snow leopard; leopard seal, leopard-skin; a leopard can't change his spots; *The Leopard* (b/f)

less smaller in quantity; to a smaller extent; minus; more haste less speed, more or less, nothing less than; *A Life Less Ordinary* (f), *Less than Zero* (b/f)

lesser minor; Lesser Antilles; *Children of a Lesser God* (f)

lesson religious reading, tuition period; driving lesson, object lesson; *The Anatomy Lesson* (pa)

lessons *see* lesson; *Lessons in Love* (s)

let hindrance, in tennis; allow, allowed, rent out, rented out; let alone, let down, let fly, let go, let in, let in on, let off, let on, let out, let-out clause, let rip, let's go, let's say, let slip, let-up, let up on; let bygones be

bygones, let it all hang out, let it be, let me see, let off steam, let sleeping dogs lie, let the cat out of the bag, let us pray, let well alone, let your hair down, let yourself go, play a let, to let, without let or hindrance; *Don't Let the Sun Go Down on Me* (s), *Let It Be* (s), *Let It Snow* (s), *Let There Be Love* (s), *Let's Face the Music and Dance* (s), *Let's Go to San Francisco* (s), *Let's Hang On* (s), *Let's Stick Together* (s), *Let's Twist Again* (s), *Let Your Love Flow* (s), *Let Yourself Go* (s), *Live and Let Die* (f/s)

lethal deadly; *Lethal Weapon* (f)

letter alphabet character, missive; begging letter, capital letter, chain letter, covering letter, dead letter, dead letter box, dear John letter, four-letter word, love letter, open letter, poison-pen letter, red-letter day; letter of credit, letter-box, letter-opener; to the letter; *Letter from America* (r/s), *Letter from an Unknown Woman* (f), *Letter to Brezhnev* (f), *The Scarlet Letter* (b/f)

letters *see* letter; literature; block letters, man of letters, woman of letters; letters patent; *Love Letters* (f/s), *Love Letters in the Sand* (s)

lettuce salad plant; iceberg lettuce, lamb's lettuce

level equal, flat; equalise, flatten, raze to the ground; rank; entry-level, eye level, eye-level grill, high-level, low-level, sea level, spirit level, split-level, street level, subsistence level, water level; level crossing, level-headed, level of attainment, level off, level-pegging, level playing field; do your level best, on the level; A Level, AS Level, O Level, Advanced Level, Ordinary Level

lever   prising-bar; prise; gear lever

liability   debt, person who causes embarrassment, state of having responsibility

liable   apt (to), legally responsible

liaisons   illicit affairs; *Dangerous Liaisons* (f)

libel   defamation; defame; 1959 Dirk Bogarde film

liberal   broad-minded, generous; former political party, member of this party; liberal arts, liberal studies; Liberal Democrats, Liberal Party

liberated   released; unbound from social convention

liberation   emancipation; animal liberation, women's liberation; liberation theology

liberties   *see* liberty; civil liberties, take liberties

liberty   freedom, presumptuous behaviour, right; statue in New York harbour; liberty bodice, liberty cap; at liberty; Statue of Liberty; *Liberty Leading the People* (pa), *The Man Who Shot Liberty Valance* (f), *The Phantom of Liberty* (f)

library   book-lending institution, large store of books; circulating library, copyright library, lending library, mobile library, reference library; *The Body in the Library* (b)

licence   freedom, official permission, official permit; driving licence, off-licence, pilot's licence, poetic licence, special licence; *Licence to Kill* (f)

licensed   authorised to sell alcohol, officially authorised; licensed victualler

lichen   moss-like plant; *Trouble with Lichen* (b)

lick   action of passing the tongue over, small amount (of paint); defeat, pass the tongue over; at a lick, lick and a promise, lick into shape

lid   container cover; skid-lid; flip your lid

lie   untruth; be situated, recline, tell an untruth; white lie; lie detector, lie doggo, lie down, lie in, lie low, lie of the land; give the lie to, let sleeping dogs lie, lie in wait, lie through your teeth; *The Great Lie* (f)

lies   *see* lie; love-lies-bleeding; see how the land lies; *My Bonny Lies Over the Ocean* (s), *My Camera Never Lies* (s), *Secrets and Lies* (f), *Sex, Lies and Videotape* (f), *True Lies* (f)

lieutenant   military rank; first lieutenant, flight lieutenant, sub lieutenant; lieutenant colonel, lieutenant commander, lieutenant-governor; Lord Lieutenant; *The French Lieutenant's Woman* (b/f)

life   existence, period from birth to death; elixir of life, family life, high life, kiss of life, long-life, love life, low life, private life, shelf life, state of life, still life, tree of life, true to life, walk of life, water of life; life assurance, life cycle, life expectancy, life force, life form, life imprisonment, life insurance, life-jacket, life member, life membership, life peer, life peerage, life raft, life savings, life sciences, life scientist, life sentence, life-sized, life-threatening; as large as life, the best things in life are free, breathe new life into, come to life, depart this life, a dog's life, the facts of life, for dear life, for the life of me, it's a fact of life, larger than life, life and death, life and limb, the life and soul of the party, life begins at forty, life is just a bowl of cherries, matter of life and death, a new lease of life, not on your life, the staff of life, take your life in your hands, that's life, that's the story of my life, university of life, variety is the spice of life, while there's life there's hope, your money or your life; Life Guards; *Back to Life* (s), *The Best Things in Life Are Free* (s), *A Bug's Life* (f), *Family Life* (f), *For Once in My Life* (s), *The Good Life* (tv), *The Happiest Days of Your Life* (f), *The High Life* (tv), *How to Save Your Own Life* (f), *It's a Wonderful Life* (f), *Last Night a DJ Saved My Life* (s), *The Life and Death of Colonel Blimp* (f), *The Life and Loves of a She-Devil* (b/tv), *Life Begins* (tv), *Life Begins at Forty* (tv), *Life Is Beautiful* (f), *Life Is Just a Bowl of Cherries* (s), *A Life Less Ordinary* (f), *A Life of Grime* (tv), *Life on Earth* (tv), *Life on Mars* (s/tv), *Life Stinks* (f), *Life, the Universe and Everything* (b), *Lust for Life* (f/s), *A Matter of Life and Death* (f), *Monty Python's Life of Brian* (f), *My Life* (b), *Private Life* (s), *The Private Life of Henry VIII* (f), *Proof of Life* (f), *The Secret Life of Walter Mitty* (f), *She's Out of My Life* (s), *The Simple Life* (tv), *The Story of My Life* (s), *That's Life* (tv), *This Is Your Life* (tv), *This Life* (tv), *This Sporting Life* (b/f), *Walk of Life* (s), *Wonderful Life* (f), *You Are the Sunshine of My Life* (s)

lift elevator, fillip, free ride; raise up; face-lift, fireman's lift, fork-lift, fork-lift truck, ski-lift, thumb a lift; lift a finger, lift attendant, lift-off

light illumination, source of illumination; ignite, illuminate; easy, insubstantial, of little weight, pale-coloured; courtesy light, first light, green light, half-light, klieg light, leading light, neon light, night light, pilot light, rear light, red light, red-light district, reversing light, strip light, tail light, Very light, white light; light ale, light as a feather, light bulb, light heavyweight, light industry, light-fingered, light-footed, light-headed, light-hearted, light infantry, light marching order, light meter, light music, light opera, light pollution, light railway, light up, light verse, light year; bring to light, the cold light of day, come to light, hide your light under a bushel, make light of, make light work of, many hands make light work, sweetness and light, travel light, trip the light fantastic; Light Brigade, Stadium of Light; *Blinded by the Light* (s), *The Charge of the Light Brigade* (po), *Light My Fire* (s), *Light of Day* (f), *Light Sleeper* (f), *Ray of Light* (s), *Travellin' Light* (s)

lighthouse coastal warning tower; *to the Lighthouse* (b)

lighting *see* light; illumination; fluorescent lighting, neon lighting, street lighting, strip-lighting; lighting-up time

lightning electrical discharge in the sky; forked lightning, sheet lightning, streak of lightning; lightning conductor, lightning strike; like greased lightning

lights *see* light; sheep's lungs; fairy lights, house lights, navigation lights, street lights, traffic lights; lights out; Festival of Lights, Northern Lights, Southern Lights; *Bright Lights* (f),

Bright Lights, Big City (b/f), *City Lights* (f), *Harbour Lights* (tv)

like   be fond of; similar to; as; Christ-like, ghost-like, sylph-like, trance-like, vice-like; like-minded; and the like, bleed like a stuck pig, drink like a fish, drop like flies, eat like a bird/horse, fit like a glove, get on/along like a house on fire, go down like a lead balloon, go down like ninepins, go like a bomb, hell hath no fury like a woman scorned, just like mother makes, just like that, laugh like a drain, like a bear with a sore head, like a bull at a gate, like a cat on a hot tin roof, like a cat on hot bricks, like a demon, like a dose of salts, like a dream, like a duck to water, like a fish out of water, like a headless chicken, like a house on fire, like a red rag to a bull, like a scalded cat, like a shot, like a ton of bricks, like anything, like as not, like billy-o, like blazes, like clockwork, like death warmed up, like father like son, like fury, like getting blood out of a stone, like greased lightning, like mad, like nobody's business, like nothing on earth, like so, like stink, like the clappers, like the devil, like there was no tomorrow, like watching paint dry, nothing succeeds like success, packed like sardines, sell like hot cakes, sleep like a log/top, smoke like a chimney, spread like wildfire, stick out like a sore thumb, swear like a trooper, tell it like it is, there's no fool like an old fool, there's no place like home, there's no time like the present, work like a Trojan, work like magic; *As You Like It* (f/pl), *Bend It Like Beckham* (f), *I'd*

Like to Teach the World to Sing (s), *I Dont Like Mondays* (s), *I Like It* (s), *Just Like a Pill* (s), *Just Like a Woman* (s), *Like a Prayer* (s), *Like a Rolling Stone* (s), *Like a Virgin* (s), *A Pretty Girl Is Like a Melody* (s), *Some Like It Hot* (f), *Take a Girl Like You* (b/tv), *There Is Nothin' Like a Dame* (s), *A Town Like Alice* (b/f), *Walk Like an Egyptian* (s)

likely   probable; as likely as not, a likely story, not likely; *The Likely Lads* (tv)

likes   *see* like; the likes of; *Somebody Up There Likes Me* (f)

lilac   fragrant shrub; shade of purple

lilies   *see* lily; *Lilies of the Field* (f), *Water Lilies* (pa)

lily   tall flower; arum lily, Lent lily, pond lily, tiger lily, water lily; lily of the valley, lily pad, lily-livered, lily-white; gild the lily; *Lily of Laguna* (s), *Lily the Pink* (s), *Pictures of Lily* (s)

limb   arm or leg, branch of a tree; life and limb, out on a limb, tear limb from limb

limber   supple; limber up

limbo   borderland of hell, state of neglect; in limbo

lime   citrus fruit, shade of green, white alkaline compound; slaked lime, vodka and lime, white lime; lime green, lime juice, lime tree; Lime Grove, Lime Street

limelight   focus of attention; Charlie Chaplin film; in the limelight

limit   boundary; confine within bounds; speed limit, time limit; over the limit, the sky is the limit; *Take It to the Limit* (s)

limited   *see* limit; restricted; public limited company; limited company, limited liability, limited partnership

limits   *see* limit; off-limits; within limits; *The Outer Limits* (tv)

limp   hobble; floppy

limpet   clinging mollusc; limpet mine

line   boundary, queue, railway branch, row, stripe, transport company; mark with creases, put a backing material on; air line, A-line, assembly line, bar line, bottom line, branch line, chorus line, clothes-line, contour line, dotted line, double white line, empire-line, firing line, fishing line, flight line, front line, front-line troops, goal line, hard line, in-line, in-line skates, in-line skating, main line, off-line, party line, picket line, plumb line, poverty line, production line, railway line, service line, tag line, three-line whip, top-line, washing-line; line dance, line dancing, line drawing, line management, line manager, line of communications, line of country, line of fire, line-out, line up; all the way down the line, draw the line, end of the line, hook, line and sinker, in a straight line, in line, lay it on the line, the line of least resistance, ship of the line, step out of line, toe the line; Bakerloo Line, Central Line, Circle Line, District Line, (International) Date Line, Jubilee Line, Maginot Line, Mason-Dixon Line, Northern Line, Piccadilly Line, Plimsoll Line, Victoria Line; *A Chorus Line* (mus), *In the Line of Fire* (f), *The Onedin Line* (tv), *Telephone Line* (s), *The Thin Blue Line* (tv), *The Thin Red Line* (f), *Walk the Line* (f), *What's My Line* (tv)

lineman   US railway worker; *Wichita Lineman* (s)

> **Line**
> Bakerloo, Central, District, International Date, Jubilee, Maginot, Mannerheim, Mason-Dixon, Northern, Piccadilly, Plimsoll, Siegfried, Victoria, White Star

linen   bedding and tablecloths, cloth made from flax; Irish linen, table linen; linen basket

liner   large ship; bin-liner, one-liner

lines   *see* line; actor's words, school punishment; hard lines; read between the lines; *Between the Lines* (tv)

ling   heather, sea-fish; ding-a-ling

lingering   staying awhile; persistent

lining   *see* line; garment's inner layer; brake lining, silver lining; every cloud has a silver lining

link   connection, loop of a chain; connect; missing link; link up; *The Weakest Link* (tv)

linked   *see* link; index-linked

links   *see* link; golf course; golf links

linseed   product of the flax plant; linseed cake, linseed oil

lion   big cat; mountain lion, sea lion; lion cub, lion-hearted, lion-tamer; the lion's den, the lion's share; *Albert and the Lion* (po), *Androcles and the Lion* (f/pl), *The Lion in Winter* (f), *The Lion King* (mus), *The Lion Sleeps Tonight* (s), *The Lion, the Witch and the Wardrobe* (b/f), *The Wind and the Lion* (f)

lions   *see* lion; British Lions

lip   impudent talk, outer part of the mouth, rim; stiff upper lip; lip-gloss, lip-read, lip-salve, lip service, lip-sync; button your lip, curl your lip, pay lip service to

lips *see* lip; my lips are sealed, pass your lips, read my lips; *Lucky Lips* (s), *My Lips Are Sealed* (s)

lipstick make-up item; *Lipstick on Your Collar* (s/tv)

liquid runny substance; easily convertible into cash, runny; washing-up liquid; liquid crystal (display), liquid paraffin

liquor alcohol; malt liquor

lisp speech impediment; be unable to pronounce the letter 's'

list itemised column; itemise, tilt; hit list, honours list, mailing list, price list, reserved list, shopping list, waiting list, wine list; list price; on the danger list; Civil List; *Schindler's List* (f), *The List of Adrian Messenger* (f)

listen prepare to hear; listen in; listen to reason; *Listen without Prejudice* (al)

listening *see* listen; easy-listening; listening post

lists *see* list; enter the lists

literal misprint; word-for-word

literary concerning books; literary critic, literary criticism, literary lunch

literate able to read and write; computer-literate, semi-literate

litmus dye that indicates pH; litmus paper, litmus test

litter animal bedding, group of newly born animals, street rubbish; scatter untidily; litter bin, litter lout

little small; little auk, little finger, little grebe, little green men, little ones, little people, little toe; great oaks from little acorns grow, I spy with my little eye, little by little, little or nothing, little wonder, mother's little helper, not a little, precious little, the little woman; Little Englander, Little Rock, Little Sisters of the Poor; *Big Trouble in Little China* (f), *Chicken Little* (f), *God's Little Acre* (b), *I Say a Little Prayer* (s), *Little Angels* (tv), *Little Big Man* (f), *Little Boy Blue* (nr), *Little Britain* (tv), *Little Buddha* (f), *Little by Little* (s), *Little Caesar* (f), *Little Dorrit* (b), *The Little Drummer Girl* (b/f), *The Little Foxes* (b/f), *Little Grey Rabbit* (b), *Little House on the Prairie* (b), *Little Jack Horner* (nr), *Little Lord Fauntleroy* (b), *The Little Match Girl* (b), *Little Men* (b), *Little Miss Muffet* (nr), *Little Orphan Annie* (com), *The Little Prince* (b), *Little Red Riding Hood* (b), *Little Red Rooster* (s), *Little Shop of Horrors* (mus), *Little Tommy Tucker* (nr), *Little Voice* (b), *Little White Bull* (s), *Little Women* (b), *Mother's Little Helper* (s), *My Little Chickadee* (f), *Stuart Little* (f), *Sweet Little Sixteen* (s), *Two Little Boys* (s), *Wake Up Little Susie* (s), *With a Little Help from My Friends* (s)

live exist, reside; happening right now; live action, live concert, live-in, live performance, live wire; go live, long live, live and breathe, live by your wits, live high on the hog, live in sin, live in the past, live it up, live off the fat of the land, live on borrowed time, live rough; Live Aid; *Alice Doesn't Live Here Any More* (f), *The Folks That Live on the Hill* (b/s), *Going Live* (tv), *I Want to Live* (f), *Live And Let Die* (f/s), *The Way We Live Now* (b), *They Live* (f), *You Only Live Twice* (f)

lived *see* live; short-lived; lived-in

lively frisky; look lively

liver internal organ; cod-liver oil; liver salts, liver sausage, liver spot; *The Liver Birds* (tv)

livery   care and feeding of horses, company's colours, distinctive uniform; livery company, livery stable

lives   *see* live and life; *The Best Years of Our Lives* (f), *Distant Voices, Still Lives* (f), *Lives of a Bengal Lancer* (f), *Private Lives* (pl)

living   *see* live; occupation; cost of living, free-living, standard of living, the living image; living room, living wage; in the land of the living, living on borrowed time, within living memory; *Design for Living* (pl), *The Living Daylights* (f), *Living Doll* (s), *Living in America* (s), *Living Next Door to Alice* (s), *Night of the Living Dead* (f), *The Return of the Living Dead* (f)

lizard   scaly reptile; Cornish headland; flying lizard, frilled lizard, lounge lizard; Lizard Point

load   cargo, large amount; charge (a gun), insert (cassette or camera film), put cargo into; abnormal load; load factor; load the dice

loaded   *see* load; charged with meaning, wealthy; spring-loaded; loaded question; *Loaded Weapon 1* (f)

loading   *see* load; loading bay

loaf   block of bread; spend time idly; cob-loaf, cottage loaf, French loaf, meat loaf, nut loaf; half a loaf is better than no bread/ none, use your loaf; Sugar Loaf Mountain

loan   money borrowed, permission to use; bank loan, bridging loan, home loan, war loan; loan shark; on loan

loathing   hating; *Fear and Loathing in Las Vegas* (b/f)

loaves   *see* loaf; loaves and fishes

lob   high hit in tennis, underarm delivery in cricket; hit high, throw

lobby   campaigning group, entrance hall; campaign (for); lobby correspondent

lobe   division of a leaf, part of the ear; ear lobe, frontal lobe, temporal lobe

lobo   US wolf; *Rio Lobo* (f)

lobster   large crustacean; lobster pot, lobster thermidor; *Rock Lobster* (s)

local   native resident, neighbourhood pub, type of anaesthetic; in the vicinity; local anaesthetic, local area network, local authority, local call, local colour, local derby, local government, local time; *Local Hero* (f)

location   film setting, specific site; *Location Location Location* (tv)

loch   Scottish lake; Loch Lomond, Loch Ness (monster)

> **Loch**
> Fyne, Katrine, Leven, Lomond, Ness, Rannock, Tay, Tummel

lock   curl of hair, fastening device, section of a canal, wrestling hold; close securely; combination lock, mortise lock, oar-lock, time lock, Yale lock; lock forward, lock in, lock-keeper, lock out, lock up; lock horns, lock, stock and barrel, pick a lock, under lock and key; *Lock, Stock and Two Smoking Barrels* (f), *Lock Up* (f), *The Rape of the Lock* (po)

locker   cupboard; locker room; Davy Jones's Locker

locking   *see* lock; central locking

loco   abbreviation for train engine; crazy; in loco parentis; *Loco in Acapulco* (s)

locomotion   power of movement; *The Locomotion* (s)

locust   pod-bearing tree, voracious

The *Puzzler* Crossword Solver's Dictionary

insect; *The Day of the Locust* (f)

locusts *see* locust; plague of locusts

lodge beaver's home, chalet, Freemason branch, gatehouse; become stuck, deposit, put forward, stay in digs

lodger paying guest; *The Lodger* (f)

lodging *see* lodge; lodging house

loft angle on a golf club, roof space

log chunk of wood, ship's record; enter into a record book; ship's log, Yule log; log cabin, log fire, log on, log-rolling; as easy as falling off a log, sleep like a log

logic art of reasoning, sound reasoning; chop logic

logical rational; *The Logical Song* (s)

loins joints of meat, pelvic region

loiter hang about; loiter with intent

lollipop sweet on a stick; lollipop lady, lollipop man; *My Boy Lollipop* (s), *On the Good Ship Lollipop* (s)

lolly icy sweet on a stick; ice lolly

lone sole; lone wolf; play a lone hand; Lone Star; *The Lone Ranger* (tv)

loneliness solitude; *The Loneliness of the Long Distance Runner* (b/f)

lonely friendless, remote; lonely hearts; *Death Is a Lonely Business* (b), *The Heart Is a Lonely Hunter* (b/f), *The Lonely Goatherd* (s), *Only the Lonely* (s), *Sgt Pepper's Lonely Hearts Club Band* (al/s)

lonesome feeling friendless; *Are You Lonesome Tonight?* (s)

long protracted, tall; yearn; daddy-long-legs, day-long; long ago, long-distance, long-case clock, long division, long-drawn-out, long-faced, long-haired, long-haul, long hop, long johns, long jump, long leg,

long-life, long off, long-player, long-range, long shot, long sight, long-sighted, long-standing, long-suffering, long suit, long-tailed tit, long-term, long-time, long trousers, long-wave, long-winded; as long as, at long last, before long, by a long chalk, in the long run, the long and the short of it, the long arm of the law, long in the tooth, long live, long time no see, night of the long knives, not by a long shot, over the long haul, so long, so long as, to cut a long story short; Long Island; *At Long Last Love* (f), *Daddy Long Legs* (mus), *The Loneliness of the Long Distance Runner* (b/f), *The Long and the Short and the Tall* (f), *The Long Arm of the Law* (s), *Long Day's Journey into Night* (f/pl), *The Long Firm* (b/tv), *The Long Goodbye* (b), *The Long Good Friday* (f), *Long-Haired Lover from Liverpool* (s), *The Long Hot Summer* (f), *The Long Kiss Goodnight* (f), *Long Tall Sally* (s), *Long Walk to Freedom* (b), *Love and Death on Long Island* (f), *So Long, Farewell* (s), *Such a Long Journey* (b),

longest *see* long; he who laughs last laughs longest; *The Longest Day* (b/f/s)

look gaze, seem; appearance, expression; dirty look, wet look; look after, look alike, look at, look daggers, look in, look into, look kindly on, look out, look over, look-see, look sharp, look up; a cat may look at a king, (don't) look a gift horse in the mouth, look a fright, look a picture, look before you leap, look down your nose at, look for trouble, look lively, look on the black side, look on the bright side, look

198

someone in the face, look straight in the eye, look the part, look to your laurels; New Look; *Always Look on the Bright Side of Life* (s), *Don't Look Now* (b/f), *Look at Me* (s), *Look Back in Anger* (f/pl), *Look Who's Talking* (f), *The Stars Look Down* (f)

looking   *see* look; forward-looking, good-looking, inward-looking;, looking-glass; *Through the Looking-Glass* (b)

lookout   sentinel; keep a lookout for, on the lookout

looks   *see* look; black looks

loom   weaving frame; approach menacingly; jacquard loom

loop   coil of a knot; tie in a circular fashion; induction loop; in the loop, loop the loop, out of the loop

loose   baggy, promiscuous, unfettered; unleash; cut loose, hang loose; loose box, loose cannon, loose change, loose covers, loose ends, loose-head prop, loose-leaf; all hell breaks loose, at a loose end, have a screw loose, on the loose, play fast and loose; *Every Which Way but Loose* (f), *Fast and Loose* (f/tv), *Loose Ends* (r), *Loose Women* (tv)

loosen   slacken; loosen up, loosen your tongue

loot   money, thief's spoils; pillage; Joe Orton play, 1970 Richard Attenborough film, free-ads paper

lop   cut off; lop-eared

lord   God, peer; law lord, liege lord, my lord, the lord's day; lord chamberlain, lord mayor; (as) drunk as a lord; Lord Advocate, Lord Chancellor, Lord Chief Justice, Lord High Chancellor, Lord High Constable, Lord Justice, Lord Justice-General, Lord Lieutenant, Lord Mayor's Show, Lord Muck, Lord of Appeal, Lord Privy Seal, Lord Provost, Lord's Taverners, Sea Lord, The Lord's Prayer; *Little Lord Fauntleroy* (b), *Lord Jim* (b/f), *Lord of the Flies* (b/f), *My Sweet Lord* (s), *The Lord of the Rings* (b/f)

lords   *see* lord; Upper House of the British Parliament; London cricket ground (Lord's); lords and ladies; House of Lords

lorry   HGV; lorry driver; off the back of a lorry

lose   be defeated, be deprived of, mislay; lose count, lose face, lose ground, lose heart, lose one's deposit, lose out, lose patience, lose time, lose weight; lose the plot, lose the way, lose your footing, lose your hair, lose your marbles, lose your rag, lose your shirt, lose your temper, lose your tongue; *How to Lose a Guy in Ten Days* (f)

loser   defeated player, no-hoper; good loser; on to a loser; *The Biggest Loser* (tv), *Every Loser Wins* (s), *I'm a Loser* (s), *Loser Takes All* (b/f)

losing   *see* lose; defeated; losing battle; *Losing My Mind* (s), *Losing My Religion* (s)

loss   defeat, deficit, demise, misplacement; dead loss, profit and loss account; loss adjuster, loss-leader; at a loss

lost   *see* lose; astray, beyond hope, engrossed, missing; tv series about plane-crash survivors; be lost on, get lost; lost cause, lost generation, lost property, lost soul, lost-property office; he who hesitates is lost, lost for words; Lost Gardens of Heligan; *I*

Lost My Heart to a Starship Trooper (s), *The Lost Boys* (f), *Lost Highway* (f), *Lost Horizon* (f), *Lost in Space* (f/tv), *Lost in Translation* (f), *The Lost Prince* (b/tv), *The Lost Weekend* (f), *The Lost World* (b/f), *Love's Labour's Lost* (f/pl), *Paradise Lost* (po), *Raiders of the Lost Ark* (f)

lot   auction item, destiny; great deal; Old Testament character; French river; job lot, parking lot; leave a lot to be desired, quite a lot, throw in your lot; *Beryl's Lot* (tv), *Salem's Lot* (b)

lotion   liquid preparation; calamine lotion, suntan lotion

lots   *see* lot; many; cast lots, draw lots

lottery   game of chance; lottery ticket

lotus   exotic flower, yoga position; sports-car make; lotus-eater, lotus position

loud   at a high volume, garish; out loud; loud-mouthed; for crying out loud

louder   *see* loud; actions speak louder than words

lounge   room with comfy seats; recline; departure lounge, transit lounge; lounge bar, lounge lizard, lounge suit; *Trees Lounge* (f)

lout   yob; lager lout, litter lout

love   great affection, zero in tennis; feel great affection for; calf love, courtly love, cupboard love, free love, labour of love, puppy love, self-love, true love; love affair, love apple, love child, love handles, love-in, love-in-a-mist, love interest, love letter, love-lies-bleeding, love life, love match, love nest, love seat; all's fair in love and war, for the love of God, not for love or money; *All You Need Is Love* (s), *Aspects of Love* (mus), *At Long Last Love* (f), *Baby Love* (s), *Because I Love You* (s), *Bye Bye Love* (s), *Can't Buy Me Love* (f/s), *Caravan of Love* (s), *Chuck E's in Love* (s), *Doctor in Love* (f), *Endless Love* (f), *Enduring Love* (b/f), *Ever Fallen in Love* (s), *From Russia with Love* (f), *Greatest Love of All* (s), *I Just Called to Say I Love You* (s), *I Love Lucy* (tv), *I Love to Boogie* (s), *I Love You Because* (s), *I'm Not in Love* (s), *In the Mood for Love* (s), *It Must Be Love* (s), *I've Got My Love to Keep Me Warm* (s), *I Was Made to Love Her* (s), *Justify My Love* (s), *Labour of Love* (s), *Lessons in Love* (s), *Let There Be Love* (s), *Let Your Love Flow* (s), *Love Actually* (f), *Love and Death on Long Island* (f), *Love Affair* (f), *Love at First Bite* (f), *The Love Bug* (f), *Love Child* (s), *Love for Lydia* (b/tv), *Love Hurts* (tv), *Love in a Cold Climate* (b), *Love Is All Around* (s), *Love Is the Drug* (s), *Love Letters* (f), *Love Letters in the Sand* (s), *The Love Machine* (b), *Love Me Do* (s), *Love Me or Leave Me* (f), *Love Me Tender* (s), *Love on the Dole* (b/f), *Love on the Rocks* (s), *Love Shack* (s), *The Love Song of J Alfred Prufrock* (po), *Love Soup* (tv), *Love Story* (b/f), *Love's Labour's Lost* (f/pl), *Love Thy Neighbour* (tv), *Modern Love* (s), *Never Love a Stranger* (b), *People Will Say We're in Love* (s), *Portrait of My Love* (s), *The Power of Love* (f), *Pride (in the Name of Love)* (s), *Punch Drunk Love* (s), *Puppy Love* (s), *Radar Love* (s), *The Sacred and Profane Love Machine* (b), *Sea of Love* (f), *Secret Love* (f), *Shakespeare in Love* (f), *Silly Love Songs* (s), *Step Inside Love* (s),

Stop! in the Name of Love (s), *Sugar Baby Love* (s), *A Teenager in Love* (s), *Tell Laura I Love Her* (s), *A Thing Called Love* (s), *To Sir with Love* (f), *True Love* (s), *True Love Ways* (s), *Tunnel of Love* (s), *When I Fall in Love* (s), *Why Do Fools Fall in Love?* (s), *Women in Love* (b/f), *You Can't Hurry Love* (s), *Your Love Is King* (s)

loved   *see* love; *Could You Be Loved?* (s), *The Loved One* (b), *The Spy Who Loved Me* (f)

lovely   adorable, very pleasant; *Farewell My Lovely* (b/f), *Isn't She Lovely?* (s), *Isn't This a Lovely Day* (s), *I've Got a Lovely Bunch of Coconuts* (s), *Lovely Day* (s), *Oh! What a Lovely War* (mus)

lover   devotee, paramour; *The Cook, the Thief, His Wife and Her Lover* (f), *Dream Lover* (s), *Easy Lover* (s), *Fifty Ways to Leave Your Lover* (s), *Lady Chatterley's Lover* (b/tv), *Long-Haired Lover from Liverpool* (s)

lovers   *see* lover; lovers' lane; *Hello Young Lovers* (s), *The Music Lovers* (f), *A Song for the Lovers* (s), *Sons and Lovers* (b/f)

loves   *see* love; misery loves company; *Everybody Loves Raymond* (tv), *How the Other Half Loves* (pl), *The Life and Loves of a She-Devil* (b/tv), *She Loves You* (s)

lovesick   pining romantically; *Lovesick Blues* (s)

lovey   affectionate form of address; lovey-dovey

loving   *see* love; affectionate; loving cup; *All My Loving* (s), *A Kind of Loving* (b/f)

low   cow's moo; moo; base, deep in pitch, depressed, humble, near the ground; lie low, run low; low comedy, low-down, low frequency, low-impact, low-key, low-level, low life, low-loader, low-lying, low-paid, low-rise, low season, low spirits, low-tech, low tide, low water, low-water mark; at a low ebb, keep a low profile; Low Church, Low Countries, Low Sunday; *Swing Low Sweet Chariot* (s)

lower   *see* low; move further down, reduce; lower case, lower chamber, lower deck, lower house; *The Lower Depths* (pl)

lowest   *see* low; lowest common denominator, lowest common multiple

loyal   faithful; loyal toast

loyalty   faithfulness; loyalty card

luck   good fortune; bad luck, beginner's luck, hard luck, hard-luck story, pot luck, stroke of luck; down on your luck, luck of the draw, no such luck, push your luck; *Good Night and Good Luck* (f), *Some Guys Have All the Luck* (s), *Stay Lucky* (tv), *Wish Me Luck* (tv)

lucky   fortuitous, fortunate; Jackie Collins novel; happy-go-lucky, third time lucky; lucky bag, lucky charm, lucky dip; I should be so lucky, thank your lucky stars; Lucky Country; *I Should Be So Lucky* (s), *Lucky Jim* (b/f), *Lucky Lips* (s), *O Lucky Man!* (f), *Strike It Lucky* (tv), *Thank Your Lucky Stars* (mus/tv)

lug   earhole; haul

luggage   bags and cases; left luggage; luggage rack

lull   period of calm; make calm

lumber   accumulated junk; lumber room

lump   protuberance; sugar lump, the lump; lump in the throat, lump sum

lunar   concerning the Moon; lunar eclipse, lunar month, lunar year

lunatic   crazy eccentric; lunatic fringe

lunch   midday meal; literary lunch, packed lunch, ploughman's lunch, working lunch; lunch-box, lunch hour; do lunch, out to lunch; *The Naked Lunch* (b/f), *The Ploughman's Lunch* (f), *Working Lunch* (tv)

luncheon   formal midday meal; luncheon meat, luncheon voucher; *Luncheon of the Boating Party* (pa)

lunge   forward thrust; thrust forward

lurch   stagger, suddenly pitch forward; leave in the lurch

lure   decoy, temptation; entice

lust   eagerness to possess; *Lust for Life* (f/s)

luxury   indulgence, opulence; non-essential; in the lap of luxury

lying   *see* lie; low-lying; lying-in-state; take lying down

lynch   execute without a lawful trial; lynch mob

lyrical   song-like; wax lyrical

M

mac   raincoat; plastic mac, whisky mac

macabre   gruesome; danse macabre; *Danse Macabre* (cl)

macaroni   tubular pasta, 18th-century dandy; macaroni cheese

mace   ceremonial staff, heavy club, offensive spray; mace-bearer

machine   automated device, system; adding machine, answering machine, automated teller machine, bathing machine, franking machine, fruit-machine, karaoke machine, pinball machine, rowing machine, sewing machine, slot machine, sub-machine gun, time machine, vending machine, washing machine, weighing machine; machine gun, machine tool, machine translation; the ghost in the machine; *The Love Machine* (b), *Mean Machine* (f), *The Sacred and Profane Love Machine* (b), *Silver Dream Machine* (s), *Silver Machine* (s), *The Time Machine* (b)

machines   *see* machine; *Those Magnificent Men in Their Flying Machines* (f/s)

mackerel   oily fish; holy mackerel; mackerel sky; a sprat to catch a mackerel

mad   crazy (about), deranged, very annoyed; go mad, hopping mad, like mad, raving mad, stark raving mad, stark staring mad; mad cow disease, mad keen; mad as a hatter; Mad Hatter's Tea Party; *Mad about the Boy* (s), *Mad Cows* (b/f), *Mad Max* (f), *Mad World* (s)

madam   courtesy title; Dear Madam; *Call Me Madam* (f)

madder   *see* mad; red-dye plant

made   *see* make; custom-made, home-made, man-made, ready-made, tailor-made, well made; made a move, made man, made to measure, made to order; rules are made to be broken; *England Made Me* (b/f), *I Was Made to Love Her* (s), *The Man Who Made*

Husbands Jealous (b), *Sweet Dreams Are Made of This* (al/s), *These Boots Are Made for Walkin'* (s)

madly in a crazy manner; *Truly, Madly, Deeply* (f)

madness folly, insanity, nonsense; *The Madness of King George* (f)

magazine periodical, stock of ammunition; parish magazine

magic prestidigitation, supernatural power; 1974 hit for Pilot; film starring Anthony Hopkins; black magic, white magic; magic carpet, magic circle, magic eye, magic lantern, magic mushroom; work like magic; Black Magic, Magic Marker; *A Kind of Magic* (s), *Black Magic Woman* (s), *The Magic Christian* (b/f), *The Magic Finger* (b), *The Magic Flute* (o), *Magic Moments* (s), *The Magic Roundabout* (f/tv), *Puff, the Magic Dragon* s

magical bewitching, enchanting; magical realism; *Magical Mystery Tour* (s)

magnetic attractive (of metal or a personality); magnetic field, magnetic north, magnetic pole, magnetic resonance imaging, magnetic storm, magnetic tape

magnetism quality of attraction; animal magnetism

magnificent splendid; *Magnificent Obsession* (f), *The Magnificent Ambersons* (f), *The Magnificent Seven* (f), *Those Magnificent Men in Their Flying Machines* (f/s)

magnifying enlarging; magnifying glass

magnitude extent, importance; order of magnitude; of the first magnitude

magnolia flowering tree, off-white colour; 1999 Tom Cruise film

magnolias *see* magnolia; *Steel Magnolias* (f)

magnum double-size champagne bottle, powerful handgun; Walls ice-cream bar; famous photographic co-operative; magnum opus; *Magnum Force* (f), *Magnum PI* (tv)

magus ancient Persian priest, any one of the Three Wise Men; *The Magus* (b/f)

maid damsel, female domestic servant; kennel-maid, lady's maid, meter maid, old maid; maid of honour; *The Fair Maid of Perth* (b), *Maid in Manhattan* (f), *Maid of Orleans* (s)

maiden girl, horse that has never won a race, non-scoring over in cricket; inaugural, initial, new, unused; iron maiden; maiden aunt, maiden flight, maiden name, maiden over, maiden speech, maiden voyage; Maiden Castle; *Death and the Maiden* (f)

mail chain armour, letters and parcels, postal system; send by post; chain mail, direct mail, fan mail, junk mail, snail mail; mail boat, mail merge, mail order, mail-order catalogue, mail van; Royal Mail; *Night Mail* (po), *You've Got Mail* (f)

mailing *see* mail; mailing list

main high sea, principal electricity, gas or water pipe; chief; ring main, water main; main clause, main course, main line, main road, main street; by main force, in the main, with might and main; Spanish Main; *Exile on Main Street* (al), *The Main Attraction* (s), *The Main Chance* (tv), *The Main Event* (f)

maintained   declared, looked after; grant-maintained

maintenance   conservation, continuation, living allowance, upkeep; maintenance contract

majesty   regal grandeur; monarch's title; 1977 Robert Lacey book; lese-majesty; Her Britannic Majesty, Her Majesty's, His Catholic Majesty, Your Majesty; *On Her Majesty's Secret Service* (f)

major   military rank; specialise (in a college subject); important; drum major, sergeant-major, trumpet major; major-domo, major general, major league, major prophet, major suit; Canis Major, Ursa Major; *Major Barbara* (pl), *The Trumpet-Major* (b)

majority   adulthood, greater part of a group; absolute majority, moral majority, silent majority; majority rule, majority verdict

make   tradename; create, coerce; make amends, make-believe, make certain, make do, make fast, make fun of, make merry, make money, make ready, make sense (of), make sure, make tracks, make up, make-up artist, make use of, make waves; doctors make the worst patients, empty vessels make most noise, fine feathers make fine birds, it takes all sorts to make a world, make a bolt for, make a clean breast of it, make a clean sweep, make a dead set at, make a fast buck, make a fist of, make a fool of, make a hash of, make a killing, make a meal of, make a mockery of, make a monkey of, make a mountain out of a molehill, make a move, make a name for yourself, make a noise, make a pig of oneself, make a pig's ear of, make a pile, make a rod for your own back, make a splash, make a stand, make a virtue of, make allowances for, make an appearance, make an example of, make an honest woman of, make an issue of, make capital out of, make ends meet, make free with, make friends with, make good time, make hay while the sun shines, make heavy weather of, make it snappy, make light of, make light work of, make mincemeat of, make no bones about, make or break, make sheep's eyes at, make the best of (a bad job), make the grade, make the most of, make the running, make up leeway, make whoopee, make your blood boil/curdle/run cold, make your flesh crawl/creep, make your hackles rise, make your hair/toes curl, make your hair stand on end, make your presence felt, make yourself scarce, make yourself useful, many hands make light work, two wrongs don't make a right; *How to Make an American Quilt* (f), *Make Mine Mink* (f)

maker   creator; mischief-maker; meet your maker

makers   *see* maker; *The Story Makers* (tv)

makes   *see* make; absence makes the heart grow fonder, haste makes waste, it makes no odds, just like mother makes, money makes the world go around, practice makes perfect, that makes two of us

making   *see* make; epoch-making, in the making, law-making, map-making, non-profit-making, shoe-making, sick-making, wine-making; be the making of, making whoopee, of your own making; *Ma, He's Making Eyes at Me* (s), *Making Whoopee* (s), *Making Your Mind Up* (s), *Stop Making Sense* (f)

male animal of the masculine gender, man; masculine; male menopause; *Deadlier than the Male* (b/f), *Deuce Bigalow: Male Gigolo* (f), *I Was a Male War Bride* (f), *Rogue Male* (b/tv)

malice evil intent, spite; Nicole Kidman and Alec Baldwin thriller; malice aforethought; *Malice Aforethought* (b), *Town Called Malice* (s)

mall shopping precinct; Pall Mall, The Mall; *Scenes from a Mall* (f)

mallet croquet or polo stick, hammer with a wooden head; croquet mallet; Shepton Mallet

malt grain treated for brewing, variety of whisky; prepare grain for brewing or distilling; single malt; malt liquor, malt whisky

malted *see* malt; malted milk

man adult male, board-game piece, humankind; operate; angry young man, best man, con man, dead man's handle, delivery man, fancy man, gingerbread man, green man, hard man, hatchet man, he-man, hit man, inner man, iron man, ladies' man, leading man, lollipop man, made man, marked man, medicine man, new man, odd man out, odd-job man, old man, old man's beard, one-man band, plain-clothes man, Portuguese man-of-war, rag-and-bone man, Renaissance man, right-hand man, sandwich man, straight man, third man, to a man, twelfth man, white-van man, yes-man; man about town, man-eating, man enough, man Friday, man-hour, man-jack, man-made, man-management, man of destiny, man of God, man of letters, man of many parts, man of straw, man of the cloth, man of the house, man of the match, man of the world, man-of-war, man overboard, man's best friend, man to man; every man jack, man from the ministry, the man in the moon, the man in the street, may the best man win, no man is an island, one man's meat is another's poison, time and tide wait for no man; Isle of Man, Long Man, Neanderthal Man, Peking Man, Piltdown Man; *Arms and the Man* (pl), *The Ascent of Man* (tv), *The Best Man* (f/pl), *The Bush Tucker Man* (tv), *Candy Man* (f), *Cinderella Man* (f), *Danger Man* (tv), *Dead Man Walking* (f), *Demolition Man* (f), *Eat Drink Man Woman* (f), *The Elephant Man* (f), *Every Man in His Humour* (pl), *Fanfare for the Common Man* (cl), *The Ginger Man* (b), *The Green Man* (b), *Handy Man* (s), *The History Man* (b/tv), *If I Were a Rich Man* (s), *The Illustrated Man* (b/f), *An Innocent Man* (s), *The Invisible Man* (b/f), *Little Big Man* (f), *Man about the House* (tv), *Man and Superman* (pl), *A Man Called Horse* (f), *A Man for All Seasons* (f/pl), *The Man from Uncle* (tv), *The Man in the Iron Mask* (b/f), *Man in the Mirror* (s), *The Man in the Moon* (f), *The Man in the White Suit* (f), *The Man of Destiny* (pl), *Man of La Mancha* (mus), *Man of Mystery* (s), *The Man of Property* (b), *The Man of the House* (f), *Man of the World* (s), *The Man Who Came to Dinner* (f), *The Man Who Fell to Earth* (f), *The Man Who*

Knew Too Much (f), *The Man Who Made Husbands Jealous* (b), *The Man Who Shot Liberty Valance* (f), *The Man Who Was Thursday* (b), *The Man Who Wasn't There* (f), *The Man without a Face* (f), *The Man with the Golden Arm* (b/f), *The Man with the Golden Gun* (f), *The Man with the X-Ray Eyes* (f), *Marathon Man* (f), *Medicine Man* (f), *Mirror Man* (s), *Mr Tambourine Man* (s), *The Music Man* (f), *My Man Godfrey* (f), *Neanderthal Man* (s), *The Nearly Man* (tv), *Nowhere Man* (s), *Odd Man Out* (f), *The Old Man and the Sea* (b), *O Lucky Man* (f/s), *The Omega Man* (f), *One-Man Band* (s), *Our Man Flint* (f), *Our Man in Havana* (b/f), *Pac-Man* (ga), *A Portrait of the Artist as a Young Man* (b), *The Punch and Judy Man* (f), *The Quiet Man* (f), *Rain Man* (f), *Rich Man Poor Man* (b/tv), *Rocket Man* (s), *The Running Man* (f), *The Six Million Dollar Man* (tv), *Soul Man* (s), *Spider-Man* (f), *Stand by Your Man* (s), *The Tenth Man* (b/tv), *There Was a Crooked Man* (f), *The Thin Man* (b/f), *The Third Man* (b/f), *The Wicker Man* (f)

manage   administer, get by; stage-manage

managed   *see* manage; managed fund

management   administration, company's bosses; anger management, database management, household management, line management, man-management, mushroom management, self-management, stage management; management committee, management company; *Anger Management* (f)

manager   administrator, boss; actor-manager, bank manager, line manager, player manager, road manager, stage manager

managing   *see* manage; managing editor

mandarin   former Chinese official, small citrus fruit, top civil servant; China's language; mandarin collar, mandarin duck, mandarin jacket, mandarin orange

mandolin   instrument like a lute; *Captain Corelli's Mandolin* (b/f), *Mandolin Wind* (s)

manger   feeding trough; dog in the manger; *Away in a Manger* (h)

mango   tropical fruit; clothing chain store; mango chutney

manic   frenzied; *Manic Monday* (s)

manifest   aeroplane's passenger list, ship's cargo list; display; easily seen

manner   behaviour, method; all manner, bedside manner; in a manner of speaking, to the manner born

mannered   artificial, behaving in a particular way; ill-mannered

manners   *see* manner; etiquette; bad manners, comedy of manners, table manners

manoeuvre   movement, stratagem; get into position; Heimlich manoeuvre

manor   large country house, police patch; manor house; Boston Manor; *To the Manor Born* (tv)

mansion   grand house; Mansion House; *The Haunted Mansion* (f)

manual   handbook; hand-operated; manual labour

manuscript   copy to be published, handwritten document; illuminated manuscript; manuscript paper

many   a large number of; a good many, how many; many a time; man of many parts, many hands make light work, many happy returns (of the day), too many cooks spoil the broth; *After Many a Summer* (b), *Many a New Day* (s)

map   area plan; chart (an area); off the map, relief map, road map, sketch map, weather map; map book, map-making, map out, map-reading, map reference; put on the map, wipe off the map

maple   Canada's leaf emblem, tree species; maple leaf, maple sugar, maple syrup; *Maple Leaf Rag* (s)

marathon   long-distance race; site of a battle in 490BC; old name for a Snickers bar; half-marathon; marathon race, marathon runner; London Marathon; *Marathon Man* (f)

marble   crystalline limestone, small glass ball used as a toy; put streaks in; marble cake; Marble Arch

marbles   *see* marble; lose your marbles; Elgin Marbles

march   advancement, public demonstration, soldier's walk; advance, demonstrate, walk in a military manner; third month of the year; Cambridgeshire town; forced march, hunger march, on the march, protest march, quick march, route march, slow march, wedding march; March hare, march past; steal a march on; *The Adventures of Augie March* (b)

marches   *see* march; border districts; Aldermaston Marches

marching   *see* march; light marching order; marching orders

---

March
Battle of Britain, Colonel Bogey, Coronation, Dead, Egyptian, Funeral, Grand, Hungarian, Oriental Festive, Persian, Pomp and Circumstance, Prince of Denmark's, Radetzky, Rakoczy, Turkish, Wedding, Wolverine

---

mare   dark area on the moon, female horse; mare's nest; Weston-super-Mare

margin   border, scope; profit margin; margin of error; *Narrow Margin* (f), *The Water Margin* (tv)

marginal   plant which grows at the edge of a pond; close to the limit, slight; marginal seat

marigold   calendula; brand of rubber gloves; marsh marigold

marine   seafaring soldier; of the sea; marine architecture

mariner   sailor; US space probe series; *The Rime of the Ancient Mariner* (po)

marines   *see* marine; tell that to the marines; Royal Marines

mark   blemish, distinguishing sign, former German currency, particular model or type of vehicle, score in a test; check (homework answers), heed, stay close to (an opponent) in a team game; black mark, exclamation mark, high-water mark, low-water mark, question mark, shelf mark, thread mark; mark down, mark off, mark time, mark up; close to the mark, overstep the mark, wide of the mark; St Mark's Square; *Mark of the Vampire* (f), *The Mark of Zorro* (f)

marked   *see* mark; marked cards, marked man

marker device for scoring, felt-tip pen, indicator of position; marker flag; Magic Marker

market buying and selling opportunity, demand for goods, place of trade; offer for sale; bear market, black market, bull market, buyer's market, cattle market, common market, flea market, free market, internal market, mass market, on the market, open market, single market, stock market; market day, market garden, market price, market research, market share, market square, market stall, market town, market value; corner the market; Market Drayton, Market Harborough

marketing promotion of goods and services; direct marketing; Milk Marketing Board

marking *see* mark; marking gauge

marks *see* mark; full marks, quotation marks; X marks the spot

maroon brownish-crimson colour; leave stranded

marriage wedlock; by marriage, civil marriage, in marriage, mixed marriage, open marriage; marriage certificate, marriage counselling, marriage counsellor, marriage guidance, marriage of convenience, marriage settlement; *Marriage à la Mode* (pa/pl), *The Marriage Settlement* (pa), *Scenes from a Marriage* (f)

married *see* marry; having a husband or wife; just married; *I Married a Witch* (f), *Married to the Mob* (f), *Peggy Sue Got Married* (f), *So I Married an Axe Murderer* (f)

marrow large edible gourd, soft inner part of bones; bone marrow, vegetable marrow; to the marrow

marry join together, take a husband or wife; *How to Marry a Millionaire* (f)

marrying *see* marry; not the marrying kind

mars planet; Roman god of war; brand-name chocolate bar; spoils; *Life on Mars* (s/tv), *Mars Attacks!* (f)

marsh area of very wet land; salt marsh; marsh fever, marsh gas, marsh harrier, marsh marigold, marsh tit; Marsh Arabs

marshal judge's clerical assistant, lawman in the Wild West, official who organises ceremonies; arrange in order; air chief marshal, air marshal, air vice-marshal, field marshal; Marshal of the Royal Air Force

marshalling *see* marshal; marshalling yard

marshals *see* marshal; *US Marshals* (f)

martial military; court martial; martial arts, martial law

martin swallow-like bird; house martin, sand martin, screech-martin; Aston Martin, St Martin-in-the-Fields; *Daniel Martin* (b), *Doc Martin* (tv), *Martin Chuzzlewit* (b)

masala Indian spice mixture; chicken tikka masala, garam masala; *Mississippi Masala* (f)

mash creamed potatoes; crush into a pulp; comedy film and series set during the Korean War; bangers and mash, sausage and mash, sour mash

mashed *see* mash; mashed potato

mask facial disguise, face protector; conceal; 1985 film starring Cher; death mask, face mask, gas mask, ski mask, stocking mask; *The Man in the Iron Mask* (f/b), *The Mask* (f), *The Mask of Zorro* (f)

masked   *see* mask; masked ball
masking   *see* mask; masking tape
mason   stone-worker; monumental mason; Mason-Dixon Line; *Perry Mason* (tv)
mass   bulk, large quantity (of), multitude; gather as a crowd; RC ceremony; critical mass, hear Mass, land-mass, relative atomic mass, requiem Mass; mass market, mass media, mass meeting, mass-produced, mass production; High Mass, Midnight Mass, Tridentine Mass, Votive Mass; *Requiem Mass* (cl)
massacre   carnage, overwhelming defeat; *The Texas Chainsaw Massacre* (f)
mast   fruit of the beech tree, large aerial, ship's pole; half mast; at half mast, before the mast, nail your colours to the mast
master   expert, original from which a copy is made, owner of a slave or animal, schoolteacher; become adept at, overcome; grand master, harbour master, jack of all trades (and master of none), old master, past master, question master; master craftsman, master key, master of ceremonies, master-stroke; Master of Philosophy, Master of the Rolls, Master of the Universe; *Master and Commander* (b/f), *The Master and Margarita* (b), *Master of the Game* (b), *The Master Builder* (pl), *The Master of Ballantrae* (b/f)
masters   *see* master; US golf tournament
mat   coaster, small rug, tangled layer (of hair); become tangled; bath mat, beer mat, on the mat, place mat, table mat

match   game, pairing, sporting contest, thin wooden stick for lighting a fire; agree, make a pair; benefit match, cup match, football match, love match, man of the match, mix and match, needle match, safety match, shouting match, slanging match, test match, wax match; match fit, match play, match point; the whole shooting match; *The Little Match Girl* (b), *Match of the Day* (tv), *Match Point* (f)
matchstick   sliver of wood with a phosphorus head; *Matchstick Men* (f), *Pictures of Matchstick Men* (s)
mate   chess move, companion, either of a pair, ship's officer, South American herbal beverage (maté); couple, make a final move in chess; cell-mate, first mate, fool's mate, room-mate, running mate, second mate, team-mate
material   cloth, substance; real, relevant; insulation material, raw material; *Material Girl* (s)
materials   equipment, substances, textiles; raw materials; materials science; *His Dark Materials* (b)
maternity   motherhood; (of clothing) made for pregnant women; maternity department, maternity leave; Maternity Allowance
mathematics   abstract science of number; pure mathematics
matinee   daytime performance; matinee idol, matinee jacket; *The Dark of the Matinee* (s)
matrix   arrangement of data in rows and columns, original mould; dot matrix; *The Matrix* (f), *The Matrix Reloaded* (f), *The Matrix Revolutions* (f)
matron   dignified married woman of

mature age, senior nurse; matron of honour; *Carry On Matron* (f)

matter affair, problem, substance; be important; grey matter, subject matter; matter of course, matter of fact, matter of opinion, matter of record; as a matter of course, as a matter of fact, crux of the matter, for that matter, in the matter of, matter of life and death, mind over matter, no laughing matter, no matter, a peg to hang a matter on; *The Heart of the Matter* (b/f), *A Matter of Life and Death* (f), *What's the Matter with Helen?* (f)

mature adult, mellow, ripe, euphemism for middle-aged or elderly; develop; mature student

may hawthorn; can, is permitted to; fifth month; May bug, May queen; be that as it may, a cat may look at a king, come what may, devil-may-care, may the best man win, much good may it do you, ne'er cast a clout till May be out, to whom it may concern; May Day, Queen of the May; *Frost in May* (b), *Maggie May* (s), *May to December* (tv), *Seven Days in May* (f), *The Darling Buds of May* (b/tv)

maybe perhaps; *Maybe Baby* (f)

mayor head of a local council; Lord Mayor, Lord Mayor's Show; *The Mayor of Casterbridge* (b)

mayoress female head of local council; Lady Mayoress

maze labyrinth; *The Moral Maze* (r)

meadow field; water meadow; meadow brown

meal eating occasion, ground grain; square meal; meal ticket; make a meal of

meals *see* meal; meals on wheels

mealy dry and powdery; mealy-mouthed

mean average; intend, signify; nasty, stingy; golden mean; mean business, mean time, mean well; Greenwich Mean Time; *Mean Girls* (f), *Mean Machine* (f), *Mean Streets* (f)

meaning *see* mean; significance; well meaning

meaningful having a serious purpose; meaningful dialogue

means *see* mean; method, resources; by means of, private means; means of subsistence, means test; by all means, by any means, by no means, the end justifies the means, a means to an end; *The Girls of Slender Means* (b)

measure amount, course of action; gauge, take the dimensions of; apothecaries' measure, beyond measure, half measure, made to measure, short measure, tape measure; for good measure, get the measure of, in large measure, take the measure of; *Measure for Measure* (pl)

meat animal flesh as food; calf's meat, easy meat, luncheon meat, red meat, sausage meat, strong meat, white meat; meat and potatoes, meat and two veg, meat-eater, meat loaf; one man's meat is another's poison

mechanical automatic, performed by habit, relating to physical forces or motion; mechanical drawing, mechanical engineer

mechanics branch of science dealing with motion, garage workers, workings; classical mechanics, quantum mechanics

mechanism process, system of parts

working together, workings; defence
mechanism, escape mechanism
medal   decoration; bronze medal, gold
medal, Olympic medal, silver medal
media   channels of mass
communication; mass media, mixed
media; media studies
medical   health check; concerned
with health care; medical certificate,
medical examination, medical officer,
medical practitioner
medicine   doctor's profession, remedy
for illness; alternative medicine,
complementary medicine,
cumulative medicine, forensic
medicine, patent medicine; medicine
ball, medicine man; laughter is the
best medicine, take your medicine;
Dr Quinn, Medicine Woman (tv),
Medicine Man (f)
meditation   deep thought, spiritual
reflection; piece from Massenet's
Thaïs; Transcendental Meditation
medium   communicator with spirits,
means; average; tv series starring
Patricia Arquette; happy medium;
medium wave
medley   jumbled mix, musical
mixture, style of swimming race;
medley relay
meek   gentle, submissive; meek and
mild
meet   assembly of huntsmen; be
introduced to, congregate, encounter,
fulfil (a need); fitting; meet halfway,
meet the case, meet up; make ends
meet, meet your maker; *Meet John
Doe* (f), *Meet Me in Battersea Park* (s),
Meet Me in St Louis (mus), *Meet the
Fockers* (f), *Meet the Parents* (f), *We'll
Meet Again* (s)
meeting   *see* meet; assembly,

rendezvous; annual general meeting,
board meeting, cabinet meeting,
mass meeting, race meeting; meeting
house
meets   *see* meet; boy meets girl
megaphone   loudhailer; megaphone
diplomacy
mellow   ripe and soft; *Mellow
Yellow* (s)
melody   tune; *A Pretty Girl Is Like a
Melody* (s), *Unchained Melody* (s)
melon   large succulent fruit;
cantaloupe melon, galia melon,
honeydew melon, musk melon
melt   soften, turn to liquid; melt
down, melt-water
melting   *see* melt; melting point,
melting pot, melting temperature;
Melting Pot (s)
member   limb, person belonging to a
group; card-carrying member,
corresponding member, founder-
member, life member, non-member,
private member, private member's
bill; Member of Parliament
membership   state of having joined a
group, those belonging to a group;
life membership
memento   keepsake; 2000 thriller
starring Guy Pearce; memento mori;
Memento Mori (b)
memoirs   autobiography; *Memoirs of a
Geisha* (b/f)
memorandum   reminder note; *The
Quiller Memorandum* (b/f)
memorial   monument of
remembrance, record of past events;
war memorial
memory   ability to recall things,
computer storage facility; hit song
from *Cats*; from memory,
photographic memory, read-only

memory; memory lane; go/walk down memory lane, in memory of, within living memory; *The Persistence of Memory* (pa), *Speak, Memory* (b), *Thanks for the Memory* (s)

men *see* man; troops; little green men, nine men's morris; dead men tell no tales; Angry Young Men; *All the King's Men* (f), *All the President's Men* (f), *Dead Men Tell No Tales* (b), *Eight Men Out* (f), *A Few Good Men* (f), *The Four Just Men* (b/tv), *G Men* (f), *Grumpy Old Men* (tv), *The Hollow Men* (po), *The Intelligence Men* (f), *Little Men* (b), *Matchstick Men* (f), *Men at Arms* (b), *Men Behaving Badly* (tv), *The Men from the Ministry* (r), *Men in Black* (f), *Of Mice and Men* (b/f), *One Hundred Men and a Girl* (f), *Pictures of Matchstick Men* (f), *Those Magnificent Men in Their Flying Machines* (f/s), *Three Men and a Baby* (f), *Three Men in a Boat* (b), *Twelve Angry Men* (f), *X-Men* (f)

menace threat; threaten; *The Phantom Menace* (f)

ménage household; ménage à trois

menagerie small zoo; *The Glass Menagerie* (f/pl)

mend repair; on the mend; mend fences; mend your ways

mental of the mind; mental block, mental cruelty

mentality mindset; siege mentality

mention reference; allude to; honourable mention; don't mention it, mention in dispatches, mention in your will, not to mention, too numerous to mention

merchant trader; scrap merchant, speed merchant, wine merchant; merchant-adventurer, merchant bank, merchant navy; *The Merchant*

of Venice (pl)

mercy forgiveness; errand of mercy; at the mercy of

merge combine; mail merge

meridian circle of constant longitude from pole to pole; south of England commercial tv company; Greenwich meridian

merrier *see* merry; the more the merrier; *The More the Merrier* (b/f)

merry cheerful, slightly drunk; make merry; merry-go-round, merry Christmas, merry Xmas; lead a merry dance, play merry hell; *Merry Christmas, Mr Lawrence* (f), *The Merry Widow* (o), *The Merry Wives of Windsor* (pl), *Merry Xmas Everybody* (s)

mess disorder, military canteen; put into disarray; officers' mess; mess about, mess hall, mess-room, mess tin, mess up

message brief communication; off-message, on-message, text message; get the message; *Message in a Bottle* (f/s)

messenger courier; *The List of Adrian Messenger* (f)

met *see* meet; hail-fellow-well-met; *Before She Met Me* (b), *When Harry Met Sally* (f)

metal broken stone for roads, hard shiny substance; base metal, heavy metal, precious metal, road metal, sheet metal; metal detector; *Full Metal Jacket* (f), *Hot Metal* (tv)

metamorphosis transformation; Kafka story; *The Metamorphosis of Narcissus* (pa)

metaphor figure of speech; mixed metaphor

meter measuring device; measure (electricity, eg); exposure meter, gas meter, light meter, parking meter; meter maid

method   procedure; method acting, method of increments

metric   of the decimal system; metric system, metric ton

metropolitan   head bishop, inhabitant of a major city; of the main city; 1990 Whit Stillman film; metropolitan county; Metropolitan Line, Metropolitan Museum of Art

mettle   pluck; be on your mettle

mice   small rodents; field mice; when the cat's away the mice will play; *Of Mice and Men* (b/f), *Three Blind Mice* (nr)

microscope   magnifying instrument; under the microscope

microwave   type of energy, type of oven; microwave oven

mid   central, halfway; silly mid-off, silly mid-on; mid-air, mid-off, mid-on; Mid Glamorgan

middle   centre; central; middle age, middle-age spread, middle-aged, middle C, middle class, middle distance, middle ear, middle ground, middle name, middle school; middle of the road, pig/piggy in the middle; Middle Ages, Middle America, Middle East, Middle England, Middle English; *In the Middle of Nowhere* (s), *Malcolm in the Middle* (tv), *Stuck in the Middle with You* (s)

middling   average; fair to middling

midi   calf-length skirt; south of France; midi system

midnight   twelve in the evening; midnight basketball, midnight blue, midnight feast, midnight oil, midnight sun; burn the midnight oil; Midnight Mass; *In the Midnight Hour* (s), *Midnight Cowboy* (f), *Midnight Express* (f), *Midnight Run* (f), *Midnight's Children* (b), *Midnight Train to Georgia* (s), *The Other Side of Midnight* (b/f), *Round Midnight* (f)

midshipman   naval rank; *Mr Midshipman Easy* (b)

midstream   halfway across a river; in midstream; don't change horses in midstream

midsummer   period on or near the June solstice; Midsummer Day; *A Midsummer-Night's Dream* (f/pl)

might   power; may; pigs might fly, with all your might, with might and main

mighty   powerful; high and mighty; *Mighty Aphrodite* (f), *The Mighty Boosh* (tv), *Mighty Joe Young* (f), *Mighty Quinn* (s)

mike   radio code word, sound-recording equipment; *Mike Hammer* (tv)

mild   variety of dark beer; meek, temperate; meek and mild; mild and bitter

mile   imperial unit of distance; country mile, four-minute mile, nautical mile, sea mile; go the extra mile, a miss is as good as a mile, run a mile, stand/stick out a mile; Royal Mile, Square Mile, Three Mile Island; *Country Mile* (s), *The Green Mile* (f)

miles   *see* mile; miles away, miles per hour; Air Miles; *I Can See for Miles* (s)

military   armed forces; of soldiers and war; military academy, military attaché, military discipline, military honours military police, military two-step; Military Cross

milk   dairy product, liquid produced by female mammals; draw from;

condensed milk, evaporated milk, malted milk, pint of milk, skimmed milk, soya milk; milk and honey, milk bar, milk bottle, milk chocolate, milk float, milk of magnesia, milk pudding, milk round, milk run, milk-shake, milk snake, milk stout, milk teeth, milk thistle, milk train; don't cry over spilt milk; Milk Marketing Board; *No Milk Today* (s), *Under Milk Wood* (pl)

milking *see* milk; milking parlour, milking stool

milky cloudy, whitish; Milky Way

mill crushing machine, machine driven by wind or water, textile factory; crush; pepper mill, run of the mill; mill-race; go/put through the mill, grist to the mill; Flatford Mill; *Flatford Mill* (pa), *The Mill on the Floss* (b)

millennium thousand years, Utopian period; 1998 Robbie Williams hit; Millennium Dome, Millennium Stadium; *The Millennium Prayer* (s)

miller flour grinder; *Davy Miller* (b), *Miller's Crossing* (f)

million first seven-figure number; thanks a million; *How to Steal a Million* (f), *Million Dollar Baby* (f), *One Million Years BC* (f), *The Six Million Dollar Man* (tv)

millionaire very rich person; *How to Marry a Millionaire* (f), *Who Wants to Be a Millionaire* (tv)

millpond calm body of water, water-wheel power source; as calm as a millpond

millstone heavy burden, heavy weight used for grinding corn; millstone grit

mince ground meat; finely chop, walk with affected delicacy; mince pies; mince your words

mincemeat dried fruit and spice filling; make mincemeat of

mind intellect; look after, object to, watch out for; UK's national association for mental health; bear in mind, frame of mind, one-track mind, open mind, presence of mind; mind-bending, mind-blowing, mind-boggling, mind games, mind-numbing, mind over matter, mind-reading, mind's eye; bored out of your mind, I don't mind telling you, know your own mind, mind the gap, mind your own business, mind your step, never mind, out of sight out of mind, speak your mind, travel broadens the mind; *Always on My Mind* (s), *A Beautiful Mind* (f), *Eternal Sunshine of the Spotless Mind* (f), *Friday on My Mind* (s), *Gentle on My Mind* (s), *Georgia on My Mind* (s), *Jealous Mind* (s), *Losing My Mind* (s), *Making Your Mind Up* (s), *Mind Your Language* (tv), *Never Mind the Quality, Feel the Width* (tv), *Out of Your Mind* (s), *Trouble in Mind* (f), *The Windmills of Your Mind* (s)

minded *see* mind; inclined; absent-minded, bloody-minded, broad-minded, evil-minded, fair-minded, high-minded, like-minded, mechanically minded, narrow-minded, open-minded, right-minded, single-minded, small-minded; *The Absent-Minded Professor* (f)

minds *see* mind; great minds think alike; *Suspicious Minds*

mine colliery, explosive device; dig (for coal and minerals); belonging to me; diamond mine, gold mine, land-mine, limpet mine, tin mine; mine host, mine-laying; *Make Mine Mink* (f), *Mine Own Executioner* (f), *Sweet Child o'Mine* (s), *This Old Heart of Mine* (s), *Vengeance Is Mine* (b)

miner pit worker; coal miner, gold miner, tin-miner; *Coal Miner's Daughter* (f)

mineral inorganic substance; mineral rights, mineral water

mines *see* mine; *King Solomon's Mines* (b/f)

mini short skirt, small car; undersized; mini-dress, mini-series

minimum least quantity; lowest; (national) minimum wage; minimum lending rate

mining *see* mine; ore extraction; gold-mining, tin mining

minister head of a government department, member of the clergy; attend (to); cabinet minister, defence minister, foreign minister, prime minister; minister of religion, minister of state; First Minister, Minister of the Crown, Minister without Portfolio; *Yes, Minister* (tv), *Yes, Prime Minister* (tv)

ministry clergy, government department; man from the ministry; *The Men from the Ministry* (r), *The Ministry of Fear* (b/f)

mink weasel-like mammal; *Make Mine Mink* (f), *That Touch of Mink* (f)

minor person under 18 years of age; insignificant, junior; minor prophet, minor suit; Asia Minor, Canis Minor, Morris Minor, Ursa Minor

minority lesser part, period before adulthood; ethnic minority; minority government, minority shareholder; *Minority Report* (f)

minstrel medieval musician; *The Lay of the Last Minstrel* (po)

mint aromatic herb, place for manufacturing money; manufacture (coins); brand new; Kendal mint cake; mint julep, mint sauce; in mint condition

minus negative sign; subtract; lacking, less than zero; minus sign

minute sixty seconds; tiny; four-minute mile, last minute; minute hand, minute steak; any minute now, at the last minute, at the minute, just a minute, a laugh a minute, up to the minute; *Just a Minute* (r), *Minute Waltz* (cl), *Two-Minute Warning* (f)

miracle marvel, supernatural event; miracle play; *The Miracle* (al), *The Miracle of Morgan's Creek* (f), *Miracle on 34th Street* (f), *Miracle Play* (b), *The Miracle Worker* (f)

mirror looking-glass; reflect; rear-view mirror, two-way mirror, vanity mirror, wing mirror; mirror image; *Daily Mirror* (n), *Man in the Mirror* (s), *The Mirror Has Two Faces* (f), *Mirror Man* (s), *Sunday Mirror* (n)

mirrors *see* mirror; hall of mirrors, smoke and mirrors

mirth laughter; *The House of Mirth* (b/f)

misadventure accident; death by misadventure

mischief naughtiness; mischief-maker; do a mischief to; *White Mischief* (f)

misery despair; 1990 film starring James Caan and Kathy Bates; Stephen King novel; misery loves company

misfits nonconformists; *The Misfits* (f)

miss failure to hit, single woman's title; be off target, fail to catch, feel the loss of, overlook; hit-and-miss, near miss; miss out, miss the boat, miss the bus; give it a miss, a miss is as good as a mile; *Driving Miss Daisy* (f), *Good Golly Miss Molly* (s), *Little Miss Muffett* (nr), *Miss Congeniality* (f), *Miss Otis Regrets* (s), *Miss Sadie Thompson* (f), *Miss Saigon* (mus), *Miss Smilla's Feeling for Snow* (b), *No Orchids for Miss Blandish* (b/f), *The Prime of Miss Jean Brodie* (b/f)

missile projected weapon; ballistic missile, cruise missile, guided missile; Cuban Missile Crisis

missing *see* miss; lacking; 1982 film starring Jack Lemmon; go missing; missing link; *The Missing* (f), *One of Our Dinosaurs Is Missing* (f)

mission assignment, religious outpost, vocation; mission statement; *The Mission* (f), *Mission: Impossible* (f/tv)

missionary person who goes abroad to preach a religion; *The Missionary* (f)

mist light fog; befog, blur; love-in-a-mist, Scotch mist

mistletoe Christmas plant; *Mistletoe and Wine* (s)

mistral Mediterranean wind; *Mistral's Daughter* (b/tv)

mistress female owner of a slave or animal, female teacher, lover, woman in authority; Mistress of the Robes

mists *see* mist; in the mists of time

misty hazy; *Play Misty for Me* (f)

mix blend; combine, meet people socially; Bombay mix, ready-mix; mix and match, mix in, mix it, mix up

mixed *see* mix; assorted, motley; ready-mixed; mixed bag, mixed blessing, mixed doubles, mixed economy, mixed grill, mixed marriage, mixed media, mixed metaphor, mixed-up

mixer any soft drink to go with a spirit, food blender, person who socialises; cement mixer, concrete mixer; mixer tap

mixture amalgam, assortment; cough mixture

mixtures *see* mixture; dolly mixtures

mob mafia, rabble; crowd round; lynch mob, rent-a-mob; mob-cap, mob-handed, mob law, mob rule; *The Lavender Hill Mob* (f), *Married to the Mob* (f)

mobile hanging ornament, portable phone; able to walk, portable, travelling; Alabama city; downwardly mobile, upwardly mobile; mobile home, mobile library, mobile phone

mobility freedom of movement; mobility allowance

moccasin soft shoe, venomous pit viper; water moccasin

mock practice examination; make fun of; imitation; mock turtle soup, mock-up

mockery derision, travesty; make a mockery of

mockingbird American thrush; *To Kill a Mockingbird* (f/b)

mod Gaelic festival, member of a 1960s youth group; mod cons; *The Mod Squad* (f)

mode fashion, manner; à la mode; *Marriage à la Mode* (pa/pl)

model mannequin, miniature version, mock-up, perfect example, person who poses for an artist; display clothes, pose, shape; ideal; financial model, role model, scale model, working model; model railway; New Model Army; *The Model* (s)

moderate   reduce in intensity, regulate; medium, reasonable

moderation   avoidance of extremes, process of re-marking exam papers to double-check; in moderation

modern   contemporary; secondary modern, ultra-modern; modern first edition, modern history, modern times; Tate Modern; *Modern Love* (s), *Modern Times* (f), *Thoroughly Modern Millie* (mus)

modified   adapted; genetically modified

module   self-contained unit; command module

mole   birthmark, burrowing mammal, long-term spy, masonry pier, Mexican sauce; Surrey river; *The Secret Diary of Adrian Mole Aged 13¾* (b)

molehill   mound thrown up by a burrowing mammal; make a mountain out of a molehill

moment   importance, instant of time; fleeting moment, of the moment, spur-of-the-moment; moment of truth; at a moment's notice, at any moment, for the moment, in the heat of the moment on the spur of the moment; *The Moment of Truth* (tv), *One Moment in Time* (s), *Perfect Moment* (s)

moments   *see* moment; *Magic Moments* (s)

monarch   sovereign; *Monarch of the Glen* (tv), *The Monarch of the Glen* (pa)

money   cash; 1984 Martin Amis novel; Pink Floyd song; beer money, big money, blood money, danger money, dirty money, easy money, even money, funny money, gate money, hush money, in the money, make money, Maundy money, on the money, paper money, pin money, pocket money, prize money, protection money, raise money, ready money, rolling in money, spending money; money-back guarantee, money box, money-grubbing, money order, money-spinner, money spider, money supply; a fool and his money are soon parted, for my money, money for jam, money for old rope, money isn't everything, money makes the world go around, money talks, not for love or money, throw good money after bad, your money or your life; *The Color of Money* (f), *Double Your Money* (tv), *Money Box* (r), *Money for Nothing* (s), *Money Money Money* (s), *The Money Pit* (f), *Take the Money and Run* (f), *The Tribute Money* (pa), *We're in the Money* (s)

monitor   computer screen, large tropical lizard, senior pupil; supervise

monk   member of a religious community of men; Buddhist monk, Trappist monk

monkey   five hundred pounds, long-tailed primate; meddle (around with); brass monkey, cheeky monkey, grease monkey, powder monkey, proboscis monkey, rhesus monkey, spider monkey, vervet monkey; monkey bars, monkey business, monkey nuts, monkey puzzle, monkey suit, monkey wrench; make a monkey of; *Monkey Business* (f), *Monkey Spanner* (s), *Monkey Trousers* (tv), *The White Monkey* (b)

monkeys *see* monkey; *Twelve Monkeys* (f)

monster huge frightening creature; gigantic; 2003 Charlize Theron film; Gila monster, green-eyed monster; Loch Ness Monster, Monster Munch; *Gods and Monsters* (f), *Monster's Ball* (f)

monsters *see* monster; *Monsters Inc* (f)

month division of a year; calendar month, lunar month; a month of Sundays, flavour of the month; *August Is a Wicked Month* (b), *A Month in the Country* (b/f/pl), *A Month of Sundays* (f)

months *see* month; *Nine Months* (f)

monument commemorative structure; pillar near Pudding Lane, London; ancient monument

mood ambience, state of mind or feeling; in the mood; *In the Mood* (s), *In the Mood for Love* (f)

moon any one of a planet's satellites, Earth's only natural satellite; present one's bare backside to public view, wander about listlessly; full moon, half-moon, half-moon spectacles, harvest moon, hunter's moon, new moon, over the moon, the man in the moon; moon boots, moon-faced, moon shot; cry for the moon, once in a blue moon; *Bad Moon Rising* (s), *Bitter Moon* (f), *Blue Moon* (s), *Brother Sun, Sister Moon* (f), *Button Moon* (tv), *Fly Me to the Moon* (s), *The Man in the Moon* (f), *The Moon and Sixpence* (b/f), *Moon River* (s), *The Moon's a Balloon* (b), *Mountains of the Moon* (f/s), *Paper Moon* (f), *Shine On Harvey Moon* (tv), *Sugar Moon* (s), *The Teahouse of the August Moon* (f)

moonlight natural illumination at night; have another job on the side; moonlight flit; *Dangerous Moonlight* (f), *Moonlight Serenade* (s), *Moonlight Shadow* (s), *Moonlight Sonata* (cl)

moonstone variety of feldspar; *The Moonstone* (b)

moot ancient English meeting of freemen, hypothetical case argued by law students; debate; arguable (point); moot point

mop bushy head of hair, floor-cleaning tool; soak (up); mop up

moral ethics, lesson of a story; ethical, virtuous; moral majority, moral support, moral victory; *The Moral Maze* (r)

morality principles of right and wrong; morality play

more greater number; additional; to a greater degree; no more, once more; more and more, more or less; bite off more than you can chew, more fool you, more haste less speed, more power to your elbow, more's the pity, the more the merrier, say no more, there's more than one way to skin a cat, what is more, you are more than welcome; *Alice Doesn't Live Here Any More* (f), *For a Few Dollars More* (f), *More Than a Woman* (s), *More Than I Can Say* (s), *The More the Merrier* (b/f), *No More Heroes* (s), *No More Mr Nice Guy* (s), *Put Out More Flags* (b), *Yesterday Once More* (s)

morgue funeral parlour; *The Murders in the Rue Morgue* (b)

morning time before midday; coffee morning; morning coat, morning dress, morning glory, morning sickness; good morning, morning, noon and night; Morning Cloud,

Morning Star; *Angel of the Morning* (s), *Good Morning* (s), *Good Morning Vietnam* (f), *Morning Glory* (al/s), *Morning Has Broken* (s), *Morning Star* (n), *Saturday Night and Sunday Morning* (b/f), *This Morning* (tv), *Touch Me in the Morning* (s)

mortal human being; deadly; mortal sin; *Mortal Kombat* (ga)

mortality death; *Old Mortality* (b)

mortar building mixture, trench weapon; bricks and mortar; mortar board

mortgage loan secured against a property; pledge (a property) as security; endowment mortgage, repayment mortgage; mortgage rate

mortified subdued by penance; embarrassed

mosquito bloodsucking insect; de Havilland bomber; mosquito net; *The Mosquito Coast* (b/f), *Mosquito Squadron* (f)

moss spongy green plant; Irish moss, peat moss, Spanish moss; moss stitch; a rolling stone gathers no moss; Moss Side

most greatest, majority of; at the most; most favoured nation status; empty vessels make most noise, for the most part, make the most of; Most Reverend

moth nocturnal flying insect; cabbage moth, emperor moth, gypsy moth, silk moth, tiger moth; moth-eaten; Gipsy Moth

mothballs strong-smelling pellets used to repel insects; puts on hold; in mothballs

mother female parent, head of a women's religious community; behave protectively towards; birth mother, earth mother, surrogate mother; Mother Carey's chicken, mother country, Mother Hubbard cloak, mother-in-law, mother-in-law's tongue, mother lode, mother-of-pearl, mother ship, mother's little helper, mother's ruin, mother-to-be, mother tongue; just like mother makes, necessity is the mother of invention; Mother Nature, Mother of Parliaments, Mother Superior, Mother's Day, Reverend Mother; *Bachelor Mother* (f), *The Mother* (f), *Mother and Child Reunion* (s), *Mother Courage and Her Children* (pl), *Mother Goose* (pan), *Mother's Little Helper* (s), *Old Mother Hubbard* (nr), *Sylvia's Mother* (s), *Your Mother Should Know* (s)

mothering *see* mother; Mothering Sunday

mothers *see* mother; *Some Mothers Do 'Ave Em* (tv)

moths *see* moth; *The Gypsy Moths* (f)

motion action, gesture, proposal in a debate; beckon; perpetual motion, slow motion, time-and-motion study; motion picture

motions *see* motion; go through the motions

motor car, engine, nerve or muscle used in movement; travel by car; outboard motor, starter motor; motor car, motor home, motor racing, motor scooter, motor sport, motor yacht; Motor Show, National Motor Museum; *'Ullo John, Got a New Motor?* (s)

motorcycle petrol-driven bike; *The Girl on a Motorcycle* (f)

motorway major road; motorway service area; *2-4-6-8 Motorway* (s)

mould   mildew, shaped container (for jellies, eg); shape; leaf mould; break the mould

mouldy   mildewed, stale; *Mouldy Old Dough* (s)

mount   glass slide, horse, peak; climb onto; mount guard; Mount Ararat, Mount Etna, Mount Everest, Mount of Olives, Mount Olympus, Mount Sinai

Mount
Ararat, Etna, Everest, Fuji, Olympus, Pleasant, Rushmore, Sinai, Snowdon, Vesuvius

mountain   huge pile, peak; mountain ash, mountain bike, mountain goat, mountain lion, mountain range; make a mountain out of a molehill; Blue Mountain Coffee, Green Mountain State; *Ain't No Mountain High Enough* (s), *Brokeback Mountain* (f), *Climb Ev'ry Mountain* (s), *Cold Mountain* (f), *Go Tell It on the Mountain* (b), *Night on a Bare Mountain* (cl), *River Deep Mountain High* (s)

mountains   *see* mountain; move mountains; Atlas Mountains, Blue Mountains, Carpathian Mountains, Great Smoky Mountains, Rocky Mountains; *Mountains of the Moon* (f/ s), *Thunder in the Mountains* (s)

Mountains
Appalachian, Atlas, Black, Blue, Blue Ridge, Carpathian, Catskill, Drakensberg, Great Smoky, Harz, Rocky, Snowy, Wicklow

mourning   lamentation; expressing

grief, regretting the passing of; in mourning; *Mourning Becomes Electra* (pl), *The Mourning Bride* (pl)

mouse   hand-held computer control, small rodent; cat and mouse, church mouse, harvest mouse; mouse deer, mouse hare, mouse-hole; (as) quiet as a mouse; *The Mouse That Roared* (f)

moustache   facial hair above the lips; handlebar moustache, horseshoe moustache, pencil moustache, toothbrush moustache, walrus moustache

mouth   entrance, organ used to eat and speak; articulate silently; bad-mouth, big mouth, foot-and-mouth disease, nil by mouth, river-mouth, roof of the mouth, word of mouth; mouth organ, mouth-to-mouth, mouth-watering; all mouth and trousers, another mouth to feed don't look a gift horse in the mouth, down in the mouth, foam at the mouth, from the horse's mouth, have a plum in one's mouth, have your heart in your mouth, keep your mouth shut, look a gift horse in the mouth; *The Horse's Mouth* (b), *Nil by Mouth* (f)

mouthed   *see* mouth; bad-mouthed, close-mouthed, foul-mouthed, loud-mouthed, mealy-mouthed

movable   transportable; movable feast

move   change of position, initiative; change position, change residence, propel, propose; make a move, on the move; move in, move mountains, move out; get a move on, move heaven and earth, move the goalposts; *Move Over, Darling* (f/s), *One False Move* (b/f)

movement   action, division of a

The *Puzzler* Crossword Solver's Dictionary

musical composition, public
campaign; pincer movement, rapid
eye movement, women's movement;
Arts and Crafts Movement, Non-
Aligned Movement, Oxford
Movement

mover proposer of a motion; prime
mover; mover and shaker

movie film; B-movie, disaster movie,
drive-in movie, home movie, road
movie, silent movie; movie-goer,
movie theatre; *The Kentucky Fried
Movie* (f), *Scary Movie* (f), *Silent
Movie* (f)

moving *see* move; poignant; moving
pavement, moving staircase

mow cut (grass); *The Barley Mow* (s)

mower grass cutter; hover-mower

mown *see* mow; cut (of grass); mown
down

much plenty; greatly; a bit much, as
much as, how much, pretty much,
too much; much good may it do you,
much of a muchness, not much cop,
so much the better; *The Man Who
Knew Too Much* (f), *Much Ado about
Nothing* (f/pl), *Thank U Very Much* (s)

muck dirt; mess (about); muck about,
muck in, muck-raking; Lady Muck,
Lord Muck; *Common as Muck* (tv)

mud soft wet earth; stick-in-the-mud;
mud pack, mud-slinging, mud
wrestling; as clear as mud, drag
through the mud, here's mud in your
eye

muddle confusion; confuse; muddle
along muddle-headed, muddle
through, muddle up

muffin cupcake; *Muffin the Mule* (tv)

mug beaker with a handle, face,
gullible person; attack and rob; a
mug's game; mug up

mugger Indian crocodile, street
robber; hugger-mugger

mulberry dark reddish-purple colour,
tree, WWII floating harbour; early
1990s sitcom starring Karl Howman;
mulberry bush, mulberry harbour;
*Here We Go Round the Mulberry
Bush* (f/s)

mule backless shoe, beast of burden;
spinning mule; (as) stubborn as a
mule; *Muffin the Mule* (tv), *Mule
Train* (f)

mules *see* mule; *Two Mules for Sister
Sara* (f)

mull Scottish promontory, soft plain
muslin; Inner Hebridean island;
heat (wine), think (over); Mull of
Kintyre; *Mull of Kintyre* (s)

mullet 1970s men's hairstyle, fish,
star in heraldry; red mullet

multiple number which can be
divided by another; numerous, of
many parts; house in multiple
occupation, lowest common
multiple; multiple-choice

multiplication increase in number,
maths procedure; 1961 Bobby Darin
song; multiplication sign,
multiplication table

mum female parent; act in a mime;
tight-lipped; keep mum; mum's the
word; *It Ain't Half Hot Mum* (tv),
Mum's on Strike (tv)

mummers actors in a traditional
masked play, silent actors; mummers'
play

mummy child's name for mother,
embalmed body; *The Mummy* (f), *The
Mummy Returns* (f)

murder intentional homicide;
assassinate, spoil by doing badly; get
away with blue murder, get away

with murder, murder will out, scream blue murder; *Blue Murder at St Trinian's* (f), *Diagnosis Murder* (tv), *Dial M for Murder* (f), *Fx: Murder by Illusion* (f), *How to Murder Your Wife* (f), *Manhattan Murder Mystery* (f), *The Murder at the Vicarage* (b), *Murder by Numbers* (f), *Murder Inc* (f/s), *Murder in the Cathedral* (pl), *Murder Most Horrid* (tv), *Murder Must Advertise* (b), *The Murder of Roger Ackroyd* (b), *Murder on the Dancefloor* (s), *Murder on the Orient Express* (b/f), *Murder She Wrote* (tv), *Murder Will Out* (b), *A Perfect Murder* (f), *A Slight Case of Murder* (f)

murderer killer; *So I Married an Axe Murderer* (f)

murders see murder; *Midsomer Murders* (tv), *The Murders in the Rue Morgue* (b)

murmur continuous mumble; speak indistinctly; without a murmur

muscle body tissue, political or financial power; force your way (in); muscle-bound, muscle in

muse creative influence; meditate; goddess of the arts

museum building housing historic items; museum piece; Ashmolean Museum, Imperial War Museum, Natural History Museum, Solomon R Guggenheim Museum, Victoria and Albert Museum; *Mystery of the Wax Museum* (f)

Museum

Ashmolean, British, Fitzwilliam, Imperial War, Natural History, Science, Victoria and Albert

---

mushroom edible fungus; expand

very rapidly; button mushroom, magic mushroom, oyster mushroom; mushroom cloud, mushroom management

music artistically organised sound; 2000 Madonna hit; chamber music, country music, early music, folk music, incidental music, light music, New Age music, piped music, sheet music, soul music, title music, world music; music box, music centre, music hall, music of the spheres; face the music, music to your ears; Bachelor of Music; *A Dance to the Music of Time* (b), *Face the Music* (al/tv), *Let's Face the Music and Dance* (s), *Music Box* (f), *The Music Box* (f), *The Music Lovers* (f), *The Music Man* (f), *My Music* (r) *The Sound of Music* (mus), *Water Music* (cl)

musical film or play with songs; melodic; musical chairs, musical comedy, musical instrument; *Musical Box* (tv)

musician player of an instrument; session musician

musk strong-smelling perfume ingredient; musk melon, musk ox

musketeers 17th-century soldiers with firearms; *The Three Musketeers* (b/f)

muslin fine cotton fabric; butter muslin

must fermenting grape juice, mouldiness, necessity; have to; must-have; needs must, the show must go on, what goes up must come down; *It Must Be Love* (s), *Murder Must Advertise* (b), *Night Must Fall* (f), *The Pope Must Die* (f), *The Show Must Go On* (s)

mustard pungent yellow condiment, plant of the cabbage family; English mustard, French mustard; mustard and cress, mustard gas, mustard plaster; (as) keen as mustard, cut the mustard

muster   assembly (of troops); gather together; pass muster

mute   trumpet-quietening device; tone down; speechless; mute swan

mutiny   open revolt against authority; rise up against authority; Indian Mutiny; *The Caine Mutiny* (b/f), *Mutiny on the Bounty* (f),

mutton   sheep meat; leg-of-mutton sleeve; mutton-chop whiskers; mutton dressed as lamb

mutual   financial institution owned by its customers; reciprocal; the feeling is mutual; *Our Mutual Friend* (b/tv)

mysteries   *see* mystery; ancient rites; *The Mysteries of Udolpho* (b)

mystery   unexplained happening; mystery play, mystery tour; *Magical Mystery Tour* (al/s), *Manhattan Murder Mystery* (f), *Man of Mystery* (s), *The Mystery of Edwin Drood* (b), *Mystery of the Wax Museum* (f), *Mystery Train* (f)

mystic   guru; supernatural; *Mystic Pizza* (f), *Mystic River* (f)

myth   old folk tale or legend; Greek myth, urban myth

N

nag old horse, shrew; harp on at

nail metal fastening spike, horny plate on a finger or toe; catch, firmly fasten; on the nail; nail-biting, nail brush, nail down, nail-file, nail polish, nail scissors, nail varnish; fight tooth and nail, hit the nail on the head, nail in the coffin, nail your colours to the mast

nails *see* nail; bed of nails; hard as nails

naked bare; stark naked; naked flame; to the naked eye; *The Naked and the Dead* (b/f), *The Naked Chef* (tv), *The Naked Civil Servant* (b/tv), *The Naked Gun* (f), *The Naked Lunch* (b/f), *Naked Video* (tv)

name appellation; designate; brand name, Christian name, code-name, domain name, family name, first name, household name, last name, maiden name, middle name, pen-name, pet name, place name, proprietary name, stage name, what's-its name; name day, name-dropping, name names; in all but name, in the name of, make a name for yourself, the name of the game, name the day, a name to conjure with, on first-name terms, take your name in vain, you name it; *Carve Her Name with Pride* (f), *A Horse with No Name* (s), *In the Name of the Father* (f), *My Name Is Earl* (tv), *The Name of the Game* (s), *The Name of the Rose* (b/f), *Name That Tune* (tv), *Pride (in the Name of Love)* (s), *Say My Name* (s), *Stop! In the Name of Love* (s)

named *see* name; *A Streetcar Named Desire* (f/pl)

names *see* name; name names; no names, no pack drill

nanny female goat, nursemaid; be overprotective towards; 1980s Wendy Craig tv series; nanny-goat; *Nanny McPhee* (f)

nap brief sleep, hot racing tip, woolly surface on cloth; sleep briefly

nappy   diaper; nappy rash

narcissus   spring flower; *Black Narcissus* (f), *The Metamorphosis of Narcissus* (pa)

nark   informer; annoy; copper's nark

narrow   restricted, slender; taper; narrow escape, narrow gauge, narrow-minded, narrow squeak; the straight and narrow; *Narrow Margin* (f)

nasty   horrid; cheap and nasty; nasty piece of work

natal   connected with birth; former Boer republic and South African province; post-natal

nation   country and its people; most favoured nation status; nation of shopkeepers, nation state; *The Birth of a Nation* (f), *Seven Nation Army* (s), *Test the Nation* (tv)

national   citizen; concerning the whole country; gross national product; national anthem, national convention, national costume, national debt, national government, national grid, national minimum wage, national park, national service; Grand National, National Assembly, National Assistance, National Audit Office, National Curriculum, National Express, National Front, National Gallery, National Guard, National Hunt, National Insurance, National Portrait Gallery, National Savings Bank, National Socialist, National Trust; *National Velvet* (f)

nationalism   advocacy of political independence for a country, feeling that one's country is superior to others; Scottish nationalism, Welsh nationalism

nations   *see* nation; League of Nations, Six Nations, United Nations; *The Wealth of Nations* (b)

native   local resident, original inhabitant; indigenous; go native; native speaker; Native American; *Native New Yorker* (s), *Native Son* (f), *The Return of the Native* (b/f)

nativity   birth, birth of Christ, Christmas festival or play; nativity play

natural   tone that is neither sharp nor flat; inborn, normal, sincere, unprocessed; 2000 S Club 7 hit; natural born, natural gas, natural history, natural law, natural philosopher, natural resources, natural sciences, natural selection; as natural as breathing; Natural History Museum; *The Natural* (f), *Natural Born Killers* (f)

nature   character, everything that is not man-made, type; back-to-nature, human nature, second nature; nature conservation, nature reserve, nature study, nature trail; the course of nature, in a state of nature, in the nature of things, nature abhors a vacuum, the nature of the beast; Mother Nature; *Human Nature* (f)

naught   failure; come to naught, set at naught

naughty   badly behaved, titillating; *Naughty Amelia Jane* (b)

nautical   of ships and sailors; nautical mile

naval   of any sea-going force; naval architect, naval officer

navel   belly-button; navel-gazing, navel orange

navigation   process of plotting a course; navigation lights

navigator   internet browser, route

plotter; *Flight of the Navigator* (f), *The Navigator* (f)

navy sea-going military force, dark blue; merchant navy; navy blue; *In the Navy* (s), *The Navy Lark* (r)

near approach; close; near at hand, near-death experience, near the knuckle, near miss, near-sighted, near thing, near to home; as near as damn it, nowhere near, sail near the wind; Near East; *Near Dark* (f)

nearly almost; not nearly; *The Nearly Man* (tv)

neat tidy, undiluted (alcoholic drink)

necessity indispensable item, inevitability; necessity is the mother of invention

neck audacity, collar of a garment, isthmus, part between the head and the shoulders, thin part of a bottle; snog, swallow quickly; cowl neck, crew neck, halter neck, polo neck, polo-neck jumper, roll neck, scoop neck, V-neck; neck and neck, neck-bone, neck of the woods; breathe down your neck, get it in the neck, pain in the neck, scruff of the neck, stick your neck out, up to your neck

neckline garment's top edge; sweetheart neckline

need poverty, requirement; require; in need; a friend in need is a friend indeed; Children in Need; *All You Need Is Love* (s), *When I Need You* (s)

needle conifer's spiked leaf, sewing or knitting implement, stylus; irritate; darning needle, knitting needle; needle in a haystack, needle match; (as) sharp as a needle; Cleopatra's Needle; *Eye of the Needle* (b/f)

needles *see* needle; pins and needles; The Needles; *Needles and Pins* (s)

needless uncalled for; needless to say

needs *see* need; special needs; needs must

negative photograph's reverse image; expressing refusal; double negative, rhesus negative; negative equity

neighbour person who lives next door; be situated next to; beggar-my-neighbour; *Beggar-My-Neighbour* (tv), *Love Thy Neighbour* (tv)

neighbourhood locality; neighbourhood watch; in the neighbourhood of

neighbours *see* neighbour; Australian tv soap

neither not one or the other; neither here nor there, neither hide nor hair; *Neither Here Nor There* (b)

neon noble gas element; neon light

nerds geeks; *Revenge of the Nerds* (f)

nerve audacity, bravery, transmitter of sensation; steel (oneself); sciatic nerve, touch a nerve; nerve centre, nerve gas, nerve-racking; *Twisted Nerve* (f)

nerves *see* nerve; anxiety; bag of nerves, bundle of nerves; get on your nerves

nervous anxious; central nervous system; nervous system, nervous wreck; *Nineteenth Nervous Breakdown* (s)

ness headland; Loch Ness, Loch Ness monster

nest bird's shelter, hotbed; build a breeding structure (of a bird), lodge and settle in one place, fit or place within one another; bird's nest, bird's-nest soup, crow's nest, hornet's nest, love nest, mare's nest, wasp's nest; nest egg, nest of tables; feather your nest; *One Flew over the Cuckoo's Nest* (b/f), *Robin's Nest* (tv)

net information superhighway, mesh for catching fish or butterflies, see-through curtain, trapeze safety precaution, tulle; snare; butterfly net, drift net, landing-net, mosquito net, safety net; net profit, net register tonnage, net surfer; slip through the net, surf the net; *The Net* (f), *Under the Net* (b)

nether lower; nether regions

nettle stinging weed; annoy; stinging nettle; nettle-rash; grasp the nettle

network grid, interconnected group or system; broadcast throughout the country, forge business contacts, link (computer terminals etc); 1976 Peter Finch film; local area network, old boy network; *Old Boy Network* (tv)

never at no time; never-ending, never-never, never-never land, never-to-be-forgotten; better late than never, cheats never prosper, faint heart never won fair lady, it never rains but it pours, never darken my door, never fear, never mind, never do a stroke of work, now or never, a watched pot never boils, well I never, a woman's work is never done, wonders will never cease; *I Never Promised You a Rose Garden* (f), *It's Now or Never* (s), *My Camera Never Lies* (s), *Never a Cross Word* (tv), *Never Been Kissed* (f), *Never Can Say Goodbye* (s), *Never Give a Sucker an Even Break* (f), *Never Mind the Quality, Feel the Width* (tv), *Never Love a Stranger* (b), *Never on Sunday* (f), *Never Say Die* (al/f), *Never Say Never Again* (f), *Never the Twain* (tv), *Tomorrow Never Dies* (f), *The Twelfth of*

Never (s), *You'll Never Walk Alone* (s)

new freshly made, hitherto unknown, modern, novel, recent, unused; brand new, pastures new; New Age music, new broom, new-laid, new man, new moon, new potatoes, new town, new wave, new year's resolution; as good as new, break new ground, breathe new life into, a new broom sweeps clean, a new lease of life, turn over a new leaf, you can't teach an old dog new tricks; Happy New Year, Jewish New Year, New Age, New Amsterdam, New Brunswick, New Caledonia, New Deal, New Delhi, New England, New Forest, New Guinea, New Hampshire, New Haven, New Hebrides, New Horizons, New Jersey, New Look, New Mexico, New Model Army, New Order, New Orleans, New Scotland Yard, New South Wales, New Stone Age, New Street, New Testament, New World, New Year, New Year's Day, New Year's Eve, New York, New Zealand, Papua New Guinea; *Brave New World* (b), *Children of the New Forest* (b), *The Emperor's New Clothes* (b), *Escape from New York* (f), *Fairy Tale of New York* (s), *Gangs of New York* (f), *The Hotel New Hampshire* (b/f), *I've Got a Brand New Combine Harvester* (s), *Many a New Day* (s), *Native New Yorker* (s), *New Faces* (tv), *New Grub Street* (b), *The New Statesman* (mag/tv), *New Tricks* (tv), *New World* (cl), *New Year's Day* (s), *The New Yorker* (mag), *New York New York* (f/s), *The Shock of the New* (b/tv), *'Ullo John, Got a New Motor?* (s)

newly recently; newly-weds

news current affairs, information; bad

news; news agency, news bulletin, news conference, news-sheet, newsstand, news vendor; bad news travels fast, no news is good news; *The Bad News Bears* (f), *Broadcast News* (f), *Have I Got News for You?* (tv), *It's Good News Week* (s), *News from Nowhere* (b), *The News Quiz* (r), *Not the Nine O'clock News* (tv), *The Shipping News* (b/f)

newspaper   daily printed journal; newspaper columnist

next   adjoining, subsequent; subsequently; high-street clothes store; the next world; next door (to), next of kin, next to, next world; next to nothing; *Living Next Door to Alice* (s), *My Wife Next Door* (tv), *Next of Kin* (f), *The Next of Kin* (f), *Star Trek: the Next Generation* (tv)

nice   fine (distinction), pleasant; city on the French Riviera; coconut-flavoured biscuit variety; have a nice day, nice work if you can get it; *It's Been Nice* (s), *Nice Work* (b/tv), *No More Mr Nice Guy* (s), *Wouldn't It Be Nice* (s)

nicety   subtle distinction; to a nicety

nick   notch, prison; arrest, make a small cut or groove in, steal; in the nick of time; Old Nick

nicotine   harmful substance in tobacco; nicotine patch

niece   brother's or sister's daughter; great-niece

nigh   imminent; well-nigh; nigh on

night   hours of darkness; all night, day and night, first night, fly-by-night, hen night, ladies' night, last night, one-night stand, opening night, stag night, the dead of night; night blindness, night light, night nurse, night owl, night porter, night safe, night school, night shift, night storage heater, night-time, night train, night-vision goggles, nightwatchman; dark night of the soul, morning, noon and night, red sky at night shepherd's delight; Bonfire Night, Burns Night, Guy Fawkes Night, Night of the Long Knives, Twelfth Night, Walpurgis Night; *The Armies of the Night* (b), *Because the Night* (s), *Black Night* (s), *Cafe Terrace at Night* (pa), *Day for Night* (f), *Good Night and Good Luck* (f), *A Hard Day's Night* (f/s), *Here Comes the Night* (s), *I Drove All Night* (s), *In the Heat of the Night* (f), *It Happened One Night* (f), *Ladies' Night* (s), *Last Night a DJ Saved My Life* (s), *Long Day's Journey into Night* (f/pl), *A Midsummer-Night's Dream* (f/pl), *Night after Night* (f), *Night and Day* (b/mus/pl/s), *A Night at the Opera* (f), *Night Fever* (s), *Night Mail* (po), *Night Must Fall* (f), *Night Nurse* (s), *The Night of the Hunter* (f), *The Night of the Iguana* (f), *Night of the Living Dead* (f), *Night on a Bare Mountain* (cl), *Night on Earth* (f), *The Night Porter* (f), *A Night to Remember* (f), *Night Train to Munich* (f), *The Night Watch* (pa), *One Night Stand* (f), *Rainy Night in Georgia* (s), *Saturday Night and Sunday Morning* (b/f), *Saturday Night Fever* (f), *Silent Night* (s), *The Sky at Night* (tv), *Strangers in the Night* (s), *Such Is the Night* (s), *Tender Is the Night* (b), *They Drive by Night* (f), *Twelfth Night* (pl), *Yield to the Night* (f)

nightdress   bedtime garment; baby-doll nightdress

nightmare   bad dream; *A Nightmare on Elm Street* (f)

nights   *see* night; white nights;

Arabian Nights (b), *Boogie Nights* (f), *Nights in White Satin* (s), *Summer Nights* (s), *White Nights* (f)

nightshade plant with poisonous berries; deadly nightshade, woody nightshade

nil zero; nil by mouth, nil desperandum; eau de Nil; *Nil by Mouth* (f)

nimble agile; nimble-fingered

nine odd number; cat-o'-nine-tails; nine-days' wonder, nine holes, nine lives, nine men's morris, nine to five; on cloud nine, a stitch in time saves nine, the whole nine yards; Ninety-Nine; *Nine and a Half Weeks* (f), *Nine Months* (f), *The Nine Tailors* (b), *Nine to Five* (f/s), *Ninety-Nine Red Balloons* (s), *Not the Nine O'clock News* (tv), *The Thirty-Nine Steps* (b/f), *The Whole Nine Yards* (f)

ninepins skittles; go down like ninepins

nineteen prime number; 1985 Paul Hardcastle hit; talk nineteen to the dozen; *Nineteen Eighty-Four* (b/f)

nineteenth ordinal number; nineteenth hole; *Nineteenth Nervous Breakdown* (s)

ninety four score and ten; Ninety-Nine; *Ninety-Nine Red Balloons* (s)

ninth ordinal number; *The Eagle of the Ninth* (b), *The Ninth Configuration* (f)

nip quick bite, small quantity of spirits; move swiftly, pinch; nip and tuck, nip in the air, nip in the bud; *Nip/Tuck* (tv)

nit fool, larva of a louse; nit-picking

noble aristocrat; blue-blooded, having fine personal qualities; noble art, noble gas, noble rot, noble savage; the noble art of self-defence; *The Two Noble Kinsmen* (pl)

nobody insignificant person, negative pronoun; nobody's fool; like nobody's business; *Ain't Nobody* (s), *The Diary of a Nobody* (b), *Nobody Does It Better* (s), *Nobody's Fool* (f)

nod head gesture, sign of agreement; doze (off), move the head in agreement; get the nod, give the nod, land of Nod, on the nod; nod off

nodding *see* nod; only slight (acquaintance); on nodding terms; nodding acquaintance, nodding donkey

nog egg drink, old strong beer, wooden peg; egg-nog

noise unpleasant sound; big noise, make a noise, white noise; empty vessels make most noise; *Beautiful Noise* (s), *White Noise* (b/f)

noises *see* noise; *Noises Off* (pl)

nominal titular, token; nominal value

none not any; bar none, second to none; half a loaf is better than none, jack of all trades (and master of none), none the worse for; *And Then There Were None* (f), *None but the Brave* (f)

nonsense absurdity; no-nonsense; nonsense verse

nook recess; every nook and cranny; *Rookery Nook* (f/pl)

noon midday; morning, noon and night; *Darkness at Noon* (b), *From Noon till Three* (f), *High Noon* (f)

noose hangman's rope, loop with a running knot; put your head in a noose

nor also not; neither here nor there, neither hide nor hair; *Neither Here Nor There* (b)

north compass direction; due north, magnetic north, true north; north-east, north-easterly, north star, north-west, north-westerly, north-western; North America, North Atlantic Drift, North Carolina, North Dakota, North Korea, North Pole, North Sea, North-West Passage; *The Angel of the North* (sc), *North and South* (b/tv), *North by Northwest* (f), *North Country* (f), *North to Alaska* (f)

North
Africa, America, Atlantic, Atlantic Drift, Carolina, Dakota, Downs, Island, Korea, Pole, Rhine-Westphalia, Sea, Shields, Star, Uist, Utsire, Wales, West Frontier Province, West Passage, Yorkshire

northern of the higher-latitude regions; northern hemisphere, Northern Ireland, Northern Lights, Northern Line, Northern Rhodesia, Northern Territory; *Northern Exposure* (tv)

nose breathing and smelling organ, wine's bouquet; cautiously go forward (in a vehicle), pry; bridge of the nose, on the nose, parson's nose, red nose, Roman nose; nose-cone, nose job, nose to tail, nose to the grindstone; by a nose, cut off your nose to spite your face, follow your nose, get up your nose, it's no skin off my nose, keep your nose clean, keep your nose out, look down your nose at, pay through the nose, poke your nose in, put one's nose out of joint, rub your nose in it, thumb your nose at, turn your nose up at, under your nose, with your nose in the air

nosed *see* nose; hard-nosed, hook-nosed, pug-nosed, toffee-nosed

noses *see* nose; rub noses

nosey over-inquisitive; nosey parker

nosh grub; eat greedily; nosh-up; *Posh Nosh* (tv)

not negating word; forget-me-not, have-not; not guilty, not least, not nearly, not out, not proven; all that glitters is not gold, as likely as not, like as not, not a dicky bird, not a hope, not a laughing matter, not a little, not a patch on, not a sausage, not all it's cracked up to be, not at all, not by a long shot, not cricket, not exactly, not for love or money, not half, not having any of it, not in the least, not in the same league, not likely, not much cop, not my cup of tea, not my scene, not on, not on your life, not on your nelly, not stand an earthly, not the full quid/shilling, not the marrying kind, not to be sneezed at, not to mention, not to put a foot right, not to put too fine a point on it, not to say, not turn a hair, not worth a damn, not worth the candle, waste not, want not; *I Am Not an Animal* (tv), *I'm Not in Love* (s), *It's Not Unusual* (s), *The Lady's Not for Burning* (pl), *Not Fade Away* (s), *Not That Sort of Girl* (b), *To Be or Not to Be* (f), *To Have and Have Not* (b/f), *What Not to Wear* (tv)

notch V-shaped cut; make a V-shaped cut; top-notch

note brief message, musical symbol; jot down, observe; cover note, delivery note, grace note, of note, promissory note, take note; hit the right/wrong note, strike the right/wrong note

notebook jotter, portable computer;

electronic notebook

notes   *see* note; compare notes, sleeve notes

nothing   void; zero; good-for-nothing; nothing but; apropos of nothing, double or nothing, for nothing, like nothing on earth, little or nothing, next to nothing, nothing doing, nothing less than, nothing of the kind, nothing succeeds like success, nothing to write home about, nothing ventured nothing gained, on a hiding to nothing, thank you for nothing, there is nothing to it, think nothing of it; *All or Nothing* (s), *I Owe You Nothing* (s), *Money for Nothing* (s), *Much Ado about Nothing* (f/pl), *Nothing Compares 2 U* (s), *Nothing Rhymed* (s)

notice   attention, declaration of intention to resign, public sign, written announcement; become aware of; D notice, enforcement notice, give notice, put on notice, serve notice; at a moment's notice, at short notice, sit up and take notice, take notice, until further notice; *Two Weeks Notice* (f)

noun   naming part of speech; collective noun, proper noun

nova   star that suddenly flares up; 1990s Vauxhall model; bossa nova; Nova Scotia

novel   fiction work in prose; original; gothic novel, graphic novel

now   at this moment, in this day and age; now and again, now and then, now or never; any minute now, every now and again/then, here and now, how now brown cow, now then, now there's a thing, now you're talking; *All Right Now* (s), *All Together Now* (s),

Apocalypse Now (f), *Both Sides Now* (s), *Don't Look Now* (f), *If You Leave Me Now* (s), *I Think We're Alone Now* (s), *It's Now or Never* (s), *Now Voyager* (f), *The Way We Live Now* (b/tv), *Who's Sorry Now?* (s), *You're in the Army Now* (f)

nowhere   out of the running, unplaced; come nowhere, from nowhere, get nowhere, go nowhere, out of nowhere; nowhere near; *A Boy from Nowhere* (s), *In the Middle of Nowhere* (s), *News from Nowhere* (b), *Nowhere Man* (s)

nowt   nothing (in the north of England); there's nowt so queer as folk

nuclear   atomic, consisting of parents and children living together (family); nuclear disarmament, nuclear family, nuclear fuel, nuclear physics, nuclear power, nuclear reactor, nuclear war, nuclear waste, nuclear winter

nudist   naturist; nudist camp

nuisance   pest, trouble; public nuisance

null   void; null and void

number   figure, quantity; amount to, count; atomic number, back number, box number, cardinal number, odd number, opposite number, ordinal number, pin number, serial number, square number, telephone number, whole number, without number, wrong number; number crunching, number one, number plates, number ten, number two, number unobtainable; do a number on, your number is up; *Any Number Can Play* (f), *The Number of the Beast* (al/b/s), *Private Number* (s)

numbers   *see* number; by numbers, cardinal numbers, E-numbers;

numbers game; *Murder by Numbers* (f)

numbing deadening; mind-numbing

numerals arithmetical symbols; Arabic numerals, Roman numerals

numerous many; too numerous to mention

nun convent member; Blue Nun; *The Flying Nun* (tv), *The Nun's Story* (f)

nurse hospital ward worker; care for the sick, look after, suckle; charge nurse, dental nurse, district nurse, night nurse, nursery nurse, staff nurse, wet nurse; nurse shark; *Carry On Nurse* (f), *District Nurse* (tv), *Night Nurse* (s), *Nurse Betty* (f)

nursery crèche, kindergarten, plant supply business; nursery nurse, nursery rhyme, nursery school, nursery slopes

nursing *see* nurse; hospital career;

nursing home, nursing officer

nut bolt's counterpart, bonce, crazy person, hard-shelled seed; butt with the head; betel nut, Brazil nut, butterfly nut, cashew nut, pine nut, wing nut; nut cutlet, nut loaf; hard/tough nut to crack; Ginger Nut

nutcracker device for breaking shells; *The Nutcracker* (bal), *The Nutcracker Suite* (cl)

nuts *see* nut; monkey nuts; nuts and bolts

nutshell hard outer husk of a seed; in a nutshell

nutty zany; (as) nutty as a fruitcake; *The Nutty Professor* (f)

nymph

woodland sprite, young insect; wood nymph; *The Constant Nymph* (b/f)

O

oak large tree; holm oak; oak apple; Oak-Apple Day; *Tie a Yellow Ribbon Round the Ole Oak Tree* (s)

oaks *see* oak; great oaks from little acorns grow; the Oaks

oar lever used to propel a boat; oarlock; stick your oar in

oars *see* oar; rest on your oars

oast kiln for drying hops; oast house

oath curse, pledge; Hippocratic oath, on oath, under oath

oaths *see* oath; commissioner for oaths

oats cereal grains; rolled oats; sow your wild oats

object aim, thing; protest (about); indirect object, no object; object lesson; *The Object of My Affection* (f)

objective aim; uninfluenced by personal feelings

objector protester; conscientious objector

obligation debt of gratitude, unavoidable requirement; day of obligation

oblige compel, put yourself out for; noblesse oblige

obscure indistinct, little-known; conceal; *Jude the Obscure* (b)

observation comment, powers of keen sight, recording of facts or data, surveillance; observation balloon, observation gallery, observation terrace

obsession idée fixe; 1976 film starring Cliff Robertson; *Magnificent Obsession* (f)

obsolescence process of becoming outdated; built-in obsolescence

obstacle impediment; obstacle race

occasion event, opportunity; cause; on occasion, take occasion; equal to the occasion, rise to the occasion

occasional happening infrequently; occasional table

occult dark arts, supernatural; esoteric; the occult

occupation activity that keeps you busy, illegal possession by foreign troops, profession; house in multiple occupation, reserved occupation

occupational work-related; occupational hazard, occupational health, occupational therapy

occupier person in possession (of a house); owner-occupier

ocean vast sea; a drop in the ocean; Antarctic Ocean, Arctic Ocean, Atlantic Ocean, Indian Ocean, Pacific Ocean, Southern Ocean; *My Bonny Lies Over the Ocean* (s), *Ocean's Eleven* (f), *Ocean's Twelve* (f)

> **Ocean**
> Antarctic, Arctic, Atlantic, Indian, Pacific

ochre yellowish pigment; burnt ochre

octane measure of the quality of motor fuel, petrol ingredient; high-octane

odd indivisible by two, occasional, strange, unpaired (socks); odd job, odd-job man, odd-jobbing, odd man out, odd number, odd one out; *The Odd Couple* (f), *Odd Man Out* (f)

oddity unusual thing; *Space Oddity* (s)

odds likelihood, prices quoted by a bookie; at odds, fixed odds, give odds, lay odds, over the odds, take odds; odds and ends, odds and sods, odds-on (favourite); against all odds, it makes no odds, shout the odds; *Against All Odds* (f/s)

ode poem; *Ode on a Grecian Urn* (po), *Ode to Billie Joe* (s)

odious abhorrent; comparisons are odious

odyssey long journey; *2001: a Space Odyssey* (f), *The Odyssey* (b)

oeuvre total output of a writer or painter; chef-d'oeuvre, hors d'oeuvre

offence crime, insult; arrestable offence, capital offence, sackable offence

offender criminal, transgressor; first offender, young offender

offensive attacking military campaign, organised forceful campaign; rude; charm offensive, on the offensive

offer bid; bid in advance, put forward; on offer, special offer; offer of amends

offering *see* offer; church collection, contribution; burnt offering, peace offering

office bureau, position of authority; booking office, box-office, head office, lost-property office, post office, registry office, seals of office, sorting office, sub-post office; office party; Foreign Office, Home Office, National Audit Office, Office of Fair Trading, Oval Office, Public Record Office, The Stationery Office; *The Office* (tv)

officer commissioned soldier, constable, person holding a position of authority; chief petty officer, executive officer, field officer, first officer, flying officer, information officer, intelligence officer, medical officer, naval officer, non-commissioned officer, nursing officer, police officer, press officer, prison officer, probation officer, returning officer, staff officer, warrant officer; *An Officer and a Gentleman* (f)

officers *see* officer; officers' mess; *Officers and Gentlemen* (b)

official administrator; authorised, representative of authority; official birthday, official secrets; Official Secrets Act

offing   horizon at sea; in the offing

offset   compensation, type of printing; balance out; lithographic offset, web offset

often   frequently; every so often

ohm   unit of electrical resistance; Ohm's Law

oil   liquid mineral, lubricant; lubricate; almond oil, castor oil, cod-liver oil, corn oil, crude oil, essential oil, hair oil, linseed oil, olive oil, salad oil, snake oil, tea tree oil, vegetable oil; oil drum, oil filter, oil-fired, oil lamp, oil of cloves, oil painting, oil paints, oil platform, oil rig, oil slick, oil-tanker, oil the wheels, oil well; burn the midnight oil, no oil painting, pour oil on troubled waters; *Lorenzo's Oil* (f)

oiled   *see* oil; well oiled

oils   *see* oil; essential oils

ointment   medicinal lotion; zinc ointment; fly in the ointment

old   advanced in years, ancient, former; age-old, the good old days, the old country, the old days; old age, old-age pension, old-age pensioner, old bean, old boy, old boy network, old chestnut, old-fashioned, old flame, old folks' home, old fruit, old girl, old gold, old guard, old hand, old hat, old lag, old maid, old man, old man's beard, old master, old pals' act, old school, old school tie, old stager, old-time, old-time dancing, old-timer, old trout, old wives' tale; (as) old as the hills, as tough as old boots, chip off the old block, money for old rope, old habits die hard, rake over old coals, the same old story, there's no fool like

an old fool, tough as old boots, up to your old tricks, you can't teach an old dog new tricks; Gloucester Old Spot, Old Bailey, Old Bill, Old English Sheepdog, Old Faithful, Old Father Time, Old Glory, Old Kent Road, Old Bill, Old Nick, Old Stone Age, Old Testament, Old Trafford, Old Vic, Old World; *Any Old Iron* (s), *Arsenic and Old Lace* (f), *The 40 Year Old Virgin* (f), *The Good Old Days* (tv), *Grumpy Old Men* (f/tv), *Grumpy Old Women* (tv), *In Old Chicago* (f), *Lavender and Old Lace* (b), *Mouldy Old Dough* (s), *My Old Dutch* (s), *Old Boy Network* (tv), *The Old Curiosity Shop* (b), *The Old Devils* (b), *The Old Grey Whistle Test* (tv), *The Old Man and the Sea* (b), *Old Mortality* (b), *Old Mother Goose* (nr), *Old Mother Hubbard* (nr), *Old Shep* (s), *The Old Wives' Tale* (b), *That Same Old Feeling* (s), *This Old Heart of Mine* (s)

oldest   *see* old; oldest trick in the book

oldie   hit song from the past; golden oldie; *The Oldie* (mag)

olive   savoury fruit, shade of green; olive branch, olive drab, olive green, olive oil; *The Olive Farm* (b)

olives   *see* olive; stuffed olives; Mount of Olives

omega   Greek letter; 1990s Vauxhall saloon model, make of wristwatch; Alpha and Omega; *The Omega Man* (f)

omelette   egg dish; Spanish omelette

omen   portent, sign of foreboding; *The Omen* (f)

omnibus   collection of stories, old public transport vehicle, screening of an entire week's soap-opera episodes; long-running BBC arts programme;

omnibus edition; the man on the Clapham omnibus

once formerly, single time; as soon as; all at once, at once, for once; once again, once more, once or twice, once-over; every once in a while, once and for all, once bitten, twice shy, once in a blue moon, once in a while, once upon a time; *For Once in My Life* (s), *Once Bitten, Twice Shy* (s), *Once in a Lifetime* (s), *Once Upon a Forest* (f), *Once Upon a Time in America* (f), *Once Upon a Time in Mexico* (f), *Once Upon a Time in the West* (f), *Once Were Warriors* (f), *Yesterday Once More* (s)

onion pungent edible bulb; cheese and onion, pearl onion, sage and onion, Spanish onion, spring onion; onion dome

onions *see* onion; pickled onions; know your onions

only sole; merely; one and only, read-only memory; only just; beauty is only skin deep, there is only one thing for it; *For Your Eyes Only* (b/f), *I Only Have Eyes for You* (s), *The One and Only* (s), *Only Angels Have Wings* (f), *Only Fools and Horses* (tv), *Only Sixteen* (s), *Only the Lonely* (s), *Only Two Can Play* (f), *Only When I Larf* (b), *Only When I Laugh* (tv), *Only You* (s), *You Only Live Twice* (f)

open unrestricted tournament; ajar, blatant, candid, exposed, ready for business, spacious; begin, undo; British golf championship; wide open; open-air, open a book, open-and-shut case, open book, open-cast, open day, open-ended, open-field system, open fire, open-handed, open-hearted, open house, open

letter, open market, open marriage, open mind, open-minded, open-necked, open out, open-plan, open prison, open question, open sandwich, open season, open secret, open sesame, open-toed, open-topped, open up, open verdict; in the open air, keep/leave your options open, under the open sky, with open arms; Open University; *Open All Hours* (tv), *Open Arms* (s), *Open Range* (f)

opened *see* open; the heavens opened

opener bottle-cap remover, first of a series, first player; bottle-opener, can-opener, eye-opener, letter-opener, tin-opener

openers *see* opener; for openers

opening *see* open; aperture, launch, opportunity; initial; opening batsman, opening night, opening time

opens *see* open; as one door closes, another opens

opera musical drama; comic opera, grand opera, light opera, soap opera; opera glasses, opera hat, opera house, opera singer; Sydney Opera House; *The Beggar's Opera* (o), *A Night at the Opera* (f), *The Phantom of the Opera* (mus), *The Threepenny Opera* (mus)

operating performing surgery, working; co-operating; operating profit, operating system, operating table, operating theatre

operative person working a machine; in use

operator machine worker, mathematical symbol, telephone exchange worker; switchboard operator, tour operator; *Smooth Operator* (s)

ophthalmic   relating to the eye; ophthalmic optician

opinion   viewpoint; matter of opinion; opinion poll; be of the opinion

opium   drug extracted from the poppy; Yves Saint Laurent perfume; opium den, opium of the people; Opium Wars

opportunity   chance, opening; photo opportunity, window of opportunity; *Opportunity Knocks* (tv)

opposite   antithesis; diametrically different, immediately facing; opposite number, opposite sex; *The Opposite of Sex* (f), *The Opposite Sex* (f)

opt   choose; opt out

optical   concerning sight; optical glass, optical illusion

optician   eye specialist; dispensing optician, ophthalmic optician

optics   pub drink dispensers, science of light and vision; fibre optics

option   alternative possibility, right to buy, selection; share option, soft option

options   *see* option; keep/leave your options open

opus   composer's numbered work; magnum opus; Opus Dei

oral   spoken exam; relating to the mouth, spoken; oral history

orange   citrus fruit, colour; mobile-phone company, royal house of the Netherlands; bitter orange, blood orange, Jaffa orange, mandarin orange, navel orange, Seville orange; orange flower water, orange juice, orange peel, orange pekoe, orange stick; Agent Orange, Orange Free State, Orange River; *A Clockwork*

Orange (b/f), *Orange County* (f)

orator   public speaker; soapbox orator

orb   small ornamental globe; orb and sceptre

orbit   eye socket, path taken by a celestial body; circle (a planet); brand of chewing gum; into orbit

orchard   fruit-tree plantation; *The Cherry Orchard* (pl)

orchestra   front stalls in a theatre, group of musicians; symphony orchestra; orchestra pit, orchestra stalls

orchid   exotic flower; bee orchid, slipper orchid

orchids   *see* orchid; *No Orchids for Miss Blandish* (b/f)

ordain   decree, enrol as a minister

ordeal   stressful experience; *The Ordeal of Gilbert Pinfold* (b)

order   body of monks or nuns, edict, neatness, sequence; arrange, arrange in sequence, command, request (goods or services); apple-pie order, banker's order, court order, exclusion order, first order, interlocutory order, law and order, light marching order, made to order, mail order, mail-order catalogue, money order, on order, out of order, pecking order, postal order, preservation order, short order, standing order, supervision order, tall order, world order; order form, order of magnitude; in apple-pie order, of the first order put your house in order; Order of the Bath, Order Paper; *Law & Order: Criminal Intent* (tv)

ordered   *see* order; what the doctor ordered

orderly   hospital attendant;

methodical; orderly room

orders *see* order; holy orders, last orders, marching orders, sealed orders; under starter's orders; *Last Orders* (b/f)

ordinal church book of forms of service; indicating position in a sequence; ordinal number

ordinary commonplace; out of the ordinary; ordinary level, ordinary seaman; *A Life Less Ordinary* (f), *Ordinary People* (f)

ordnance department concerned with military equipment; ordnance department; Ordnance Survey

ore mineral-bearing rock; village near Hastings; iron ore

organ any vital body part, keyboard instrument; barrel organ, mouth organ, pipe organ; organ transplant, organ-grinder; Hammond organ

organiser person arranging an event or activity; personal organiser

oriel windowed recess; Oxford University college; oriel window

orient the East; align with reference to the points of a compass; Orient Express, Leyton Orient; *Murder on the Orient Express* (b/f)

original master copy, prototype; existing from the beginning, first, innovative; original sin; *Original Sin* (f/s)

orphan child whose parents are dead; *Little Orphan Annie* (com)

orthodox adhering strictly to religious or political doctrines, conventional, relating to the Eastern Church; Greek/Russian Orthodox Church

other additional, alternative; every other, one or other, the other place; other half, other ranks, other woman, other world, other-worldly; at each other's throats, the boot is on the other foot, have other fish to fry, have other irons in the fire, one after the other, one or the other, on the other hand, the shoe is on the other foot, this, that and the other, turn the other cheek; *How the Other Half Loves* (pl), *John Bull's Other Island* (pl), *The Other 'Arf* (tv), *The Other Side of Midnight* (b/f)

others alternatives, those remaining; *The Others* (f)

otter semi-aquatic mammal; *Tarka the Otter* (b)

ottoman low backless sofa; royal house of the Turkish empire; Ottoman Empire

ounce snow leopard, small unit of weight; fluid ounce

ourselves us personally; between ourselves, just between ourselves; *Honey, We Shrunk Ourselves* (f), *Just between Ourselves* (pl)

outdoor alfresco; outdoor pursuits

outer external ring on a target; exterior; outer space; Outer Hebrides; *The Outer Limits* (tv)

outfit business set-up, gang, set of clothes; provide with equipment; repair outfit

outing excursion; *The Bottle Factory Outing* (b)

outgoing expenditure; sociable

outlaw bandit; prohibit; *The Outlaw* (f), *The Outlaw Josey Wales* (f)

outside external surface; external, remote (chance); beyond the limits of, in the open air; outside broadcast, outside chance, outside interests, outside of; at the outside, get outside of, think outside the box; *Baby It's Cold Outside* (s)

outsider excluded person, long-odds racehorse, stranger; *The Outsider* (b)

outskirts peripheral areas (of a town); on the outskirts

outward exterior, superficial; going away from a place; outward bound, outward visible sign; Outward Bound

oval ellipse; egg-shaped; the Oval, Oval Office

ovation enthusiastic applause; standing ovation

oven cooker, furnace; microwave oven; oven gloves, oven-ready; have a bun in the oven

overboard from within a ship into the water; 1987 comedy film with Goldie Hawn; go overboard, man overboard

overcome defeat, surmount; defeated; *We Shall Overcome* (s)

overdo go too far with; don't overdo it

overgrown full of weeds; overgrown schoolboy

overhead transparency for use with a projector; directly above; overhead projector

overload excessive burden; burden excessively; information overload

overlook disregard, have a general view of

overplay ham up, make too much of; overplay your hand

overstep transgress (a limit); overstep the mark

owe be in debt; *I Owe You Nothing* (s)

owing *see* owe; still to be paid; owing to

owl nocturnal bird of prey; barn owl, night owl, screech owl, snowy owl, tawny owl; Brown Owl; *The Owl and the Pussycat* (f), *The Owl Service* (b/tv)

own admit, possess; belonging to the person mentioned, personal; on your own; own brand, own goal, own up; at your own risk, blow your own trumpet, come into your own, dig your own grave, do your own thing, a fox smells its own lair first, get your own back, have a will of your own, hoist by your own petard, keep your own counsel, know your own mind, left to your own devices, make a rod for your own back, mind your own business, of your own accord, of your own making, off your own bat, on your own ground, on your own initiative, stew in your own juice, under your own steam; *From Our Own Correspondent* (r), *How to Save Your Own Life* (b), *Mine Own Executioner* (f), *My Own Private Idaho* (f)

owner possessor; part-owner; owner-driver, owner-occupier; *The Sweet-Shop Owner* (b)

owning *see* own; land-owning

oxbow horseshoe-shaped bend in a river; oxbow lake; *The Oxbow Incident* (f)

oxygen atmospheric gas; oxygen tent

oyster pearl-producing shellfish; London travelcard; prairie oyster; oyster mushroom, oyster sauce; the world is your oyster

ozone form of oxygen, fresh sea air, protective layer of the atmosphere; ozone-friendly, ozone layer

P

pace   single step, tempo; walk up and down; with due respect to; pace bowler, pace car, pace-setter; force the pace, keep pace with, off the pace, stand the pace, stay the pace

pacemaker   electronic heart-regulator; speed-setter in a race

paces   *see* pace; handbags at ten paces

pacific   peaceful; Earth's largest ocean; Cathay Pacific, Pacific Ocean, South Pacific; *Across the Pacific* (f), *Pacific Heights* (f), *South Pacific* (mus), *Union Pacific* (f)

pacifier   appeaser; *The Pacifier* (f)

pack   deck (of cards), group of wolves, group of Cubs or Brownies, kitbag, small carton; cram, put things in a suitcase, stow; face pack, flat-pack, ice pack, mud pack, power pack, six-pack, vacuum-pack, wolf pack; pack animal, pack drill, pack heat, pack ice, pack of cards, pack up; the joker in the pack, no names, no pack drill, pack a punch, pack it in, pack

your bags; Brat Pack, Rat Pack; *Leader of the Pack* (s)

package   composite scheme or offer, computer program, parcel; package deal, package holiday

packed   *see* pack; crowded; action-packed, flat-packed, jam-packed, pre-packed, vacuum-packed; packed lunch, packed out; packed like sardines

packet   cardboard container, large sum of money, mail boat; pay packet

packing   *see* pack; charge for the cost of wrapping paper, joint sealant, wadding; packing-case; send packing

pact   agreement; Warsaw Pact

pad   apartment, block of paper, foot of an animal, pillow, sportsman's leg-guard, wodge of soft material; fill out, walk softly; brake pad, drum pad, hard pad, knee-pad, launching pad, lily pad, scratch pad, scribbling pad, shin-pad, touch pad; pad out

padded   *see* pad; cushioned; padded cell

paddle short oar; walk in shallow water; doggy-paddle; paddle steamer, paddle wheel; up the creek without a paddle

paddling *see* paddle; paddling pool

paddock field for horses, parade area at a racecourse

paddy fit of temper, rice field; in a paddy; paddy field

pads *see* pad; shoulder pads

pagan follower of a pre-Christian religion; relating to pre-Christian religions; *A Pagan Place* (b/s)

page leaf of a book, boy attendant; summon by bleeper; home page, web page; page boy, page-turner; on the same page; Page Three; *The Front Page* (f)

pages *see* page; Yellow Pages

paid *see* pay; duty-paid, low-paid; paid-up; put paid to

pain ache, anguish, pest; pain in the neck

pains *see* pain; meticulous care; growing pains

paint liquid colouring material; apply colouring material to; coat of paint, emulsion paint, gloss paint, poster paint, war paint; paint pot, paint shop; like watching paint dry, paint the town red; *Paint It Black* (s), *Paint Your Wagon* (f)

painted *see* paint; painted lady; *Behind a Painted Smile* (s), *The Painted Veil* (b/f)

painter artist; portrait painter

painting *see* paint; picture; action painting, face-painting, finger-painting, oil painting, wall painting; no oil painting

paintings *see* paint and painting; cave paintings

paints *see* paint; face paints, oil paints

pair set of two; au pair, carriage and pair; pair of compasses, pair of scissors, pair of shoes, pair off, pair up

paisley swirly pattern; town near Glasgow

pal friend; pen pal; *Pal Joey* (f)

palace royal residence; picture palace; palace revolution; Blenheim Palace, Buckingham Palace, Crystal Palace, Doge's Palace, Lambeth Palace; *Picture Palace* (b), *White Palace* (f)

Palace
Blenheim, Buckingham, Crystal, Doge's, Lambeth, Scone, St James's

---

palate roof of the mouth, sense of taste, wine's flavour; soft palate

pale fence post, light in colour; go white; pale ale; beyond the pale; *A Pale View of Hills* (b), *Pale Rider* (f), *A Whiter Shade of Pale* (s)

palette paint-mixing board; palette knife

pall cloth spread over a coffin, gloomy atmosphere; become tedious; pall-bearer; Pall Mall

palm centre of the hand, tropical tree; conceal in the hand; itching palm; grease the palm of, in the palm of your hand; Palm Beach, Palm Sunday, West Palm Beach; *The Palm Beach Story* (f)

palms *see* palm; *Wild Palms* (tv), *The Wild Palms* (b)

pals *see* pal; old pals' act

pampas South American grasslands; pampas grass

pampers mollycoddles; nappies' brand name

pan   cooking utensil; criticise, swing (a camera); Greek god; frying pan, warming pan; pan-fry, pan pipes; flash in the pan, go down the pan; pan-American, Tin Pan Alley; *Peter Pan* (b/f/pan), *Tai-Pan* (b), *Tin Pan Alley* (mus)

pancake   dish of eggs and flour; Scotch pancake; pancake race; as flat as a pancake; Pancake Day

panda   black and white bear-like animal; giant panda; panda car

panel   group of experts, wooden board; solar panel; panel beater, panel game, panel pin

panic   feeling of anxiety and fear; feel anxious or fearful; panic attack, panic button, panic stations; *Panic in the Streets* (f), *Panic Room* (f)

pans   *see* pan; pots and pans

panther   black wild cat; black panther; *The Pink Panther* (f)

panthers   *see* panther; Black Panthers

pants   trousers; gasps; capri pants, cargo pants, hot pants, palazzo pants, ski pants, stirrup pants; by the seat of one's pants, caught with your pants down, have ants in your pants; *Fancy Pants* (f)

papa   dad, radio code word; *Papa Don't Preach* (s), *Papa Was a Rollin' Stone* (s)

paper   news sheet, treatise, writing material; decorate (walls); ballot paper, blotting paper, carbon paper, cartridge paper, cigarette paper, corrugated paper, crêpe paper, daily paper, emery paper, graph paper, green paper, litmus paper, manuscript paper, rice paper, scrap paper, tissue paper, toilet paper, tracing paper, waste paper, waxed paper, wrapping paper, writing paper; paper boy, paper-chain, paper chase, paper-clip, paper hat, paper-knife, paper money, paper over, paper round, paper tiger, paper trail; on paper, paper over the cracks; Order Paper, White Paper; *Paper Moon* (f)

paperback   soft-covered book; *Paperback Writer* (s)

papers   *see* paper; *The Aspern Papers* (b), *The Pickwick Papers* (b), *The Rachel Papers* (b/f)

par   golfer's average score, state of equality; below par; par avion, par excellence; on a par, par for the course

parachute   skydiver's canopy; jump from an aircraft under a canopy; golden parachute; parachute jump

parade   procession; flaunt; hit parade, identity parade; parade ground; on parade; *The Big Parade* (f), *Easter Parade* (mus), *Footlight Parade* (f), *Privates on Parade* (f/pl)

paradise   idyllic place; bird of paradise, fool's paradise; *Another Day in Paradise* (s), *Halfway to Paradise* (s), *Laughter in Paradise* (f), *The Paradise Club* (tv), *Paradise Lost* (po), *Paradise Postponed* (b), *Paradise Regained* (po), *Stranger in Paradise* (s), *This Side of Paradise* (b), *Trouble in Paradise* (f)

paraffin   domestic fuel; liquid paraffin; paraffin stove

parallax   optical effect; *The Parallax View* (f)

parallel   analogy, line of latitude; continuously equidistant (lines); parallel bars

parasite   bloodsucking insect, sponger

parcel   package; divide into portions and distribute, put into a package;

part and parcel, pass the parcel
parched seared by the Sun; very thirsty
pardon amnesty; absolve; request asking a speaker to repeat something; free pardon, general pardon; I beg your pardon, pardon me, pardon my French
pare trim; pare to the bone
parent mother or father; act as guardian towards; foster-parent, single parent; *The Parent Trap* (f)
parents *see* parent; *Meet the Parents* (f)
paring *see* pare; cheese-paring
parish church district; parish council, parish magazine, parish register

---

Park

Battersea, Bletchley, Cardiff Arms, Celtic, Central, Croke, Ewood, Finsbury, Fontwell, Fratton, Goodison, Green, Holland, Home, Hyde, Lingfield, Ninian, Pride, Queen's, Regent's, Richmond, Selhurst, St James', St James's, Sunninghill, Upton, Villa, Windsor

---

park urban green area; leave a car; amusement park, business park, car park, caravan park, deer park, double-park, national park, safari park, science park, theme park, trailer park, zoological park; park-and-ride, park bench, park-keepers; Battersea Park, Cardiff Arms Park, Central Park, Finsbury Park, Fontwell Park, Goodison Park, Green Park, Holland Park, Hyde Park, Hyde Park Corner, Lingfield Park, Park Lane, Park Royal, Queen's Park Rangers, Ravenscourt Park, Regent's Park, Richmond Park, Roker Park, St James Park, St James's

Park, Windsor Park; *Barefoot in the Park* (f/pl), *Gorky Park* (b/f), *Gosford Park* (f), *Itchycoo Park* (s), *Jurassic Park* (f), *MacArthur Park* (s), *Mansfield Park* (b), *Meet Me in Battersea Park* (s), *South Park* (tv), *Spring in Park Lane* (f)
parking *see* park; free parking; parking fee, parking lot, parking meter, parking ticket
parliament legislative body; European Parliament, Houses of Parliament, Member of Parliament, Parliament Hill
parlour drawing room; beauty parlour, funeral parlour, ice-cream parlour, milking parlour; parlour game
parody satirical imitation; imitate satirically; self-parody
parrot colourful bird; parrot-fashion; sick as a parrot; *Flaubert's Parrot* (b)
parsley culinary herb; cow parsley
parsnips root vegetables; fine words butter no parsnips
parson vicar; parson's nose
part actor's role, section; divide, go separate ways; bit part, take part; part company, part of speech, part with, part-owner, part-song, part-time, part-timer; the best part, the better part, for the most part, in large part, in part, look the part, part and parcel, part of the furniture, take the part of; *Part of the Union* (s), *Till Death Us Do Part* (tv)
parted *see* part; a fool and his money are soon parted
partial biased, fond, incomplete; partial eclipse
particle small piece of matter; elementary particle; particle accelerator, particle physics
particular listed detail; fussy,

noteworthy, specific; in particular

parting   *see* part; line in the hair; leave-taking; parting shot; parting is such sweet sorrow, parting of the ways

partition   division of a state, room divider; divide into smaller units

partner   close associate; sleeping partner, sparring partner

partners   *see* partner; partners in crime

partnership   association, business owned by two or more people; civil partnership, limited partnership

partridge   game-bird; *The Partridge Family* (tv)

parts   *see* part; man of many parts

party   political group, celebratory get-together, one side mentioned in a contract; enjoy oneself with others; bachelor party, birthday party, boarding party, concert party, dinner party, garden party, Halloween party, hen party, house party, office party, search party, stag party, street party, tea party, third party, working party; party-goer, party line, party piece, party political, party politics, party-pooper, party popper, party wall; the life and soul of the party, a party to; Boston Tea Party, Conservative Party, Green Party, Labour Party, Liberal Party, Mad Hatter's Tea Party; *Abigail's Party* (pl), *Bachelor Party* (f), *The Birthday Party* (pl), *The Cocktail Party* (pl), *It's My Party* (s), *Luncheon of the Boating Party* (pa), *Noel's House Party* (tv), *24 Hour Party People* (f)

pass   entry document, exam success, route between mountains; elapse, exceed, hand over, move, overtake, spend (time), succeed in an exam; boarding pass, bus pass; pass by, pass

judgement, pass key, pass muster, pass on, pass out, pass over, pass rate, pass through, pass your lips; bring to pass, come to pass, pass the buck, pass the hat round, pass the parcel, pass the time of day; Brenner Pass, Khyber Pass; *Breakheart Pass* (b/f)

passage   corridor, duct, extract from a text, journey; bird of passage, purple passage, rite of passage, secret passage; passage of arms; work your passage; North-West Passage; *A Passage to India* (b/f), *Rites of Passage* (b)

passenger   public-transport traveller; passenger pigeon, passenger train; *Passenger 57* (f)

passing   *see* pass; demise; passing resemblance, passing shot; in passing

passion   ardour; passion flower, passion fruit; Passion Play, Passion Sunday; *The Passion of the Christ* (f), *The Pride and the Passion* (f), *St Matthew Passion* (cl)

passive   verb voice; unresisting; passive resistance, passive role, passive smoking

passport   travel document; passport photograph; *Passport to Pimlico* (f)

past   time gone by; former; beyond; fly-past, march past; past it, past master, past tense; a quarter past, first past the post, live in the past; *Remembrance of Things Past* (b)

paste   adhesive, glass for making artificial gems, sandwich spread, viscous substance; fix with glue; almond paste; cut and paste

pastel   chalk drawing, chalky crayon, light colour

pastry   flour and water crust, small cake; choux pastry, Danish pastry, flaky pastry, puff pastry, shortcrust pastry; pastry-cook

pasture grazing land; put out to pasture

pastures *see* pasture; pastures new

pasty doughy pie; pale-faced; Cornish pasty

pat portion (of butter); touch lightly; glib; children's tv postman; pit-a-pat, stand pat; pat-a-cake; off pat, a pat on the back; *Postman Pat* (tv)

patch eye cover, mending square, small plot; mend temporarily; bad patch, nicotine patch, purple patch; patch pocket, patch test, patch up; not a patch on; *Patch Adams* (f), *A Patch of Blue* (f)

patchwork craft of sewing together small pieces of cloth, medley; patchwork quilt

pate head, meat spread; pâté de foie gras

patent inventor's copyright, shiny leather; obvious; letters patent; patent leather, patent medicine

path course of action, walkway; bridle path, flare path, flight path, primrose path; the path of least resistance

paths *see* path; *Paths of Glory* (f)

patience card game for one, willingness to wait; Gilbert & Sullivan opera; lose patience; patience is a virtue

patient receiver of medical attention; willing to wait; in-patient; *The English Patient* (b/f)

patients *see* patient; doctors make the worst patients

patio garden terrace; patio doors

patriot nationalist; US missile; *A Patriot for Me* (pl), *The Patriot* (f), *Patriot Games* (f)

patrol mobile observation unit; walk around checking security; patrol car

patron customer, sponsor; patron saint

patter glib sales talk, light drumming; walk lightly

pattern decorative design, knitting or dressmaking instructions, template; holding pattern, willow pattern

pauper needy person; *The Prince and the Pauper* (b/f)

pause brief stop; stop briefly; pause for thought

pave lay concrete slabs on; pave the way

pavement roadside walkway; moving pavement; pavement artist; *Angel Pavement* (b)

pavilion cricket-ground building, exhibition building, large tent; Royal Pavilion

pavilions *see* pavilion; *The Far Pavilions* (b/tv)

paving *see* pave; crazy paving

paw animal's foot; maul

pawn chess piece, person controlled by others; put up as security

pay salary; be profitable, give money to; back pay, severance pay, sick pay, strike pay, take-home pay; pay attention, pay channel, pay court to, pay day, pay dearly, pay-dirt, pay in, pay off, pay out, pay packet, pay tv, pay the bill, pay up; the devil to pay, in the pay of, pay as you earn, pay lip service to, pay through the nose, pay your dues, pay your respects, rob Peter to pay Paul, there will be hell to pay; *Pay It Forward* (f)

paying *see* pay; paying guest

paymaster financial controller; Paymaster-General

payment remittance; down payment, suspend payment

payments *see* payment; balance of payments

pays *see* pay; he who pays the piper calls the tune

pea small green vegetable; marrowfat pea, snow pea, sweet pea; pea-brain, pea-brained, pea coat, pea green, pea-shooter, pea soup, pea-souper; *The Princess and the Pea* (b)

peace absence of war, tranquillity; peace dividend, peace envoy, peace-keepers, peace-keeping, peace offering, peace pipe, peace sign, peace treaty; at peace, breach of the peace, keep the peace, no peace for the wicked, rest in peace; Justice of the Peace, Prince of Peace; *Pipes of Peace* (s), *War and Peace* (b/f)

peaceful free from strife, tranquil; peaceful co-existence

peach fleshy fruit; peach brandy, peach Melba; *Eat the Peach* (f), *James and the Giant Peach* (b/f)

peaches *see* peach; peaches and cream

peacock bird with bright plumage; peacock butterfly; proud as a peacock; Peacock Throne; *The White Peacock* (b)

peak flap on a cap, highest point, mountain; off-peak, widow's peak; peak period; Peak District; *Peak Practice* (tv)

peaks *see* peak; *Twin Peaks* (tv)

peal set of bells, sound of bells; chime

peanut edible seed; peanut butter

peanuts *see* peanut; paltry sums of money; Schulz cartoon; salted peanuts

pear droplet-shaped fruit; alligator pear, avocado pear, prickly pear; pear tree, pear-drop; go pear-shaped

pearl oyster's stone; mother-of-pearl; pearl barley, pearl diver, pearl diving, pearl fishing, pearl onion; Pearl Harbor; *Girl with a Pearl Earring* (b/f), *The Pearl Fishers* (b/o), *Pearl Harbor* (f), *Pearl's a Singer* (s)

pearls *see* pearl; string of pearls; cast pearls before swine; *A String of Pearls* (s)

pearly white and translucent; pearly king, pearly queen; Pearly Gates

pears *see* pear; apples and pears

peas *see* pea; black-eyed peas, garden peas, split peas, sugar-snap peas

peasants people who work the land; Peasants' Revolt

peat fuel dug from bogs; peat-bog, peat moss

pebble small stone; pebble-dashed

peck hasty kiss, old measure of weight; nibble, nip with the beak

pecker beak; keep your pecker up

pecking *see* peck; pecking order

peculiar belonging exclusively (to), odd; funny peculiar; *A Very Peculiar Practice* (tv)

pedal foot lever; propel a bicycle; back-pedal, soft-pedal; pedal-pushers, pedal steel guitar

pedestrian person walking along the street; uninspired; pedestrian crossing, pedestrian precinct

peel rind; take the rind off; orange peel; peel off

peep discreet glance, sound; sneak a glance; peep show; *Peep Show* (tv)

peeping *see* peep; peeping Tom

peer an equal, House of Lords member, member of the same age and social group; look through narrowed eyes; life peer; peer group, peer of the realm; without peer; *Peer Gynt* (b/cl)

peg   coat hook, lower limb, wooden pin; fasten with pins; clothes peg, hat-peg, square peg, tent peg, tuning peg; peg leg, peg out; off the peg, a peg to hang a matter on, a square peg in a round hole, take down a peg or two; *Jake the Peg* (s), *The Square Peg* (f)

pegging   *see* peg; level-pegging

pelican   large water-bird; pelican crossing; *The Pelican Brief* (b/f)

pellet   small ball, particularly of shot; slug pellet

pelt   animal hide; bombard, pour with rain; at full pelt

pen   female swan, small enclosure, writing implement; coop (up), write; ballpoint pen, felt-tip pen, fountain pen, ink pen, poison-pen letter; pen and ink, pen-friend, pen-holder, pen-name, pen pal, pen-pusher; slip of the pen

penal   concerning punishment; penal servitude, penal settlement

penalty   fine, punishment, soccer spot-kick; death penalty; penalty area, penalty box, penalty kick, penalty spot, penalty try; under penalty of

pence   divisions of a pound; fifty pence, fifty-pence piece, ten pence, twenty pence; Peter's pence

pencil   writing implement; blue-pencil, chinagraph pencil, coloured pencil, eyebrow pencil, lead pencil, propelling pencil, styptic pencil; pencil moustache, pencil sharpener, pencil skirt

pendulum   clock's weighted rod; *Foucault's Pendulum* (b), *The Pit and the Pendulum* (f)

penguin   Antarctic seabird; emperor penguin

peninsula   land that is almost an island; Antarctic Peninsula

peninsular   relating to a near-island; Peninsular War

pennies   British coins; pennies from heaven; *Pennies from Heaven* (mus/tv)

penny   hundredth of a pound; ten a penny, the penny dropped, turn an honest penny; penny dreadful, penny-farthing, penny-pincher, penny-pinching, penny post, penny whistle, penny wise; cost a pretty penny, in for a penny in for a pound, penny for the guy, a penny for your thoughts, penny wise and pound foolish; Penny Black; *Penny Lane* (s), *Penny Serenade* (f), *Will Penny* (f)

pension   Continental guest house, retirement income; non-contributory pension, old-age pension, personal pension, retirement pension, stakeholder pension; pension off; *In a German Pension* (b)

pensioner   retired person; old-age pensioner; Chelsea Pensioner

people   folks; flower people, little people; people carrier, people person; opium of the people; *The Bone People* (b), *Common People* (s), *Crazy People* (f), *Eating People Is Wrong* (b), *An Enemy of the People* (pl), *Liberty Leading the People* (pa), *Ordinary People* (f), *The People Versus Larry Flynt* (f), *People Will Say We're in Love* (s), *Ruthless People* (f), *Smiley's People* (b/tv), *Some People* (s/f), *Sunset People* (s), *24 Hour Party People* (f), *Used People* (f), *Wonderful World, Beautiful People* (s)

pep   vigour; pep pill, pep talk

pepper capsicum, condiment; sprinkle liberally; cayenne pepper, green pepper, Jamaica pepper, red pepper, salt-and-pepper, sweet pepper; pepper mill, pepper pot, pepper spray; *Sgt Pepper's Lonely Hearts Club Band* (s)

peppercorn spice berry; peppercorn rent

perception discernment; extra-sensory perception; *The Doors of Perception* (b)

perch bird's resting pole, freshwater fish, old measure of length; sit

perfect verbal tense; complete, faultless; make flawless; future perfect, word-perfect; perfect binding; practice makes perfect; *My Perfect Cousin* (s), *Perfect Moment* (s), *A Perfect Murder* (f), *A Perfect Spy* (b), *The Perfect Storm* (f), *A Perfect Stranger* (b)

perform act or play in front of an audience, carry out

performance accomplishment, artistic production, vehicle's capacity at speed; 1970 Mick Jagger film; concert performance, live performance, (royal) command performance; performance artist

performing *see* perform; performing arts

perfume aroma, fragrance in a bottle; Patrick Süskind novel

peril danger; *Peril at End House* (b)

period interval of time, teaching session, US full stop; cooling-off period, peak period; period piece; Glacial Period

periodic occurring at intervals; periodic table

perish die, rot; perish the thought

perk fringe benefit; perk up

permanent everlasting; permanent wave; Permanent Secretary

permeable porous; gas-permeable

permission authorisation; planning permission

permit authorisation document; allow; entry permit, work permit

perpetual never-ending; perpetual calendar, perpetual motion

persecution constant harassment; persecution complex

persistence dogged continuation; *The Persistence of Memory* (pa)

person human being; first person, first-person shooter, people person, second person, third person, shooter; in person; *Absurd Person Singular* (pl)

personal individual, of private concern; personal ad, personal appearance, personal assistant, personal best, personal column, personal computer, personal effects, personal equity plan, personal organiser, personal pension, personal pronoun, personal property, personal stereo; *Personal Best* (f), *Personal Services* (f), *Up Close and Personal* (f)

personnel human resources department, workforce; personnel carrier

persuasion art of coaxing, set of beliefs; Jane Austen novel

pest annoying person, destructive insect

pet domestic animal, favourite, fit of the sulks; caress; teacher's pet; pet hate, pet name, pet shop; *Ace Ventura: Pet Detective* (f), *Auf Wiedersehen, Pet* (tv), *Pet Rescue* (tv), *Teacher's Pet* (tv)

petard old explosive device; hoist by your own petard

peter criminal slang for a safe; fade (out); Peter's pence, Peters projection; rob Peter to pay Paul; Blue Peter, Peter Principle, St Peter Port; *Blue Peter* (tv), *Peter and the Wolf* (cl), *Peter Grimes* (o), *Peter Pan* (b/pan), *Peter Simple* (b), *The Tale of Peter Rabbit* (b)

petition list of objectors' signatures, application to a court of law; make a formal request to

petrify paralyse with fear, turn to stone

petrol fuel for vehicles; lead-free petrol; petrol can, petrol pump, petrol station, petrol tank; run out of petrol

petroleum mineral oil; petroleum jelly

pets *see* pet; *Pets Win Prizes* (tv)

petticoat underskirt; *The Iron Petticoat* (f)

petty trivial; chief petty officer; petty cash, petty sessions

pew bench; box pew

phantom ghost; Rolls-Royce model; *The Phantom Menace* (f), *The Phantom of Liberty* (f), *The Phantom of the Opera* (b/mus)

phase period of time, stage of development; phase out

pheasant game bird; golden pheasant

philanderer womaniser; *The Philanderer* (pl)

philosopher person who pursues wisdom and knowledge; natural philosopher; philosopher's stone; *Harry Potter and the Philosopher's Stone* (b/f), *The Philosopher's Pupil* (b)

philosophy attitude to life, pursuit of wisdom and knowledge; hermetic philosophy; Doctor of Philosophy, Master of Philosophy

phoenix mythical bird; capital of Arizona; *The Phoenix and the Carpet* (b)

phone handset for transmitting and receiving sound; ring up; car phone, mobile phone; phone book, phone booth, phone box, phone-in; *Phone Booth* (f)

phoney false; Phoney War

photo snapshot; take a picture of; photo call, photo-finish, photo opportunity, photo-story; *One Hour Photo* (f)

photograph snapshot; take a picture of; passport photograph; photograph album

photographic relating to cameras; photographic memory

photography art of using a camera; Kirlian photography

phrase group of words; put into particular words; phrase book; to coin a phrase

physical concerning the body, fitness examination, involving bodily effort; Olivia Newton-John single; physical education, physical geography, physical jerks, physical sciences

physics study of matter and energy; nuclear physics, particle physics

pianist keyboard musician; concert pianist; *The Pianist* (f)

piano keyboard instrument; softly, in music; grand piano, upright piano; piano accordion, piano recital, piano roll, piano stool, piano tuner; *The Piano* (f)

pick digging tool, plectrum; choose, gather, open (a lock); cherry-pick, hand-pick, ice pick, nit-pick; pick a fight, pick a lock, pick and shovel, pick holes in, pick-me-up, pick out, pick up, pick-up truck; pick and choose, pick out of a hat, pick up steam, pick up the pieces, pick up the tab, take your pick; *Pick Up the Pieces* (s), *Take Your Pick* (tv)

picked *see* pick; hand-picked

picket group of strikers, pointed stake: blockade a workplace; flying picket; picket line

picking *see* pick; cherry-picking, cotton-picking, hop-picking, nit-picking; picking out

pickle awkward situation, salad relish; preserve in vinegar; dill pickle; in a pickle

pickled *see* pickle; pickled onions

picnic outdoor meal; 1955 William Holden film; picnic basket, picnic hamper; no picnic; *Picnic at Hanging Rock* (f)

picture cinema film, visual image; imagine; motion picture, word picture; picture book, picture palace, picture postcard, picture rail, picture restorer, picture window; (as) pretty as a picture, every picture tells a story, get the picture, look a picture, a picture is worth a thousand words; *Every Picture Tells a Story* (al), *The Kid Stays in the Picture* (f), *The Last Picture Show* (f), *The Picture of Dorian Gray* (b/f), *A Picture of You* (s), *Picture Palace* (b), *Picture This* (s), *The Rocky Horror Picture Show* (mus)

pictures *see* picture; *Pictures of Lily* (s), *Pictures of Matchstick Men* (s)

pie dish with a pastry crust; apple pie, apple-pie bed, apple-pie order, banoffee pie, cherry pie, cottage pie, custard pie, mince pie, pork pie, pork-pie hat, shepherd's pie; pie chart, pie-eyed; eat humble pie, have a finger in the pie, in apple-pie order,

pie in the sky; *American Pie* (f), *Can She Bake a Cherry Pie?* (f), *Pie in the Sky* (tv)

piece artistic composition, game token, portion; a piece of cake, all of a piece, conversation piece, fifty-pence piece, in one piece, museum piece, nasty piece of work, one-piece, party piece, period piece, say your piece, set piece, three-piece suite, two-piece; piece by piece, pièce de résistance, piece of cake, piece together

pieces *see* piece; bits and pieces; pieces of eight; go to pieces, in pieces, pick up the pieces, pull to pieces, shot to pieces, take to pieces, tear to pieces; *Bits and Pieces* (s), *Five Easy Pieces* (f), *Pick Up the Pieces* (s)

pied dappled; foot in French; pied noir, pied-à-terre

pier jetty; *The Road to Wigan Pier* (b)

piers *see* pier; *Piers Plowman* (po)

piercing bodily puncture; perforating; shrill; body piercing, ear-piercing

piffle nonsense; *Balderdash and Piffle* (tv)

pig farm animal, greedy person; guinea pig, Vietnamese pot-bellied pig; pig farmer, pig iron, pig out, pig-headed, pig-ignorant, pig's trotters; bleed like a stuck pig, buy a pig in a poke, make a pig of oneself, make a pig's ear of, pig in the middle; *Babe: Pig in the City* (f), *Leon the Pig Farmer* (f)

pigeon bird of the dove family; carrier pigeon, clay pigeon, clay pigeon shooting, passenger pigeon, stool pigeon, wood pigeon; pigeon-chested, pigeon-hole, pigeon-toed; *Stool Pigeon* (s)

pigeons *see* pigeon; put the cat among the pigeons

piggy little porker; resembling a porker; piggy-bank, piggy in the middle

pigs *see* pig; pigs might fly; Bay of Pigs

pike freshwater fish, jacknife position in diving, spear-like weapon; Scafell Pike

pikestaff weapon shaft; (as) plain as a pikestaff

pile heap, large quantity, nap of a carpet; make a pile, slush pile; pile up, pile-up

pilgrim traveller for religious reasons; Pilgrim Fathers; *The Pilgrim's Progress* (b)

pill tablet; form small balls of fluff; bitter pill, pep pill, sleeping pill; pill-popping; sugar the pill, sweeten the pill; *Just Like a Pill* (s)

pillar column; pillar-box; from pillar to post, pillar of strength

pillars *see* pillar; *Seven Pillars of Wisdom* (b)

pillow bed cushion; pillow book, pillow fight, pillow talk; *The Pillow Book* (f), *Pillow Talk* (f), *Tears on My Pillow* (s)

pills *see* pill; slimming pills, vitamin pills

pilot aviator; steer; automatic pilot, co-pilot, fighter pilot, test pilot; pilot light, pilot's licence, pilot whale

pimpernel plant of the primrose family; *The Scarlet Pimpernel* (b/f/tv)

pimples spots; goose pimples

pin metal fastener; hold (down); cash-card code (PIN as abbrev); bobby pin, cotter pin, drawing-pin, hat-pin, panel pin, rolling pin, safety pin, split pin; pin down, pin money, pin number, pin-striped suit, pin-up; pin your ears back, pin your hopes on

pinafore apron; pinafore dress; *HMS Pinafore* (o)

pinball amusement arcade game; pinball machine; *Pinball Wizard* (s)

pincer claw of a crustacean, gripping tool; pincer movement

pinch very small quantity; nip with the finger and thumb, steal; at a pinch, feel the pinch, take with a pinch of salt

pinching *see* pinch; penny-pinching

pine coniferous tree, furniture wood; yearn; bristlecone pine, Chile pine, Scots pine, umbrella pine; pine cone, pine marten, pine nut, pine tree; *The Trail of the Lonesome Pine* (s)

pineapple tropical fruit; pineapple juice; *Pineapple Poll* (bal)

ping high ringing sound; ping-pong

pinhole tiny aperture; pinhole camera

pink carnation-like flower, light red shade; cut in a zigzag pattern; salmon pink, shocking pink, tickled pink; pink elephants, pink gin; in the pink; *Lily the Pink* (s), *Pink Cadillac* (f), *The Pink Panther* (f), *Pink String and Sealing Wax* (f), *Pretty in Pink* (f)

pinking *see* pink; pinking shears

pins *see* pin; legs; pins and needles; *Nedles and Pins* (s)

pint liquid measure; cuckoo pint; pint of milk, pint-sized

pinto piebald horse; pinto beans

pioneer early settler, trail-blazer; be at the forefront

pip small seed, spot on a playing card; defeat by a small margin; pip to the post

pipe smoker's tube, long tube, simple wind instrument; convey by tube or cable, play a wind instrument; clay pipe, exhaust pipe, peace pipe, reed pipe, soil pipe, waste pipe, water pipe; pipe cleaner, pipe down, pipe dream, pipe organ, pipe up

piped   *see* pipe; piped music

pipeline   supply channel; in the pipeline

piper   military musician; he who pays the piper calls the tune; Maris Piper

pipes   *see* pipe; Scottish instrument; pan pipes, uillean pipes; *Pipes of Peace* (s)

piping   *see* pipe; decorative furnishing cord, tubing; very hot; lead piping; piping hot

pirate   shipboard robber; make illegal copies of; pirate radio station

pirates   *see* pirate; *The Pirates of Penzance* (o), *Pirates of the Caribbean* (f)

pirouette   ballet twirl; twirl round

piste   ski-run; off-piste

pistol   gun; air pistol, starting pistol, water pistol

piston   car-engine component; piston ring

pit   bed, coalmine, fruit stone, hole, orchestra's area in a theatre, pockmark, refuelling area at a racetrack; make hollows in; bear pit, bottomless pit, coal-pit, orchestra pit, the pit of the stomach; pit-a-pat, pit bull terrier, pit pony, pit prop, pit saw, pit stop, pit viper; *The Money Pit* (f), *The Pit and the Pendulum* (b/f)

pitch   angle (of a roof), sports playing area, tar residue, vocal tone; throw; concert pitch, fever pitch; pitch-black, pitch in; queer your pitch; *Fever Pitch* (b/f)

pitched   *see* pitch; high-pitched; pitched battle

pitcher   baseball player, large jug; pitcher plant

pith   essence, inner skin of a citrus fruit; pith helmet

pity   sympathy; feel sorry for; self-pity; for pity's sake, more's the pity; *Town without Pity* (f)

pivot   crucial person or point, turning point; twist around

pizza   Italian dish; *Mystic Pizza* (f)

place   location; put; another place, assisted place, take place, the other place; place card, place kick, place mat, place name; between a rock and a hard place, in place, in the first place, pride of place, place a premium on, there's no place like home; the Other Place; *Heaven Is a Place on Earth* (s), *A Pagan Place* (al/b/s), *A Place in the Sun* (f/tv), *Peyton Place* (tv)

placebo   dummy medicine; placebo effect

placement   positioning, temporary work posting; product placement

places   *see* place; go places; *Changing Places* (b), *Trading Places* (f)

plague   affliction, deadly disease, swarm; cause distress to, pester; bubonic plague; plague of locusts; Great Plague of London; *Journal of the Plague Year* (b), *The Plague* (b), *The Plague Dogs* (f)

plain   open tract; clearly evident, homely in appearance, unadorned; flood plain; plain chocolate, plain-clothes man, plain flour, plain Jane, plain sailing; (as) plain as a pikestaff; *The Plain Dealer* (pl), *Virginia Plain* (s)

plains   *see* plain; *High Plains Drifer* (f)

plait   weave of hair; braid; French plait

253

plan blueprint, map, scheme of action; design, intend; game plan, open-plan, personal equity plan

plane aircraft, flat surface, smoothing tool, tall tree; smooth (wood); jet plane, London plane, ski-plane; *Leavin' on a Jet Plane* (s)

planes *see* plane; *Q Planes* (f)

planet celestial body; what planet are you on?; The Red Planet; *The Blue Planet* (tv), *Planet of the Apes* (f), *Red Planet* (f), *The Red Planet* (b)

plank piece of timber; walk the plank; *The Plank* (f)

planks *see* plank; (as) thick as two short planks

planned *see* plan; planned economy

planner designer, organiser; town planner; *The Wedding Planner* (f)

planning *see* plan; organisation; family planning, town planning; planning permission

plant factory, heavy machinery, vegetable organism; put in the ground; bedding plant, cheese plant, curry plant, desalination plant, house plant, ice plant, pitcher plant, pot plant, power plant, rubber plant, spider plant, Swiss cheese plant, tobacco plant, umbrella plant

planter colonist, flowerpot; planter's punch

plaster adhesive dressing, wall-lining material; spread thickly; mustard plaster, sticking plaster; plaster cast, plaster of Paris

plastic synthetic substance; plastic bag, plastic explosive, plastic mac, plastic surgeon, plastic surgery

plate dental fixture, flat dish; cover with a thin metal coating; South American river; collection plate, gold plate, Sheffield plate, silver plate, tin-plate; plate glass, plate tectonics, plate-layer; on a plate, on your plate

plated coated with a thin metal; armour-plated, silver-plated, tin-plated

plates *see* plate; L-plates, number plates, registration plates

platform raised stage, walkway alongside a rail track; oil platform; platform ticket

platinum precious metal; platinum blonde; *Platinum Blonde* (tv)

platter large flat serving-dish; on a silver platter

play dramatic work, fun; act out, have fun, perform on a musical instrument; child's play, fair play, foul play, match play, miracle play, morality play, mummers' play, mystery play, nativity play, power play, Restoration play, role play, school play, state of play; play-acting, play a let, play along, play around, play back, play ball, play by ear, play dirty, play down, play false, play God, play-goer, play gooseberry, play hardball, play hookey, play-off, play possum, play safe, play-scheme, play up; play a lone hand, play ducks and drakes with, play for time, play havoc with, play it by ear, play merry hell, play second fiddle, play the devil with, play the field, play the game, play the giddy goat, play to the gallery, play with fire, play your cards right, two can play at that game, when the cat's away the mice will play; Passion Play; *Any Number Can Play* (f), *Foul Play* (f), *Miracle Play* (b), *Only Two Can Play* (f), *Play It Again, Sam* (f), *Play Misty for Me* (f),

Play Your Cards Right (tv), *See Emily Play* (s)

playboy   pleasure-seeking young man; *The Playboy of the Western World* (pl)

player   actor, game participant; card player, cassette player, darts player, long-player, polo player, record player, team player, tennis player; player-manager; *The Guitar Player* (pa), *The Player* (f)

players   see player; old cigarette brand (Player's); strolling players; *The Chess Players* (b/f)

playground   recreation area; adventure playground

playing   see play; level playing field, role playing; playing-cards, playing for time

plea   earnest request; plea-bargaining, plea of tender

plead   address a lawcourt, entreat

please   polite request word; make satisfied; Pet Shop Boys album, U2 hit; eager to please, fares please, hard to please, please yourself; *No Sex Please, We're British* (f/pl), *Please Don't Tease* (s), *Please Mr Postman* (s), *Please Please Me* (s), *Please Sir!* (tv)

pleased   satisfied; well pleased; (as) pleased as punch

pleasing   satisfying; delightful; *Ain't No Pleasing You* (s)

pleasure   feeling of joy; pleasure-seeker; business before pleasure; *Welcome to the Pleasure Dome* (s)

pleat   garment fold; make a fold in; box pleat, kick pleat

pledge   solemn promise; make a promise; brand-name furniture polish

plenty   abundance; 1985 Meryl Streep film; horn of plenty

plight   predicament; promise; plight your troth

plimsoll   gym shoe; Plimsoll line

plonk   cheap wine; set down carelessly

plot   conspiracy, piece of land, storyline; mark on a chart, scheme secretly; sub-plot; lose the plot, the plot thickens; Gunpowder Plot

plough   farming machine; group of seven stars; plough back; *The Plough and the Stars* (pl)

ploughman   farm worker; ploughman's lunch; *The Ploughman's Lunch* (f)

pluck   bravery; remove the feathers from

plug   electrical connector, sink stopper; give publicity to, seal; spark plug; plug in

plughole   sink draining aperture; go down the plughole

plum   fleshy stoned fruit; excellent; Victoria plum; plum duff, plum pudding, plum tomato; have a plum in one's mouth; Sugar Plum Fairy

plumb   lead weight; exactly vertical; assess the depth of; plumb bob, plumb line

plume   feather; nom de plume

plumed   feathered; *The Plumed Serpent* (b)

plump   opt (for); chubby

plunder   booty; steal

plunge   submerge; plunge pool; take the plunge

plus   addition sign, additional factor; with the addition of; eleven-plus; plus fours, plus sign; plus ça change, plus c'est la meme chose

plush   rich fabric; opulent; plush velvet

ply   layer of laminated wood, strand of

wool; travel to and fro; work steadily at; cross-ply

pneumatic   using air; pneumatic drill

poach   cook in hot water, steal game or fish

pocket   compartment in a bag or garment; take for yourself; air pocket, handkerchief pocket, patch pocket; pocket guide, pocket handkerchief, pocket knife, pocket money, pocket watch; burn a hole in your pocket, in pocket, out of pocket, put your hand in your pocket; *Brass in Pocket* (s), *A Pocket Full of Rye* (b)

pod   plant's seed shell; shell (peas); senna pod

poem   literary composition; tone poem

poet   writer of verse; performance poet; Poet Laureate

poetic   expressed in verse, lyrical; poetic justice, poetic licence

poets   *see* poet; Lake Poets

point   compass division, electricity socket, full stop, item in a discussion, meaning, objective, precise moment, sharp tip; indicate; boiling point, break point, breaking point, cardinal point, cover point, decimal point, dew point, focal point, freezing point, game point, gros point, interrogation point, match point, melting point, moot point, petit point, power point, pressure point, reference point, saturation point, selling point, set point, sore point, strong point, talking point, three-point turn, triangulation point, trigger point, vanishing point, vantage point; point blank, point break, point duty, point of departure, point of honour, point of no return,

point of view, point-to-point; at point-blank range, in point of fact, labour the point, not to put too fine a point on it, stretch a point; Lizard Point, St Catherine's Point, West Point; *Breaking Point* (b/ga), *Deception Point* (b), *Grosse Point Blank* (f), *Match Point* (f), *Point Blank* (f), *Point Break* (f), *Point Counter Point* (b), *Vanishing Point* (f), *Zabriskie Point* (f)

Point
Dodman, Hartland, Lizard, Start, St Catherine's, West

---

points   *see* point; brownie points

poise   composure; balance steadily

poison   toxic substance; contaminate; 1989 Alice Cooper hit; rat poison; poison ivy, poison pen, poison-pen letter; one man's meat is another's poison; *Poison Ivy* (f)

poisoned   *see* poison; poisoned chalice

poisoning   *see* poison; blood poisoning, food poisoning, lead poisoning

poke   elbow jab, sack; prod; buy a pig in a poke, poke fun at, poke your nose in

poker   gambling card game, rod for stirring a fire; red-hot poker, strip poker, stud poker; poker dice, poker-faced

polar   of the ice regions; polar bear, polar cap; *The Polar Express* (f), *Polar Star* (b)

pole   end of a magnet, rod, top or bottom of the Earth; native of a Central European country; barber's pole, greasy pole, magnetic pole, telegraph pole, totem pole; pole position, pole vault; up the pole; North Pole, Pole Star, South Pole; *Pole to Pole* (tv)

poles *see* pole; poles apart

police law enforcers; military police, secret police, thought police; police box, police car, police commissioner, police constable, police dog, police force, police inspector, police officer, police sergeant, police state, police station; *Police Academy* (f), *Police Squad* (tv), *Police Woman* (tv)

policeman male law-enforcement officer; community policeman, military policeman, sleeping policeman; *The Third Policeman* (b)

policewoman female law-enforcement officer; military policewoman

policy course of action, insurance document; endowment policy, insurance policy, scorched-earth policy; honesty is the best policy

polish elegance, cleaning substance; buff up; relating to a Central European country, Slavonic language; French polish, nail polish, shoe polish; polish off; spit and polish

politic prudent; body politic

political active in a party, government-related; party political; political correctness, political economist, political economy, political prisoner, political science, political scientist

politically in a way that relates to government; politically correct

politics science and art of government; party politics, sexual politics

polka lively dance; polka dots; *Itsy Bitsy Teeny Weeny Yellow Polka Dot Bikini* (s)

poll head, survey, voting process; record the opinion of; deed poll, exit poll, Gallup poll, opinion poll, straw poll; poll tax; *Pineapple Poll* (bal)

pollen flower's fertilising powder; pollen count

pollination botanic fertilisation; cross-pollination, self-pollination

polling *see* poll; polling booth, polling day, polling station

polo equestrian sport; brand-name mint, Jilly Cooper novel, Ralph Lauren brand, Volkswagen model; water polo; polo neck, polo-neck jumper, polo player, polo shirt

polythene tough light plastic; polythene bag

pommel part of a saddle; pommel horse

pond small lake; duck pond, fish-pond; pond lily, pond skater; big fish in a small pond; *On Golden Pond* (f)

pong bad smell; smell badly; ping-pong

pontoon flat-bottomed boat, floating bridge, gambling card game; pontoon bridge

pony small horse, £25; Dartmoor pony, Jerusalem pony, one-trick pony, pit pony, Shanks's pony, Shetland pony; pony and trap, pony-trekking; ; Pony Express; *One-Trick Pony* (s/f), *Smack the Pony* (tv)

pooh expression of contempt; pooh-pooh; *The House at Pooh Corner* (b)

pool combined fund, mini-snooker, small body of water; combine (resources); birthing pool, car-pool, gene pool, paddling pool, plunge pool, rock pool, swimming pool, typing pool

pools *see* pool; football gambling

competition; football pools; win the pools

poor needy, unsatisfactory; time-poor; poor box, poor relation; in poor health; Little Sisters of the Poor; *Poor Cow* (b/f), *Poor Folk* (b), *Rich Man Poor Man* (b)

poorly ill; badly

pop dad, lemonade, modern music genre, small explosive sound; burst; soda pop, vox pop; pop art, pop culture, pop-eyed, pop festival, pop off, pop record, pop song, pop-top, pop-up; pop the question, pop your clogs, take a pop at; *Pop Idol* (tv)

pope head of the RC Church; is the pope a catholic?; *The Pope Must Die* (f)

poplar tall tree; former London borough; Lombardy poplar, trembling poplar

popper party explosive, press stud; party popper

popping *see* pop; body-popping, pill-popping

poppy wild flower; California poppy, Flanders poppy; Poppy Day

pops *see* pop; *Top of the Pops* (tv)

popular prevailing, widely favoured; popular front

population inhabitants; floating population

pore skin opening; read intently

pork meat from a pig; leg of pork; pork chop, pork pie, pork-pie hat, pork scratchings; *Pork Chop Hill* (f)

porridge oat-based breakfast dish, prison stretch; Ronnie Barker sitcom; do porridge

port fortified wine, ship's left side, town with a harbour; free port, sally port; port of call, port of entry; Cinque Port, Ellesmere Port, Port

Elizabeth, Port Louis, Port Moresby, Port Salut, Port Talbot, Port Vale, Port Vila, Port-au-Prince, Port-of-Spain, St Peter Port

porter dark beer, doorkeeper, luggage handler; hall porter, night porter, prêt-à-porter; *The Night Porter* (f), *Oh, Mr Porter* (f)

porterhouse old inn; porterhouse steak; *Porterhouse Blue* (b/tv)

portfolio document case, government minister's area of responsibility; Minister without Portfolio

portmanteau large travelling-bag; portmanteau word

portrait picture of a person; full-length portrait, self-portrait; portrait gallery, portrait painter; National Portrait Gallery; *The Arnolfini Portrait* (pa), *The Portrait of a Lady* (b/f), *Portrait of Dr Gachet* (pa), *Portrait of My Love* (s), *A Portrait of the Artist as a Young Man* (b)

pose masquerade, stance; put forward, sit for an artist, strike an attitude; pose a problem

posh upper-class; *Posh Nosh* (tv)

position attitude, job, place, state of affairs; put; first position, lotus position, pole position, recovery position

positive photographic image; absolutely certain, affirmative, constructive; proof positive, rhesus positive; positive discrimination, positive vetting

possessed owned; taken over by an evil spirit; self-possessed; what possessed you?

possession item of property, ownership; AS Byatt novel, 2002

Gwyneth Paltrow film; self-possession, vacant possession

possessions belongings; worldly possessions

possessive grammatical case; controlling and demanding, unwilling to share; possessive pronoun

possible achievable, potential; the art of the possible

possum marsupial; play possum

post employment position, mail, military base, stake; announce, pin up, put into position, send by mail; finishing post, first post, first-class post, fly-post, lamp-post, last post, listening post, penny post, registered post, staging post, starting post, sub-post office, trading post, winning post; post horn, post meridiem, post office, post-chaise, post-dated, post-feminism, post-free, post-haste, post-house, post-mortem, post-natal, post-op, post-war; deaf as a post, first past the post, from pillar to post, pip to the post; Post-Impressionism

postage mail carriage fee; postage stamp

postal relating to mail; postal order

postcard pictorial token sent by mail; picture postcard

postcards *see* postcard; *Postcards from the Edge* (f)

posted *see* post; informed; keep posted

poster paper picture; fly-poster, four-poster bed, wanted poster; poster paint

posting *see* post; foreign assignment; fly-posting

postman mail carrier; postman's knock; *Please Mr Postman* (s), *The*

Postman (f), *The Postman Always Rings Twice* (f), *Postman Pat* (tv)

postmaster man who runs a mail office; sub-postmaster; postmaster general

postponed put off till a later date; *Paradise Postponed* (b)

posture deportment, stance; adopt an attitude

pot marijuana, plant container, pool (of money), saucepan; plant in a container, sink (a snooker ball); chamber pot, chimney pot, coffee pot, lobster pot, melting pot, paint pot, pepper pot, Vietnamese pot-bellied pig; pot-au-feu, pot-bellied, pot-bellied stove, pot belly, pot-boiler, pot-bound, pot-herb, pot-house, pot luck, pot of gold, pot plant, pot-pourri, pot roast, pot shot; go to pot, keep the pot boiling, a watched pot never boils, *Melting Pot* (s), *Pot Black* (tv)

potato root vegetable; couch potato, hot potato, jacket potato, mashed potato, seed potato, sweet potato; Potato Famine; *The Potato Eaters* (pa)

potatoes *see* potato; duchesse potatoes, French fried potatoes, new potatoes, small potatoes; meat and potatoes

potential quality not yet developed; in the making; potential energy

pots *see* pot; pots and pans

potter clay worker; amble; *Harry Potter and the Goblet of Fire* (b/f), *Harry Potter and the Half-Blood Prince* (b), *Harry Potter and the Philosopher's Stone* (b/f)

potteries earthenware factories; five Staffordshire towns

potting *see* pot; potting compost, potting shed

potty   baby's loo; daft; potty-trained

pounce   fine dust for drying ink, sudden jump; jump suddenly

pound   currency unit, enclosure, imperial unit of weight; beat repeatedly; pound cake, pound of flesh; in for a penny in for a pound, penny wise and pound foolish, pound the beat

pour   dispense (liquid), gush, rain hard; pour oil on troubled waters, pour with rain

pours   *see* pour; it never rains but it pours

pout   sullen expression; look sullen

poverty   lack of money; poverty line, poverty-stricken

powder   fine grains; pulverise, sprinkle; baking powder, chilli powder, curry powder, dusting powder, face powder, itching powder, lemonade powder, soap powder, talcum powder, tooth powder, washing powder; powder blue, powder keg, powder monkey, powder puff, powder room

power   ability, authority, energy, strength; supply energy to; balance of power, flower power, nuclear power, sea power, solar power, staying power, water power, world power; power-assisted, power broker, power cut, power of attorney, power pack, power plant, power play, power point, power shower, power station, power steering; corridors of power, in power, more power to your elbow; *Absolute Power* (f/tv), *The Corridors of Power* (b), *The Power and the Glory* (b), *The Power Game* (tv), *The Power of Love* (f)

powered   *see* power; high-powered,

nuclear-powered, water-powered

powers   *see* power; the powers that be; *Earthly Powers* (b)

practical   functional, hands-on, realistic; practical joke, practical joker

practically   nearly, realistically

practice   dry run, habitual action, professional business, repeated exercise; choir practice, general practice, private practice, restrictive practice, sharp practice; out of practice, practice makes perfect; *Peak Practice* (tv), *A Very Peculiar Practice* (tv)

practise   carry out, follow (a profession), make a habit of, rehearse; practise what you preach

practitioner   one actively engaged in a discipline; general practitioner, medical practitioner

prairie   grassy plain; prairie dog, prairie oyster, prairie schooner, prairie wolf; *Little House on the Prairie* (b/tv)

praise   commendation, exaltation; extol; damn with faint praise, praise be; *Praise Be* (tv), *Songs of Praise* (tv)

prattle   idle chat; witter on

prawn   small crustacean; Dublin Bay prawn, king prawn, tiger prawn; prawn cocktail, prawn cracker; *The Amorous Prawn* (f/pl)

pray   entreat, speak to God; let us pray

prayer   appeal to God; prayer rug, prayer shawl, prayer wheel; on a wing and a prayer; The Lord's Prayer; *I Say a Little Prayer* (s), *Like a Prayer* (s), *The Millennium Prayer* (s), *My Prayer* (s), *Save a Prayer* (s)

praying   *see* pray; praying mantis

preach   deliver a sermon; practise what you preach; *Papa Don't Preach* (s)

precinct cathedral surroundings, pedestrianised area, US police district; pedestrian precinct; *Assault on Precinct 13* (f), *The Last Precinct* (b)

precious cherished, valuable; semi-precious; precious few, precious little, precious metal, precious stone; *Precious Bane* (b)

precipitate substance formed from a solution, bring on prematurely; occurring suddenly, over-hasty

precise exact, scrupulous

predict foretell; *I Predict a Riot* (s)

preface introduction; introduce

prefect French police chief, school monitor; old Ford model

prefer like better; *Gentlemen Prefer Blondes* (b/f)

preference card game, first choice; preference shares

pregnant expecting a baby, significant

prejudice bias, unreasonable dislike; make biased; without prejudice; *Bride and Prejudice* (f), *Listen without Prejudice* (al), *Pride and Prejudice* (b/f/tv)

preliminary first-round event; introductory; preliminary to

premier head of government; most important; premier cru

premiere first performance; film premiere

premises assumptions, building with its land

premium bonus, insurance policy payment, surcharge; of high quality; at a premium, place a premium on; Premium Bonds

prenuptial occurring before marriage; prenuptial agreement

prep homework; prep school

preparatory introductory; preparatory school, preparatory to

prepared cooked, made ready; ready; be prepared

presence attendance, strong personal aura; presence of mind; make your presence felt; *Weak in the Presence of Beauty* (s)

present current time, gift; existing, in attendance; birthday present; present arms, present day; at present, at the present time, for the present, there's no time like the present; *Clear and Present Danger* (b/f), *Present Laughter* (pl)

presentation appearance, performance, speech

preservation maintenance, protection; self-preservation; preservation order

preserve foodstuff such as jam, place where game is protected; maintain, save from destruction; game preserve

president chair, head of a republic; vice-president; *All the President's Men* (f), *The American President* (f)

press newspapers collectively, printing apparatus; flatten, iron, push down, urge; bench press, gutter press, printing press, stop press, trouser press; press agent, press box, press charges, press conference, press gallery, press gang, press officer, press on, press release, press stud, press-up; go to press, hot off the press, press ahead; Cambridge University Press, Hogarth Press, Oxford University Press

pressed *see* press; hard-pressed; pressed for time

pressing *see* press; urgent

pressure constraining force, stress;

coerce; atmospheric pressure, blood pressure; pressure cooker, pressure group, pressure point, pressure suit; under pressure; *Under Pressure* (s)

pretence   claim, make-believe

pretend   claim, make believe; imaginary

pretender   claimant to a throne or title; *The Great Pretender* (s)

pretty   attractive; fairly; sitting pretty; pretty good, pretty much; (as) pretty as a picture, cost a pretty penny, pretty kettle of fish; *Dirty Pretty Things* (f), *Oh Pretty Woman* (s), *Pretty Flamingo* (s), *A Pretty Girl Is Like a Melody* (s), *Pretty in Pink* (f), *Pretty Vacant* (s), *Pretty Woman* (f), *Sitting Pretty* (mus)

prevailing   having the upper hand, widespread; prevailing wind

prevention   avoidance; prevention is better than cure

previous   former; previous to

prey   object of a hunt; Michael Crichton novel; bird of prey

price   cost; set the cost of; asking price, cost price, cut-price, list price, market price, reserve price, retail price index, starting price, trade price; price list, price tag; at a price, at any price, price on your head; *The Price Is Right* (tv)

prick   act of piercing, little puncture; pierce slightly; *Prick Up Your Ears* (b/f)

prickly   easily annoyed, thorny; prickly heat, prickly pear

pricks   *see* prick; kick against the pricks

pride   group of lions, self-respect, vanity; pride and joy, pride of place; London Pride; *Carve Her Name with Pride* (f), *Pride and Prejudice* (b/f/tv), *The Pride and the Passion* (f), *Pride (in the Name of Love* (s)

priest   RC minister; 1994 Linus Roache film; high priest; priest's hole; *Zadok the Priest* (cl)

prim   stiffly formal; prim and proper

primal   fundamental; *Primal Fear* (f)

primary   first, fundamental; primary care, primary colour, primary school; *Primary Colors* (f)

primate   high-ranking churchman, tree-dwelling mammal; Primate of All England

prime   heyday; most important, of the highest quality; prepare; prime minister, prime mover, prime suspect, prime time; *Prime Cut* (f), *The Prime of Miss Jean Brodie* (b/f/tv), *Prime Suspect* (tv), *Yes, Prime Minister* (tv)

primordial   original; primordial soup

primrose   spring flower; evening primrose; primrose path; Primrose Hill

prince   monarch's son; crown prince; prince consort, prince of the blood, Prince of Wales check; Port-au-Prince, Prince Edward Island, Prince of Darkness, Prince of Peace, Prince of Wales, Prince Regent; *The Black Prince* (b), *The Fresh Prince of Bel-Air* (tv), *Harry Potter and the Half-Blood Prince* (b), *The Little Prince* (b), *The Lost Prince* (b/tv), *Pericles, Prince of Tyre* (pl), *The Prince and the Pauper* (b/f), *The Prince and the Showgirl* (f), *Prince Charming* (s), *Prince Igor* (o), *Prince of Darkness* (f), *Prince of the Blood* (b), *The Prince of Tides* (f), *Prince Regent* (tv), *Some Day My Prince Will Come* (s), *The Student Prince* (mus)

princess monarch's daughter; crown princess; princess of the blood; Princess Royal; *The Princess and the Pea* (b), *The Princess Bride* (f), *Princess Daisy* (b/tv), *Princess Ida* (o), *The Princess Diaries* (f)

principal capital sum, college head; chief; principal boy

principle fundamental cause, guiding theory or belief, high moral standards; pleasure principle; in principle, on principle; Archimedes Principle, Peter Principle

principles *see* principle; first principles

print lithograph, positive photograph, typeface; reproduce on paper, stamp, write in block capitals; fine print, small print; print run; (appear) in print, out of print

printed *see* print; printed circuit

printer company producing written text, computing machine producing text, typographer; bubblejet printer, ink-jet printer, laser printer, line-at-a-time printer; printer's devil

printing *see* print; printing press

prior senior monk; earlier; prior to

prison jail; open prison; prison camp, prison cell, prison officer; in prison; Fleet Prison; *Prison Break* (tv)

prisoner jail inmate; political prisoner; prisoner of conscience, prisoner of war; *The Prisoner* (tv), *Prisoner: Cell Block H* (tv), *The Prisoner of Second Avenue* (f/pl), *Prisoner of War* (f), *The Prisoner of Zenda* (b/f)

prisoners *see* prisoner; take no prisoners

private lowest-ranking soldier; personal, secret; private company, private detective, private enterprise, private eye, private income, private life, private means, private member, private member's bill, private practice, private school, private secretary, private sector, private view, private war; in private; *My Own Private Idaho* (f), *Private Benjamin* (f), *Private Dancer* (s), *Private Eye* (mag), *A Private Function* (f), *Private Life* (s), *The Private Life of Henry VIII* (f), *Private Lives* (pl), *Private Number* (s), *Private's Progress* (f), *Saving Private Ryan* (f)

privates *see* private; *Privates on Parade* (f)

privilege advantage; executive privilege

privy toilet; knowing secrets; privy counsellor, privy purse, privy seal; Lord Privy Seal, Privy Council

prize award; value highly; booby prize, consolation prize; prize money, prize-winner; Booker Prize, Nobel Prize, Pulitzer Prize; *The Prize* (f)

prizes; *The Glittering Prizes* (b/tv), *Pets Win Prizes* (tv)

pro argument in favour, non-amateur; in favour of; pro-am, pro forma, pro rata; ora pro nobis, quid pro quo, pro tem; *Ora Pro Nobis* (po)

probability likelihood; in all probability

probation release from prison of an offender, trial period; probation officer

probe detailed investigation, unmanned spacecraft; investigate; space probe

problem difficult matter, puzzle; knotty problem; no problem, pose a problem

proceeds profits; goes along

process method, summons, system; treat; Bessemer process, due process

processing   *see* process; central processing unit, data processing, word processing

processor   refining machine; data processor, food processor, word processor

procrastination   postponement; procrastination is the thief of time

procurator   old Roman finance agent, Scottish legal officer; procurator fiscal

prodigal   extravagant; prodigal son; *The Prodigal Daughter* (b), *The Return of the Prodigal Son* (pa)

produce   foodstuffs; bring about, manufacture; mass-produce

producers   film financiers, manufacturers; *The Producers* (mus)

product   commodity, outcome, result of multiplication; by-product, end product, gross domestic product, gross national product; product placement

production   making of a film, play or disc, output; co-production, mass production; production line

profane   blasphemous; *The Sacred and Profane Love Machine* (b)

profession   declaration, occupation; *Mrs Warren's Profession* (pl)

professional   competent person, person competing for money; competent, non-amateur; non-professional, semi-professional; professional foul

professionals   *see* professional; *The Professionals* (tv)

professor   declarer, high-ranking academic; Regius professor; *The Absent-Minded Professor* (f), *The Nutty Professor* (f)

profile   short biography, side-view; describe; in profile, keep a low profile

profit   advantage, financial gain; bring or gain advantage, make money; net profit, non-profit-making, operating profit; profit and loss account, profit margin, profit-sharing

programme   booklet sold at shows, schedule, television show; arrange; television programme, twelve-step programme

progress   advancement; go forward; *Private's Progress* (f), *The Pilgrim's Progress* (b), *A Rake's Progress* (pa), *The Rake's Progress* (o)

progression   forward movement; arithmetic progression, geometric progression; *The Aquitaine Progression* (b)

prohibition   ban; 1920-33 alcohol ban in the USA

project   scheme; forecast, jut out, throw outwards; *The Blair Witch Project* (f)

projection   forecast, jutting-out feature, mapping technique, showing of an image on a screen; back-projection, gnomonic projection, Mercator projection, Peters projection

projector   film- or slide-showing machine; overhead projector

promenade   seafront walkway; stroll; promenade concert, promenade deck

prominent   bulging, noticeable, well known

promise   potential, solemn pledge; give your word; breach of promise; lick and a promise; *Promise Me* (s)

promised   *see* promise; promised land; Promised Land; *I Never Promised You a Rose Garden* (f)

promising   *see* promise; up-and-coming

promote encourage, publicise, raise to a higher rank
prompt cue; give a cue to, instigate; punctual; prompt book
prone lying flat, susceptible; accident-prone
pronoun part of speech; personal pronoun, possessive pronoun
pronounced sounded (a word); very noticeable
pronunciation way of speaking; received pronunciation
proof evidence, test print; resistant; burden of proof, damp-proof, draught-proof, tamper-proof; proof positive, proof spirit, proof-read; *Proof of Life* (f), *Rabbit-Proof Fence* (f)
prop clothes-line support, inanimate stage object, rugby forward; shore (up); clothes-prop, loose-head prop, pit prop; prop forward, prop jet, prop up
propelled pushed forward; jet-propelled, self-propelled
propelling *see* propelled; propelling pencil
proper appropriate, correct, real, seemly; proper noun; prim and proper
property belongings, characteristic, premises; government property, intellectual property, lost property, lost-property office, personal property; property ladder; *The Man of Property* (b), *Property Ladder* (tv)
prophecy prediction; self-fulfilling prophecy
prophet visionary; major prophet, minor prophet
proportion part, ratio; inverse proportion, sense of proportion; blow out of all proportion, in proportion, out of proportion

proposal offer; *Indecent Proposal* (f)
propose make an offer of marriage, suggest
proposition suggestion; make an offer to; business proposition
pros *see* pro; pros and cons
prose writings not in verse; purple prose
prosecution attempt to convict, carrying out; *Witness for the Prosecution* (b/f)
prosecutor person instigating legal action; crown prosecutor, public prosecutor
prospect outlook, potential customer, view; explore (for gold)
prosper thrive; cheats never prosper
protection safe keeping; data protection, password protection; protection money
protective sheltering, watchful; protective custody
protector guardian, temporary regent; Lord Protector
protein nutritional compound; textured vegetable protein
protest demonstration, objection; demonstrate, make objections; protest march
protocol code of practice; *The Fourth Protocol*
proud full of satisfaction, projecting slightly, self-respecting, vain; house-proud; (as) proud as a peacock, (as) proud as punch; *Proud Mary* (s), *The Proud One* (s)
proverbs sayings; Old Testament book
proves shows to be true, rises (of dough); the exception proves the rule
provided supplied; on the condition (that)

providence divine intervention, foresight; Rhode Island state capital; tempt providence

provident prudent; Provident Society

provider supplier; service provider

provincial person living outside the capital; narrow-minded, referring to regions outside the capital

proving *see* proves; proving ground

provision action of supplying, clause in law, measure taken beforehand

provoke annoy, arouse

provost Scottish magistrate; Lord Provost

prudence caution, wisdom; Jilly Cooper novel; *Dear Prudence* (s)

prune dried plum; cut back

psychic one with clairvoyant abilities; clairvoyant

psychological relating to the mind; psychological warfare

psychologist person who studies mind and behaviour; clinical psychologist, sports psychologist

psychology mindset, study of the mind and behaviour; analytical psychology, clinical psychology, social psychology;

pub inn; pub crawl

public people in general; belonging to the people, unrestricted; public address system, public bar, public company, public enemy, public house, public lending right, public limited company, public nuisance, public prosecutor, public purse, public relations, public school, public sector, public servant, public-spirited, public transport, public utility, public works; go public, in public; Great British Public, Joe Public, Public Record Office; *The Public Enemy* (f)

publishing book trade; producing books, putting in print; desktop publishing, electronic publishing

pudding cooked dessert, doughy steamed dish; black pudding, cabinet pudding, Christmas pudding, milk pudding, plum pudding, rice pudding, sponge pudding, suet pudding, summer pudding, white pudding, Yorkshire pudding; pudding basin; in the pudding club, over-egg the pudding; Pudding Lane

puddings *see* pudding; queen of puddings

puff gust of air or smoke; breathe heavily, smoke; cream puff, powder puff; puff adder, puff pastry, puff-puff, puff sleeves; puff and blow; *Puff, the Magic Dragon* (s)

puffing *see* puff; Puffing Billy

pug small breed of dog; pug dog, pug-nosed

pull attraction, influence; attract, haul; leg-pull, ring pull; pull back, pull in, pull out, pull rank, pull strings, pull through, pull up; pull a fast one, pull out all the stops, pull to pieces, pull your finger out, pull your socks up

pulp liquidised mass, unprocessed paper; liquidise; pulp fiction; *Pulp Fiction* (f)

pulse edible seed, regular beat; throb; feel the pulse, have your finger on the pulse, take the pulse

pump inflating device, light shoe, machine for moving water; force along, interrogate; air pump, bicycle pump, petrol pump, stirrup pump, suction pump, water pump; pump-action, pump iron, pump up

pumping *see* pump; *Pumping Iron* (f)

pumpkin large gourd; pumpkin seeds; *The Pumpkin Eater* (b)

pun wordplay; make a joke using wordplay

punch boxer's blow, hole-making machine, mixed drink; hit with the fist; card-punch, knockout punch, planter's punch, rabbit punch, sucker punch, Suffolk punch; punch-drunk, punch-up; (as) pleased as Punch, pack a punch, proud as Punch, punch above your weight, punch the clock; Punch and Judy; *The Punch and Judy Man* (f), *Punch-Drunk Love* (f), *Punch the Clock* (al)

puncture hole in a tyre; pierce; slow puncture

punishment harsh treatment, penalty; capital punishment, corporal punishment; a glutton for punishment; *Crime and Punishment* (b/f/tv)

punitive disciplinary; punitive damages

punk 1970s youth culture, style of rock music; punk rock

punt flat-bottomed boat, former Irish currency unit; kick, steer a boat with a pole

pup young dog or seal; buy/sell a pup

pupil centre of the eye, learner; star pupil; *The Philosopher's Pupil* (b)

puppet doll; glove puppet; *Puppet on a Chain* (b/f), *Puppet on a String* (s)

puppies *see* puppy; Hush Puppies

puppy young dog; puppy fat, puppy love; *Puppy Love* (s)

purchase item bought; buy; compulsory purchase, hire purchase; purchase tax

pure untainted; pure-bred, pure mathematics; (as) pure as the driven snow; *The Pure Hell of St Trinian's* (f)

purge removal from a group; rid

purple colour between red and blue; purple emperor, purple heart, purple passage, purple patch, purple prose; born to the purple; *The Color Purple* (f), *Purple Rain* (s), *The Purple Rose of Cairo* (f)

purpose intention, reason, resolution; general-purpose, multi-purpose; on purpose, to the purpose

purse prize of money, wallet; pucker (the lips); privy purse, public purse, shepherd's purse; hold the purse strings

pursue engage in (an activity), follow

pursuit activity, chase, quest, type of cycle race; in hot pursuit; Trivial Pursuit; *Trivial Pursuit* (tv)

pursuits *see* pursuit; outdoor pursuits

push jostle, press forward, urge; push-start; at a push, get the push, give the push, when push comes to shove, push the boat out, push your luck

pushing *see* push; pen-pushing; pushing up daisies

puss cat; *Puss in Boots* (pan)

pussy *see* puss; pussy willow

put place, placed, submit, submitted; shot-put, stay put; put across, put away, put by, put down, put-down, put off, put on, put on notice, put out, put paid to, put the shot, put to bed, put to death, put to rout, put to sea, put to shame, put up, put-up job, put-upon, put-you-up; (don't) put all your eggs in one basket, (don't) put the cart before the horse, not to put a foot right, not to put too fine a point on it, put a damper on, put a foot wrong, put a sock in it, put an end to, put back the clock, put down roots, put flesh on the bones, put in an appearance, put on a charge, put on the map, put on the spot, put on your thinking cap, put one over on, put one's nose out of joint, put out to grass, put out to pasture, put out to tender, put the boot in, put the cat among the pigeons, put the fear of God into, put the finger on, put the flags out, put the frighteners on, put the mockers on, put the question, put the record straight, put the skids under, put the squeeze on, put the wind up, put through the hoops, put through the mill, put to the sword, put to the torch, put two and two together, put up or shut up, put your best foot forward, put your feet up, put your foot down, put your foot in it, put your hand in your pocket, put your hands together, put your hands up, put your head in a noose, put your head on the block, put your house in order, put your shirt on, put your shoulder to the wheel; *Put Out More Flags* (b)

putter   golf club, sound of a small engine; chug away; shot-putter

putting   *see* put; golfing stoke; hitting (a golf ball); off-putting; putting green

putty   window sealant; putty in your hands

puzzle   brain-teaser, enigma; baffle; Chinese puzzle, crossword puzzle, jigsaw puzzle, monkey puzzle

pyjamas   nightwear; cat's pyjamas

pyramid   pointed Egyptian monument; pyramid selling

python   snake; reticulated python; *Monty Python and the Holy Grail* (f), *Monty Python's Flying Circus* (tv), *Monty Python's Life of Brian* (f)

Q

quack fake doctor, duck's noise; make a duck's noise

quad college courtyard, one of four children born together; quad bike

quail partridge-like bird; tremble with fear

qualify make the grade, render capable

quality excellence, trait; air quality; quality control, quality time; Quality Street; *Never Mind the Quality, Feel the Width* (tv), *Quality Street* (f/pl)

quandary difficult situation; in a quandary

quantity amount, value that may be expressed in numbers; unknown quantity; quantity surveyor

quarantine period of isolation; isolate on medical grounds; in quarantine

quarry place where stone is dug, prey; extract (stone)

quarter 25 US cents, area of a town or city, fourth, mercy, three-month financial period; cut into four equal parts; a quarter past, a quarter to; quarter day, quarter of an hour, quarter-final, quarter-pounder; Empty Quarter, Quarter Horse

quarters *see* quarter; military accommodation; at close quarters, three-quarters

quartet foursome; Jean Rhys novel, 1981 Merchant-Ivory film; string quartet; *The Alexandria Quartet* (b), *The Raj Quartet* (b)

quaver half a crotchet; speak in a trembling voice, vibrate

queen female monarch, most powerful chess piece, only fertile female in an ant or bee colony, picture playing-card; beauty queen, carnival queen, drag queen, May queen, pearly queen; queen bee, queen of puddings; turn Queen's evidence; Queen of Hearts, Queen of the May, Queen's Bench, Queen's Counsel, Queen's English, Queen's Guide, Queen's Park Rangers,

Queen's Scout, Queen's Speech; *The African Queen* (b/f), *Dancing Queen* (s), *God Save the Queen* (s), *Killer Queen* (s), *Queen Christina* (f), *Queen Mab* (po), *The Queen of Spades* (b/o), *The Snow Queen* (b)

queer odd; in Queer Street, queer your pitch, there's nowt so queer as folk; *Queer as Folk* (tv), *Queer Eye for the Straight Guy* (tv)

quench extinguish (a fire), slake (thirst), stifle

question issue, statement requiring an answer; cross-examine, quiz, throw doubt upon; burning question, cross-question, in question, indirect question, leading question, loaded question, open question, rhetorical question; question mark, question master; beg the question, bring into question, come into question, out of the question, pop the question, put the question; West Lothian Question; *A Question of Sport* (tv), *Question Time* (tv)

questions *see* question; *Any Questions?* (r)

queue line of people awaiting their turn; wait in line; queue-jumping, queue up; jump the queue

quiche savoury egg and cheese flan; quiche Lorraine

quick clever, fast; double quick; quick-fire, quick fix, quick march, quick-tempered, quick-witted; cut to the quick, get rich quick, in double quick time, in quick succession, kiss-me-quick, quick and dirty, quick as a flash, a quick one, quick on the draw, quick on the uptake; *The Quick and the Dead* (f), *The Quick Draw McGraw Show* (tv)

quicken accelerate; quicken up

quid lump of tobacco for chewing, slang word for one pound; quid pro quo; not the full quid

quids *see* quid; quids in

quiet calm, silent; pacify; keep quiet, on the quiet; (as) quiet as a mouse; *All Quiet on the Western Front* (b/f), *And Quiet Flows the Don* (b), *The Quiet American* (b/f), *The Quiet Man* (f)

quilt padded bed covering; continental quilt, patchwork quilt; *How to Make an American Quilt* (f)

quintet group of five; *The Trout Quintet* (cl)

quite rather; completely; quite a bit, quite a few, quite a lot; quite the contrary

quits abandons, departs; all square, clear of debt; call it quits, double or quits

quiver case for holding arrows; shake; an arrow in the quiver

quiz question-answering contest; interrogate; *The News Quiz* (r), *Quiz Show* (f)

quota proportional share; full quota

quotation estimated price, famous saying, repetition of someone else's words; quotation marks

quote citation, estimated price; cite, estimate (a price); *Quote Unquote* (r)

quotient mathematical ratio; intelligence quotient

R

rabbit   hare-like mammal; chat; angora rabbit, bunny rabbit, jack rabbit; rabbit hutch, rabbit punch, rabbit warren; *Little Grey Rabbit* (b), *Rabbit-Proof Fence* (f), *Rabbit Redux* (b), *Rabbit, Run* (b), *The Tale of Peter Rabbit* (b), *White Rabbit* (s), *Who Framed Roger Rabbit?* (f)

rabble   disorderly crowd; rabble-rouser

race   competitive trial of speed, ethnic group; run quickly; arms race, bicycle race, boat race, drag race, egg-and-spoon race, flat race, human race, marathon race, mill-race, obstacle race, one-horse race, pancake race, rat race, relay race, sack race, three-legged race, two-horse race; race against time, race-goer, race meeting, race relations; be in the race; *Bicycle Race* (s), *Death Race 2000* (f), *The Great Race* (f)

racecourse   track for horses; greyhound racecourse

racer   competitor, fast car or bicycle; boy racer, drag racer; *Silver Dream Racer* (f)

races   *see* race; relay races; *A Day at the Races* (f), *Wacky Races* (tv)

racing   *see* race; equestrian sport; drag racing, flat racing, greyhound racing, horse racing, motor racing, stock-car racing; racing car, racing correspondent, racing driver

rack   instrument of torture, joint (of lamb), slatted shelf; draw off (wine) from the sediment; coat-rack, luggage rack, roof rack, toast rack; rack your brains

racket   din, illegal enterprise, tennis bat; tennis racket

radar   aircraft location and warning system; radar beacon, radar gun, radar trap; *Radar Love* (s)

radical   political or social extremist; revolutionary; *Felix Holt, the Radical* (b)

radicals   *see* radical; free radicals

radio broadcasting medium, wireless; send a message over the air; CB radio, clock radio, pirate radio station, talk radio; radio astronomy, radio-controlled, radio frequency, radio ham, radio station, radio telescope, radio waves; *Radio Days* (f), *Radio Ga Ga* (s), *Radio Times* (mag), *Talk Radio* (f), *Video Killed the Radio Star* (s)

raffle prize draw; dispose of by lottery; raffle ticket

raft floating platform; sail on a makeshift boat; life raft

rag disreputable newspaper, scrap of cloth, students' festivity; tease; rag-and-bone man, rag day, rag doll, rag-roll, rag trade, rag week; like a red rag to a bull, lose your rag; *Maple Leaf Rag* (s), *Rag Doll* (s), *The Rag Trade* (tv)

rage anger, craze; vent anger (about); all the rage, road rage; fly into a rage; *Rage of Angels* (b)

ragged teased; tattered; ragged robin

raging *see* rage; *Raging Bull* (f)

rags *see* rag; old worn-out clothes; glad rags

ragtime jazz piano style; *Alexander's Ragtime Band* (f/s)

raid attack; make a sudden surprise attack; air-raid, air-raid shelter, air-raid warden, ram raid

raider invader; corporate raider, ram-raider; *Lara Croft: Tomb Raider* (f), *Tomb Raider* (ga)

raiders *see* raider; *Raiders of the Lost Ark* (f)

rail form of transport, horizontal support bar, waterside bird, train track; complain bitterly (at); dado rail, guard rail, picture rail; British Rail

railing *see* rail; grille

rails *see* rail; on the rails; go off the rails

railway mode of transport, track for trains; cable railway, light railway, model railway, scenic railway; railway bridge, railway carriage, railway cutting, railway line, railway terminus; Great Western Railway; *The Railway Children* (b/f)

rain pluvial weather; pour down; Somerset Maugham story; acid rain, pour with rain; rain check, rain down, rain gauge, rain tree; (as) right as rain, rain cats and dogs, take a rain check; *Black Rain* (f), *Fire and Rain* (s), *Flowers in the Rain* (s), *Hard Rain* (f), *Here Comes the Rain Again* (s), *Purple Rain* (s), *Rain Man* (f), *Rain, Steam and Speed* (pa), *Singin' in the Rain* (s/f)

rainbow coloured arc in the sky, species of trout; 1980s children's tv programme; rainbow coalition, rainbow trout; Rainbow Warrior; *Finian's Rainbow* (f), *Gravity's Rainbow* (b), *Over the Rainbow* (s), *The Rainbow* (b), *Rainbow Valley* (s), *The Serpent and the Rainbow* (f)

rained *see* rain; rained off

rains *see* rain; it never rains but it pours; *The Rains Came* (f)

rainy showery; rainy day; *Rainy Night in Georgia* (s)

raise pay increase; assemble, bring up, increase, lift; raise money; raise an eyebrow, raise Cain, raise hell, raise the ante, raise the roof, raise the standard, raise your eyebrows, raise your voice; *Raise the Titanic* (f)

raising *see* raise; fire-raising, fund-raising, hair-raising, self-raising flour; *Raising Arizona* (f), *Raising Helen* (f)

rake garden implement, libertine;

dredge (up), sift (through); muck-rake; rake in, rake-off; (as) thin as a rake, rake and scrape, rake over old coals, rake over the ashes; *A Rake's Progress* (pa), *The Rake's Progress* (o)

rally mass gathering, road race, series of strokes in tennis; make a recovery, unite for a cause; rally-cross; Monte Carlo Rally

ram male sheep; thrust; 1971 No.1 album for Paul and Linda McCartney; battering ram; ram raid

rambling talking aimlessly, walking; *Rambling Rose* (f)

ran *see* run; 1985 Kurosawa film; also-ran; *When Time Ran Out* (f)

ranch large US cattle farm; rear cattle on a large farm; dude ranch

random haphazard; Random House; *The Adventures of Roderick Random* (b)

range assortment, chain of mountains, old cooking stove, place for shooting practice, scope; extend, roam at large; driving range, free-range, long-range, mountain range, rifle range, short-range; at close range, at point-blank range; *At Close Range* (b), *Open Range* (f)

ranger forest warden, Texas lawman; senior Guide; US lunar probe of the 1960s; forest ranger; Sloane Ranger; *The Lone Ranger* (tv)

rangers *see* ranger; Scottish football team; Queen's Park Rangers

rank cab stand, line of soldiers, social or military status; be classified, classify; foul-smelling; cab rank, keep rank, pull rank, taxi rank; rank and file

ranking *see* rank; world-ranking

ranks *see* rank; break ranks, close ranks, other ranks; reduce to the ranks

ransom money demanded by a kidnapper; demand hostage payment; 1996 Mel Gibson kidnap film; hold to ransom, king's ransom

rant tirade; rave; rant and rave

rap criminal charge, hip-hop vocal style, sharp blow or knock; hit sharply, tell off; gangsta rap; beat the rap, rap on/over the knuckles, take the rap

rapid quick; in rapid succession; rapid eye movement

rapture bliss; 1980 Blondie hit; rapture of the deep

rare scarce, very lightly cooked (meat); rare bird, rare earth, rare gas

rash outbreak, skin eruption; ill-considered, impetuous; heat rash, nappy rash, nettle-rash

raspberry red summer fruit, rude spluttering noise; raspberry jam; *Raspberry Beret* (s)

rat deserter, informer, long-tailed rodent; grass (on); 2000 Imelda Staunton film; brown rat, kangaroo rat, rug rat, sewer rat, water rat; rat-a-tat, rat-catcher, rat poison, rat race, rat run, rat trap; smell a rat; Rat Pack; *King Rat* (b/f)

rate price, speed; be worthy of, appraise, think highly of; bank rate, basal metabolic rate, base rate, birth rate, cheap rate, exchange rate, first-rate, minimum lending rate, mortgage rate, over rate, pass rate, second-rate, strike rate, third-rate, work rate; rate-cap, rate of exchange; at a rate of knots, at any rate, at this rate

rating *see* rate; classification, ordinary seaman; credit rating

rations fixed quantities (of food); apportions; iron rations

rats *see* rat; rats desert a sinking ship; Desert Rats

rattle baby's noisy toy; fluster, vibrate; rattle sabres; *Shake, Rattle and Roll* (s)

rattlesnake venomous N American reptile; diamond rattlesnake

rattling *see* rattle; sabre-rattling

rave huge wild party; enthuse (about), talk irrationally or excitedly; rant and rave; rave-up; *Rave On* (s)

raving *see* rave; delirious; (stark) raving mad

raw bitterly cold, lacking experience, inflamed, uncooked, unprocessed; a raw deal, in the raw; raw materials; *Raw Deal* (f)

ray beam of light, skate-like fish; 2004 biopic starring Jamie Foxx; cathode ray (tube), X-ray; ray gun, ray of sunshine; Ray-Bans; *The Man with the X-Ray Eyes* (f), *Ray of Light* (al/s)

rays *see* ray; cosmic rays, gamma rays, ultraviolet rays

razor shaving implement; cut-throat razor, safety razor; razor blade, razor cut, razor shell, razor wire; *The Razor's Edge* (b)

razzle drinking spree; razzle-dazzle; on the razzle

reach scope, stretch of water; arrive at, communicate with; reach out; *Reach for the Sky* (f), *Reach Out I'll Be There* (s)

reaching *see* reach; far-reaching

reaction change in an opposite direction, chemical process involving change, response; chain reaction; *Chain Reaction* (s)

reactor nuclear generator; fast-breeder reactor, nuclear reactor, pressurised water reactor

read interpret written characters, look at (a book), looked at (a book), studied or study (a subject) at university; lip-read, proof-read, sight-read, well-read; read aloud, read-only memory, read out, read through; read between the lines, read my lips, read the Riot Act to, take (it) as read

reader book user, decoder, university lecturer; lay reader, mind-reader; *Reader's Digest* (mag)

reading *see* read; interpretation, sermon; Berkshire town; first reading, map-reading, second reading, third reading; reading age; *The Ballad of Reading Gaol* (po)

ready prepared, willing; prepare (yourself); camera-ready, get ready, make ready, oven-ready, rough and ready; ready-made, ready-mixed, ready money, ready reckoner, ready-to-wear; at the ready, ready to drop; Ever Ready; *Get Ready* (s), *Ready Steady Cook* (tv), *Ready, Steady, Go* (tv)

real Brazilian currency unit; actual, genuine; for real; real ale, real estate, real tennis, real thing, real time; Real Madrid; *The Real Glory* (f), *The Real McCoy* (tv), *The Real Thing* (pl)

realism facing of facts, naturalistic portrayal, practicality; magical realism, social realism, socialist realism

reality genuineness, true life; virtual reality; reality check, reality tv; *Reality Bites* (f), *A Separate Reality* (b)

really genuinely, indeed; The Really Useful Company; *Is She Really Going Out with Him?* (s), *Really Saying Something* (s), *You Really Got Me* (s)

realm   kingdom; peer of the realm; *Defence of the Realm* (f)

reaper   harvest gatherer, harvesting machine; Grim Reaper; *Don't Fear the Reaper* (s)

rear   back, bottom; bring up, rise up on hind legs (of a horse), tend; rear admiral, rear light, rear-view mirror, rear-wheel drive; bring up the rear; *Rear Window* (f)

rearguard   conservative element, defending players, soldiers at the back; rearguard action

reason   cause, logic, power of thought, purpose; argue rationally, think logically; by reason of, it stands to reason, listen to reason, without rhyme or reason; Age of Reason; *The Age of Reason* (b), *Bridget Jones: the Edge of Reason* (b/f), *Reason to Believe* (s)

reasons   *see* reason; *Reasons to be Cheerful* (s)

rebel   insurgent, nonconformist; defy authority; *The Rebel* (f), *Rebel Rebel* (s), *Rebel without a Cause* (f), *Rebel Yell* (s)

rebound   process of springing back; backfire, gather a failed basketball shot; on the rebound

recall   ability to remember things; bring to mind, summon back; beyond recall; *Total Recall* (f)

receive   accept, acquire; it is better to give than to receive

received   *see* receive; received pronunciation

receiving   *see* receive; on the receiving end

reception   formal party, hotel's check-in area, quality of radio or tv signals, welcome; reception desk, reception room

recess   alcove, court's adjournment, Parliamentary break; adjourn, indent

recital   performance of classical music or speech, repetition from memory; piano recital

reckon   calculate, consider, estimate; reckon up

reckoned   *see* reckon; to be reckoned with

reckoner   calculator; ready reckoner

reckoning   *see* reckon; calculation; day of reckoning, dead reckoning; out of the reckoning

recognition   acknowledgement, appreciation; speech recognition

record   best-ever performance, chronicle, music disc before the CD; note down, put on tape; gold record, gramophone record, matter of record, on record, pop record, track record; record-breaking, record player; for the record, hold the record, in record time, off the record, on the record, put the record straight; Public Record Office

recorded   *see* record; pre-recorded; recorded delivery

recorder   registrar, wooden wind instrument; descant recorder, flight recorder, tape recorder, video recorder

recording   *see* record; audio or video transcription; tape recording, video recording; recording studio

recount   additional check (of numbers of votes, eg); narrate, tot up again

recovery   golf shot from a bunker, return to good health, upswing; recovery position

recreation   leisure, simulation; recreation ground

red   communist, primary colour; brick

red, go red, in the red, Rhode Island red, see red; red admiral, red alert, red blood cells, red-blooded, red cabbage, red card, red carpet, red cells, red deer, red dwarf, red ensign, red eye, red-faced, red flag, red giant, red grouse, red-handed, red herring, red hot, red-hot poker, red-letter day, red light, red-light district, red meat, red mullet, red nose, red pepper, red rose, red salmon, red setter, red shift, red snapper, red squirrel, red tape, red wine; (as) red as a beetroot, caught red-handed, like a red rag to a bull, paint the town red, red sky at night shepherd's delight; Great Red Spot, Red Army, Red Berets, Red Crescent, Red Cross, Red Devils, Red Duster, Red Leicester, Red Planet, Red River, Red Sea, Red Sox, Red Square; *The Bride Wore Red* (f), *The Hunt for Red October* (b/f), *Little Red Riding Hood* (b), *Little Red Rooster* (s), *Ninety-Nine Red Balloons* (s), *The Red Badge of Courage* (f), *Red Cap* (tv), *Red Cavalry* (b), *Red Dawn* (f), *Red Dragon* (b/f), *Red Dress* (s), *Red Dust* (f), *Red Dwarf* (tv), *Red Eye* (f), *The Red Flag* (s), *Red Gauntlet* (b), *Red Harvest* (b), *Red Heat* (f), *Red Planet* (f), *Red Red Wine* (s), *Red River* (f), *Red Rock West* (f), *The Red Shoes* (f), *Red Shift* (b), *Red Sonja* (f), *Red Square* (b), *The Thin Red Line* (f)

redress compensation; make amends for; redress the balance

reds *see* red; faction in the Russian Civil War, low-value snooker balls; 1981 Warren Beatty film; reds under the bed

reduce make thicker (a sauce), decrease; reduce to the ranks

reduced *see* reduce; reduced circumstances

reed aquatic plant, vibrating strip in a wind instrument; reed bed, reed bunting, reed pipe, reed warbler

reef ridge of rock or coral under the sea, double knot; barrier reef; reef knot; Great Barrier Reef; *Donovan's Reef* (f)

reefer cigarette containing marijuana, jacket; reefer jacket

reeks smells awful; Macgillicuddy's Reeks

reel lively folk dance, spool; stagger; cotton reel, eightsome reel, hose-reel; reel off, reel-to-reel

refectory communal dining room; refectory table

refer allude (to), turn for information (to); cross-refer; refer to drawer

reference allusion, citation, information source, testimonial; cross reference, frame of reference, map reference, terms of reference, with reference to; reference library, reference point

reflecting contemplating, mirroring, portraying; reflecting telescope

reflections mirror images; *Reflections in a Golden Eye* (f)

reflex angle exceeding 180°, instinctive action; instinctive; single-lens reflex

reform improvement; change for the better, construct again; reform school

reformation improvement; religious change in 16th-century Europe; Counter-Reformation

reformed *see* reform; Reformed Church

refreshment light snack or drink,

renewed strength or spirit;
refreshment room

refugee displaced person; refugee
camp

refusal non-acceptance; first refusal

refuse rubbish; turn down

regained got back; *Paradise
Regained* (po), *Titmuss Regained* (b)

regard admiration, view; consider,
observe

regardless no matter what; regardless
of; *Carry On Regardless* (f)

regards *see* regard; best wishes; as
regards, kind regards

regency interim rule by a stand-in;
Regency buck; *Regency Buck* (b)

regent monarch's stand-in; Prince
Regent, Regent Street, Regent's Park;
Prince Regent (tv)

regime Government, programme;
ancien régime

region area; in the region of

regions *see* region; nether regions

register official list, range of a voice,
tone of language; make an
impression, record, sign in or on;
cash register, parish register; Lloyd's
Register

registered *see* register; registered post

registrar hospital doctor, official
recorder of births, marriages and
deaths, university official; senior
registrar

registration act of noting in the
records, enrolment, roll-call;
registration fee, registration plates

registry church room, official
archives office; registry office

regrets feelings of remorse; feels
sorry about; no regrets; *Miss Otis
Regrets* (s), *No Regrets* (s)

regular habitual customer, soldier; at

constant intervals, usual; regular
soldier; (as) regular as clockwork

rehearsal practice session; dress
rehearsal

reign monarch's period in office; rule;
reign of terror

rein horse's bridle strap; curb; free
rein; keep a tight rein on

reinvent alter radically; reinvent the
wheel

rejection brush-off, renunciation;
rejection slip

rejoin answer, put back together, take
up membership again

relate associate, narrate; marriage-
guidance charity

relation family member, link,
narrative, ratio; blood relation, in
relation to, poor relation

relations *see* relation; dealings;
industrial relations, public relations,
race relations; *Our Relations* (f)

relative family member;
compared (to); blood relative

relay race run in stages; broadcast,
send on; medley relay; relay race

release liberation, newly distributed
film or record; issue, set free; drugs
advisory organisation; day release,
press release, release on bail, re-
release; release date; *Release Me* (s)

relief aid to the needy, alleviation,
projection (in sculpture); bas-relief,
comic relief, in relief, on relief; relief
map, relief road; Comic Relief

religion faith; minister of religion;
Losing My Religion (s)

relish enthusiasm, spicy sauce; greatly
enjoy; Gentleman's Relish

rely depend (on); rely on

remains ashes, leftovers, ruins; stays
behind; *The Remains of the Day* (b/f)

remand committal to custody; keep (in custody); on remand; remand in custody

remedies treatments; makes better, puts right; Bach flower remedies; *Desperate Remedies* (b/f)

remember bring to mind, commemorate, keep information in the mind; *I Remember It Well* (s), *I Remember You* (s), *A Night to Remember* (f), *Remember the Time* (s), *Remember You're a Womble* (s)

remembrance act of honouring the dead, recollection; garden of remembrance; Remembrance Day, Remembrance Service, Remembrance Sunday; *Remembrance of Things Past* (b)

remit area of responsibility; desist from, dispatch, pay

remote tv or video control device; aloof, distant, isolated; remote control, remote-controlled

removal displacement, elimination; removal van

renaissance rebirth; post-medieval European cultural development; Renaissance man

rend split; tear asunder; rend the air

rendered caused to be, melted down (fat), plastered with a first coat, provided; for services rendered

rending *see* rend; heart-rending

renewal extension (of a licence, eg), overhaul; urban renewal

rent large tear, payment to a landlord; hire out, lease; torn; 1996 rock musical; for rent, ground rent, peppercorn rent; rent-a-mob, rent book

repair maintenance; fix, go; repair outfit

repairs *see* repair; running repairs

repayment sum of money reimbursed, type of mortgage; repayment mortgage

repeats encores, tv programmes that have been shown before; reiterates; history repeats itself

repellent substance used to drive away insects; loathsome; water-repellent

repentance remorse; deathbed repentance

repertory store of information, theatre company; repertory company

repetitive monotonous; repetitive strain injury

replacement substitute, successor; hormone replacement therapy

replay follow-up match; listen to again, show (part of a video) again; action replay

reply response; respond; reply coupon

report account of an event, sound of a gun; give an account of; on report; report card, report stage; *The Frost Report* (tv), *Minority Report* (f)

reported *see* report; reported speech

reporter journalist; cub reporter, roving reporter

representative agent, commercial traveller, person elected to a legislative assembly; serving as a symbol (of), typical (of); sales representative

representatives *see* representative; House of Representatives

reproach admonish; beyond reproach

republic country with an elected head of state; banana republic; Central African Republic, Czech Republic, Dominican Republic, Republic of Ireland, Weimar Republic; *Banana*

Republic (s), *The Republic* (b)

request application, polite demand; ask for; request stop

requiem Mass for the souls of the dead; musical work by Mozart or Verdi; requiem Mass; *Requiem for a Dream* (b/f), *Requiem Mass* (cl)

rescue liberation; save from danger; air-sea rescue; *Emotional Rescue* (s), *Pet Rescue* (tv), *Rescue Me* (s/tv)

research academic investigation; investigate; market research, operations research; research and development, research chemist

researcher investigator, person conducting experiments; market researcher

resemblance likeness; passing resemblance

reservation advance booking, doubt, land set aside for Native Americans, proviso; central reservation

reserve substitute (player), timidity; book in advance; animal reserve, gold reserve, nature reserve; reserve price; Federal Reserve

reserved *see* reserve; shy; reserved list, reserved occupation

reserves *see* reserve; club's second team, spares; gold reserves, hidden reserves

reservoir artificial lake; *Reservoir Dogs* (f)

residence dwelling, length of stay somewhere; artist in residence, writer-in-residence

resident occupant; in-house; *Resident Evil* (f/ga)

resignation giving up of a job, passive acceptance

resigned left your job, stood down; acquiescent

resistance body's ability to fight disease, opposition, opposition to the conductance of electricity; WWII French underground movement; consumer resistance, electrical resistance, non-resistance, passive resistance, pièce de résistance; the line/path of least resistance

resolution degree of detail visible in an image, determination, firm decision made at New Year, formal proposal; conflict resolution, New Year's resolution

resort option, tourist centre; arrange again, turn (to); health resort, last resort, seaside resort; as a last resort

resources available supplies; provides money for; natural resources

respects messages of esteem; esteems; pay your respects

respiration mechanism of breathing; artificial respiration

respite breathing space; respite care

rest relaxation, remainder; take a break; back-rest, come to rest, day of rest, lay to rest; rest cure, rest home, rest in peace; a change is as good as a rest, no rest for the wicked, the rest is history, rest on your laurels, rest on your oars

restaurant eating-place; restaurant car; *Alice's Restaurant* (f), *The Restaurant at the End of the Universe* (b)

restoration bringing back (of a previous practice), process of repairing a building; Charles II's reign; tv programme with Griff Rhys Jones; Restoration play

restorer craftsman; hair restorer, picture restorer

results consequences, scores; ends (in), ensues; get results

resume   summary, US curriculum vitae; start up again

retail   sale of goods; sell to the public; retail price index, retail therapy

retainer   fee to secure future services, long-standing servant

retirement   seclusion, time after your working life; semi-retirement; retirement pension

retiring   giving up work for good, going to bed; shy

retort   distillation vessel, quick witty answer; answer back

retreat   secluded private place, withdrawal; withdraw; beat a (hasty) retreat; *No Retreat, No Surrender* (f)

retriever   breed of hunting dog; golden retriever

retro   redolent of an earlier era; retro-active, retro-rocket

retrospect   contemplation of the past; in retrospect

return   computer's enter key, homecoming, profit, recurrence, round-trip ticket, (tax) statement; come back, elect to Parliament, give back; by return, carriage return, day return, sale or return, tax return; return ticket; point of no return return the compliment; *Return of the Jedi* (f), *The Return of the Living Dead* (f), *The Return of the Native* (b), *The Return of the Prodigal Son* (pa), *Return to River Cottage* (tv), *Return to Sender* (s)

returning   *see* return; returning officer

returns   *see* return; many happy returns (of the day); *Batman Returns* (f)

reunion   get-together; Indian Ocean island; family reunion; *The Family Reunion* (pl), *Mother and Child Reunion* (s), *Romy and Michele's High School Reunion* (f)

rev   cycle of the internal combustion engine; increase an engine's speed; rev counter, rev up

revenge   eye for an eye; ship commanded by Admiral Grenville; Montezuma's revenge; revenge is sweet; *Revenge of the Nerds* (f), *Star Wars: Episode III – Revenge of the Sith* (f)

revenue   income; Inland Revenue

reverend   vicar's title; clerical; Most Reverend, Reverend Mother, Right Reverend, Very Reverend

reverse   'backwards' gear of a car, setback, tails side of a coin; drive (a car) backwards, turn around; opposite; reverse arms, reverse gear; reverse the charges; *King Midas in Reverse* (s)

reversing   *see* reverse; reversing light

review   appraisal; assess; judicial review

revisited   called on again, went back to; *Brideshead Revisited* (b/tv)

revolt   insurgency; disgust; Peasants' Revolt

revolution   dramatic change, recurrence in cycles, single complete orbit; Beatles song; counter-revolution, industrial revolution, palace revolution; Cultural Revolution, French Revolution, Velvet Revolution; *Children of the Revolution* (s)

Revolution

American, Bulldozer, Carnation, Cedar, Cultural, February, French, Glorious, Hungarian, Industrial, October, Orange, Rose, Tulip, Velvet

---

revolutionary political rebel; involving dramatic change; counter-revolutionary

revolutions *see* revolution; *The Matrix Revolutions* (f)

revolving rotating; revolving door

rhapsody emotional piece of music, expression of ecstatic enthusiasm; *Bohemian Rhapsody* (s), *Rhapsody in Blue* (cl)

rhesus factor found in blood, species of monkey; rhesus factor, rhesus monkey, rhesus negative, rhesus positive

rhetorical relating to the art of effective speaking, requiring no answer (question); rhetorical question

rhinoceros large ungulate; play by Eugène Ionesco; rhinoceros beetle

rhyme verse; have the same end-sound (of a line of verse); nursery rhyme; without rhyme or reason

rhymed *see* rhyme; *Nothing Rhymed* (s)

rhyming *see* rhyme; Cockney rhyming slang; rhyming slang

rhythm musical beat, section of a dance band; circadian rhythm; rhythm and blues, rhythm section; *Hit Me with Your Rhythm Stick* (s), *I Got Rhythm* (s), *Rhythm of My Heart* (s), *Star Spangled Rhythm* (f)

rib bone of the torso; tease; floating rib, skinny-rib; rib-eye, rib-tickling; *Adam's Rib* (f), *Spare Rib* (mag)

ribbon hair tie, stripe of colour; streak; ribbon development; *She Wore a Yellow Ribbon* (f), *Tie a Yellow Ribbon Round the Ole Oak Tree* (s)

ribbons *see* ribbon; cut/tear to ribbons; *Scarlet Ribbons* (s)

ribs *see* rib; spare ribs

rice cereal grass; basmati rice, brown rice, fried rice, wild rice; rice paper, rice pudding

rich abounding (in), creamy, fertile, opulent, wealthy; rich pickings; get rich quick; *If I Were a Rich Man* (s), *Rich and Famous* (f), *Rich Man Poor Man* (b)

riddance disposal of an unwanted person or thing; good riddance

riddle puzzle, sieve; fill with holes; *The Riddle of the Sands* (b)

ride fairground attraction, journey; travel on an animal or by vehicle; free ride, park-and-ride; ride roughshod over; Dial-a-Ride; *Morningtown Ride* (s), *Ride a White Swan* (s), *Ride on Time* (s), *Ticket to Ride* (s)

rider clause added to a document, jockey; dispatch rider; *Easy Rider* (f), *Knight Rider* (tv), *Pale Rider* (f), *Whale Rider* (f)

rides *see* ride; *Destry Rides Again* (f), *The Devil Rides Out* (b/f), *Rural Rides* (b)

ridge apex of a roof, narrow top or crest, raised strip; wrinkle; ridge tent, ridge tile

riding *see* ride; equestrianism; former division of Yorkshire; horse riding; riding crop, riding habit, riding school; *Little Red Riding Hood* (b)

riff repeated musical phrase played on a guitar; play a musical refrain repeatedly; riff-raff

rifle firearm; rummage; air rifle, Winchester rifle; rifle range

rifles *see* rifle; *The Eton Rifles* (s)

rift breach, split; cleave; rift valley; Great Rift Valley

rig costume, oil platform, sailing tackle; fit with sails, fraudulently organise, kit out; oil rig; Rig Veda

rigged *see* rig; square-rigged

right entitlement, prerogative, side of the House inclined towards Conservatism; rectify; correct; correctly; all right, just right, public lending right; right about, right angle, right away, right back, right hand, right-hand drive, right-hand man, right-handed, right-minded, right of abode, right of way, right on, right-thinking, right whale, right wing, right-winger; (as) right as rain, at right angles, a bit of all right, the customer is always right, divine right of kings, err on the right side, get off on the right foot, hit the right note, not to put a foot right, on the right side of, play your cards right, right as rain, right up your street, right, left and centre, serves you right, start off on the right foot, strike the right note, two wrongs don't make a right; Mr Right, Right Honourable, Right Reverend; *All Right Now* (s), *The Divine Right of Kings* (po), *Do the Right Thing* (f), *Have I the Right* (s), *He Knew He Was Right* (b/tv), *I'm All Right Jack* (f), *Play Your Cards Right* (tv), *The Price Is Right* (tv), *Right By Your Side* (s), *Right Said Fred* (s), *The Right Stuff* (b/f), *Walk Right Back* (s)

rights *see* right; bill of rights, civil rights, human rights, mineral rights; rights issue

ring boxing or circus arena, cartel, circle, finger-band, telephone call; call by phone, encircle, chime; boxing ring, diamond ring, engagement ring, eternity ring, fairy ring, growth ring, key-ring, piston ring, signet ring, teething ring, three-ring circus, wedding ring; ring a bell, ring binder, ring-dotterel, ring-dove, ring fence, ring finger, ring main, ring off, ring out, ring ouzel, ring pull, ring road, ring round, ring-tailed lemur, ring up; hold the ring, ring the changes, throw your hat into the ring; Avebury Ring, Pacific Ring of Fire; *Brown Girl in the Ring* (s), *The Ring* (f/o), *Ring-a-Ring-o'-Roses* (s), *Ring My Bell* (s), *Ring of Bright Water* (b/f)

ringer campanologist, impostor, lookalike; bell-ringer, dead ringer; *Dead Ringer* (f), *Dead Ringer for Love* (s)

ringers *see* ringer; quoits; *Dead Ringers* (f/r/tv)

ringing *see* ring; bell-ringing, change-ringing; *The Singing, Ringing Tree* (tv)

rings *see* ring; gymnastics apparatus; engagement rings, fairy rings, growth rings; run rings round; *The Lord of the Rings* (b/f), *The Postman Always Rings Twice* (b/f)

ringside spectators' area at a boxing match; ringside seat

rink ice-skating venue; ice rink, skating rink

rinse temporary hair-tint; wash out in clean water; blue rinse; rinse out

riot striking display (of colour), violent public disturbance, wildly enjoyable event; go on the rampage; run riot; riot gear, riot squad; read the Riot Act to; Riot Act; *I Predict a Riot* (s)

riotous boisterous, wildly funny; *Riotous Assembly* (b)

rip dangerous undercurrent, tear; tear

open; let rip; rip current, rip off, rip-roaring, rip up

ripping   *see* rip; dated term meaning 'excellent'; *Ripping Yarns* (tv)

rise   increase (in salary, eg); ascend, get out of bed, grow; 2000 Gabrielle chart-topper; high-rise, low-rise, on the rise; make your hackles rise, rise and shine, rise from the ashes, rise to the bait, rise to the occasion; *The Fall and Rise of Reginald Perrin* (tv), *Lark Rise to Candleford* (b), *The Resistible Rise of Arturo Ui* (pl)

rises   *see* rise; *The Sun Also Rises* (b)

rising   *see* rise; insurrection; rising damp, rising sun; Easter Rising; *Bad Moon Rising* (s), *House of the Rising Sun* (s), *Rising Damp* (tv)

risk   danger, gamble; chance, endanger; 1978 Dick Francis novel; board-game; at risk, fire risk, run a risk, take a risk; at your own risk

rites   ceremonial acts, sacraments; last rites; rites of passage; *Rites of Passage* (b)

rivals   challengers; stands in competition with; 1988 Jilly Cooper novel; *The Rivals* (pl)

river   large stream of fresh water; river-mouth; sell down the river, up the river; Crocodile River, Red River, Yellow River; *The Bridge on the River Kwai* (f), *Moon River* (s), *Mystic River* (f), *Ol' Man River* (s), *Red River* (f), *Return to River Cottage* (tv), *The River* (f), *River Deep Mountain High* (s), *A River Runs through It* (f), *Up the River* (f)

rivers   *see* river; *Rivers of Babylon* (s)

riveter   metalworker; *Rosie the Riveter* (f)

road   thoroughfare; A-road, high road, main road, middle of the road, off-road, on the road, relief road, ring road, Roman road, service road, side road, slip road, trunk road; road hog, road-holding, road hump, road manager, road map, road metal, road movie, road rage, road sign, road tax, road test, road user; down the road, the end of the road, gentleman of the road, hit the road, knight of the road, one for the road, rule of the road; Abbey Road, Caledonian Road, Edgware Road, Elland Road, Euston Road, Gloucester Road, Goldhawk Road, Holloway Road, Lansdowne Road, Maine Road, Old Kent Road, Tottenham Court Road, Yellow Brick Road; *Abbey Road* (al), *The Crow Road* (b), *The Famished Road* (b), *Goodbye Yellow Brick Road* (s), *Hit the Road Jack* (s), *King of the Road* (s), *The Long and Winding Road* (s), *On the Road* (b), *On the Road Again* (s), *Road House* (f), *Road to Bali* (f), *Road to Hong Kong* (f), *Road to Morocco* (f), *Road to Rio* (f), *Road to Singapore* (f), *The Road to Wigan Pier* (b), *Road to Zanzibar* (f), *Take the High Road* (tv), *Tobacco Road* (b/f/s)

Road

Abbey, Burma, Caledonian, Carrow, Edgware, Euston, Gloucester, Goldhawk, Great North, Holloway, Lansdowne, Loftus, Old Kent, Portman, Tottenham Court, Vicarage, Yellow Brick

---

roads   *see* road; all roads lead to Rome; *The Roads to Freedom* (b), *Take Me Home Country Roads* (s)

roadshow   promotional tour; *Antiques Roadshow* (tv)

roan   horse of mixed colour; strawberry roan

roared   bellowed, laughed loudly; *The Mouse That Roared* (f)

roaring   *see* roared; a roaring trade, rip-roaring; The Roaring Forties; *The Roaring Twenties* (f)

roast   joint of meat; bake in the oven, severely criticise, swelter; pot roast, spit-roast; roast beef, roast duck, roast turkey

rob   deprive (of), steal from; rob Peter to pay Paul; *Rob Roy* (b/f)

robber   thief; grave robber; robber baron

robbery   theft; 1967 Stanley Baker film; daylight robbery; Great Train Robbery

robe   long loose outer garment, official gown; dress; *Black Robe* (f), *The Robe* (f)

robes   *see* robe; Mistress of the Robes

robin   red-breasted songbird; ragged robin, round robin; robin redbreast; Robin Hood's Bay; *The Adventures of Robin Hood* (f/tv), *Robin's Nest* (tv)

robot   android; *I Robot* (b/f), *Robot Wars* (tv)

rock   boulder, hard seaside sweet, mass of stone, style of pop music; gently sway, shake; folk rock, glam rock, hard rock, punk rock, stick of rock; rock bottom, rock cake, rock climbing, rock face, rock garden, rock pool, rock salmon, rock salt, rock singer, rock solid, rock-steady; between a rock and a hard place, (don't) rock the boat; Ayers Rock, Bishop Rock, Little Rock, Rock of Gibraltar, Wolf Rock; *Bad Day at Black Rock* (f), *Brighton Rock* (b/f), *Crocodile Rock* (s), *Don't Rock the Boat* (s/tv), *The Hot Rock* (f), *I Am a Rock* (s), *Jailhouse Rock* (s/f), *Picnic at Hanging Rock* (f), *Red Rock West* (f), *Rock Around the Clock* (s), *Rock DJ* (s), *Rock Follies* (tv), *Rock Lobster* (s), *Rock Me Amadeus* (s), *Rock of Ages* (s), *Rock the Boat* (s), *The School of Rock* (f), *Third Rock from the Sun* (tv), *Will Success Spoil Rock Hunter?* (f)

rocker   leather-clad 1960s teenager, swaying chair; rocker switch; off your rocker

rockers   *see* rocker; mods and rockers

rocket   leafy salad vegetable, missile, soaring firework, spacecraft; shoot up rapidly, soar; Stephenson's famous locomotive; retro-rocket; rocket scientist; *Rocket Man* (s)

rocking   *see* rock; rocking chair, rocking horse; *Rocking All Over the World* (s)

rocks   *see* rock; on the rocks; *The Hand That Rocks the Cradle* (f), *Love on the Rocks* (s)

rocky   stony, unsteady; 1976 Sylvester Stallone film; Rocky Mountains; *The Rocky Horror Picture Show* (mus), *The Rocky Horror Show* (mus)

rod   angling pole, long stick; Aaron's rod, connecting rod, divining rod, dowel rod, fishing rod, golden rod, hot rod, stair rod; rod of iron; kiss the rod, make a rod for your own back, rule with a rod of iron; Black Rod; *Spare the Rod* (f)

roe   fish-eggs, species of deer; soft roe; roe deer

rogue   animal driven from its herd, scoundrel; rogue elephant; *Rogue Male* (b/tv), *Rogue Trader* (f), *Rogue Traders* (tv)

rogues   *see* rogue; rogues' gallery

role dramatic part, function in life; cameo role, passive role, title role; role model, role playing

roll bap, list of names, spinning movement; move like a ball, move on wheels, turn (over); anti-roll bar, barrel roll, bread roll, bridge roll, drum roll, electoral roll, Eskimo roll, fig roll, finger roll, French roll, kitchen roll, piano roll, rag-roll, sausage roll, spring roll, Swiss roll, toilet roll, victory roll, western roll; roll back, roll-call, roll neck, roll-on, roll-on roll-off, roll over, roll-top desk, roll up; *Roll Over Beethoven* (s), *Roll with It* (s), *Shake, Rattle and Roll* (s)

rolled *see* roll; rag-rolled; rolled gold, rolled oats

roller big wave, hair-curler, painting tool, road-levelling machine, tumbler pigeon; high roller, holy roller; roller blind, roller skates, roller-skating, roller-towel; *Holy Roller* (s)

rolling *see* roll; log-rolling; rolling pin, rolling stock, rolling stone; get/keep the ball rolling, rolling in money, rolling in the aisles, a rolling stone gathers no moss, set/start the ball rolling; *Like a Rolling Stone* (s)

rolls *see* roll; Master of the Rolls, Rolls-Royce

romance love, love affair, love story; woo; language family; *A Fine Romance* (tv), *True Romance* (f)

rood crucifix, old land measure; rood screen

roof top of a building or car; cover the top of (a building); roof garden, roof of the mouth, roof rack; go through the roof, hit the roof, like a cat on a hot tin roof, raise the roof; Roof of the World; *Cat on a Hot Tin Roof* (f/pl), *Fiddler on the Roof* (mus)

rook crow-like bird, chess piece; swindle

rookery overcrowded area, penguins' breeding colony; *Rookery Nook* (pl)

rookie new recruit; *The Rookie* (f)

room chamber, space; auction room, back room, barrack-room lawyer, chat room, common room, day room, delivery room, dining room, dining-room table, drawing room, dressing-room, elbow-room, engine room, fitting room, green room, grill room, incident room, junior common room, ladies' room, living room, locker room, lumber room, mess-room, operations room, orderly room, powder room, reception room, refreshment room, senior common room, shelf room, sitting room, tea room, utility room, waiting room; room service, room temperature, room-mate; no room to swing a cat, room for improvement; *Barrack-Room Ballads* (po), *Giovanni's Room* (b), *The L-Shaped Room* (b/f), *Panic Room* (f), *Room 101* (tv), *Room at the Top* (b/f), *Room for Improvement* (tv), *Room Service* (f), *A Room with a View* (b/f), *The Shuttered Room* (f), *The Women's Room* (b)

rooms *see* room; assembly rooms; *Changing Rooms* (tv)

roost bird's perch; sleep on a perch (bird); rule the roost; *Home to Roost* (tv)

rooster cockerel; *Little Red Rooster* (s), *Rooster Cogburn* (f)

root source, underground part of a plant; cheer (for), rummage; cube root, square root, take root; root and branch, root beer, root canal, root cause, root out, root vegetable

rooted   *see* root; embedded; deep-rooted; rooted to the spot

roots   *see* root; heritage; 1977 tv saga based on an Alex Haley book; grass roots; put down roots

rope   string (of pearls), thick cord; tether; 1948 Hitchcock thriller; guy-rope, Indian rope-trick, skipping rope, tow-rope; rope in, rope ladder, rope of sand; money for old rope

ropes   *see* rope; know/learn the ropes

rose   fragrant garden flower, pink wine (rosé), watering can's nozzle; ascended, got out of bed; China rose, Christmas rose, compass rose, damask rose, dog rose, English rose, red rose, tea rose, Tudor rose, white rose, yellow rose; rose bowl, rose bush, rose garden, rose of Sharon, rose-tinted, rose water, rose window; Marie Rose, Mary Rose; *Kiss from a Rose* (s), *Mary Rose* (pl), *The Name of the Rose* (b/f), *The Purple Rose of Cairo* (f), *Ramblin' Rose* (s), *Rambling Rose* (f), *The Rose* (f), *Rose Garden* (s), *The Rose of Tralee* (s), *The Rose Tattoo* (f/pl), *Second Hand Rose* (s), *The Slipper and the Rose* (f), *The Yellow Rose of Texas* (s)

rosehip   berry-like fruit; rosehip syrup

rosemary   herb; *Rosemary and Thyme* (tv), *Rosemary's Baby* (f)

roses   *see* rose; bed of roses, dog roses; come up smelling of roses; Wars of the Roses; *Days of Wine and Roses* (f/s), *Good Year for the Roses* (s), *Ring-a-Ring-o'-Roses* (s), *The War of the Roses* (f)

rot   damaging fungus, nonsense; go bad or mouldy; dry rot, foot rot, gut-

rot, noble rot, wet rot; stop the rot; *Dry Rot* (f/pl)

rotary   moving around an axis, type of circular washing line; Rotary Club

rotten   bad, mouldy; rotten apple, rotten borough; Rotten Row; *Dirty Rotten Scoundrels* (f)

rouge   powder for the cheeks; Baton Rouge, Khmer Rouge, Moulin Rouge; *Moulin Rouge* (f), *Le Rouge et le Noir* (b)

rough   crude preliminary sketch, hooligan; approximate, coarse, harsh, unwell; in the rough, live rough, sleep rough; rough and ready, rough and tumble, rough cut, rough diamond, rough edges, rough guide rough-hewn, rough idea, rough it, rough justice, rough stuff; take the rough with the smooth; *Rough Cut* (f), *Rough Guide* (tv)

roulette   casino game; Russian roulette; roulette wheel

round   amount of ammunition, circular song, division in a boxing match etc, drinks for a group, regular trip made by a postman or milkman, eg, stage of competitions; finish (off), make circular; circular, whole (number); all-round, gather round, merry-go-round, milk round, paper round, ring round, scout round, turn round, whip-round, year-round; round dance, round robin, round-shouldered, round table, round the bend, round the clock, round the twist, round trip, round up; get your tongue round, go round in circles, go round the bend, go round the houses, pass the hat round, run rings round, run round in circles, a square peg in a round hole; *Here We Go Round the Mulberry Bush* (f/s), *Round*

Midnight (f), *Round the Horne* (r)

roundabout   carousel, road junction, circumlocutory; *The Magic Roundabout* (f/tv)

rounded   *see* round; circular, plump; well rounded

rounder   complete circuit in a game like baseball; more circular; all-rounder

rousing   awakening, lively; rabble-rousing

rout   overwhelming defeat; defeat and put to flight; put to rout

route   course of travel; en route, escape route; route march

routine   daily habits, entertainer's act; run-of-the-mill

rover   wanderer; make of car; Land Rover

rovers   *see* rover; Blackburn Rovers, Doncaster Rovers, Bristol Rovers, Raith Rovers, Tranmere Rovers; *Roy of the Rovers* (mag)

> **Rovers**
> Albion, Blackburn, Bristol, Doncaster, Raith, Tranmere

roving   wandering; roving reporter

row   argument, hubbub, line, tier; have an argument, propel (a boat) with oars; back row, skid row; Rotten Row, Savile Row; *The Boat That I Row* (s), *Cannery Row* (b/f), *Front Row* (r), *King's Row* (f)

rowing   *see* row; Olympic water sport; rowing boat, rowing machine; *Rowing in Eden* (b/po)

royal   of the monarchy; battle royal; royal assent, royal blue, royal box, royal command performance, royal flush, royal icing, royal jelly, royal

standard, royal warrant, royal yacht; Ark Royal, Astronomer Royal, Marshal of the Royal Air Force, Park Royal, Princess Royal, Royal Academy, Royal Academy of Arts, Royal Air Force, Royal Albert Hall, Royal Artillery, Royal Ascot, Royal Commission, Royal Courts of Justice, Royal Engineers, Royal Festival Hall, Royal Gala, Royal Mail, Royal Marines, Royal Mile, Royal Pavilion, Royal Society, Royal Tunbridge Wells; *The Royal* (tv), *The Royal Tenenbaums* (f)

rub   impediment, massage; chafe, massage, polish up; rub down, rub it in, rub noses, rub out, rub shoulders; rub of the green, rub salt into the wound, rub up the wrong way, rub your hands, rub your nose in it

rubber   bridge session, eraser, latex; burn rubber, India rubber; rubber band, rubber bullets, rubber gloves, rubber plant, rubber stamp, rubber tree; *Rubber Bullets* (s), *Rubber Soul* (al)

rubbing   *see* rub; impression of a design on brass or stone; brass-rubbing

ruby   red gemstone; ruby wedding; *Ruby Tuesday* (s)

rude   impolite, roughly made; rude boy

ruffian   thug; *The Ruffian on the Stair* (pl)

rug   floor mat, travelling blanket; hearth-rug, prayer rug, scatter rug; rug rat

rugby   team sport played with an oval ball; Midlands town and public school; rugby ball, rugby fives, rugby league, rugby union

ruin   crumbling building, downfall;

wreck; mother's ruin

ruins *see* ruin; old remains of buildings; in ruins

rule maxim, measuring-strip, regulation, reign; be prevalent, draw (a straight line) with a measuring-strip, reign; golden rule, ground rule, home rule, majority rule, mob rule, self-rule, slide rule, work to rule; rule of law, rule of the road, rule of thumb, rule out, rule the roost, rule with a rod of iron; as a rule, divide and rule, the exception proves the rule, run the rule over; *Everybody Wants to Rule the World* (s), *Rule Britannia* (s)

rules *see* rule; conditions of a game; ground rules; rules are made to be broken; Australian Rules, Queensberry Rules; *The Cider House Rules* (b/f)

ruling *see* rule; *The Ruling Class* (f)

rum spirit made from sugar cane; odd; Inner Hebrides isle; Jamaica rum; rum baba, rum butter

rumble noise of thunder; discover (a plot); rumble strip; *Rumble Fish* (f)

rummage stowage (of casks) in a ship's hold, thorough search; poke around; rummage sale

rump cut of beefsteak, hindquarters, remnant; Parliament of 1648; rump steak

run circuit of duty, enclosure for chickens etc, ladder in tights or stockings, race, score in cricket, series, stretch, theatre success, trip; be in charge of, control, flee, flow, hurry, manage, organise, smuggle, sprint, stand (for office); chicken run, close-run thing, cut and run, dry run, dummy run, fun run, home run, milk run, on the run, print run, rat

run, sheep-run, ski run, tip-and-run, trial run; run a blockade, run a mile, run a risk, run amok, run around, run away, run down, run in, run into, run low, run of the mill, run off, run out, run riot, run the gamut, run through, run-time, run up, run wild; in the long run, learn to walk before you run, make your blood run cold, run a tight ship, run out of petrol, run out of steam, run rings round, run round in circles, run the rule over, still waters run deep; Cresta Run; *Band on the Run* (s), *Chicken Run* (f), *Logan's Run* (f), *Midnight Run* (f), *Rabbit, Run* (b), *Run for Home* (s), *Run Lola Run* (f), *Run to You* (s), *Still Waters Run Deep* (s), *Take the Money and Run* (f), *Young Hearts Run Free* (s)

runaway deserter; overwhelming; Del Shannon hit; runaway train; *Runaway Bride* (f), *The Runaway Bus* (b), *Runaway Jury* (b/f), *Runaway Train* (f)

rung *see* ring; step of a ladder

runner blade of a sedge, jogger, messenger, narrow strip of carpet; distance runner, front-runner, marathon runner, scarlet runner; runner beans, runner-up; do a runner; Bow Street Runner; *Blade Runner* (f), *The Loneliness of the Long Distance Runner* (b/f)

running *see* run; continuous, in operation; up and running; running battle, running-board, running commentary, running costs, running knot, running mate, running repairs, running scared, running stitch; hit the ground running, in the running, make the running, out of the running, take up the running, running on empty; *Keep On Running* (s), *The Running Man* (f), *Running on Empty* (f), *Running Scared* (f/s)

runs *see* run; *A River Runs through It* (f)

rush grass-like plant, haste, sudden demand; hurry; 1991 film about undercover cops and drugs; gold rush; rush hour, rush of blood; rush of blood to the head, rush your fences; *After the Gold Rush* (al), *The Gold Rush* (f), *Rush Hour* (f), *Sugar Rush* (b/tv)

rust iron oxide, reddish-brown colour; become inefficient through inaction, corrode; rust-bucket

rusticated banished to the country, covered with large blocks and a roughened surface (building), suspended temporarily from university

rustle soft crackling sound; steal (cattle); rustle up

rut groove, humdrum existence, mating season for deer; in a rut

ruthless hard-hearted; *Ruthless People* (f)

rye cereal crop; East Sussex town; rye bread, rye grass; *The Ballad of Peckham Rye* (b), *The Catcher in the Rye* (b), *A Pocket Full of Rye* (b)

S

sabre sword; sabre-rattling, sabre-toothed tiger; *Sabre Dance* (cl)
sabres *see* sabre; rattle sabres
sac internal pouch; air sac, cul-de-sac; *Cul-de-Sac* (f)
sack bag, dismissal, dry Spanish wine; dismiss, plunder; stuff sack; sack race; hit the sack
sackcloth hessian; sackcloth and ashes
sacred holy; sacred cow; *The Sacred and Profane Love Machine* (b)
sad unhappy; *The Ballad of the Sad Cafe* (f)
saddle lamb cut, seat on a horse or bicycle; burden (with); in the saddle, side-saddle; saddle soap, saddle-sore, saddle stitch
saddles *see* saddle; *Blazing Saddles* (f)
safari wildlife expedition; on safari; safari jacket, safari park, safari suit
safe strongbox; out of harm's way, secure; fail-safe, night safe, play safe; safe and sound, safe bet, safe-breaker,

safe-cracker, safe conduct, safe house, safe keeping, safe seat; better safe than sorry, to be on the safe side; *Fail Safe* (f)
safety freedom from danger; safety belt, safety cage, safety catch, safety curtain, safety deposit, safety first, safety glass, safety lamp, safety matches, safety net, safety pin, safety razor, safety valve
saffron orange-yellow colour, spice; Saffron Walden
saga lengthy tale, Norse legend; holiday company for older people; *The Forsyte Saga* (b/tv)
sage
herb, shade of green, wise person; wise; sage and onion, sage-green; Sage Derby
said *see* say; easier said than done, enough said, that said, when all is said and done; Port Said; *All the Things She Said* (s), *Right Said Fred* (s)
sail cloth on a boat; travel on water;

set sail, under sail; sail along; sail close to the wind, sail near the wind, sail under false colours

sailing   *see* sail; maritime pursuit; Rod Stewart hit; plain sailing; sailing boat, sailing ship

sailor   seafarer; sailor suit; *Sailor Beware* (f), *Sinbad the Sailor* (f)

sailors   *see* sailor; sailors' hornpipe

sails   *see* sail; take the wind out of your sails, trim your sails

saint   canonised person; patron saint; saint's day; Nuits-Saint-Georges; *Blue Murder at St Trinian's* (f), *The Pure Hell of St Trinian's* (f), *The Saint* (f/tv), *St Elsewhere* (tv)

saints   *see* saint; Southampton FC nickname; All Saints, All Saints' Day, Latter-Day Saints

sake   behalf, Japanese rice wine; art for art's sake, for Pete's sake, for pity's sake, for the sake of argument; *Art for Art's Sake* (s), *For Pete's Sake* (f)

salad   cold dish of raw vegetables; Caesar salad, fruit salad, Russian salad, side salad, Waldorf salad; salad cream, salad days, salad dressing, salad oil; *Salad Days* (mus)

sale   auction, exchange of items for money, period of reduced prices; Greater Manchester town; bill of sale, bring and buy sale, car boot sale, clearance sale, fire sale, for sale, garage sale, jumble sale, on sale, rummage sale; sale or return; *Sale of the Century* (tv)

sales   *see* sale; January sales; sales assistant, sales clerk, sales representative

salesman   commercial traveller, vendor; travelling salesman; *Death of a Salesman* (pl)

sally   attack; go forth; sally port; Aunt Sally, Sally Lunn; *Long Tall Sally* (s), *When Harry Met Sally* (f)

salmon   pink-fleshed fish, pinkish-orange colour; red salmon, rock salmon; salmon pink

salon   beauty parlour, social gathering of writers or artists, reception room; beauty salon

saloon   bar in a pub, enclosed motor car, public room on a ship; saloon car

salsa   Latin American dance, spicy Mexican sauce; salsa verde

salt   chemical compound, common condiment, sailor; season; rock salt, sea salt; salt and pepper, salt and vinegar, salt cellar, salt flats, salt lake, salt marsh, salt spoon, salt water; rub salt into the wound, sit below the salt, take with a pinch of salt, the salt of the earth; Salt Lake City

salted   *see* salt; salted peanuts

salts   *see* salt; bath salts, Epsom salts, liver salts, smelling salts; like a dose of salts

salute   military greeting; hail in military manner; clenched-fist salute

salvation   redemption, rescue; Salvation Army

salve   ointment; soothe; lip-salve

same   identical; all the same, at the same time, by the same token, cut from the same cloth, in the same boat, just the same, not in the same league, on the same page, same again, same difference, same here, same to you, the same old story, speak the same language, tar with the same brush; *That Same Old Feeling* (s)

sample   specimen; try; free sample

samurai   Old Japanese warrior(s); *The Last Samurai* (f), *The Seven Samurai* (f)

sanction   official permission, penalty for breaking laws; authorise, endorse; *The Eiger Sanction* (b/f)

sanctum   holy or private place; inner sanctum; sanctum sanctorum

sand   tiny particles on the beach; polish with abrasive material; rope of sand; sand dune, sand iron, sand martin, sand-snake, sand-trap, sand wedge; bury your head in the sand; *Blood and Sand* (f), *The Sand Pebbles* (f)

sands   *see* sand; beaches; the sands of time; Goodwin Sands; *The Riddle of the Sands* (b), *Sands of Iwo Jima* (f), *Sands of the Kalahari* (f)

sandwich   snack of bread with a filling; place between two layers; Cinque Port; club sandwich, knuckle sandwich, open sandwich, Victoria sandwich; sandwich board, sandwich course, sandwich man, Sandwich tern

sandy   yellowish-beige in colour; Bedfordshire town; song from *Grease*; Great Sandy Desert

sap   fool, plant's juice, wartime trench; drain, weaken

sapphire   blue gemstone; *Sapphire and Steel* (tv)

sardines   young pilchards; packed like sardines

sash   sliding window frame, waist or shoulder band; sash cord, sash window

sat   *see* sit; *By Grand Central Station I Sat Down and Wept* (b)

satanic   devilish; *The Satanic Verses* (b)

satellite   body orbiting around a planet, subordinate state; communications satellite; satellite dish, satellite telephone, satellite television

satin   smooth glossy fabric; satin stitch; *Nights in White Satin* (s)

satisfaction   pleasure, redress; Rolling Stones song; job satisfaction, self-satisfaction

saturation   state of being thoroughly wet, very full extent; saturation point

sauce   cheek, dressing poured over food; make piquant; apple sauce, barbecue sauce, Béarnaise sauce, black bean sauce, bread sauce, brown sauce, hoisin sauce, hollandaise sauce, mint sauce, mornay sauce, oyster sauce, soy sauce, tartare sauce, white sauce, Worcester sauce; sauce boat

saucer   part of a tea set, shallow dish; cup and saucer, flying saucer

sausage   meat product; Cumberland sausage, liver sausage, not a sausage; sausage and mash, sausage dog, sausage meat, sausage roll

savage   ferocious; maul; noble savage; *Savage Messiah* (f)

save   prevention (of a goal); keep, prevent (a goal), put money by regularly, rescue, update (a computer file); with the exception of; save face, save the day, save up; save your bacon, save your breath, save your skin; Save the Children Fund; *God Save the Queen* (s), *How to Save Your Own Life* (b), *Save a Prayer* (s), *Save the Last Dance for Me* (s), *Save the Tiger* (f), *Save Your Kisses for Me* (s)

saved   *see* save; saved by the bell; *Last Night a DJ Saved My Life* (s)

saver   investor; face-saver, screen saver

saves   *see* save; a stitch in time saves nine

saving   *see* save; face-saving, labour-saving; saving grace; *Saving Grace* (f),

Saving Private Ryan (f)

savings   economies, nest eggs; life savings; savings account, savings bank; National Savings Bank

saw   *see* see; proverb, toothed cutting implement; use a cutting tool; 2004 horror film with Cary Elwes; buzz saw, circular saw, coping saw, pit saw, see-saw, tenon saw; *What the Butler Saw* (pl)

sawdust   wood shavings; spit-and-sawdust

sawed   *see* saw; see-sawed

sawn   *see* saw; sawn-off

say   chance to express an opinion; put into words; for example; say-so; how say you, I dare say, let's say, needless to say, not to say, say cheese, say no more, say the word, say when, say your piece, suffice it to say, they say, to say the least, wouldn't say boo to a goose, you can say that again, you don't say; *Don't Say a Word* (f), *I Just Called to Say I Love You* (s), *I Say a Little Prayer* (s), *I Say No* (b), *More Than I Can Say* (s), *Never Can Say Goodbye* (s), *Never Say Die* (s), *Never Say Never Again* (f), *People Will Say We're in Love* (s), *Say My Name* (s)

saying   *see* say; adage; as the saying goes, that goes without saying, there is no saying; *Really Saying Something* (s)

scab   crust on a wound, strike-breaker; work during a strike

scalded   injured by hot liquid, plunged into boiling water; like a scalded cat

scale   extent, graduated series of musical notes, index, part of a fish's or reptile's skin, proportion, residue left by hard water, weighing device; ascend, remove incrustation from; Beaufort scale, economy of scale, full-scale, in scale, Kelvin scale, large-scale, Richter scale, sliding scale, small-scale, to scale; scale model

Scale
Baumé, Beaufort, Binet-Simon, Brix, Celsius, Fahrenheit, Kelvin, Likert, Mercalli, Mohs', Pythagorean, Rankine, Réaumur, Richter, Scoville

scales   *see* scale; bathroom scales; scales of justice; tip the scales

scallop   bivalve mollusc, curved pattern on an edge

scaly   flaky; scaly anteater

scan   medical check; be metrically correct (of poetry), examine medically, read quickly, view carefully; CAT scan

scandal   malicious gossip, public disgrace or outrage; 1989 film starring John Hurt; scandal sheet; *The School for Scandal* (pl)

scarce   in short supply; make yourself scarce

scared   frightened; afraid; running scared; scared stiff; *Running Scared* (f/s)

scarlet   rich red colour; scarlet fever, scarlet runner, scarlet woman; *Captain Scarlet and the Mysterons* (tv), *The Scarlet Empress* (f), *The Scarlet Letter* (b), *The Scarlet Pimpernel* (b/f), *Scarlet Ribbons* (s), *Scarlet Woman* (b), *A Study in Scarlet* (b)

scary   frightening; *Scary Movie* (f)

scatter   disperse, sprinkle; scatter cushions, scatter rug

scene   landscape, place of action, spectacle, subdivision of a play;

change of scene, mise en scène; scene of the crime; appear/arrive/come on the scene, not my scene

scenes *see* scene; behind the scenes; *Scenes from a Mall* (f), *Scenes from a Marriage* (f)

scenic picturesque (view); scenic railway

sceptre ceremonial staff; orb and sceptre

schedule timetable; plan; according to schedule, on schedule

scheduled *see* schedule; scheduled flight

scheme plan of action; make plans, plot; colour scheme, play-scheme

scholar learned person, student; Rhodes Scholar

scholarship academic study, bursary; Rhodes Scholarship

school educational establishment, group of fish, university faculty; educate; approved school, boarding school, charm school, church school, comprehensive school, day school, direct-grant school, drama school, elementary school, finishing school, grammar school, high school, infant school, junior school, middle school, night school, nursery school, old school, old school tie, prep school, preparatory school, pre-school, primary school, private school, public school, reform school, riding school, special school, state school, summer school, Sunday school, upper school; school bag, school fees, school of thought, school play, school uniform; school of hard knocks; *Crime School* (f), *Romy and Michele's High School Reunion* (f), *The School for Scandal* (pl), *The School of*

Athens (pa), *The School of Rock* (f)

schoolboy male pupil; overgrown schoolboy; schoolboy howler; *The Honourable Schoolboy* (b)

schooldays period of education, term times; *Tom Brown's Schooldays* (b/f)

schooner fast sailing ship, sherry glass; prairie schooner

science branch of knowledge; behavioural science, computer science, domestic science, information science, materials science, political science, rocket science, the dismal science; science fiction, science park; Christian Science; *Weird Science* (f)

sciences *see* science; earth sciences, life sciences, natural sciences, physical sciences, social sciences

scissor cut with shears, pass in rugby; scissor cut

scissors *see* scissor; jointed cutting tool; nail scissors, pair of scissors

scoff eat greedily, jeer

scone plain cake; Scottish palace; drop scone

scoop exclusive news story, ice-cream server, shovelling spoon; dig or hollow (out); Evelyn Waugh novel; scoop neck

scooter two-wheeled toy, small motorbike; motor scooter

scorched singed; scorched-earth (policy)

score musical arrangement, points total, twenty; get a goal, keep a tally, scratch (a line); final score; score a goal; know the score, on that score, settle a score; *Final Score* (tv)

scorned scoffed at and ignored; hell hath no fury like a woman scorned

scot tax; scot-free

scotch quash (a rumour); whisky; Scotch bonnet, Scotch broth, Scotch egg, Scotch mist, Scotch pancake, Scotch tape, Scotch whisky

scoundrels rascals; *Dirty Rotten Scoundrels* (f)

scout reconnaissance person or vehicle; reconnoitre; member of a youth movement; talent scout; scout round; Boy Scout, Kinder Scout, Queen's Scout, Sea Scout, Venture Scout; *The Last Boy Scout* (f)

scrag bony part of the neck; seize roughly by the neck or collar; scrag-end

scrambled beat and cooked (eggs), clambered hastily, jammed (a message) electronically, mixed up, ordered (aircraft) to take off immediately; unintelligible; scrambled eggs

scrap fragment, punch-up, waste (metal, eg); cancel, discard, fight; scrap heap, scrap merchant, scrap paper

scrape minor skirmish, superficial wound, tricky predicament; grate, graze; bow and scrape, rake and scrape; scrape the barrel

scratch slight skin injury, zero golf handicap; delete, graze, rub an itch, withdraw (from a contest); from scratch, up to scratch; scratch pad; scratch the surface, scratch your head

scream loud cry, wildly funny thing; yell loudly; spoof horror film with Courteney Cox; scream blue murder; *The Scream* (pa)

screech shrill piercing cry; shout piercingly; screech-martin, screech owl

screen film projection surface, front of a tv set or computer, room divider; hide, medically check for illness, show (a film), televise, vet; rood screen, sight screen, silk screen, silver screen, split screen, the big screen, the silver screen, the small screen, touch screen; screen saver, screen test

screw metal pin, ship's propeller, slang for a prison warder; cheat, twist; Allen screw, cross-head screw, wood screw; screw cap, screw top, screw-worm; have a screw loose, tighten the screw, turn the screw; *The Turn of the Screw* (b/o)

scribbling drawing carelessly, writing hurriedly; scribbling pad

scroll furled parchment, ornamental spiral; move through text on a computer screen; scroll bar

scrolls *see* scroll; Dead Sea Scrolls

scrub brushwood; delete, scour; body scrub; scrub up

scrubbing *see* scrub; scrubbing brush

scrubs *see* scrub; hospital sitcom with Zach Braff; Wormwood Scrubs

scruff back of the neck, dirty and untidy person; scruff of the neck

scrum disorderly struggle, rugby huddle; form a rugby huddle; scrum half

scrunch noise of paper being crumpled; style (hair) to give a tousled look; scrunch-dry

scuba diving equipment; scuba diver, scuba diving

scum floating waste matter; worthless people; 1979 film about borstal life

scuttle domestic coal container, opening in a ship's side; ruin (plans), scamper, sink (a ship) deliberately; coal scuttle

sea salt-water expanse; maritime; air-sea rescue, at sea, deep-sea, deep-sea diver, go to sea, inland sea, put to sea; sea anchor, sea anemone, sea bass, sea biscuit, sea bream, sea breeze, sea cadet, sea change, sea chest, sea cow, sea cucumber, sea dog, sea eagle, sea floor, sea hawk, sea-island cotton, sea kale, sea lane, sea legs, sea level, sea lion, sea mile, sea power, sea salt, sea serpent, sea shanty, sea slug, sea snail, sea snake, sea trout, sea urchin, sea wall, sea wasp; all at sea; Adriatic Sea, Baltic Sea, Black Sea, Caspian Sea, Clacton-on-Sea, Coral Sea, Dead Sea, Dead Sea Scrolls, Ionian Sea, Irish Sea, North Sea, Norwegian Sea, Red Sea, Sargasso Sea, Sea Lord, Sea of Azov, Sea of Galilee, Sea of Okhotsk, Sea Scout, South China Sea, Southend-on-Sea, Timor Sea, Tyrrhenian Sea, Yellow Sea; *Beyond the Sea* (f), *The Cruel Sea* (b/f), *Deep Blue Sea* (f), *The Deep Blue Sea* (pl), *Doctor at Sea* (f), *The Old Man and the Sea* (b), *Sea Fever* (po), *The Sea Hawk* (f), *Sea of Love* (f), *Sea of Souls* (tv), *The Sea the Sea* (b), *Twenty Thousand Leagues under the Sea* (b/f), *Voyage to the Bottom of the Sea* (f), *Wide Sargasso Sea* (b/f)

seagull marine bird; *Jonathan Livingston Seagull* (b), *The Seagull* (pl)

seal aquatic mammal, closing device, piece of stamped lead or wax; close off, conclude (a deal), make airtight, stick down (an envelope); elephant seal, fur seal, grey seal, leopard seal, Solomon's seal, set the seal on; seal of approval, seal off; seal your fate; (Lord) Privy Seal; *The Seventh Seal* (f)

sealed *see* seal; hermetically sealed; sealed orders; my lips are sealed; *My Lips Are Sealed* (s), *Sealed with a Kiss* (s)

sealing *see* seal; self-sealing; sealing wax; *Pink String and Sealing Wax* (f)

seals *see* seal; seals of office

seam dressmaker's join, stratum of ore or coal; deviate after pitching (of a cricket ball); French seam; seam bowling

seaman sailor; able seaman, ordinary seaman

seams *see* seam; bulging at the seams, bursting at the seams, come apart at the seams, fall apart at the seams

seance spiritualist meeting; *Seance on a Wet Afternoon* (f)

search hunt; frisk, hunt (for); search engine, search fee, search party, search warrant; search me; *Call Off the Search* (al), *In Search of the Castaways* (f), *Six Characters in Search of an Author* (pl)

searching *see* search; quizzical (look); heart-searching, soul-searching

seas *see* sea; high seas, seven seas, the seven seas; half seas over; South Seas; *Seven Seas of Rhye* (s)

seaside beach, coastal area; seaside resort

season time of year; add condiments to; close season, high season, low season, off season, open season, summer season, the silly season; season ticket; *A Dry White Season* (b/f)

seasons *see* season; *The Four Seasons* (cl), *A Man for All Seasons* (f/pl), *Seasons in the Sun* (s)

seat bench or chair, MP's constituency, (country) residence or estate; accommodate on chairs; Spanish car manufacturer; back seat, back-seat driver, booster seat, bucket seat, country seat, ejector seat, hot seat, love seat, marginal seat, ringside seat, safe seat, take a seat, window seat; seat belt; by the seat of one's pants, in the driver's/driving seat, take a back seat

seated   *see* seat; in a chair; deep-seated; *Lady Seated at a Virginal* (pa)

seaway   ship's route; St Lawrence Seaway

second   boxer's aide, sixtieth of a minute; endorse (a nomination); after the first; split second; second ballot, second best, second chamber, second class, second cousin, second-generation, second-guess, second hand, second-hand shop, second-in-command, second mate, second nature, second person, second-rate, second reading, second slip, second string, second thoughts, second to none, second wind; at second hand, play second fiddle, without a second thought; Second Coming; *Every Second Counts* (tv), *King Richard the Second* (pl), *The Prisoner of Second Avenue* (f/pl), *Second Hand Rose* (s), *The Second Coming* (po), *The Second Sex* (b), *Second Thoughts* (tv)

secondary   auxiliary, type of school; secondary colour, secondary modern, secondary picketing

seconds   *see* second; extra helpings; 1966 John Frankenheimer film; *Gone in Sixty Seconds* (f), *Thirty Seconds over Tokyo* (f)

secret   confidence; clandestine, confidential; keep a secret, official secret, open secret, top secret, trade

secret; secret agent, secret ballot, secret passage, secret police, secret service, secret society; *On Her Majesty's Secret Service* (f), *The Secret Agent* (b/f), *Secret Army* (tv), *The Secret Diary of Adrian Mole Aged 13¾* (b), *The Secret Garden* (b/f), *The Secret Life of Walter Mitty* (f), *Secret Love* (s), *The Secret of My Success* (f), *Secret Window* (f), *Top Secret* (f)

secretary   clerical worker, government minister; club secretary, private secretary, social secretary; secretary bird; Foreign Secretary, Home Secretary, Permanent Secretary, Secretary General, Secretary of State; *The Secretary Bird* (pl)

secrets   *see* secret; official secrets; Official Secrets Act; *The Divine Secrets of the Ya-Ya Sisterhood* (b/f), *Secrets and Lies* (f)

section   department, part; commit to a psychiatric hospital, divide into pieces; Caesarean section, cross section, rhythm section

sector   branch of the economy, zone; private sector, public sector

secure   attach firmly, make safe; firmly fixed, safe; secure arms

security   pledge, protection, safety of a state or organisation; collateral security, social security; security blanket, security check, security guard, security of tenure

sedan   big old American car, chair carried on poles; sedan chair

sedate   tranquillise; calm and dignified

sedation   administration of calming drugs; under sedation

sedge   grass-like swamp plant; sedge warbler

297

seduction enticement; *The Last Seduction* (f)

see diocese; have the power of vision, perceive, understand; look-see; see daylight, see fit, see off, see over, see red, see-saw, see stars, see the sights, see-through, see to; be glad to see the back of, let me see, long time no see, see eye to eye, see here, see how the land lies, see someone coming, see the error of your ways, see which way the cat jumps, see you; Holy See; *I Can See for Miles* (s), *See Emily Play* (s), *See My Baby Jive* (s), *See You* (s)

seed grain, plant embryo, ranked player (in tennis, eg); produce pips, rank (players) in a tournament; go to seed; seed cake, seed potato; *The Tamarind Seed* (f), *The Wanting Seed* (b)

seeds *see* seed; pumpkin seeds; *The Seeds of Time* (b)

seeing *see* see; far-seeing; seeing things; seeing is believing; *Seeing is Believing* (s)

seek look for; hide-and-seek; seek out; *Hide and Seek* (f)

seekers people looking for something; pleasure seekers; *The Shell Seekers* (b)

seeking *see* seek; heat-seeking, self-seeking; *Desperately Seeking Susan* (f)

seems appears to be; *Sorry Seems to Be the Hardest Word* (s)

seen *see* see; *Have You Seen Her* (s)

seize capture, grab; seize the day; *Seize the Day* (b)

select choose; elite; pre-select; select committee

selection assortment, choice; natural selection, pre-selection

sell betray, give in exchange for money, portray favourably; buy and sell, hard sell, soft sell; sell a pup, sell-by date, sell off, sell out, sell short; sell a dummy to, sell down the river, sell like hot cakes, sell the pass, sell your soul

selling *see* sell; best-selling, pyramid selling; selling point

senator ancient Roman state councillor, US politician, MP in certain countries; *The American Senator* (b)

send dispatch; send off, send up, send word; send for an early bath, send packing, send to Coventry; *Send in the Clowns* (s)

sender dispatcher; *Return to Sender* (s)

senior someone older or higher in rank; higher in rank, older; senior citizen, senior common room, senior nursing officer, senior registrar, senior service

sensation extraordinary happening, feeling; *New Sensation* (s)

sense feeling, logic, meaning, perception; detect, instinctively feel; common sense, dress sense, horse sense, make sense, make sense of, sixth sense; sense of proportion; *Sense and Sensibility* (b/f), *A Sense of Guilt* (b/tv), *Smilla's Sense of Snow* (f), *Stop Making Sense* (f), *The Sixth Sense* (f)

sensibility discernment; *Sense and Sensibility* (b/f)

sensory relating to external stimulation; extra-sensory (perception); sensory deprivation

sent *see* send; heaven-sent

sentence grammatical unit, prison

term; pass judgement on; life sentence; sentence to death; *A Five Year Sentence* (b)

sentiment feeling, mawkishness, opinion

sentimental nostalgic, self-indulgently emotional; sentimental value; *Sentimental Education* (b), *A Sentimental Journey* (b)

sentry soldier on guard duty; sentry box

separate part company, pull apart; unconnected; *A Separate Reality* (b), *Separate Tables* (f/pl)

separation detachment, marital division; judicial separation, legal separation; separation of powers; *Six Degrees of Separation* (f)

septic infected (wound); septic tank

sequence chronological list; Fibonacci sequence; sequence dancing

serenade romantic song; sing to; James M Cain novel; *Moonlight Serenade* (s), *Penny Serenade* (f)

sergeant military or police rank; colour sergeant, drill sergeant, police sergeant, staff sergeant; sergeant-major; *Carry On Sergeant* (f), *Sgt Pepper's Lonely Hearts Club Band* (al/s), *Sergeant York* (f)

serial set of things in succession, story or programme in instalments; episodic; serial number; *Serial Mom* (f)

series string of events; mini-series; World Series

seriously earnestly, significantly; take seriously

serpent historical wind instrument, snake; sea serpent; *The Plumed Serpent* (b), *The Serpent and the Rainbow* (f)

servant domestic employee; civil servant, public servant; *The Naked Civil Servant* (b/tv), *The Servant* (f)

serve tennis stroke; attend to (customers), begin a tennis game, be of use, dish up (food), hold office; serve notice, serve time, serve up; *In Which We Serve* (f), *To Serve Them All My Days* (tv)

served *see* serve; first come first served; *Are You Being Served?* (tv)

server central computer, person starting a game in tennis, priest's assistant; time-server

serves *see* serve; serves you right

service assistance, church occasion, complete set of dishes, employment, opening shot in a tennis match, routine maintenance; overhaul; active service, answering service, be of service, Christingle service, civil service, community service, dinner service, health service, in service, intelligence service, lip service, motorway service area, national service, room service, secret service, self-service, senior service, silver service, skeleton service, yeoman service; service area, service book, service charge, service dress, service industry, service line, service provider, service road, service station; at your service, pay lip service to; Remembrance Service; *On Her Majesty's Secret Service* (f), *The Owl Service* (b/tv), *Room Service* (f)

serviceman member of the armed forces; ex-serviceman, national serviceman

services *see* service; armed forces, motorway rest area; social services; for services rendered; *Personal Services* (f)

serving *see* serve; food portion; time-serving

servitude subjugation; penal servitude

sesame oil-yielding seed; open sesame; *Sesame Street* (tv)

session court or parliamentary sitting, designated period; session musician; Court of Session

sessions *see* session; petty sessions

set complete collection, film location, play props and scenery, group, part of a tennis match; fix in position, lay (a table), present (an example), sink below the horizon (sun), solidify; determined, ready, solidified; chemistry set, companion set, crystal set, dead set, deep-set, dinner set, film set, jet set, tea set, television set, train set; set alight, set aside, set at naught, set back, set by, set fire to, set free, set off, set on, set out, set piece, set point, set sail, set square, set store by, set-to, set up; make a dead set at, set a thief to catch a thief, set the ball rolling, set the seal on, set the stage, set the Thames on fire, set the world on fire, set your teeth on edge; *Do Not Adjust Your Set* (tv), *Set Me Free* (s), *The Set Up* (f)

settee sofa; *A Cream Cracker under the Settee* (tv)

setter breed of hunting dog, compiler; English setter, Irish setter, jet-setter, pace-setter, red setter

setting *see* set; jewellery mounting, level of power, surroundings; jet-setting, pace-setting; *Setting the World on Fire* (b)

settle bench; decide (upon), make yourself comfortable, pay up, put down roots, reach agreement; N

Yorkshire market town; settle a score, settle down, settle on, settle up; settle your hash

settlement community, end of a dispute, payout; marriage settlement, penal settlement; Act of Settlement

settles *see* settle; when the dust settles

seven odd number; 1995 Brad Pitt film; dance of the seven veils; seven-a-side, seven deadly sins, seven seas; Seven Years War, The Seven Wonders of the World; *Blake's Seven* (tv), *The House of the Seven Gables* (b/f), *The Magnificent Seven* (f), *Seven against Thebes* (pl), *Seven Days in May* (f), *Seven Nation Army* (s), *The Seven-Per-Cent Solution* (f), *Seven Pillars of Wisdom* (b), *The Seven Samurai* (f), *Seven Seas of Rhye* (s), *Seven Wonders* (s), *The Seven Year Itch* (f), *Snow White and the Seven Dwarfs* (b/f)

seventeen prime number; 1979 hit song for the Regents; *Sixteen Going On Seventeen* (s)

seventh ordinal number; in seventh heaven; Seventh-Day Adventist; *The Seventh Seal* (f)

seventy three score and ten; seventy-eight; *Seventy-Six Trombones* (s)

severance redundancy, split; severance pay

severed cut off; *A Severed Head* (b/f)

sewage effluent; sewage farm

sewer person using needle and thread, underground waste channel; sewer rat

sewing needlework; using a needle and thread; sewing machine

sewn (had) stitched; hand-sewn; sewn up

sex gender, intimate relations; opposite sex, the fair sex, the opposite sex; sex appeal, sex bomb, sex symbol; *No Sex Please, We're British* (f/pl), *The Opposite of Sex* (f), *The Opposite Sex* (f), *The Second Sex* (b), *Sex Bomb* (s), *Sex, Lies and Videotape* (f), *Sex and the City* (tv), *The Weaker Sex* (f)

sexual of gender or intimate relations; sexual politics

shack hut; *Love Shack* (s)

shade darkness out of the sun, degree of colour, slight amount; protect from the sun; *A Whiter Shade of Pale* (s)

shadow darkness out of the sun, silhouette cast by sunlight, vestige; follow closely; five o'clock shadow; shadow-boxing, shadow cabinet, shadow theatre; *Cast a Dark Shadow* (f), *Cast a Giant Shadow* (f), *Moonlight Shadow* (s), *Shadow of a Doubt* (f)

shaft arrow, light ray, long handle, vertical mine entrance; treat in a harsh and unfair way; 1971 Richard Roundtree film remade in 2000; Isaac Hayes film theme; propeller shaft

shag carpet, coarse tobacco, cormorant-like bird, US dance

shaggy bushy and matted; shaggy-dog story

shake frothy milk drink, quivering movement; cause to vibrate; milk-shake; shake hands, shake off, shake up; shake a leg; *Hippy Hippy Shake* (s), *Shake, Rattle and Roll* (s)

shaker device for mixing drinks, salt or flour dispenser; one of an American religious sect; mover and shaker

shakes *see* shake; in two shakes of a lamb's tail, no great shakes; *Shake Your Booty* (s)

shall will; *Shall We Dance?* (f/s), *We Shall Overcome* (s)

shambles complete mess, old slaughterhouse; walks awkwardly; medieval street in York

shame embarrassment, humiliation; disgrace; 1983 Salman Rushdie novel; 1978 Evelyn 'Champagne' King single; put to shame; shame on you; *Ain't That a Shame?* (s), *Shame Shame Shame* (s)

shandy beer and lemonade mixture; *Tristram Shandy* (b)

shanghai kidnap; Chinese city; *The Lady from Shanghai* (f), *Shanghai Express* (f), *Shanghai Noon* (f), *Shanghai Surprise* (f)

shanks cuts of meat, lower legs; mishits (a golf ball); Shanks's pony

shanty dilapidated hut, sailor's song; sea shanty; shanty town

shape outward form of an object; mould; in good shape, in the shape of, out of shape, take shape; shape-shifting, shape up; knock/lick/whip into shape; *Bend Me, Shape Me* (s), *The Shape of Things to Come* (b)

shaped *see* shape; (go) pear-shaped; *The L-Shaped Room* (b/f)

share portion, small part of the capital stock of a company; divide up, have in common; job-share, market share, the lion's share; share index, share option, share out; share and share alike

shared *see* share; a trouble shared is a trouble halved

shareholder investor in a company; minority shareholder

shares *see* share; securities; preference shares, stocks and shares

sharing *see* share; job-sharing, profit-sharing

shark large predatory fish, swindler;

basking shark, great white shark, loan shark, nurse shark, tiger shark, whale shark; *Shark Tale* (f)

shark   *see* shark; *Swimming with Sharks* (f)

sharp   note raised by a semitone; capable of cutting, perceptive, well defined; card sharp; sharp-featured, sharp practice, sharp-tongued, sharp-witted; as sharp as a needle, look sharp

shattering   breaking into small pieces, destroying, devastating, exhausting; earth-shattering

shave   trim; pare off (a slice), remove hair with a razor; close shave; *A Close Shave* (f)

shaven   *see* shave; free of hair; clean-shaven

shaver   barber, razor, young lad; electric shaver

shaving   *see* shave; shaving cream

shawl   woollen shoulder wrap; prayer shawl; shawl collar

she   feminine pronoun, that woman or girl; 1999 Elvis Costello hit; Charles Aznavour song; H Rider Haggard novel; she-devil; *Before She Met Me* (b), *Is She Really Going Out with Him?* (s), *The Life and Loves of a She-Devil* (b/tv), *Murder, She Wrote* (tv), *She Bangs* (s), *She-Devil* (f), *She Done Him Wrong* (f), *She Loves You* (s), *She's Out of My Life* (s), *She Stoops to Conquer* (pl), *She Wore a Yellow Ribbon* (f)

shears   large-sized scissors; pinking shears

sheath   blade-covering; sheath knife

shed   garden outhouse; cast off, got rid of; football stand at Chelsea; potting shed; shed a tear, shed tears

sheep   fleecy farm animal or animals; black sheep, count sheep, flock of sheep; sheep-dip, sheep-run, sheep-shearer, sheep-shearing, sheep-wash; make sheep's eyes at, a wolf in sheep's clothing

sheepdog   collie, eg; sheepdog trials; Old English sheepdog

sheer   downright, see-through (fabric), very steep; deviate

sheet   broad continuous expanse, item of bed linen, piece of paper; fall heavily (rain); balance sheet, clean sheet, crime sheet, dust sheet, news-sheet, scandal sheet, tear sheet, time sheet; sheet bend, sheet lightning, sheet metal, sheet music, sheet of ice; keep a clean sheet; *Crime Sheet* (tv)

sheets   *see* sheet; three sheets to the wind

shelf   ledge, sandbank; continental shelf, ice shelf, off the shelf, on the shelf; shelf life, shelf mark, shelf room

shell   hard outer casing, projectile; bombard, prepare (peas); global fuel company; razor shell; shell company, shell shock, shell-shocked, shell suit; come out of your shell; *The Shell Seekers* (b)

shelter   refuge; find refuge, protect; charity for the homeless; air-raid shelter, Anderson shelter, bus shelter, Morrison shelter; *Gimme Shelter* (s/f)

sheltered   *see* shelter; sheltered housing

sheltering   *see* shelter; *The Sheltering Sky* (b/f)

shelve   arrange (books) in a library, postpone, slope gradually

shepherd   person who tends flocks; guide; German shepherd; shepherd's pie, shepherd's purse; red sky at night shepherd's delight; Shepherd's Bush

sheriff   chief officer of the Crown in a county, US law officer; high sheriff; sheriff court; *I Shot the Sheriff* (s)

sherry   fortified Spanish wine; 1962 Four Seasons hit; cream sherry, dry sherry; sherry trifle

shield   means of defence; protect; heat shield

shift   move, shapeless dress, work period; alter position; graveyard shift, night shift, red shift, split shift; shift worker; shift your ground; *Red Shift* (b), *Swing Shift* (f)

shilling   old British coin; not the full shilling

shin   front of the lower leg; climb (up); shin-pad; Shin Bet

shine   gloss; polish, radiate; 1996 Geoffrey Rush film; rise and shine, take a shine to, take the shine off; *Shine On Harvey Moon* (tv)

shines   *see* shine; make hay while the sun shines

shining   *see* shine; knight in shining armour; *The Shining* (f)

ship   sea-going vessel; send by sea, transport commercially; abandon ship, factory ship, mother ship, sailing ship, sinking ship, tall ship; ship canal, ship of the desert, ship of the line, ship's biscuit, ship's company, ship's log, ship-to-shore; rats desert a sinking ship, run a tight ship, when your ship comes in; *On the Good Ship Lollipop* (s), *Ship of Fools* (b/f/pa)

shipping   *see* ship; sea-going vessels collectively, transport of goods by sea; shipping agent; *The Shipping News* (b/f)

shire   county, large draught horse; shire horse

shirt   front-fastening top; dress shirt, hair shirt, polo shirt, stuffed shirt, t-shirt; shirt dress; keep your shirt on, lose your shirt, put your shirt on, the shirt off your back

shirtsleeves   arms of a man's buttoned top; in your shirtsleeves

shiver   small fragment; tremble; shiver my timbers

shock   impact, mass of thick shaggy hair, nasty surprise, trauma; horrify; culture shock, electric shock, shell shock; shock absorber, shock-headed, shock tactics, shock therapy, shock troops, shock waves; *Future Shock* (b), *The Shock of the New* (b/tv)

shocking   *see* shock; scandalous; shocking pink

shoe   camera socket, casino card dispenser, item of footwear; put a cover on (a horse's hoof); brake shoe, gym shoe, hot shoe, soft-shoe shuffle; shoe-making, shoe polish, shoe tree; the shoe is on the other foot; *Hole in My Shoe* (s)

shoes   *see* shoe; ballet shoes, court shoes, goody two shoes, pair of shoes, tap shoes, track shoes; *Ballet Shoes* (b), *Blue Suede Shoes* (s), *Crocodile Shoes* (tv), *Goody Two Shoes* (s), *The Red Shoes* (f), *The Shoes of the Fisherman* (b/f)

shook   *see* shake; *All Shook Up* (s)

shoot   filming or photo session, meeting to hunt with guns, young plant growth; fire, germinate, dart forward, take pictures, try for a goal; shoot the sun, shoot-out; shoot down in flames, shoot from the hip; *Stop! Or My Mom Will Shoot* (f), *They Shoot Horses, Don't They?* (f)

shooter   basketball team member,

gun, small glass of spirits; first-person shooter, pea-shooter, six-shooter, third-person shooter

shooting   *see* shoot; clay pigeon shooting, grouse shooting, straight-shooting, the whole shooting match; shooting gallery, shooting star, shooting stick; *Shooting Stars* (tv)

shoots   *see* shoot; bamboo shoots

shop   retail outlet; betray, buy things; barber-shop, betting shop, body shop, bucket shop, closed shop, coffee shop, cop shop, corner shop, factory shop, junk shop, paint shop, pet shop, second-hand shop, shut up shop, swap shop, talking shop, tea shop, thrift shop, toy shop, tuck shop, window-shop; shop around, shop assistant, shop floor, shop-soiled, shop steward, shop window; bull in a china shop; *Beauty Shop* (f), *Little Shop of Horrors* (mus), *Multi-Coloured Swap Shop* (tv), *The Old Curiosity Shop* (b), *The Sweet-Shop Owner* (b)

shopkeepers   retail managers; nation of shopkeepers

shopper   retail customer, wheeled basket; window shopper

shopping   *see* shop; window-shopping; shopping arcade, shopping bag, shopping centre, shopping list, shopping spree

shore   coastline; prop (up); ship-to-shore; shore leave; *The Fatal Shore* (b), *Shore Leave* (s), *Stranger on the Shore* (s)

short   any brief film, glass of spirits; blow a fuse; below average height, brief, deficient, terse; cut short, for short, sell short; short and sweet, short back and sides, short change, short circuit, short cut, short fuse,

short-handed, short haul, short-lived, short measure, short order, short-range, short shrift, short sight, short-sighted, short-staffed, short story, short temper, short-term, short time, short wave; (as) thick as two short planks, at short notice, by a short head, draw the short straw, the long and the short of it, to cut a long story short, win by a short head; *The Long and the Short and the Tall* (f), *Short Circuit* (f), *Short Cuts* (f)

shortening   pastry fat; reducing in length

shorthand   rapid writing system; shorthand typist

shorts   *see* short; thigh-length trousers; Bermuda shorts, boxer shorts

shot   *see* shoot; athlete's metal ball, goal-scoring attempt, lead pellets, photo, small glass of alcohol; big shot, dead shot, drop shot, long shot, Moon shot, Parthian shot, parting shot, passing shot, pot shot, put the shot, slap shot; shot glass, shot-putter; get shot of, give it your best shot, like a shot, not by a long shot, shot across the bows, a shot in the arm, shot in the dark, shot to pieces; *The Golden Shot* (tv), *I Shot the Sheriff* (s), *A Shot in the Dark* (f)

shotgun   firearm; shotgun wedding; *Shotgun Wedding* (s)

should   ought to; I should be so lucky; *I Should Be So Lucky* (s), *Your Mother Should Know* (s)

shoulder   arm joint, edge of the road; jostle, take on (a burden); cold shoulder, drop shoulder, frozen shoulder, hard shoulder, the cold shoulder; shoulder arms, shoulder bag, shoulder belt, shoulder blade, shoulder pads, shoulder strap; have a chip on your shoulder, put your shoulder to the wheel, shoulder to cry on, shoulder to shoulder, straight from the shoulder; *Shoulder to Shoulder* (tv), *Standing on the Shoulder of Giants* (al)

shouldered *see* shoulder; round-shouldered

shoulders *see* shoulder; rub shoulders

shout loud cry, turn to buy the drinks; yell; 1984 Tears for Fears single; Lulu's first hit; shout the odds; give a shout to, in with a shout; *Shout at the Devil* (f), *Twist and Shout* (s)

shouting *see* shout; shouting match; all over bar the shouting

shove rough push; push roughly; shove-halfpenny; get the shove, when push comes to shove

shovel broad spade-like tool; scoop up; pick and shovel

show exhibition, spectacle; demonstrate, display; chat show, dog show, fashion show, floor show, game show, gang show, ice show, no-show, peep show, talk show; show business, show home, show of hands, show off, show-stopping, show the way, show trial, show up; the show must go on, show your true colours, steal the show; Lord Mayor's Show, Motor Show; *The Benny Hill Show* (tv), *The Clothes Show* (tv), *The Culture Show* (tv), *The Fast Show* (tv), *The Goon Show* (r), *The Greatest Show on Earth* (f), *The Huckleberry Hound Show* (tv), *The Last Picture Show* (f), *The Late Show* (f), *The Morecambe and Wise Show* (tv), *The Muppet Show* (tv),

Peep Show (tv), *The Phil Silvers Show* (tv), *The Quick Draw McGraw Show* (tv), *Quiz Show* (f), *The Rocky Horror Picture Show* (f), *Show Boat* (mus), *Show Business* (f), *The Show Must Go On* (s), *The Sketch Show* (tv), *The South Bank Show* (tv), *The Truman Show* (f), *The Woody Woodpecker Show* (tv)

shower group of disreputable people, short burst of rainfall, vertical washing booth; distribute liberally, rain briefly; power shower

showers *see* shower; April showers; *April Showers* (f)

shredded grated; Shredded Wheat

shrew scolding woman, small mouse-like mammal; elephant shrew; *The Taming of the Shrew* (f/pl)

shrift absolution; short shrift

shrink colloquial word for a psychiatrist; reduce in size; shrink-wrapped

shrinking *see* shrink; shrinking violet

shrivel wither; shrivel up

shroud burial cloth; envelop; Turin Shroud

shrove gave absolution; Shrove Tuesday

shrug shoulder gesture; raise the shoulders; shrug off

shrugged *see* shrug; *Atlas Shrugged* (b)

shrunk *see* shrink; pre-shrunk; *Honey, I Shrunk the Kids* (f), *Honey, We Shrunk Ourselves* (f)

shuffle act of jumbling up (cards, eg), dance step, evasion; behave shiftily, drag (the feet), jumble up; soft-shoe shuffle; *Harlem Shuffle* (s)

shut close, closed; open-and-shut case; shut down, shut-eye, shut in, shut out, shut up, shut up shop; keep your mouth shut, put up or shut up; *Eyes Wide Shut* (f)

shutter hinged window cover, part of a camera; shutter speed

shuttle short-distance transport, spacecraft designed to be used more than once, tool used in weaving; travel backwards and forwards; space shuttle; shuttle diplomacy

shy recoil, throw; timid; camera shy, coconut shy, work-shy; fight shy of, once bitten twice shy; *Once Bitten, Twice Shy* (s), *Shy Boy* (s), *Too Shy* (s), *Twice Shy* (b)

sick ill, nauseous, tired (of); car-sick, travel-sick; sick bay, sick building syndrome, sick leave, sick-making, sick pay; sick as a parrot, sick to your stomach

sickle cutting tool; hammer and sickle

sickness ill health, nausea; altitude sickness, car-sickness, decompression sickness, morning sickness, travel sickness; sickness benefit; *In Sickness and in Health* (tv)

side edge, flank, left or right half of the body, pretentious air, team, tv channel; ally yourself (with); subsidiary (issue); blind side, B-side, distaff side, five-a-side, flip side, off side, on the side, seven-a-side, sunny-side up; side arm, side by side, side dish, side drum, side effects, side issue, side-on, side road, side-saddle, side salad, side-slip, side-splitting, side street, side whiskers, side wind; bit on the side, err on the right side, err on the side of caution, from side to side, get out of bed on the wrong side, look on the black side, look on the bright side, on the right side of,

on the side of the angels, on the wrong side of, thorn in the side, to be on the safe side; Moss Side; *Always Look on the Bright Side* (s), *The Other Side of Midnight* (b/f), *Right by Your Side* (s), *This Side of Paradise* (b), *Thorn in My Side* (s), *Walk on the Wild Side* (s), *West Side Story* (mus)

sided *see* side; four-sided, one-sided

sides *see* side; short back and sides, take sides; split your sides; *Both Sides Now* (s)

siege blockade; lay siege to, under siege; siege mentality; *The Siege* (f), *Under Siege* (f)

sierra mountain range in the Americas, radio code word; Ford saloon model; Sierra Leone, Sierra Madre; *High Sierra* (f), *The Treasure of the Sierra Madre* (f)

sighs soft sounds of relief or boredom; exhales audibly; Bridge of Sighs

sight faculty of vision, spectacle, targeting device, tourist attraction, view; glimpse; at first sight, in sight, know by sight, long sight, short sight, telescopic sight; sight-reading, sight screen, sight unseen; out of sight, out of mind; *Out of Sight* (f), *Sight Unseen* (b)

sighted *see* sight; able to see; clear-sighted, far-sighted, long-sighted, near-sighted, short-sighted

sights *see* sight; see the sights

sign emblem, indication, notice; use gestures to communicate with deaf people, write your name; birth sign, call sign, dollar sign, equals sign, minus sign, multiplication sign, outward visible sign, peace sign, plus sign, road sign, star sign; sign in, sign language, sign on, sign up; *The Sign of Four* (b/f), *The Sign of the Cross* (f)

signal indication, indicator; convey by gesture, indicate; remarkable; brand-name toothpaste; distress signal, smoke signal, time signal; signal box

signature autograph, characteristic mark, indication of key in music; key signature, time signature; signature tune

signet official seal, style of ring; signet ring

silence absence of sound; gag; be quiet!; conspiracy of silence; silence in court, silence is golden; *Silence is Golden* (s), *The Silence of the Lambs* (b/f)

silent noiseless; silent films, silent majority, silent movie; *Jay and Silent Bob Strike Back* (f), *Silent Movie* (f), *Silent Night* (s), *Silent Witness* (tv)

silicon element used in making microelectronic chips; silicon chip; Silicon Valley

silk cocoon thread, fine smooth fabric, QC's gown, Queen's Counsel; watered silk, wild silk; silk moth, silk screen; *Silk Stockings* (f)

silly daft; the silly season; silly-billy, silly mid-off, silly mid-on; *Silly Love Songs* (s)

silver Olympic second prize, precious shiny white metal; sterling silver; silver birch, silver jubilee, silver lining, silver medal, silver-plated, silver screen, silver service, silver spoon, silver-tongued, silver wedding; every cloud has a silver lining, on a silver platter; Silver Ghost; *Silver Dream Machine* (s), *Silver Dream Racer* (f), *Silver Lady* (s), *Silver Machine* (s), *Silver Streak* (f), *The Silver Tassie* (pl)

simmer temperature just below boiling point; boil gently; simmer down

simple easy, naive; simple time; *Blood Simple* (f), *Peter Simple* (b), *The Simple Life* (tv), *A Simple Twist of Fate* (f)

simulator computer modeller; flight simulator

simultaneous synchronous; simultaneous equations

sin moral wrong; offend against God; cardinal sin, deadly sin, live in sin, mortal sin, original sin; sin bin; *It's a Sin* (s), *Original Sin* (f/s), *Sin City* (f), *The Sin Eater* (b)

since because, from that time on; ever since; the best thing since sliced bread; *Since You've Been Gone* (f/s), *Since You Went Away* (f)

sincerely honestly, in good faith; yours sincerely

sing use the voice melodically; 2001 Travis hit; sing-song; sing for your supper; *Hark the Herald Angels Sing* (s), *I'd Like to Teach the World to Sing* (s), *Sing as We Go* (f), *Sing When You're Winning* (s)

singer vocalist; sewing-machine manufacturer; carol-singer, folk singer, opera singer, rock singer, torch singer; *The Folk Singer* (s), *The Jazz Singer* (f), *Pearl's a Singer* (s), *Torch Singer* (f), *The Wedding Singer* (f)

singing *see* sing; carol-singing, community singing, folk singing; all-singing all-dancing; *The Grass Is Singing* (b), *The Singing Detective* (tv), *The Singing, Ringing Tree* (tv)

single one-tune record, one-way ticket; one, unmarried; single-breasted, single combat, single cream, single-decker, single file, single-handed, single-lens reflex, single malt, single market, single-minded, single parent; *Single White Female* (f)

sings   *see* sing; *I Know Why the Caged Bird Sings* (b)

singular   odd, one-off; *Absurd Person Singular* (pl)

sinister   ominous; bend sinister; *Bend Sinister* (b)

sink   basin; diminish, submerge; kitchen sink, kitchen-sink drama; sink in, sink or swim; *Sink or Swim* (tv), *Sink the Bismarck!* (f)

sinker   weight attached to a fishing line; hook line and sinker

sinking   *see* sink; sinking ship; rats desert a sinking ship, that sinking feeling; *That Sinking Feeling* (f)

sins   *see* sin; seven deadly sins; for my sins

siphon   pump, soda-water bottle; draw (liquid) by tube; soda siphon

sir   knight's or teacher's title; *Days with Sir Roger de Coverley* (b), *Please Sir!* (tv), *To Sir with Love* (f), *Yes Sir, I Can Boogie* (s)

sire   male parent of a horse, old form of address; beget

siren   temptress, warning device; siren song

sister   female sibling, nun, senior nurse; twin sister, ward sister; sister-in-law; *Brother Sun, Sister Moon* (f), *The Killing of Sister George* (f), *Sister Act* (f), *Two Mules for Sister Sara* (f)

sisterhood   sorority; *The Divine Secrets of the Ya-Ya Sisterhood* (b/f)

sisters   *see* sister; Little Sisters of the Poor; *Hannah and Her Sisters* (f), *Sisters Are Doin' It for Themselves* (s),

The Three Sisters (pl)

sit   be in session, be sedentary, pose (for an artist), undergo (an exam); house-sit; sit down, sit-down strike, sit-in, sit out, sit tight, sit up, sit-ups, sit well; sit below the salt, sit on the fence, sit up and take notice; *Sit Down* (s)

site   building plot, location; locate; bomb site, building site, caravan site; World Heritage Site

sitter   artist's model, childminder, easy shot; house-sitter

sitting   *see* sit; session, specific mealtime; sitting duck, sitting pretty, sitting room, sitting tenant; *Sitting Pretty* (mus)

situation   position, set of circumstances; situation comedy; chicken and egg situation, no-win situation

situations   *see* situation; situations vacant

six   even number; six-gun, six-pack, six-shooter; hit for six, knock for six, six feet under, six of the best; Six Day War, Six Nations; *Seventy-Six Trombones* (s), *Six Characters in Search of an Author* (pl), *Six Degrees of Separation* (f), *Six Feet Under* (tv), *Six-Five Special* (tv), *The Six Million Dollar Man* (tv)

sixes   biggest cricket hits; at sixes and sevens

sixpence   old British coin; turn on a sixpence; *Half a Sixpence* (mus), *The Moon and Sixpence* (b/f)

sixteen   number; *Only Sixteen* (s), *Sixteen Going On Seventeen* (s), *Sweet Little Sixteen* (s)

sixth   ordinal number; sixth form, sixth-form college, sixth sense; *The*

Inn of the Sixth Happiness (f), *The Sixth Sense* (f)

sixty number; *Gone in Sixty Seconds* (f)

size bulk, dimensions, glue; measure; king-size, life-size; size up; cut down to size, that's about the size of it; *Super Size Me* (f)

skater ice performer; figure-skater, free-skater, ice-skater, pond skater

skates boots with blades or wheels, ray-like fish; glides on ice; ice skates, in-line skates, roller skates; get your skates on

skating *see* skates; ice-rink sport; figure-skating, free skating, ice-skating, in-line skating, roller-skating; skating rink

skeleton framework of bones; skeleton key, skeleton service, skeleton staff; skeleton at the feast, skeleton in the closet/cupboard

sketch rough drawing, short comedy scene; draw roughly; thumbnail sketch; sketch map, sketch out; *The Sketch Show* (tv)

skew oblique angle; bias; awry; skew-whiff

ski runner for snow travel; travel across snow; brand-name yogurt; après-ski, jet ski, water-ski; ski-bob, ski jump, ski-lift, ski mask, ski pants, ski-plane, ski run, ski slope; *Ski Sunday* (tv)

skid sideways slippage (of a vehicle); slide out of control; skid-lid, skid row

skids *see* skid; downward path; hit the skids, on the skids, put the skids under

skies heavens; hits high into the air; to the skies; *Blue Skies* (mus/s)

skiffle music style of the late 1950s; skiffle group

skiing *see* ski; winter sport; jet-skiing, water-skiing

skills talents; interpersonal skills

skimmed brushed (the surface), perused hastily, removed floating matter (from a surface); low-fat (milk); semi-skimmed; skimmed milk

skin body covering, outer layer; flay, peel; banana skin, leopard-skin, under the skin; skin and blister, skin and bone, skin-deep, skin-diver, skin test, skin-tight; beauty is only skin deep, by the skin of one's teeth, have a thick/thin skin, it's no skin off my nose, save your skin, soaked to the skin, there's more than one way to skin a cat; *The Skin of Our Teeth* (pl)

skinned *see* skin; thick-skinned

skinny very thin; skinny-dipping, skinny-rib

skip large container for rubbish; jump with a rope, omit, step lightly from one foot to the other; hop, skip and jump; *My Dog Skip* (f)

skipping *see* skip; skipping rope

skirt female garment; edge past; grass skirt, hobble skirt, pencil skirt, ra-ra skirt

skirting *see* skirt; wainscoting; skirting-board

skittle ninepin; knock down; skittle alley

skittles *see* skittle; alley game; beer and skittles

skull cranium; skull and crossbones; out of your skull

sky heavens, shade of blue; hit high into the air; satellite tv channel; blue-sky, mackerel sky; sky-blue; pie in the sky, red sky at night shepherd's delight, the sky is the limit, under the open sky; Sky Blues; *Blue Sky* (f), *Cabin in the Sky* (f), *Lucy in the Sky with Diamonds* (s), *Mr Blue Sky* (s), *Pie in the Sky* (tv), *Reach for the Sky* (f), *The Sheltering Sky* (b/f), *The Sky at Night* (tv), *Sky Captain and the World of Tomorrow* (f), *Spirit in the Sky* (s), *Vanilla Sky* (f)

slacken ease off, loosen; slacken off

slacks loose-fitting trousers; idles

slag waste matter from a mine; deride; slag heap

slaked quenched; slaked lime

slalom downhill zigzag ski race; giant slalom

slam twelve or thirteen tricks at bridge, wrestling move; bang down or shut, criticise fiercely; grand slam; slam dunk; Grand Slam

slammer prison; tequila slammer

slang informal language; back slang, (Cockney) rhyming slang

slap sharp blow with the hand; daub, hit with the palm of the hand; slap bang, slap-happy, slap shot, slap-up; slap and tickle, slap in the face, slap on the back, slap on the wrist

slapping *see* slap; thigh-slapping

slash long sweeping cut, stroke in printing; cut drastically, slit; slash-and-burn

slate dull dark blue, bluish-grey rock, drinks tab, roofing tile; review scathingly; clean slate; wipe the slate clean

slaughterhouse abattoir; *Slaughterhouse-Five* (b/f)

slave forced labourer; work hard; wage slave; slave-driver, slave labour, slave trade

slayer killer; *Buffy the Vampire Slayer* (tv)

sleep nocturnal rest; slumber; 1963 Andy Warhol film; beauty sleep, get to sleep, go to sleep; sleep in, sleep over, sleep rough; goodnight, sleep tight, sleep like a log/top; *The Big Sleep* (b/f)

sleeper overnight railway carriage, rail track crossbar, secret agent, slumbering person; *Light Sleeper* (f)

sleeping *see* sleep; sleeping bag, sleeping car, sleeping draught, sleeping partner, sleeping pill, sleeping policeman; let sleeping dogs lie; *Sleeping Beauty* (b/f), *The Sleeping Beauty* (bal), *Sleeping with the Enemy* (f), *While You Were Sleeping* (f)

sleepless suffering from insomnia; *Sleepless in Seattle* (f)

sleeps *see* sleep; *The Lion Sleeps Tonight* (s)

sleepy dozy; *The Legend of Sleepy Hollow* (b), *Sleepy Hollow* (f)

sleeve arm-piece of a garment, cover for a record, windsock; cap sleeve, leg-of-mutton sleeve; sleeve notes; ace up your sleeve, have a card up your sleeve, laugh up your sleeve, up your sleeve, wear your heart on your sleeve

sleeves *see* sleeve; dolman sleeves, puff sleeves

sleigh snow vehicle; sleigh bells, sleigh ride

slender lean; *The Girls of Slender Means* (b)

slice piece (of bread, cake etc), poor golf shot; carve; fish slice; slice up

sliced *see* slice; the best thing since sliced bread

slick nautical oil spill; glib, well presented; oil slick

slicker *see* slick; city slicker

slickers   *see* slick; *City Slickers* (f)

slide   hair clip, photographic transparency, playground chute; lapse, skid, slip smoothly; water slide; slide guitar, slide rule, slide trombone, slide valve

sliding   *see* slide; sliding scale; *Sliding Doors* (f)

slight   snub; insult (someone); very little; *A Slight Case of Murder* (f)

slimming   dieting; slimming pills

sling   alcoholic drink, catapult, support for an injured arm; throw; gin sling; sling your hook

slinging   *see* sling; mud-slinging

slip   cricket fielding position, error, landslide, liquid clay, petticoat, pillowcase, small piece of paper; glide out of control, lapse; betting slip, compliments slip, Freudian slip, give the slip, leg slip, let slip, rejection slip, second slip, side-slip; slip case, slip knot, slip on, slip-ons, slip road, slip stitch, slip up; slip of the pen, slip of the tongue, slip through the net

slipped   *see* slip; slipped disc

slipper   indoor shoe; carpet slipper, glass slipper; slipper orchid; *The Glass Slipper* (b/f), *The Slipper and the Rose* (f)

slippery   evasive, smooth and slimy; slippery elm, slippery slope

sloe   blackthorn fruit or bush; sloe gin

slog   blow, strenuous work; hit hard, work hard (at)

sloop   sailing vessel; sloop-of-war; *Sloop John B* (s)

slop   pig food, spilled liquid; spill, walk carelessly in water, wash away; slop out

slope   incline; tilt; dry slope, nursery slope, ski slope, slippery slope; slope arms

sloppy   baggy (clothes), maudlin, slipshod, watery; sloppy joe

slot   aperture for a coin, niche; insert into a narrow space; slot machine

sloth   idleness, tree-dwelling mammal

slow   decelerate; leisurely, sluggish; go-slow; slow cooker, slow down, slow handclap, slow march, slow motion, slow puncture, slow up, slow-worm; slow but sure, slow on the uptake; *On a Slow Boat to China* (s)

slug   air-gun pellet, gastropod; hit; sea slug; slug pellets

sluice   floodgate; wet copiously; sluice gate

slur   calumny; speak unclearly

slush   liquid mud or snow, sentimental drivel; wash by throwing water; slush fund, slush pile

sly   cunning; on the sly

smack   rough kiss, sharp blow, small fishing vessel; slap; *Smack the Pony* (tv)

small   little; feel small, great and small, the small screen; small arms, small beer, small change, small claims court, small fortune, small fry, small hours, small intestine, small-minded, small of the back, small potatoes, small print, small-scale, small talk, small-time, small-town, small wonder; big fish in a small pond, it's a small world, no small wonder, sweat the small stuff; *All Creatures Great and Small* (tv), *It's a Small World* (f), *A Small Family Business* (pl), *Small Is Beautiful* (b), *Small Town Boy* (s), *Small Town Girl* (f), *A Small Town in Germany* (b), *Small World* (b)

smart be sore; clever, well dressed; smart Alec, smart card; *Get Smart* (tv)

smash collision, resounding success, tennis stroke; break; brand-name creamed potato mixture; smash and grab, smash hit, smash up

smashing *see* smash; excellent

smear smudge; daub, defame; smear campaign

smell aroma, one of the five senses; give off an (unpleasant) odour, sniff; smell a rat; *Sweet Smell of Success* (f)

smelling *see* smell; smelling salts; come up smelling of roses

smells *see* smell; a fox smells its own lair first; *Smells Like Teen Spirit* (s)

smelt *see* smell; fish of the salmon family; separate metal from ore

smile happy expression; beam with pleasure; *Behind a Painted Smile* (s), *A Certain Smile* (b/f)

smiley emoticon; *Smiley's People* (b/tv)

smith worker in metals; forge; Granny Smith; *Alas Smith and Jones* (tv), *Alias Smith and Jones* (tv), *Citizen Smith* (tv), *Mr and Mrs Smith* (f), *Mr Smith Goes to Washington* (f), *Nevada Smith* (f)

smoke fumes; emit vapour, preserve (food) using fumes, use tobacco; 1995 Harvey Keitel film; chain-smoke; smoke alarm, smoke signal; go up in smoke, no smoke without fire, smoke and mirrors, smoke like a chimney; *Holy Smoke* (f), *Smoke Gets in Your Eyes* (s), *Smoke on the Water* (s)

smoker compartment in which cigarettes are allowed, fish curer, tobacco user; chain-smoker, non-smoker

smoking *see* smoke; tobacco use; no smoking, non-smoking, passive smoking; smoking compartment, smoking gun, smoking jacket; *Lock, Stock and Two Smoking Barrels* (f)

smoky full of tobacco fumes, greyish in colour; smoky bacon; Great Smoky Mountains

smooth glib, level, silky; flatten; smooth-bore, smooth snake, smooth-talking, smooth-tongued; take the rough with the smooth; *Smooth Operator* (s)

snag drawback; catch

snail gastropod; sea snail; snail mail

snake serpent; crawl sinuously, twist; coral snake, garter snake, grass snake, milk snake, sand-snake, sea snake, smooth snake, tiger snake; snake charmer, snake eyes, snake oil; snake in the grass; *Snake Eyes* (f), *Union of the Snake* (s)

snakes *see* snake; snakes and ladders

snap children's card game, quick photo; crack, photograph informally, speak brusquely; brandy snap, ginger snap, sugar-snap peas; snap up; snap your fingers

snapper fish, impromptu photographer, turtle species; red snapper; *The Snapper* (b/f)

snappy irritable, quick, smart, trendy; make it snappy

snare animal trap, side drum; catch in a trap; snare drum

snarl vicious growl; growl, speak angrily; snarl up

sneak telltale; move furtively, tell tales; sneak up

sneezed exhaled violently; not to be sneezed at

snip bargain, quick cut; cut

snipe bird related to the woodcock;

make nasty comments, shoot (at) from cover

snobbery pretension; inverted snobbery

snooze brief sleep; nod off; snooze button

snow frozen crystals of rain; fall in white flakes; snow blindness, snow-boots, snow bunting, snow-capped, snow goose, snow leopard, snow pea; (as) pure as the driven snow; *Let It Snow* (s), *Miss Smilla's Feeling for Snow* (b), *Smilla's Sense of Snow* (f), *Snow Falling on Cedars* (b/f), *The Snow Goose* (b/f), *The Snow Queen* (b), *Snow White and the Seven Dwarfs* (f)

snowed *see* snow; snowed in

snowman icy figure with a carrot nose; Abominable Snowman; *The Snowman* (b/f)

snowy white and wintry; snowy owl

snuff powdered tobacco for inhaling; put out (a candle); up to snuff

snuggle settle into a comfy position; snuggle up

soaked drenched; soaked to the skin

soaking steeping; drenched; soaking wet

soap cleansing substance, popular tv serial; wash with lather; saddle soap, soft soap, sugar soap; soap dish, soap opera, soap powder

soapbox improvised speaking platform; soapbox orator

sob convulsive cry; weep loudly; 1981 Blake Edwards film; sob story

sober sedate, temperate; sober up; (as) sober as a judge

social informal party; convivial, relating to the community; social anthropology, social climber, social contract, social democrat, social

sciences, social scientist, social secretary, social security, social services, social studies, social work, social worker; *Buena Vista Social Club* (f), *The Social Contract* (b)

socialist left-winger; left-wing; champagne socialist; socialist realism; National Socialist

society association, community, haut monde; alternative society, building society, cafe society, co-operative society, friendly society, high society, plural society, re-enactment society, secret society; Oxford Union Society, Provident Society, Royal Society, Society Islands, Theosophical Society; *Cafe Society* (f), *Dead Poets' Society* (f), *High Society* (f)

Society
Cambridge Union, Oxford Union, Provident, Royal, Temperance, Theosophical

---

sock hosiery item; thump; put a sock in it

socket concavity, receptacle for a plug; ball-and-socket joint; socket wrench

socks *see* sock; bobby socks; blow/ knock the socks off, pull your socks up

sod clump of turf; under the sod; Sod's Law

soda carbonated water; baking soda, bicarbonate of soda, caustic soda, club soda, cream soda, ice-cream soda, washing soda; soda bread, soda fountain, soda pop, soda siphon, soda water

sods *see* sod; odds and sods

sofa settee; sofa bed

soft gentle, malleable; soft-boiled, soft-centred, soft focus, soft fruit, soft furnishings, soft-hearted, soft option, soft palate, soft pedal, soft roe, soft sell, soft-shoe, soft-shoe shuffle, soft soap, soft target, soft-top, soft touch; have a soft spot for

soften alleviate, make less hard, relent, tone down; soften up; soften the blow

softener fabric conditioner; water softener

softly gently, quietly; softly-softly; *Softly Softly* (tv)

software computer programs; application software; software engineering

soil earth; besmirch; soil pipe

soiled *see* soil; shop-soiled

sol old French coin, personification of the sun, Peru's currency unit; sol-fa; Costa del Sol

solar of the sun; solar eclipse, solar energy, solar flare, solar panel, solar plexus, solar power, solar system

sold *see* sell; sold out

soldering fusing with molten alloy; soldering iron

soldier member of an army; serve in the army; foot soldier, regular soldier, tin soldier; soldier of fortune, soldier on; Unknown Soldier; *Buffalo Soldier* (s), *The Good Soldier* (b/tv), *Soldier Blue* (f), *Soldier of Fortune* (f), *Tinker, Tailor, Soldier, Spy* (b/tv), *Universal Soldier* (s/f)

soldiers *see* soldier; *Buffalo Soldiers* (f), *The Virgin Soldiers* (b/f)

sole bottom of a foot or shoe, marine flatfish; lone; shipping forecast area; Dover sole, lemon sole; *O Sole Mio* (s)

solicitor lawyer; Solicitor General

solid hard, three-dimensional; rock solid; solid gold; *Solid Gold Easy Action* (s)

solitary hermit; lonely, single; solitary confinement

solitude isolation; *One Hundred Years of Solitude* (b), *Solitude Standing* (al)

solo unaccompanied performance, variety of whist; alone; single-handedly; 1981 Felicity Kendal sitcom; fly solo; solo whist

solstice longest or shortest day of the year; summer solstice, winter solstice

solution answer to a problem, liquid mixture; developing solution; *The Seven-Per-Cent Solution* (f)

solvent diluting agent; able to pay all debts; solvent abuse

some a few, unspecified amount; some day; and then some, some hope; *Some Day My Prince Will Come* (s), *Some Day You'll Be Sorry* (s), *Some Enchanted Evening* (s), *Some Guys Have All the Luck* (s), *Some Like It Hot* (f), *Some Mothers Do 'Ave Em* (tv), *Some People* (s/f)

somebody important person; any person; *Somebody Help Me* (s), *Somebody Killed Her Husband* (f), *Somebody Up There Likes Me* (f)

someone any person, unspecified person; look someone in the face, see someone coming, thank someone kindly; *Someone Else's Baby* (s), *Someone to Watch Over Me* (s/f)

something unspecified object; Beatles song; forty-something, start something, thirty-something; something else; *I'm into Something Good* (s), *Really Saying Something* (s), *Something Else* (s), *Something Happened* (b), *There's Something about Mary* (f)

somewhere   indefinite location; in an unknown place; get somewhere

son   male child; favourite son, prodigal son; son et lumière, son-in-law, son of a gun; like father like son; *Dombey and Son* (b), *Matthew and Son* (s), *Native Son* (f), *The Return of the Prodigal Son* (pa), *Saturn Devouring His Son* (pa), *A Son at the Front* (b), *Son of My Father* (s), *Son of Paleface* (f), *Steptoe and Son* (tv)

sonata   musical composition; *Moonlight Sonata* (cl), *The Ghost Sonata* (pl), *The Kreutzer Sonata* (b)

song   bird call, words set to music; drinking song, folk song, on song, part-song, pop song, sing-song, siren song, theme song, torch song; song cycle, song thrush; going for a song, a song and dance; Song of Solomon; *Annie's Song* (s), *The Banana Boat Song* (s), *The Birdie Song* (s), *Carla's Song* (f), *The Chicken Song* (s), *The Desert Song* (mus), *Elephant Song* (b), *Going for a Song* (tv), *The Logical Song* (s), *The Love Song of J Alfred Prufrock* (po), *The Pushbike Song* (s), *A Song for the Lovers* (s), *Song for Whoever* (s), *The Song of Bernadette* (f), *Song of Solomon* (b), *This Is My Song* (s), *Torch Song Trilogy* (f/pl), *The Trolley Song* (s), *Your Song* (s)

songs   *see* song; *Silly Love Songs* (s), *Songs of Innocence and Experience* (po), *Songs of Praise* (tv)

sonic   relating to noise; sonic boom; *Sonic the Hedgehog* (ga)

sons   *see* son; *Sons and Lovers* (b/f/tv), *The Sons of Katie Elder* (f), *Sons of the Desert* (f)

soon   before long; a fool and his money are soon parted, get well soon

sooner   earlier, preferably; sooner or later

sop   bread soaked in liquid, propitiatory gift; soak (up)

sopranos   female opera singers, female voices of the highest pitch; mezzo-sopranos; *The Sopranos* (tv)

sorcerer   magician; 1977 remake of *The Wages of Fear*; *The Sorcerer's Apprentice* (cl), *The Sword and the Sorcerer* (f)

sore   ulcer or boil; painful; cold sore, saddle-sore; sore point; like a bear with a sore head, stick out like a sore thumb

sorrel   horse with a light reddish-brown coat, plant of the dock family; reddish-brown; wood sorrel

sorrow   sadness; 1973 David Bowie hit; parting is such sweet sorrow

sorry   apologetic, pitiful; excuse me!; 1980s Ronnie Corbett sitcom; better safe than sorry; *I'm Sorry I Haven't a Clue* (r), *Some Day You'll Be Sorry* (s), *Sorry Seems to Be the Hardest Word* (s), *Who's Sorry Now?* (s)

sort   type; categorise; sort out; *Not That Sort of Girl* (b)

sorting   *see* sort; sorting office

sorts   *see* sort; out of sorts; it takes all sorts to make a world

sought   searched for; sought after

soul   inner spirit, person, style of music; body and soul, life and soul, lost soul; soul-destroying, soul food, soul music, soul-searching; brevity is the soul of wit, dark night of the soul, keep body and soul together, the life and soul of the party, sell your soul, upon my soul, windows of the soul; *Heart and Soul* (s), *Rubber Soul* (s), *Soul Man* (s)

The *Puzzler* Crossword Solver's Dictionary

souls *see* soul; All Souls Day; *Dead Souls* (b), *Sea of Souls* (tv)

sound noise, strait; measure depth, probe; in good condition, trustworthy; Dolby sound, safe and sound; sound barrier, sound bite, sound-check, sound effects, sound engineer, sound system, sound waves; (as) sound as a bell; *The Sound and the Fury* (b), *Sound and Vision* (s), *The Sound of Music* (f), *Wired for Sound* (s)

sounding *see* sound; echo-sounding; sounding board

soup broth; alphabet soup, bird's-nest soup, duck soup, mock turtle soup, oxtail soup, pea soup, primordial soup, tomato soup, vegetable soup; soup kitchen, soup spoon; in the soup; *Animal Crackers in My Soup* (s), *Duck Soup* (f), *Love Soup* (tv), *There's a Girl in My Soup* (f)

sour spoil; acid; sweet-and-sour, turn sour, whisky sour; sour cream, sour grapes, sour mash; *Sour Sweet* (b)

source origin; at source

sources *see* source; *Manon des Sources* (f)

South
Africa, America, Atlantic, Australia, Bank, Carolina, China Sea, Dakota, Downs, Georgia, Glamorgan, Island, Kensington, Korea, Pacific, Pole, Sandwich Islands, Sea Bubble, Sea Islands, Seas, Shields, Tyrone, Uist, Utsire, Wales, Yorkshire

---

south compass direction; south-east, south-easterly, south-eastern, south temperate zone, south-west, south-westerly, south-western; Deep South, New South Wales, South Africa,

South America, South Bank, South Carolina, South China Sea, South Dakota, South Downs, South Glamorgan, South Kensington, South Korea, South Pacific, South Pole, South Seas, South Yorkshire; *Due South* (tv), *Goin' South* (f), *North and South* (b/tv), *The South Bank Show* (tv), *South Pacific* (mus), *South Park* (tv)

southern austral; southern-fried, southern hemisphere; Southern Comfort, Southern Lights, Southern Ocean; *Southern Comfort* (f)

sovereign monarch, old gold coin; possessing supreme power; half-sovereign

sow female pig; scatter (seeds); sow your wild oats

soya protein-rich bean; soya bean, soya milk

spa curative mineral spring, health resort; Belgian resort and Grand Prix circuit; Leamington Spa

space area outside the Earth, empty area, gap, room; arrange gaps in; breathing space, deep space, in space, inner space, outer space; space age, space bar, space cadet, space capsule, space probe, space shuttle, space station, space traveller, space walk; waste of space; *Inner Space* (f), *Lost in Space* (f/tv), *Space Invaders* (ga), *Space 1999* (tv), *Space Oddity* (s), *2001: A Space Odyssey* (f)

spaceman astronaut; 1996 Babylon Zoo hit; *I'm the Urban Spaceman* (s)

spade black playing-card, garden digging tool; bucket and spade; call a spade a spade

spades *see* spade; ace of spades, in spades; *Ace of Spades* (s), *The Queen of Spades* (b/o)

spaghetti stringy variety of pasta; spaghetti Bolognese, spaghetti carbonara, spaghetti straps, spaghetti western

spam junk email, tinned meat product

span breadth, bridge's width, distance between wing tips, duration, hand measure; extend across; spick and span

spaniel floppy-eared breed of dog; cocker spaniel, King Charles spaniel

spanner wrench for nuts and screws; box spanner; spanner in the works; *Monkey Spanner* (s)

spar nautical beam; practise boxing; supermarket chain

spare duplicate kept for emergencies; be merciful towards, part with voluntarily; extra, frugal, meagre; go spare, to spare; spare ribs, spare time, spare tyre; spare no expense; *Brother, Can You Spare a Dime* (s), *Spare Rib* (mag), *Spare the Rod* (f)

spared *see* spare; no expense spared

sparing *see* spare; frugal

spark electrical discharge, flash; set off; bright spark; spark plug; *The Vital Spark* (tv)

sparkling bubbly (wine), glittering; sparkling wine; *Sparkling Cyanide* (b/tv)

sparring boxing practice; arguing; sparring partner

sparrow small common brown bird; hedge sparrow, house sparrow; sparrow-hawk

spat shoe gaiter, tiff; ejected saliva

spate sudden flood; in spate

speak communicate with the voice; speak up, speak volumes; actions speak louder than words, speak evil of, speak ill of, speak in tongues, speak of the devil, speak the same language, speak your mind; *Speak, Memory* (b)

speaker orator, part of a PA system, person talking; House of Commons presiding officer; native speaker

speakers *see* speaker; Speakers' Corner

speaking *see* speak; non-English-speaking; speaking clock; in a manner of speaking, on speaking terms

special distinctive; extra-special; special agents, special case, special constable, special delivery, special effects, special licence, special needs, special offer, special school; Special Branch; *Six-Five Special* (tv), *Special Branch* (tv)

specific precise; non-specific; specific gravity

spectacles exhibitions, eye-glasses, shows; half-moon spectacles

speech act of talking, language, lecture; direct speech, figure of speech, maiden speech, part of speech, reported speech; speech day, speech recognition, speech therapy; Mansion House Speech, Queen's Speech

speed amphetamine, velocity; drive too fast, expedite; 1994 Keanu Reeves film; at speed, ground speed, high-speed train, shutter speed; speed bump, speed camera, speed limit, speed trap, speed up; full speed ahead, more haste less speed, up to speed; *Rain, Steam and Speed* (pa)

speedy fast; *Speedy Gonzales* (s)

spell magical formula, period of time; read out letter by letter, signify; cast a spell, dizzy spell

spelling   *see* spell; spelling bee

spender   buyer; 1990s Jimmy Nail drama series; *Big Spender* (s)

spending   passing (time), paying out; spending money

spent   paid out, passed (time); exhausted; well spent

sphere   ball-like shape, field; armillary sphere

spheres   *see* sphere; harmony of the spheres, music of the spheres

spice   excitement, food flavouring; add zest to; five-spice; variety is the spice of life; Old Spice; *Spice World* (f), *Sugar and Spice* (s)

spider   arachnid, snooker rest; 2002 Ralph Fiennes film; bird-eating spider, funnel-web spider, money spider, trapdoor spider, wolf spider; spider crab, spider monkey, spider plant, spider's web; *Along Came a Spider* (f), *Spider-Man* (f), *The Spider's Web* (f)

spike   ear (of corn), power surge, sharp pointed object; impale, reject (a newspaper story), ruin

spill   overflow, thin taper; pour out accidentally; spill blood, spill over; spill the beans

spills   *see* spill; thrills and spills

spilt   *see* spill; don't cry over spilt milk

spin   short car journey, slant in a news story, style of bowling in cricket; whirl; flat spin, leg spin, off spin; spin a yarn, spin bowler, spin bowling, spin doctor, spin-dry, spin dryer, spin-off, spin out; in a flat spin; *Spin City* (tv)

spinal   backbone-related; cerebro-spinal system; spinal column, spinal cord, spinal tap; *This Is Spinal Tap* (f)

spine   back of a book, row of backbones, sharp-backed mountain or ridge, thorn; spine-chilling, spine-tingling

spinner   drying machine, fishing lure, specialist bowler, type of ball at cricket, yarn maker; leg-spinner, money-spinner, off-spinner

spinning   converting threads into yarn, whirling; money-spinning; spinning a yarn, spinning jenny, spinning mule, spinning top, spinning wheel

spiny   prickly; spiny anteater

spiral   twisting helical shape; move in decreasing circles; coiled; spiral-bound, spiral staircase

spirit   disposition, distilled alcoholic drink, enthusiasm, ghost, soul, vital principle; evil spirit, in spirit, kindred spirit, proof spirit, surgical spirit, team spirit, white spirit; spirit lamp, spirit level; in spirit and in truth; Holy Spirit; *Blithe Spirit* (f/pl), *Smells Like Teen Spirit* (s), *Spirit in the Sky* (s), *Surgical Spirit* (tv)

spirited   headstrong, lively; high-spirited, public-spirited

spirits   *see* spirit; mood; high spirits, low spirits, methylated spirits; *The House of the Spirits* (b/f)

spit   coastal ridge of sand, exact replica, rotisserie; eject saliva, rain lightly; cuckoo spit; spit and polish, spit-and-sawdust, spit blood, spit-roast; be the (dead) spit of, spit into the wind, spit it out

spite   malice; thwart; in spite of; cut off your nose to spite your face

spitting   *see* spit; spitting image; *Spitting Image* (tv)

splash   sensational news story, sound of an object hitting water; bespatter;

1984 Tom Hanks film; splash out; make a splash; *A Bigger Splash* (f/pa)

splice   join; splice the mainbrace

spliced   *see* splice; get spliced

splinter   fragment of wood or metal; break into small sharp fragments; splinter group

split   crack; break up, burst open, divide; forced apart; Croatian city and port; banana split, lickety-split; split decision, split ends, split hairs, split infinitive, split-level, split peas, split pin, split screen, split second, split shift, split the vote, split up; split the difference, split your sides

splits   *see* split; *The Banana Splits* (tv)

splitting   *see* split; bad (headache); ear-splitting, hair-splitting, side-splitting

spoil   material cast out in excavation, remains of an animal body; go bad, overindulge, ruin; too many cooks spoil the broth; *Will Success Spoil Rock Hunter?* (f)

spoils   *see* spoil; booty; *The Spoils of Poynton* (b)

spoilt   *see* spoil; spoilt for choice

spoke   *see* speak; one of the radiating bars of a wheel

spoken   *see* speak; oral; be spoken for, well spoken

sponge   absorbent item for the bath, light cake, sea creature, steamed pudding; live off others; sponge bag, sponge cake, sponge pudding; throw in the sponge

spontaneous   impromptu; spontaneous combustion

spooks   ghosts, spies; frightens; BBC drama series about MI5

spoon   cutlery item, fishing lure; court in a sentimental way, scoop with a

ladle; apostle spoon, egg-and-spoon race, greasy spoon, runcible spoon, salt spoon, silver spoon, soup spoon, wooden spoon; spoon-feed

sport   athletic activities; wear ostentatiously; blood sport, contact sport, indoor sport, motor sport; be a sport, the sport of kings; *A Question of Sport* (tv), *Tie Me Kangaroo Down, Sport* (s)

sporting   *see* sport; magnanimous in defeat; sporting chance; *This Sporting Life* (b/f)

sports   *see* sport; contact sports, water sports, winter sports; sports car, sports jacket, sports psychologist

spot   mark, particular place, pimple; catch sight of; beauty spot, black spot, blind spot, high spot, hot spot, in a spot, leaf spot, liver spot, on the spot, penalty spot, tight spot, trouble spot; spot check, spot kick, spot on, spot the ball, spot-welder; have a soft spot for, hit the spot, put on the spot, rooted to the spot, X marks the spot; Gloucester Old Spot, Great Red Spot; *The Hot Spot* (f)

spotless   clean, pure; *Eternal Sunshine of the Spotless Mind* (f)

spots   *see* spot; hit the high spots, knock spots off, a leopard can't change his spots

spotted   *see* spot; speckled; spotted dick

spotter   look-out person, observer; talent spotter

spout   funnel, jet (of water), teapot's pouring part; gush; up the spout

sprat   small species of herring; a sprat to catch a mackerel

spray   aerosol, mist from crashing waves, small bunch of flowers;

sprinkle; fly-spray, pepper spray; spray gun

spraying *see* spray; crop-spraying

spread
array of food, extent, paste-like food; distribute, expand, scatter, unfold, widen; extended; centre spread, middle-age spread; spread betting, spread eagle, spread out; spread like wildfire, spread your wings

spree jaunt, wild fling; carouse; Berlin river; shopping spree

spring coiled wire, natural water source, vernal season; help (a prisoner) escape, jump; hot spring, thermal spring; spring a leak, spring balance, spring chicken, spring-clean, spring-cleaning, spring greens, spring-loaded, spring onions, spring roll; full of the joys of spring; *Black Spring* (b), *The Roman Spring of Mrs Stone* (f), *Spring Awakening* (pl), *Spring in Park Lane* (f)

springs *see* spring; hope springs eternal; Alice Springs, Colorado Springs

sprite fairy; brand-name soft drink

sprouts buds, shoots, small cabbage-like vegetables; germinates; bean sprouts, Brussels sprouts

spruce long-coned fir tree; smarten (up); dapper; Norway spruce

spud narrow-bladed spade, potato; spud-bashing

spun *see* spin; woven; fine-spun; spun sugar

spur incentive, rider's goading instrument; encourage; spur-of-the-moment; on the spur of the moment; *Fame Is the Spur* (b/f)

spy secret agent; notice, secretly observe; I-spy; I spy with my little

eye, spy out the land; *Confessions of a Nazi Spy* (f), *I-Spy* (f/tv), *A Perfect Spy* (b/tv), *Spy Game* (f), *Spy Hard* (f), *Spy Kids* (f), *The Spy Who Came In from the Cold* (b/f), *The Spy Who Loved Me* (f), *Tinker, Tailor, Soldier, Spy* (b/tv)

spyglass small telescope; *The Amber Spyglass* (b)

squad group of workers, soldiers or sportspeople; bomb squad, firing squad, flying squad, riot squad; squad car; *The Mod Squad* (f), *Police Squad* (tv)

squadron military unit; squadron leader; *Mosquito Squadron* (f), *633 Squadron* (b/f)

Square
Berkeley, Bloomsbury, Cadogan, Cavendish, Eaton, Hanover, Leicester, Portman, Red, Russell, Sloane, Soho, St Mark's, Tiananmen, Times, Trafalgar, Washington

---

square four-sided shape, open space in a city, product of a quantity multiplied by itself; balance (an account), be compatible (with); equitable, four-sided, old-fashioned, satisfying (meal); at right angles, solidly; all square, fair and square, four-square, market square, set square, T-square; square-bashing, square dance, square-dancing, square deal, square-eyed, square leg, square meal, square number, square peg, square-rigged, square root; back to square one, a square peg in a round hole; Berkeley Square, Bloomsbury Square, Leicester Square, Red Square, Russell Square, Sloane Square, Square Mile, St Mark's Square, Tiananmen

Square, Times Square, Washington Square; *Berkeley Square* (f), *Hangover Square* (b/f), *Red Square* (b), *The Square Peg* (f), *Washington Square* (b)

squarely   *see* square; fairly and squarely

squares   *see* square; *Celebrity Squares* (tv)

squash   fruit cordial, indoor racket sport, marrow-like vegetable; flatten; butternut squash, lemon squash; squash court

squat   house occupied without permission, weight-lifting movement; occupy illegally, sit on your heels; low and broad; diddly-squat

squeak   high-pitched cry, narrow escape; make a mouse noise; bubble and squeak, narrow squeak

squeaky   high-pitched (cry), needing oiling; squeaky clean

squeeze   boyfriend or girlfriend, informally; compress, hug; squeeze-box; put the squeeze on

squib   short piece of satire, small noisy firework; lampoon; damp squib

squid   sea creature; giant squid

squirrel   bushy-tailed rodent; stash (away); flying squirrel, grey squirrel, ground squirrel, red squirrel; *The Tale of Squirrel Nutkin* (b)

squirt   irritatingly pretentious person, jet of water; throw out (liquid) in a jet

stab   attempt, knife wound, sharp pain; injure or pierce with a knife; stab in the back, stab in the dark; have a stab

stabbing   *see* stab; knifing incident; back-stabbing

stable   collection of racehorses,

horse's shelter; provide shelter for (horses); constant, firmly fixed, well balanced; livery stable; stable companion, stable door, stable lad

stack   pile, tall chimney; pile (up); chimney stack; stack up

stacked   *see* stack; Pamela Anderson sitcom

stadium   sports arena; Millennium Stadium, Stadium of Light, Wembley Stadium

---

Stadium
Britannia, Emirates, Ibrox, Madejski, Millennium, Pride Park, Reebok, Riverside, Walkers, Wembley

---

staff   rod, workforce; provide employees for; chief of staff, general staff, skeleton staff, the staff of life; staff college, staff nurse, staff officer, staff sergeant

staffed   *see* staff; short-staffed

stag   male deer, men-only party; 1970s Triumph sports model; stag beetle, stag do, stag night, stag party; *Stag at Bay* (pa)

stage   leg (of a journey), phase, theatre platform; put on (a play); apron-stage, centre stage, committee stage, landing stage, off-stage, report stage; stage by stage, stage directions, stage door, stage fright, stage management, stage-manage, stage manager, stage name, stage struck, stage whisper; hold the stage, set the stage; Key Stage; *The Deadwood Stage* (s), *Stage Beauty* (f), *Stage Door* (f), *Stage Fright* (f), *Stage Struck* (f)

staging   *see* stage; scaffold in a theatre, theatre production; staging post

stain dirty mark, dye; tarnish; wood stain; *The Human Stain* (b/f)

stained *see* stain; stained glass

stainless immaculate, rust-free; stainless steel

stair one of a flight of treads; stair rods; *The Ruffian on the Stair* (pl)

staircase flight of steps; moving staircase, spiral staircase

stairs *see* stair; below stairs, flight of stairs

stake interest, sharpened post, wager; deposit as a wager, mark (out) the bounds with posts, risk; stake a claim, stake out

stakeholder independent party in a wager, person with an interest in an enterprise; stakeholder pension

stalk plant stem; pursue stealthily

stalking *see* stalk; stalking horse

stall booth; cut out (of an engine), deliberately delay; market stall

stalls *see* stall; theatre seating area; orchestra stalls

stamp distinguishing sign, postage token; imprint, tread heavily; date stamp, newspaper stamp duty, postage stamp, rubber stamp, trading stamp; stamp album, stamp collecting, stamp collection, stamp duty, stamp of approval, stamp out

stamping *see* stamp; rubber-stamping; stamping ground

stand batting partnership, kiosk, position, spectators' enclosure; be a candidate, be upright, put up with; coat-stand, news-stand, on stand-by, one-night stand, umbrella stand; stand a chance, stand-alone, stand at ease, stand bail, stand by, stand down, stand easy, stand guard, stand in, stand off, stand-off half, stand

out, stand pat, stand surety, stand to, stand to attention, stand up, stand-up comedian; make a stand, make your hair stand on end, not stand an earthly, stand on ceremony, stand on your dignity, stand out a mile, stand the pace, stand the test of time, stand your ground; *One Night Stand* (f), *Stand and Deliver* (s), *Stand by Me* (f/s), *Stand by Your Man* (s)

standard flag, norm; normal; bog-standard, double standard, gold standard, lamp standard, non-standard, royal standard; standard assessment task, standard-bearer, standard deviation, standard lamp, standard of living, standard time; raise the standard; Eastern Standard Time, Standard Grade; *Evening Standard* (n)

standing *see* stand; reputation; upright; free-standing, hard standing, long-standing; standing joke, standing order, standing ovation, standing stone; in good standing, leave standing; *I'm Still Standing* (s), *Solitude Standing* (al), *Standing on the Shoulder of Giants* (al)

stands *see* stand; it stands to reason

staple main element, main item of trade, piece of wire used to secure papers; fasten with a metal clip; basic (diet), fundamental; staple gun

star asterisk, celebrity, heavenly body, leading performer; play the leading role (in); 1968 Julie Andrews film; child star, dog star, evening star, falling star, film star, five-star, four-star, neutron star, shooting star; star anise, star-crossed, star pupil, star sign, star-spangled, star-struck, star-studded, star turn; hitch your wagon to a star; Death Star, Evening Star, Lone Star, Morning Star, North Star, Pole Star, Star Chamber, Star of Bethlehem, Star of David, Star-Spangled Banner; *Dark Star* (f), *The Evening Star* (f), *Morning Star* (n), *Polar Star* (b), *A Star Is Born* (f), *Star-Spangled Banner* (s), *Star Spangled Rhythm* (f), *Star Trek* (tv), *Star Wars* (f), *Video Killed the Radio Star* (s)

staring gaping, watching fixedly; stark staring mad

stark austere, bleak, downright, grim, harsh, sharply evident, unadorned; 1989 debut novel by Ben Elton; stark naked; stark raving mad, stark staring mad

starred *see* star; ill starred

starry full of heavenly bodies, twinkly; starry-eyed; *Starry Eyed* (s), *Starry Night* (pa)

stars *see* star; see stars; thank your lucky stars; Stars and Bars, Stars and Stripes; *The City and the Stars* (b), *The Plough and the Stars* (pl), *Shooting Stars* (tv), *Stars and Bars* (b/f), *The Stars Look Down* (b/f), *Thank Your Lucky Stars* (mus/tv)

start beginning, entry point, onset; begin, jump in fright, set out, spring forward; bump-start, false start, flying start, head start, jump-start, kick-start, push-start; start out, start over, start up; for a start, start off on the right/wrong foot, start something, start the ball rolling, to start with; *Start Me Up* (s), *Start the Week* (r), *We Didn't Start the Fire* (s)

started *see* start; *It Started with a Kiss* (s)

starter beginner, competitor in a race, first course, ignition switch,

racecourse official; fire starter, non-starter, self-starter, under starter's orders; starter home, starter motor

starters *see* starter; for starters

starting *see* start; starting blocks, starting gate, starting pistol, starting post, starting price; *Starting Over* (f)

starts *see* start; bump-starts, fits and starts

starve deprive of food, go hungry; feed a cold, starve a fever

state government, nation, region within a federal republic, set of circumstances; declare; head of state, lying-in-state, minister of state, nation state, police state, welfare state; state of affairs, state of emergency, state of grace, state of life, state of play, state-of-the-art, state school; in a state of nature; Empire State, Empire State Building, Garden State, Green Mountain State, Irish Free State, Orange Free State, Secretary of State, State Department, State of the Union; *Enemy of the State* (f), *Garden State* (f), *State Fair* (mus), *State of Grace* (f), *State of the Union* (f)

stately dignified; stately home

statement declaration; bank statement, mission statement; *The Strawberry Statement* (f)

states *see* state; Jersey parliament; Trucial States, United States, United States of America

statesman respected senior politician; elder statesman; *The New Statesman* (mag/tv)

station depot, local police office, railway stop, rank, tv or radio channel; appoint to a post; bus station, coach station, comfort station, filling station, fire station, generating station, hill station, lifeboat radio station, petrol station, pirate radio station, police station, polling station, power station, radio station, service station, space station, tracking station, weather station; station wagon; *By Grand Central Station I Sat Down and Wept* (b), *Ice Station Zebra* (b/f)

stationery writing materials; the Stationery Office

stations *see* station; action stations, battle stations, panic stations, pirate radio stations; Stations of the Cross

statistics numerical data; vital statistics

statue sculpted figure; Statue of Liberty

status prestige, rank; most favoured nation status; status quo, status symbol; *Status Anxiety* (b)

statute decree; statute book, statute law

staunch stem (bleeding, eg); steadfast

stave barrel slat, ladder rung, lines for music notation, long stick; ward (off)

stay corset support, deferment, sojourn; remain; 1992 Shakespear's Sister hit; stay in, stay of execution, stay over, stay put, stay the course, stay the distance, stay the pace, stay up; *Stay Another Day* (s), *Stay Lucky* (tv), *Stay with Me* (s)

staying *see* stay; staying power; *Staying Alive* (f/s), *Staying On* (b)

stays *see* stay; *The Kid Stays in the Picture* (f)

steady balanced, regular; go steady, rock-steady; ready steady go, steady on; *Ready Steady Cook* (tv), *Ready Steady Go* (tv)

steak thick slice of fish or meat; fillet steak, minute steak, porterhouse steak, rump steak, T-bone steak; steak tartare

steal bargain; take illegally, tread silently; steal a march on, steal the show; *How to Steal a Million* (f)

steam vapour from boiling water; cook by means of water vapour, emit water vapour; steam bath, steam engine, steam iron, steam train, steam turbine; blow off steam, full steam ahead, get up steam, let off steam, pick up steam, run out of steam, under your own steam; *Rain, Steam and Speed* (pa)

steamed *see* steam; steamed up

steamer cooking vessel, old-fashioned ship; paddle steamer

steamy erotic, hot and humid, misty; *Steamy Windows* (s)

steel hard alloy of iron and carbon; harden (oneself); damask steel, pedal steel guitar, Sheffield steel, stainless steel, tungsten steel; steel band, steel drum, steel engraving, steel wool; *Blue Steel* (f), *Sapphire and Steel* (tv), *Steel Magnolias* (f)

steep leave to soak; exorbitant, sharply inclined

steer bullock; guide (a vehicle); steer clear of

steering *see* steer; car's guiding mechanism; power steering; steering column, steering committee, steering wheel

stem base of a wine glass, plant stalk; originate, restrain; stem cell, stem ginger, stem stitch; from stem to stern

step dance movement, gait, part of a staircase, phase; pace; Boston two-step, change step, false step, goose-step, hop step and jump, in step, military two-step, one step, out of step, twelve-step programme, two-step; step aerobics, step by step, step down, step in, step up; mind your step, step into the breach, step on it, step out of line, watch your step; *One Step Beyond* (s), *Step Inside Love* (s)

stepping   *see* step; stepping stone; *Stepping Out* (mus)

steps   *see* step; small ladder; *The Thirty-Nine Steps* (b/f), *Three Steps to Heaven* (s)

stereo   hi-fi unit, two-way sound system; personal stereo

sterling   British currency; genuine; sterling silver

stern   ship's rear end; strict; from stem to stern

stew   casserole, state of anxiety; cook slowly in liquid; Irish stew; stew in your own juice

steward   crowd attendant, domestic manager, flight or cruise attendant, race-meeting official; marshal; shop steward

stick   criticism, rod; adhere, jam; cocktail stick, crab stick, French stick, hockey stick, joss stick, non-stick, orange stick, pogo stick, shooting stick, swagger stick, swizzle stick, walking stick; stick insect, stick-in-the-mud, stick of rock, stick together, stick up; (caught) in a cleft stick, stick at it, stick in your craw/throat, stick out a mile, stick out like a sore thumb, stick the knife in, stick to your guns, stick your neck out, stick your oar in; *Hit Me with Your Rhythm Stick* (s), *Let's Stick Together* (s)

sticking   *see* stick; sticking plaster

sticks   *see* stick; backwoods, rural

areas; in front of the sticks, up sticks

sticky   adhesive, awkward, glutinous, gummy, humid, tacky; sticky-fingered, sticky fingers, sticky wicket; come to a sticky end; *Sticky Fingers* (al)

stiff   corpse; rigid, strong (alcoholic drink); bored stiff, frozen stiff, scared stiff; stiff-necked, stiff upper lip

stifling   suffocating; oppressively hot

still   apparatus for making liquor, photograph; silence; motionless; nevertheless; stock-still; still life, still water; still waters run deep; *All Stood Still* (s), *The Day the Earth Stood Still* (f), *Distant Voices, Still Lives* (f), *I'm Still Standing* (s), *Still Crazy* (f), *Still Waters Run Deep* (s), *You're Still the One* (s)

stilts   long-legged wading birds, poles used for walking

sting   elaborate con, poisonous barb of a plant or animal, smarting pain; smart; a sting in the tail; *The Sting* (f)

stinging   *see* sting; hurtful; stinging nettle

stink   bad smell; smell bad; like stink; stink bomb; stink to high heaven

stinking   *see* stink; fetid; cry stinking fish

stinks   *see* stink; *Life Stinks* (f)

stir   commotion, prison; begin to move, cause trouble, mix (in); stir crazy, stir-fried, stir-fry, stir up; stir up a hornets' nest; *Stir Crazy* (f)

stirrup   rider's foot-support, type of pump; stirrup cup, stirrup pants, stirrup pump

stitch   loop of thread, sharp pain; sew; blanket stitch, blind stitch, buttonhole stitch, cable stitch, chain stitch, cross stitch, garter stitch, moss stitch, running stitch, saddle stitch, satin stitch, slip stitch, stem stitch, stocking stitch, tent stitch; a stitch in time saves nine

stitches   *see* stitch; surgical sutures; in stitches

stock   basis of soups, capital of a company, farm's animals, goods for sale, gun handle, lineage, stored material, trunk or main stem; provide (goods); bankrupt stock, joint-stock company, laughing stock, rolling stock, take stock; stock car, stock-car racing, stock cube, stock exchange, stock-in-trade, stock market, stock-still, stock-taking; lock, stock and barrel; *Lock, Stock and Two Smoking Barrels* (f)

stockbroker   buyer and seller of shares; stockbroker belt

stocking   *see* stock; hosiery item; body stocking; stocking filler, stocking mask, stocking stitch

stockings   hosiery items; *Silk Stockings* (f)

stocks   *see* stock; stocks and shares

stoke   attend to a fire; Staffordshire city; Stoke Poges

stole   *see* steal; woman's shoulder wrap

stomach   belly, digestive organ; endure; strong stomach; stomach ache; the pit of the stomach, sick to your stomach

stone   hard-shelled seed of a fruit, rock, small rock or pebble, unit of weight; throw rocks at; coping stone, dry-stone walling, fire stone, foundation stone, kidney-stone, philosopher's stone, Portland stone, precious stone, rolling stone, standing stone, stepping stone; stone circle, stone curlew, stone fruit; kill

two birds with one stone, leave no stone unturned, like getting blood out of a stone, a rolling stone gathers no moss, stone me, stone the crows, a stone's throw; Blarney Stone, New Stone Age, Old Stone Age, Rosetta Stone, Rufus Stone, Stone Age; *Harry Potter and the Philosopher's Stone* (b/f), *Like a Rolling Stone* (s), *Papa Was a Rollin' Stone* (s), *Romancing the Stone* (f), *The Roman Spring of Mrs Stone* (f), *The Sword in the Stone* (b/f)

Stone

Black, Blarney, Coronation, Maiden, Picardy, Rocking, Rosetta, Rufus

---

stony   expressionless, rocky; stony broke, stony-faced; fall on stony ground; Stony Stratford

stood   *see* stand; *All Stood Still* (s), *The Day the Earth Stood Still* (f), *Fair Stood the Wind for France* (b)

stool   backless seat; bar stool, ducking stool, milking stool, piano stool; stool pigeon; *Stool Pigeon* (s)

stools   *see* stool; fall between two stools

stoops   verandas; crouches, submits; *She Stoops to Conquer* (pl)

stop   cessation, obstacle, set of organ pipes; finish, prevent; 1998 hit for the Spice Girls; bus stop, full stop, glottal stop, non-stop, pit stop, request stop, truck stop, whistle-stop (tour); stop press; stop it, stop the rot; *Bus Stop* (f/s), *Fried Green Tomatoes at the Whistle Stop Cafe* (f), *Stop! in the Name of Love* (s), *Stop Making Sense* (f), *Stop! or My Mom Will Shoot* (f)

stoppage   break in supply, strike; stoppage time

stopper bung; conversation stopper, show-stopper

stopping *see* stop; heart-stopping, show-stopping

stops *see* stop; pull out all the stops, the buck stops here

storage accommodation (for goods); cold storage, (night) storage heater

store cache, place to keep things, shop; stockpile; chain store, cold store, convenience store, department store, dime store, discount store, general store, in store; store card; set store by; *Trouble in Store* (f)

storey floor of a building; multi-storey, upper storey

stories *see* story; *Just So Stories* (b)

storm commotion, violent outburst of bad weather; launch an assault upon, rant; dust storm, electric storm, eye of a storm, magnetic storm, tropical storm; storm clouds, storm drain, storm petrel, storm troops, storm warning; go down a storm, a storm in a teacup, take by storm; Storm Trooper; *The Ice Storm* (f), *The Perfect Storm* (f)

stormy tempestuous; *Stormy Weather* (s/f)

story plot, tale; cock-and-bull story, detective story, fairy story, ghost story, hard-luck story, photo-story, shaggy-dog story, short story, sob story, success story, tall story; every picture tells a story, a likely story, the same old story, the story of my life, to cut a long story short; *The Colditz Story* (f), *Every Picture Tells a Story* (al), *Ghost Story* (f), *Love Story* (b/f), *The Nun's Story* (f), *The Palm Beach Story* (f), *The Philadelphia Story* (f), *The Story Makers* (tv), *The Story of My*

Life (s), *The Straight Story* (f), *Toy Story* (f), *West Side Story* (mus)

stout strong dark beer; plump, robust; milk stout; stout-hearted

stove oven; paraffin stove, pot-bellied stove

stow pack away; stow away

straight poker hand; direct, heterosexual, honest, in good order, level; back straight, go straight, home straight; straight away, straight-cut, straight edge, straight face, straight fight, straight flush, straight man, straight-shooting, straight up; in a straight line, keep a straight face, look straight in the eye, put the record straight, the straight and narrow, straight as a die, straight from the shoulder; *Going Straight* (tv), *Queer Eye for the Straight Guy* (tv), *The Straight Story* (f)

straighten align, make tidy, unbend; straighten out

strain breed, section of a melody, tension; overexert, sieve; eye strain, repetitive strain injury; *The Andromeda Strain* (b/f)

strait narrow channel of water; narrow; strait-laced; Bass Strait, Bering Strait, Cook Strait, Menai Strait, Strait of Hormuz, Torres Strait

straits *see* strait; hardships; dire straits

strand beach, thread; maroon; The Strand; *Do the Strand* (s), *The House on the Strand* (b), *The Strand* (mag)

strange odd; strange to tell; *Strange Bedfellows* (f), *Strange Fruit* (s), *Stranger in a Strange Land* (b)

stranger outsider, unknown person; more odd; *Beautiful Stranger* (s), *Dance with a Stranger* (f), *Never Love a Stranger* (b), *A Perfect Stranger* (b), *The*

Stranger (f), *Stranger in a Strange Land* (b), *Stranger in Paradise* (s), *Stranger on the Shore* (s)

strangers   *see* stranger; *Strangers in the Night* (s), *Strangers on a Train* (b/f)

strap   thong; bind (an injury), fasten or punish with a belt; shoulder strap; strap-hang

strapped   *see* strap; strapped for cash

straps   *see* strap; spaghetti straps

stratagem   scheme; *The Beaux' Stratagem* (f)

straw   dried corn stalks, tube for sucking up a beverage; man of straw, the final straw, the last straw; straw in the wind, straw man, straw poll; draw the short straw; *Straw Dogs* (f)

strawberry   soft red summer fruit; strawberry blonde, strawberry jam, strawberry roan; *Strawberry and Chocolate* (f), *Strawberry Fields Forever* (s), *The Strawberry Statement* (f)

straws   *see* straw; cheese straws; clutch at straws

strays   ownerless cats and dogs; gets lost; waifs and strays

streak   irregular line, swift dash; run naked in a public place, travel at great speed; winning streak; streak of lightning; *Silver Streak* (f), *The Streak* (s)

stream   school grouping, small river, torrent; flow copiously, separate by ability in schools; jet stream, main stream, on stream; stream of consciousness; against the stream; Gulf Stream; *Islands in the Stream* (s)

street   urban thoroughfare; Somerset town; back street, civvy street, easy street, high street, main street, one-way street, side street, two-way street;

street cred, street furniture, street lamp, street legal, street level, street lighting, street lights, street party; in Queer Street, the man in the street, (right) up your street; Baker Street, Baker Street Irregulars, Bond Street, Bow Street, Bow Street Runners, Cannon Street, Carey Street, Carnaby Street, Chester-le-Street, Downing Street, Ermine Street, Fleet Street, Great Portland Street, Grub Street, Harley Street, High Street Kensington, Lime Street, Liverpool Street, Lombard Street, New Street, Oxford Street, Quality Street, Regent Street, Threadneedle Street, Wall Street, Wall Street Crash, Warren Street, Watling Street; *Alphabet Street* (tv), *Baker Street* (s), *Coronation Street* (tv), *Dancing in the Street* (s), *The Duchess of Duke Street* (tv), *Easy Street* (f), *Exile on Main Street* (al), *Hill Street Blues* (tv), *Miracle on 34th Street* (f), *New Grub Street* (b), *A Nightmare on Elm Street* (f), *Quality Street* (f/pl), *Sesame Street* (tv), *Street Fighter* (f/ga), *Street Legal* (al), *Up Your Street* (tv), *Wall Street Journal* (n)

Street
Baker, Bond, Bow, Cannon, Carey, Carnaby, Downing, Ermine, Fleet, Goodge, Great Portland, Grub, Harley, Lime, Liverpool, Lombard, New, Old, Oxford, Quality, Regent, Threadneedle, Wall, Warren, Watling

---

streetcar   US tram; *A Streetcar Named Desire* (f/pl)

streets   *see* street; on the streets; streets ahead; *Mean Streets* (f), *Panic in* the Streets (f), *Streets of London* (s), *The Streets of San Francisco* (tv)

strength   power; from strength, in strength, industrial-strength, pillar of strength, tensile strength, tower of strength; strength of character; go from strength to strength, on the strength of; *Tower of Strength* (s)

strengthen   reinforce; strengthen your hand

stress   emphasis, nervous tension; emphasise; *Executive Stress* (tv)

stretch   period in prison; extend; home stretch; at a stretch, at full stretch, stretch a point, stretch your legs, stretch your wings; *Two-Way Stretch* (f)

stretcher   brick laid lengthwise, carrying-frame for casualties, frame for a painting, rod joining chair legs; stretcher-bearer

stricken   afflicted; grief-stricken, horror-stricken, poverty-stricken; stricken in years

strictly   exactly, severely; strictly for the birds; *Strictly Ballroom* (f), *Strictly Come Dancing* (tv), *Strictly Dance Fever* (tv)

stride   single long step; walk with long paces; take in your stride

strife   conflict; trouble and strife; *Troubles and Strife* (tv)

strike   attack, good skittles shot, missed hit in baseball, withdrawal of labour; chime, down tools in protest, forcibly impress, hit, light (a match), take down (a tent); dock strike, general strike, hunger strike, lightning strike, on strike, sit-down strike, wildcat strike; strike-breaker, strike down, strike force, strike home, strike out, strike pay, strike rate; strike a balance, strike a bargain, strike a blow against/for, strike a chord, strike the right/wrong note, strike while the iron is hot; *Jay and Silent Bob Strike Back* (f), *Mum's on Strike* (tv), *Strike It Lucky* (tv)

striker   football centre-forward, rough band on a matchbox, worker withdrawing his or her labour; hunger striker

strikes   *see* strike; *The Empire Strikes Back* (f)

string   cord, part of a violin or cello, series; thread, tie (up); G string, on a string, second string; string along, string bag, string beans, string of pearls, string quartet, string vest; another string to your bow; *Air on a G String* (cl), *Pink String and Sealing Wax* (f), *Puppet on a String* (s), *A String of Pearls* (s)

strings   *see* string; orchestra section; apron strings, pull strings; hold the purse strings, no strings attached

strip   long narrow piece, soccer team's outfit; disrobe, peel off (an outer layer); comic strip, landing strip, rumble strip; strip cartoon, strip light, strip poker; tear a strip off, tear off a strip; Gaza Strip; *77 Sunset Strip* (tv)

stripe   chevron, narrow band, variety; mark with bands

striped   streaked; candy-striped, pin-striped (suit)

stripes   *see* stripe; 1981 Bill Murray comedy; Stars and Stripes

stripper   exotic dancer, paint remover; asset-stripper, wire stripper

stroke   blow, first oarsman, swimming style; caress; at a stroke, butterfly stroke, master-stroke, two-stroke; stroke of genius, stroke of luck; never do a stroke of work

strokes *see* stroke; *Brush Strokes* (tv), *Diff'rent Strokes* (tv)

strolling sauntering; strolling players

strong powerful, pungent, robust; strong-arm, strong meat, strong on, strong point, strong stomach, strong suit; come on strong, going strong; *I'm Gonna Be Strong* (s)

strop leather piece for sharpening razors, temper tantrum; sharpen (a razor)

struck *see* strike; smitten; horror-struck, stage-struck, star-struck; *Stage Struck* (f)

struggle conflict, tough endeavour; progress with difficulty, put up a fight; class struggle

strung *see* string; highly strung

strut confident walk, supporting beam or brace; brace, walk swaggeringly; strut your stuff

stub cheque counterfoil, cigarette end; accidentally strike (your toe)

stubble stalks of reaped corn, unshaven facial hair; designer stubble

stubborn obstinate; (as) stubborn as a mule

stuck *see* stick; baffled, unable to move; stuck at it, stuck up; bleed like a stuck pig, get stuck in; *Stuck in the Middle with You* (s)

stud breeding stallion, fastener, horse-breeding farm, knob on the sole of a football boot, small simple earring, version of poker; rivet, set at intervals; press stud; stud book, stud farm, stud poker; *The Stud* (b/f)

studded *see* stud; star-studded

student person in education; mature student; *The Student Prince* (mus)

studies research, rooms for academic work; examines, meditates on, reads carefully, researches; business studies, liberal studies, media studies, social studies, women's studies

studio artist's or photographer's workshop, broadcasting or film-making premises; recording studio; studio couch, studio flat

studios *see* studio; Elstree Studios

study home office, investigation; research; case study, nature study, time-and-motion study; in a brown study; *A Study in Scarlet* (b)

stuff material, things; pack tightly, practise taxidermy; hot stuff, rough stuff; stuff sack; strut your stuff, sweat the small stuff, that's the stuff; *The Boys from the Black Stuff* (tv), *Hot Stuff* (s), *The Right Stuff* (b/f)

stuffed *see* stuff; overate; stuffed olives, stuffed shirt

stuffing *see* stuff; flavouring inside poultry; knock the stuffing out of

stuffy airless, prim and proper

stumbling losing your footing, walking unsteadily; stumbling block

stump part of a wicket, remnant of a tree; baffle; off stump, on the stump; Boston Stump

stun momentarily daze, shock; stun gun

stunned *see* stun

stunning *see* stun; very attractive

stupid daft; *Somethin' Stupid* (s), *Stupid Cupid* (s)

style elegance, fashion, manner, type; design; grand style, international style, Mediterranean-style; cramp your style; *Divorce American Style* (f)

styptic agent that stops bleeding; astringent; styptic pencil

sub advance payment, club

membership payment, long bread roll, replacement player; assist in newspaper editing, lend (money); sub-aqua, sub-clause, sub-heading, sub judice, sub lieutenant, sub-machine gun, sub-plot, sub-post office, sub-postmaster, sub-zero

subject citizen, school topic, topic under discussion; make liable to; dependent, liable; subject matter

subliminal unconscious (perception); subliminal advertising

submarine underwater craft; under the sea; *Yellow Submarine* (s/f)

submit capitulate, present for appraisal

subordinate person of lower rank; place in a lower order; lower-ranking; subordinate clause

subscribe assent, pay for regular delivery of a publication, sign up

subsistence livelihood; means of subsistence; subsistence allowance, subsistence farming, subsistence level

substance essence, importance, material; in substance; *A Woman of Substance* (b/tv)

suburb outlying area of a city or town; Hampstead Garden Suburb

succeeds does well, follows; nothing succeeds like success

success achievement, favourable outcome, prosperity; 1978 Martin Amis novel; success story; nothing succeeds like success; *The Secret of My Success* (f), *Sweet Smell of Success* (f), *Will Success Spoil Rock Hunter?* (f)

succession collective line of heirs, sequence; apostolic succession, in succession (to); in quick/rapid succession

such of the kind described; such as,

such-and-such; no such luck, parting is such sweet sorrow, such as it is; *A Fool Such As I* (s), *Such a Long Journey* (b), *Such a Night* (s), *Such Good Friends* (f)

suck draw in (air) like a vacuum cleaner, draw into the mouth; teach your grandmother to suck eggs

sucker adhesive rubber pad, gullible person, new plant shoot; sucker punch; *Never Give a Sucker an Even Break* (f)

suction adhesion by reducing air pressure; suction pump

sudden abrupt; sudden death; all of a sudden; *Sudden Death* (f), *Sudden Impact* (f)

suddenly *see* sudden; all at once; *Suddenly Last Summer* (f/pl)

suede soft brushed leather; *Blue Suede Shoes* (s)

suet hard animal fat; suet pudding

sufferance lack of objection; on sufferance

suffering distress; experiencing pain or unpleasantness, tolerating; long-suffering

suffice be adequate; suffice it to say

suffrage franchise; universal suffrage

sugar sweet substance; sweeten; barley sugar, blood sugar, brown sugar, cane sugar, caster sugar, demerara sugar, fruit sugar, granulated sugar, icing sugar, maple sugar, spun sugar; sugar beet, sugar-coated, sugar cane, sugar cube, sugar daddy, sugar loaf, sugar lump, sugar rush, sugar-snap peas, sugar soap; sugar the pill; *Brown Sugar* (s), *Sugar and Spice* (s), *Sugar Baby Love* (s), *Sugar Coated Iceberg* (s), *Sugar Me* (s), *Sugar Moon* (s), *Sugar Rush* (b/tv)

suggestion proposal, trace (of); auto-suggestion

suit formal matching outfit, legal action, set of thirteen playing cards; be appropriate, be becoming; bathing suit, birthday suit, boiler suit, diving suit, flying suit, follow suit, long suit, lounge suit, major suit, minor suit, monkey suit, pin-striped suit, pressure suit, safari suit, sailor suit, shell suit, strong suit, trouser suit, zoot suit; suit down to the ground, suit the action to the word; *The Man in the White Suit* (f)

suite musical sequence, set of furniture or hotel rooms; bridal suite, en suite, three-piece suite; *California Suite* (f), *Karelia Suite* (cl), *Mother Goose Suite* (cl), *The Nutcracker Suite* (cl), *Plaza Suite* (pl)

sulky light horse-drawn vehicle; moody

sultans Muslim rulers; *Sultans of Swing* (s)

sultry hot and humid, sensual

sum result of addition, total; add; dim sum, lump sum, tidy sum; sum total, sum up; *The Sum of All Fears* (b/f), *The Sum of Us* (f)

summary précis; without unnecessary formalities or delay

summer warm season; spend the warm season; Indian summer; summer camp, summer holiday, summer house, summer lightning, summer pudding, summer school, summer season, summer solstice; British Summer Time; *After Many a Summer* (b), *Cruel Summer* (s), *Here Comes Summer* (s), *Indian Summer* (f), *Last of the Summer Wine* (tv), *The Long Hot Summer* (f), *Suddenly Last Summer* (f/pl), *Summer Holiday* (f/s),

Summer in the City (s), *Summer Nights* (s)

summertime warm season; *Porgy and Bess* song; 1955 David Lean film; *In the Summertime* (s), *Summertime Blues* (s)

summit apex, high-level conference; Earth Summit

summon muster, send for; summon up

summoned *see* summon; *Summoned By Bells* (po)

summons *see* summon; official order to attend court; county court summons

sun Earth's nearest star; tabloid newspaper; against the sun, midnight sun, rising sun, shoot the sun, under the sun, with the sun; sun-baked, sun-blind, sun bonnet, sun-cream, sun deck, sun god, sun hat, sun-kissed, sun-up, sun visor; make hay while the sun shines; *Brother Sun, Sister Moon* (f), *Don't Let the Sun Go Down on Me* (s), *Empire of the Sun* (f), *Evil under the Sun* (b/f), *Here Comes the Sun* (s), *House of the Rising Sun* (f), *Island in the Sun* (b/f/s), *A Place in the Sun* (tv), *Seasons in the Sun* (s), *The Sun Also Rises* (b), *Third Rock from the Sun* (tv), *A Walk in the Sun* (f)

sundry assorted, various; all and sundry

sunflowers tall plants; Van Gogh painting

sunny bright and cloudless (weather), cheerful; 1977 Boney M hit; Nissan saloon model; sunny-side up; Sunny Delight; *Sunny Afternoon* (s)

sunrise dawn; early-morning tv show; tequila sunrise; *Before Sunrise* (f), *Impression: Sunrise* (pa), *Tequila Sunrise* (f)

sunset   dusk; 1988 Bruce Willis film; *Before Sunset* (f), *77 Sunset Strip* (tv), *Sunset Boulevard* (f/mus), *Sunset People* (s), *Waterloo Sunset* (s)

sunshine   bright weather; ray of sunshine; *Bring Me Sunshine* (s), *Eternal Sunshine of the Spotless Mind* (f), *The Sunshine Boys* (f), *Sunshine Superman* (s), *You Are My Sunshine* (s), *You Are the Sunshine of My Life* (s)

suntan   browning of the skin; suntan lotion

super   actor without a speaking part; excellent, first-rate, marvellous; super-duper; Weston-super-Mare; *Super Mario Brothers* (f), *Super Size Me* (f), *Super Trouper* (s)

superhighway   US dual carriageway; information superhighway

superior   person of higher rank; better, higher in rank, upper; largest of the Great Lakes; Lake Superior, Mother Superior

superiority   advantage, better quality, higher rank, lead, pre-eminence; superiority complex

supervision   direction, guidance, inspection, management; supervision order

supper   evening meal; sing for your supper; Last Supper; *The Last Supper* (pa)

supplement   addition, additional charge, magazine sold with a newspaper; add to; colour supplement

supplementary   additional, extra; supplementary benefit

supply   amount of goods provided; provide with; money supply; supply and demand, supply teacher

support   back-up, encouragement; give backing to, maintain, prop up, reinforce; income support, moral support; Child Support Agency

supporters   backers, fans; supporters' club

supremacy   state of being the best; Act of Supremacy; *The Bourne Supremacy* (b/f)

supreme   sauce served with chicken; above all others; Supreme Court, Supreme Soviet

sure   certain; certainly; 1994 Take That chart-topper; make sure; sure enough, sure-fire, sure-footed, sure thing; as sure as death, as sure as eggs is eggs, for sure, slow but sure, to be sure

surety   guarantee; stand surety

surf   tidal foam; ride the waves on a board, search (the internet); brand-name soap powder; surf 'n' turf, surf the net

surface   outside or upper layer; come to the top, materialise; surface tension, surface-to-air; scratch the surface

surfer   wave rider; net surfer

surgeon   doctor who performs operations, Royal Navy medical officer; dental surgeon, plastic surgeon, tree surgeon, veterinary surgeon; surgeon general; *The Surgeon's Daughter* (b)

surgery   branch of medicine, doctor's consulting room; cosmetic surgery, dental surgery, keyhole surgery, plastic surgery

surgical   concerning medical operations, precise; surgical spirit; *Surgical Spirit* (tv)

surplus   overabundance; more than required; government surplus, trade surplus

surprise astonishment, unexpected event; startle; take by surprise; *Shanghai Surprise* (f)

surrender capitulation, renunciation; give in, relinquish; 1961 Elvis Presley hit; 1987 film with Sally Field and Michael Caine; cash surrender value, unconditional surrender; surrender to bail, surrender value; *No Retreat, No Surrender* (f), *Sweet Surrender* (s), *Unconditional Surrender* (f)

surrey old US horse-drawn carriage; English county; *The Surrey with the Fringe on Top* (s)

surrogate stand-in; surrogate mother

survey opinion poll, property inspection; examine in detail; Ordnance Survey

surveyor buildings or land inspector, overseer; quantity surveyor

survival continued existence; survival kit; survival of the fittest

survive last, live through danger; *I Will Survive* (s)

suspect possible guilty party; believe to be guilty, mistrust; dodgy; 1987 film starring Cher; prime suspect; *Prime Suspect* (tv)

suspects *see* suspect; *The Usual Suspects* (f)

suspend adjourn, hang; suspend payment

suspended *see* suspend; suspended animation, suspended ceiling

suspender stocking fastener; suspender belt

suspension car springs, mixture containing particles, postponement, type of bridge; suspension bridge; Clifton Suspension Bridge

suspicion distrust, inkling; 1941 Hitchcock thriller; above suspicion, under suspicion; *Above Suspicion* (f), *Under Suspicion* (f)

suspicious doubtful, mistrustful; *Suspicious Minds* (s)

suss realise; suss out

swab absorbent cotton pad; mop (the decks)

swaddling wrapping (a baby) tightly; swaddling clothes

swagger strutting walk; boast, strut; swagger stick

swallow bird; gulp; swallow dive

swallows *see* swallow; *Swallows and Amazons* (b/f)

swamp marsh; overwhelm; swamp fever

swan aquatic bird; move (around) aimlessly; Naomi Campbell's novel; Bewick's swan, black swan, mute swan; swan-necked, swan-upping; *The Black Swan* (f), *Dying Swan* (cl), *Ride a White Swan* (s), *Swan Lake* (bal)

swap instance of bartering; exchange; swap shop; *Multi-Coloured Swap Shop* (tv), *Wife Swap* (tv)

swat sharp blow (to kill a fly); hit (a fly); fly swat

swathe band of mown ground, strip of material; wrap in layers; cut a swathe through

sway influence; have influence on, rock gently; hold sway

swear promise on oath, utter expletives; swear blind, swear in, swear word; swear like a trooper

sweat perspiration; perspire; break sweat; sweat blood, sweat buckets; blood sweat and tears, in a cold sweat, no sweat, sweat it out, sweat the small stuff

sweated *see* sweat; sweated labour

swede root vegetable; Scandinavian

sweep long gentle curve, lottery, person who cleans chimneys; extend in a long arch, use a broom; chimney sweep, clean sweep; make a clean sweep, sweep the board, sweep under the carpet

sweeper broom-wielder in curling, carpet cleaner, defensive footballer; carpet-sweeper

sweeps *see* sweep; a new broom sweeps clean

sweepstake form of lottery; Irish Sweepstake

sweet dessert, piece of candy; cute, sugary; bitter-sweet, boiled sweet, keep sweet, short and sweet; sweet-and-sour, sweet-briar, sweet cicely, sweet nothings, sweet pea, sweet pepper, sweet potato, sweet talk, sweet tooth, sweet William; parting is such sweet sorrow, revenge is sweet; *Bitter-Sweet* (mus), *Bitter Sweet Symphony* (s), *My Sweet Lord* (s), *Sour Sweet* (b), *Sweet Bird of Youth* (f/pl), *Sweet Caroline* (s), *Sweet Charity* (f), *Sweet Child o' Mine* (s), *Sweet Dreams* (f), *Sweet Dreams (Are Made of This)* (al/s), *Sweet Home Alabama* (f), *Sweet Little Sixteen* (s), *Sweet Smell of Success* (f), *Sweet Talkin' Guy* (s), *The Sweet-Shop Owner* (b), *Sweet Surrender* (s), *Sweet Valley High* (tv), *Sweet William* (b/f), *Swing Low Sweet Chariot* (s)

sweeten add sugar to, mitigate; sweeten the pill

sweetheart beloved; sweetheart neckline; *Goodnight Sweetheart* (tv), *Sweetheart of the Campus* (f)

sweetie piece of confectionery, term of endearment; 1989 Jane Campion film

sweetness charm, sugary quality; sweetness and light

swelling bulge; dilating, surging

swells *see* swelling; fashionable persons; *A Couple of Swells* (s)

swift swallow-like bird; rapid

swim act of moving through water; move through water; in the swim; swim bladder; sink or swim; *Sink or Swim* (tv)

swimmer bather; Channel swimmer; *The Swimmer* (f)

swimming *see* swim; water sport; synchronised swimming; swimming costume, swimming pool, swimming trunks; *Swimming to Cambodia* (f), *Swimming with Sharks* (f)

swine contemptible person, pig, pigs; swine fever; cast pearls before swine; Gadarene Swine

swing form of jazz, golfing action, playground apparatus; influence the result of (an election, eg), sway back and forth; swing-bin, swing bridge, swing door; no room to swing a cat; *Sultans of Swing* (s), *Swing Low Sweet Chariot* (s), *Swing Shift* (f), *Swing Time* (f)

swipe sweeping stroke; hit, steal; card swipe; swipe card

switch electrical on and off control, exchange, slender whip; change round; form of debit card; dimmer switch, dip switch, rocker switch, time switch, toggle switch, trip switch; switch on; *Switch Bitch* (b)

switchboard apparatus for making or breaking an electric current, telephone exchange; switchboard operator

swivel ring that turns on a pin; turn on an axis; swivel chair

swizzle disappointment, fraud, mixed rum drink; mix (a cocktail) with a glass rod; swizzle stick

swoop sudden descent, surprise raid; rush down in flight; in one fell swoop

sword bladed weapon; sword-bearer, sword fight, sword-swallower; put to the sword; Sword of Damocles; *The Sword and the Sorcerer* (f), *The Sword in the Stone* (b/f)

sworn *see* swear; under oath; sworn in

swot excessively studious pupil; revise hard for exams; swot up

sylph slender person, spirit of the air; sylph-like

symbol emblem, representation; sex symbol, status symbol

sympathy fellow-feeling; *Sympathy for Mr Vengeance* (f), *Sympathy for the Devil* (s), *Tea and Sympathy* (f)

symphony orchestral composition; symphony orchestra; *Bitter Sweet Symphony* (s)

synchronised style of swimming; tallied; coinciding exactly; synchronised swimming

syndicate group of business interests or punters, news association; publish in several newspapers at once; newspaper syndicate

syndrome pattern of symptoms; China syndrome, sick building syndrome; *The China Syndrome* (f)

synod church assembly; General Synod

syrup thick sugary liquid or topping; golden syrup, maple syrup, rosehip syrup; syrup of figs

system process, prevailing social order, set of things working together; central nervous system, cerebro-spinal system, exhaust system, metric system, midi system, nervous system, open-field system, operating system, public address system, solar system, sound system; *System Addict* (s)

systems *see* system; systems analyst; all systems go

T

table chart, item of furniture; put forward for discussion; billiard table, bird-table, captain's table, card table, coffee table, coffee-table book, dining table, dining-room table, dressing table, gateleg table, high table, league table, multiplication table, occasional table, operating table, periodic table, refectory table, round table, times table, trestle table, water table; table d'hôte, table football, table linen, table manners, table mat, table tennis, table top, table wine; drink under the table, lay your cards on the table, on the table, under the table; *An Angel at My Table* (f), *The Captain's Table* (f), *Ten Times Table* (pl)

tableau striking scene; tableau vivant

tables *see* table; nest of tables; turn the tables; *Separate Tables* (f/pl)

tablet pill, stone slab; *The Tablet* (mag)

tabs *see* tab; keep tabs on

tack carpet nail, direction; fasten, stitch roughly, zigzag; hard tack; Blu-Tack

tackle equipment, sporting challenge; confront, get to grips with; block and tackle, fishing tackle

tacks *see* tack; brass tacks; get down to brass tacks

tacky sticky, vulgar

tactics strategies; shock tactics

tag chasing game, electronic surveillance marker, label, nickname; add, follow, put a label or electronic device on; dog tag, price tag; tag line, tag team, tag wrestling

tail appendage, back end; follow; turn tail; tail end, tail-end Charlie, tail fin, tail light, tail off; in two shakes of a lamb's tail, nose to tail, on my tail, a sting in the tail, with your tail up

tailor garment-maker; customise; tailor-made, tailor's dummy; *The Tailor of Panama* (b/f), *Tinker, Tailor, Soldier, Spy* (b/tv)

tailors *see* tailor; *The Nine Tailors* (b)

tails *see* tail; cat-o-nine-tails, coat-tails, lamb's-tails; heads and tails, heads or tails

take film scene; bring, consume, gain possession of, receive, remove, seize, steal; double take, out-take; take after, take aim, take apart, take away, take back, take breath, take care, take care of, take charge, take counsel, take courage, take cover, take down, take exception, take five, take flight, take fright, take guard, take heed, take-home pay, take in, take in hand, take liberties, take note, take notice, take occasion, take odds, take off, take on, take on board, take out, take over, take part, take place, take root, take seriously, take shape, take sides, take stock, take to, take turns, take up, take wing; give and take, sit up and take notice, take a back seat, take a bow, take a chance, take a dim view of, take a fancy to, take a heavy toll, take a hike, take a pop at, take a rain check, take a risk, take a seat, take a shine to, take a tumble, take account of, take advantage, take as read, take by storm, take by surprise, take delivery of, take down a peg or two, take for granted, take in your stride, take into consideration, take issue with, take it amiss, take it as read, take it easy, take it from me, take it on the chin, take it or leave it, take its toll, take lying down, take no prisoners, take the air, take the biscuit, take the bull by the horns, take the consequences, take the field, take the fifth, take the gilt off the gingerbread, take the measure of, take the mickey (out of), take the part of, take the plunge, take the pulse, take the rap, take the rough with the smooth, take the shine off, take the veil, take the wind out of one's sails, take to heart, take to pieces, take to task, take to the cleaners, take to your heels, take up the baton, take up the cudgels, take up the gauntlet, take up the running, take with a pinch of salt, take your breath away, take your chance, take your hat off to, take your leave, take your life in your hands, take your medicine, take your name in vain, take your pick, take your time; *Every Breath You Take* (s), *Out-Take TV* (tv), *Take a Chance on Me* (s), *Take a Girl Like You* (b/tv), *Take Five* (s), *Take It from Here* (r), *Take It to the Limit* (s), *Take Me Home Country Roads* (s), *Take On Me* (s), *Take the High Road* (tv), *Take the Money and Run* (f), *Take These Chains from My Heart* (s), *Take Your Pick* (tv), *You Can't Take It with You* (f)

takes *see* take; have what it takes, it takes all sorts to make a world, it takes two to tango; *It Takes Two* (s), *Loser Takes All* (b/f), *Winner Takes All* (tv), *The Winner Takes It All* (s)

taking *see* take; leave-taking, mickey-taking, stock-taking; for the taking; *The Taking of Pelham One Two Three* (f)

tale story; blood-and-thunder tale, fairy tale, folk tale, old wives' tale, tall tale, traveller's tale; a tale of a tub; *A Bronx Tale* (f), *Fairy Tale of New York* (s), *The Handmaid's Tale* (b/f), *A Knight's Tale* (f), *The Old Wives' Tale* (b), *Shark Tale* (f), *A Tale of a Tub* (b), *The Tale of Peter Rabbit* (b), *The Tale of Pigling Bland* (b), *The Tale of Squirrel Nutkin* (b), *A Tale of Two Cities* (b/f), *The Winter's Tale* (pl)

talent innate ability, old Greek and Roman coin; talent scout, talent spotter

talented having an innate ability; *The Talented Mr Ripley* (b/f)

tales *see* tale; cautionary tales, fairy tales, tell tales; dead men tell no tales; *Cautionary Tales* (b), *Dead Men Tell No Tales* (b), *The Canterbury Tales* (b/tv), *Tales from the Vienna Woods* (cl), *The Tales of Hoffmann* (f/o), *Tales of the Jazz Age* (b), *Telling Tales* (b)

talk speech; speak; fast-talk, pep talk, pillow talk, small talk, smooth-talk, sweet-talk; talk big, talk over, talk radio, talk show, talk turkey; chalk and talk, talk nineteen to the dozen, talk of the devil, the talk of the town, talk the hind leg off a donkey, talk through your hat; *Happy Talk* (s), *Pillow Talk* (f), *The Talk of the Town* (f), *Talk Radio* (f)

talkie early sound film; walkie-talkie

talking *see* talk; smooth-talking; talking book, talking head, talking point, talking shop, talking-to; hark who's talking, now you're talking; *Look Who's Talking* (f), *Talking Book* (al), *Talking Heads* (pl/tv)

talks *see* talk; money talks; *Money Talks* (f)

tall high, unlikely (story); walk tall; tall order, tall ship, tall story, tall tale; tall, dark and handsome; *The Long and the Short and the Tall* (f), *Long Tall Sally* (s), *The Tall Guy* (f), *Walk Tall* (s)

tally ongoing score; correspond; tally-ho

tamarind tropical tree; *The Tamarind Seed* (b/f)

tambourine percussion instrument;

Green Tambourine (s), *Mr Tambourine Man* (s)

tame domesticate; domesticated, dull

taming *see* tame; *The Taming of the Shrew* (f/pl)

tan darkening of the skin in the sun, light brown colour; go brown in the sun, prepare (leather), thrash; black and tan

tandem bicycle for two; in tandem

tang piquant flavour; *P'tang Yang Kipperbang* (f/pl)

tangle intertwine; intertwined mess

tango Latin American dance, radio code word; dance in a Latin American style; brand-name orangeade; it takes two to tango; *Last Tango in Paris* (f), *Tango & Cash* (f)

tank armoured vehicle, vat; Churchill tank, fish-tank, flotation tank, fuel tank, petrol tank, septic tank, think tank; tank engine, tank top; *Tank Girl* (f), *Thomas the Tank Engine* (b), *Thomas the Tank Engine and Friends* (tv)

tanker oil-carrying ship or lorry; oil-tanker

tanner leather-worker, old sixpence

tap sink fixture, style of dancing; bug (a phone line), draw off, knock gently; hot tap, mixer tap, spinal tap; tap-dancing, tap shoes; on tap; *This Is Spinal Tap* (f)

tape cassette, long thin strip; record on video; gaffer tape, insulating tape, magnetic tape, masking tape, red tape, Scotch tape, ticker tape; tape deck, tape measure, tape recorder; *Krapp's Last Tape* (pl)

taper thin candle; become narrower; taper off

tapestry ornamental textile; Carole

King album; Bayeux Tapestry

tapping   *see* tap; toe-tapping, wire-tapping

tar   coal distillate, sailor; cover with a bituminous substance; coal tar, Jack tar; tar and feather, tar baby; tar with the same brush; *Tar Baby* (b)

target   object aimed at; aim; soft target; off target, on target

tart   flan; sour; Bakewell tart, custard tart, jam tart

tartar   formidable person, hard scaly deposit on teeth; follower of Genghis Khan; cream of tartar

tartare   served raw; steak tartare; tartare sauce

task   job; task force; take to task

taste   flavour, sense of style; savour; acquired taste; taste bud; there's no accounting for taste; *A Taste for Death* (b), *A Taste of Honey* (f/pl)

tasting   *see* taste; wine tasting

tat   shoddy goods; make knotted lace; rat-a-tat; tit for tat

tatters   rags; in tatters

tattle   idle talk; chatter idly; tittle-tattle

tattoo   indelible marking of the skin, military pageant; mark indelibly on the skin; *The Rose Tattoo* (f/pl)

taunt   mocking remark; tease viciously

taw   large marble; treat (leather); Devon river

tawny   shade of brown, species of owl; tawny owl

tax   government levy; charge a levy on, make heavy demands on; capital gains tax, capital transfer tax, corporation tax, council tax, direct tax, income tax, inheritance tax, poll tax, pre-tax, purchase tax, road tax, value added tax, wealth tax, windfall tax, window tax; tax avoidance, tax break, tax collector, tax-deductible, tax disc, tax evasion, tax exile, tax-free, tax haven, tax return, tax year

taxi   car for hire; move slowly along a runway; taxi driver, taxi rank; hail a taxi; *Big Yellow Taxi* (s), *Taxi Driver* (f)

tea   beverage; beef tea, China tea, cream tea, cup of tea, green tea, herbal tea, high tea, iced tea, jasmine tea, lemon tea; tea bag, tea break, tea caddy, tea-cake, tea ceremony, tea chest, tea clipper, tea cloth, tea cosy, tea dance, tea garden, tea kettle, tea lady, tea leaves, tea party, tea room, tea rose, tea set, tea shop, tea towel, tea tray, tea tree, tea tree oil, tea trolley, tea urn; not my cup of tea; Boston Tea Party, Mad Hatter's Tea Party; *Honey for Tea* (tv), *Tea and Sympathy* (f), *Tea for Two* (mus/s), *Tea with Mussolini* (f)

teach   educate; teach your grandmother to suck eggs, you can't teach an old dog new tricks; *I'd Like to Teach the World to Sing* (s)

teacher   educator; head teacher; teacher's pet; *Carry On Teacher* (f), *Teacher's Pet* (tv)

teaching   *see* teach; teaching hospital

teacup   drinking vessel; a storm in a teacup

teal   greenish-blue colour, species of duck

team   group working together, sporting side; come together; tag team; team player, team spirit, team-mate; *The A-Team* (tv), *Time Team* (tv)

tear   water-droplet from the eye; rip, rush; tear apart, tear down, tear duct, tear gas, tear-jerker, tear off, tear sheet, tear up; shed a tear, tear a strip off, tear limb from limb, tear off a strip, tear to pieces, tear to ribbons, tear your hair out, wear and tear

tears *see* tear; vale of tears; blood sweat and tears, crocodile tears, in tears, shed tears; *The Bitter Tears of Petra von Kant* (f), *French without Tears* (f/pl), *The Tears of a Clown* (s), *Tears on My Pillow* (s), *The Tracks of My Tears* (s)

tease mocking person; poke fun at, untangle; *Please Don't Tease* (s)

teaser puzzle; brain-teaser; *Teaser and the Firecat* (al)

technical scientific, specialised; technical college, technical difficulty, technical knockout

technician skilled worker; dental technician

technique method, skill; Alexander technique

technology applied science; information technology; technology transfer; City Technology College

teddy lingerie item, toy bear; teddy bear, teddy boy

tee golf peg, marker in curling and quoits; tee-hee, tee off

teem abound, pour with rain

teen adolescent; *Smells Like Teen Spirit* (s), *Teen Wolf* (f)

teenage adolescent; *I Was a Teenage Werewolf* (f), *Sabrina, the Teenage Witch* (tv), *Teenage Kicks* (s), *Teenage Mutant Ninja Turtles* (f)

teenager adolescent; *A Teenager in Love* (s)

teeny very small; teeny-bopper, teeny-weeny; *Itsy Bitsy Teeny Weeny Yellow Polka Dot Bikini* (s)

teeth *see* tooth; buck-teeth, eye-teeth,

false teeth, milk teeth, wisdom teeth; armed to the teeth, by the skin of one's teeth, fed up to the back teeth, get your teeth into, give your eye teeth, in the teeth of, kick in the teeth, lie through your teeth, set your teeth on edge; *The Skin of Our Teeth* (pl), *White Teeth* (b/tv)

teething growing pearlies; teething ring, teething troubles

telegraph message-wiring system; bush telegraph; telegraph pole; *The Daily Telegraph* (n)

telephone communication device; ring up; satellite telephone; telephone bill, telephone book, telephone box, telephone directory, telephone exchange, telephone kiosk, telephone number; *Hanging on the Telephone* (s), *Telephone Line* (s)

telescope large magnifying device; radio telescope, reflecting telescope, refracting telescope

television broadcasting medium; cable television, closed-circuit television, satellite television; television programme, television set

tell count (votes), inform, narrate; tell off, tell tales, tell the time, tell the truth, tell your fortune; dead men tell no tales, kiss and tell, strange to tell, tell it like it is, tell me about it, tell that to the marines, time will tell, to tell the truth, truth to tell; *Dead Men Tell No Tales* (b), *Go Tell It on the Mountain* (b), *Tell Her about It* (s), *Tell Laura I Love Her* (s), *Tell Them Willie Boy Is Here* (f), *William Tell* (o)

teller cashier; automated teller machine, fortune teller

telling *see* tell; fortune telling; telling-off, telling tales; I don't mind telling

The Puzzler Crossword Solver's Dictionary

you, that would be telling, there is
no telling, you're telling me; *Telling
Tales* (b)

tells *see* tell; every picture tells a story;
Every Picture Tells a Story (al)

telly goggle-box; *Telly Addicts* (tv)

temper fit of anger, mood;
harden (steel), moderate; bad temper,
short temper; keep your temper, lose
your temper

temperance moderation, teetotalism;
temperance hotel

temperate abstemious, mild;
temperate zone

temperature degree of heat or cold;
absolute temperature, room
temperature

tempest storm; a tempest in a teapot;
The Tempest (f/pl)

temple place of worship, side of the
forehead; London Underground
station; Temple Meads; *Indiana Jones
and the Temple of Doom* (f)

tempt entice; tempt fate, tempt
providence

temptation enticement; 1961 Everly
Brothers hit; *The Last Temptation of
Christ* (f)

ten number; ten pence, ten-gallon
hat; handbags at ten paces, ten a
penny, ten out of ten, ten to one;
Number Ten, Ten Commandments;
How to Lose a Guy in Ten Days (f), *The
Ten Commandments* (f), *Ten Times
Table* (pl), *The Whole Ten Yards* (f)

tenant leaseholder; sitting tenant;
tenant farmer; *The Tenant* (f), *The
Tenant of Wildfell Hall* (b)

tend be inclined, care for

tender bid, coal wagon, supply ship;
offer; easy to chew, gentle, painful to
the touch, sensitive; legal tender;

tender mercies, tender-hearted; plea
of tender, put out to tender; *Love Me
Tender* (s/f), *Tender Is the Night* (b/f),
Tender Mercies (f), *The Tender Trap* (f/s)

tendon fibrous tissue; Achilles'
tendon

tennis racket sport; lawn tennis, real
tennis, table tennis; tennis ball,
tennis court, tennis elbow, tennis
player, tennis racket

tenon carpentry joint; tenon saw

tenor singing voice; counter-tenor

tense verb form; nerve-racking, on
edge, tightly stretched; past tense,
present tense

tension emotional strain, tautness;
surface tension

tent canvas shelter; bell tent, frame
tent, oxygen tent, ridge tent; tent
peg, tent stitch

tenth decimal fraction; *Tenth Avenue
Angel* (f), *The Tenth Man* (b/tv)

tenure occupancy, period of
occupancy; security of tenure

term division of the school year,
expression, limited period; dub; half-
term, half-term holiday, long term,
long-term, Michaelmas term, short-
term, Trinity term

terminal airport building, computer
device, electrical circuit end, end of a
transport route; final; air terminal;
The Terminal (f)

terminus end of a transport route;
Roman god of boundaries; bus
terminus, railway terminus

terms *see* term; conditions; come to
terms with, contradiction in terms,
easy terms, in no uncertain terms, on
first-name terms, on nodding terms,
on speaking terms; terms of
reference; *Terms of Endearment* (f)

342

terrace   patio, row of houses, standing area at a stadium; observation terrace; *Cafe Terrace at Night* (pa)

terrible   awful; enfant terrible

terrier   dog breed; Airedale terrier, Bedlington terrier, bull terrier, fox terrier, Irish terrier, Lakeland terrier, pit bull terrier, Scottish terrier, Sealyham terrier, Skye terrier, Staffordshire bull terrier, Welsh terrier, West Highland terrier, wheaten terrier, Yorkshire terrier

territorial   concerning a locality, protective of a habitat, related to ownership; army reservist; territorial waters; Territorial Army

territory   land; Northern Territory

terror   extreme fear; reign of terror

terrorist   user of violence for political ends; *The Good Terrorist* (b)

terry   towelling fabric; *Terry and June* (tv)

test   cricket match, exam, trial; examine, try out; Hampshire river; acid test, bench test, breath test, crash test, driving test, field test, ink-blot test, litmus test, means test, patch test, road test, Rorschach test, screen test, skin test; test bed, test card, test case, test cricket, test drive, test flight, test match, test pilot, test tube, test-tube baby; stand the test of time, test the water; *The Old Grey Whistle Test* (tv), *Test the Nation* (tv)

testament   evidence, section of the Bible, will; New Testament, Old Testament; *Testament of Youth* (b/tv)

tested   *see* test; road-tested; tried and tested

testing   *see* test; testing ground

tether   restricting-rope; tie with a rope

text   printed matter; send a message by mobile phone; text message

textured   patterned on the surface; textured vegetable protein

thank   express gratitude to; thank goodness, thank heavens, thank you; thank someone kindly, thank you for nothing, thank your lucky stars; *Thank U Very Much* (s), *Thank You* (s), *Thank Your Lucky Stars* (mus/tv)

thanks   *see* thank; word of gratitude; thanks to; no thanks to, thanks a million; *Thanks for the Memory* (s)

thanksgiving   expression of gratitude to God; Thanksgiving Day

that   the one there; which; all that glitters is not gold, and all that, and all that jazz, be that as it may, bite the hand that feeds you, come to that, for that matter, hair of the dog that bit you, how's that, I'll drink to that, just like that, leave it at that, on that score, take that, tell that to the marines, that goes without saying, that makes two of us, that's about the size of it, that said, that sinking feeling, that's life, that's that, that's the idea, that's the story of my life, that's the stuff, that's torn it, that will be the day, that would be telling, the powers that be, this and that, this, that and the other, two can play at that game, with that, you can say that again; *Ain't That a Shame* (s), *All's Well That Ends Well* (pl), *All That Jazz* (mus), *And All That Jazz* (s), *The Boat That I Row* (s), *Carry On ... Follow That Camel* (f), *The Folks That Live on the Hill* (b/s), *Goodbye to All That* (b), *How About That* (s), *I Guess That's Why They Call It the Blues* (s), *I Want That House* (tv), *The Mouse That*

Roared (f), *Name That Tune* (tv), *Not That Sort of Girl* (b), *1066 and All That* (b), *That'll be the Day* (s/f), *That Same Old Feeling* (s), *That Sinking Feeling* (f), *That's Life* (tv), *That Touch of Mink* (f), *Who's That Girl?* (s)

thatched having a thick head of hair, roofed with straw; thatched cottage

thaw melting process; melt; thaw out

theatre hospital operating room, playhouse; coup de théâtre, movie theatre, operating theatre, shadow theatre; theatre-goer; Theatre of the Absurd; *Theatre of Blood* (f)

theme recurring melody, subject; theme park, theme song; *Theme for a Dream* (s)

then afterwards, at that time; and then some, but then again, (every) now and then, now then, then and there, there and then; *And Then There Were None* (f), *Then He Kissed Me* (s)

theorem logical proposition; 1968 Pasolini film; Fermat's last theorem, Pythagoras' theorem; *Fermat's Last Theorem* (b)

theory hypothesis; conspiracy theory, quantum theory; in theory; *Conspiracy Theory* (f)

therapy treatment; alternative therapy, aversion therapy, cognitive therapy, group therapy, hormone replacement therapy, occupational therapy, retail therapy, shock therapy, speech therapy

there in that place; word of comfort; all there, here and there, like there was no tomorrow, neither here nor there, now there's a thing, over there, then and there, there and then, there is no help for it, there is no knowing, there is no saying, there is no telling, there is nothing to it, there is only one thing for it, there will be hell to pay, there's more than one way to skin a cat, there's no accounting for taste, there's no fool like an old fool, there's no place like home, there's no time like the present, there's nowt so queer as folk, where there's a will there's a way, while there's life there's hope, who goes there; *And Then There Were None* (f), *Are We There Yet?* (f), *Being There* (b/f), *Let There Be Love* (s), *The Man Who Wasn't There* (f), *Neither Here Nor There* (b), *Over There* (s/tv), *Reach Out, I'll Be There* (s), *Somebody Up There Likes Me* (f), *There Is Nothin' Like a Dame* (s), *There's a Girl in My Soup* (f), *There's a Hole in My Bucket* (s), *There's Something about Mary* (f), *There Was a Crooked Man* (f)

thermal current of warm air; insulating (of clothing), pertaining to heat; British thermal unit; thermal imaging, thermal spring

thermals *see* thermal; warm underwear

these plural of 'this'; one of these days, these days; *Take These Chains from My Heart* (s), *These Boots Are Made for Walkin'* (s), *These Dangerous Years* (f), *These Days* (s), *These Foolish Things* (s)

thick stupid, very friendly, wide; thick-headed, thick-skinned; (as) thick as thieves, (as) thick as two short planks, get a thick ear, give a thick ear to, have a thick skin, the thick of it, thick and fast, through thick and thin; *The Thick of It* (tv)

thickens makes or grows more dense; the plot thickens

thicker   *see* thick; blood is thicker than water

thief   robber; 1981 James Caan film; cattle thief; procrastination is the thief of time, set a thief to catch a thief; *The Cook, the Thief, His Wife and Her Lover* (f), *The Thief* (f), *The Thief of Bagdad* (f), *The Thief's Journal* (b), *To Catch a Thief* (f)

thieves   *see* thief; den of thieves; (as) thick as thieves; *Ali Baba and the Forty Thieves* (b/pan), *Bicycle Thieves* (f)

thigh   top of the leg; thigh bone, thigh boots, thigh-slapping

thimble   finger-cover; hunt the thimble

thin   narrow, slim; wafer-thin, wear thin; (as) thin as a rake, have a thin skin, have a thin time, on thin ice, thin end of the wedge, thin on the ground, thin on top, through thick and thin, vanish into thin air; *The Thin Man* (f), *The Thin Blue Line* (tv), *The Thin Red Line* (f)

thing   object; close thing, close-run thing, first thing, last thing, near thing, real thing, sure thing; be on to a good thing, the best thing since sliced bread, do your own thing, have a thing about, now there's a thing, there is only one thing for it; *Do the Right Thing* (f), *A Funny Thing Happened on the Way to the Forum* (mus), *The Real Thing* (pl), *The Thing* (f), *A Thing Called Love* (s), *The Thing from Another World* (f), *The Twisted Thing* (b), *Wild Thing* (s)

things   *see* thing; 1962 Bobby Darin hit; all good things come to an end, all things considered, first things first, hear things, in the nature of things, seeing things, the best things in life are free; things to come; *All the Things She Said* (s), *All Things Bright and Beautiful* (h), *The Best Things in Life are Free* (s), *Dirty Pretty Things* (f), *Just One of Those Things* (s), *My Favourite Things* (s), *Remembrance of Things Past* (b), *The Shape of Things to Come* (b), *These Foolish Things* (s), *Things to Come* (f), *Very Bad Things* (f)

think   believe, ponder; think aloud, think back, think big, think fit, think over, think tank, think through, think twice, think up; come to think of it, great minds think alike, have another think coming, think better of it, think ill of, think nothing of it, think outside the box, think the world of; *I Think We're Alone Now* (s), *They Think It's All Over* (tv), *Think Twice* (s)

thinker   philosopher; *The Thinker* (sc)

thinking   *see* think; good thinking, right-thinking; thinking cap; put on your thinking cap

third   fraction; in the bronze-medal position; third age, third degree, third estate, third man, third party, third person, third-person shooter, third-rate, third reading, third way; third time lucky; Third Reich, Third World; *King Richard the Third* (f/pl), *The Third Man* (b/f), *The Third Policeman* (b), *Third Rock from the Sun* (tv)

thirteen   number; 2003 Holly Hunter film; *Assault on Precinct 13* (f)

thirty   number; thirty-something; *A Woman of Thirty* (b), *The Thirty-Nine Steps* (b/f), *Thirty Is a Dangerous Age, Cynthia* (f), *Thirty Seconds Over Tokyo* (f)

this   the one here; this instant; at this rate, depart this life, in this connection, out of this world, this and that, this that and the other, this way up, what's all this in aid of; *Bless This House* (tv), *Isn't This a Lovely Day* (s), *Picture This* (s), *This Gun for Hire* (f), *This Happy Breed* (f/pl), *This Is My Song* (s), *This Is Spinal Tap* (f), *This Is Your Life* (tv), *This Life* (tv), *This Morning* (tv), *This Old Heart of Mine* (s), *This Ole House* (s), *This Side of Paradise* (b), *This Sporting Life* (b/f), *This Wheel's on Fire* (s)

thistle prickly plant; milk thistle; Knight of the Thistle

thither to that place; hither and thither

thorn plant prickle; thorn in the flesh/side; *The Thorn Birds* (b/tv), *Thorn in My Side* (s)

thorns *see* thorn; crown of thorns

thoroughly completely; *Thoroughly Modern Millie* (mus)

those plural of 'that'; one of those days; *Just One of Those Things* (s), *Those Barren Leaves* (b), *Those Magnificent Men in Their Flying Machines* (s/f), *Those Were the Days* (s)

thou old-fashioned word for 'you'; holier-than-thou; *O Brother, Where Art Thou?* (f)

though despite the fact that; however; even though

thought *see* think; deliberation, idea; school of thought; thought police, thought transference; food for thought, (give) pause for thought, perish the thought, without a second thought

thoughts *see* thought; second thoughts; a penny for your thoughts; *Second Thoughts* (tv)

thousand large number; Thousand

Island dressing; a picture is worth a thousand words; One Thousand Guineas, Two Thousand Guineas; *Anne of the Thousand Days* (f), *Twenty Thousand Leagues under the Sea* (b/f)

thousands *see* thousand; hundreds and thousands; *Hundreds and Thousands* (al)

thrash defeat thoroughly, flog

thread cotton, groove of a screw; pass or weave through; thread mark; hang by a thread

threat intimidatory remark, source of danger

threatening looking as if it will rain, menacing; life-threatening

three number; three cheers, three-card trick, three-dimensional, three-legged race, three-line whip, three-piece suite, three-point turn, three-quarters, three-ring circus, three-wheeler; the best of three, three sheets to the wind, two's company three's a crowd; Page Three, Three Mile Island, Three Wise Men; *From Noon Till Three* (f), *Knock Three Times* (s), *The Taking of Pelham One Two Three* (f), *Three Blind Mice* (nr), *The Three Caballeros* (f), *Three Coins in the Fountain* (s/f), *The Three-Cornered Hat* (bal), *Three Days of the Condor* (f), *The Three Faces of Eve* (f), *The Three Graces* (al/pa/sc), *Three Kings* (f), *Three Men and a Baby* (f), *Three Men in a Boat* (b/f), *The Three Musketeers* (b/f), *Three of a Kind* (tv), *The Three Sisters* (pl), *Three Steps to Heaven* (s), *Three Times a Lady* (s), *Three Weeks* (b), *Three Wheels on My Wagon* (s), *We Three Kings* (s)

thrift careful economy, cliff-growing plant; thrift shop

thrilled excited; thrilled to bits

thrills exciting experiences; thrills and spills

throat front part of the neck, narrow part of a vase; cut-throat, cut-throat razor; force down your throat, have a frog in your throat, lump in the throat, stick in your throat

throb vibration; beat strongly; heart-throb

throes spasms; in the throes of

throne seat of power; heir to the throne; ascend the throne

throng crowd of people; gather en masse

through finished; by means of, from end to end, via; break through, drive-through, follow through, get through, leaf through, muddle through, pass through, pull through, read through, run through, see-through, think through, walk-through; through train; cut a swathe through, drag through the mud, go through fire and water, go through hoops, go through the mill, go through the motions, go through the roof, lie through your teeth, pay through the nose, put through the hoops, put through the mill, slip through the net, talk through your hat, through and through, through thick and thin; *Break On Through* (s), *A River Runs through It* (f), *Through the Keyhole* (tv), *Through the Looking-Glass* (b), *Tiptoe through the Tulips* (s), *Until the Time Is Through* (s)

throw act of flinging, light blanket-like cover; disconcert, fling; free throw; throw away, throw back, throw-in, throw out; a stone's throw, throw caution to the wind, throw down the gauntlet, throw good money after bad, throw in the sponge, throw in the towel, throw in your lot, throw the baby out with the bathwater, throw the book at, throw to the wolves, throw up your hands, throw your hand in, throw your hat into the ring, throw your weight about/around; *Throw Momma from the Train* (f)

thrower person who flings; discus thrower, flame-thrower, hammer thrower, javelin thrower; *The Discus Thrower* (sc)

throwing *see* throw; throwing event

thrush songbird; mistle thrush, song thrush

thrust driving force; force forward; cut and thrust

thumb first digit; flick through (pages), hitch-hike; ball of the thumb, miller's thumb, rule of thumb; thumb index; stick out like a sore thumb, thumb a lift, thumb your nose at

thumbed *see* thumb; dog-eared; well thumbed

thumbnail brief representation, small computer image, tip of the first digit; thumbnail sketch

thumbs *see* thumb; all fingers and thumbs, all thumbs, thumbs down, thumbs up, twiddle your thumbs

thump heavy blow; hit heavily

thumping *see* thump; whopping; Bible-thumping, tub-thumping

thunder noise following lightning; boom; blood and thunder; *Days of Thunder* (f), *Thunder in the Mountains* (s)

thunderbolt noisy flash of lightning, powerful blow, unexpected news; *The Titfield Thunderbolt* (f)

347

thyme   garden herb; *Rosemary and Thyme* (tv)

tic   nervous twitch; tic-tac, tic-tac-toe

tick   bloodsucking mite, credit, sound of a clock, mark indicating correctness; make the sound of a clock, mark as correct; tick off, tick over; half a tick, on tick

ticker   heart, telegraphic instrument; ticker tape

ticket   receipt for entry or to travel, tag; all-ticket, dream ticket, hot ticket, lottery ticket, meal ticket, parking ticket, platform ticket, raffle ticket, return ticket, season ticket; ticket collector, ticket inspector; just the ticket; *Ticket to Ride* (s)

ticking   *see* tick; mattress fabric; ticking off

tickle   touch which causes laughter; amuse by touching; slap and tickle, tickle the ivories

tickled   *see* tickle; amused; tickled pink, tickled to death

tickling   *see* tickle; rib-tickling

tidal   relating to the movement of the sea; tidal wave

tide   movement of the sea; ebb tide, flood tide, high tide, lee tide, low tide, neap tide; time and tide wait for no man; *Crimson Tide* (f), *Ebb Tide* (f), *The Tide Is High* (s)

tides   *see* tide; *The Prince of Tides* (f)

tidy   orderly; clear up; tidy sum; clean and tidy, keep Britain tidy

tie   bond, dead heat, neckwear item, restraint; draw, fasten with a bow, link, restrict, tether; black tie, bow tie, cup-tie, kipper tie, old school tie, white tie; tie-back, tie-break, tie-breaker, tie clip, tie down, tie-dye, tie in, tie up; tie the knot, tie up in

knots; *Tie a Yellow Ribbon round the Ole Oak Tree* (s), *Tie Me Kangaroo Down, Sport* (s)

tied   *see* tied; hog-tied, tongue-tied; tied cottage; fit to be tied

ties   *see* tie; family ties; *Family Ties* (tv)

tiger   striped big cat; paper tiger, sabre-toothed tiger, Siberian tiger; tiger balm, tiger lily, tiger moth, tiger prawn, tiger's-eye, tiger shark, tiger snake; Tiger Bay; *Crouching Tiger, Hidden Dragon* (f), *Eye of the Tiger* (s), *Save the Tiger* (f), *Tiger Feet* (s)

tight   fairly drunk, in short supply, miserly, too close-fitting; sit tight, skin-tight; tight corner, tight-fisted, tight head, tight-knit, tight-lipped, tight spot; goodnight, sleep tight, keep a tight rein on, run a tight ship

tighten   apply constraints to, fix more firmly; tighten the screw, tighten your belt

tile   thin wall slab; apply wall slabs; ridge tile

tiles   *see* tile; on the tiles

till   cash register; cultivate; up to the time of; ne'er cast a clout till May be out, till kingdom come, till the cows come home; *From Noon till Three* (f), *Till Death Us Do Part* (f/tv)

tilt   slope; lean, thrust when jousting; at full tilt, tilt at windmills

timber   wood; lumberjack's warning call; timber-framed

time   epoch, hour of the day, occasion, prison sentence; measure how long (an activity) takes; call at the end of drinking hours; US current affairs weekly; all-time, any time, beat time, buy time, closing time, core time, dead time, do time, double time, drinking-up time, extra time, first-time buyer, free time, full-time, good-time, half-time, injury time, kill time, lead time, lighting-up time, local time, long-time, lose time, mark time, mean time, night-time, old-time, old-time dancing, one-time, opening time, part-time, prime time, quality time, real time, run-time, serve time, short time, simple time, small-time, spare time, standard time, stoppage time, triple time, two-time, waste time; time-and-motion study, time bomb, time capsule, time-consuming, time frame, time-honoured, time lag, time-lapse, time limit, time lock, time machine, time off, time out, time-poor, time-serving, time sheet, time signal, time signature, time switch, time travel, time trial, time warp, time-wasting, time-worn, time zone; about time too, ahead of its time, ahead of time, all in good time, all the time, all the time in the world, another time, at one time, at the present time, at the same time, at the time, behind time, bide your time, big time, the big time, every time, for the time being, from time to time, have a thin time, have a whale of a time, in double quick time, in good time, in jig time, in no time, in record time, in the fullness of time, in the mists of time, in the nick of time, in time, just in time, live on borrowed time, long time no see, make good time, many a time, of all time, on time, once upon a time, one at a time, pass the time of day, play for time, pressed for time, procrastination is the thief of time, race against time, the sands of time, stand the test of time, a stitch in time saves nine, take your time, tell the

time, there's no time like the present, third time lucky, time after time, time and a half, time and tide wait for no man, time flies when you're having fun, time is a great healer, time is of the essence, time will tell, waste of time; British Summer Time, Eastern Standard Time, Greenwich Mean Time, Old Father Time; *As Time Goes By* (s/tv), *Child of Our Time* (tv), *A Dance to the Music of Time* (b), *Dee Time* (tv), *From Time to Time* (b), *Injury Time* (b), *The Land That Time Forgot* (f), *The Last Time* (s), *Marguerita Time* (s), *Once Upon a Time in America* (f), *Once Upon a Time in Mexico* (f), *Once Upon a Time in the West* (f), *One Moment in Time* (s), *Question Time* (tv), *Remember the Time* (s), *Ride on Time* (s), *The Sands of Time* (b), *The Seeds of Time* (b), *Swing Time* (f), *The Time Machine* (b/f), *Time after Time* (s), *Time Bandits* (f), *Time Out* (mag), *Time's Arrow* (b), *Time Team* (tv), *A Time to Dance* (tv), *A Time to Kill* (b/f), *Time Traveller* (al), *Time Tunnel* (tv), *Until the Time is Through* (s), *We Have All the Time in the World* (s), *When Time Ran Out* (f), *Wonderful Christmas Time* (s)

timer   clock-like device; egg-timer, full-timer, old-timer, part-timer, small-timer, two-timer

times   *see* time; daily newspaper; hard times, modern times; times table; at the best of times, at times, in between times; Times Square; *Financial Times* (n), *Hard Times* (b), *Knock Three Times* (s), *Modern Times* (f), *Radio Times* (mag), *Ten Times Table* (pl), *Three Times a Lady* (s)

timing   *see* time; co-ordination of

opportunity; bad timing; *Bad Timing* (f)

tin food or paint can, metallic element; biscuit tin, mess tin; tin can, tin hat, tin mine, tin-opener, tin-plate, tin soldier, tin whistle; have a tin ear, like a cat on a hot tin roof; Tin Pan Alley; *Cat on a Hot Tin Roof* (f/pl), *Tin Cup* (f), *The Tin Drum* (b/f), *Tin Pan Alley* (mus)

tinge slight trace of colour; colour slightly

tingle shiver of excitement; prickle

tingling *see* tingle; light itching sensation; spine-tingling

tinker mender of pots and pans, rascal; potter; *Tinker Tailor Soldier Spy* (b/tv)

tint hair dye, shade; colour

tinted *see* tint; rose-tinted

tip end point, gratuity, hint, rubbish dump; give a gratuity to, lean, overturn; felt-tip pen, filter tip, fly-tip; tip-and-run, tip off, tip-top, tip-up; on the tip of your tongue, tip of the iceberg, tip the balance, tip the scales, tip the wink

tipping *see* tip; *Tipping the Velvet* (b/tv)

tipple alcoholic drink; drink frequently, pour with rain

tipsy slightly drunk; tipsy cake

tiptoe walk on the balls of the feet; (walk) on tiptoe; *Tiptoe through the Tulips* (s)

tired weary; made weary; dog-tired; tired out; *Tired of Waiting for You* (s)

tissue bodily flesh, gauzy fabric, network, paper handkerchief, thin paper; connective tissue, toilet tissue; tissue paper

tit small bird; blue tit, coal tit, great tit, long-tailed tit, marsh tit; tit for tat

titan bigwig; Greek god, Saturn's satellite

titanic huge; ill-fated liner; 1997 Kate Winslet film; *Raise the Titanic* (f)

tithe old church tax, tenth part; donate 10% of income; tithe barn

title designation, heading, ownership; designate; title deeds, title music, title role

titter furtive laugh; laugh furtively

toad frog-like amphibian; giant toad, horned toad, natterjack toad; toad-in-the-hole; *Toad of Toad Hall* (pl)

toady sycophant; creep

toast formal drink, grilled bread; drink to the health of; beans on toast, egg on toast, French toast, loyal toast, Melba toast; toast rack; (as) warm as toast

toasting *see* toast; toasting fork

tobacco plant whose leaves are smoked; tobacco plant; *Tobacco Road* (b/f/s)

today this 24 hours; former newspaper, Radio 4 morning programme; today week; *The Day Today* (tv), *No Milk Today* (s)

toddy alcoholic drink; hot toddy

toe digit on the foot; big toe, hammer toe, little toe, tic-tac-toe; toe-clip, toe-tapping; on tippy-toe, toe the line

toes *see* toe; make your toes curl, turn up your toes

toffee sticky confection; toffee apple, toffee-nosed

together in unison; mentally composed; club together, get-together, hang together, piece together, stick together; together with; all together, birds of a feather flock together, get it together, keep body and soul together, put two and two together, put your hands together; *All Together Now* (s), *Come Together* (s), *Get It Together* (s), *Happy Together* (s), *Let's Stick Together* (s), *Together in Electric Dreams* (s), *Together We Are Beautiful* (s)

toggle computer on/off switch, wooden button; switch between facilities on a computer; toggle switch

toil hard work; work hard

toilet lavatory; toilet bag, toilet paper, toilet roll, toilet tissue, toilet water

toilette grooming process; eau de toilette

token slot-machine disc, symbol, voucher; symbolic; book token, gift token; by the same token

told *see* tell; all told, I told you so, if truth be told

tolerance ability to endure, open-mindedness, permissible range of variance; zero tolerance

toll levy, number of casualties, sound of a bell; ring in mourning; toll-booth, toll-bridge, toll-gate; take a heavy toll, take its toll; *When Eight Bells Toll* (f)

tolls *see* toll; *For Whom the Bell Tolls* (b/f)

tom male cat; ginger tom, peeping Tom; tom-tom; every Tom, Dick and Harry; Tom Collins; *The Adventures of Tom Sawyer* (b/f), *Peeping Tom* (f), *Tom and Jerry* (f/tv), *Tom Brown's Schooldays* (b/f), *Tom, Dick or Harry* (s), *Tom Jones* (b/f), *Uncle Tom's Cabin* (b)

tomato bright shade of red, red salad food; beef tomato, cherry tomato, plum tomato; tomato ketchup, tomato soup

tomb grave; *Lara Croft: Tomb Raider* (f), *Tomb Raider* (ga)

tomorrow in 24 hours' time; song from *Bugsy Malone*; jam tomorrow; tomorrow week; like there was no tomorrow, tomorrow is another day; *The Day after Tomorrow* (f), *It Happened Tomorrow* (f), *Sky Captain and the World of Tomorrow* (f), *Tomorrow Belongs to Me* (s), *Tomorrow Never Dies* (f), *Tomorrow's World* (tv)

ton imperial unit of weight; metric ton; ton-up; like a ton of bricks

tone shade of colour, quality of sound; harmonise; dialling tone, half-tone, touch-tone; tone-deaf, tone down, tone poem

tongs gripping utensil, hair-curling device; curling tongs; hammer and tongs

tongue language, muscular organ in the mouth, shoe flap; play on a wind instrument; adder's tongue, hart's tongue, mother tongue, mother-in-law's tongue, ox-tongue, silver tongue; tongue-lashing, tongue-tied, tongue-twister; bite your tongue, find your tongue, get your tongue round, loosen your tongue, lose your tongue, on the tip of your tongue, slip of the tongue, tongue and groove, tongue-in-cheek

tongues *see* tongue; speak in tongues, the gift of tongues

tonic first note of a musical scale, pick-me-up, spirit mixer; gin and tonic; tonic water

tonight this evening; West Side Story song, 1960s tv series presented by

Cliff Michelmore; *Are You Lonesome Tonight* (s), *The Lion Sleeps Tonight* (s)

too   also, excessively; too much, too-too; about time too, go too far, not to put too fine a point on it, too big for your boots, too clever by half, too close for comfort, too hot to handle, too many cooks spoil the broth, too numerous to mention; *A Bridge Too Far* (f), *Father Came Too!* (f), *It's Too Late* (s), *The Man Who Knew Too Much* (f), *Too Darn Hot* (s), *Too Shy* (s)

tool   working instrument; machine tool; tool-bag, tool kit

tools   *see* tool; down tools; a bad workman blames his tools

tooth   hard structure in the mouth; canine tooth, dog-tooth, eye-tooth, fine-tooth comb, milk tooth, sweet tooth, wisdom tooth; tooth fairy, tooth powder; fight tooth and nail, long in the tooth

toothbrush   bristled dental cleaner; electric toothbrush; toothbrush moustache

tooting   peeping a horn; South London district; Tooting Bec, Tooting Broadway

top   garment for the upper body, lid, spinning toy, summit, upper surface; cover, outdo; big top, crop top, double top, flat-top, flip-top, pop-top, roll-top desk, screw top, soft-top, spinning top, table top, tank top, tip-top; top brass, top copy, top dog, top-down, top-drawer, top dressing, top-flight, top gear, top hat, top-heavy, top-hole, top-line, top-notch, top secret, top up; blow your top, go over the top, on top, on top of the world, over the top, sleep like a top, thin on top, top the bill, top

whack; *Curly Top* (f), *Girls on Top* (tv), *Room at the Top* (b/f), *The Surrey with the Fringe on Top* (s), *Top Cat* (tv), *Top Gear* (tv), *Top Gun* (f), *Top Hat* (f), *Top of the Pops* (tv), *Top Secret* (f), *You're the Top* (s)

topped   *see* top; open-topped

topping   *see* top; food sauce; first-rate; topping up

torch   portable lamp; set alight; Olympic torch; torch singer, torch song, torch-bearer; carry a torch for, put to the torch; *Torch Singer* (f), *Torch Song Trilogy* (f/pl)

torment   agony; agonise, pester

torn   (had) ripped; in two minds, ripped; 1997 Natalie Imbruglia hit; war-torn; that's torn it; *Torn Curtain* (f)

torpedo   underwater missile; destroy; torpedo boat

torque   ancient necklace, twisting force; 2004 biker thriller; torque wrench

torrid   hot and dry, intensely passionate; torrid zone

tortilla   Mexican pancake; *Tortilla Flat* (b/f)

torture   great suffering, infliction of bodily pain; inflict bodily pain on; torture chamber

toss   flip of a coin; flip, move from side to side, throw; full toss; toss-up; argue the toss

tossing   *see* toss; tossing the caber

tot   measure of spirits, small child; add (up); tot up

total   final amount; complete; add up; grand total, sum total; total eclipse; *Total Eclipse of the Heart* (s), *Total Recall* (f)

tote   betting system; carry; tote bag

totem   symbol; totem pole
touch   smattering, tactile sense; affect, come into contact with, feel; finishing touch, Midas touch, soft touch; touch-and-go, touch a nerve, touch base, touch down, touch judge, touch pad, touch screen, touch-tone, touch-type; in touch, touch wood, a woman's touch; *Invisible Touch* (f), *That Riviera Touch* (f), *That Touch of Mink* (f), *The Gentle Touch* (tv), *Touch Me* (s), *Touch Me in the Morning* (s), *A Touch of Class* (f), *Touch of Evil* (f), *A Touch of Frost* (tv), *A Woman's Touch* (s)
touching   see touch; *Touching Evil* (tv)
tough   ruffian; difficult, robust, rugged; hang tough; (as) tough as old boots, tough it out, tough nut to crack; *Tough Guys* (f)
tour   excursion; travel around; coach tour, conducted tour, Cook's tour, grand tour, lecture tour, mystery tour, whistle-stop tour; tour de force, tour of duty, tour operator; Tour de France; *Magical Mystery Tour* (s), *Tour of Duty* (tv)
touring   see tour; touring car
tourist   holidaymaker; tourist class; *The Accidental Tourist* (b/f)
tout   illegal ticket seller; solicit for custom; tout de suite
tow   pull along; tow-rope; in tow
towed   see tow; *Towed in a Hole* (f)
towel   cloth for drying; hand-towel, roller-towel, tea towel; throw in the towel
tower   tall structure; be very high; bell tower, clock tower, conning tower, control tower, cooling tower, ivory tower, Martello tower, water tower; tower block, tower of strength;

Blackpool Tower, Eiffel Tower, Leaning Tower of Pisa, Sears Tower, Spinnaker Tower, Telecom Tower, Tower Bridge, Tower Hill, Tower of Babel, Tower of London, Victoria Tower Gardens; *The Black Tower* (b), *Tower of Strength* (s)
towering   see tower; *The Towering Inferno* (f)
towers   see tower; Alton Towers, Barchester Towers (b), Fawlty Towers (tv), Lord of the Rings: The Two Towers (f), The Towers of Trebizond (b)
town   urban area; county town, ghost town, home town, man about town, market town, new town, one-horse town, shanty town, small-town; town clerk, town council, town councillor, town crier, town hall, town house, town planning; go to town, paint the town red, the talk of the town; Acton Town, Camden Town, Canning Town, Cape Town, George Town, Kentish Town; *The Boys Are Back in Town* (s), *Boys' Town* (f), *Ghost Town* (s), *Mr Deeds Goes to Town* (f), *On the Town* (mus), *Small Town Boy* (s), *Small Town Girl* (f), *A Small Town in Germany* (b), *Town Called Malice* (s), *A Town Like Alice* (b/f), *The Talk of the Town* (f), *Town without Pity* (f)

Town
Acton, Camden, Canning, Cape, George, Grimsby, Huddersfield, Ipswich, Kentish, Luton, Macclesfield, Swindon, Yeovil

towns   see town; *Anna of the Five Towns* (b)
toxic   poisonous; toxic waste

toy miniature (dog), plaything; trifle (with); toy boy, toy shop; *Toy Story* (f)

trace indication, smidgen; draw an outline of, locate; trace element

traces *see* trace; kick over the traces

tracing *see* trace; tracing paper

track one item on a disc, path, racecourse, railway line; follow; backing track, dirt track, fast track, keep track, multi-track, one-track mind; track down, track events, track record, track shoes; off the beaten track

tracker follower; tracker dog

tracking *see* track; tracking station

tracks *see* track; make tracks; *The Tracks of My Tears* (s)

tract area of land, pamphlet; respiratory tract

traction grip of a car tyre, pulling power; traction engine

tractor farm vehicle; tractor driver

trade commerce, occupation; do business, swap; balance of trade, board of trade, fair trade, free trade, horse-trade, rag trade, slave trade, stock-in-trade; trade deficit, trade discount, trade gap, trade in, trade off, trade price, trade secret, trade surplus, trade union, trade winds; a roaring trade, tricks of the trade; *The Rag Trade* (tv)

trader dealer; rogue trader, slave trader; *Rogue Trader* (f)

traders *see* trader; *Rogue Traders* (tv)

trades *see* trade; jack of all trades (and master of none); Trades Union Congress

trading *see* trade; horse-trading; trading estate, trading post, trading stamps; Office of Fair Trading; *Trading Places* (f)

traditional long-established; traditional jazz

traffic illicit commerce, vehicles; do business illegally; 2000 Michael Douglas thriller; air traffic control; traffic calming, traffic island, traffic jam, traffic lights, traffic warden

tragedy classical drama, very sad event; Bee Gees and Steps hit; Greek tragedy; *An American Tragedy* (b/f), *A Yorkshire Tragedy* (pl)

tragic very sad; tragic flaw

trail path; drag along; nature trail, paper trail, vapour trail; trail arms, trail bike; blaze a trail, trail your coat; Oregon Trail; *The Trail of the Lonesome Pine* (s)

trailer film preview, towed vehicle; trailer park

train aim (a gun), column (of camels), part of a garment dragging along the ground, railway vehicle; instruct, practise; boat train, bullet train, down-train, express train, freight train, ghost train, goods train, gravy train, high-speed train, house-train, milk train, night train, passenger train, potty-train, road train, runaway train, steam train, through train, up-train, wagon train; train set; in train; *Big Train* (tv), *The Ghost Train* (f/pl), *Last Train to Clarksville* (s), *Midnight Train to Georgia* (s), *Mule Train* (f), *Mystery Train* (f), *Night Train to Munich* (f), *Runaway Train* (f), *Stamboul Train* (b), *Strangers on a Train* (f), *Throw Momma from the Train* (f), *The Train* (f), *Wagon Train* (tv)

trainer instructor, sports shoe; animal trainer

training *see* train; circuit training,

corrective training, weight training; training college; in training

trains *see* train; *Mr Norris Changes Trains* (b)

tramlines area for tennis doubles, rigid principles, streetcar rails

tramp vagrant; hike, walk heavily; *Lady and the Tramp* (f)

transfer relocation; hand on, relocate; capital transfer tax, credit transfer, technology transfer; transfer fee

transit act of carrying, act of passage; pass through; Ford van; transit lounge, transit visa; in transit, sic transit gloria mundi

translation act of expressing in another language, text put into another language; free translation, machine translation; *Lost in Translation* (f)

transpire become known, give off water vapour (of plants), happen

transplant removal of an organ to another body; remove and put elsewhere; organ transplant

transport conveyance; convey, enrapture; public transport; transport cafe

trap light carriage, snare; ensnare; booby-trap, death trap, fire trap, gin trap, pony and trap, radar trap, rat trap, sand-trap, speed trap; *The Parent Trap* (f), *The Tender Trap* (s/f)

trapdoor ceiling or floor panel; trapdoor spider

trapeze circus swing; 1956 Burt Lancaster film; flying trapeze; trapeze artist

trash rubbish; vandalise; 1970 Warhol film; trash can

travel globetrotting; go on a journey; time travel; travel agency, travel

agent, travel light, travel sickness; travel broadens the mind; *Have Gun Will Travel* (tv)

traveller itinerant, person on a journey; 1950s Morris estate car; commercial traveller, fellow-traveller, space traveller, time traveller; traveller's cheque, traveller's joy, traveller's tale; *Time Traveller* (al)

travelling *see* travel; fellow-travelling; travelling salesman

travels *see* travel; bad news travels fast; *Gulliver's Travels* (b), *Travels with My Aunt* (b/f)

travesties poor imitations; Tom Stoppard play

trawl thorough search; drag a fishing net, search thoroughly

tray platter; in-tray, out-tray, tea tray

treacle thick dark syrup; *Brimstone and Treacle* (f/pl)

tread sound of footsteps, tyre grip, upper surface of a step; walk; tread the boards, tread water; fools rush in where angels fear to tread; *Where Angels Fear to Tread* (b/f)

treason act of betrayal; high treason

treasure hidden valuables; cherish; treasure chest, treasure hunt, treasure trove; *The Treasure of the Sierra Madre* (f), *Treasure Hunt* (tv), *Treasure Island* (b/f)

treasury store of valuables; government finance department; treasury bench; Lords of the Treasury

treat special pleasure; behave towards, medicate, pay for, process; Dutch treat, ill-treat; trick or treat

treatment medical care, process; heat treatment, ill-treatment

treaty pact; peace treaty; Lateran Treaty, Maastricht Treaty

treble boy's singing voice, dartboard ring; multiply by three; treble chance, treble clef

tree chart with a branching structure, woody plant; apple tree, cedar tree, Christmas tree, family tree, flame tree, gum tree, Joshua tree, lime tree, pear tree, pine tree, rain tree, rubber tree, shoe tree, tea tree, tea tree oil, walnut tree, Xmas tree; tree fern, tree frog, tree house, tree of knowledge, tree of life, tree surgeon; bark up the wrong tree, out of your tree, up a gum tree, up a tree; *The Joshua Tree* (al), *The Singing, Ringing Tree* (tv), *Tie a Yellow Ribbon round the 'Ole Oak Tree* (s), *Under the Greenwood Tree* (b)

trees *see* tree; *The Flame Trees of Thika* (b/tv), *Trees Lounge* (f)

trek arduous journey; footslog; *Star Trek* (f/tv)

trekking *see* trek; pony-trekking

tremble small shiver; quiver; all of a tremble

trembling *see* tremble; trembling poplar

tremor minor earthquake; earth tremor

trench ditch; trench coat, trench warfare

trespass wrongful entry; encroach, enter illegally, sin

trestle supporting framework; trestle table

trial court hearing, ordeal, test; clinical trial, fair trial, field trial, show trial, time trial; trial run; on trial, trial and error; *The Trial* (b/f), *Trial by Jury* (f/o)

trials *see* trial; sheepdog trials

triangle three-sided shape; 1980s Kate O'Mara tv serial; equilateral triangle, eternal triangle; Bermuda Triangle

tribunal arbitration board; industrial tribunal

tribute expression of admiration; *The Tribute Money* (pa)

trick clever deception; deceive; con trick, confidence trick, hat-trick, Indian rope-trick, one-trick pony, three-card trick; trick cyclist; do the trick, every trick in the book, oldest trick in the book, trick or treat; *One-Trick Pony* (s/f)

tricks *see* trick; bag of tricks; how's tricks, tricks of the trade, up to your old tricks, you can't teach an old dog new tricks; *New Tricks* (tv)

tried *see* try; tried and tested

trifle cold dessert, insignificant thing; toy (with); sherry trifle

trigger cause, gun lever; activate; hair trigger; trigger finger, trigger happy, trigger point; *Trigger Happy TV* (tv)

trilogy series of three books; *The Balkan Trilogy* (b), *Torch Song Trilogy* (f)

trim quick haircut; cut; neat and tidy, slender; in trim, trim your sails

trinity group of three; Father, Son and Holy Spirit; Cambridge University college, Dublin college, university term; Leon Uris novel, 2002 Wesley Snipes film; Trinity term; Trinity College, Trinity House, Trinity Sunday

trip outing; cause to stumble, disconnect automatically, stumble, walk daintily; coach trip, day trip, ego trip, field trip, guilt trip, round trip; trip switch, trip the light fantastic, trip up

triple threefold; multiply by three;

triple crown, triple jump, triple time; Triple Alliance, Triple Entente

tripper   person on an outing; day tripper; *Day Tripper* (s)

triumph   victory; prevail; British car and motorcycle manufacturer; Triumph Herald; *The Triumph of Death* (pa), *Triumph of the Will* (f)

trivial   inconsequential; Trivial Pursuit; *Trivial Pursuit* (tv)

trodden   *see* tread; well trodden

trolley   table, basket or bed on wheels; tea trolley; off your trolley; *The Trolley Song* (s)

trombone   brass instrument; slide trombone

trombones   *see* trombone; *Seventy-Six Trombones* (s)

troop   army unit, group; flock (in), plod; troop carrier; troop the colour

trooper   cavalry soldier; swear like a trooper; Storm Trooper; *I Lost My Heart to a Starship Trooper* (s)

troops   *see* troop; soldiers; front-line troops, shock troops; Storm Troops

trophy   victory award; trophy wife

tropical   hot and humid; tropical storm

trot   horse's pace; move briskly; turkey trot; trot out; on the trot

troth   fidelity; plight your troth

trotters   pigs' feet; Bolton Wanderers' nickname; pigs' trotters

trouble   disturbance, inconvenience; put to inconvenience, worry; trouble and strife, trouble spot; ask for trouble, cause trouble, in trouble, look for trouble, a trouble shared is a trouble halved; *Big Trouble in Little China* (f), *The Trouble with Girls* (f), *The Trouble with Harry* (f), *Trouble in Mind* (f), *Trouble in Paradise* (f),

Trouble in Store (f), *Trouble with Lichen* (b)

troubled   *see* trouble; uneasy; pour oil on troubled waters; *Bridge over Troubled Water* (al/s)

troubles   *see* trouble; problems; teething troubles; *Troubles and Strife* (tv)

trough   animal feed-container, gully, low point

trouper   experienced performer, reliable person; *Super Trouper* (s)

trouser   relating to pants; pocket; trouser press, trouser suit

trousers   leg-covering garment; pockets; combat trousers, long trousers, pyjama trousers; all mouth and trousers, anything in trousers, caught with your trousers down, wear the trousers; *Baggy Trousers* (s), *Monkey Trousers* (tv), *The Wrong Trousers* (f)

trout   game fish; brown trout, old trout, rainbow trout, sea trout; *Paris Trout* (f), *The Trout Quintet* (cl)

trove   store of valuable items; treasure trove

trowel   gardening tool; lay on with a trowel

troy   system of weights; ancient city; 2004 Brad Pitt film

truck   dealings, lorry; dumper truck, fork-lift truck, pick-up truck, utility truck; truck driver, truck stop

truckle   barrel-shaped cheese; behave obsequiously; truckle bed

true   correct, faithful, genuine; true-blue, true love, true north; come true, out of true, show your true colours, true to form, true to life; *True Blue* (al/s), *True Crime* (tv), *True Grit* (f), *True Lies* (f), *True Love* (s), *True*

Love Ways (s), *True Romance* (f)

truly *see* true; well and truly, yours truly; *Truly, Madly, Deeply* (f)

trump card of the master suit; go one better than; trump card

trumpet brass instrument, elephant's cry; announce, roar; ear-trumpet; trumpet major; blow your own trumpet; *The Trumpet-Major* (b)

trumps *see* trump; come up trumps, no trumps

trunk elephant's proboscis, large chest, stem of a tree, torso, US car boot; trunk call, trunk road

trunks *see* trunk; swimming shorts; swimming trunks

truss surgical support; tie up

trust confidence, holding fund; have confidence in; brains trust, hospital trust, investment trust, unit trust; trust company, trust fund; National Trust

truth fact, veracity; half-truth, home truth, moment of truth, tell the truth; truth drug; economical with the truth, if truth be told, in spirit and in truth, in truth, to tell the truth, truth is stranger than fiction, truth to tell; *The Moment of Truth* (tv), *The Truth about Cats and Dogs* (f), *The Truth about Charlie* (f)

try rugby touchdown, attempt; hear in court, sample; penalty try; try on, try out; try your hand at, try it on

trying *see* try; irksome

tub clumsy boat, old bath, open food container; bran tub, dolly tub, hot tub, twin-tub; tub-thumping; a tale of a tub; *A Tale of a Tub* (b)

tuba brass instrument; *Tubby the Tuba* (s)

tubby plump; *Tubby the Tuba* (s)

tube cylindrical vessel, tv set; London Underground; boob tube, cathode ray tube, inner tube, test tube, test-tube baby; go down the tube; *The Tube* (tv)

tubular cylindrical; *Tubular Bells* (al)

tuck grub, stitched fold; fold under; nip and tuck; tuck-box, tuck in, tuck shop; *Nip/Tuck* (tv)

tucker Aussie food; best bib and tucker; *The Bush Tucker Man* (tv), *Little Tommy Tucker* (nr)

tug harbour boat, sharp pull; pull hard; tug-of-war, tug your forelock

tulip spring flower; *The Black Tulip* (b)

tulips *see* tulip; *Tiptoe Through the Tulips* (s)

tumble sudden fall; fall headlong; tumble-dry, tumble-dryer; rough and tumble, take a tumble

tumbler acrobat, tall glass

tummy stomach; tummy button

tune melody; adjust; fine-tune, signature tune; tune in; call the tune, change your tune, dance to your tune, he who pays the piper calls the tune, in tune, out of tune, to the tune of; *I Whistle a Happy Tune* (s), *Name That Tune* (tv)

tuner adjustment knob, person who adjusts a piano; piano tuner

tunes *see* tune; brand-name throat sweets; *Tunes of Glory* (f), *Your Hundred Best Tunes* (r)

tuning *see* tune; tuning fork, tuning peg

Tunnel
Blackwall, Box, Channel, Mersey, Severn, Simplon

tunnel underground passage; dig an

underground passage; wind tunnel; tunnel vision; Blackwall Tunnel, Channel Tunnel, Mersey Tunnel; *Time Tunnel* (tv), *Tunnel of Love* (s), *Tunnel Vision* (s)

turbine rotary engine; gas turbine, steam turbine

turf grass, horse racing; cover with grass, throw (out); surf 'n' turf; turf accountant, turf out

turkey flop, large fowl; country in both Europe and Asia; cold turkey, roast turkey, talk turkey; turkey trot

turn change of direction, music-hall act, stroll; become sour, change direction, spin, transform; about-turn, Buggins's turn, good turn, out-turn, star turn, three-point turn, U turn; turn about, turn around, turn back, turn down, turn in, turn off, turn out, turn over, turn round, turn sour, turn turtle, turn up; not turn a hair, one good turn deserves another, turn a blind eye, turn a deaf ear, turn an honest penny, turn on a sixpence, turn on your heel, turn over a new leaf, turn Queen's evidence, turn up your toes, turn your nose up at, turn-up for the books; *The Turn of the Screw* (b/f/o), *U Turn* (f)

turned *see* turn; turned the heat on, turned the tables

turner lathe operator; page-turner; Turner Prize; *Turner and Hooch* (f)

turning *see* turn; head-turning, wood-turning; *Turning Japanese* (s)

turns *see* turn; take turns

turquoise bluish-green colour, gemstone

turtle marine reptile; leatherback

turtle, loggerhead turtle, mock turtle, mock turtle soup, turn turtle; turtle dove

turtles *see* turtle; *Teenage Mutant Ninja Turtles* (f)

tut exclamation of rebuke; say disapprovingly; tut-tut

tutor teacher; teach

tuxedo dinner jacket; *The Tuxedo* (f), *Tuxedo Junction* (cl)

twang nasal tone, plucking noise

tweed woollen cloth; river on the England/ Scotland border; Harris tweed; Berwick-upon-Tweed

twelfth ordinal number; twelfth man; Glorious Twelfth, Twelfth Night; *Twelfth Night* (f/pl), *The Twelfth of Never* (s)

twelve dozen; twelve o'clock, twelve-step programme; *Ocean's Twelve* (f), *Twelve Angry Men* (f/pl), *The Twelve Chairs* (b/f), *Twelve Monkeys* (f)

twenties post-WWI decade, scores; *The Roaring Twenties* (f)

twenty score; twenty pence, twenty-four-hour clock, twenty-one, twenty-twenty; *Twenty-Four* (tv), *Twenty Thousand Leagues under the Sea* (b/f)

twice double, on a couple of occasions; think twice; once bitten twice shy, once or twice; *Once Bitten Twice Shy* (s), *The Postman Always Rings Twice* (f), *Think Twice* (s), *Twice Shy* (b), *You Only Live Twice* (f)

twiddle toy (with); twiddle your thumbs

twig small branch; understand

twilight dusk; twilight zone; *The Twilight Zone* (tv)

twill thick fabric; cavalry twill

twin one of a pair; exactly matching; identical twin; twin beds, twin brother, twin sister, twin-tub; *Twin Peaks* (tv)

twine string; interlace

twinkling flickering; in a twinkling, in the twinkling of an eye

twins *see* twin; 1988 Danny DeVito film

twist roll (of tobacco), rotation, surprise ending in a story; distort, sprain, turn, wind together; 1960s dance; get your knickers in a twist, round the twist, twist in the wind, twist your arm; *Let's Twist Again* (s), *Oliver Twist* (b/f), *A Simple Twist of Fate* (f), *Twist and Shout* (s)

twisted *see* twist; *Twisted Nerve* (f), *The Twisted Thing* (b)

twister swindler, tornado; 1996 Helen Hunt film; tongue-twister

twisting *see* twist; arm-twisting

twitch nervous spasm; move spasmodically

twitter chirp, prattle; in a twitter

two low number; Boston two-step, goody two shoes, meat and two veg, military two-step, number two, one or two, one-two; two-bit, two-dimensional, two-faced, two-hander, two-horse race, two-piece, two-reeler, two-seater, two-step, two-stroke, two-timer, two-way, two-way mirror, two-way street, two-wheeler; (as) thick as two short planks, fall between two stools, have two left feet, in two shakes of a lamb's tail, it takes two to tango, kill two birds with one stone, put two and two ·

together, take down a peg or two, that makes two of us, two by two, two can play at that game, two heads are better than one, two up two down, two wrongs don't make a right, two's company three's a crowd; Formula Two, Two Thousand Guineas, World War Two; *Goody Two Shoes* (s), *It Takes Two* (s), *A Kid for Two Farthings* (f), *Lock, Stock and Two Smoking Barrels* (f), *Lord of the Rings: The Two Towers* (f), *The Mirror Has Two Faces* (f), *Only Two Can Play* (f), *The Taking of Pelham One Two Three* (f), *A Tale of Two Cities* (b/f), *Tea for Two* (mus/s), *The Two Drovers* (b), *Two Fat Ladies* (tv), *The Two Gentlemen of Verona* (pl), *Two Hearts* (s), *The Two Jakes* (f), *Two Little Boys* (s), *Two-Minute Warning* (f), *Two Mules for Sister Sara* (f), *The Two Noble Kinsmen* (pl), *The Two of Us* (tv), *The Two Ronnies* (tv), *Two's Company* (tv), *Two Up, Two Down* (tv), *Two Weeks Notice* (f), *Two-Way Stretch* (f), *Two Women* (f), *Under Two Flags* (f)

type printed characters, sort; write via a keyboard; touch-type

typewriter old office machine; electric typewriter

typing *see* typing; typing pool

typist keyboard user; audio typist, copy typist, shorthand typist, touch-typist

tyre rubber wheel-surround; Lebanese port; bicycle tyre, flat tyre, spare tyre; tyre gauge; *Pericles, Prince of Tyre* (pl)

U

ugly   unattractive; ugly duckling; *Coyote Ugly* (f), *The Good the Bad and the Ugly* (f), *The Ugly Duckling* (b/s), *Ugly Betty* (tv)

ultimate   final, maximum; *Ultimate Force* (tv)

ultra   Latin word meaning 'beyond'; very; brand-name washing powder; code-name for the WWII decoding operations at Bletchley Park; ultra-high frequency, ultra-modern; ne plus ultra, ultra vires

unbearable   intolerable; *The Unbearable Lightness of Being* (b/f)

umbrella   wet-weather parasol; umbrella pine, umbrella plant, umbrella stand

uncertain   doubtful, hesitant; in no uncertain terms

unchained   released the fetters from; *Unchained Melody* (s)

uncle   aunt's husband, pawnbroker; Dutch uncle, great-uncle; bob's your uncle; Uncle Sam; *The Man from Uncle* (tv), *Uncle Buck* (f), *Uncle*

Silas (f), *Uncle Tom's Cabin* (b), *Uncle Vanya* (pl)

unconditional   absolute; unconditional surrender; *Unconditional Surrender* (b)

unconscious   deepest level of the psyche; asleep or comatose; collective unconscious

under   below, junior to, less than; buckle under, go under, up-and-under; under a cloud, under-age, under arms, under arrest, under canvas, under consideration, under control, under cover, under debate, under fire, under oath, under penalty of, under pressure, under sail, under-represented, under-resourced, under-run, under sedation, under siege, under suspicion, under way, under wraps; come under the hammer, drink under the table, hide your light under a bushel, hot under the collar, keep under your hat, put the skids under, reds under the bed, sail under false colours, six feet under, sweep under the carpet, under lock and key, under no circumstances, under starter's orders, under the auspices of, under the circumstances, under the influence, under the knife, under the microscope, under the open sky, under the counter, under the hatches, under the skin, under the sod, under the sun, under the table, under the weather, under the wire, under your belt, under your breath, under your feet, under your nose, under your own steam, under your wing, water under the bridge; Ashton-under-Lyne, Down Under, Newcastle-under-Lyme; *Courage under Fire* (f), *A Cream Cracker under the Settee* (tv), *Down Under* (s), *Evil under the Sun* (b/f), *Six Feet Under* (tv), *Twenty Thousand Leagues under the Sea* (b/f), *Under Milk Wood* (pl), *Under Pressure* (s), *Under Siege* (f), *Under Suspicion* (f), *Under the Boardwalk* (s), *Under the Greenwood Tree* (b/po), *Under the Net* (b), *Under the Volcano* (b/f), *Under Two Flags* (f)

underneath   side facing the ground; below; *Underneath the Arches* (s)

unearned   not deserved; unearned income

unemployment   joblessness; unemployment benefit

unification   merger; Unification Church

uniform   official clothing worn by members of a group, radio code word; consistent; school uniform; *Girls in Uniform* (f)

union   marriage, merger, students' club, workers' organisation; credit union, customs union, rugby union, trade union; union flag; Act of Union, Christian Democratic Union, European Union, Oxford Union Society, State of the Union, Trades Union Congress, Union Jack; *Part of the Union* (s), *State of the Union* (f), *Union City Blue* (s), *Union of the Snake* (s), *Union Pacific* (f), *World in Union* (s)

unison   agreement, several voices singing together; public-sector workers' organisation; in unison

unit   kitchen fitment, measure of alcohol intake, military division, single element or item; British thermal unit, central processing unit, vanity unit, visual display unit, waste-disposal unit; unit trust

unitary   individual; unitary authority

united   combined; 1960s tv soap about football; Dundee United, Hartlepool United, Leeds United, Manchester United, Newcastle United, Peterborough United, Scunthorpe United, Sheffield United, United Arab Emirates, United Artists, United Kingdom, United Nations, United States (of America), West Ham United

universal   cosmic, global, omnipresent; Hollywood film studios; universal indicator, universal joint, universal suffrage; Universal City; *Universal Soldier* (f/s)

universe   cosmos; *Life, the Universe and Everything* (b), *The Restaurant at the End of the Universe* (b)

university   institution of higher learning; university of life; Cambridge University Press, Open University, Oxford University Press; *University Challenge* (tv)

unknown anonymous, not yet discovered; unknown quantity; Unknown Soldier; *Letter from an Unknown Woman* (f)

unobtainable inaccessible; number unobtainable

unseen unprepared passage for translation; invisible; sight unseen; *Sight Unseen* (b)

unskilled lacking training, not calling for specific training (of a job); unskilled labour

unstuck loosened, thrown into a state of disorganisation; come unstuck

unsuitable inappropriate; *An Unsuitable Job for a Woman* (b/tv)

until as far as, up to the time of; until further notice, until hell freezes over; *Until the Time Is Through* (s), *Wait Until Dark* (f)

unto as far as; be a law unto yourself; *Unto Us a Child Is Born* (s)

unusual atypical, rare; *It's Not Unusual* (s)

unwashed dirty; the great unwashed

upholstered padded and stuffed (furniture); well upholstered

upon atop; put-upon; cast bread upon the waters, once upon a time, upon my honour, upon my soul; Berwick-upon-Tweed, Kingston-upon-Thames, Newcastle-upon-Tyne, Richmond-upon-Thames, Stratford-upon-Avon; *Composed upon Westminster Bridge* (po), *Once upon a Time in America* (f), *Once upon a Time in Mexico* (f), *Once upon a Time in the West* (f)

upper top part of a shoe; higher, top; stiff upper lip; upper case, upper chamber, upper class, upper crust, upper house, upper school, upper storey; gain/have the upper hand; *The Upper Hand* (tv)

uppers *see* upper; drugs producing euphoria; on one's uppers

upping increasing; swan-upping

upright perpendicular, type of piano, vertical (goalpost); respectable, vertical; bolt upright; upright piano

ups high points; press-ups, sit-ups, slip-ups; ups and downs; ups-a-daisy

upset shock; cause distress to, disrupt, tip over; distressed, spilt; upset the apple cart

upside positive aspect; upside down, upside-down cake; *Upside Down* (s), *The Upside of Anger* (f)

upstairs on a higher storey; kick upstairs; *Upstairs Downstairs* (tv)

uptake mental agility, proportion accepting an offer; quick/slow on the uptake

urban of a town or city; urban myth, urban renewal; *I'm the Urban Spaceman* (s), *Urban Cowboy* (f)

urchin dirty ragged child; sea urchin

urn large tea-making vessel, vase for the ashes of the dead; Grecian urn, tea urn; *Ode on a Grecian Urn* (po)

use application, function, purpose; consume, operate, take advantage of; ill-use, make use of, of use; use-by date, use up; use your loaf; *Use Your Illusion* (al)

used *see* use; accustomed, second-hand; used cars; *Used People* (f)

useful beneficial, convenient; make yourself useful

user consumer, drug addict, operator; end-user, road user; user-friendly

usher cinema attendant, courtroom or wedding official, guide; direct people (at a wedding, eg); Yeoman

Usher; *The Fall of the House of Usher* (b)

usual customary, ordinary; as usual, the usual; as per usual, business as usual; *The Usual Suspects* (f)

utility practicality, public commodity or service; functional rather than attractive; make of functional WWII clothing and furniture; public utility; utility room, utility truck

utter speak out; downright

V

vacancies gaps, hotel rooms available, job openings; no vacancies

vacant expressionless, unoccupied; situations vacant; vacant possession; *Pretty Vacant* (s)

vacuum empty space; clean by sucking up dust; in a vacuum; vacuum cleaner, vacuum flask, vacuum-packed; nature abhors a vacuum

vague blurred, unclear; Nouvelle Vague

vain conceited, futile; in vain; take your name in vain; *You're So Vain* (s)

vale lowland area; Latin for 'farewell'; vale of tears; Ebbw Vale, Maida Vale, Port Vale

valentine card sent in February; *My Funny Valentine* (s), *Shirley Valentine* (f/pl)

valley lower ground between hills; lily of the valley, rift valley; Death Valley, Happy Valley, Silicon Valley, Thames Valley, Valley Forge, Valley of the Kings; *Happy Valley* (b), *How Green*

Was My Valley (b/f), *Rainbow Valley* (s), *Sweet Valley High* (tv), *Valley of the Dolls* (b/f), *Valley of the Kings* (f)

> **Valley**
> Death, Happy, Loire, Napa, Rhondda, Silicon, Taff, Thames

value item's worth; appreciate, assess; calorific value, cash surrender value, face value, food value, market value, nominal value, pH value, rateable value, sentimental value, surrender value; value added, value added tax, value judgement

values *see* value; moral principles; family values; *Addams Family Values* (f)

valve old wireless component, regulating device; escape valve, safety valve, slide valve

vamp alluring seductress, simple musical introductory passage, upper front part of a shoe; flirt, improvise a musical accompaniment, patch (up)

vampire bloodsucking creature of European legend; vampire bat; *Buffy the Vampire Slayer* (tv), *Interview with the Vampire* (f), *Mark of the Vampire* (f)

van forefront, light delivery vehicle; delivery van, furniture van, guard's van, mail van, removal van, white-van man; Van de Graaff generator; Van Allen Belt, Van Diemen's Land; *Van der Valk* (tv), *Van Helsing* (f)

vane propeller or windmill blade, weathercock; weather-vane

vanilla flavouring extract; *Vanilla Sky* (f)

vanish disappear; brand-name stain remover; vanish into thin air

vanishes see vanish; *The Lady Vanishes* (f)

vanishing see vanish; vanishing cream, vanishing point; *Vanishing Point* (f)

vanities follies; *The Bonfire of the Vanities* (b/f)

vanity conceit, futility; vanity case, vanity mirror, vanity unit; *Vanity Fair* (b/f/tv)

vapour gaseous form of a liquid; vapour trail

variety assortment, diversity, theatrical show; American entertainment magazine; variety is the spice of life

varnish lacquer; embellish (the truth), glaze; nail varnish

vault arched structure, gym jump, underground chamber; leap over; barrel vault, pole vault

vaulting see vault; arched work on a roof or ceiling; pole-vaulting; vaulting horse

veg greens; chill (out); veg out; meat and two veg

vegetable dull inactive person, plant grown for food; relating to plant life; root vegetable, textured vegetable protein; vegetable marrow, vegetable oil, vegetable soup

vegetarian person who eats no meat or fish; eating no meat or fish, non-meat (meal); lacto-ovo-vegetarian, lacto-vegetarian; vegetarian diet

vehicle means of transport; all-terrain vehicle, commercial vehicle

veil face covering; conceal; draw a veil over, take the veil; *The Painted Veil* (b/f), *The Seventh Veil* (f)

veils see veil; dance of the seven veils

vein blood vessel, manner, seam of ore, thin line in a leaf; jugular vein

velvet plush fabric; black velvet, crushed velvet, plush velvet; an iron fist in a velvet glove; *Blue Velvet* (s/f), *International Velvet* (f), *National Velvet* (b/f), *Tipping the Velvet* (b/tv), *Velvet Goldmine* (f)

vending selling; vending machine

vendor seller; news vendor

vengeance retribution; with a vengeance; *Die Hard with a Vengeance* (f), *Sympathy for Mr Vengeance* (f), *Vengeance Is Mine* (b)

vent air duct, outlet, volcano shaft; release; give vent to, vol-au-vent

venture exploit; dare; venture capital; Venture Scout

ventured see venture; nothing ventured nothing gained

verb word signifying an action; phrasal verb

verdict ruling; majority verdict, open verdict; *The Verdict* (f)

vernal   happening in spring; vernal equinox

verse   division of a Biblical chapter, group of lines in a song or poem, poetry; blank verse, free verse, heroic verse, light verse, nonsense verse; chapter and verse

verses   *see* verse; *The Satanic Verses* (b)

version   particular form; Authorised Version; *The Browning Version* (f/pl)

versus   against; *Joe versus the Volcano* (f), *Kramer versus Kramer* (f), *The People versus Larry Flynt* (f)

very   actual; extremely; very good, very light, very well; all very well, at the very least, the very idea; Very Reverend; *Thank U Very Much* (s), *Very Bad Things* (f), *A Very Peculiar Practice* (tv)

vessels   containers, ships and boats; blood vessels; empty vessels make most noise

vest   undergarment, US waistcoat; clothe, endow; bulletproof vest, string vest

vested   *see* vest; vested interest

veteran   ex-serviceman, old hand, very old car; long-serving, pre-1905 (car); veteran car

veterinary   relating to animal health; veterinary surgeon

vetting   carefully checking; positive vetting

via   by way of; Via Dolorosa

vicar   minister of religion; *The Vicar of Bray* (s), *The Vicar of Dibley* (tv), *The Vicar of Wakefield* (b)

vicarage   rectory; *The Murder at the Vicarage* (b)

vice   bad habit, sin, tool for gripping; air vice-marshal; vice-admiral, vice-chairman, vice-chancellor, vice-like, vice-president, vice versa; *Miami Vice* (f/tv), *Vice Versa* (f)

vicious   cruel; vicious circle

victim   casualty, prey; 1961 Dirk Bogarde film; fall victim to, fashion victim

victor   radio code word, winner; victor ludorum; Victor Gollancz

victory   triumph; Nelson's flagship; moral victory; victory roll; *Dark Victory* (f), *Escape to Victory* (f)

victualler   supplier of provisions; licensed victualler

video   film on a cassette, tv recorder; record off the tv; video camera, video game, video recorder, video recording; *Naked Video* (tv), *Video Killed the Radio Star* (s)

view   opinion, panorama; examine; aerial view, bird's-eye view, in full view, in view, in view of, on view, point of view, private view, rear-view mirror, world view, worm's-eye view; take a dim view of, with a view to; *A Pale View of Hills* (b), *The Parallax View* (f), *A Room with a View* (b/f), *A View from the Bridge* (pl), *View on the Stour near Dedham* (pa), *A View to a Kill* (f)

vile   despicable; *Vile Bodies* (b)

villa   holiday home; Roman villa; Aston Villa

village   small rural settlement; global village; village green, village hall; Greenwich Village; *The Village* (f), *Village of the Damned* (f)

vine   grape-producing plant; Russian vine

vinegar   liquid condiment; balsamic vinegar, salt and vinegar

vintage   old car, season's wine yield;

best of its type, classic; vintage car

violet bluish-purple colour, purple flower; African violet, gentian violet, Parma violet, shrinking violet

viper snake; pit viper

virgin chaste person; Richard Branson's airline and chain of record shops; extra virgin, vestal virgin; *The 40 Year Old Virgin* (f), *Like a Virgin* (s), *The Virgin and the Gypsy* (b/f), *The Virgin Soldiers* (b/f)

virginal old instrument like a harpsichord; chaste; *Lady Seated at a Virginal* (pa)

virtual almost real; virtual reality; *Virtual Sexuality* (f)

virtue goodness, good quality; make a virtue of, of easy virtue, patience is a virtue

virus destructive computer bug, disease-carrying micro-organism; computer virus

visa travel permit; credit card; transit visa

vision ability to see, dream; double vision, field of vision, night-vision goggles, tunnel vision; *Sound and Vision* (s), *Tunnel Vision* (f), *Vision On* (tv)

visions *see* vision; hallucinations; *Visions in Blue* (s), *Visions of China* (s)

visit short stay; go to see (a person or place); flying visit

visiting *see* visit; visiting card

visitor guest; health visitor

visor part of a helmet, peak of a cap; sun visor

vista view narrowing towards the horizon; hasta la vista; *Buena Vista Social Club* (f)

visual pertaining to sight; audio-visual; visual display unit

vital essential, full of life; vital force, vital statistics; *The Vital Spark* (tv)

vitamin essential nutrient; vitamin A, vitamin B, vitamin C, vitamin D, vitamin E, vitamin K, vitamin pills

viva oral examination; Spanish cry of acclaim; 1960s Vauxhall model; *Viva Las Vegas* (s/f), *Viva Zapata* (f)

vocal articulate, designed for singing, forthright; vocal cords

vodka Russian spirit; vodka and lime

vogue fashion; dance while adopting fashion-model poses; 1990 Madonna chart-topper

voice passive or active verb form, power of speech, singing register; say; in voice; voice box, voice-over; raise your voice, voice in the wilderness; *Little Voice* (f)

voices *see* voice; *Distant Voices, Still Lives* (f)

void empty space; nullify; empty, invalid; null and void

volatile explosive, unpredictable; sal volatile

volcanic liable to erupt; volcanic glass

volcano erupting mountain, pointed firework; 1997 Tommy Lee Jones disaster movie; active volcano, dormant volcano, extinct volcano; *Joe versus the Volcano* (f), *Under the Volcano* (b/f)

vole mouse-like rodent; water vole

volley salvo, spectacular hit or kick; discharge in quick succession, return a ball before it touches the ground; half-volley

volumes books, large amounts; speak volumes

vote ballot, suffrage; take part in an election; block vote, card vote, casting vote, free vote; vote in, vote

of (no) confidence; split the vote,
vote with your feet
voter   one of the electorate; floating
voter
voucher   coupon; gift voucher,
luncheon voucher
voyage   sea journey; maiden voyage;
bon voyage; *Fantastic Voyage* (b/f),
Voyage of the Damned (f), *The Voyage*

Out (b), *A Voyage round My Father* (pl/
tv), *Voyage to the Bottom of the Sea* (f)
voyager   ship's passenger; American
space probe launched in 1977; *Star
Trek* series; *Now, Voyager* (f)
vulgar   coarse, tasteless; vulgar
fraction
vulture   large carrion-eating bird;
culture vulture

W

wacky   zany; wacky baccy; *Wacky Races* (tv)

wafer   thin crisp biscuit; communion wafer; wafer-thin

waffle   crisp batter cake, empty talk; speak trivially at length; waffle iron

wag   witty person; shake (a tail); *Wag the Dog* (f)

wage   payment for work; conduct (a war); average wage, basic wage, living wage, (national) minimum wage; wage slave, wage war

wages   *see* wage; *The Wages of Fear* (f)

wagon   horse-drawn cart, railway goods truck; station wagon; wagon-lit, wagon train, wagon wheel; hitch your wagon to a star, on the wagon; Wagon Wheel; *The Band Wagon* (mus), *Paint Your Wagon* (f), *Three Wheels on My Wagon* (s)

wagons   *see* wagon; circle the wagons

waifs   urchins; waifs and strays

wailing   crying; Wailing Wall

wain   cart; *The Hay Wain* (pa)

waist   middle of the body; drop waist

wait   delay; linger, serve at table; lie in wait; wait a while, wait up; time and tide wait for no man; *Don't Wait Up* (tv), *Heaven Can Wait* (f), *Wait until Dark* (f)

waiter   restaurant worker; dumb waiter, head waiter; *The Dumb Waiter* (pl)

waiting   *see* wait; gentleman-in-waiting, lady-in-waiting; waiting list, waiting room; an accident waiting to happen; *Tired of Waiting for You* (s), *Waiting for God* (tv), *Waiting for Godot* (pl)

wake   aftermath, funeral party, ship's stern trail; rouse from sleep; in the wake of; wake up; *Finnegan's Wake* (b), *Hereward the Wake* (b), *Wake Up Little Susie* (s)

wakes   *see* wake; *The Kraken Wakes* (b)

waking   *see* wake; *Waking the Dead* (tv)

walk   excursion made on foot; go on foot; cock of the walk, space walk;

walk it, walk of life, walk-on, walk out, walk tall, walk the plank, walk the wards, walk through, walk up and down; learn to walk before you run, walk down memory lane, walk on air, walk on eggshells, walk on tiptoe, you have to crawl before you can walk; *The Lambeth Walk* (s), *Long Walk to Freedom* (b), *Walk Away Renee* (s), *A Walk in the Sun* (f), *Walk Like an Egyptian* (s), *Walk of Life* (s), *Walk On By* (s), *Walk on the Wild Side* (f/s), *Walk Right Back* (s), *Walk Tall* (s), *Walk the Line* (f), *You'll Never Walk Alone* (s)

Walk
Addison's, Birdcage, Cheyne, Coast to Coast, Five Weirs, Lambeth, Lyke Wake

---

walker hiker; baby walker, fell-walker, fire-walker, tightrope walker, wire-walker; *Riddley Walker* (b)

walking *see* walk; fell-walking, fire-walking, hill-walking; walking encyclopedia, walking stick, walking wounded; *Dead Man Walking* (f)

wall barrier, partition; enclose, fortify; brick wall, cavity wall, climbing wall, drystone wall, fly on the wall, garden wall, hole in the wall, party wall, retaining wall, sea wall; wall bars, wall-chart, wall-eyed, wall game, wall hanging, wall painting, wall-to-wall, wall up; drive up the wall, go to the wall, hit the wall, off the wall, the writing is on the wall; Berlin Wall, Great Wall of China, Hadrian's Wall, Wailing Wall, Wall of Death, Wall Street, Wall Street Crash; *Another Brick in the Wall* (s), *Wall Street* (f), *Wall Street Journal* (n)

wallop beer, heavy blow; thrash

wallpaper decorating material; paste up decorating material; upmarket design and style magazine; flock wallpaper

walls *see* wall; climbing the walls, walls have ears; *Within These Walls* (tv)

wally fool, pickled gherkin; *La Wally* (o)

walnut edible fruit of a tree, furniture wood; walnut tree

walrus tusked seal-like mammal; walrus moustache; *I Am the Walrus* (s), *The Walrus and the Carpenter* (po)

waltz ballroom dance; dance with a partner; Viennese waltz; *The Cuckoo Waltz* (tv), *Invitation to the Waltz* (b/cl), *The Last Waltz* (s), *Minute Waltz* (cl), *The Waltz King* (f), *Waltz of the Toreadors* (f)

waltzing *see* waltz; *Waltzing Matilda* (s)

wander walk aimlessly; wander off

wanderers nomads; Bolton Wanderers, Wolverhampton Wanderers, Wycombe Wanderers

wane decline; diminish; on the wane

want need; desire, lack; waste not want not; *Don't You Want Me* (s), *Girls Just Want to Have Fun* (s), *I Want That House* (tv), *I Want to Break Free* (s), *I Want to Hold Your Hand* (s), *I Want to Live!* (f), *Whatever You Want* (s), *What Women Want* (f)

wanted *see* want; sought by the authorities; wanted poster

wanting *see* want; *The Wanting Seed* (b)

wants *see* want; *Everybody Wants to Rule the World* (s), *Who Wants to Be a Millionaire?* (tv)

war armed conflict; wage battle; 1970 Edwin Starr hit; all-out war, civil war, cold war, council of war, holy war, man-of-war, nuclear war, Portuguese man-of-war, post-war, pre-war, prisoner of war, private war, sloop-of-war, tug-of-war, wage war, world war; war baby, war chest, war clouds, war crimes, war cry, war dance, war games, war graves, war hero, war loan, war memorial, war paint, war-torn; all's fair in love and war; Boer War, Crimean War, Gulf War, Falklands War, Imperial War Museum, Korean War, Peninsular War, Phoney War, Seven Years War, Six Day War, Trojan War, Vietnam War, World War One, World War Two; *The Dogs of War* (b/f), *A Family at War* (tv), *Fortunes of War* (b/tv), *Foyle's War* (tv), *Hart's War* (f), *How I Won the War* (f), *I Was a Male War Bride* (f), *Oh! What a Lovely War* (mus), *Prisoner of War* (f), *War and Peace* (b/f), *The War Cry* (mag), *War Games* (f), *The War of the Roses* (f), *War of the Worlds* (f), *The War of the Worlds* (b/f/r), *The Winds of War* (b)

War
Boer, Cod, Cold, Crimean, Falklands, Gulf, Hundred Years, Korean, Opium, Peninsular, Phoney, Punic, Seven Years, Six Day, Trojan, Vietnam, Zulu

warbler songbird; reed warbler, sedge warbler, willow warbler
ward electoral district, hospital dormitory, person under the protection of a guardian; fend (off); ward of court, ward off, ward sister; *Emergency Ward 10* (tv)
warden custodian; air-raid warden, fire warden, game warden, traffic warden; *The Warden* (b)
warder prison guard; Yeoman Warder
wardrobe collection of clothes, cupboard; *The Lion, the Witch and the Wardrobe* (b/f)
wards *see* ward; walk the wards
ware items of merchandise, pottery goods; Hertfordshire town
warehouse building for storing goods; fashion chain store; bonded warehouse
warfare armed conflict; germ warfare, psychological warfare, trench warfare
warm heat (up); friendly, moderately hot; warm and fuzzy, warm-blooded, warm front, warm-hearted, warm up; (as) warm as toast, cold hands warm heart, warm the cockles of your heart; *I've Got My Love to Keep Me Warm* (s), *A Warm December* (f)
warmed *see* warm; like death warmed up
warmer *see* warm; hot drink on a cold day, thing that provides heat; bed-warmer, body warmer
warming *see* warm; global warming, heart-warming, house-warming; warming pan
warning danger signal, threat; alerting; cautionary; storm warning; *Two-Minute Warning* (f)
warp distortion, lengthwise yarn on a loom; distort, lose shape; time warp
warpath hostile expedition; on the warpath
warrant judicial writ; justify; death warrant, royal warrant, search warrant; warrant card, warrant officer

warren   rabbit colony or dwelling; rabbit warren; Warren Street; *Mrs Warren's Profession* (pl)

warrior   fighter, soldier; eco-warrior; Rainbow Warrior

warriors   *see* warrior; *Once Were Warriors* (f)

wars   *see* war; in the wars; Opium Wars, Wars of the Roses; *Robot Wars* (tv), *Star Wars* (f)

warts   skin growths; warts and all

wash   act of cleansing with water; bathe, cleanse with water; inlet between Lincolnshire and Norfolk; car wash, pre-wash, sheep-wash; wash down, wash up; come out in the wash, wash your hands of; *Car Wash* (s/f)

washed   *see* wash; washed out

washer   machine for cleaning clothes or dishes, metal or rubber connecting ring; washer-dryer

washing   *see* wash; laundry; washing-line, washing machine, washing powder, washing soda, washing up, washing-up liquid

wasp   stinging insect; organisation in *Stingray*; sea wasp; wasp-waisted; *The Wasp Factory* (b)

wasps   *see* wasp; wasps' nest

waste   unwanted material; squander, use uneconomically; go to waste, nuclear waste, toxic waste; waste away, waste-disposal unit, waste land, waste paper, waste pipe, waste time; haste makes waste, waste not want not, waste of space, waste of time, waste your breath; *The Waste Land* (po)

waster   good-for-nothing; time-waster

wasting   *see* waste; decaying; time-wasting

watch   guard duty, timepiece, vigil; gaze at, look after; clock-watch, death-watch beetle, dog-watch, fob-watch, keep watch, neighbourhood watch, on the watch, pocket watch; watch chain, watch out, watch over; watch the birdie, watch the clock, watch your back, watch your step; Black Watch; *The Night Watch* (pa), *Someone to Watch Over Me* (s/f), *Watch on the Rhine* (f)

watched   *see* watch; a watched pot never boils

watcher   viewer; clock-watcher, weight-watcher

watching   *see* watch; clock-watching, weight-watching; watching brief; like watching paint dry; *Watching the Detectives* (s)

watchman   caretaker, sentry; night-watchman

water   most common liquid on Earth; irrigate; barley water, distilled water, gripe water, heavy water, high-water mark, holy water, hot water, hot-water bottle, lavender water, low water, low-water mark, melt-water, mineral water, orange flower water, rose water, salt water, soda water, still water, toilet water, tonic water, tread water, white water; water-based, water-bird, water birth, water biscuit, water boatman, water-borne, water buffalo, water butt, water cannon, water chestnut, water clock, water closet, water cooler, water cure, water-divining, water gate, water ice, water jug, water jump, water level, water lilies, water main, water meadow, water moccasin, water of life, water pipe, water pistol, water polo, water-powered, water pump, water rat, water-repellent, water-resistant, water-skiing, water slide, water softener, water sports, water table, water tower, water vole, water wheel, water wings; blood is thicker than water, come hell or high water, dead in the water, fish out of water, go through fire and water, in deep water, in hot water, like a duck to water, like a fish out of water, of the first water, test the water, water off a duck's back, water under the bridge; Bourton-on-the-Water, Rydal Water, Southampton Water; *Bridge over Troubled Water* (al/s), *Dark Water* (f), *Knife in the Water* (f), *Ring of Bright Water* (b/f), *Smoke on the Water* (s), *The Water-Babies* (b), *Water Lilies* (pa), *The Water Margin* (tv), *Water Music* (cl)

watered *see* water; watered down, watered silk

waterfront part of a town bordering a river or the sea; *On the Waterfront* (f)

watering *see* water; mouth-watering; watering can, watering hole

waters *see* water; territorial waters; cast bread upon the waters, pour oil on troubled waters, still waters run deep; *Esther Waters* (b), *Still Waters Run Deep* (s)

wattle Australian acacia, flap on a bird's neck, primitive building material; plait twigs; wattle and daub

wave gesture of greeting or farewell, sea ripple, sudden surge; move the arm in greeting, undulate; body wave, long wave, medium wave, Mexican wave, new wave, permanent wave, short wave, sound wave, tidal wave; on the crest of a wave; *The Last Wave* (f)

wavelength distance between crests, particular radio frequency, person's characteristic way of thinking; dominant wavelength; be on the same wavelength

waves *see* wave; radio waves, shock waves, sound waves; make waves; *Above Us the Waves* (f), *The Waves* (b)

wax bees' produce, candle-making material, ear substance; depilate, increase, polish; sealing wax; wax jacket, wax lyrical, wax match; the whole ball of wax; *House of Wax* (f), *Mystery of the Wax Museum* (f), *Pink String and Sealing Wax* (f)

waxed *see* wax; waxed jacket, waxed paper

way direction, method; each-way (bet), gather way, give way, in the way, lead the way, lose the way, on the way, one-way (street), pave the way (for), right of way, show the way, third way, two-way, two-way mirror, two-way street, under way; way out; all the way down the line, by the way, every which way, get in the way, in a bad way, in a big way, in the family way, no way, out of harm's way, rub up the wrong way, see which way the cat jumps, there's more than one way to skin a cat, this way up, the way the cookie crumbles, wend your way, where there's a will there's a way, wing your way; Appian Way, Fosse Way, Milky Way; *Any Which Way You Can* (f), *Blackberry Way* (s), *Carlito's Way* (f), *Cutter's Way* (f), *Every Which Way but Loose* (f), *The Family Way* (f), *A Funny Thing Happened on the Way to the Forum* (mus), *Going My Way* (f), *Howards' Way* (tv), *Just the Way You Are* (s), *My Way* (s), *No Way Out* (f),

Two-Way Stretch (f), *The Way Ahead* (f), *The Way of the World* (pl), *The Way We Live Now* (b/tv), *The Way We Were* (s/f), *The Way of All Flesh* (b), *Way Out West* (f), *Working My Way Back to You* (s)

> **Way**
> Appian, Cleveland, Fosse, Great White, Milky, North Downs, Pennine, Pilgrim's, South Downs

ways *see* way; mend your ways, parting of the ways, see the error of your ways, (you can't) have it both ways; *Fifty Ways to Leave Your Lover* (s), *True Love Ways* (s)

wayside road's edge; fall by the wayside

weak feeble, watery; weak-kneed; (as) weak as a kitten, weak at the knees; *Weak in the Presence of Beauty* (s)

weaker *see* weak; *The Weaker Sex* (f)

weakest *see* weak; *The Weakest Link* (tv)

wealth profusion, riches; wealth tax; *The Wealth of Nations* (b)

weapon instrument used in fighting; *Lethal Weapon* (f), *Loaded Weapon 1* (f)

wear clothing, durability, erosion; be dressed in, erode, resist the ravages of time, show signs of age; Sunderland's river; ready-to-wear; wear and tear, wear away, wear down, wear off, wear out, wear thin; if the cap fits wear it, wear the trousers, wear your heart on your sleeve, the worse for wear; *What Not to Wear* (tv), *You Wear It Well* (s)

weary tired; world-weary

weasel stoat-like mammal; weasel words

weather meteorological conditions; overcome; fair-weather friend; weather balloon, weather-beaten, weather forecast, weather glass, weather map, weather station, weather-vane; keep a weather eye on, make heavy weather of, under the weather; *It's Always Fair Weather* (f), *Stormy Weather* (s/f)

weave texture of a fabric; produce cloth on a loom, zigzag; bob and weave

weaving *see* weave; get weaving

web internet, network, skin between the toes of waterfowl, snare, spider's construction; funnel-web spider, spider's web; web-footed, web offset, web page; World Wide Web; *Charlotte's Web* (b/f), *The Spider's Web* (f)

wed marry; married; newly-wed

wedding espousal, marriage ceremony; marrying; diamond wedding, golden wedding, ruby wedding, shotgun wedding, silver wedding, white wedding; wedding breakfast, wedding cake, wedding dress, wedding march, wedding ring; *Blood Wedding* (pl), *Delta Wedding* (b), *Muriel's Wedding* (f), *My Best Friend's Wedding* (f), *My Big Fat Greek Wedding* (f), *The Wedding Banquet* (f), *Wedding Crashers* (f), *The Wedding Planner* (f), *The Wedding Singer* (f), *White Wedding* (s)

weddings *see* wedding; *Four Weddings and a Funeral* (f)

wedge chock, golf club; become jammed; sand wedge; drive a wedge between, thin end of the wedge

weeds unwanted plants; filters (out), uses a hoe; widow's weeds

week seven days; rag week, today

week, tomorrow week; week in week out; Cowes Week, Holy Week; *Eight Days a Week* (s), *It's Good News Week* (s), *Start the Week* (r)

weekend Saturday and Sunday; 1961 Eddie Cochran hit; *Dirty Weekend* (f), *The Lost Weekend* (f), *Weekend at Bernie's* (f)

weeks *see* week; *Nine and a Half Weeks* (f), *Three Weeks* (b), *Two Weeks' Notice* (f)

weeping *see* weeps; weeping willow

weeps cries; *While My Guitar Gently Weeps* (s)

weevil species of beetle; boll weevil

weigh check the heaviness of, evaluate, raise (anchor); weigh anchor, weigh-in

weighing *see* weigh; weighing machine

weight heaviness, influence, significance; make heavier; apothecaries' weight, carry weight, lose weight; weight training, weight-watching; punch above your weight, throw your weight about/around, worth your weight in gold

weird bizarre; after word comes weird; *Weird Science* (f)

welcome greeting, reception; receive warmly; gladly received, gratifying; you are more than welcome; *Welcome to the Jungle* (f), *Welcome to the Pleasure Dome* (s), *Welcome to Sarajevo* (f)

welder metalworker; spot-welder

welfare health and comfort; welfare state

well source of water or oil; healthy; in a good manner; alive and well, as well, do well, doing well, mean well, ne'er-do-well, oil well, sit well, very well, wishing-well; well advised, well

appointed, well behaved, well-being, well-bred, well disposed, well-done, well dressing, well earned, well fed, well head, well heeled, well informed, well-intentioned, well known, well made, well matched, well meaning, well-nigh, well off, well oiled, well placed, well pleased, well preserved, well read, well rounded, well spent, well spoken, well thumbed, well-to-do, well travelled, well trodden, well upholstered, well-wisher, well worn; all very well, be well up on, get well soon, hail-fellow-well-met, leave well alone, let well alone, well and truly, well done, well I never, well out of it; *All's Well That Ends Well* (pl), *I Know Him So Well* (s), *I Remember It Well* (s), *Wishing Well* (s), *You Wear It Well* (s)

wellington rubber boot; capital of New Zealand; wellington boots; Beef Wellington

wells *see* well; Somerset cathedral city; oil wells; Llandrindod Wells, (Royal) Tunbridge Wells, Sadler's Wells, Wells Fargo; *Wells Fargo* (tv)

wend make (your way); wend your way

wept *see* weeps; *By Grand Central Station I Sat Down and Wept* (b)

went departed; *Since You Went Away* (f)

werewolf fictional monster; *An American Werewolf in London* (f), *I Was a Teenage Werewolf* (f)

west compass direction; due west, north-west, south-west; North-West Passage, West Bank, West Bromwich Albion, West Country, West End, West Germany, West Ham, West

Highland Terrier, West Indies, West Lothian Question, West Midlands, West Palm Beach, West Point, West Sussex, West Virginia, West Yorkshire, Wild West; *The Ghost Goes West* (f), *How the West Was Won* (f), *Once upon a Time in the West* (f), *Red Rock West* (f), *Way Out West* (f), *West Side Story* (mus), *The West Wing* (tv), *Wild West* (tv), *Wild Wild West* (f)

West
Africa, Bank, Bromwich, Bromwich Albion, Drayton, End, Ham, Ham United, Indies, Lothian, Midlands, Palm Beach, Point, Sussex, Virginia, Wales, Yorkshire

---

westerly   wind blowing towards the east; north-westerly, south-westerly

western   cowboy film; occidental; country and western, north-western, south-western, spaghetti western; western hemisphere, western roll; Great Western Railway, Western Australia, Western Sahara, Western Samoa; *All Quiet on the Western Front* (b/f), *The Playboy of the Western World* (pl)

westward   in the direction of the setting sun; Westward Ho!; *Westward Ho!* (b)

wet   moisture, rain; moisten; damp, rainy, sodden, wimpish; soaking wet; wet blanket, wet fish, wet look, wet nurse, wet rot; wet behind the ears, wet the baby's head, wet your whistle; *Seance on a Wet Afternoon* (f)

whack   share, sharp blow; hit smartly; full whack, out of whack, top whack

whale   large sea mammal; hunt large sea mammals; baleen whale, blue

whale, humpback whale, killer whale, pilot whale, right whale, sperm whale, toothed whale, white whale; whale shark; have a whale of a time; *Whale Rider* (f)

whammy   intense powerful event; double whammy

what   interrogative pronoun; what if, what's-its-name; what do you know, what goes around comes around, what goes up must come down, what is more, what of it?, what planet are you on?, what possessed you?, what's cooking?, what's eating you?, what's the damage?, what the doctor ordered; *Oh, What a Beautiful Mornin'* (s), *Oh! What a Lovely War* (mus), *What a Carve Up!* (b), *What a Wonderful World* (s), *What Becomes of the Broken Hearted?* (s), *What Ever Happened to Baby Jane?* (f), *What Katy Did* (b), *What Kind of Fool Am I?* (s), *What Maisie Knew* (b), *What Not to Wear* (tv), *What Price Glory?* (f), *What's Eating Gilbert Grape?* (f), *What's My Line* (tv), *What's the Matter with Helen?* (f), *What's Up Doc?* (f), *What the Butler Saw* (pl), *What Women Want* (f), *You Are What You Eat* (tv)

whatever   anything that, of any kind; regardless; *Whatever Will Be, Will Be* (s), *Whatever You Want* (s)

wheat   cereal grain; bulgar wheat, cracked wheat, durum wheat; Shredded Wheat; *Wheat Field with Crows* (pa)

wheaten   made from cereal flour, pale yellow-beige in colour; wheaten terrier

wheel   circular frame on an axle; roll along; balance wheel, big wheel, Catherine wheel, daisy wheel, emery wheel, Ferris wheel, four-wheel drive, front-wheel drive, paddle wheel, prayer wheel, rear-wheel drive, roulette wheel, spinning wheel, steering wheel, wagon wheel, water wheel; wheel and deal, wheel clamp, wheel of fortune; put your shoulder to the wheel, reinvent the wheel; Wagon Wheel; *This Wheel's on Fire* (s), *Wheel of Fortune* (b/tv)

wheelie bicycle trick; wheelie bin

wheels *see* wheel; meals on wheels, on wheels; oil the wheels, wheels within wheels; *Three Wheels on My Wagon* (s)

wheeze chesty sound, clever amusing scheme; breathe with difficulty

when during the time that, question word denoting time; say when, time flies when you're having fun, when all is said and done, when in Rome do as the Romans do, when push comes to shove, when the balloon goes up, when the cat's away the mice will play, when the chips are down, when the dust settles, when your ship comes in; *Only When I Larf* (b), *Only When I Laugh* (tv), *Sing When You're Winning* (al), *When Eight Bells Toll* (b/f), *When Harry Met Sally* (f), *When I Fall in Love* (s), *When I Need You* (s), *When Time Ran Out* (f), *When the Boat Comes In* (tv), *When Will I Be Famous?* (s)

where question word denoting place; home is where the heart is, where there's a will there's a way; *Car 54, Where Are You?* (s/f), *O Brother, Where Art Thou?* (f), *Where Angels Fear to Tread* (b/f), *Where Eagles Dare* (b/f), *Where the Boys Are* (s/f), *Where the Heart Is* (tv)

whey part of milk; curds and whey; whey-faced

which relative pronoun; consumer advice magazine; every which way, see which way the cat jumps; *Any Which Way You Can* (f), *Every Which Way but Loose* (f), *In Which We Serve* (f)

whiff gust of air, inhalation, odour, slight trace; smell; skew-whiff

while period of time; pass (time) in a leisurely way; during the time that, whereas; wait a while; while away; every once in a while, fiddle while Rome burns, make hay while the sun shines, once in a while, strike while the iron is hot, while the going is good, while there's life there's hope; *While My Guitar Gently Weeps* (s), *While You Were Sleeping* (f), *Whistle While You Work* (s)

whip order to MPs to vote, political party official, riding crop; flog, make frothy and light; chief whip, government whip, three-line whip; whip-round; crack the whip, fair crack of the whip, the whip hand, whip into shape

whipping *see* whip; cord which binds the end of a rope, corporal punishment with a lash, defeat; whipping boy, whipping cream

whirl round of intense activity, spiralling pattern; spin; in a whirl; give it a whirl

whisk kitchen utensil; beat (eggs), move smartly; balloon whisk, egg-whisk; whisk away

whiskers facial hair; cat's whiskers, mutton-chop whiskers, side whiskers; the cat's whiskers

whiskey Irish spirit; *Whiskey in the Jar* (s)

whisky   radio code word, Scotch; malt whisky, Scotch whisky; whisky mac, whisky sour; *Whisky Galore* (b/f)

whisper   low hushed voice; talk in a quiet voice; stage whisper; *Careless Whisper* (s)

whispering   *see* whisper; whispering campaign; Whispering Gallery; *Whispering Grass* (s)

whispers   *see* whisper; Chinese whispers

whist   card game; solo whist; whist drive

whistle   high-pitched shrill sound, referee's device, simple wind instrument; make a shrill high-pitched sound; penny whistle, tin whistle, wolf whistle; whistle and flute, whistle-blower, whistle-stop (tour); (as) clean as a whistle, blow the whistle on, wet your whistle, whistle Dixie, whistle down the wind, whistle in the dark; *Fried Green Tomatoes at the Whistle Stop Cafe* (f), *I Whistle a Happy Tune* (s), *The Old Grey Whistle Test* (tv), *Whistle Down the Wind* (f), *Whistle While You Work* (s)

whistles   *see* whistle; bells and whistles

whit   tiny amount; seventh Sunday after Easter; tu-whit tu-whoo; Whit Monday, Whit Sunday

white   lightest of colours; pale; black and white, cabbage white, double white line, egg white, flake white, great white shark, lily-white, off-white, snow white; white admiral, white ant, white bread, white cells, white-collar, white dwarf, white elephant, white ensign, white feather, white fish, white flag, white gold, white goods, white heat, white knight, white-knuckle, white lie, white light, white lime, white magic, white meat, white nights, white noise, white-out, white paper, white pudding, white rose, white sauce, white spirit, white tie, white-van man, white water, white wedding, white whale, white witch; knight on a white charger; White City, White Friar, White Hart Lane, White Horse, White House, White Lady, White Russian; *Black or White* (s), *A Dry White Season* (b/f), *The Lair of the White Worm* (b/f), *Little White Bull* (s), *The Man in the White Suit* (f), *Nights in White Satin* (s), *Ride a White Swan* (s), *Single White Female* (f), *Snow White* (f), *Snow White and the Seven Dwarfs* (b/f), *White Chicks* (f), *White Christmas* (f/s), *The White Devil* (pl), *White Fang* (b/f), *White Feather* (f), *White Flag* (s), *The White Girl* (pa), *White Heat* (f), *White Horses* (s), *The White Hotel* (b), *White Hunter Black Heart* (f), *White Mischief* (f), *The White Monkey* (b), *White Nights* (f), *White Noise* (b/f), *White Palace* (f), *The White Peacock* (b), *White Rabbit* (s), *White Teeth* (b/tv), *White Wedding* (s), *The Woman in White* (b/mus)

whites   cricketing gear, pale laundry items, parts of eggs or eyes

whittle   pare with a knife, scale (down); whittle away

whizz   hissing sound, talented person; make a hissing sound, move rapidly; whizz-bang, whizz-kid

who   question word denoting people, relative pronoun; hark who's talking, he who hesitates is lost, he who laughs last laughs longest, he who pays the piper calls the tune, who dares wins, who goes there; *Doctor Who* (tv), *Guess Who's Coming to Dinner* (f), *Look Who's Talking* (f), *The Goat or Who Is Sylvia* (pl), *The Man Who Came to Dinner* (f), *The Man Who Knew Too Much* (f), *The Man Who Made Husbands Jealous* (b), *The Man Who Was Thursday* (b), *The Man Who Wasn't There* (f), *The Spy Who Came In from the Cold* (b/f), *The Spy Who Loved Me* (f), *Who Dares Wins* (f), *Who Framed Roger Rabbit?* (f), *Who's Afraid of Virginia Woolf?* (f/pl), *Who's Sorry Now?* (s), *Who's That Girl?* (s/f), *Who's Who* (b), *Who Wants to Be a Millionaire?* (tv)

whoever   anyone at all; *Song for Whoever* (s)

whole   totality; entire; whole number; as a whole, go the whole hog, on the whole, the whole ball of wax, the whole enchilada, the whole nine yards, the whole shooting match; *The Whole Nine Yards* (f), *The Whole Ten Yards* (f)

whoop   shout of joy; shout out; whoop it up

whoopee   cry of joy; make whoopee; whoopee cushion; *Making Whoopee* (s/tv)

whooping   *see* whoop; whooping cough

whoops   *see* whoop; exclamation of concern; *Whoops Apocalypse* (f)

whopping   thrashing; really big

why   question word; the how and why; *I Guess That's Why They Call It the Blues* (s), *I Know Why the Caged Bird Sings* (b), *Why Do Fools Fall in Love?* (s)

wick   candle's inner thread; town of NE Scotland; get on your wick

wicked   evil, fantastic; no peace for the wicked, no rest for the wicked; *August Is a Wicked Month* (b), *The Wicked Lady* (f)

wicker   basket material; made of osiers; *The Wicker Man* (f)

wicket   cricket stumps, small gate; sticky wicket; wicket-keeper; at the wicket, leg before wicket

wide   cricket penalty; broad; far and wide; wide-angle (lens), wide awake, wide boy, wide-eyed, wide open; give a wide berth to, wide of the mark; World Wide Web; *Eyes Wide Shut* (f), *Wide Eyed and Legless* (s), *Wide Sargasso Sea* (b/f)

widow   woman whose husband has died; black widow, grass widow; widow's peak, widow's weeds; *The Merry Widow* (o)

widowers   men whose wives have died; *Widowers' Houses* (pl)

width   breadth; *Never Mind the Quality, Feel the Width* (tv)

wife   married woman; Caesar's wife, trophy wife; the world and his wife; *The Cook, the Thief, His Wife and Her Lover* (f), *The Country Wife* (pl), *How to Murder Your Wife* (f), *My Favorite Wife* (f), *My Wife Next Door* (tv), *Wife Swap* (tv)

wild   uncultivated region; savage, uncultivated, unrestrained, untamed; run wild; wild boar, wild card, wild duck, wild geese, wild-goose chase, wild hyacinth, wild rice, wild silk; sow your wild oats, wild and woolly; Wild West; *Aces Wild* (f), *Born to be Wild* (s), *The Call of the Wild* (b), *Hog Wild* (f), *The Joker Is Wild* (f), *Walk on the Wild Side* (f/s), *Wild at Heart* (f), *The Wild Bunch* (f), *The Wild Geese* (f),

Wild in the Country (f), *The Wild One* (f), *Wild Palms* (tv), *The Wild Palms* (b), *Wild Strawberries* (f), *Wild Thing* (s), *Wild West* (tv), *Wild Wild West* (f)

wildcat   exploratory oil well, quick-tempered woman, undomesticated feline; sudden and unofficial (strike); wildcat strike

wilderness   desolate uninhabited region; (voice) in the wilderness

wildfire   combustible substance used in warfare; spread like wildfire

will   testament, volition; bequeath, is going to; at will, free will, good will, ill-will, with a will; will-o'-the-wisp; bear ill will, boys will be boys, have a will of your own, the fur will fly, I will, mention in your will, murder will out, that will be the day, there will be hell to pay, time will tell, when the cat's away the mice will play, where there's a will there's a way, with the best will in the world, wonders will never cease; *Act of Will* (b), *Any Dream Will Do* (s), *Boys Will Be Boys* (f), *Good Will Hunting* (f), *Have Gun Will Travel* (tv), *I Will Survive* (s), *Murder Will Out* (f), *My Heart Will Go On* (s), *People Will Say We're in Love* (s), *Stop! or My Mum Will Shoot* (f), *Triumph of the Will* (f), *Whatever Will Be, Will Be* (s), *When Will I Be Famous?* (s), *Will and Grace* (tv), *Will Penny* (f), *Will Success Spoil Rock Hunter?* (f), *Yes I Will* (s)

willing   *see* will; amenable; God willing

willow   Chinese porcelain pattern, cricket-bat wood, drooping tree; pussy willow, weeping willow; willow pattern, willow warbler

willows   *see* willow; Newton-le-Willows; *The Wind in the Willows* (b/f)

win   victory; be victorious; no-win situation; may the best man win, win by a short head, win the day, win the pools; *Pets Win Prizes* (tv), *So You Win Again* (s), *You Win Again* (s)

wind   current of air, intestinal gas, orchestra section; burp (a baby), punch hard in the solar plexus, twist round; ill wind, prevailing wind, second wind, side wind, trade winds; wind chill, wind-chill factor, wind chimes, wind farm, wind gauge, wind instrument, wind tunnel, wind up; before the wind, get wind of, put the wind up, sail close to/near the wind, spit into the wind, straw in the wind, take the wind out of your sails, three sheets to the wind, throw caution to the wind, twist in the wind, whistle down the wind; *Blowin' in the Wind* (s), *Candle in the Wind* (s), *Gone with the Wind* (b/f), *Fair Stood the Wind for France* (b), *A High Wind in Jamaica* (b/f), *Mandolin Wind* (s), *Whistle Down the Wind* (f), *The Wind and the Lion* (f), *The Wind in the Willows* (b/f)

winded   *see* wind; out of breath; long-winded

windfall   fruit blown from a tree, surprise financial gain; windfall tax

windmills   breeze-driven flour-grinding buildings; tilt at windmills; *The Windmills of Your Mind* (s)

window   framed area on a computer screen, opening in a wall; bay window, bow window, lattice window, oriel window, picture window, rose window, sash window, shop window; window box, window

381

cleaner, window dressing, window frame, window ledge, window of opportunity, window seat, window shopping, window sill, window tax; go out of the window; *Confessions of a Window Cleaner* (f), *Rear Window* (f), *Secret Window* (f), *The Woman in the Window* (f)

windows   *see* window; computer operating system; French windows; windows of the soul; *Steamy Windows* (s)

winds   *see* wind; to the four winds; *The Winds of War* (b)

windscreen   glass front of a car; windscreen wiper

windy   breezy, scared; Windy City; *Just Blew in from the Windy City* (s)

wine   alcoholic drink; barley wine, bread and wine, dessert wine, elderberry wine, Madeira wine, red wine, sparkling wine, table wine; wine bar, wine box, wine cellar, wine glass, wine-grower, wine gums, wine list, wine-making, wine merchant, wine tasting; *Days of Wine and Roses* (s/f), *Last of the Summer Wine* (tv), *Mistletoe and Wine* (s), *Red Red Wine* (s)

wing   aeroplane part, feathered flying limb, part of a car's bodywork, player at the side of the pitch, section of a large building; move speedily; delta wing, left wing, on the wing, right wing, take wing; wing chair, wing collar, wing commander, wing mirror, wing nut; on a wing and a prayer, under your wing, wing your way; *Green Wing* (tv), *The West Wing* (tv)

winger   attacking player; left-winger, right-winger

wings   *see* wing; 1927 film of early aerial combat; buffalo wings, water wings; clip the wings of, in the wings, spread/stretch your wings; *Only Angels Have Wings* (f), *Wings of Desire* (f), *Wings of a Dove* (s), *The Wings of the Dove* (b/f)

wink   quick movement of one eyelid; close and open one eye quickly; in the wink of an eye, tip the wink

winking   *see* wink; as easy as winking

winkle   small edible sea snail; force (out) little by little; winkle-pickers

winks   *see* wink; forty winks

winner   victor; prize-winner; *Winner Takes All* (tv), *The Winner Takes It All* (s)

winning   *see* win; charming; 1969 Paul Newman film; winning post, winning streak; *Sing When You're Winning* (al)

wins   *see* win; who dares wins; *Every Loser Wins* (s), *Who Dares Wins* (f)

winter   cold season; pass the cold season (at or in); nuclear winter; winter garden, winter solstice, winter sports; Winter Gardens, Winter Olympics; *Before Winter Comes* (f), *The Lion in Winter* (f), *The Winter's Tale* (pl)

wipe   clean with a cloth; wipe out; wipe off the map, wipe the floor with, wipe the slate clean; *Wipe Out* (s)

wire   cable, metal thread, telegram; send a telegram, supply (an area or building) with cables; barbed wire, chicken wire, fuse wire, high-wire (act), hot-wire, live wire, razor wire; wire brush, wire-haired, wire stripper, wire-tapping, wire-walker, wire wool; go down to the wire, under the wire; *Barb Wire* (f), *A Bouquet of Barbed Wire* (b/tv)

wired   *see* wire; electrically connected, fitted with a concealed microphone; hard-wired; *Wired for Sound* (s)

wisdom   sagacity; wisdom teeth; *The Getting of Wisdom* (b/f), *Seven Pillars of Wisdom* (b)

wise   knowledgeable; penny wise, worldly-wise; wise guy; be wise after the event, penny wise and pound foolish; *The Morecambe and Wise Show* (tv), *Wise Blood* (f), *Wise Guys* (f)

wish   desire; want; death wish; wish-fulfilment; I wish; *Death Wish* (f), *I Wish* (s), *Wish I Could Fly* (s), *Wish Me Luck* (tv), *Wish You were Here* (al/f/tv)

wishes   *see* wish; best wishes

wishing   *see* wish; wishing-well; *Wishing Well* (s)

wisp   fine strand; will-o'-the-wisp

wit   humorist, humour, mental agility; brevity is the soul of wit

witch   sorceress; white witch; witch doctor, witch hazel, witch hunt; *The Blair Witch Project* (f), *The Lion, the Witch and the Wardrobe* (b/f), *I Married a Witch* (f), *Sabrina, the Teenage Witch* (tv), *Witch Hunt* (f)

witches   *see* witch; witches' sabbath; *The Witches* (b/f), *The Witches of Eastwick* (b/f)

within   enclosed by; wheels within wheels, within an ace of, within limits, within living memory; *Within These Walls* (tv)

without   lacking; without cease, without ceremony, without compare, without fail, without number, without peer, without prejudice; no

smoke without fire, that goes without saying, up the creek without a paddle, without a murmur, without a second thought, without batting an eyelid, without fear or favour, without let or hindrance, without rhyme or reason; Minister without Portfolio; *French without Tears* (f/pl), *The Man without a Face* (f), *Me without You* (f), *Not without My Daughter* (f), *Rebel without a Cause* (f), *Town without Pity* (f)

witness   person who testifies, spectator; attest, see (a crime); 1985 Harrison Ford film; bear witness, eye-witness; witness box; Jehovah's Witness; *Death of an Expert Witness* (b/tv), *Silent Witness* (tv), *Witness for the Prosecution* (b/f)

wits   *see* wit; mental faculties; at your wits' end, gather your wits, live by your wits

wives   *see* wife; old wives' tale; *The First Wives Club* (f), *Footballers' Wives* (tv), *Good Wives* (b), *Hollywood Wives* (b), *Husbands and Wives* (f), *The Merry Wives of Windsor* (pl), *The Old Wives' Tale* (b), *The Stepford Wives* (f), *Wives and Daughters* (b)

wizard   sorcerer; *Pinball Wizard* (s), *The Wizard of Oz* (f), *The Wonderful Wizard of Oz* (b)

wobble   unsteady movement; quiver; wobble-board

woe   sorrow; woe betide, woe is me

wolf   wild dog-like mammal; devour quickly; 1994 Jack Nicholson film; cry wolf, lone wolf, prairie wolf, Tasmanian wolf; wolf cub, wolf pack, wolf spider, wolf whistle; big bad wolf, keep the wolf from the door, a wolf in sheep's clothing; Wolf Rock;

Cry Wolf (b/s), *Peter and the Wolf* (cl), *Teen Wolf* (f)

wolfhound   large rough-coated dog; Irish wolfhound

wolves   *see* wolf; nickname of the Midlands 'Wanderers' soccer team; throw to the wolves; *The Company of Wolves* (f), *Dances with Wolves* (f)

woman   adult female person; John Lennon 1981 No.1 hit; fancy woman, kept woman, other woman, police woman, scarlet woman; woman of letters; hell hath no fury like a woman scorned, the little woman, make an honest woman of, a woman's touch, woman to woman, a woman's work is never done; *Dr Quinn, Medicine Woman* (tv), *Eat Drink Man Woman* (f), *The Edible Woman* (b), *The French Lieutenant's Woman* (b/f), *Just Like a Woman* (s), *Letter from an Unknown Woman* (f), *More than a Woman* (s), *Oh Pretty Woman* (s), *Police Woman* (tv), *Pretty Woman* (f), *Scarlet Woman* (b), *An Unsuitable Job for a Woman* (b/tv), *The Woman in the Window* (f), *The Woman in White* (b/mus), *A Woman of No Importance* (pl), *A Woman of Substance* (b/tv), *Woman of the Year* (f), *A Woman of Thirty* (b), *A Woman's Touch* (s), *Woman to Woman* (f), *Wonder Woman* (tv)

women   *see* woman; women's liberation, women's movement, women's studies; Women's Institute; *Grumpy Old Women* (tv), *Honky Tonk Women* (s), *Little Women* (b/f), *Loose Women* (tv), *The Trojan Women* (pl), *What Women Want* (f), *The Women* (f), *Two Women* (f), *Women Beware Women* (pl), *Women in Love* (b/f), *The Women's Room* (b)

won   *see* win; monetary unit of Korea; hard-won; faint heart never won fair lady; *How I Won the War* (f), *How the West Was Won* (f)

wonder   awe, marvel; be amazed (at), cogitate; boy wonder, chinless wonder, nine-days' wonder, one-hit wonder; I shouldn't wonder, little wonder, no small wonder, no wonder, small wonder; Golden Wonder; *The Wonder of You* (s), *Wonder Woman* (tv), *The Wonder Years* (tv)

wonderful   marvellous; *It's a Wonderful Life* (f), *What a Wonderful World* (s), *Wonderful Christmas Time* (s), *Wonderful Copenhagen* (s), *Wonderful Land* (s), *Wonderful Life* (f), *The Wonderful Wizard of Oz* (b), *Wonderful World* (al/s), *Wonderful World, Beautiful People* (s)

wonderland   place full of marvellous things; *Alice in Wonderland* (b/f), *Boogie Wonderland* (s)

wonders   *see* wonder; work wonders; wonders will never cease; The Seven Wonders of the World; *Seven Wonders* (s)

wood   golf club, projectile in the game of bowls, small forest, timber; dead wood, gopher wood, mechanical wood pulp; wood anemone, wood-cutting, wood engraving, wood nymph, wood pigeon, wood screw, wood sorrel, wood stain, wood-turning; knock on wood, touch wood; St John's Wood, Wood Green; *The Babes in the Wood* (b/pan), *Ed Wood* (f), *Knock on Wood* (s), *Norwegian Wood* (s), *Under Milk Wood* (pl)

wooden made of timber; wooden spoon; *Wooden Heart* (s), *The Wooden Horse* (f)

woodpecker climbing bird; green woodpecker; *The Woody Woodpecker Show* (tv)

woods *see* wood; neck of the woods, out of the woods; *Tales from the Vienna Woods* (cl)

woodwork carpentry; come out of the woodwork

woody resembling timber, tree-covered; woody nightshade; *The Woody Woodpecker Show* (tv)

wool knitting yarn, sheep's fleece; cotton wool, glass wool, steel wool, wire wool; wool-fat, wool-gathering; dyed in the wool, wrap in cotton wool

woolly knitted garment; fleecy, vague; woolly bear; wild and woolly

word news, promise, sentence component, short chat; express; four-letter word, household word, portmanteau word, send word, swear word, the last word; word association, word blindness, word of mouth, word-perfect, word picture, word processing; after word comes weird, from the word go, get a word in edgeways, mum's the word, my word, say the word, suit the action to the word, word for word; *Don't Say a Word* (f), *The F Word* (tv), *Never a Cross Word* (tv), *Sorry Seems to Be the Hardest Word* (s)

words *see* word; disagreements, lyrics; 1968 Bee Gees hit; bandy words, have words, weasel words; actions speak louder than words, eat your words, famous last words, fine words butter no parsnips, lost for words,

mince your words, a picture is worth a thousand words

wore *see* wear; *The Bride Wore Black* (f), *The Bride Wore Red* (f), *She Wore a Yellow Ribbon* (f)

work composition, job, labour; be employed, function, toil; dirty work, donkey work, fancy-work, nice work, out of work, Protestant work ethic, social work; work-bag, work camp, work ethic, work experience, work of art, work out, work permit, work rate, work-shy, work-to-rule, work wonders; all in a day's work, make light work of, many hands make light work, nasty piece of work, never do a stroke of work, nice work if you can get it, a woman's work is never done, work like a Trojan, work like magic, work your fingers to the bone, work your passage; *Dirty Work* (f/pl), *Nice Work* (b/tv), *We Can Work It Out* (s), *Whistle While You Work* (s)

worker bee that collects pollen, employee; shift worker, social worker; *Daily Worker* (n), *Miracle Worker* (f)

workers *see* worker; workers' co-operative

working *see* work; in employment, in running order; working capital, working class, working lunch, working model, working party; *Working Girl* (f), *Working Lunch* (tv), *Working My Way Back to You* (s)

workman labourer; a bad workman blames his tools

works *see* work; factory, inner mechanisms, literary output; clerk of the works, public works; works council; spanner in the works

world any planet, Earth; global; next world, other world, the next world;

world-beater, world-class, world fair, world-famous, world music, world order, world power, world-ranking, world view, world war, world-weary; all the time in the world, around the world, dead to the world, it takes all sorts to make a world, it's a small world, man of the world, money makes the world go around, on top of the world, out of this world, set the world on fire, think the world of, with the best will in the world, the world and his wife, the world is your oyster; First World, Miss World, New World, Old World, Roof of the World, The Seven Wonders of the World, Third World, World Cup, World Heritage Site, World Series, World War One, World War Two, World Wide Web, World's End; *All Around the World* (s), *Around the World in Eighty Days* (b/f/tv), *The Biggest Aspidistra in the World* (s), *Brave New World* (b), *Cool World* (f), *A Different World* (tv), *Everybody Wants to Rule the World* (s), *Gardeners' World* (tv), *Ghost World* (f), *I'd Like to Teach the World to Sing* (s), *It's a Small World* (f), *The Lost World* (b/f), *Man of the World* (s), *New World* (cl), *The Playboy of the Western World* (pl), *Rocking All Over the World* (s), *Setting the World on Fire* (b), *Sky Captain and the World of Tomorrow* (f), *Small World* (b), *Spice World* (f), *The Thing from Another World* (f), *Tomorrow's World* (tv), *Wayne's World* (f), *The Way of the World* (pl), *We Are the World* (s), *We Have All the Time in the World* (s), *What a Wonderful World* (s), *Wonderful World* (al/s), *Wonderful World, Beautiful People* (s), *The World*

According to Garp (b/f), *World in Action* (tv), *World in Union* (s), *The World of Apu* (f)

worldly   materialistic, urbane; other-worldly; worldly goods, worldly possessions, worldly-wise

worlds   *see* world; the best of both worlds; *The War of the Worlds* (b/f/r), *War of the Worlds* (f)

worm   computer bug, long burrowing invertebrate, spiral gear-shaft; treat (a dog, eg) for parasites, winkle (out), wriggle stealthily; glow-worm, screw-worm, slow-worm; worm cast, worm-eaten, worm's-eye view; the early bird catches the worm; *The Lair of the White Worm* (b/f)

worms   *see* worm; German 'Diet' town; can of worms

worn   *see* wear; haggard, threadbare; time-worn, well worn; worn out

worry   anxiety; be anxious, pester; worry beads, worry-guts

worse   more inferior or severe; worse off; fate worse than death, for better or worse, his bark is worse than his bite, none the worse for, the worse for drink, the worse for wear

worship   adoration, religious ceremony; attend a church service, venerate; devil worship, hero-worship; Your Worship

worst   get the better of; most inferior or severe; at worst; do your worst, doctors make the worst patients, if the worst comes to the worst

worth   value; deserving, equal in value to; self-worth; for what it is worth, not worth a damn, not worth the candle, a picture is worth a thousand words, worth your weight in gold

wound   *see* wind; injury; injure; flesh wound; rub salt into the wound
wounded   *see* wound; walking wounded
wow   expression of wonder; excite and impress; bow-wow; wow factor
wrap   shawl; cover (gifts), envelop; body wrap, bubble wrap, gift wrap, shrink-wrap; wrap-around, wrap-over, wrap up; wrap in cotton wool
wrapping   *see* wrap; packaging; wrapping paper
wraps   *see* wrap; under wraps
wrath   anger; *The Grapes of Wrath* (b/f), *The Wrath of Khan* (f)
wreak   bring about; wreak havoc
wreck   ruined ship or person; ruin; nervous wreck
wrecking   *see* wreck; wrecking ball
wrench   large spanner, violent twist; pull with a twist, sprain; monkey wrench, socket wrench, torque wrench
wrestle   get to grips (with), grapple; arm-wrestle
wrestling   *see* wrestle; fighting sport; all-in wrestling, arm-wrestling, mud wrestling, tag wrestling; *Jacob Wrestling with the Angel* (pa)
wring   twist in opposite directions; wring your hands
wrist   lower arm joint; slap on the wrist
writ   legal document; writ large; Holy Writ

write   compose, put pen to paper; write off, write-up; nothing to write home about
writer   author; writer-in-residence, writer's block, writer's cramp; *Paperback Writer* (s)
writing   *see* write; penmanship; automatic writing, in writing; writing-desk, writing paper; the writing is on the walls
written   *see* write; written all over one's face
wrong   instance of harm; harm; bad, incorrect; incorrectly; go wrong, in the wrong; wrong-foot, wrong-headed, wrong number; bark up the wrong tree, get off on the wrong foot, get out of bed on the wrong side, hit the wrong note, on the wrong side of, put a foot wrong, rub up the wrong way, start off on the wrong foot, strike the wrong note; *Eating People Is Wrong* (b), *I've Been Wrong Before* (s), *She Done Him Wrong* (f), *The Wrong Box* (f), *The Wrong Trousers* (f)
wrongful   unjust; wrongful arrest
wrongs   *see* wrong; two wrongs don't make a right
wrote   *see* write; *Murder She Wrote* (tv)
wrought   forged into shape; wrought iron

Y

yacht sailing boat; sail in a light pleasure boat; motor yacht, royal yacht; yacht club

yachting *see* yacht; maritime leisure activity and sport; yachting cap

yak Tibetan pack animal; prattle; yackety-yak; *Yakety Yak* (s)

yard imperial measure, enclosed outdoor space; by the yard, exercise yard, knacker's yard, marshalling yard; yard of ale; New Scotland Yard

yards *see* yard; the whole nine yards; *The Whole Nine Yards* (f), *The Whole Ten Yards* (f)

yarn anecdote, spun thread; spin a yarn

yarns *see* yarn; *Ripping Yarns* (tv)

year twelve months; calendar year, financial year, fiscal year, gap year, leap year, light year, lunar year, New Year's resolution, tax year, the year dot; year-on-year, year-round; a year and a day, year in year out; Happy New Year, Jewish New Year, New Year, New Year's Day, New Year's Eve; *A Five Year Sentence* (b), *The 40 Year Old Virgin* (f), *The Garrick Year* (b), *Good Year for the Roses* (s), *Holding Back the Years* (s), *Journal of the Plague Year* (b), *Last Year at Marienbad* (f), *New Year's Day* (s), *The Seven Year Itch* (f), *Woman of the Year* (f), *The Year of the Dragon* (f)

years *see* year; donkey's years; years ago; stricken in years; Seven Years' War; *The Best Years of Our Lives* (f), *One Hundred Years of Solitude* (b), *One Million Years BC* (f), *These Dangerous Years* (f), *The Years* (b)

yell loud shout; shout loudly; island in the Shetlands; *Rebel Yell* (s)

yellow primary colour; cowardly; Coldplay hit; cadmium yellow, canary yellow, clouded yellow; yellow-bellied, yellow card, yellow fever, yellow flag, yellow jersey; Yellow Pages, Yellow River, Yellow Sea; *Big Yellow Taxi* (s), *The Clouded*

Yellow (f), *Crome Yellow* (b), *Goodbye Yellow Brick Road* (s), *Itsy Bitsy Teeny Weeny Yellow Polka Dot Bikini* (s), *Mellow Yellow* (s), *She Wore a Yellow Ribbon* (f), *Tie a Yellow Ribbon round the Ole Oak Tree* (s), *Yellow River* (s), *The Yellow Rose of Texas* (s), *Yellow Submarine* (f/s)

yen desire, Japanese currency unit; desire

yes affirmative answer; yes-man; *Yes I Will* (s), *Yes, Minister* (tv), *Yes, Prime Minister* (tv), *Yes Sir, I Can Boogie* (s)

yesterday 24 hours ago; Beatles song, 1965 Matt Munro hit; yesterday's news; I wasn't born yesterday; *Born Yesterday* (f), *Yesterday Once More* (s)

yet besides, however, up until now; yet again; *Are We There Yet?* (f)

yield financial return, output; give way; *Yield to the Night* (f)

yoga Hindu system of exercises and meditation; hatha yoga

yogurt dairy product; yogurt pots

young offspring; of tender years; young at heart, young blood, young offender; Angry Young Men, Young Turk; *Dying Young* (f), *Forever Young* (f), *Hello Young Lovers* (s), *Mighty Joe Young* (f), *A Portrait of the Artist as a Young Man* (b), *Young*

Adam (f), *Young and Innocent* (f), *Young at Heart* (s/f), *Young Frankenstein* (f), *Young Guns* (f), *Young Hearts Run Free* (s), *Young Mr Lincoln* (f), *The Young Ones* (f/s/tv), *The Young Visiters* (b/tv), *Young Winston* (f)

younger *see* young; *Younger Than Springtime* (s)

yours not mine; magazine for the over 60s; you and yours; yours faithfully, yours sincerely, yours truly; *Unfaithfully Yours* (f), *You and Yours* (r)

yourself emphatic personal pronoun; beside yourself, despite yourself, do-it-yourself, enjoy yourself; be a law unto yourself, dig yourself into a hole, go and chase yourself, left to yourself, let yourself go, make a name for yourself, make yourself scarce, make yourself useful, please yourself; *Consider Yourself* (s), *Express Yourself* (s), *Let Yourself Go* (s)

youth period of immaturity, teenage boy; youth club, youth hostel, youth leader; Hitler Youth; *Sweet Bird of Youth* (f/pl), *Testament of Youth* (b/tv)

yule Christmas season; Yule log

yuppie 1980s City careerist; yuppie flu

Z

zebra   striped horse-like animal; zebra crossing; *Ice Station Zebra* (b/f)

zero   nil; homed (in on), set at nought; absolute zero, sub-zero; zero hour, zero tolerance; *Less Than Zero* (b/f), *Zero Hour!* (f), *Zero Tolerance* (ga)

zest   enthusiasm, outer citrus skin

zinc   metallic element; zinc ointment

zip   fastener with interlocking teeth, oomph; move swiftly; zip code, zip-fastener

zone   district, geographical region; crumple zone, demilitarised zone, drop zone, enterprise zone, no-fly zone, north temperate zone, smokeless zone, south temperate zone, temperate zone, time zone, torrid zone, twilight zone; *The Dead Zone* (f), *Drop Zone* (f), *The Twilight Zone* (tv)

zoological   relating to animals; zoological garden, zoological park

zoom   telephoto lens; go fast; zoom lens